ARCHAEOLOGICAL SURVEY OF INDIA.

REVISED LISTS OF ANTIQUARIAN REMAINS IN THE BOMBAY PRESIDENCY

AND THE NATIVE STATES OF BARODA, PALANPUR, RADHANPUR, KATHIAWAD, KACHH, KOLHAPUR, AND THE SOUTHERN MARATHA MINOR STATES.

ARCHAEOLOGICAL SURVEY OF INDIA.

REVISED LISTS OF ANTIQUARIAN REMAINS IN THE BOMBAY PRESIDENCY

AND THE NATIVE STATES OF BARODA, PALANPUR, RADHANPUR, KATHIAWAD, KACHH, KOLHAPUR, AND THE SOUTHERN MARATHA MINOR STATES.

ORIGINALLY COMPILED BY

JAS. BURGESS, C.I.E., LL.D., F.R.G.S., M.R.A.S.,

Mem. De La Soc. Asiat.,

LATE DIRECTOR-GENERAL, ARCHAEOLOGICAL SURVEYS.

REVISED BY

HENRY COUSENS, M.R.A.S.,

SUPERINTENDENT, ARCHAEOLOGICAL SURVEY, BOMBAY

GYAN

Published by

Gyan Publishing House
5, Ansari Road
Daryaganj, New Delhi-110002
Phone: 011-47034999, 9811692060
E-mail: books@gyanbooks.com

Distribution Network
gyanbooks.com
India, USA, Canada, UK, Australia, France

ISBN : 978-81-212-2428-4 (HB)
First Published, 1897

2nd Impression 2021

Printed at: Gyan Press, Delhi.

Revised Lists of Antiquarian Remains
in the
Bombay Presidency
Author: Jas. burgess, Henry Cousens

ARCHÆOLOGICAL SURVEY OF INDIA.

REVISED LISTS OF ANTIQUARIAN REMAINS

IN THE

BOMBAY PRESIDENCY

AND THE NATIVE STATES OF BARODA, PALANPUR, RADHANPUR, KATHIAWAD, KACHH, KOLHAPUR, AND THE SOUTHERN MARATHA MINOR STATES.

ORIGINALLY COMPILED BY

JAS. BURGESS, C.I.E., LL.D., F.R.G.S., M.R.A.S., Mem. De La Soc. Asiat.,
LATE DIRECTOR-GENERAL, ARCHÆOLOGICAL SURVEYS.

REVISED BY

HENRY COUSENS, M.R.A.S.,
SUPERINTENDENT, ARCHÆOLOGICAL SURVEY, BOMBAY.

BOMBAY:
PRINTED AT THE GOVERNMENT CENTRAL PRESS.
1897.

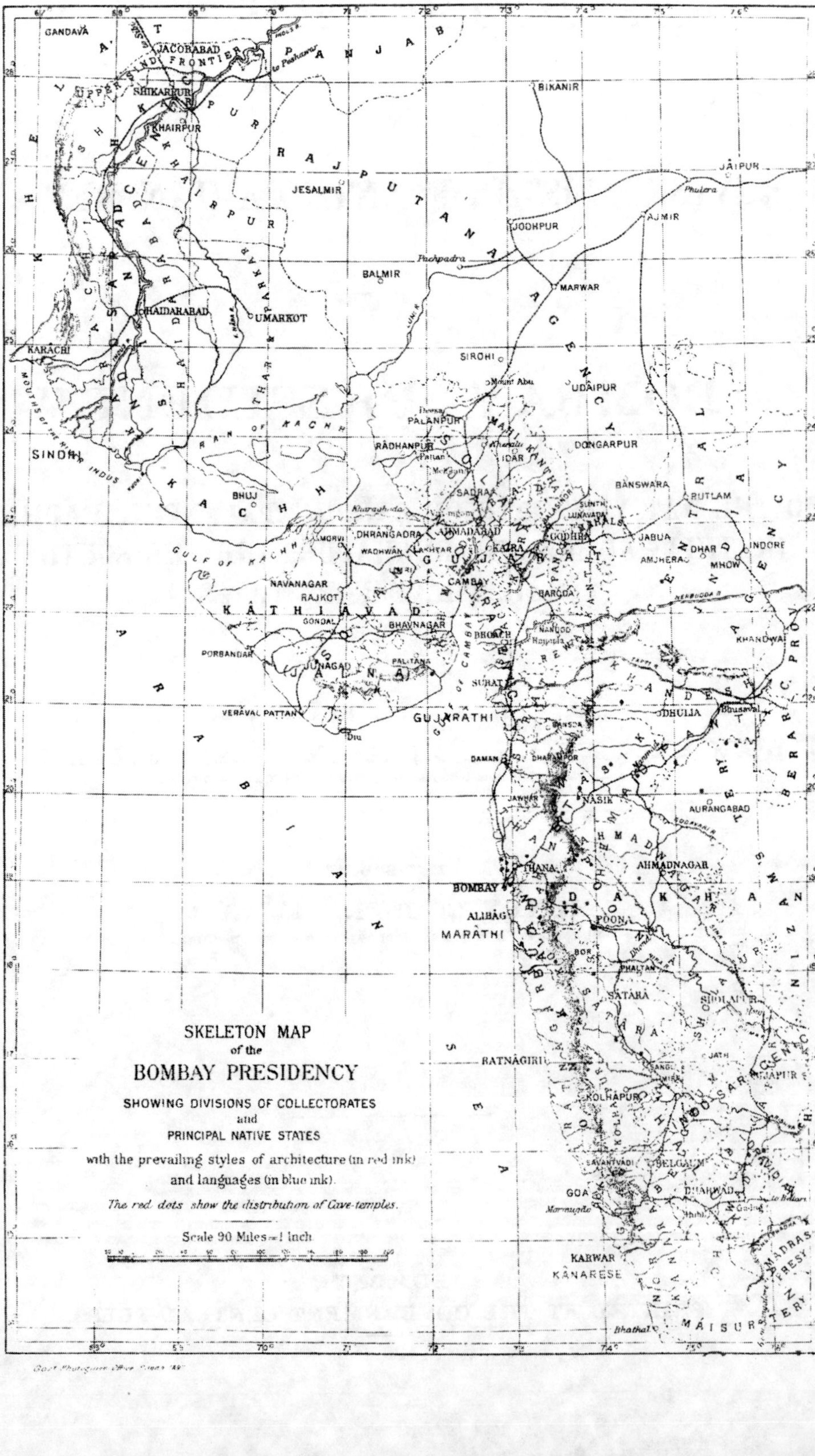
SKELETON MAP
of the
BOMBAY PRESIDENCY
SHOWING DIVISIONS OF COLLECTORATES
and
PRINCIPAL NATIVE STATES
with the prevailing styles of architecture (in red ink)
and languages (in blue ink).
The red dots show the distribution of Cave-temples.
Scale 90 Miles = 1 Inch
GANDAVA
JACOBABAD
UPPER SIND FRONTIER
SHIKARPUR
KHAIRPUR
HAIDARABAD
KARACHI
UMARKOT
SINDHI
BIKANIR
JAIPUR
JESALMIR
JODHPUR
AJMIR
BALMIR
MARWAR
SIROHI
UDAIPUR
PALANPUR
RADHANPUR
IDAR
DONGARPUR
BANSWARA
RUTLAM
BHUJ
MORVI
DHRANGADRA
AHMADABAD
GODHRA
JABUA
DHAR
MHOW
INDORE
KAIRA
CAMBAY
NAVANAGAR
RAJKOT
KATHIAVAD
BHAVNAGAR
BARODA
BROACH
PORBANDAR
JUNAGAD
PALITANA
SURAT
VERAVAL PATTAN
GUJRATHI
DHULIA
DAMAN
NASIK
AURANGABAD
THANA
AHMADNAGAR
BOMBAY
ALIBAG
MARATHI
POONA
SATARA
SHOLAPUR
RATNAGIRI
KOLHAPUR
BELGAUM
SAVANTVADI
GOA
DHARWAD
KARWAR
KANARESE
MAISUR
GULF OF KACHH
RAN OF KACHH
GULF OF CAMBAY
ARABIAN SEA

ARCHÆOLOGICAL SURVEY OF INDIA.

(NEW IMPERIAL SERIES.)

VOLUME XVI.

REVISED LISTS OF ANTIQUARIAN REMAINS

IN THE

BOMBAY PRESIDENCY.

VOLUME VIII.

PREFATORY NOTE TO THE FIRST EDITION.

THE Lists of the Antiquarian Remains in the Bombay Presidency, Sindh and Berár contained in this volume have been prepared in compliance with the orders of the Government of India (Circular letter No. 34—1888 to 1897 of 12th November 1875). Owing to frequent interruptions they have been for a long time in the press, and are not of equal merit throughout. But in most cases the materials have been supplied by subordinate district officers, always hard-wrought, and but rarely with any very clear ideas what exactly should be entered and what omitted from their returns. These returns were mostly made in tabular form; but to have printed them in this form would have been a work of needless extra expense and bulk. In preparing the Lists from such returns I have had often to deal with most untractable materials. A constantly recurring entry was, "The temple consists of stones placed one upon another." Where two returns for the same place were available, their unsatisfactoriness became most palpable: one described a temple of Mailarlinga as 27½ feet long by 20 wide and the roof supported by 60 pillars; the other made it "85 feet long and 37 wide" with 96 pillars. A temple at Kaginelli is said in one return to be 31 feet by 16 and 11 high, with 20 columns; the other says it is 195 feet by 65 and 24 feet high, with 36 columns. Of a temple at Kalkeri it is said, "the temple is 66 feet long and 48 feet wide. The temple contains 361 stone pillars," the narrator being seemingly unconscious that so many pillars would fill up the whole space and leave no floor area. A temple is described as "about 500 years old," and yet in another place we are told it was built in 1530 A.D. Whatever else is omitted (and the position of the place was very frequently not given) we are generally told, even of temples six hundred years old, what they cost: "This temple" (at Hángal) cost three lákhs of rupees in building," says the writer, though evidently he knew nothing whatever about it. Fortunately some of the returns were creditable, and personal knowledge and references to the higher officers have supplied many details. The delay in carrying the Lists through the Press has further enabled me to fill up blanks and add to the information contained in the returns.

The inscriptions given from various places are not critically edited, but are simply copied from the returns. Those in the Appendix from Girnár have been to some extent revised through the kindness of Colonel J. W. Watson; the Persian and Arabic series from Ahmadâbâd and other places in Gujarát, however, have all been prepared by E. Rehatsek, Esq., from facsimiles made by the Archæological Survey and forwarded to that scholar.

Some additions will doubtless have to be made to the Lists in the following pages, and some entries probably ought not to have been made; but it is believed they include nearly all that is at present known as deserving of any special notice. Of only a small proportion of these monuments is conservation or restoration desirable and possible; of very many of them an archæological survey and delineation might be desirable, but even of these only a selection can be made.

The Government of India in a Resolution of the Home Department (Archæology), under date Calcutta, the 26th November 1883, No. 3—168-83, gave the following orders:—

"3. The Governor General in Council desires that each local Government will now, with as little delay as possible, take up the lists of ancient monuments for its province as given in Major Cole's report for the year 1882-83, and, as regards Northern, Eastern and Central India, in communication with General Cunningham, and as regards Madras and Bombay, in communication with the Archæological Surveyor of Southern and Western India, prepare classified lists and a detailed report showing—

I.—Those monuments which from their present condition and historical or archæological value ought to be maintained in permanent good repair.

II.—Those monuments which it is now only possible or desirable to save from further decay by such minor measures as the eradication of vegetation, the exclusion of water from the walls, and the like.

III.—Those monuments which from their advanced stage of decay or comparative unimportance it is impossible or unnecessary to preserve.

"4. The monuments in classes I and II should be further sub-divided, thus—

I (a) and II (a).—Monuments in the possession or charge of Government, or in respect of which Government must undertake the cost of all measures of conservation.

I (b) and II (b).—Monuments in the possession or charge of private bodies or individuals.

"In respect of classes I (a) and II (a), the report should show what arrangements it is proposed to make for the due carrying out of the necessary measures of conservation. Definite provision should be made for the proper custody and upkeep of each monument in these classes. The Government of India do not wish to interfere in the details of these arrangements, but they desire to be satisfied that each local Government has at its disposal the means for the intelligent and judicious treatment of any questions that may arise in connection with the preservation of buildings of such importance. The Governor General in Council considers that the cost of these measures is a legitimate charge upon the Public Works allotment of each province, but will be prepared to consider in very special cases whether any further assistance should be granted from Imperial funds.

"In respect of classes I (b) and II (b), it should be reported what funds are available for their conservation; and whether the custodians can be induced to allow the inspection, direction, and control of Government officers in such matters. It may be advisable in some instances to offer small subsidies in view to securing the necessary amount of supervision, but this should only be proposed where the monument is one of primary importance and its due conservation cannot be otherwise secured. In general, it may be hoped that the local officers and the local Government will be able to induce those interested to take proper steps for maintaining the buildings in their charge.

"5. If hereafter it should become apparent that the local Governments require advice or instructions with reference to the proper mode of preserving or treating any monument, the Government of India will be happy to arrange for procuring this from the best available authorities.........

"6. In the annual administration reports of each province full information should be given as to the measures of conservation carried out during the year and as to the condition of all monuments in classes I and II."

Without great trouble it was found practically impossible to comply fully with this order for the Bombay Presidency, but provisional lists were supplied in January 1884, pending the completion of the present volume.

Again in the Resolution of the Home Department (Archæology) No. 5—170-82 of 22nd August 1885, the Government of India minutes as follows :—

"Lists of objects of antiquarian interest were called for with a view to the preparation of a general amalgamated list for the whole of India. As, however, the lists submitted by the several local Governments and Administrations have not been drawn up in any uniform plan, it has been found impracticable to amalgamate them in a satisfactory manner, and it has accordingly been decided to abandon the attempt, especially as the preparation of a general list appears now to be unnecessary, in view of the instructions contained in Home Department Resolution of the 26th November 1883. Under the operation of those instructions, detailed and properly classified lists will be prepared of the ancient monuments which exist in the several provinces. The Governor General in Council is accordingly pleased to direct that all the lists received in manuscript be returned to the local Governments and Administrations concerned, as they may be found useful in the compilation of the lists to be prepared in accordance with the orders above cited.

"2. The Government of India will now wait until the local Governments and Administrations, in consultation with the newly constituted Archæological Department, can prepare classified lists for each province in Upper India and Bengal in accordance with the instructions contained in the Resolution of November 1883. These lists should be drawn up in the form* annexed to this Resolution.

"The lists for the Madras and Bombay Presidencies and for the Hyderabad Assigned Districts should be prepared under the direction of Dr. Burgess, and be edited by that officer.

"ORDER.—Ordered, that a copy of this Resolution be forwarded to local Governments and Administrations for information and guidance, manuscript lists being returned; and that a copy be forwarded to the Director General of the Archæological Survey of India for information.

"Also that a copy be forwarded to the Foreign Department, with a request that that Department will be good enough to consider whether similar lists might not with advantage be obtained from Native States."

The lists now printed will render practicable the preparation of classified lists of monuments for conservation, whether in the tabular form now proposed or in that suggested in the former Resolution quoted above. The insertion, however, of a column calling for "any local history or tradition" may well be omitted: it has appeared in so many previous returns that its claim to a place may itself be regarded as traditional rather than important But much local information as to the claimants, custody or present use and precise state of preservation will still have to be collected in order to render further lists worth publication. The present show how wealthy the Bombay Presidency is in Ancient Remains.

J. BURGESS,
Archæological Surveyor,
Western and Southern India.

Bharoch, 24th November 1885.

---

* Form referred to :—

"*List of objects of antiquarian interest in the*

No.	District.	Locality.	Name of object.	Any local history or tradition regarding it.	Custody or present use.	Present state of preservation.	Whether restoration is desirable and possible.	Whether photographs, plans or drawings of the building exist.	Remarks.
									"

PREFACE TO THE REVISED EDITION.

The orders of Government for the revision of the Lists of Antiquarian Remains in the Bombay Presidency are contained in the Government of Bombay Resolutions No. 31 of the 6th January 1892 and No. 2601 of the 12th July 1894. The circumstances under which the original lists were compiled are stated in Dr. Burgess' Prefatory Note, which is retained. The classes for conservation purposes are also described there, and it is in accordance with these that the indication opposite each entry in the lists is now made.

As epigraphy forms a special and important branch of Archæology, I have, for the benefit of those more especially interested in this subject, had the word **Inscription**, wherever it occurs in the text, printed in Old English type so as to catch the eye.

A glossary of terms and proper names is added where explanations are given of all vernacular and other terms occurring in italics in the body of the Lists; and, at the end, all monuments in classes I*a*., I*b*., II*a*. and II*b*. are gathered together in classified lists.

In the original lists Dr. Burgess freqently acknowledged, in footnotes, special assistance which he received from various Government officers and other gentlemen. As I have omitted these footnotes in the revised edition, I here record the names mentioned, *viz*., Messrs. J. F. Fleet, C.I.E., C. P. B. Wiltshire, A. B. Steward, E. C. Ozanne, A. T. Crawford, G. H. Johns, A. F. Woodburn, W. F. Sinclair and J. G. White, of the Bombay Civil Service; Messrs. Little, West, Anding, Martineau, Mahâdev Vâsudev Barve, C.I.E., and Mathurâdâs Amṛitalâl; Colonel J. W. Watson, the Reverend S. Baromian, Râo Sâheb Gopâlji Sûrbhâi Desâi and Pandit Bhagwânlâl Indraji, Ph.D.

HENRY COUSENS,

Superintendent, Archæological Survey, Bombay.

Camp, Khâtgun, 1st December 1897.

CONTENTS.

Errata.

Page 101, line	*1,*	IIa.	*should read*	III.
" "	*3,*	IIa	"	III.
" *136,*	*26,*	1860	"	1160.
" "	*43,*	Ia.	"	Ib.

Addenda.

(*See page 20.*)

BHOR STATE.

3. Gomrâshi, a cave consisting of a single cell about 15′ × 7′ with an image of Buddha (Ind. Ant., Vol. XX., p. 121).

4. Pâli, a fort and caves.

5. Bhorap, a fort.

6. Râireshvar, a small rock-cut cell.

7. Nâdsur, 6 miles from Pâli. In the hills close by is a series of plain Buddhist caves.

8. Karsambla, 6 miles south of Nadsur. In the hills close by is another series of old Buddhist caves. (These two series were brought to notice by Rev. J. E. Abbott, and were surveyed and described by the Archæological Survey.)

Abbreviations.

J. B. B. R. A. S. ... ... Journal of the Bombay Branch of the Royal Asiatic Society.
Arch. Sur. Report ... ... Archæological Survey Report.
Epig. Ind. ... ... Epigraphia Indica.
Fergusson's I. and E. Arch. ... Fergusson's Indian and Eastern Architecture.
Journ. A. S. Bengal ... ... Journal of the Asiatic Society of Bengal.
J. R. A. S. ... ... Journal of the Royal Asiatic Society.
Elliot MS. Coll. ... ... Elliot Manuscript Collection.
P. S. and O. C. Ins. ... ... Pâli, Sanskrit and Old Canarese inscriptions.
Bom. Sel. ... ... Bombay Government Selections.
Ind. Ant. ... ... Indian Antiquary.

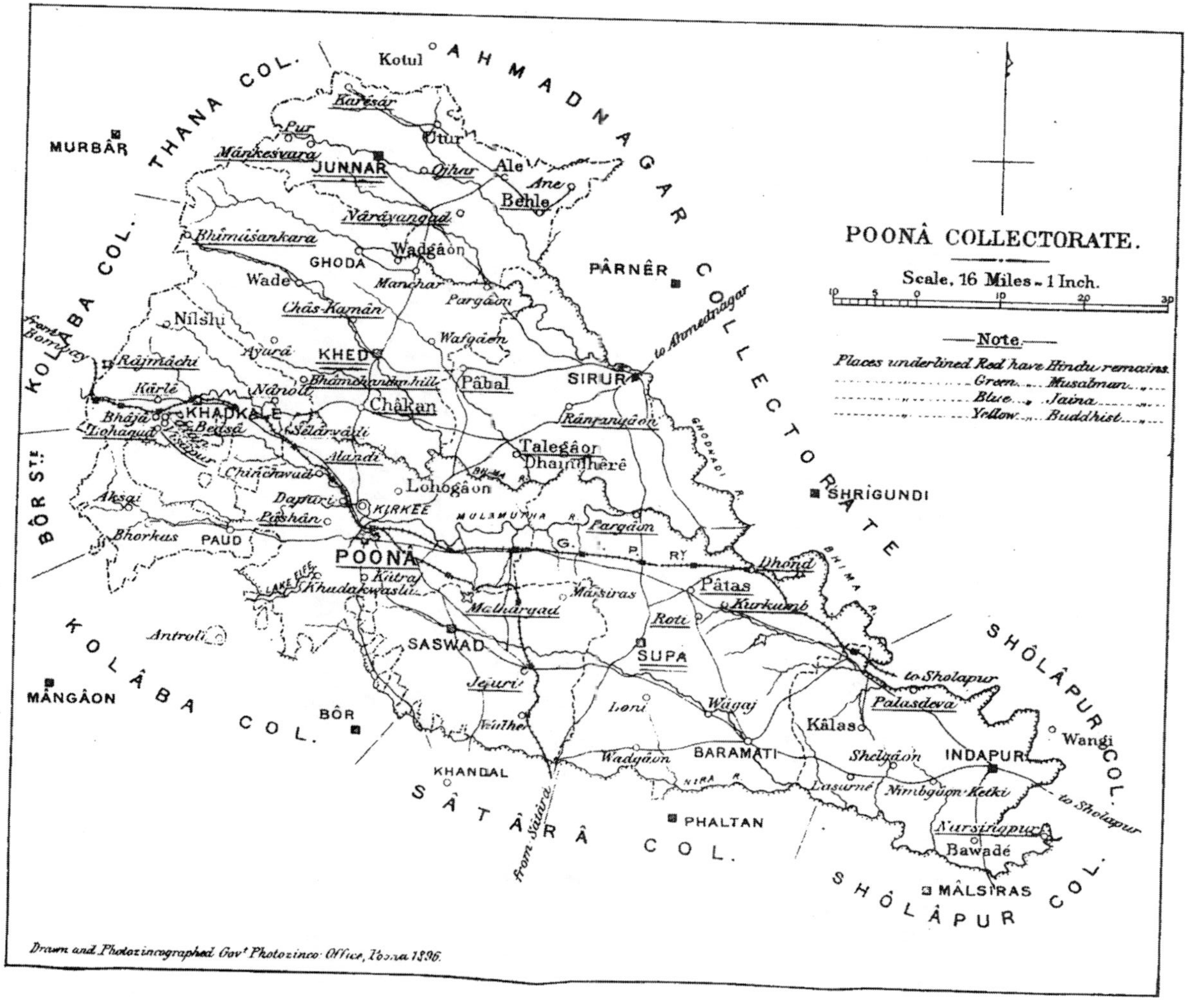
POONÂ COLLECTORATE.
Scale, 16 Miles = 1 Inch.
Note
Places underlined Red have Hindu remains.
Green Musalman
Blue Jaina
Yellow Buddhist
AHMADNAGAR COLLECTORATE
THANA COL.
KOLÂBA COL.
BÔR STE
SÂTÂRÂ COL.
SHÔLÂPUR COL.
POONÂ
JUNNAR
SIRUR
KHED
SASWAD
SUPA
BARAMATI
INDAPUR
KIRKEE
KHADKALE
GHODA
PAUD
PÂRNÊR
SHRIGUNDI
PHALTAN
MÂLSIRAS
KHANDAL
BÔR
MÂNGÂON
MURBÂR
Kotul
to Ahmednagar
to Sholapur
from Sâtâra
from Bombay
Drawn and Photozincographed Govt Photozinco Office, Poona 1896.

I.—CENTRAL DIVISION.

I.—POONA ZILLA.

I.—Poona and Haveli Tâlukâs.

1. **Poona.**—The principal temples in and about the city of Poona are the following :—

A.—Ṡaiva temples :—Parvatî, Pâshân, Vṛiddheśvara, Bhairava at Yeraudâ, Pañchâleśvara or the Cave temple at Bhâmburde, Oṁkâreśvara, Hari-Hareśvara, Amṛiteśvara, Nâgeśvara, Sômeśvara, Râmeśvara, and Sangameśvara Mahâdeva.

B.—Vaishṇava temples :—Bâlâji, Narsobâ, Khunyâ Muralîdhara, Vishṇu in Gosâvipurâ, Tulasîbâg Râma, Belbâg Vishṇu, and Viṭhobâ at Lakḍipul.

C.—Of Devî :—Bhavânî and Tâmbadi Jogeśvarî.

D.—Of Gaṇapati in Kasbâ.

III. (1.) Parvati.—On a hill south-west of Poona at about a distance of a mile, there is a collection of temples, approached by a spacious flight of rough cut-stone steps with a wooden hand-rail on the left side. From the entrance, which is on a level with the second plateau on the hill, to the right, there is another flight of steps leading to the upper plateau, on which is an irregular octagonal enclosure of vaulted, terraced roof buildings. Within this enclosure there is a cut-stone kerbed platform 72′ × 66½′; on this the temple of Pârvatî and S'ambhu is built of brick and lime masonry 33½′ × 27½′ and 45½ feet high, having open verandahs on three sides and a spire above, with stucco ornaments, surmounted by five ornamental copper-sheeted domes, with finials plated with gold, the centre one being the higher and larger. At the four corners of this platform are 4 small temples with spires of burnt brick and lime-masonry, each 6′ × 6′ and 16½ feet high, dedicated to Devî Pârvatî, Gaṇapati, Vishṇu, and Sûrya Nârâyaṇa, respectively. In front of this, to the east side of the platform, is a fountain and a stone shed for Nandi 7¼′ × 7¼′ and 10 feet high. Opposite and outside the enclosure is an upper-storeyed building called the *nagârkhâna*. On the plateau is a *vâdâ*, or enclosure of plain buildings chiefly occupied by the devotees of the *Saṁsthâna*.

In rear of the *vâdâ*, in a small quadrilateral enclosure measuring 83′ × 53½′, is a temple of Kârtika Svâmi, of cut-stone and burnt brick and lime, with a stucco ornamental pinnacle, surmounted with a dome of the same material and a finial. The measurements of this temple are 14½′ × 14½′ and 32 feet high. A *jatrâ* is held every year on Kârtika Pûrṇimâ in honour of this god. Women are prohibited from worshipping it.

To the south of the temple of Kârtika Svâmi is the temple of Vishṇu. The exterior dimensions of this temple are 35½′ × 35½′ and 65½ feet high, on a platform of cut-stone 41½′ × 52½′ and 2 feet high. To the south and west side of this temple, is the ruin of an upper-storeyed burnt brick and lime masonry building, called the *Divânkhâna*, said to have been burnt down by lightning in 1815 A.D. These temples were erected by Peśvâ Bâlâji Bâjirâv, in the year 1758 A.D. The annual Government grant for this *Saṁsthâna* is said to be Rs. 18,000.

III. (2.) Pâshân Hâveli.—Five miles to the north-west of Poona is a temple of Someśvara Mahâdeva, on the bank of a small river called Râmnadî. The temple is in a walled courtyard. The exterior dimensions of the temple are 17′×17′. It is built with a cut-stone facing up to a cornice 9½ feet high; from this the dome commences, which is of burnt brick and plaster; the spire is 20 feet high. Attached to this temple is a *maṇḍapa* of cut-stone up to the cornice. The exterior measurements are 24′×21′; the cornice is surmounted with corbels, projecting about a foot. The building has a vaulted roof, surmounted with cut-stone parapet and cornice, rather ruinous. About 3 feet from this in front is another *maṇḍapa*. The plinth is 2 feet high of cut-stone, and 22½′×21½′. On this is built a brick domed building measuring inside 16′ 3″ × 15′ 9″, with four pointed arches, one on each side; the inside height, being 16 feet, is plastered with chunam; the walls and stuccoed ceiling are painted with pictures of different deities and anchorites. The vault of this building is surmounted with a parapet having four octagonal minarets, one at each corner, with domes; the outside stucco plaster is highly ornamented, but in a very dilapidated state. In front of this second *maṇḍapa* is a shed for Nandi, supported on stone pillars, with a vault surmounted with masonry dome. Further in front at the distance of 8 feet, on a stone platform 28′×21′8″ there is a temple of Mâruti, 6½′×6′ of plain cut-stone with cornice. Behind this temple is an unfinished *dîpamâla* of the form of a frustum of a cone, of stone up to 6 feet, the whole height being 30 feet; the upper 24 feet is of brick and lime; the top is approached by a winding flight of steps inside. On both sides of this column are small temples of Gaṇapati and Bhairava, of equal size, 8¼′×8¼′, of plain cut-stone, surmounted with masonry spires or domes with stucco-plaster ornament. Above this platform, 7 feet high, is the entrance platform approached by steps recessed; this platform is partly paved. The entrance is a flat arched vestibule with horse-shoe form arches. Near the entrance is a *dharmaśâlâ* of common sun-dried brick and mud consisting of one open hall enclosed on three sides and 28′×11½′. In the courtyard is a square unfinished *kachcha* building, intended for *homakuṇḍa* now in ruins; the roof is nothing but bare rafters. This temple of Pâshân was built by the mother of S'âhû Mahârâja about the year 1726 A.D. The annual Government grant for this *Saṁsthâna* is Rs. 1,013. The first *maṇḍapa* is said to have been built by the Daphles, and the second by a Bhaṭa named Chitrâo. These *maṇḍapas* were built about eighty years ago.

III. (3.) Vṛiddheśvara.—To the north of the city of Poona near the village of Bhâmburḍe, on the bank of the river Mulâ, is the temple of Vṛiddheśvara, which is approached from the river bank by a flight of steps 25½ feet broad called a *ghâṭ*, with circular bastions on both sides of the several landings, leading to an enclosure 70′×51′. The enclosing wall is of stone and brick, pointed outside and plastered inside, with an entrance door from the river side, set in cut-stone framing; the floor of the enclosure is paved with rough stone. The temple is 28′×19½′ built of ashlar masonry up to about 12 feet, with vaulted roof and pinnacle of stucco, ornamental and surmounted with domes and finials. In front of this temple is a *maṇḍapa*, 25½′×23′ on a stone plinth; the roof is terraced, supported on heavy posts and post-plates, joists and planking; there is a sacred bull placed in this *maṇḍapa*.

In the same enclosure 3½ feet apart, is another temple dedicated to *Siddheśvara*, built on a plinth 4 feet high and 38′×20′; the front portion of this temple is of stone and lime masonry, and plastered. The rear portion has a stone superstructure; the roof over the front portion is vaulted, surmounted with low dome and finial; the roof over the rear portion is also vaulted, a cut-stone cornice projecting over corbels, surmounted with a pinnacle and domes with finials, ornamented with stucco. Next to this temple, on the north side, is a *dharmaśálá*, not worthy of note.

Opposite the temple of Siddheśvara is a sacred bull under a canopy supported on four pillars. The east side entrance to the enclosure of these temples is ornamented with stucco plaster, with horse-shoe arch over it, approached by a flight of steps; near the steps is a masonry *dîpamâla*.

This temple with *ghâṭ* and *dharmaśálá* is said to have been built by one Vallabhdâs Tânksâli, a Gujarâti, in the time of the Peśvâs.

III. (4.) Temple of Bhairava at Yeraudâ.—To the north of Poona, on the left bank of the river Mulâ Muṭhâ, on a hill near the village of Yeraudâ, is the temple of Bhairava, consisting of a shrine and vestibule; the former is 29′×20′ and 7 feet high cut into the rock. The vestibule has a flat slabbed roof, with thin pointed arches and pillars 8 feet broad; and has an open shed in front on posts and post-plates with flat terraced roof on planks and joists. It is 17′×16½′ and 8½ feet high, and contains an image of Nandi. In front is a *dîpamâla*. There are one or two small temples besides within the enclosure wall. The temple is reached by a paved flight of steps 5 feet broad, through an entrance door under an archway.

II*b*. (5.) Cave Temples of Bhâmburde.—To the west of Poona near the village of Bhâmburde, is a cave temple cut in the rock under ground, and called Pañcha Pâṇḍavâchî Guhâ. In the cave temple are the images of Sâmba, Devî Ambîkâ, Viṭhobâ, Rakhmâî, and Gaṇapati. The cave is 77′ × 74′ and 10½ feet high. It is a hall supported on thirty pillars, 2½ feet square, and is open on one side. The enclosure in front is open, and in the centre of it is a round shed supported on 14 pillars; a portion of it with two pillars has fallen down. In this shed is a Nandi. The bases of the pillars are slightly ornamented. (*Ind. Ant.* VI. 98; *B. B. R. A. S.* Part XIII. p. 55; and *Cave Temples of India.*)

III. (6.) Temple of Omkâreśvara is on the south bank of the river Mulâ in Śanivâr Peth, in a closed courtyard. It is about 55′ square; in the centre is a shrine 24′ × 24′ (external dimensions) in which is the *liṅga* of Sâmba. This whole building is divided into nine rooms, one enclosed in the centre and eight round it, with archways between each other, which are narrowed and pointed at the crowns. The rooms have separate vaulted roofs of cut-stone beautifully carved in the inside. The body of the building is of cut-stone, with plain projecting cornice supported on ornamental corbels. The top of each of the vaulted compartments is surmounted by domes, with finials of brick and stucco-plaster, which is out of repair in places; the middle dome is the highest. On each side of the temple the courtyard enclosure contains rows of rooms for the use of devotees, but now vacant. In the courtyard opposite the temple is the image of Nandi in a small building on a platform. The courtyard is paved, and a portion in front is raised. The entrance to this courtyard is in three compartments, with archways recessed on the sides and between each other, the former having raised platforms under them for sitting in. Each compartment has a cut-stone vaulted roof with ornamented cornice, with diamond-shaped spaces at the corners. The front enclosure of the courtyard has also rows of rooms on the inside, on both sides of the entrance, and on the outside vaulted roofed compartments (two on each side of the entrance) having open archways, narrow, pointed at the crowns; in front, the compartments on one side contain the images of

Mâruti and Śani, and in one of the two on the other side is the image of Ashtabhujâ Devi; the second is vacant. The entrance and the temple is strong and highly finished. In front of the entrance, outside, is a small *dharmaśálá* used by the Hindus for performing ceremonies after the dead bodies have been burnt on the river bank, which is approached by two flights of steps. There is also a small temple of Vishṇu, of a very inferior description. Behind it is a small cut-stone *dîpamâla* and a few tombs of various sizes and shapes. This temple is said to have been constructed by one S'ivarâma Janârdana Chitrâv, a Bhikshuka in the time of the Peśvâs, about 160 years ago. The whole temple has been repaired (1893) by public subscription.

III. (7.) The temple of Hari-Hareśvara is in Śanivâr Peth, in a small courtyard, and consists of a shrine and enclosed octagonal vestibule with three horse-shoe-shaped small archways on three sides. The shrine is surmounted with a dome of brick and stucco-plaster, and ornamented like the other temples. The vestibule has a terraced roof. In front is an image of Nandi, on a platform under a canopy supported on four pillars and archways surmounted with small domes, now in ruins. The courtyard is partially paved. In one corner of it is a small upperstoreyed building occupied by a devotee; on the top of the doorway is a small rough stone *dîpamâla*.

(8.) The temple of Amriteśvara is situated in Śanivâr Peth, on the bank of the river Mulâ, on a high platform in a paved courtyard, the walls of which are of cut-stone below and brick and lime with a round chunam coping neatly finished. The temple consists of a shrine and open vestibule, the latter being supported on three archways of horse-shoe-shape and pillars. The body of the temple is of cut-stone; the shrine is vaulted and surmounted with a dome of stucco-plaster ornamented. The platform on which the shrine and vestibule stand is 28 feet by 19 feet and 4 feet high. In front of the vestibule is the image of Nandi under a canopy, supported on four pillars, over a platform of the same height as that of the temple, which is approached by steps on each side, the space between the vestibule and Nandi forming a landing. The entrance to the courtyard is also reached by a flight of steps. On the river side of this temple is another courtyard about 3 feet lower, in which is a temple of Sâmba nearly of the same size, but less ornamental. To the north of this is a verandah, open in front, in which are marble images of Vishnu and Lakshmi and of Garuḍa opposite to them. The platform of this courtyard is about 25 feet above the bed of the river, which is approached by a flight of steps and sloping ground. These temples were constructed by Śivarâma Janârdana Chitrâv over a century ago.

III. (9.) The temple of Nágeśvara consists of a shrine and enclosed room in front, of stone, and dome of stucco-plaster, much out of order. A *sabhá maṇḍapa* in front is chiefly of wood work, 38½′ long and 24′ 8″ broad, with ornamental wooden ceiling and gallery all round. In front is an image of Nandi in the *maṇḍapa*. At the entrance is an upper storey for a *nagárkhána*, and on the walls figures of *Rishis*, &c., are painted.

III. (10.) The temple of Someśvara is situated in Kápadganja near Aditvâr Peth, in an enclosure partly paved. It consists of a shrine and vestibule, open in front, supported on two stone pillars. The body of the temple is of rough stone, surmounted with a brick and chunam dome; the entrance door frame and shutters of the shrine are covered with ornamental brass sheets. The temple is 19½′ × 14′; in front is a *sabhá maṇḍapa* 29′ × 28′, open, supported on square wooden posts and ornamented plank ceiling with terraced roof. In the *maṇḍapa* on a small platform of decayed stones is the image of Nandi, with a plain little shrine over it. On both sides of the temple are other shrines, smaller in dimensions, 8′ 4″ × 8′ 4″, with small open verandahs in front; in one is the image of Gaṇapati of common stone and in the other is that of Pârvatî. These small shrines are surmounted with domes of brick and stucco plaster, set with different images. In the principal temple is the symbol of Sâmba, a *pindi*. In the courtyard are open long buildings used as *dharmaśâlâs*, and a fountain. This temple is said to have been constructed by Ganapatrâo Nátu, a Sâvkâr, in the time of the Peśvâs, about a century ago. At the entrance is a *nagârkhâna* of stone and timber; this is a recent addition. The courtyard has a small garden near the fountain and some trees.

III. (11.) The temple of Rámeśvara is in Śukravâr Peth, near the Reay Market, and consists of a shrine, on a platform 25′ × 25′. In front and attached to it is another platform 25′ × 25½′, on which is an enclosed *maṇḍapa*. The body of the shrine is of brick and lime plastered, and that of the *maṇḍapa* is of cut-stone; the walls inside are painted with pictures of *Ṛishis* and gods; the shrine is surmounted with a spire of brick and stucco-plaster ornamented; the latter has a smaller plain dome at the top. In front is another open *sabhâ maṇḍapa* on square wooden posts 29½′ × 27½′, with a gallery on three sides, approached by a staircase on the outside. In this *maṇḍapa*, in front, is an image of the sacred bull on a small low platform under a canopy, supported on four pillars, surmounted with cornice and a dome with finial. The courtyard is partly paved; the entrance and portion of front wall is of fine cut-stone with a small doorway. This temple is said to have been constructed by Bhâu Sâheb Khâsgivâle in the time of the Peśvâs, about a century ago. The open *sabhâ maṇḍapa* was added about eighteen years ago by Mr. Govind Raghunâth, a contractor. In the courtyard, on one side, is a long open building used by the devotees, and a large well on the other side.

III. (12.) Sangameśvara Mahádeva.—This temple, as its name signifies, is at the confluence of the rivers Mulâ and Muṭhâ to the north-west of Poona, and on the south bank of the Mulâ-Muṭhâ. It is dedicated to Mahâdeva, and is approached by a flight of steps or *ghât*. The temple consists of a shrine and open verandah on stone pillars. The body of the structure is of stone, and the shrine is surmounted by a double spire of brick and stucco-plaster. Over the entrance door is a high *gopura* approached by steps inside the structure. The *gopura* is set with human and animal images, and is much out of repair now. On the left as you enter is a small shrine in which is a large image of Mâruti. Behind the temple is a tomb said to be of some member of the Holkar family; the enclosure is a garden containing orange and plantain trees. On the platform of the *ghâṭ* abutting upon the temple enclosure, outside, are two open verandahs used as *dharmaśâlâs*. The tomb is an excellent specimen of good cut-stone work, and is surmounted with a low stone dome. The temple is said to have been constructed by a tailor, and the *ghâṭ*, *gopura*, and enclosure wall by Harinâmgir Gosâvi, the former about a century ago, and the latter about fifty years ago. In front of the temple is the image of Nandi on a platform. In the shrine is the image of Ashtabhujá Devî of marble. In the vestibule is the image in stone of Gaṇapati.

III. (13.) Bâlâji.—This temple is situated in the same peth opposite to that of Bhavânî on the other side of the road, a little to the east, on a platform 33′ 9″ × 32, and consists of a shrine and vestibule; the former is 19¾ feet square; the superstructure up to the cornice is of cut-stone, the roof is vaulted, surmounted with a *śikhara* and domes with finials, ornamented with stucco-plaster, and contains images of different deities. This temple is in a *malá* (garden) with a well. In front is an enclosed *manḍapa* of common materials, very dark inside, and rather ruinous. The entrance to this temple has an upper storey over a stone vestibule called the *nagárkhâna*, in front of which is a fine *dîpamâla*. This temple is said to have been constructed by one Godaddâs Bairâgi about a century ago. The expenses are defrayed by the product of the *malá* in which it is situated. The temple is said to have been struck with lightning some thirty-five years ago, and received slight damage. Close to and in front of this temple are two *dharma-śálás*, one on each side; on the other side of the road are three small temples of Gaṇapati, Mâruti, and Bhairava.

III. (14.) Narsobâ.—The temple of Narsobâ is situated in Peth Sadâśiv Kârkolpurâ, near Kâlevâvar, and consists of a shrine, surmounted with a dome. The body of the temple is of stone; the *śikhara* is of bricks and stucco-plaster. In front is a *sabhá manḍapa* on wooden posts and post-plates, with wooden cusped arches and tiled roof wooden plank ceiling, with ornamental cornice. The length of the *manḍapa* is 40 feet, and breadth 28 feet; the temple itself is 17′ × 9′ × 15′ 3″, and is within a paved court-yard. To the left is a long hall 51′ × 9½′ open on the inner side, the rear being enclosed with a wall painted with pictures. This temple is said to have been built by one Nârâyana Vâman Josi, a priest, about a century ago. In the shrine is the marble image of Narsobâ.

III. (15.) Khunyâ Muralidhara.—This temple is in the same street, to the north, within a partly paved courtyard. The entrance to it from the east side is of neat cut-stone, and has an upper storey for a *nagárkhâna*. The temple consists of a shrine and a vestibule, the latter supported on ornamental stone pillars with three horse-shoe shaped arches. The body of the temple is of stone; the roof is surmounted by polygonal domes of sizes, ornamented, of brick and stucco-plaster. In front of the vestibule is the *sabhá manḍapa* in which is a small shrine on a stone platform with an image of Garuḍa made of marble. In the temple is the image of Vishnu also of marble. The temple is 28′ × 23¼′, and the *sabhá manḍapa* 45½′ × 30½′. It is said to have been built by one Dâdâ Gadre, one of the Peśvâ's Kârbhâris, about a century ago.

III. (16.) The temple of Vishṇu is situated in Gosâvi Purâ, Somavâr Peth, in a court-yard, and consists of a shrine and vestibule. The vestibule is supported on highly ornamental stone pillars and three horse-shoe arches; the body of the temple, as usual, is of cut-stone; the shrine is vaulted, surmounted with a stucco dome, ornamented and painted. In front of the vestibule is a *sabhá manḍapa* on posts and post-plates; in the courtyard is a small fountain of water, with some trees round it. This temple was constructed by Gosâvi Narpatgîr, some forty years ago. The courtyard wall is finished off with ornamented stucco plaster all round. In the court are other buildings; in the shrine is a marble image of Vishṇu and in the vestibule is an image of Garuḍa. The domes, small and large, are all surmounted with gold gilt finials.

III. (17.) Tulasîbâg Temples.—Tulasîbâg is situated in Budhavár Peth in an enclosed yard. These temples are of very long standing, but the principal shrine dedicated to Râma has been renewed with additions to its dome and sides. The *sabhâ manḍapa* is 48′×41′; the shrine is 19′×19′, with an open vestibule. The body of the shrine is of cut-stone as usual, and the top of it is surmounted with a high spire, set with columns and domes of sizes of stucco-plaster. In the shrine are the images of Râma, Lakshmaṇa, and Sîtâ. On each side are smaller shrines of Gaṇapati and Sâmba. Behind the large shrine are small temples of Śeshaśâyi, containing small images of Mâruti, Gaṇapati, and Viṭhobâ and Rakhamâî. In front of the principal temple, on a high platform, in a shrine, is a large stone image of Mâruti. This temple is said to have been constructed by Nâro Appâji, the Peśvâ's Daftardâr, about 130 years ago. The present additions have been made by one Mr. Nandrâm Sundarji Nâik, a contractor. The entrance has a *nagârkhâna*. This temple is approached by a paved lane, from under a treble-storeyed building. In the courtyard are other small temples not worthy of note. It has the finest *śikhara* in the city.

III. (18.) Belbâg, near the city library, is an old temple consisting of a shrine and a very small simple *maṇḍapa*. The shrine is of the usual construction and contains marble images of Vishṇu and Lakshmî; on each side of it are smaller shrines of Gaṇapati and Sâmba. In front is the image of Garuḍa in a shrine like that of Mâruti in Tulasîbâg. In the courtyard is a well and small houses for devotees to live in. This temple is said to have been constructed by Nânâ Phaḍanavîs, the Peśvâ's Kârbhâri, about a century ago. Has been repaired (1893) with the addition of a *sabhâ maṇḍapa*.

III. (19.) The temple of Vithoba is situated in Nârâyaṇa Peth, in a small courtyard to the south-east of the Nârâyana Peth Bridge called Lakḍipul, and consists of a shrine and an open vestibule supported on pillars and arches of ornamented cut-stone. The shrine is surmounted by a spire of stucco-plaster, highly ornamented, and set with images of *Ṛishis* and animals. In the shrine is the image of Viṭhobâ and Rakhmâî, and in the vestibule are those of Gaṇapati, Vishṇu, Lakshmî, and other deities. The platform on which the shrine and vestibule are constructed is 24′×16′. Attached to the shrine is an enclosed *sabhâ maṇḍapa* with a tiled roof, 53′×39′. The entrance to the courtyard is of stone and has a small upper storey for the *nagârkhâna*. In front of the *sabhâ maṇḍapa* is a small shrine in which an image of Garuḍa is set. This temple is said to have been constructed by one Joti Bâvâ Bhikshuka about a century and a half ago.

III. (20.) Bhavânî.—The temple of Bhavânî is situated in Bhavânî Peth, in the city, in an enclosure 97′×58′ on a stone plinth 3 feet high and 16′ 7″×25′ 9″. The temple is 12′ 9″ square; the superstructure is of stone 12 feet high, with fine cornice projecting on corbels; roof vaulted, surmounted with a *śikhara* and finial. In front is a vestibule, 14′×10′, supported on stone pillars, with scolloped arches. In front of this is a *maṇḍapa* 24¼′×21½′ terraced and with tiled roof, supported on posts. In front of this is a small *dîpamâla*. Near the temple is a well or *bâva*, with steps, and two *dharmaśâlâs* of common structure on one side, and on the other a long tiled building, occupied by the devotees of the temple. Over the entrance is a small upperstoreyed room for a *nagâr-khâna*. This temple is said to have been built by one Rangnâth Sadâsiva Satvane, a shroff, about a century ago.

III. (21.) The temple of Tâmbadi Jogeśvari is situated in Budhavâr Peth and consists of a shrine and open vestibule supported on three arches and pillars. The courtyard is very small, and contains two other small shrines dedicated to Vishṇu and Mahâdeva. In front of the latter is the image of the sacred bull under a small canopy. Besides, there are small temples of Gaṇapati and Mahâdeva. To the left of the shrine is a verandah open in the front. The frame-work of the entrance to the shrine is covered with ornamented sheet brass. In the shrine is the image of Jogeśvarî; in the vestibule are the images of Nâgobâ, Vithobâ, Rakhamâî, and Gaṇapati.

III. (22.) The temple of G a ṇ a p a t i is situated in Kasbâ Peth, in a courtyard, and consists of a shrine and enclosed room on a platform 35′×23′; in front of this is a *sabhâ maṇḍapa* 28′×23′, supported on posts and post-plates of wood, beautifully carved ceiling, with tiled roof. In front, on a high stone platform, is a small plain enclosed temple in which there is an image of the rat (Undîr). Behind this is a cut-stone *dîpamâla* in ruins. At the entrance side of the temple is an upperstoreyed building; the lower storey is open in front; the rear and end walls are decorated with pictures; occasionally used as a dining room. Has been lately repaired (1893).

II*a*. 2. O l d E u r o p e a n t o m b s.—In and about Poona are some old cemeteries and tombs. Tombs of French officers in native service at Ghorpadi and on the Pârvati Hill road. The graves of the Europeans who fell in the battle of Kirkee on the river bank about 250 yards to the north-west of the College of Science. Old grave-yard near St. Paul's Church and another in East Street.

II.—Mâval Tâlukâ.

I*a*. 1. **Ka'rle.**—The cave temples at Kârle are well known. They are situated high up in a spur of the range of hills running along parallel with, and about two and a half miles north of the railway line. They are about two and a half miles from the Kârle station and five from Lanauli. They consist of a large *chaitya* and several *vihâras*—some of the latter much ruined. The *chaitya* is, without exception, the largest and finest, as well as the best preserved of its class. In and about the cave there are many inscriptions and fragments of inscriptions, The date of the *chaitya* cave is placed slightly anterior to the Christian Era.* Outside the cave is a small Hindu temple, but neither it nor its attendants have anything to do with the caves which are Buddhist, and a few years ago a stop was made to their red-leading and using the cave as a *dharmaśâla*, when iron gates were added to the entrances. (Inscriptions *J.B.B. R.A.S.*, Part XX. p. 426; Part XIII. p. 48; *Arch. Sur. Report*, Vol. IV). (**Surveyed.**)

I*a*. 2. **Bha'ja'.**—The cave temples of Bhâjâ, 3½ miles south of the Kârle Caves, and about one mile from the Kârle station, are situated in the hill side, a short distance above the village of Bhâjâ, and are a small series of very early Buddhist caves. There are about eighteen excavations, among which is a quaint old *chaitya* with sloping pillars. It is one of the most interesting in India, and certainly one of the most important to be found anywhere for the history of cave architecture. These caves are as early or earlier than 200 B.C. A fresh cave was discovered here about fourteen years ago by Mr. Cousens of the

* For full account see *Cave Temples of India* by Fergusson and Burgess, p. 232.

Archæological Survey. (**Inscriptions** *J.B.B. R.A.S.*, Part XVIII. p. 51; Part VII. p. 438; *Arch. Sur. Report*, Vol. IV.; *Cave Temples of India*, pp. 223 and 513.) (**Surveyed.**)

I *a.* 3. **Bedsa'.**—The Cave Temples of Beḍsâ, 6 miles south-east from the Kârle Caves, are another small group of Buddhist caves. They are also known as Karunj-Bedsâ from the two villages in the plain just below them. They consist of a *chaitya* cave and *vihâra* with some *dágobas*, wells, and cells. Some years ago the Mámlatdár of Karkála was instructed to have them cleaned out when he promptly whitewashed them inside and out. (**Inscriptions** *B.B. R.A.S.*, Part XXIV. p. 222, Part XIII. p. 52, Part VII. p. 438; *Cave Temples of India*). (**Surveyed.**)

III. 4. **Patan,** one mile south-east from Kârlê station; a rude unfinished cave with a *dâgoba* in it, and the beginning of another cave. (**Surveyed.**)

III. 5. **Ayara,** 3 miles west from Taḷegâon Dâbhâḍê : some caves, unvisited.

III. 6. **Na'noli,** 3 miles north of Taḷegâon Dâbhâḍê, on the left bank of the Indrâyaṇi :—Caves in the escarpment of the hill, a mile north of the village. A steep climb three-fourths up the hill brings the visitor to the base of a high scarp facing south-west, skirting which a cistern and a cell are first passed, and then a high flight of steps rudely cut and well worn is reached; ascending them a square flat-roofed cave is entered about 18′ × 18′, with a height of upwards of 7 feet; this excavation is now used as a temple to Feringâbâi; a small cell is caverned out of the south side wall. Further on, the escarpment is hollowed out into two small cells. (*Ind. Ant.* V. 252.) (**Surveyed.**)

II *a.* 7. **Sela'rva'di** excavations are high up in a hill about two miles to the south-east of Taḷegâon Dâbhâḍê, and are most of them in the village limits of Gahunjê and facing south-west. The north-west caves are in Sêlárvâḍi, which is a hamlet of Taḷegâon, and consist each of two or three cells only; they are nearly inaccessible and have some fine Champa trees (*Mesua ferrea*) near them. The south-west excavations possess more merit; at the base of the scarp, out of which they are hollowed, is a narrow foot-path, pursuing which a two-celled cave high up in the cliff is first passed and then a fine cistern; two cells succeed, one with an **inscription** of 5 lines cut on its outer face (see No. 10), close to which, but further south, is a large excavation consisting of a nave or vestibule 24 feet by 18 feet, with four cells on either side and of an inner shrine, near the end of which are what would seem to be the remains of a *dâgoba*, viz., an abacus of four slabs, the lower the smaller, pendent from the roof, and an indistinctly traced base of the drum, the latter is now occupied by a *śalunkâ* and *liṅga*. The roof is flat and about 9 feet from the ground. The entrance to this cave is now walled up with two round arched doorways as means of ingress. Further on, are a cistern and well. (*Ind. Ant.* V. 252; *B. B. R. A. S.*, Part XIII. p. 54; *Cave Temples of India.*) (**Surveyed.**)

II *a.* 8. **Lohagad,** 4 miles south of Kârlê. The Fort is on a striking hill in the same range as the neighbouring Fort of Visâpur. At the foot of the escarpment below the fortifications is the hamlet of Lohavâḍi, embosomed in trees and plentifully supplied with water. The fortifications consist of an outer and inner line of defence, and are entered through four formidable gateways in succession called the Gaṇeśa, the Nârâyaṇa, the Hanumân, and the Mahâ gates, the last introducing to the summit of the hill. The hill is a fine plateau of great extent, and was once extensively built over, as is shown by the ruined walls and foundations still existing. There is no lack of cisterns and water.

Lohagaḍ is a fortress of some antiquity and importance: in 1485 Malik Ahmad, the founder of the Nizâmshâhi dynasty at Ahmadnagar, successfully besieged it; and a century and a half later, during the struggle which ultimately led to the establishment of the Marâṭhâ power by Śivâji, Lohagaḍ was not overlooked as a place of strength; in 1648 Śivâji surprised it, but eighteen years later had to surrender it to Aurangzib's Lieutenant, Jaysing,—retaking it, however, in 1670. When the Marâṭha rule was firmly established its strength and position marked Lohagaḍ out as a suitable place for a Kamâvisdâr's Treasury and *kacheri*. The hill is the scene of an *urus* each Pausha full-moon, to the tomb of Sheikh Umar, who is supposed to have been a celebrity on the hill and to have been buried there before Lohagaḍ became a fortress. The long, narrow north-west spur of the hill is called "Bichu Kânta" from its supposed resemblance to a scorpion's sting.

IIa. 9. **Visa'pur.**—The fort which crowns an adjoining and higher hill is of larger area than that of Lohagaḍ, but not so strong either artificially or naturally. It is said to have been constructed by Bâlâji Viśvanâth Peśvâ. Its entrance gateway is now in ruins, but the walls encircling the hill are in tolerable preservation. On the east there is a well-built tank, and there are other tanks and cisterns on the hill. A small temple of Mahâdeva within the fortifications is supported by a *devasthâna* allowance; this temple is not far from the Peśvâ's residence, now a ruin.

IIa. 10. **Ra'jma'chi** is a fortress on the crest of the Sahyâdri range, a few miles north of the Bhor Ghâṭ. It is more than once mentioned in Marâṭhâ history during the struggles of Śivâji and his successors with the Moghals.

III.—Khed Tâlukâ.

III. 1. **Khed**, 23 miles north from Poona. Here the places of interest from an architectural or archæological point of view are—the tomb and mosque of Dilâwar Khân, an old temple at Tukâivâḍi, and the recently built shrine of Siddheśvara on the left bank of the Bhîmâ.

(1) Dilâwar Khân's tomb and mosque are situated on the north of the town just outside the Delhi gate, and are surrounded by a wall enclosing a spacious compound, the greater portion of which is put each year under cultivation. The *dargâh* is on a raised platform of some height, the upper part of which is ornamented all round with a pendent wreath of sculptured foliage. Within the *dargâh*, which is domed, are two tombs said to contain the remains of Dilâwar Khân and of his brother; a third brother is said to have been buried at Rahimatpur. The inscription over the entrance of the *dargâh* shows that it was built in the year of *Hijra* 1022, *i. e.* A.D. 1613, or early in Jahângir's reign. The exterior is quadrangular, with a minaret flanking the dome at each corner; the four walls are decorated each with a double row of blank arches, three in number, the central arch in the lower and the two side arches in the upper row being minutely cusped. The mosque on the west is a graceful specimen of Musalmân carved stonework. It is small, on an elevated platform, and has a double row of arches.

(2) The temple of Tukâi Devi at Tukâivâḍi is a few yards to the east of the Poona and Nâsik road. It is entered on the east through a small porch with wall and pillars on either side, which expands into a *manḍapa* containing 12 columns, in rows of three, and guarded by a high parapet wall, surmounted by short pillars. The pillars through-

out the building are rude and massive; half-way up they are square and are then chamfered off so as to be octagonal, returning quickly however to their quadrangular form which again becomes eight-sided, the shaft ending in a series of round members, surmounted by a square abacus, which is itself topped by a heavy bracket with four projections: they support a flat stone roof which, receding slightly between each set of four pillars, is relieved somewhat of its flat monotony. The pillars are monolithic as is also the *dîpamâla* at the entrance. The external roof of the *maṇḍapa* or nave is flat with a *kalaśa* at each of the four corners, and at the junction with the *gâbhârâ* has a small spire. The *gâbhârâ* is itself surmounted by an egg-shaped dome, with a rude minaret at each of the four corners. This temple must be some centuries old, but it is impossible to arrive at its age from local inquiry and there is no inscription discoverable.

(3) The temple of Siddheśvara is picturesquely built among trees on the banks of the Bhîmâ, about half a mile to the east of the town of Khêḍ. On the north-east of the temple is a corridor *dharmaśâlâ* of brick and chunam, now somewhat out of repair; it is rectangular, the eastern side consisting of four cusped arches, and the north of seven arches, the middle one of which only is cusped; the roof, which is flat, is ornamented with a pierced cornice. On the north of the temple is a small tank with flights of steps on east, north, and south, the west side being occupied by a corridor supported by 8 pillars and 2 pilasters in its frontage towards the tank. The steps on the north are interrupted by two small shrines facing similar shrines on the south. The temple, which consists of nave, transept, and *gâbhârâ*, is entered from the north through a small vestibule, the roof of which is supported by two pillars; a canopied Nandi and several *dîpamâlas* face the entrance. The *gâbhârâ* is surmounted by a pyramidal and fluted or ribbed roof, with a dome above, some snake ornaments adorning the ribs on the east and west; there is a smaller dome over either transept and a tiny one over the nave. The projecting entablature of the temple is adorned underneath with ribs terminating in what resembles a drop, and with an occasional figure. There is an inscription over the doorway in Sanskṛit, which shows that the temple was built by a Vâṇi—Trimbak Mâdhava—in the year Viśvâvasu, which, if considered as a year of the 3rd Saṁvatsara from the present, will make the building about 150 years old, *i. e.*, the age assigned by local tradition. The date, *Śaka* 1647, is however discoverable in the last four words of the third line of the inscription. At *Śivarâtri* there is a small *jatrâ* here.

III. Besides the three buildings above mentioned there is a temple dedicated to Vishṇu on the south of Khêḍ on the bank of the Bhîmâ built by Chandirâm, a Sâdhu, about 50 years ago, to which the neighbourhood resorts in small numbers on Gokula Ashṭami.

III. 2. **Bhima's'ankara**, 27 miles north-west from Khêḍ, is a temple built at the source of the river Bhîmâ near the crest of the Ghâṭs and is within the village limits of Bhauargiri. The temple, which is dedicated to Mahâdeva, was built by Nânâ Phadanavîs on the site of an older one, and his widow built the spire. The entrance portal is elaborately carved. Well-built cisterns near it afford a good water-supply the whole year round; at a distance from the temple towards the north-west is a small cistern which is pointed out as marking the exact source of the sacred river. At this spot, so Hindu mythology relates, Bhîmaka, king of Ayodhyâ, of the Solar line, did (*tapaścharyâ*) penance before Mahâdeva and implored his pardon on account of having, during a hunting expedition, wounded two deer, into whose bodies the souls of two *Ṛishis* had transmigrated : the god pardoned Bhîmaka and offered to grant him any wish he might mention, and Bhîmaka asked that the sweat of Mahâdeva's brow might be converted into a river for the benefit of himself and of mankind. Mahâdeva had just then been engaged in a successful but fatiguing contest with the Râkshasa Tripurásura, and, wearied out by the conflict, was resting from his labours when Bhîmaka addressed him: from the sweat of Mahâdeva's brow was thus produced the river Bhîmâ. The conjunction of the names Bhîmâ and Sankara, the latter being a synonym of Mahâdeva, is probably due to this tradition. There is an annual *jatrâ* here on *Śivarâtri* (Mâgha Vad 14) when as many as 20,000 persons collect together from the neighbouring parts of the Dakhan and Koṅkaṇ.

III. 3. **Bha'mchandra hill**, 7 miles west of Châkan within the village limits of Sindê, close to the boundary of Bhâmboli. The hill rises steep from the plain on the south and west, and in the escarped southern side are the caves in question. After a somewhat arduous climb a cistern is passed on the right; the villagers call it Sîtâ's bath. A little further on, after rounding a promontory, the principal cave of the series is reached; it is small, faces south-west, and is now dedicated to Bhâmchandra Mahâdeva. There is a cistern on the left as one enters. The entrance which is 8 feet in height by 13 feet wide is now built up, leaving a small arched doorway in the centre. The temple is very nearly square, rather more than 14 feet long by 15 feet wide; the height is 7 feet and the roof is flat. Four pillars, two on either side, divide the cave into three compartments, the side compartments being each adorned with two pilasters similar to the pillars, and having each a niche with pillared jambs and canopy. There is a *chhatri* frame carved in the roof. The pillars are massive and square, but half-way up are chamfered so as to be octagonal. The capitals have massive brackets. This temple has an inner shrine occupied by a *liṅga* and an image. The inner is separated from the outer cave by an elaborately sculptured doorway, the opening being 2 feet by 4 feet high; the carvings are chiefly of human figures. There are no Buddhist ornaments about the cave. The rock, of which this hill is composed, is of a soft character and the screen or doorway dividing the two shrines has had to be cemented or mortared by the villagers to keep it in its place. Further on is a cell or rather cavern, and at some little distance, and in the middle of an escarpment, and therefore reached with difficulty is a cave, at the end of which is a winding cavernous road, low and narrow, said to permeate the hill and to be many *kos* in length. There are one or two inaccessible caves higher up; and beyond, on the west, is also a small cave. The Gurava of Bhâmchandra Mahâdeva is supported by *inâm* land in Bhâmboli.

III. 4. **Alaṇdi**, on the Indrâyaṇi, is a small municipal town possessing a population of 1,649 persons and an annual municipal revenue of about Rs. 3,500. This income is chiefly derived from the poll-tax levied on the pilgrims who resort to Jñânobâ or Jñânêśvara's shrine on Kârtika Vadya 11 and following days. There are small *jatrâs* on the Vadya Ekâdaśi of every month, but that of Kârtika witnesses the assembling of a very large concourse at Aḷandi, as many as 50,000 being the estimated average attendance at the *jatrâ*. The town is a *Devasthâna* with a revenue of Rs. 1,080, and the management of the temple is in the hands of six administrators elected by the inhabitants, the election being subject to the confirmation of the Collector, and conferring a life tenure on the elected. The temple of Jñânêśvara is not picturesquely situated, being surrounded by houses. It is entered through three chief doorways named Chandulâl's, Sindia's, and the Gâikvâd's, the second being the principal and fronting the Bâzâr. The temple enclosure has an arched corridor running all round, which is now divided into separate compartments used as dwelling houses. The *mandapa* is large and arched, and built of basalt or trap, and between it and the shrine is an unwalled covered way; the shrine itself consists of a small vestibule and a *gâbhârâ*, in the latter of which is Jñânobâ's tomb or "Samâdhi," over which in a sitting posture is the image of the Sâdhu dressed in red, and behind him are figures of his patron gods Vithobâ and Rakhmâi, Jñânêśvara being regarded as an incarnation of Vishṇu; both night and day is the *gâbhârâ* kept lighted. The shrine is said to have been built three centuries ago by Ambekar Deśpâṇḍê and the large *mandapa* by Râmchandrarâo Śenvî, a Divân of Sindia's, 125 years ago. The west wall and corridor were erected a century and a quarter since at the Peśvâ's expense and the balcony or *nagârkhânâ* over the west gateway was constructed by Gaṇpatrâv Gâikvâd at an outlay of Rs. 2,000 some thirty years back; hence the west entrance bears the name of "Gâikvâdi." A century and a half ago a descendant of the founder Ambekar Deśpâṇḍê built the east and south wall and corridor, and the balcony over the east entrance being erected by Chandulâl, a Divân of the Nizâm, he gave his name to that doorway. The north corridor has been in existence for a century and a quarter, being constructed at the expense of Sindia and Kâśi Pilâji Vâgholkar. The balcony over the gateway is due to Bâḷâji Govind, one of Sindia's followers, seventy-five years ago, at a cost of Rs. 8,000.

Some account of Jñânêśvara will not be out of place here:—

This celebrated Sâdhu was, with his brothers Nivṛiti and Sopâna and their sister Muktâbâi, born about six centuries ago in the Nâsik district. His father was a Sanyâsi and called Chaitanya, and as marriage is forbidden to devotees of that class, Jñânêśvara and his brothers and sister were regarded as illegitimate and outcastes. They, however, being desirous of admission into the caste of their father, left their native place and made a pilgrimage to Paiṭhan on the Godâvarî, a town held in high veneration among Hindus, to beseech the Brâhmaṇs of that place to absolve them from the crime of illegitimacy and to admit them within the pale of the "twice-born." The Brâhmaṇs of Paiṭhan at first strenuously refused to listen to their supplication, but were at length convinced by a miracle performed by Jñânêśvara that he and his brethren were not ordinary mortals, but were *avatâras* of Vishṇu and Śiva, and that therefore no expiatory rites were necessary. The miracle performed was that of endowing a he-buffalo with speech and causing him to recite the Vedas! Some Brâhmaṇs still doubted, and a second miracle becoming necessary, Jñânêśvara took advantage of a Śrâddha festival to call down from heaven "the manes" of the host's ancestors, who duly appeared, did justice to the viands offered them, and then vanished. Jñânêśvara and his brethren now bethought them of proceeding to Aḷandi, and during their journey thither the Veda-speaking buffalo died; they duly performed the Samâdhi ceremonies, and gave him the name of Mhasobâ. This occurred at Kolvâḍi, a hamlet of Alê in the Junnar Tâlukâ, and to this day his Samâdhi there is worshipped by a large number of devotees on Chaitra S'uddha 11. Jñânobâ's most notable miracle after arriving at Aḷandi was on the occasion of the Sâdhu Chângadeva's visit to that town. The latter came riding through the air on a tiger and using a snake for a whip; but Jñânobâ determining not to be outdone, went with his brethren to the wall of the town, and striding on it with them caused a portion of it to move forward and meet

Châṅgdeva; this wall is still pointed out, and at present surrounds a small temple of Viṭhobâ on the river-bank.

III. 5. **Chakan**, 18 miles north from Poona, was a place of some importance so far back as the Bâhmani rule when Malik-al-Tijâr in Alâu'd-din the II.'s reign made it his head-quarters (*circ.* A.D. 1445) during the seven or eight years that he was engaged in reducing the Koṅkaṇ and the Western Ghât regions to the subjection of the Bâhmani Sultân. The fort, which has been dismantled, is nearly square and is strengthened by towers at the four corners: each front too is bastioned; the entrance is from the east and through more than one gateway; the walls are high and the moat at their base deep. There are also the remains of a mud out-work protected by a ditch, which were probably once a portion of the mud fort constructed centuries ago, tradition says, by an Abyssinian polygar and strengthened by Malik-al-Tijâr in the middle of the fifteenth century. It sustained a memorable siege in 1662, when Phirangaji Narsâla, one of S'ivâji's officers, held his own for nearly two months against the Moghal army under Shayishteh Khân, one of Aurangzib's generals.

III. 6. **Chas-Kaman**, on the Bhîmâ, 6 miles north-west from Khêḍ, with a population of 2,200. In the Peśvâ's time it was a place of some importance, especially in the middle of the last century, when Rakhmâbâi, the daughter of Bâḷâji Bajirâv Peśvâ and the sister of Bâlâji and Raghunâthrâv, became the wife of Kṛishṇarâv Mâdhav Joshi of Châs, who is said to have perished at the battle of Pânipat. Rakhmâbâi expended a large fortune on the town and constructed a fine *ghât* to the river, besides building a notable temple on the west near the river, dedicated to Mahâdeva under the name of Somêśvara. The temple is surrounded by a quadrangular enclosure, the exterior walls of which terminate in blank petal-shaped battlements and are bastioned at the four corners; the battlements of the south-east bastion bear each a snake ornament. The enclosure contains some goodly trees; its chief entrance is by the east doorway, fronting which, and inside, is a very striking *dîpamâla* or round *stambha* of basalt, ending in an elaborately carved capital with a square abacus above; the receptacles for the lights, a few of which bear sculptured figures in alto-relievo on their front, are said to number 350; this *dîpamâla* is lighted on the full-moon of Kârtika only. Beyond the *dîpamâla* and facing the temple is a Nandi on a raised platform and under a domed canopy; the latter has below the dome and on each of the four sides a fine cusped arch slightly ogeed; the Nandi, however, is not worthy of its baldacchino. The temple itself is oblong, consisting of the ordinary *maṇḍapa* and *gâbhârâ*, the latter being surmounted by a chunam and brick dome, the sides of which are adorned with niches, figures, and miniature domes so usually the adjuncts of a Dakhan temple. Three elaborately pierced and small apertures in the wall-veil admit light into the sanctum, while three square-headed doorways permit access into the *maṇḍapa*, those on the north and south having each a grotesquely carved human head, the *kirttimukha*, as a stepping-stone. This town is usually styled Châs Kamân to distinguish it from Châs Nârodi in the north of the *tâlukâ*, Kamân and Nârodi being villages adjoining the two towns of Châs respectively.

IV.—Junnar Tâlukâ.

I *a*. 1. **Junnar** (19° 12′; 73° 56′). There are about 140 caves in some six groups round Junnar, which have been described in the *Ind. Ant.* Vol. VI. p. 32, and *Cave Temples of India*. **Inscriptions**. **(Surveyed.)**

II *b*. Among the Muhammadan remains the Jami Masjid is said to be 500 years old, and there is no doubt that it occupies the site of an old Hindu temple. It is approached through a narrow gateway surmounted by an arch which is flanked by four *minârs*; the gateway is recent, as the year 1235 (Hijra) is engraved below the arch; the roof of the mosque is flat and wooden, and is supported by 18 stone pillars; these pillars are plainly Hindu,—a fact admitted by the Musalmân in charge; the outermost row of pillars, six in number, are assisted in supporting the roof by beautifully carved wooden brackets, which are taken by the goldsmiths of the town as patterns in carving their ornaments; the front is surmounted by six minarets.

II *a*. The present fort of S'ivneri outside the town on the south-east is of Musalmân origin. It is accessible on the south side only, where a steep ascent conducts to the entrance gateway, which is massive and flanked by towers; several other gateways, all strongly built and bastioned, are passed through before the first of a triple line of fortifications is entered, and when the fortress proper is gained and the summit of the hill, which is near 1,000 feet above Junnar, reached, the thought can scarcely fail to present itself that nature and art combined have created here one of the most impregnable of mountain strongholds. The present fort was built about A.D. 1445 by Malik-al-Tijar, the lieutenant of the Bâhmani king Alâu'd-din II., but doubtless additions were frequently made to the fortifications under subsequent rulers. It played a not unimportant part during the earlier Marâṭhâ period, and is celebrated as being the birthplace of S'ivâji. A memorable night attack was made on it in 1680, near the close of S'ivâji's career. The most striking of its remains is a mosque with two flanking minarets, the latter being united by a graceful flying arch. This mosquo is built over a rock-hewn tank, the water of which outlasts the hot season, as does also that of several of the other reservoirs on the hill. On the summit of the plateau is an *idgâh*, and the tomb of Adam Subhedâr.

III. Perhaps the most interesting buildings are those outside the town on the east; and the most ancient of these is a *dargâh* close to and on the right of the high road as one goes from Junnar to Nârâyaṇagâon. It is plainly built and has three entrances, and some of the stones used seem taken from a Hindu temple. North of this *dargâh* and near the Delhi Ves is an old mosque, said to be of the time of Shâh Jahân.

III. About a couple of miles east of Junnar is a garden of some extent called the Âfiz Bâgh. More than one solution is given of the name, but perhaps the most plausible is that which makes Âfiz a corruption of Habshi, this garden and its mansion having, tradition states, been in the possession of, if not founded by, an Abyssinian chief. The mansion is a substantial and not inelegant building: three balcony windows on the south side overlook a small tank; these windows are supported by somewhat heavy-looking brackets, and are canopied; the east and west sides have each a bay window; the entrance is on the north, the steps being flanked by bay windows similar in adornment to those on the other three sides; there is an upper storey to the house; the roof of the ground floor is arched, and ornamented with lozenge-shaped mouldings.

III. At a little distance west of the garden, and therefore nearer Junnar, is a fine *dargâh* or *gumbaz* which is supposed to contain the ashes of the Habshi founder of the Âfiz Bâgh. This mausoleum has a domed roof, and within it are nine tombs said to be those of the Habshi, his wife, six children, and a servant. There are entrances on the south and east.

The south entrance is beautifully carved and pierced; it is flat-headed, with pierced work above, and sculptured jambs, and is contained within an ogee arch; there is an inscription above the lintel. The east is a narrow doorway under a pointed arch. The interior is an octagon, and every other octagonal side is embrasured and arched; the west is covered with texts from the Qurân. The exterior walls form a quadrangular figure; the upper portion of the wall-veil terminates in an artistic cornice of brick and chunam, consisting of pointed arches resting on tiny pedestals and interlacing each other; a small minaret graces each of the four corners of the building. The walls are, as regards ornament, divided into two series of blank and arched windows, the upper consisting of five and the lower of three windows, the middle lower panel on the south and east walls being exchanged for a doorway.

To the west of this large mausoleum is a small *dargâh*, with a pyramidal roof.

III. 2. **Behle**, 21 miles E.S.E. from Junnar (19° 7'; 74° 15'), contains a fine Hemâḍpanti *bâvadi*. This tank is about 20 yards square, and is entered by two flights of ten steps each on opposite sides; the walls are adorned with 18 canopied niches, of which four ornament each of the sides where the steps are, and five each of the remaining sides. These niches are somewhat under 3 feet high, and are 1½ feet wide by 1 foot deep; they are square-headed with carved jambs, and their finial is a canopy knobbed at the top. There was an inscription on the south wall, but it has been worn away.

II *b*. 3. **Pur**, 10 miles W.N.W. from Junnar:—Temple of Kukaḍêśvara at the source of the Kukaḍi, a few miles east from the Nânâ Ghâṭ, and attracts an assemblage of from one to two thousand persons on Mâgha Vadya 14 (*Śivarâtri*). It is situated within the village limits of Pur, and is supported by a *Devasthâna* allowance of Rs. 76 per annum. The abrupt mountain fortress of Châwand, three miles to the east, and an amphitheatre of hills which encircle it on the south and west, combine to make the site of Kukaḍeśvara very picturesque. The temple itself is in the Hemâḍpanti style and in fair preservation; its court is strewn with portions of the carved work which have from time to time fallen, their places in the structure being filled in with plain masonry. The position of much of the carved stone work on the exterior of the building would lead to the impression that at one time the temple was partially in ruins (possibly rendered so by Musalmân fanaticism) and in its restoration somewhat careless or unskilful hands pieced it together. The elaboration of the sculpture and the size of the stones used are striking. The west and only entrance is especially worthy of notice. Those in charge are peculiarly jealous of the intrusion of strangers, and even the *manḍapa* is closed to heretical footsteps. From the doorway, however, may be seen six fine pillars, three on either side, dividing the *manḍapa* into nave and aisles with a seventh column at the entrance to the *gâbhârâ*. These pillars bear sculptured figures on their capitals. On the north-west of the temple is a small shrine, now in ruins, dedicated to Bhairava; either jamb of the doorway bears a *dvârapâla* in relief. The temple itself is protected from the severity of the weather by a thatched roof supported on a wooden structure.

III. 4. **Ma'nkes'vara** is a small village a few miles west of Junnar. Its only claims to notice are a few remains of what must once have been a Hemâḍpanti temple of great merit; the remains now visible are three or four artistically sculptured pillars without base or capital, some fragments of capitals, and two large Nandis. Probably, if the mound on which the ruin is were excavated, a large portion of the old temple might be discovered. The belief of the villagers is that the Musalmâns during their rule destroyed the building, and this belief is rather strengthened by the fact that within a stone's throw on the south is a Pîr's tomb.

III. 5. **Nârâyangad,** 10 miles south-east from Junnar and 3 miles east of Nârâyaṇgâon. The hill is isolated and rises abruptly from the plain on the north-west and south. The fortifications are almost completely dismantled; portions of four bastions, however, and part of the north wall remain, though in a ruined state. This fort, said to have been built by the first great Peśvâ, Bâlâji Viśvanâtha, was given as a *saranjâm* to Sayâji Povâr at the end of the last or the beginning of this century, with the duty of keeping the neighbouring country in a quiet state and in the interest of the Peśvâ. There is a tradition in the neighbourhood that Nârâyaṇgaḍ surrendered to the British after only one shell or cannon ball had reached the interior of the fortifications. There is a small shrine to Hastabâi on the extreme summit of the hill. Water is plentiful, being supplied by two *ṭâkâs* or spring cisterns and by several *hauds*; the former are full of water even in May, and of them the Nârâyaṇa Tâkâ is the more famous. In this *ṭâkâ*, Nârâyaṇa Deva is said to have appeared, though invisible to the uninitiated, forty years ago, on which occasion the hill was for two or three years the scene of a weekly Somavâra *jatrâ* attracting some thousands of persons. There are some ruins on the hill, but the only one worth mentioning is a stone doorway bearing on its lintel a figure of Gaṇapati and two attendant tigers.

III. 6. **Ojhar,** east from Junnar, is the supposed scene of one of the Ashṭa Vinâyaka *avatâras*. The present temple is modern, being only a century old. It is in an enclosure which is entered under a somewhat interesting looking gateway; the sides of the gateway bear sculptured *dvârapâlas*, and a row of four musicians in bas-relief adorns the lintel; these figures are all gorgeously painted. On entering the enclosure two fine *dîpamâlas* first attract attention; they are in front of an extremely fine corridor of seven cusped arches; this corridor serves the purpose of a *dharmaśâlâ*. The temple itself is entered by three doors, each of which is sculptured on the jambs and lintel; the east entrance is the chief, and bears in relief over the lintel a figure of Gaṇapati with parrots and monkeys disporting themselves in trees. A small dome flanked by four minarets surmounts the *maṇḍapa*, and over the *gâbhârâ* is a *śikhara* adorned with the ordinary rows of niches and figures. This temple is very little frequented. For the other Ashṭa Vinâyaka's temples see Rânjaṇgâon in Sirur Tâlukâ.

III. 7. **Kareśar,** 3 miles north-west from Maḍh—a very interesting temple of perhaps the eleventh century, falling to ruins.

V.—Sirur Tâlukâ.

III. 1. **Rânjangaon**, at the junction of the Bhimâ and Muṭhâ-Mulâ. Temple of Gaṇapati. The village is supposed to be the scene of one of the Ashṭa Vinâyaka *avatâras* of that divinity. The other seven Ashṭa Vinâyaka temples are situated at Morgâon, Theur, Lenâdri, and Ojhar in the Poona Collectorate, at Pâli in the Pant Sachiv's territory, at Maḍh in the Thâna District, and a t Siddhaṭek in the Collectorate of Ahmadnagar. The present temple at Rânjangâon occupies, it is said, the site of an old Hemâdpanti edifice, of which four pillars remain, two of them at the entrance to the enclosure. The present shrine is said to have been constructed by Chintâmaṇa Mahârâja Dêva, two centuries back, and on the north side there is a fine corridor with a façade of 15 arches, each arched compartment being vaulted in a low conical form. This arcade is due to the Povâr family, and is contemporary with the present temple. A flight of steps leads to the roof of the corridor which is flat and a pleasant place of resort during the *jatrâ* season, *i. e.* at Gaṇeśa Chaturthi. The temple consists of a *maṇḍapa* with rows of wooden pillars and an outer and inner *gâbhârâ*; a stone rat is stationed at the entrance of the *maṇḍapa*, as the usual *vâhana* of the elephant-snouted god. The outer *gâbhârâ* is surmounted by a small *śikhara* and the sanctuary by a more imposing one; both *śikharas* are somewhat rude; the larger rises in four storeys, the lowest being the widest, and the three higher ones being each ornamented with a frieze; a small *kaḷasa*, flanked by four *minars* completes the spire. There is a tiny shrine dedicated to Mahâdeva on the extreme west, *i. e.* beyond the *gâbhârâ* and joined to it. The cornice of both temple and corridor is supported by brackets of the Phallic symbol type.

III. 2. **Pâbal**, 25 miles N.N.E. from Poona. Old temple of Nâgeśvara Mahâdeva on the west of the town, said to have been built five centuries ago by Kânhu Râjpâṭak. The *maṇḍapa* is divided into three small aisles by two rows of three pillars each, the outermost pillars being slightly sculptured. In front and on the east is a small tank in the Hemâḍpanti style, constructed, according to tradition, by Kânhu's favourite dancing girl. Flights of steps lead down to the water and the side walls contain small niches with sculptured jambs. On the north-east of the temple is a fine *stambha*; its shaft, which stands on a lofty pedestal and supports a massive capital, is monolithic. (2) Mastân Bâi's tomb, to which a mosque is attached, is situated among some fine trees in an enclosure on the north of Pâbal. This lady received as *saranjâm* Pâbal and the neighbouring villages of Kendur and Loni from Bâjirâv Peśvâ, and though she died in the Śanivâra Palace at Poona, she was buried in her *inâm* town of Pâbal. She was probably a native of the north of India, and is said to have been taken captive by Sindia in his wars in Hinduṣthân and to have been made by him a present to the Peśvâ. There is nothing of architectural merit in her tomb or its surroundings.

III. 3. **Talegaon-Dhamdhere**, 20 miles north-east from Poona (18° 40′; 74° 12′). Of the many temples in this town the most remarkable are: (1) Siddhêśvara, a large Śaiva shrine enclosed by lofty battlemented walls and built on an elevation. A Kulkarṇi of Talegâon, who was also Sindia's Diván, is said to have erected it. On the east and west there are high flights of steps leading into the temple inclosure. (2) Gaṇapati's temple owes its existence to the Dhamdhêrê family. The *śikhara* surmounting the *gâbhârâ* is profusely adorned with quaint little figures in niches, and the vestibule is entered on the east and south through arched openings, and has a vaulted roof. (3) Nátha's shrine is built on the bank of the river and is dedicated to the Sádhu whose name it bears. On *S'ivarâtri* there is a *jatrâ* of about 3,000 persons to this shrine. Nâtha lived in Sivâji's time, and was a friend of Itnâk Bâvâ, whose tomb is in the Musalmân cemetery to north-east of the town. The townsfolk have a tradition that Nâtha and Itnâk were great card-players, and spent most of their spare time in playing together. This shrine is supported by *inâm* land assessed at Rs. 49, and is the scene of a *jatrâ* of about 2,000 persons on Mâgha Vadya 13. (4) Uttarêśvara temple was built by one of the Mahâjan family about two centuries back. There is a fine well on the north side, and an ancient *dîpamâla* outside the enclosure. (5) Tâkleśvara is an old building dedicated to Mahâdeva and is to the west of that of Gaṇapati. There is an old *dharmaśâlâ* opening into the bâzâr through which this temple is entered. Besides these sanctuaries, there is a temple outside the town, about half a mile to the north-west, dedicated to Bhairava,—a quaint old structure, enclosed by walls; its *maṇḍapa* is divided into three aisles by two rows of low stone pillars supporting brick arches.

VI.—Purandar Tâlukâ.

III. 1. **Malha'rgad,** 5 miles north from Sâsvaḍ, fort built by Bhivarâv Yasavant and Krishṇaji Mâdhavrâv Phânsê about 1775 A.D. There is an outer line of fortification taking the triangular shape of the plateau, and an inner square one. It contains temples of Khaṇḍobâ and Mahâdeva. The main entrance is at the north-east corner.

III. 2. **Jejuri,** 10 miles E.S.E. from Sâsvaḍ. Temple of Khaṇḍobâ-Malhârî-Mârtaṇḍa-Bhairava-Mhâlasâkânta,—Khaṇḍobâ, because he has a dagger; Malhâri, because he killed the demon Maṇimalla. The temple was built by Malhârrâv Holkar and completed by Ahalyâbâî. There are several short inscriptions, all modern.

VII.—Bhimathadi Tâlukâ.

III. 1. **Dhond,** 8 miles E.N.E. from Pâṭas, on the Bhîmâ. (1) A temple of Bhairavadêva said to have been built by Mâdhavji Sinde, to whom the village was given as an *inâm*. It is of stone with a superstructure of brick. (2) Temple of Viṭhobâdeva, by the same; also in the village a large door called "Ves" of polished stone.

III. 2. **Pa'tas,** about 2 miles from the railway station. Temple of Nâgeśvara Mahâdeva is said to have been built about 200 years ago. It is constructed of hewn, polished stones, and has an audience-hall with verandahs on both sides.

III. 3. **Supa',** 8 miles S.S.W. from Pâṭas. (1) *Dargâh* of Shaman Shur Pîr, with a *dharmaśâlâ*. A large fair is held on the 16th Zilkâd. (2) Temple of Tukobâdêva built by Aṇṇâji Râv Marâṭhâ.

III. 4. **Kurkamb,** 5 miles south-east from Pâṭas. (1) Temple of Phirangâi Devî. (2) A similar but smaller one to the same idol stands on a hill near the village; in this latter there is an inscription dated 1681 :—

> श्री चरणीं तत्पर वंश निरंतर वणगोजी नाईक निंबाळकर त्याचे पुत्र मुधोजी नाईक त्याचे पुत्र संभाजी नाईक त्याचे पुत्र तुकाराम नाईक त्याचे पुत्र अमृतराव शाहाजी व पिराजी नाईक निंबाळकर त्याचे पुत्र संभाजी नाईक निंबाळकर देशमुख प्रांत फलटण देश याणीं श्रीचे आहेवरून देवालय समग्र सिद्ध केलें. शके १६८१ सौम्य नाम संवत्सरे. श्रावण शुद्ध पंचमी. श्रीरस्तु.

III. 5. **Roti,** 3 miles south of Pâṭas. Temple of Tukâidêvî built by the Medhê family.

III. 6. **Pa'rgaon,** 11 miles north-west from Pâṭas. A temple to the same idol, which is said to have been brought from Tuljâpur.

VIII.—Indâpur Tâlukâ.

III. 1. **Palasdeva** on the Bhîmâ, 13 miles north-west from Indâpur (18° 15′; 74° 57′), formerly called Ratnâpur. The temple of Śiva is built of stone below, and the upper portion is brick.

III. 2. **Narsingpur**, 12 miles south-east from Indâpur at the junction of the Bhîmâ and Nîrâ. Temple of Śrî Lakshmî-Narasinha, built by the Vinchurkar about 150 years ago. It is octagonal and built of black stone. The apex is of copper, gilt with gold. It is 70 feet high.

Pilgrimages are held in the month of Vaiśâkha. The idol of this temple is known by the name of Śrî Lakshmî-Narasinha, whence it is called the temple of Narasingpur. A fable is given in the *Purânas* called the *Narasinha Mahâtmya.* It is as follows:—Narasinha became incarnate for the sake of one of his votaries called Pralhâda. Pralhâda made a sand *pinḍi* for worship and through mistake left it there, and it afterwards became established. The reason for the name of Śrî Lakshmî-Narasinha is that the god was represented with a lion's face and man's body, and with a woman by him.

Bhor State.

III. 1. **Sirval**, 39 miles north from Sâtârâ. Temple of Kedâreśvara, built by Ambâji Devji Dêśpâṇḍê about 200 years ago, is a large and fine building about 200 years old: it was struck by lightning about six years ago. There is a series of seventeen Buddhist caves about two miles south-west from the town, one of them with a *dâgôba.* They are of the same plain type as those at Karâḍ (*Cave Temples of India.*)

III. 2. **Ra'nje**, 14 miles south-west from Poona: a Vaishṇava temple dedicated to Lakshmî-Nârâyaṇa.

Inscription:—On the temple, dated Śaka 1684.

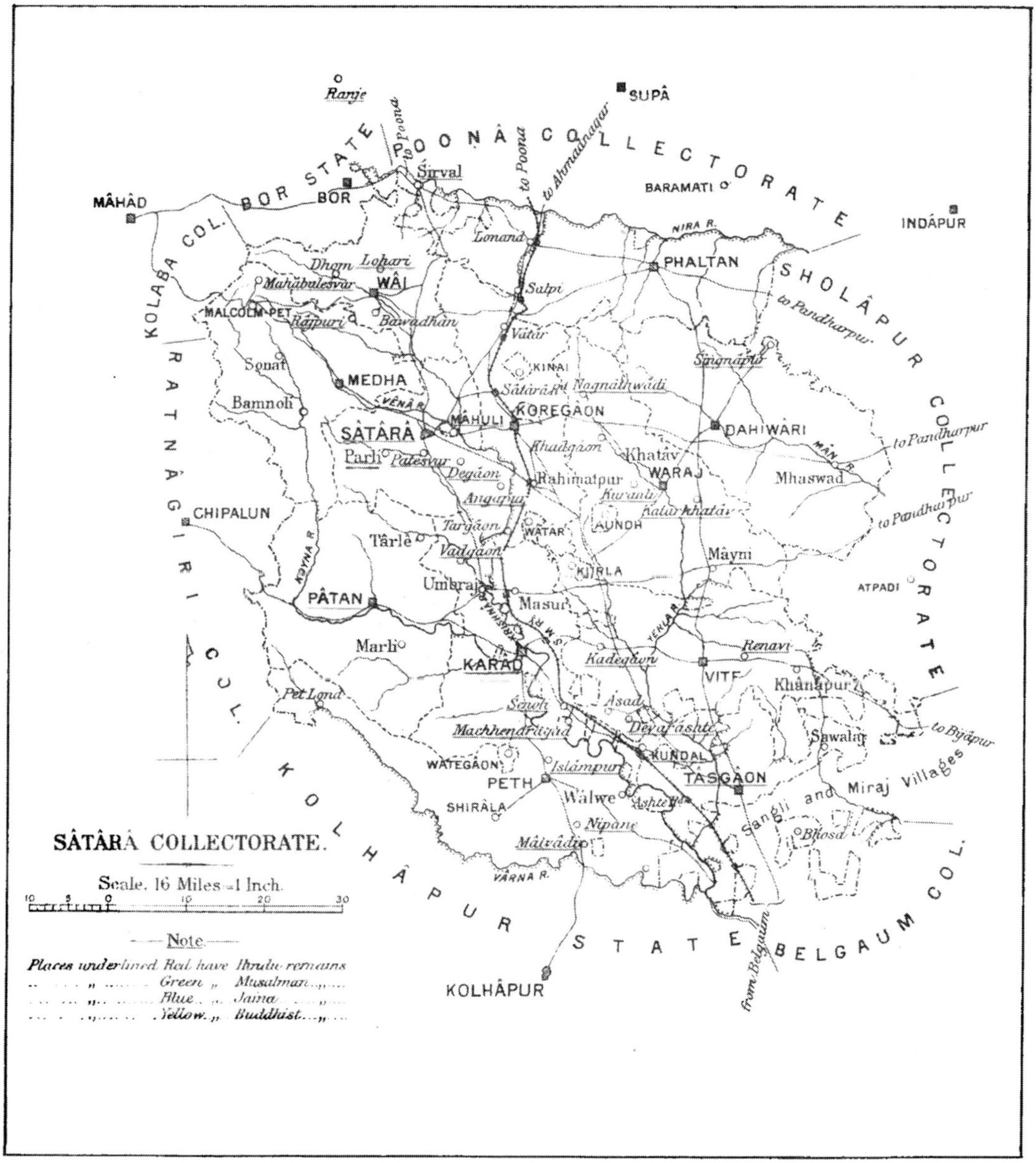
SÂTÂRÂ COLLECTORATE.
Scale, 16 Miles=1 Inch.
Note.
Places underlined Red have Hindu remains
" " Green " Musalman "
" " Blue " Jaina "
" " Yellow " Buddhist "
POONA COLLECTORATE
SHOLÂPUR COLLECTORATE
BOR STATE
KOLABA COL.
RATNÂGIRI COL.
KOLHÂPUR STATE
BELGAUM COL.
Sangli and Miraj Villages
Ranje
SUPÂ
BARAMATI
INDÂPUR
MÂHÂD
BOR
Sirval
to Poona
to Ahmadnagar
NIRA R.
Lonand
PHALTAN
Dhom
Lohari
Mahâbalesvar
WÂI
MALCOLM PET
Râjpuri
Bawadhan
Salpi
Vatar
to Pandharpur
Singnâpur
KINAI
Sonat
MEDHA
Sâtârâ Rd
Nagnâthwâdi
Bamnoli
VENÂ R.
SÂTÂRÂ
MÂHULI
KOREGAON
DAHIWÂRI
MÂN R.
Parli
Patesvar
Degâon
Khatâv
WARAJ
Mhaswad
Rahimatpur
Angapur
Kurauli
Kalar khatâv
CHIPALUN
Târle
Targâon
WATAR
AUNDH
Vadgaon
Mâyni
KIRLA
KOYNA R.
Umbraj
ATPADI
PÂTAN
Masur
YERLA R.
Renavi
Marli
KARAD
Kadegaon
VITE
Khânâpur
Pet Lond
Sowh
Asad
Machhendragad
Devarâshte
to Bijâpur
Sawalaj
KUNDAL
WATEGAON
Islâmpur
PETH
TASGÂON
Walwe
Ashte
SHIRÂLA
Nipane
Bhosa
Mâlvâdi
VÂRNA R.
from Belgaum
KOLHÂPUR

II.—SÂTÂRÂ ZILLÂ.

I.—Sâtârâ Tâlukâ.

III. 1. **Sa'ta'ra'**: Palace and Gardens form a quadrangular block of building occupying several acres, and the large open space of ground in front admits of their being seen to advantage. There is nothing very imposing about the façade, the white plastered surface of which is only broken by numerous large square windows and their wooden framework. A low verandah on wooden pillars runs along the ground floor. There is some carving on the wood-work, but it is too minute to produce any general effect on the building; a gateway leads into the courtyard, round which there is a broad colonnade. The walls are covered with paintings of mythological subjects and hunting scenes. It would be tedious to go into an enumeration of all the rooms, of which there are said to be 52, as a large portion of the building necessarily consists of the apartments of the Râṇî and royal retinue. On one side of the quadrangle is the hall of audience, at the upper end of which is a shrine dedicated to the great goddess of the Marâṭhâs, Bhavânî. It was built by Appâ Sâheb about 1844 A.D. It is 83 feet long, 45 feet broad, and 25 feet high. The roof is supported on two parallel longitudinal rows of teak pillars, 16 in each row, with horse-shoe arches between the pillars. The roof is hung with lamps. Outside are fountains. In a small room opening from the colonnade above mentioned, are the thrones of Râjas Appâ Sâheb and Shâhû. The carving in this room is exceedingly rich. The palace, although apparently one building, is really two, called respectively the old and new palaces. The former was built in 1820-21 by the Râja Pratâpsiñha. The latter, to which the rooms above described belong, was built about 1838 to supersede the Rangamahâl, another palace of less pretensions situated immediately under the fort. The old and new gardens and pleasure-house, to which the Râjâ was wont to repair in the hot weather, are separate from the palace and each other. The old ones were laid out about A.D. 1824-25 by Pratâpsiñha. The house is a plain building of one storey, with a large basin for fountains in front. It has one room, of which the wall and ceilings are covered with looking-glass. The new gardens, which are somewhat larger, were laid out in the same year for the Râjâ's brother, Appâ Sâheb. The pleasure-house is of two storeys, and has, besides the mirror room, a room hung with pictures, mostly works of native art: some, however, would seem to have been brought from England, and that, too, at no very distant date. (Copperplate grant *J.B.B.R.A.S.*, part viii., p. 3.)

II. 2. **Ma'huli** is about 3 miles east of Sâtârâ: owing to its situation at the confluence or *saṅgama* of the Kṛishṇâ and Vêṇâ rivers it is considered a place of great sanctity, and the dead from Sâtârâ and the surrounding villages are brought there to be burned. It is divided into,—(1) *Kshetra Mâhuli*, on the east bank of the Kṛishṇâ in British territory; (2) *Vasti Mâhuli*, on the west bank of that river, which is the property of the Pant Pratinidhi, by whose family most of the temples were built. (1.) Descending the river, the first temple that meets the eye is one on the east bank in Kshetra Mâhuli, dedicated to Râdhâ Śankara. It was built about 1825 A.D. by Bâî Sâheb Sachiv, the great-grandmother of the present Bhor Pant. The temple stands on what is called the Giri Ghâṭ, a long handsome platform of stone built by one Bâpu Bhaṭ *bin* Gôvind Bhaṭ about 1780 A.D. It is of basalt, and consists of a shrine and vestibule, or, perhaps as it ought to be called in this instance, a verandah supported by three small horse-shoe scolloped arches. The dome is of brick and, as far as it has any geometrical form at all, is conical; but it is broken up into gradually diminishing rows of stucco ornamentation, in which are niches filled with images. On each side of the entrance there is a *dîpamâla*. (2.) On the same side of the river is the temple of Bilveśvara Mahâdeva built about 1742 A.D. by Śrîpatrâv Pant Pratinidhi. The absence of Muhammadan forms shows that it is much older than the last. It consists of a vestibule and shrine, but the vestibule is square or nearly so, and has no opening but a low door. The roof is supported by a few pillars, each of which is in alternate portions square, round, or octagonal. The front is about 30 feet long, and plain. The sides gradually contract by a series of offsets, which run up nearly to the top of the dome, so that the back wall is only 5 or 6 feet long. With the exception of the upper portion of the dome, which is of brick covered and ornamented with stucco, this temple is built of grey stone, and has a very solid appearance. It is not enclosed in any way. The bull is so close to the door of the vestibule that there is hardly room to enter. It is surmounted by a square stone canopy supported on each side by a broad low pointed arch, and its style seems to indicate a later date than the temple. In front are a few tombs where Gosâvîs and other holy men have been buried. The *ghâṭ* near this spot was built by Anandrâv Bhivrâv Dêshmukh Angâpurkar about four years before this temple. (3.) The next is on the same bank as the last two, but at some distances from them and the village, and close to the Sâtârâ and Koregâon road, which in fact skirts it. It was built and dedicated to Râmeśvara by Paraśurâma Nârâyaṇa Ângal of Dehgâon about 1700 A.D. Looking at it from the opposite bank, the chief object that attracts the observer's notice is the very fine flight of steps leading up to it from the river-bed. One flight with its broad platform was commenced by Bâjirâv II., but never finished. Though forming part of the whole structure, it would lead, if finished, rather to the side of the temple than to the temple itself. The other flight begins nearly where the first leaves off, and at an angle to it, and is said to be also the work of Paraśurâma Ângal. Half-way up it on either side is a small cloister of two arches, which would be perfectly circular but for a small notch in the keystone. The roof is domed and formed by concentric layers of stone, each projecting over the one below, and so diminishing in circumference till only a small hole is left sufficient to admit one stone. At the top of the steps are two *dîpamâlas*, one on either side; on the right is a small shrine with an image of the Trimûrti. In front is a bull with his face towards the door of the vestibule. He is very richly ornamented with chains and bells. Between his feet is a small *liṅga* overshadowed by the cobra, with two women paying adoration to it. The canopy is supported at the corners by pillars, which are square and round or octagonal in alternative courses. Above is a low octagonal dome on two courses—the lower plain, the upper with a few figures. Above this, again, is a representation of the lotus, but the stucco has fallen off. The doorway consists of a porch of stone supported on half pillars. The vestibule is too small to require any support for its roof. The only light it receives is from the low door by which it is entered. There are three domes: the lowest is over the vestibule; next comes one a little higher; and adjoining it the highest of all. They are, as usual, of brick and stucco surmounted by a representation of the lotus. Behind the temple is a cloister of five arches like those already described. A small door leads into a shrine with five small figures in black basalt. The central one is a representation of Śiva and Pârvatî. At one end is Hanumân in an upright position with his hands clasped together. (4.) Temple of Sangameśvara Mahâdeva is, as its name indicates, close to the junction of the two rivers, on the west bank of the Krishna and the north bank of the Vênâ and nearly opposite No. 2. From the bank of the Krishṇâ two flights of steps lead up to the courtyard wall, in which there is a small door opening into the quadrangular court in which the temple is situated. The temple consists of a small open verandah, in which there is a roughly executed painting of Lakshmi, and a vestibule and shrine. In front is the sacred bull under a canopy supported by four pillars. The breadth at the back is gradually diminished by a series of offsets which are carried up into the dome. The architecture is pure Hindu. The pillars are round or octagonal and square in alternate courses, and the roof is formed of long stones which stretch diagonally from pillar to pillar so as to form a series of lozenge or diamond-shaped spaces, filled in with square stones of less size. The flying buttresses to the platform of the sacred bull and the top of the dome deserve notice. As usual the body of the building is of basalt and the dome of brick and stucco, like No. 2. It is said to have been built by Śrîpatrâv Pant Pratinidhi, and its date may be approximately fixed at 1679 A.D. Just below this temple, and at the actual junction of the rivers, is a triangular plot of ground occupied by several tombs built over the burial-places of a Gosâvi (named Banśapuri) and his disciples. The largest, under which the Gosâvi himself is said to be buried, is an octagonal building of grey basalt, surmounted by a low dome. The sides are open, and the triangular heads of the openings are scolloped and richly carved above; a broad ledge is carried round supported on elegant scrolls. Inside is a *liṅga* and sacred bull. The next in size is square with a horse-shoe opening about 6 feet high and carved pilasters on each side. The dome is of brick plastered and fluted: *liṅga* and bull inside. The third is a mere canopy supported on square pillars over the *liṅga* and bull; the dome is fluted. There are two others which do not deserve any special notice. (5) Viśveśvara Mahâdeva, the largest of the Mâhuli temples on the south side of the Venâ, at its confluence with the Krishṇâ, is said to have been built by Śrîpatrâv Pant Pratinidhi about 1735 A.D. It is of basalt, and enclosed by an irregular-shaped courtyard, open on the side of the river, from which it is approached by a flight of steps. The high platform on which it is raised; the low colonnade which runs round the greater part of it; the short thick pillars in alternate courses of round, octagonal, and square; the lozenge-figured stone roof, the breadth increasing from the front by offsets, and then decreasing in a similar way behind, show that it is a building of purely Hindu architecture. The length from back to front is about 50 feet. The greatest breadth is 20 feet, the least 5 feet. The interior consists of a vestibule and shrine. In the wall of the former there are two images of Gaṇapati and Lakshmi respectively. The latter is of marble. The dome is of the usual material. The squareness of the form in this and other domes of the same period contrasts with the round domes of a later one. The animal forms, carved in the capitals of the pillars and the cornices, deserve notice. The sacred bull is on the usual platform surmounted by a canopy and octagonal dome, the niches of which are filled with mythological figures, and are divided from each other by figures of men on elephants. On two sides of the courtyard are cloisters with broad low pointed arches and square pillars; they are for cooking purposes, or hostelries for visitors to the temple. On another side is a building of a similar kind but incomplete. The arches of it are narrower and more pointed. At the entrance of the vestibule is a fine bell on which there is apparently no writing, but the date, in English figures, of 1744. I could not glean any information as to its history; but it was, I suspect, taken by the Marâthâs from a Portuguese church in the Konkan. In one of the temples on the Krishṇâ at Menavali, near Wâi, there is a bell which is said to have been presented by the builder of the temple, the great Nânâ Phaḍnavîs. There is a tradition in that case that it was taken from the Portuguese, a tradition which is almost converted into fact by the inscription "Bene sonantibus cymbalis laudate Dominum." A similar bell is said to have been brought by Ṅânâ Phaḍnavîs out of Mâhuli Fort and given to the temple at Bhimâ Śankara, where it now is. (6) Temple of Râmachandra at the back of the last, to which it is very inferior in every respect, is of basalt, and said to have been built by Trimbak Viśvanâth Pêthê in 1772 A.D. It is very small, and consists merely of verandah and shrine. In the latter are figures, in brass, of Râma, Lakshmaṇa, and Sîtâbâî. The wall behind them is panelled with broad low arches and painted with flowers, &c. The dome consists of only two polygonal courses. (7) Temple of Vithobâ built by Jotipant Bhâgvat of Chinchnerâ about A.D. 1730. It originally consisted of a small verandah, with carved wooden pillars opening into the shrine by a low Muhammadan arch. A hall or vestibule, with wooden pillars and door all round was added fifteen or twenty years ago. The roof is hung with lamps. (8) Temple of Kṛishṇâbâî, built by Kṛishṇa Dikshit Chiplûnkar about 1754 A.D., does not deserve particular notice. (9) Temple to Kṛishṇêśvara Mahâdeva built by Kṛishṇa Dikshit Chiplûnkar, about 1790 A.D. (10) Temple to Bhairavadeva, built by Krishnabhat Tâtkê about 1770 A.D. It is on a very small scale, and consists of shrine and open vestibule or verandah with three small arches. A hall with wooden pillars like that in No. 7 has been recently added. (11) A temple with a handsome flight of steps from the river, begun by the Râṇî of Sâtârâ in 1865. It is on the right of the road from Sâtârâ. Besides these temples there are, on each side of the road leading to the ferry, several tombs or cenotaphs to members of the late royal family of Sâtârâ and others. There is some simple but handsome stone carving on one or two of them. The figure of a dog sitting, which is to be seen on one of them, is said to mark the burial-place of a favourite dog of Râjâ Shâhu called the "Veḍâ Râjâ" from his eccentricities. It is probably the one which on one occasion he dressed in gold brocade, and exhibited in full *darbâr*, and for whose use he kept up a palanquin establishment. The dog had once saved him from a tiger (*vide* Grant Duff's *History of the Marâthâs*, vol. II. page 30). (12) The temple of Bhârgavarâma, in the small shrine of which are the images of Paraśurâma, his father Jamadagni, and his mother Reṇukâ. It has *inâm* land attached to it.

3. **Parli** is the name given to an isolated hill about 6 miles west of Sâtârâ. The fort at the top is called Sajjanagaḍ, and was built by one of the Emperors of Dehli about 700 years ago. Additions were made by one Nâro Ballâl Soni, Mâmlatdâr, in 1775 A.D. It is now very much out of repair: over the doorway is a Persian inscription,—not translated. The temple was built about 1860 A.D. by Akâbâi and Divâkar Gosâvi, disciples of Śivâji's spiritual guide, Râmdâs Svâmi, to whom the temple is dedicated and who lies buried here. Paraśurâm Bhâu Śrigâṅvkar repaired and ornamented this temple in 1800 and 1830 A.D., and Vaijnâth Bhâgvat, of Yavateśvara, built the verandah. It is of basalt with dome of brick and chunam.

III. 4. **Anga'pur.**—The temple, which is dedicated to Gaṇapati, was built by Anandrâv Bhivrâv, Deśmukha of Angâpur, in 1779 A.D. It is of stone, with a dome of brick and stucco.

III. 5. **Pa'tes'vara,** 6 miles south-east from Sâtârâ. Near the summit of a hill called Pâtêśvara are some five caves. Besides the caves and buildings attached to them there are three or four temples almost on the summit of the hill. One of them, sacred to Mahâdeva, is of moderate size, enclosed in a courtyard with a fine flight of steps leading down to a tank close adjoining. The other temples are small, sacred to Mahâdeva and other idols.

The caves are now, with the exception of No. 4, crowded with *liṅgas* cut out of detached blocks of stone, some of very large size. Including those in the temples, 43 were counted altogether. These caves were probably of Brahmanical origin (see *Jour. B. B. R. A. Soc.*, vol. III. Part II. p. 68).

III. 6. **Degaon.**—Temple of Śrî Pâtêśvara with large *sabhā-maṇḍapa* and *śikhara*.

III. 7. **Khadgaon.**—An excavation to the west called Morghal.

II.—Jâvli Tâlukâ.

III. 1. **Mahâbaleśvara.**—Temple described *J. B. B. R. A. Soc.*, Vol. IX. p. 250; vol. X. pp. 1-18.

III. 2. **Râjpuri**, 4 miles south-west from Wâi and about 3 west of Bâwadhan. A group of rudely cut Brahmanical caves, about 1,300 feet above the valley. They communicate with one another by a passage inside the rock. They face eastward and extend about 100 feet in length.

Ia. **Inscription.**—A detached slab of stone, leaning against the front of the cave, bears an inscription in old Devanâgarî characters.

III.— Wâi Tâlukâ.

III. 1. **Bâwadhan**, 4 miles south-east of Wâi. Two small caves at about 600 feet above the level of the valley and very difficult of access; the most southerly is a cell 9′ by 7′, with bed-place at the back and a stone bench on the right side; the other is similar and about 65 yards northward.

III. 2. **Lohâri**, 4 miles north of Wâi. On the south-western face of a short lofty spur are eight excavations in a line extending about a furlong along the hill, and at an elevation of at least 400 feet above the valley. The four largest are evidently early Buddhist monastic residences, and one of these has had two rows of pillars, three in each, from front to back, and the remains of some sculpture on the right hand wall, which, however, may possibly have been an after insertion; another, close to it, has a *dâgoba* in a shrine 10 feet square at the back, a cell on each side of it, and four in the right wall, with rock beds.

III. 3. **Wâi.**—At this place there are 49 temples built by the Râste family alone, besides others of older date; as it is unnecessary to particularize each, only those of importance are mentioned. Commencing from above, the first group of buildings is on the north bank of the Kṛishṇâ, and consists of a *ghâṭ vâdâ* and temple. (1) The *ghâṭ* goes by the name of Gangâpuri and is a flight of 12 steps. The first portion, 200 feet in length, was built by Gangâdhar Râste of cut-stone in 1789. To this, one Bhâu Jośi added 76 feet and Bâjirâv II. 80 feet. There is now, therefore, an unbroken length of 350 feet. At the back of this is a plain brick wall through which a door opens into the street with the Gangâpuri Vâdâ (now the Munsif's Court) on the left and the temple of Umâ Mahêśvara Panchâyatana on the right. The temple on the right was, like the *ghâṭ*, built by Gangâdhar Râste and about five years before it. It consists of a vestibule and shrine, and is about 40 feet high. It has all the Muhammadan forms of architecture common at the period. In the four corners are separate shrines dedicated to Vishṇu, Lakshmî, Gaṇpati, and Sûrya;—Vishṇu's is on the left on entering, and has a wooden *maṇḍapa*, the back wall of which is covered with figures, so are also the outer walls. The great cluster of river temples begins at some distance nearly opposite to the travellers' bungalow. (2) A shrine with dome containing a marble bull and the image of Mahâdeva Dhâkleśvara. It stands on a low *ghâṭ*, 75 feet long. (3) In a line with it, but near the bank on an upper ledge of the same *ghâṭ*, is another temple to Gaṇgârâmeśvara Mahâdeva, built by Gaṇgâdhar Râste about 1780 A.D. It is of basalt, and consists of an open verandah with 3 scolloped arches and a shrine. The breadth in front is 32 feet. The length from front to back is about 26 feet, with the dome, which is of brick and stucco with blank panels; the height is probably about 40 feet. In front is the sacred bull with a plain canopy. (4) A temple to Gaṇapati built by Gaṇpatrâv Bhikâji Râste in 1762 at a cost of Rs. 1,50,000, and a *ghât* 163 feet in length, built by Anandrâv Bhikâji. Besides the usual verandah and shrine, in which is a huge image of Gaṇapati painted red, there is a covered court or *maṇḍapa* 60 feet by 30. The roof is flat, and composed of square cut stones cemented with chunam. The walls are of the unusual thickness of 4 feet, which gives considerable dignity to the small arches, 5 on a side and 3 at the end, with which they are pierced. Except the dome, which is pyramidal or conical and of brick covered with white plaster and fluted, the material used is grey basalt. The total height is about 70 feet. (5) Ascending the bank is a temple to Kâśi Viśveśvara Mahâdeva, standing in a quadrangular court 216 feet by 95 feet, surrounded by a wall. The temple was built by Anandrâv Bhikâji in 1757 A.D., and consists of vestibule and shrine. Its length from front to back is 49 feet. The façade is about 28 feet from side to side. In style the Muhammadan forms prevail to a considerable extent. The spire has three rows of figures and a Muhammadan dome; the *maṇḍapa* of the temple is domed. The large bull in front, under a plain canopy with plain scolloped arches, is carved out of a magnificent piece of black basalt; the bells and flowers with which it is decorated are very finely cut. The most conspicuous part of this building, however, is a covered Kuṇḍa *maṇḍapa* at the east entrance, the roof of which is of squared stone cemented with chunam, and supported on 16 lofty pillars 10 feet apart, with neat semicircular moulded arches between them. On each side is a *dîpamâla*. (6) Temple to Mahâlakshmî built by Anandrâv Bhikâji in 1778 A.D. at a cost of Rs. 2,75,630. It is away from the river, on the east side of the bâzâr. It is about 70 feet high, and consists of a vestibule and shrine, which together measure about 70 feet from back to front. The façade is 39 feet from side to side. The vestibule is open in front with two pillars and pilasters *in antis*. The corners at the top are rounded off by scolloped work. There is a trap-door in the floor, and the roof is formed of large slabs stretching from lintel to lintel. The *maṇḍapa* has two doors on each side, and the porch is wider than the *maṇḍapa*. The *maṇḍapa* has 5 pillars in depth with 2 in width, and on a lower step an additional range over a stylobate approached by three steps and tread. (7) Temple to Vishṇu, built in 1774 A.D. by Ânandrâv Bhikâji Râste at a cost of Rs. 2,16,250. A covered court 48′×′18 with a roof of cut stone without intermediate support leads to a raised verandah with three small Muhammadan arches, behind which is the shrine. The walls are very thick, 5 scolloped arches on each side and 3 in front—a small *chhatri* of Garuḍa in front and a marble image.

The following temples are enumerated to complete the list of those on the river, but do not call for any special mention. The date is a clue to the style of architecture. The prevalence of Muhammadan forms may be assumed in those that are less than a century old. (8) The temple to Mahâdeva, built by Govindpant Velankar about 1744 A.D., east of Kâśi Viśveśvara. (9) Temple to the same by Bâbâ Appâ Sâheb Sâthê, 1854 A.D. (10) Temple to the same with *dharmâśâlâ* attached by Chimanrâv Nârâyana. (11) Temple to Dattâtreya, built by a mendicant named Venkobâ Bâvâ in 1861 A.D. on a *ghât* made by Ânandrâv Bhikâji, 1785 A.D. (12) Temple to Mahâdeva by Chimaṇbhat Dhirulkar about 1808 A.D. (13) To the same, built about 1760 A.D. (14) To the same, built by Meghaśyâm-Nâyak Megrek about 1740 A.D. (15) Temple to Vithobâ by Bâi Sâheb, the great-grandmother of the Bhor Pant, mentioned as the builder of a temple at Mâhuli. (16) Temple to Mahâdeva, built by Vishṇu Bhat Dikshit about 1760 A.D. (17) Temple to Mahâdeva, built by Venkambhaṭ Dhakne about 1760 A.D. (18) The Râste's Vâḍâs.—Of these there are several in and about the town of Wâi. The only one that requires special notice is the Moti Bâgh, which is about 1½ miles out of Wâi, standing in a large garden with water-tower and fountains. The *vâḍâ* was built about 1789 A.D. by Ânandrâv Bhikâji Râste, and is said to have cost Rs. 1,02,000. The interior walls are covered with paintings, the colour of which is unfortunately rapidly disappearing. The ceiling is very elaborately painted and gilded. (*J. B. B. R. A. S.*, Part XIII. p. 55, Wâi Caves ; *Cave Temples of India.*)

III. 4. **Menavali.**—About two miles from Wâi. Temple of Krishṇâbâi (*see* also end of entry " Mâhuli ").

III. 5. **Dhom.**—On the north bank of the Kṛishṇâ, about 5 miles above Wâi ; the principal temple is between the village and the river, and is dedicated to Mahâdeva. It is built of basalt, and consists of a shrine with a verandah in front of three small Saracenic scolloped arches supported on pillars about 6 feet high. The arches are covered with leaves and what appear to be fir-cones. Beyond the arches there is on each side of the façade a broad band of wall carved in arabesques. The height of the building, including the dome, is probably not more than 40 feet. Opposite the entrance is a bull of polished basalt under a canopy surmounted by a dome. It is seated upon the back of a turtle (which is found in nearly all the temples above mentioned) represented in the act of swimming. To complete the illusion, it is intended that the surrounding basin should be filled with water, which does not appear to be now done. Around this principal temple are four others dedicated, respectively, to Narasiṅha, Gaṇapati, Lakshmî, and Vishṇu. Several of the images in these temples are of yellow marble, said to have been brought from Âgrâ. One, which stands outside by itself, is a representation of the S'iva Panchâyatana. Four heads look to the four cardinal points of the compass, and the fifth to the sky. The five temples were built about 1780 A.D. by one Mahâdevarâv S'ivarâma, Sâvkâr of Poona, where his descendants now live. A side door from the courtyard of this temple leads to a *ghât* built by one Nârâyaṇrâv Vaidya about 100 years ago. On the right is a small temple to Râma attributed to Bâjirâv II. The conical dome has been broken short off by the fall of a tree. Below this, and facing the river, is a sort of cloister containing an image of Gaṇapati. The arches are pointed. The date probably about 1780 A.D.

III. About half a mile up the river is a small temple to Mahâdeva, built by the Râjâ Śâhû, who reigned at Sâtârâ between 1708 and 1750 A.D., and came to Dhom to bathe in the Kṛishṇâ.

II *b*. 6.—**Mhasva.** Two banyan trees. There is no record whatever of the age of these trees. They are known to be at least 200 years old, and they are probably double that age. Although the centres have decayed, the outer trunks do not show the slightest signs of any diminution in their vitality. The larger tree is 450 yards in circumference; the smaller about 100 yards less.

IV.—Koregâon Tâlukâ.

III. **Dhuma'lva'di,** close to the Sâtârâ Road railway station. A cave in which is an image of Pârśvanâtha about two and a half feet high with the head broken off. The cave is very irregular in shape and is nearly filled with water. About half-way up the hill is an excavation known as the "Khâmb tâki," originally no doubt a cave temple, now filled with mud and water to within three feet of the roof. The roof is supported by massive pillars. These, where intact, bear a simple ornamentation. On the top of the hill are the remains of an old fort, and the entrance to the upper cave is enclosed within the wall which defends the gate. The most important remains on the top of the hill are a substantially built *mâsjid* and a simple stone-building which may have been a bomb proof magazine. There is a tomb of a Musalmân Pîr still kept in repair.

V.—Mân Tâlukâ.

III. 1. **S'ingna'pur,** about 44 miles E.N.E. of Sâtârâ (17° 51′; 74° 43′), the scene of a large yearly Hindu festival held in honour of Śambhu Mahâdeva, or Kamaleśvara, to which as many as 40,000 people go. The temple is on a hill, and thus forms a striking object from some distance. It is built on a plan similar to that of many of the temples of the Dakhan, and consists of a courtyard, an ante-chamber, and an idol chamber. It was rebuilt in 1708 by one Basvant Raikhogai in the time of Śivâji II. The courtyard is an oblong, about 129 feet long and 92 broad, entered from all four sides by gateways, and contains, besides the temple proper, various small rooms, a *nagárkhána* and a small temple of Nandi. The temple itself consists of an oblong ante-chamber, 46 feet by 49 feet, entered from the north, south, and east by three small doorways, about 3¼ feet square. To the west is another doorway, 4 feet wide by 6 feet high, communicating with the idol chamber. This room is about 11 feet long and wide and 17 feet high, and in it is the image of Mahâdeva Śambhu. Over the temple is a spire of brick, the rest of the temple being of stone; throughout it are carved images of gods and mythological beings, and also coloured representations of animals.

III. 2. **Katarkhata'v,** 35 miles E.S.E. from Sâtârâ (17° 34′; 74° 35′). The temple of Śri Kâtareśvara; the walls and pillars are of stone and carved. It is said to be very old, and measures 45′ by 28′. The upper portion is of brick.

Inscription:—On the front is a Dêvanâgarî inscription weather-worn.

III. 3. **Kurauli,** 4 miles S.S.E. from Khatâv. A similar old temple, but larger; repaired in late times.

Inscription:—On the pavement, but much effaced.

III. 4. **Wadgaon,** 24 miles south-east from Sâtârâ. Temple of Jayarâm Svâmi, with some inscriptions.

III. 5. **Na'gna'thva'di,** 20 miles east from Sâtârâ. Temple of Nâganâtha, partly cut in the rock; a genuine Snake temple, with an old inscription.

III. 6. **Sangames'vara,** 36 miles east of Sâtârâ. An old Śaiva temple, with carved pillars and effaced inscription.

VI.—Khatav Tâlukâ.

(No returns sent in.)

VII.—Khânâpur Tâlukâ.

III. 1. **Devara'shte,** 16 miles north-west from Tâsgâon (17° 10'; 74° 27'). An old octagonal temple of Sâgareśvara, with three reservoirs of water.

III. 2. **Kadegaon,** 10 miles N.N.E. from Devarâshṭê. Four temples of Eknâth, one of Mâruti, and two of Viṭhobâ; one of the latter with a *manḍapa* in front.

III. 3. **Kundal,** 4 miles south-east from Devarâshṭê and 14 W.N.W. from Tâsgâon. Close to this village are the Kunḍal Caves of which there are two groups; the principal one of thirteen caves is in the north-eastern face of the hill, the other of three caves is in the southern face. In the first, Cave 1 measures 16′ by 15′; No. 2, 12′ 6″ by 7′ 6″; No. 3, 27′ 6″ by 22′, having a row of 3 plain square pillars across the centre; No. 4 measures 14′ 6″ by 9′; No. 5 is a water-tank 11′ square, with steps within, leading down to the water; No. 6 is another cistern 5′ by 11′ with a doorway, and having a large moulded pilaster, or half pillar carved on the left wall: the partition between this and No. 5 is cut away at half its height, leaving a half column in the centre corresponding to the pilaster opposite. This is the only original ornament in the group. No. 7 measures 26′ 6″ by 17′ 6″; Nos. 8, 9, and 10 are smaller rooms. No. 11 is a wide passage round a shrine, behind which is a deep cistern. In the second group, No. 14 is a room 19′ by 15′ with a recess 7′ square at the back, on the back wall of which is a rude modern bas-relief covering the whole. On the right hand portion of the back wall of the main room are remains of two old figures, life-size and in high relief; nothing remains of one but the feet, and the other is much worn. No. 16 seems to be partially a natural cavern, with a deep cistern in one corner and a built front; an artificial ceiling within is supported by 15 rude stone pillars. These caves are evidently Brahmanical. (**Surveyed.**)

III. 4. **A'sad,** 6 miles north-west from Kunḍal. In a *khind* leading to Yerê is a small tank cut in the solid rock, the front said to be supported by a pillar.

III. 5. **Senoli,** 5 miles west from Âsad. In the hill over the village is a small natural cavern under a low scarp; a rude masonry cell has been built in it, and several little wooden bulls and other idols lie about.

III. 6. **Rena'vi,** 18 miles north-east from Kunḍal (17° 17′; 74° 40′). On the edge of the tableland near the village, in a projecting summit of laterite, is a small irregular cell with an entrance only about 2 feet high. There are several temples round about: one rather ancient.

Inscription:—In Dêvanâgarî on the door-sill of the portico of this temple.

VIII.—Tâsgâon Tâlukâ.

III. 1. **Ta'sgaon,** 60 miles south-east from Sâtâra and 15 north of Miraj (17° 1′; 74° 40′). A temple of considerable size and celebrity, dedicated to Gaṇapati. It was begun in 1779 by Paraśurâm Bhâu Patavardhan, and finished in 1799 by Appâ Sâheb, his son. It consists of a courtyard and a temple inside. The most striking feature is the *gopura* or tower, over the principal entrance to the courtyard, consisting of seven storeys, gradually decreasing till they culminate in a mere ridge. The lower storey is of stone and the remainder of brick. In the courtyard is the temple itself, over which is a brick spire. The body of the temple is of stone undecorated with sculpture, but on the walls outside are rude paintings of mythological subjects. In the temple there are images of Gaṇapati, Vishṇu, Sûrya, and a goddess. Some of the devotees reside in the courtyard.

III. 2. **Bhosa,** 9 miles south-east from Tâsgâon, 10 miles N.N.E. from Miraj (16° 57′; 74° 46′). On the top of a high hill near the village are a number of curious cave-temples with Kanarese inscriptions on slabs. On the very summit of the hill is a tower with a stair inside; it is a station of the Trigonometrical Survey.

IX.—Vâlvâ Tâlukâ.

III. 1. **Nipa'ni (Yede).** A fine temple of Mallikârjuna on a hill.

III. 2. **Machhindragad** (17° 9; 74° 20). A temple of Machhindranâtha.

X.—Karâd Tâlukâ.

IIa. **Kara'd,** about 30 miles S.S.E. from Sâtârâ at the junction of the Koyanâ and Krishṇâ rivers (17° 17′; 74° 14′). (1) About 3 miles S.S.W. from the town, at the angle of the junction of the Kṛishṇâ and Koyanâ valleys, is a group of about fifty-four Buddhist caves, of a very plain and probably mostly early type, generally resembling the groups at Kuḍâ, Mahâḍ and elsewhere south of Poona and Bombay (described in *Jour. Bom. B. R. As. Soc.*, Vol. III. Pt. II. p. 58; Pt. XIII. p. 58; *Arch. Sur. Report*, IV.; and in *Cave Temples of India*). **(Surveyed.)**

IIb. (2) The Jami Masjid with two lofty dome-crowned minarets stands in the middle of the town. It was built, according to an inscription in the interior, by one Ibrâhim Khân, son of Kamalkhân, probably a Thânedâr in the years 1566-69, during the reign of Ali Adil Shâh of Bijâpur, when the kingdom of Bijâpur was still flourishing. The mosque and minarets stand on a stone platform about 50 feet square and 31 feet high; the latter rise to a height of about 40 feet above this platform, and are dome-shaped. For 8 feet they are made of stone, and the remainder of the structure is of brick-work, considerably cracked and unsound. One minaret in particular is in an unsafe condition, owing to a curb of wood, which had been inserted at a considerable height from the ground, having become rotten. The mosque itself is an ordinary stone structure of considerable size. Both it and the minarets are decorated with carving and covered with plaster, but not painted. In the mosque, on the arches and pillars, are several inscriptions in Persian and Arabic. The following are translations made by the Oriental Translator:—(1) On a pillar: "Ibrâhim Khân *bin* Kamil Khân *bin* Ismâel Khân, servant in the house of God." (2) Round a pillar: When the assistance of God shall come and the victory and they shall see the people enter into the religion of God by troops, celebrate the praise of thy Lord, and ask pardon of him, for he is inclined to forgive." (3) "During the time of Shâh Ali Adil Shâh, the shelter of all the people and the shadow of the favour of God—may he continue faithful and enjoy health and Khital (or grant) to Ibrâhim Kamil Khân, a friend of the family." (4) On another pillar: "The beggarly, powerless and dustlike and powerless Pehelvân Ali *bin* Ahmad Ispahâni, a servant of God in this house of God. Sunah 963. Titled (?) Tuzyet Khân completed on this date. Pray for the welfare of the builder of this mosque." (5) An Arabic inscription on a pillar: "May God forgive its builder for the sake of Muhammad and his descendants." (6) An Arabic inscription on the top of an arch: "I bear witness that there is certainly no God but God, that he is only one and that he has no sharers, and I bear witness that Muhammad is certainly his servant and prophet." (7) There is an inscription at the foot of an arch in Kufic characters which cannot be made out (a rubbing is desiderated). (8) On the top there are the following inscriptions: "O Ali, there is nobody young but Ali. There is no sword but the 'Zul Fikr.' God send blessing to Muhammad the chosen [of God], Ali the approved, Hassan the elect (of God), Husain who became a martyr at Kerbalâh, Zainu'l Abidin, Muhammad Bâkar, Jâfar Sadik Musa-ul-Kâzim, Muhammad Taki Ali Naki, Hasan Ashkâri, Muhammad Madhi: the most high and glorious God hath said. But he only shall visit the temples of God who believeth in God and the last day and is constant at prayer, and payeth the legal alms, and feareth God alone. These perhaps may become of the number of those who are rightly directed." "Do ye reckon the giving drink to the pilgrims and the visiting of the holy temple *to be actions as meritorious as those performed* by him who believeth in God and the last day and fighteth for the religion of God? The most high and glorious God hath said—Regularly perform thy prayer at the declension of the sun, at the first darkness of the night, and the prayer of daybreak; for the prayer of daybreak is borne witness unto *by the angels*, and watch *some part* of the night in the same exercise as a work of supererogation, for peradventure the Lord will raise thee to an honourable station. And say—O Lord, cause me to enter with a favourable entry and cause me to come forth with a favourable coming forth; and grant me from thee an assisting power."

XI.—PÂTAN TÂLUKÂ.

II *a*. **Pa'tan**, 21 miles S.S.W. from Sâtârâ and 20 miles W.N.W. from Karâd. Two or three miles to the north-west of Pâtan, in the hills bounding the Keḍa valley on the west, are two Buddhist caves. They are in a ravine under the main hills; their position is marked by a large thatched temple on a spur above at a considerably higher elevation. They are cut in a small overhanging scarp in the *nâlâ* bed and the water falls over in front. The platform in front has been broken and worn away till it now leaves a scarcely practicable path from one to the other. The larger cave consists of a room 19 feet by 18; the front, much ruined, has had a doorway with a window 3 feet wide on each side. On the right hand side near the front is a recess 2¾ feet above the floor and 5½ feet long. In the left angle at the back is a seat 9' long and 2½' broad. At the back are two cells 6½ square; the left one containing a bed or bench 1 foot in height. Between them, in the middle of the back, is a recess 2¾ feet from the ground, 6' wide and 2' deep. Close to this, on the right side, is the other cave 10' wide near the front, 12' at the back, and about 15' deep and 9½ ft. high. It contains a very perfect *dágoba* of the plain pattern found in the earlier caves, with the *chhatra* carved on the roof. The doorway is 4' wide.

III.—AHMADNAGAR ZILLA.

I.—AHMADNAGAR TÂLUKÂ.

1. **Ahmadnagar.** A few only of its old Muhammadan buildings remain, among
I b. which, perhaps, the little Damri Masjid is the most interesting, though the great octagonal
II a. tomb of Salâbat Khân is best known. Beside these two buildings, there are the Faria-
II a. bâgh, the tomb of Nizâm Ahmad Shâh, the Bihisti Bâgh, Alamgir's Dargâh, and a few other buildings of lesser note, together with the fort. The little Damri Masjid is a small building of very neat design, and is decorated with surface ornament, much after the style of the Andu Masjid and similar buildings at Bijâpur. It is, perhaps, not generally known that Alamgir, or Aurangzib, was buried in two tombs, one of which is at Ahmadnagar. The other is the well-known tomb at Rauza above the Elura caves and not far from Daulatâbâd. It would seem that his body was embalmed after death, when his heart and intestines were buried at Ahmadnagar. Over these has been built a large platform upon which is a masonry tomb. Beside it is the usual mosque and other accompanying buildings, and the whole is surrounded by a wall. It lies some distance outside the city on the east. (**Surveyed.**)

II a. 2. **Mehekri,** 7 miles east from Ahmadnagar. Salâbat Khân's tomb, commonly called Chând Bîbî's Mahâl, an octagonal dome surrounded by a three-storeyed verandah: it is 100 feet high and about the same in maximum diameter; now used as a military sanitarium. (**Surveyed.**)

II.—PÂRNER TÂLUKÂ.

II a. 1. **Dhoke,** near Tâkli, 12 miles north of Pârnêr :—The Dhokêśvara Cave is a large hall with triple cells, on the east side of one of two rugged hills rising from a stony plateau. The largest is 20 yards deep and 15 wide, the front open and supported by two massive square pillars and two pilasters; a little inside of these another similar row supports a great architrave running right across the temple; and within this, again, is the shrine, hollowed out of a rectangular block left standing from floor to roof, and surrounded by a dark passage.

The chief object of worship is a mean little *liṅga* in the central shrine; but there is another to the right of it, faced by a large Nandi carved *in situ* on the same side; and nearer the light, in a sort of chapel, is a four-armed figure grasping several weapons. One is a live cobra; another, perhaps, the *damaru* or drum, the others indistinguishable. This figure is worshipped under the name of Kâla Bhairava. Opposite him are eight *dêvts* called Ashtamâtarah (one has the head of a pig) accompanied by Bhringi and Gaṇapati. They appear in the Dhumar Lena at Elurâ, and in the chapel in the east wing of the great cave at Elephanta. Besides, there are giant *dvârapâlas*, Lakshmi attended by elephants (on the central architrave), and a multitude of other figures; some cut *in situ*, others on detached or even imported stones, and evidently of various ages up to the present. The lesser cave is a triple cell; the inner part separated from the outer by a dwarf partition without gap or doorway. It is approached by a risky stair in

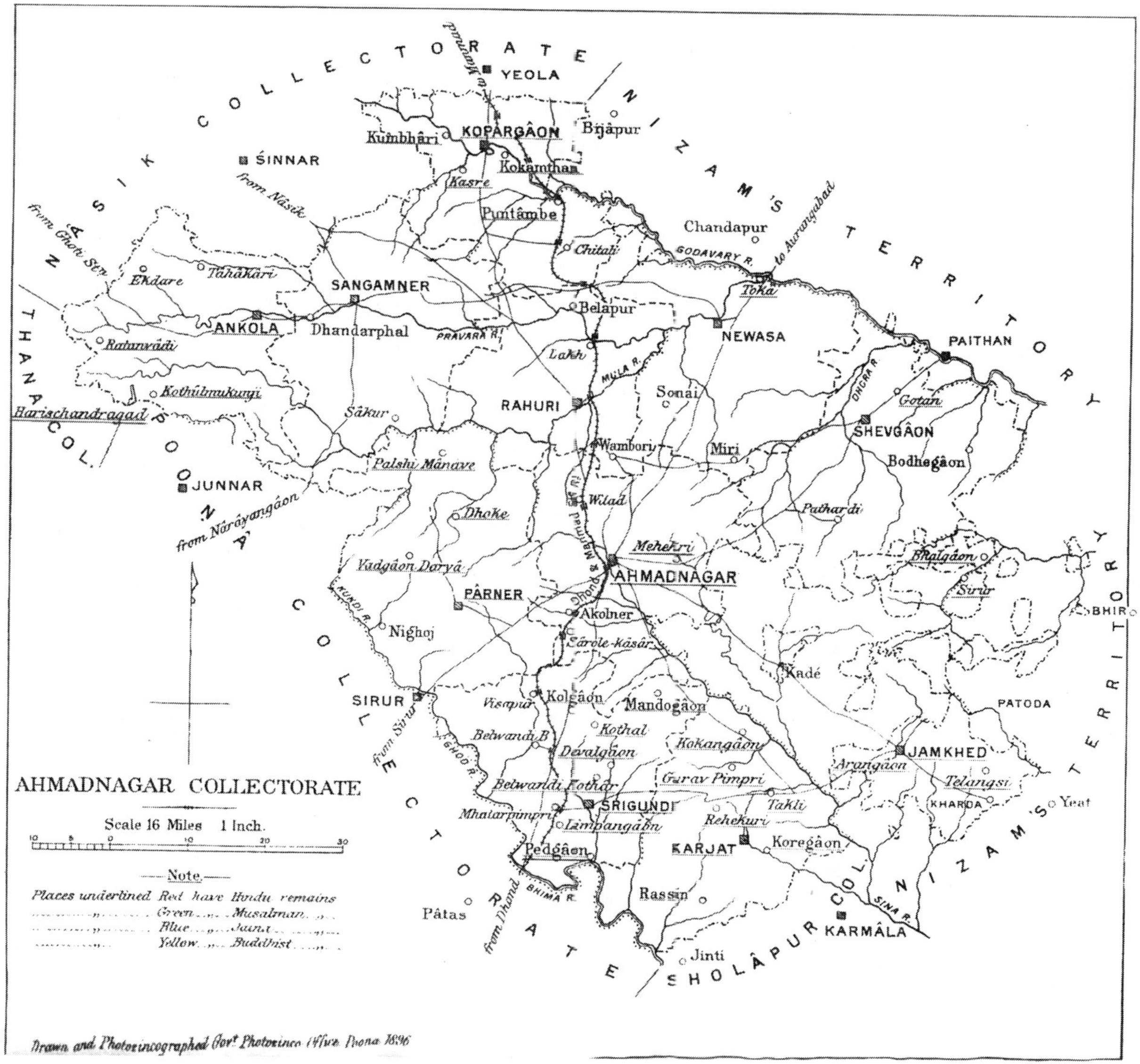
AHMADNAGAR COLLECTORATE
Scale 16 Miles 1 Inch.
Note.
Places underlined Red have Hindu remains
Green Musalman
Blue Jain
Yellow Buddhist
NASIK COLLECTORATE
NIZAM'S TERRITORY
THANA COL.
POONA COLLECTORATE
SHOLÂPUR COL.
AHMADNAGAR
KOPARGÂON
SANGAMNER
ANKOLA
RAHURI
NEWASA
SHEVGÂON
PAITHAN
PÂRNER
SIRUR
SRIGUNDI
KARJAT
JAMKHED
KARMÂLA
JUNNAR
SINNAR
YEOLA
PATODA
BHIR
Drawn and Photozincographed Govt Photozinco Office Poona 1896

the rock, south of the big cave; between them is a larger cistern full of good water. There is no inscription except an unimportant one in modern Marâthi on a small *thadage* outside the large cave. This cave may perhaps be ascribed to the latter part of the 8th century A.D. (*Ind. Ant.* V. 11.; *Cave Temples of India.*) (**Surveyed.**)

III. 2. **Vadgaon Darya'**, 9 miles north-west from Pârner. Enclosed in the wild beauty of a little glen, are some natural caverns under a cliff by a waterfall, which have been altered by modern masonry. There are a few coarse sculptures on the rock and on detached stones, but no architectural interest attaches to the place.

III. 3. **Pa'rner**, 20 miles west by south from Ahmadnagar. Temple of Sangameśvara or Tryambakeśvara at the junction of two small *nâlâs*. The ground plan is the normal double-broken diamond or square; not very much facetted, there being only three superior re-entering angles on the front sides of the *maṇḍapa* and one lesser similar angle near the front porch. There have been three porches, as usual. All of them are now in ruins, the front one least so. Its door strongly resembles the inner door of Temple No. II. at Belgâum, but has not the pierced flanking panels. The pillars are more in the style of temple No. I. at Belgâum. Four large pillars, with the help of the walls and surviving pilasters, support the roof, composed of nine small rough domes. This would appear to have been the original plan, but the whole roof has been destroyed (tradition says by the first Musalmân invaders) and restored from a height of about nine feet above the ground. This is shown by the use of mortar in the restored portion and by the inverted position of some of its decorations. The lower or ancient part is of dry stonework in receding embedded courses of very large blocks, and the *liṅga* is enshrined in a deep pit. The whole exterior is covered with a decoration representing in low relief, sometimes an arch, sometimes a dome. This is observable also in a large "*bârav*" now attached to a modern mosque east of the town of Pârnêr (which has probably usurped the site of a temple), and in the remains of a small temple between the town and river at Palshî (20 miles north of Pârnêr) in the same *tâlukâ*. The roof has been destroyed, but a few fragments of cornice seem to indicate that it was Dravidian in style; like that of Malai Devî at Nighoj, 10 miles south-west of Pârnêr. The pillars of this temple closely resemble the two shown in the front of the temple figured in Plate I. of the *Archæological Report* for 1874. The Nandi in front of the principal entrance now rests at the bottom of a pit lined with modern masonry, and partly covered by a rough dome constructed of the débris of the porch, and perhaps of a destroyed pavilion. On this rests a stone representing apparently an inverted bunch of grapes, which the people call a *liṅga*, but do not worship; probably it was a finial of the pavilion or of one of the porches. Several slender pillars of a broken square section have been built into a small modern temple in the middle of the place, which is, however, chiefly now admired as possessing a relief, in moulded clay coloured and gilt, of Chaṇḍikâ Devi in strife with the buffalo demon, the work of a local artist, a *pâtil* of the village of Renavâdi. Under a *pipal* tree before this temple are several fragments of sculpture, among which are a huge gargoyle in the form of a monster's head, and a great stone *rânjana*, or vase, the superior and inferior portions of which have been hewn separately and afterwards fitted together. It is of the still popular form of an egg truncated at both ends, and is 4½ feet both in height and in external diameter. It is very rough; its simple ornamentation does not correspond with that of any of the other remains; and it might have been made at any period by the stone-cutters who hew out oil-presses. (*Ind. Ant.* V. 12). (**Surveyed.**)

III. The old temple of Nâganâtha Mahâdeva to the east of the Nagar gate has also a *bârav* or well.

Inscription:—In the *bârav*, at the Nâganâtha temple is an inscription in Devanâgarî dated *Saka* 1015.

III. 4. **Palshi Ma'ndve.**—Two fine modern temples.

III. Śrigonda Tâlukâ.

III. 1. **S'rigonda,** 20 miles W.N.W. from Karjat and 32 miles south from Ahmadnagar. (1) Temple of Vithobâ of Hemâdpanti masonry, *i. e.* of large blocks of stones without cement, in imbedded courses. *Maṇḍapa* of nine domes supported on six pillars; shrine—one dome; portico in front—one dome; shrine on a lower level than the *maṇḍapa*. There is an **inscription** on the door step in front of the temple, but the steps appear to be modern. Round the door of the shrine are two rows of figures. The inner row represents females, and the outer one monkeys. On the raised block forming the threshold of the shrine are carved two tigers' heads, one on each side. Projecting from the top of the entrance to the shrine, and from the middle of the front of the *maṇḍapa* are carved blocks, resembling those in the temple of Lakshmi-Nârâyaṇa at Mândavgan. The length of the *maṇḍapa* is about 28 feet and width about 21. The pillars are similar to those of the temple of Lakshmî-Nârâyaṇa at Mândavgan. Externally also the two temples are similar, but what carving there is on the latter gives the shrine the appearance of being built of a succession of pillars packed together, while in the former, being perfectly plain, this effect
III. is not produced. (2) Temple of Rakhmâi adjoins the above and is in the same style,
III. but on a smaller scale; both temples have a good deal of carving. (3) Temple of Mahâdeva Hatkeśvara, the same as the above as to the number of domes. A *liṅga* in a pitlike shrine. Style plainer than any of the above. The front of the *maṇḍapa* is built up
III. with bricks. (4) Temple of Mahâlakshmî, the same as the above as to number of domes. The shrine has been built up, and parts of the *maṇḍapa* also. It is not used for worship and is in a horrible state of filth. The work appears superior to that of the preceding two.

II *b*. Some very good wood-carving decorates the façades of two houses at Śrigonda, of the style, though not so old, that is found in such abundance in North Gujarât.

2. **Pedgaon,** 8 miles south of Śrigonda. The village occupies a long strip of land, which, with the river on the other side, hems in an old Musalmân fortified enclosure which is roughly a quarter of a mile square, and is now almost completely overrun by prickly pear, which, in most parts, grows so thick and so high as to hide from view the ruins it so jealously guards. The fort is said to have been built by Khân Jahân in 1673,
III. when it was called Bahâdurgaḍ. The Muhammadan buildings, which, judging from the great amount of débris, must have been very extensive, have almost entirely disappeared, the most complete being the Bibi Mahâl, occupying a delightful position upon the ramparts overlooking the river. There is also a *nal* for bringing water from the Bhimâ to the village. The water was raised from the river by an elephant *mot* still in existence. The *nal* seems to be in good repair outside. But, although nearly three times the age of

the Muhammadan remains, and despite the devastating work of the spoiler's hand, there still remain, within the precincts of the fort, the ruins of five old Hemâdpanti temples, one
I a. of which, that of Lakshmi-Nârâyana, is a perfect little gem. It is most profusely decorated both within and without, and its outer walls are thickly covered with figure sculpture. It has, though in less degree than some of the others, suffered severely from the hand of man. It is a Vaishṇava temple facing west, built on a high part of the bank overlooking the river, and whose spire, now absent, was, like many of this class, probably constructed in brickwork. The basement mouldings are studded with little figures of horses, elephants, and men, and a very rarely occurring moulding is here found, viz., the *aśvathara* or horse moulding. The walls above the basement, the pillars, and door frames are richly wrought, the pillars being of rather a different type from those generally met with. (**Surveyed.**)

III. The other temples are those of Bâleśvara, Râmeśvara, Kholeśvara, and Bhairavanâtha's, originally a Jaina temple. The shrines of Bâleśvara and Kholeśvara are sadly ruined and dismantled, the shrine only in each case standing, while the halls are but heaps of ruins. Pedgâon must have been a place of importance long before the advent of the Muhammadans and perhaps, owing to its position upon the Bhimâ, it may have been a centre of special sanctity. At this point the Sarasvati river runs into the Bhimâ, and it is upon the bank of the former that Śrigonda stands.

III. 3. **Limpangaon.**—At the village of Limpangâon, five miles south-west from Śrigonda, is the large, plain, but substantially built temple of Siddheśvara. On either side of the main porch is a large perforated screen wall, neatly designed in imitation of cross bars, and slightly decorated. The building looks heavy and massive, and the pillars of the hall are very well proportioned. The temple is, in every respect, a much better one than any of those at Srigonda and is better built. It is in use. (**Surveyed.**)

III. 4. **Kothal,** 10 miles north of Śrigoṇḍa. Temple of Khaṇḍobâ on the top of hill; the roof supported by six pillars in octagonal and square sections. The date is unknown, but there is an inscription on an old temple behind the principal one which might be made out. The temple has been struck by lightning, which has left the marks of its course, but has not injured the building materially. In front of the temple is a place where the *Pâtil* says he used to see people swung round on a pole by a rope with a hook on Mârgaśirsha Śuddha 6th and Pausha Śuddha 6th.

III. 5. **Belvandi Kothar,** 4 miles north of Śrigoṇḍa—Hemâḍpanti *bârav* or well quite perfect. A Hemâḍpanti temple projects into the *bârav* on one side. There are two doors to the *maṇḍapa* and one to the shrine, all uncarved; also a dome over the bull, in front of the door. Above this dome is a place for raising water to the top, and a stone waterway running the length of the temple on the roof, and emptying into an old water trough. The shrine is on the same level as the *maṇḍapa*, and has a *liṅga* in it; no carving. The *bârav* is not used, as it is supposed to be haunted, a man having been drowned in it once. There is a good deal of mud in it.

III. 6. **Kolgaon**, 12 miles north-west of Śrigoṇḍa. Hemâḍpanti temple of Vâlukeśvara Mahâdeva, with nine domes; *liṅga* in a sunk shrine; pillars much carved, with figures on the capitals, but they are all covered with chunam. Two recesses, unused, one on each side of the *maṇḍapa*. In front of door the remains of a verandah built of large blocks of stones let into each other in receding courses. A new shrine with a *liṅga* on the left of the verandah. In front of the verandah, a Nandi under a dome supported by four pillars. Over the shrine of the temple is a brick and chunam dome in the usual style. In front of the temple a brick *dîpamâla* with staircase inside. The original outside of the temple has evidently been removed and replaced by modern masonry.

II *b*. 7. **Ma'ndavgan Katra'ba'd**, 20 miles north of Śrigoṇḍa. Temple of Dêvî, formerly of Lakshmî-Nârâyaṇa; *maṇḍapa* of nine plain domes, supported by four pillars and eight pilasters. The pillars are in square, octagon, and round sections; on their capitals are various figures, with cobras on the brackets of the pilasters. The shrine is a sunken one with an image of Dêvî; also a large mutilated one of Lakshmî-Nârâyaṇa about 5 feet high. The *maṇḍapa* has three entrances, and the shrine door and main door of the *maṇḍapa* are well carved. In front is a pavilion on 4 pillars. The outside has not much carving except string courses of lozenge ornament. The outline is broken by a succession of right angles. The *maṇḍapa* is 24 feet square inside.

III. 8. About 4 or 5 miles south-west of Mândavgan, on the northern slope of the hills, there is a curious old tank attributed to the Gavali Râjâs, and another somewhat similar on the east side of the road from Pissorekhand to Mândavgan, a mile or two from the former place.

III. 9. **Devalgaon**, 8 miles north from Śrigoṇḍa. An old Hemâḍpanti well, which has been repaired in later times and the old stones broken up, so as to make them manageable, by the modern Wadars.

IV.—Karjat Tâlukâ.

III. 1. **Karjat**, 42 miles S.S.E. from Ahmadnagar:—(1) Temple Mallikârjuna (Naktiche dêval) with nine domes and the shrine, the centre dome being cut smooth. The pillars are a good deal cut. The door is opposite the shrine, and on each side of the *maṇḍapa* are shrines containing images. In the main shrine, which is on a slightly lower level than the *maṇḍapa*, is a *liṅga*. In the wall on each side of the door are a good many carved figures, principally obscene. In front of the door is a bull under a dome, and on the left-hand side of the door is a detached shrine with a *liṅga*. (2) Temple of Mahâdeva, adjoining the above has 9 domes to the *maṇḍapa*, and a *liṅga* in a pit-like shrine. There is no carving about it. (3) The temple of Nâgeśvara, across the stream, has a shrine whose floor is six feet below the floor of the hall, and is approached by a flight of steps leading down to it from inside the shrine doorway. The antechamber to the shrine is about two feet lower than the hall floor. The temples, though old, are of no particular merit. (**Surveyed**.)

III. 2. **Ta'kli**, 6 miles north of Karjaṭ. Temple of Khanḍêśvara Mahâdeva (Hemâḍpanti) in ruins. The stones are said to have been taken to build the fort at Parainda (?) between Bârsi and Karmâla.

III. 3. **Rehekuri**, 6 miles north-west from Karjat. Temple of Komnâtha Mahâdeva has 12 domes to the *maṇḍapa*, one to the shrine, and one door, under which is a bull, beside which is a cobra on a detached stone. It is surrounded by a wall which is capped with big stones.

III. 4. **Koregaon**, 2 miles east of Karjat. (1) West of the village is an old Hemâḍpanti temple of 9 domes to the *maṇḍapa*; *liṅga* in the shrine. (2) Temple of Koreśvara Mahâdeva, old, said to be a Hemâḍpanti temple. The shrine only is left. In it are a *liṅga*, Nandi and figures of Gaṇapati and Pârvatî, all in white marble. The *piṇḍi* of the *liṅga* is composed of four faces of Mahâdeva adorned with snakes, and there is a snake on the narrow part of the *śâluṅkâ*. One Bâburâv Gôvind Vakil is said to have brought these figures to Karmâla from Hindusthân about 100 or 150 years ago; and they were brought from Karmâla by Râvaji Lakshmaṇ, father of the present Kuḷkarṇi of Koregâon.

III. 5. **Ra'ssin**, 10 miles south-west from Karjat. (1) Hemâḍpanti temple of Mahâdeva (*Kâledêval*): nine domes to the *maṇḍapa*, one dome to the shrine, and one dome to porch. The pillars are a good deal carved. In the centre of each dome is a carved stone, something like a star; figures on the capitals of the pillars. Three shrines; the main one opposite the door, and one on each side of the *maṇḍapa*. The main shrine is a pit with a *liṅga* in it. A stone platform runs round the temple, about the level of the floor. (2) Temple of Ḍêvî, said to have been built, with two or three other temples here, by a Vâṇia about 100 years ago. On the site of the present temple there is said to have been an old brick one 200 or 300 years old, the brick *dîpamâlas* and well attached to which still remain. One of the *dîpamâlas* has a stair inside, and a man at the top can make it oscillate perceptibly. It is 43 feet high, and 22 feet in circumference at the top. The well is of brick, where devotees bathe and make the water most filthy.

III. 6. **Gurav Pimpri**, 8 miles north from Karjat. Temple of Pimpreśvara Mahâdeva. Nine domes to the *maṇḍapa*; and a *liṅga* in a pit-like shrine. The work is all plain; an extra pillar, put in to support one of the stone cross-beams which is cracked, has an inscription on it. There is also an inscription under the door of the compound. There is a ruined temple of Râmêśvara Mahâdêva in the village (apparently modern) with a ruined *bârav* and drinking trough attached to it.

III. 7. **Kokangaon**, 14 miles north of Karjat. Hemâḍpanti temple and well, both in ruins. Of the temple nothing is left but the shrine. The villagers say the stones were taken for the forts at Nagar, Parainda, and Karmâla, and for the Nimbâḷkar's Vâḍâ at Mirajgâon.

V.—Jâmkhed Tâlukâ.

III. 1. **Arangaon**, 10 miles west of Jâmkhêḍ. Hemâḍpanti temple of Araṇeśvara Mahâdeva, rather larger than usual, but plain. An inscription.

III. 2. **Ja'mkhed**, 45 miles south-east from Ahmadnagar (18° 43′; 75° 22′). (1) Hemâḍpanti temple of Mallikârjuna Mahâdeva. The shrine only left, the pillars of the *maṇḍapa* lie about. (2) Hemâḍpanti temple of Jaṭâśankara Mahâdeva was long buried under the earth and is in good preservation; it resembles the one at Araṅgâon.

B 1169—10

III. 3. **Telangsi,** 11 miles east from Jâmkhêḍ. Hêmâḍpanti temple of Jaṭâśankara Mahâdeva; nine domes to the *manḍapa*; cobra in pit-like shrine. Cobras on capitals of pillars: no carving. Not far off is a Hemâḍpanti *bârav*. Four stairs descend from the middle of the four sides. Between the stairs in the wall are niches. The *bârav* is broken at one corner.

III. 4. **S'irur,** 24 miles north of Jâmkhêḍ. Temple of Siddheśvara Mahâdeva; nine domes; cobras on the capitals of the pillars. Shrine opposite the door. The front (on both sides of the door) and the entrance to the shrine are nicely carved. There is also a shrine on the left side of the *manḍapa*. In front of the door is a single dome with a Nandi. Roof of temple modern, of chunam.

III. 5. **Bha'lgaon,** 26 miles north by east of Jâmkhêḍ and 3 miles north-east from Śirur. Temple of Bhâleśvara Mahâdeva; 9 domes on fairly carved pillars with lozenge shaped ornaments on the faces. One shrine in ruins, another has a *manḍapa*.

VI.—Shevagâon Tâlukâ.

III. **Ghotan,** 6 miles north-east of Shevagâon. In the *Journal of the Bombay Branch of the Royal Asiatic Society* for January, 1850, in a paper by the Rev. Dr. Wilson, is mention of temples at Ghotan and Miri. In quoting Dr. Gibson's account, he writes: "I may mention, of those I have seen, a temple at Miri below the Diwar Ghât on the road from Ahmadnagar to Paithan, and a similar one at Bâmini and a third near Kopargâon." The temple at Ghotan, seen by Dr. Gibson, is now so masked by modern walls and other improvements (?) in chunam and whitewash that little can be seen of the original temple. What little is seen, however, shows that the building is of a very old type, perhaps older than the general run of so-called Hemâḍpanti temples. In and near the village are two other old temples, both more or less in ruins. (**Surveyed**.)

VII.—Nevâsa Tâlukâ.

III. 1. **Miri,** 18 miles south by east from Nevâsa. At Miri there is a Hemâḍpanti well, possibly the one mentioned by Dr. Gibson as being on the road to Paithan. It is now in a very ruinous condition, the whole of the four sides leaning dangerously inwards and ready, at the least further subsidence of any part, to be precipitated bodily into the pit. Notwithstanding the danger, the well is still in use, and the villagers descend to its lowest depths, whence escape would be impossible, with little concern for their own safety. There is also a much older step-well cut in the rock, a short distance south-west from the village, lately unearthed. It is now partly full of water, but the Jâghirdâr of Miri says that, when the water was lower, he saw an inscription below with a Jaina figure near it. Dr. Wilson mentions in his paper, quoted from above, several Buddhist temples, but this is a mistake, for, so far as is now known, there is not a structural Buddhist temple in Western India left standing, those so called by him being Jaina. (**Surveyed**.)

III. 2. **Toka,** 8 miles north-east of Nevâsa on the Godâvari, is an old sacred place with some interesting temples.

VIII.—Râhuri Tâlukâ.

III. **Ba'mini**, 6 miles east of Râhuri, a large square Hemâḍpantî tank partly in ruins. (**Surveyed.**)

IX.—Kopargâon Tâlukâ.

II *b*. 1. **Kokamtha'n**, about 5 miles down the river from Kopargâon. Upon what appears to be an artificial embankment, projecting out into the stream, and upon the north-east outskirts of the village, is an exceedingly interesting old temple. It consists of the usual shrine and *maṇḍapa*, and seems, originally, to have had three porches, one of which, that on the east, has been afterwards converted into a side shrine. The general plan of both shrine and *maṇḍapa* is star-shaped, the numerous corners, which always give such a pretty effect to these buildings, being the corners of superimposed squares upon a common centre. Curious additions to the three outer walls of the shrine are half *śikharas*, each with its own walls and basement mouldings. Each of these looks like half a small temple, which has been cut down the middle, and stuck on to each of the three middle projecting faces of the shrine. From external appearances one would be led to think each of these additions contained a small shrine or cell off the main shrine, but this is not the case. The lower portion of the temple, *i.e.* between the cornices and the ground, has been built of stone, while the upper part, or *śikharas* of the shrine and *maṇḍapa*, is built of brick. The whole has been plastered, and the ornament and figures, first finished in stone, have been reproduced in the plaster which overlays them. On the brickwork the whole of the decoration is in plaster. The brickwork seems to be original, and it was probably with the object of having the lower part of the building in keeping with the plastered *śikhara* that that part of the work was also plastered. The temple at present contains, in the small side shrine, a shapeless stone, bedaubed with red paint, which the villagers call Jagadambâdevi, and which now appears to be the principal object of worship. In the main shrine is the usual *liṅga*, but set up behind it on end is Vishṇu on Śesha. (*Ind. Ant.* V. 5.) (**Surveyed.**)

III. 2. **Kopargaon**, 60 miles north of Ahmadnagar on the Godâvari: Temples of Śakreśvara and Kacheśvâra, repaired by the Peśvâ's Government: the temple of Vishṇu was built by one of the Peśvâs. (*Ind. Ant.* V. 4.)

III. 3. **Kumbha'ri**, about 6 miles up stream from Kopargâon. Has a temple which is much plainer and more massive looking than that at Kokamthân. At present it contains the *liṅga*. The main shrine holds an *âsana* or throne, an ornamental figure on which is worshipped as Lakshmi (*Ind. Ant.* V. 6.) (**Surveyed.**)

III. 4. **Kasre**.—Here is an ugly mean temple of Bhairava beside a *nâlâ*. It has Hemâḍpantî foundations, probably one of the oldest pieces of *built* stone-work in the district, as the ground plan, a rectangular *maṇḍapa* with a shrine forming a very slightly broken square, is exceedingly archaic.

III. 5. **Punta'mbe**, on the Godâvari, 12 miles south-east from Kopargâon, has numerous temples, mostly recent; one of them is to Châṅgadeva, a famous saint said to have had 1,400 disciples; the temple is said to belong to the middle of the 17th century. There are also temples here of Kaśi-Viśveśvara, Jagadambâ, Bâḷâji, Kâla-Bhairava, Râmachandra, Keśavarâja, Gopâla-Kṛishṇa, Viṭhala, Annapûrṇâ, Bhadrakâlîśankara, Tryambakeśvara,

Rámeśvara, Mahârudraśankara; also a *ghâṭ* built by Ahalyâbâi of Indore, and another by Shivarâma Dumal.

X.—Sangamner Tâlukâ.

Sangamner.—Two sets of copper-plates were obtained here in December 1891. One, in Sanskrit, is dated *śakasamvat* 922, and records a grant made by the Mahásámanta Bhillana of the Yâdava of Seunadeśa. These plates are in the possession of Ganpat Sing *valad* Nârâyan Sing Patevála. (*Epig. Ind.* Vol. II., Part XII., p. 212.) The other grant was in Persian and does not appear to be of any great age. (Other Persian inscriptions, *Ind. Ant.* IV. 349.)

XI.—Akolâ Tâlukâ.

II *b*. 1. **Akola'.**—Situated to the east of the town, some little distance above the bank of the Pravarâ river, is the old temple of Siddheśvara. A short account of it is given in the *Journal of the Bombay Branch of the Royal Asiatic Society*, No. XIII. Vol. III. January 1850, and a more detailed one in the *Indian Antiquary*, Vol. V. p. 8; but in neither of these accounts, which describe temples in the neighbourhood, is mention made of the fine old temples at Ratanvâdi and Tâhâkari, twenty and eight miles west and north-west respectively from Akolâ. In the above accounts the temple of Siddheśvara is said to have been buried for a considerable period. If buried it must have been with the accumulation of earth washed down from the hillocks which overtop it on the south. Its basement is even now partly buried, the earth being deeper on the side of the hillocks, there being some four feet on that side and two feet on the side nearest the river. Owing to the elevation of the temple above the river and its distance from it, it seems impossible for it to have been covered up with silt from the latter.

The plan of the temple is peculiar, insomuch that it has a porch and doorway opening into the back of the shrine in addition to the usual door between the *maṇḍapa* and the shrine. This is very unusual. It occurs also in the temple at Ratanvâdi, and there is a small ruined temple at Sinnar, which seems also to have had the same back door arrangement. The general plan consists of a *maṇḍapa* with three porches, and the shrine with its antechamber on one side and porch upon the other. The temple, as regards decoration, is comparatively plain, but the few bands of ornament that are used are sparingly and tastefully applied. The whole of the roofing of the temple is comparatively new from the beams upwards, excepting the ceiling of the eastern porch, which is original. The west porch, before the main entrance, has been entirely rebuilt, and when these repairs were carried out, the walls were "pointed" with chunam, the raw white lines of which being no improvement upon the general appearance of the interior. The shrine doorways, which are both alike, are fairly well carved, and Gaṇapati presides above them. The entrance doorway has, with its porch, been entirely rebuilt, the side jambs and threshold of the original being included in the new work. Upon the outside of the shrine, on the north and south, is a niche containing figures of Kâlikâ Mâtâ and the *Tâṇḍava*, respectively.

In the account of the temple given in the *J. B. B. R. A. S.*, Dr. Gibson is quoted as having said, "On the side of one of the verandah pillars is a long inscription in the Sanskrit character. I regret I had not time to copy it:" and in the *Indian Antiquary*

Mr. Sinclair says, "unfortunately the front porch has been restored, by some pious blockhead, in the Saracenic style of a handsome modern temple in the village, so that it is not available for purposes of comparison. More than that the Vandal threw away the ruins of the old porch, on one of which was a long Sanskrit inscription observed, but not copied, by Dr. Gibson twenty-five years ago. After long search I found that the fragment on which it was, had been turned face-up under a *nim* tree, and used as a seat by the idlers of the village, who had with their barbarous hinder parts obliterated the inscription (never very deep or clear cut) beyond all hope of transcription or estampage, though it is possible that a competent Sanskrit scholar, with time and the stone itself before him, might decipher a few words." The portion of a pillar bearing the worn-out inscription mentioned is (1893) in the old *kacheri* enclosure lying before the entrance to the Subordinate Judge's Court-house. The letters are almost entirely obliterated. Above the inscription are engraved the sun and the moon. The inscribed pillar is totally different from those of the east porch, and it is probable that the east and west porches were alike in design. Possibly the pillar had been used in the porch to prop up some broken beam and was not an integral part of the building, having been brought from the ruins of some other building for that purpose. (*Ind. Ant.* V. 8; *J. B. B. R. A. S.*, Pt. XIII. p. 85.) (**Surveyed.**)

II *b*. 2. **Ratanvâdi**, 20 miles west of Akolâ. The temple of Amriteśvara at Ratanvâdi is on almost precisely the same plan as that of Siddheśvara at Akolâ, having the same unusual doorway and porch at the back of the shrine, the only difference in the plan being the absence of the side porches of the *mandapa*; in their places are gratings or windows set in shallow recesses, one on each side of the hall. The closing of the sides and the substitution of these windows was a precaution probably necessitated by the wild and mountainous nature of the country around, to keep out wild beasts which might otherwise prove unwelcome visitors to the shrine. The roof of the *mandapa* has disappeared leaving its inner lining, but the *śikhara* over the shrine is almost entire and is very ornamental. The temple is of the same style as that of Gondeśvara at Sinnar. The walls are decorated in the same manner as those of Siddheśvara at Akolâ but slightly varied in detail. There is no figure sculpture on the walls save what was in the two niches on the shrine walls similar to those on the Akolâ shrine. Near the temple, and coeval with it, is an old square *kunda* or well. (**Surveyed.**)

III. 3. **Tâhâkari**, a small hamlet amongst the hills, eight miles to the north-west of Akolâ. Here is the old triple-shrined temple of Bhavâni or Devi, in the principal shrine of which there is installed a figure of Mahâlakshmi, whilst upon the dedicatory block above the shrine doorway presides a *devi*. The exterior walls of the temple are ornamented with decorative bands similar to that of Siddheśvara at Akolâ, but in each of the recessed panels around the principal shrine is a female figure, and in each of three niches—one on each face of the back wall of the shrine—is a figure. The *śikharas*, which were built of brick, like that of the Kokamthân temple, are very dilapidated and partly destroyed. The rest of the building below the cornice is of stone masonry. In the central *mandapa*, which is common to the three shrines, is a well decorated domical ceiling. The ceiling of the porch is also a very good piece of work. Both are adorned with those bracket figures of musicians which are so very ornamental a feature in these ceilings. Upon the pillar of the *mandapa* of a small ruined shrine, between the main temple and the river, is a Sanskrit inscription. (**Surveyed.**)

III. 4. **Ekdare,** 15 miles north-west from Akolâ, two caves in Mahâkâli hill, apparently of no particular interest.

III. 5. **Kothulmkunji,** 16 miles south-west from Akolâ: the ruins of the temple of Nârâyaṇeśvara, with a fine doorway; foundations of the temple of Koṭeśvara.

II *a*. 6. **Harischandragad,** with a group of late Brahmanical caves. A little below the row of caves is a large Hemâdpanti *bârav* or reservoir, with steps, along the southern side of which is a row of little niches or shrines, some still occupied by images. This is surrounded by small temples and *thadagi* or tombs. Below the reservoir is a small temple in a pit, half cave half building, consisting merely of a cell with a shrine at each side, one of which contains the socket of a departed *liṅga*. Below it again is a deep hollow or pit, formed by cutting away the rock at the head of a ravine, so as to leave a small level space, in the centre of which rises a structural temple with a central spire. It has a very ancient appearance, probably contributed to by the tremendous rainfall of these highlands, but it is also remarkable for its plan. There is no *maṇḍapa*; the shrine is under the tall spire, which is of the Northern form, and the *liṅga* within is worshipped from any one of four doors with porches. Another shrine containing the image of some goddess is half built, half hewn, in the south-east corner of the pit, and the western side is occupied by caves used as *dharmaśâlâs*, two or three in number, for they are much mixed up together. **(Surveyed.)**

About 50 yards down the ravine is the best cave in the place, a great cistern about forty feet square, the centre of which is occupied by a huge *liṅga* surrounded by four pillars,—something resembling in pattern those of the chief cave at Elephanta, but much more slender. The worshippers swim and wade round this, splashing it. There is a good relief to the left, and a small chamber above the water. (*Ind. Ant.* V. 10; *Arch. Sur. Report,* Vol. V.; *Cave Temples of India.*)

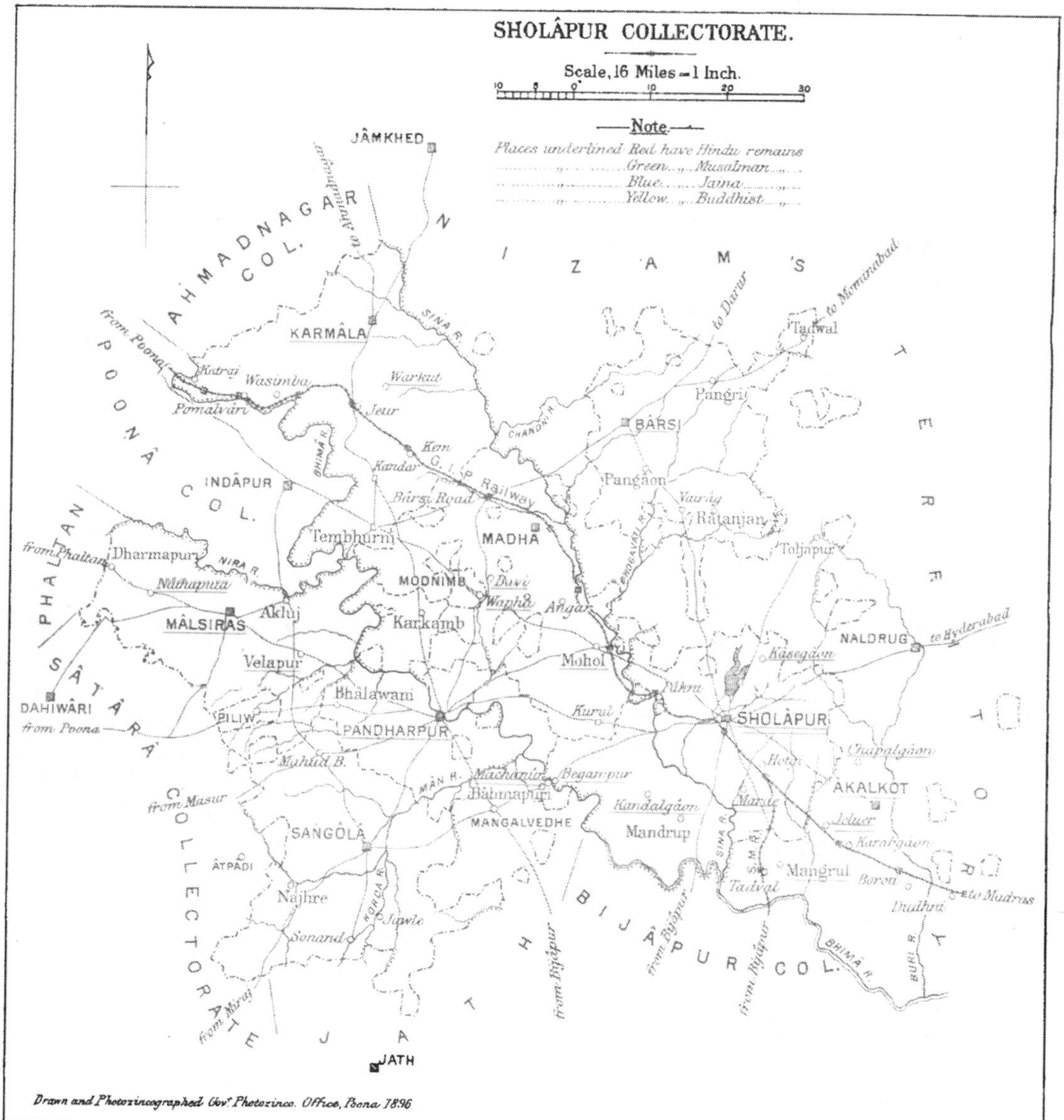
SHOLÂPUR COLLECTORATE.
Scale, 16 Miles = 1 Inch.
Note.
Places underlined Red have Hindu remains
Green Musalman
Blue Jaina
Yellow Buddhist
JÂMKHED
AHMADNAGAR COL.
NIZAM'S TERRITORY
POONA COL.
PHALTAN
SÂTÂRA COLLECTORATE
JATH
BIJÂPUR COL.
KARMÂLA
BÂRSI
INDÂPUR
MADHA
MODNIMB
MÂLSIRAS
DAHIWÂRI
PILIW
PANDHARPUR
SANGOLA
ÂTPADI
MANGALVEDHE
SHOLÂPUR
NALDRUG
ÂKALKOT
Tembhurni
Karkamb
Mohol
Mandrup
Mangrul
Pangaon
Ratanjan
Tuljapur
Tadwal
Pangri
G. I. P. Railway
Bârsi Road
Drawn and Photozincographed Govt. Photozinco. Office, Poona 1896

IV.—SHOLÂPUR ZILLA.

I.—Sholâpur Tâlukâ.

II a. 1. **Shola'pur**; the fort contains some Persian and Marâthi inscriptions.

III. 2. **Kandalgaon**, 14 miles south-west from Sholâpur and 6 miles north-west of Mandrup. A Hemâḍpanti temple of Kedâralinga Mahâdeva. The porch has 3 pillars on each side and the *maṇḍapa* 5 on each side in continuation of those in the porch. There are side shrines to Mahâdeva and Mallikârjuna.

III. 3. **Marde**, 8 miles south of Sholâpur;—a mosque which was originally a Śaiva Hemâḍpanti temple; also the remains of a fine old Hemâḍpanti well, which must have had a good deal of curious sculpture about it.

III. 4. **Ka'segaon**, 8 miles north-east from Sholâpur. Hemâḍpanti temple of Kâśeśvara Mahâdeva, approached by a flight of steps from the courtyard; some carving and figures on the left side of the entrance. The *maṇḍapa* has 8 pillars.

II a. 5. **Begampur**, (Ghoḍeśvara) on the Bhîmâ, 23 miles W.S.W. from Sholâpur. Tomb of Begami, a young daughter of Aurangzib, who died while he was encamped at Machanûr opposite. It is in danger of destruction from the river.

II.—Bârsi Tâlukâ.

III. **Ba'rsi**, 20 miles E.N.E. from Bârsi Road Station:—a fine large temple to Bhagavân, well ornamented.

III.—Mâdha Tâlukâ.

II b. 1. **Wapha**, a large stone slab 7′ by 3′, with an old inscription in Devanâgarî upon it.

III. 2. **Bavi**, some apparently very old half underground temples, said to be Hemâḍpanti; they are very rude, unlike any others in the district, and disused.

III. 3. **Mohol**, 18 miles S.S.E. from Mâdha; a temple of Hanumân, in which the image has four heads. Inscription in unknown characters.

IV.—Pandharpur Tâlukâ.

III. 1. **Pandharpur**, 48 miles west from Sholâpur;—Great temple of Vithobâ (see *Tenth Annual Report of Sanitary Commissioner*, also *Ind. Ant.* II. 272, IV. 22, and XI. 149; *B. B. R. A. S. Journ.* XIII. 87.)

III. 2. **Machanur**, on the Bhîmâ opposite Begampur, 23 miles W.S.W. from Sholâpur; a fort built by Aurangzib; and higher up near Bâhmapuri, a temple of Siddheśvara, enclosed in a paved court and said to be old.

V.—Sângola Tâlukâ.

(*No Returns.*)

VI.—Mâlsiras Tâlukâ.

III. 1. **Ma'lsiras**, 11 miles W.N.W. from Veḷâpur; an old Hemâḍpanti temple of Someśvara.

II b. 2. **Vela'pur**, 20 miles north-west from Paṇḍharpur;—a large Hemâḍpanti temple of Śiva, with an image of Hara-Nareśvara. There are two inscriptions here, dated *Śaka* 1222, of which the following are copies by the Mâmlatdâr:—

(1). ॥ स्वस्ति श्रीशके १२२२ प्रमनामसंवत्सरे मार्गशीर्षमासे सोमे अद्यह श्रीमत् प्रौढप्रतापचक्रवर्ती श्री रामचंद्रदेवविजयवान् श्री तत्पादवंदनोपजीवी सचवसांति अंबीकाविग्रहरतत्प्रसादेयो रुद्रे अनादिसिद्धदैवतदेवालय शिखरबाने देवक्षत्रस्य ॥ जोगेश्वर द्विजोत्तम यानी पुरातन स्थापन केलें. जीर्णोद्धार देवराव विख्यातदानधर्म हवनं कृत्वा त्रैलोक्यविख्यात जीर्णोद्धार केला. प्रख्यातयशःकीर्तिमान् अस्तु. शुभं भवतु ॥

(2). ॥ स्वस्ति श्रीशके १२२२ प्रमनामसंवत्सरे मार्गशीर्षमासे सोमे अद्य श्रीमत् प्रौढप्रतापचक्रवर्ती श्री रामचंद्रदेवविजयवान् श्री तत्पादवंदनोपजीवी सचवसंती अंबीकाविग्रहार एतत्प्रसादेयो रुद्रे अनादि सिद्धदैवत देवालय शिखर देवक्षत्रस्य ॥ जोगेश्वरद्विजोत्तम यानी पुरातन स्थापन केले त्याचा जीर्णोद्धार देवराव विख्यात् दानधर्महवनं कृत्वा नृपविख्यात जीर्णोद्धार केला प्रख्यात यशःकीर्तिमान् शुभं भवतु ॥

(बारवेंत जातांना उजवेबाजूस दगडावर लिहिलें आहे त्याचा उतारा.)

स्वस्ति श्री शके १२२१ विश्वावसुनामसंवत्सरे मार्गशीर्ष वद ९ सोमे अद्यह श्रीमत् प्रौढप्रताप चक्रवर्ती श्री रामचंद्र देव विजयवान् जयश्री तत्पादवंदुमोपजीवीवान् देशस्थ सचवसंती अंबिका विग्रहार देव याणि अस्मिन्काले वर्तमाने वेळापुरस्यकुलदैवत् अनादिसिद्धदैवत देवालय शिखरस्थान शिरस्थकीयदेवसंपुज्य होते ते या प्रक्षणात् तत्प्रसादात् वेळापुरकुनाट देवतालोकवासपुरी लोकः स्थित व लेखांकितकेसतमृत्तिकाकेककशांतर जपहोमहवनब्राह्मणभोजनकतुदानप्रदान देवब्रह्मेंद्रादिहवनं कृत्वा बलीयद्यः रिंवदु पापपुण्यभो हारण कीर्तिभान याजला जो गिरीश अंबिकाकैलासवार्ती वर्तमान महिमागजगजधर्मब्रह्मेंद्राचितंससंतोष कीर्तिकलावान् ॥

III. 3. **Na'thaputa,** 11 miles W.N.W. from Mâlsiras;—two large carved temples of Girijâpati and Parvateśvara, very old.

VII.—Karmâla Tâlukâ.

III. 1. **Karma'la,** 11 miles north from Jeur station:—a large temple of Ambâbâî.

III. 2. **Warkut:** a half built, but old, temple with 21 sculptured slabs in excellent preservation arranged along the wall.

Akalkot State.

III. 1. **Akalkot,** 23 miles south-east from Sholâpur. Outside the Maindurgi gate and adjoining the Sukhibansi is a small but chaste mosque attributed to the times of the Dakhan kings. It has but one arch and two low minarets, and much plain but delicate stone work.

III. 2. **Jeluer,** 8 miles south-east of Akalkoṭ, near the railway;—(1) a mosque with some simple decoration said to have been built by one Farâs Khân, Vazîr to some king; (2) the temple of Mâruti at the gate is Hemâḍpanti; the pillars in the *manḍapa* run parallel to the front, and form a portico; (3) a small temple of S'ėshaśâyî in the court of Kâśilinga Mahâdeva's has some figure carving about it. There is a fine well in the same court.

III. 3. **Mangrul,** 14 miles south-west of Akalkoṭ, and 3 miles south-west of Karabgâon station;—shrine of Pîr Shekh Bâbâ; and at its south-west corner is a tomb, built "by a Vazîr," with a good deal of plain decoration. It stands on a platform raised some 10 feet from the ground on arches.

4. At a village south from Karabgâon are some very old Kanarese inscriptions.

III. 5. **Chapalgaon,** 6 miles north of Akalkoṭ. A Hemâḍpanti temple of Mallikârjuna Mahâdeva, cruciform in shape or with three shrines, and about 60 feet long. The front is covered with carved figures, and the roof supported by columns.

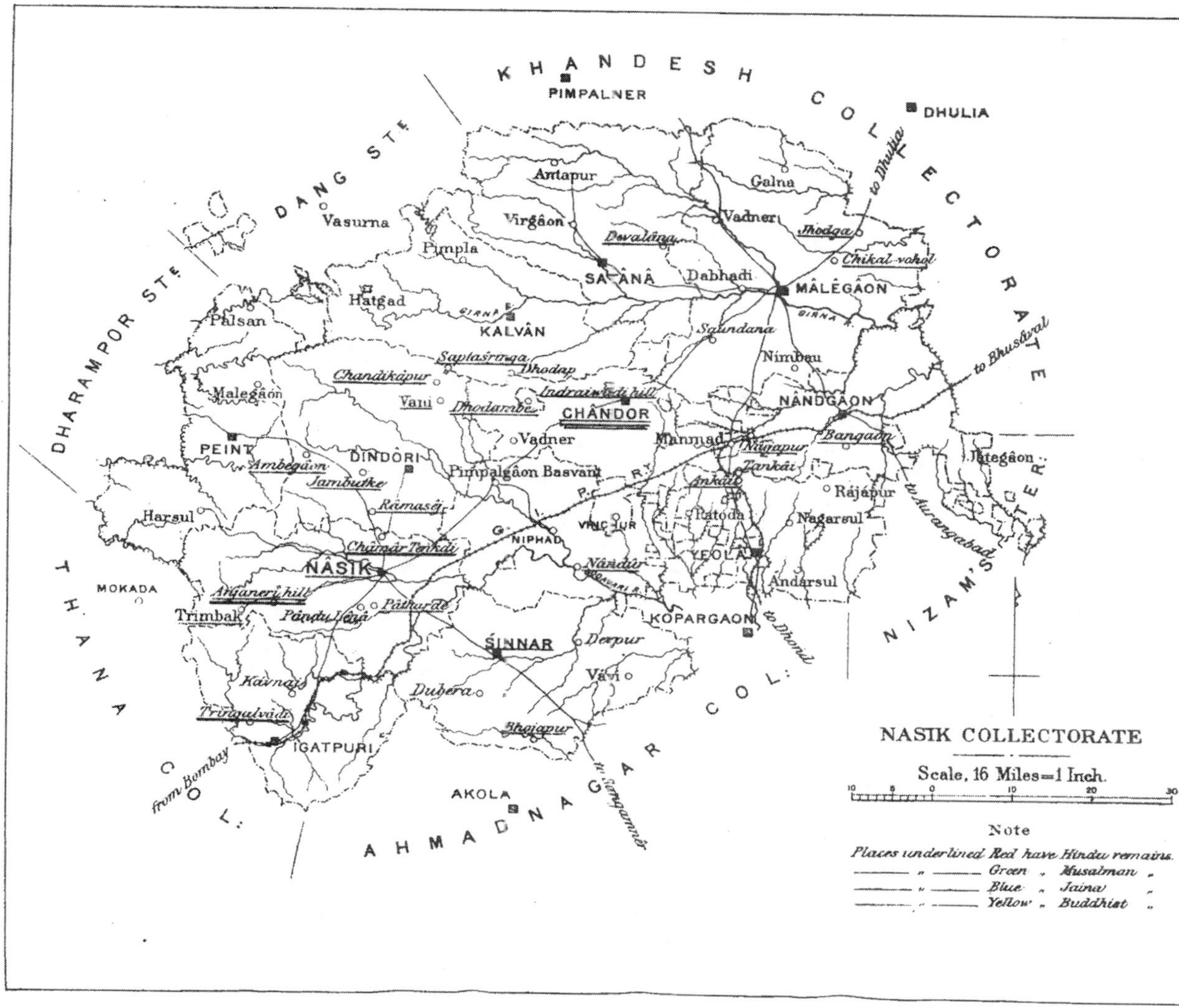

NASIK COLLECTORATE

Scale, 16 Miles = 1 Inch.

10 5 0 10 20 30

Note

Places underlined Red have Hindu remains.

" Green " Musalman "

" Blue " Jaina "

" Yellow " Buddhist "

V.—NÂSIK ZILLA.

I.—NÂSIK TÂLUKA.

1. **Na'sik** is situated in the upper valley of the Godâvari river, and is four miles off the railway leading from Bombay to Calcutta. The town is a place of great antiquity and sanctity, being associated with the legend of Râma, who is said to have spent part of his exile at Pañchavaṭi, a suburb of Nâsik on the north side of the Godâvari or Gangâ river. It is to a large extent a Brâhmanical town, and may be regarded as the Benares of Western India. It is mentioned under its present name by Ptolemy, and, situated as it is just above one of the few easily accessible passes up the Ghâts, and in the middle of a fertile plain interspersed with isolated hills, it must always have been a place of note. Nâsik has now a large number of temples but mostly dating from last century and not remarkable for their architectural beauty. No very accurate or detailed information as to their history or dimensions has been obtained as yet. The
III. principal are :—(1) Temple of Srî Râma, in Pañchavaṭi, said to have been built by Rangarâv Oḍhekar about 1782. It is a large stone temple with a handsome dome, and stands in the middle of a court with a *nagârkhâna* over the entrance. (2) Temple of Râmêśvara Mahâdêva, in Pañchavaṭi, built about 1754 by Nârośankar Râjebahâdar, a noted chief under the Peśvâ Bâlâji Bâjirâv (1740-1762). (3) Temple of Kapâlêśvara, in Pañchavaṭi, said to be the oldest here (*Jour. Bom. B. R. As. Soc.* Vol. III. Pt. II. p. 87). (4) Temple of Sundara Nârâyaṇa on the Nâsik bank of the river, is dedicated to Lakshmî-Nârâyaṇa. It is uncertain when it was erected, some say about 1748. It enjoys a large *inâm* managed by the *pujâris*. Opposite to it is the Râmakuṇḍa or Astivilaya Tîrtha. (5) The Sîtâ Gumphâ or Cave of Sîtâ. (6) Temple of Venkatêśa, or Bâḷâji as it is commonly known, a pretty large building, enjoys a *jâhgîr* worth Rs. 20,000. (7) The temple of Gorâ Râma close to the river, built by Ahalyâbâi of Indor. (8) Temple of Muralidhara, with an image exactly like that of Khunyâ Muralidhara at Poona. (9) Temple of Bhadrakâlî. (10) Bhaṭjibâvâ's Maṭha built by an ancestor of the Vinchurkar. (11) Palaces of the Pêśvâ and Nârośankar. Besides which there are many others, besides *ghâṭs*, &c.

I *a*. 2. **Pa'ndu Lena or Triras'mi**, 5 miles south from Nâsik. A well known series of Bauddha caves with many inscriptions of the Ândhra, Kshatrapa, and other kings. They are situated in one of three isolated hills, called in the inscriptions Triraśmi, close to the Bombay road. They were first described by Captain James Delamaine who visited them in 1823, and afterwards by Dr. T. Wilson and Mr. West. The caves are 17 in number, and though small, are a very interesting group. For further description see *Cave Temples of India* and *Ind. Ant.* XII. 139 for inscriptions. (*J. B. B. R. A. S.*, Pt. XIII. p. 65; XVI. 35; XXII. 37; *Archæol. Survey Report*, Vol. IV. (**Surveyed.**)

III. 3. **Trimbak**, 20 miles west from Nâsik. Temple of Trimbakêśvara or Tryambakeśvara, built by Sadâśivarâv *alias* Bhâu Sâheb, about 1750, has a Government endowment of Rs. 12,000 per annum, under the charge of the *pujâris* (*Jour. Bom. B. R. As. Soc.*, Vol. III. Pt. II. p. 86). There is also a temple built by Ahalyâbâi of Indor in 1779, and five others. There is, however, close to the east wall of the enclosure, outside, a small plain Hemâdpanti shrine, now of little account, but which probably was part of an older temple that existed before the present one was built.

4. **Anjaneri or Anjani-giri**, 14 miles west of Nâsik on the Trimbak Road, is a small village, on the lower slopes of the hill upon which is, or was, a fort of the same name. Just below the village, in the plain, scattered over an area of about half a square mile, have been innumerable small shrines, sixteen of which now stand in whole or in part, while the rest are represented by the mounds where they stood, upon many of which lie heaps of their material—columns, figures, beams, and carved blocks. The most striking feature about all these is the small scale upon which they have been built, and they are all independent shrines and not satellites to a larger one. They all appear to rest upon brick foundations. They have been dedicated to various deities, the more important ones being Jaina; two are Vaishṇava, while the rest are Śaivite. They face all directions of the compass. They are not used, nor do they seem ever to have been much used. The shattered condition they are now in seems to point to wanton destruction by the hand of man, but trees, cactus bushes and other plants grow most luxuriantly upon them. Beside the temples there appear to have been extensive masonry tanks, none of which, beyond their pits, and a few bits of stone-work, remain. There is one group of Jaina shrines,
II *b*. which on account of their better preservation than the rest, and the presence in one of a very finely engraved and important inscription, might be considered the principal group. Dated inscriptions upon temples are so very few and rare that when they are found they are of the utmost importance in fixing a style of architecture definitely, and giving a fixed point around which to group its variations. The inscription at Anjaneri records that in *Śakasamvat* 1063 Seuṇachandra III. gave three shops in the city (probably Anjaneri) for maintaining the temple of Chandraprabha, and that a rich merchant named Vatsarâja, with two others, Lâhada and Daśaratha, gave a shop and house for the same purpose. (*Ind. Ant.* XII. 126; *J. B. B. R. A. S.*, Pt. XIII. p. 86.) (**Surveyed.**)

III. Upon the very highest plateau of Anjaneri hill is a small roughly built temple dedicated to Anjani, who is here represented by the usual red-bedaubed rough stone image. The shrine is built up of material from an older and better built temple. In the upper cliff, below the topmost plateau, to the north-east, just above the pond and bungalows, is a small roughly cut Jaina cave with a roughly cut seated Jina within. A small doorway, with coarsely cut figures on either side, gives access to a long verandah room off which, again, is the shrine. In the lower cliff, in the side of the gorge through which the rough ascent passes, is another small Jaina cave with better finished sculpture than in the one above. Pârasnâtha flanks the doorways. These belong to the Digambara Jains, whose images are always nude. Attached to the cave is a water cistern. (**Surveyed.**)

III. 5. **Cha'ma'r Tenkdi**, a hill about 600 feet high, 5 or 6 miles north from Nâsik: A few small Jaina caves, of no great age or merit. They are at a height of about 450 feet from the base of the hill, and face about S.S.W. The upper part of the ascent is by a stair of roughly dressed stone, containing 173 steps of varying heights, and with a parapet on each side. At the 163rd step a path leads to two rock-cut tanks on the right,—one having the top broken in and the other with two square openings. Above the built steps the stair is continued by 16 more steps, cut in the scarp, landing on the terrace. The excavations, beginning from the left or west, are :—(1) In a slight recess is a tank with two openings broken into one. (2) A cave, the verandah of which has four columns; the left one and left pilaster are left square in the rough, the others plain octagons. On the rock over the cave is built a lotus-bud cupola like those on structural temples. In the left end of the verandah is a covered cell; in the back, at the left side, a door has been begun but not cut through the wall; next to it is a plain rectangular window; the central doorway is plain with a raised sill, and has Tîrthankaras or *dvârapâlas* by the sides of it; Gautama, on the left, is 5′ 2″ high and is attended by two female figures about 3½ feet high. Over the door is a Jina seated cross-legged, about 14″ high on a throne with three lions on the front of it, with a male *chauri* bearer 21″ high on each side. To the left of this is a fat figure seated on a kneeling elephant; and to the right, a female (Ambikâ) is also squatted on some couching animal, and holding a child on her knee. Pârśvanâtha stands on the right of the door with the five-hooded snake canopying his head. On his right a female attendant, about 3′ high, has a single *nâga* hood over her head; and to his right a male kneels on one knee. To the right of this is another window, and then a side door leading into a rough part of the cave walled off from the rest. In the right end of the verandah is an unfinished cell with a bench, and over the door a sculpture, very like that over the central door but somewhat larger. All the sculpture, however, being in a very coarse spongy rock, is rough and seems to have been touched up at a comparatively late date. The interior is but roughly hewn and not properly squared. At the left end is a group of figures in a slight recess and consisting of,—a Tîrthankara seated cross-legged, 10″ high, on a cushion on a throne bearing the bull, the *chinha* of Âdinâtha, in the centre; to its left a squatted figure, and then two standing males, 5″ high,—the other side below is unfinished. Outside each of the Jina's arms is another, similarly seated, 5″ high; and over each of the three heads is a painted canopy with a male figure 3½″ high on the central one, and a similar one at each side of him. Around this group are 21 shallow recesses 1¼ inch square, each containing a seated Jina: five down each side, three sloping upwards on each side towards one in the centre at the top of all, one under each of the lowest on the slopes and in line with the upper ones in the sides and one over each shoulder of the larger figure; these make in all the 24 Tîrthankaras or Jinas. A bench goes round three sides of the cave. On the back wall, above the bench, is a group of figures: in the centre is a seated Pârśvanâtha, 3′ 2″ high, on a throne with three lions below; his head is canopied by a seven-hooded snake. Above is a small seated figure and on each side a standing figure 2′ 9″ high with high cap and *chauri*. On each side of this is a large seated figure with high ornamental cap, necklaces, earrings: the left one is a male on a kneeling elephant with foliage below; the right one is Ambikâ on a crouching lion or tiger and at her knee is a reclining female figure. Beyond each of these is a seated male 3′ 5″ high, similar to the central figure and with similar standing males at each side, but also with a triple umbrella upheld by Vidyâdharas over the seven-hooded snake. The right group has Gautama standing under foliage and with no other canopy. To the extreme right is part of a standing male figure and of others unfinished. (3) About ten yards to the right is a recess as if for the beginning of a cave, and seven yards farther is the third excavation, with an open verandah. On the left wall is a figure 2′ high, squatted on an animal, with a canopy above and pilasters down each side of the compartment. On the right wall, in a similar recess, is Ambikâ on her tiger with a child on her left knee and a standing figure 1 foot high below her right knee and behind the tiger; figures also stand by the pilasters and appear in the canopy overhead. In the back of the verandah is an ornamental central doorway with raised sill having two griffins or lions' heads in front; an ornamental pilaster is on each side, and a cornice over the lintel with small standing males above over each pilaster and the centre of the door. To the left of the door is Pârśvanâtha Śeshaphaṇi, with two smaller attendants, and an ornamental pilaster down each side of the panel, on which are carved some small standing figures. On the right side of the door is Gautama but much defaced, with decayed seated attendants below on each side, and several small figures on the side pilasters. The hall is 8 or 9 feet square. On the left wall is a group, containing two seated Jinas, 10″ high, on a cushion with two lions below each; right and left of them are Ambikâ and Indra with attendants. To the left of each Jina is a standing male. The canopies and 21 very small seated Jinas are nearly the same as before. By the sides of the central figures are three males in a row with triple *chhatris* over their heads very rudely cut. The back wall has a built bench in front and 3 male figures standing, the central one 3′ 5″ and the side ones 3′ 3″ high with four ornamental pilasters between and at the sides of the compartments they occupy; and at the base of each pilaster is a standing Jina. Overhead is scroll work and figures. The base of each pilaster contains a small standing male with his arms down and the capital a very small squatting Jina. Beyond the outer pilasters are other standing figures 15″ high. To the left of this group is another squatting figure 14″ high with clasped hands and a large back knot of hair. On each side of each of the three large male figures in the lower corners are very small kneeling female figures with large back knots of hair. On the right wall are two small seated Jinas and to the right is Ambikâdêvî, 12″ high, on her *vâhana*, with a child on her left knee and the stem of a tree (mango) behind and above her head with a bunch of fruit hanging on each side, and a small seated male above. (4) About 10 feet to the right is a recess 15 feet wide and 7′ deep. In the centre of the back wall, in high relief, is the upper part of an unfinished gigantic seated Pârśvanâtha, 7′ from the top of the head to the waist and with a polycephalous snake canopying his head. Just to the right of this the rock is undercut and on the top of the projecting part are three half lotuses carved on the level surface. The middle one 4′ 6″ in diameter and the side ones half the size and 5′ from centre to centre. A square socket for a flagstaff is sunk in the centre of each lotus, and two raised *pâdukâs* or footprints are sculptured on the flat centre of the middle lotus. A recess has been commenced just to the right of these and over the top of the stair. All the carving is of a very inferior character. (**Surveyed**.)

II.—Igatpuri Tâlukâ.

III. 1. **Tringalvadi.**—Six miles from Igatpuri, under the hill fort of the same name, is the little village of Tringalvâdi. Not far from it, situated in the foot of the hill side, is a Jaina cave which, though now very much the worse for the weathering it has passed through, was once a very fine cave. It consists of a large hall about 35 feet square, off the back of which is an antechamber and shrine, and before which is a long verandah the length of the width of the hall. Along the front of the verandah is a low parapet wall from which rise two pillars, one on either side of the entrance, supporting the outer eave of the verandah. Opposite these two pillars are two pilasters, and between the latter is the main doorway to the hall. On either side of these pilasters, between them and the ends of the verandah and piercing the partition wall between the verandah and the hall, is a barred window neatly decorated. In the centre of the verandah ceiling before the doorway is a group cut in relief representing five human figures in a circle. The middle figure appears to be assisted (or carried through the air) by one on either side, while two others help beneath. Over the doorway, on the dedicatory block, is a Jina.

Within, the hall ceiling is, or was, supported by four columns set square in the centre. The walls and ceilings are plain. Only one pillar now remains intact, the others being more or less destroyed. Round the two sides in the south-west and north-east corners are high benches (not altars). The shrine doorway is much corroded too, but was not so elaborate as the hall doorway. Above it, one above the other on three bands of mouldings, are three Jinas. Within the shrine, which is quite plain, and measures 13 feet by 12 feet, upon an altar against the back wall, are the remains of a colossal Jina. The chest, head, and umbrella have been smashed and thrown away, but the legs and cushion are left. In the middle of the cushion is the bull, shewing the figure to have been that of Ṛishabhadeva, while on either side of it is an inscription dated *Samvat* 1266 (A.D. 1210).

There was a very fine inscription upon the wall in the north end of the cave, only a very small fragment of which now remains. The rest has flaked off. The letters were small and well cut, the inscribed panel measuring, perhaps, four to five feet across, the depth being uncertain. The front of the cave, with the main doorway, was originally painted, traces of which still remain. The partition wall between the verandah and the hall has been entirely built of great irregular masses well fitted together. (**Surveyed**.)

III. 2. **Met Chandra'chi**, with three caves, much filled in.

3. **Nirpan**, copper-plate grant, *Ind. Ant.* IX. 123.

III.—Sinnar Tâlukâ.

1. **Sinnar**, twenty miles south of Nâsik. Here there is the largest and most complete Hemâdpanti temple in the Dakhan—the temple of Gondeśvara, or, as it is sometimes erroneously called, Govindeśvara. There is also on the north-west of the town a very interesting and exquisitely carved little temple in the Châlukyan style. This example of the style that is almost exclusively confined to the Kânarese districts, is the furthest north yet found.

I *b*. (1). The temple of Gondeśvara is a Śaivite shrine, surrounded by four other smaller shrines, and known as a *Śivapanchâyatana* temple. All these five shrines, with the Nandi pavilion before the main entrance, stand upon a raised platform, and the whole is surrounded by a masonry wall with two entrances, one on the south and the other on the east. The main temple faces east, and, with the exception of the crowning members of the finial, which have been rebuilt in a very barbarous fashion,* it is practically complete in all its parts. It is however a great deal shattered, more especially the three porches. It is built of the ordinary amygdaloidal trap rock of the locality, and this has not weathered well, the surface having become more or less honeycombed, and the smaller carving has consequently suffered much on this account. The temple and its minor shrines are sculptured with decorative ornament from ground line to finial. Of figure sculpture there is very little, and in this respect it forms a strong contrast with the smaller but richly carved temple of Lakshmi-Nârâyaṇa at Pedgâon. They are each good specimens of the two styles of decoration—the one adorned chiefly with bands and panels of arabesque and other ornament, the other mainly covered with figure sculpture which forms the chief decoration. Figure sculpture enters more largely into the decoration of the pillars, and in this they are more like those of the Pedgâon temple.

* A new finial in keeping with the rest of the building is being substitued for this.

The whole group is built upon high ground, a short distance outside the town to the north-east, and is seen for miles around. Close beside it, on the east, is a large tank to which steps lead down from the eastern portico, and which appears to have been the quarry out of which the stone was excavated with which the temple was built. The temple has been repaired in recent times, when stone props were inserted in the porches and doorways to support broken beams, a new flight of steps was added to the front porch and, unfortunately, a new, but alien, finial was built upon the top of the spire to supply the place of the fallen one.

The four central pillars of the *maṇḍapa* or hall are very richly carved, in fact all the elaboration of the interior seems to be concentrated upon them. Another fine piece of work is the gargoyle projecting from the north wall of the shrine, and through which the water from the washings of the *liṅga* in the shrine flows. It is fashioned to the shape of the conventional *makara* with a very florid tail, the water passing out from the open mouth.

I *a*. (2). The shrine of Aeśvara upon the north-west of the town, just above the rivulet, is the remains of a Châlukyan temple. It consists now of the shrine, with but part of the first storey of the *śikhara*, and eight columns standing out before it in two groups of four each, one beyond the other. These pillars are polygonal in plan and are similar to those at Nâregal, Dambal, and other places in the Dhârwâr District, four being eight-sided and four six-sided with recessed corners. From the remains of foundations around the present walls, it would seem that the shrine had had a *pradakshiṇâ* or circumambulatory passage about it. A most superb piece of carving spans the entrance to the antechamber and is one of the finest pieces of chiselled decorative work to be found in any shrine in Western India. The central portion of this great slab is a group representing the *tâṇḍava*, the figures being remarkably well and boldly cut. On either side of this is the conventional *makara* from whose mouths an arch of little figures rises over the heads of the figures in the group, and whose tails curl up above their bodies in the most wild exuberance of whorls and rolls of the richest arabesque.

Within the antechamber is an *ashṭadikpâla* ceiling, such as is so frequently met with in Châlukyan shrines; but curiously, a mistake has been made in the location of two of the *dikpâlas*. The ceiling, which is divided into nine equal divisions by crossbars, has in the eight bays surrounding the central one the *ashṭadikpâlas* or regents of the eight points of the compass. These are so arranged that each occupies the position north, south, north-east, &c., assigned to him; but in this particular ceiling the positions of Kubera and Agni have been interchanged by some blunder of the sculpture or designer. The whole ceiling is in one slab. Over the shrine door, which is fairly well carved, is a row of dancing figures representing the *saptamâtarah* or seven mothers. Altogether this temple has been a perfect gem, rich in the very best workmanship, the bas-reliefs being exceedingly well carved.

III. (3) and (4). Beside the temples of Gondeśvara and Aeśvara, there are two old ones of no particular interest in the village. A peculiar feature in one of these is the presence of four doors to the shrine. (5) Out in the fields, about a mile east of the town, is a small Hemâdpanti shrine partly in ruins. Just outside the east gate, by a well, are two colossal Jaina figures. (*J. B. B. R. A. S.* Part XIII. p. 86.) (**Surveyed.**)

2. **Dubera**, 6 miles south-south-west from Sinnar. Krishnarâv Gopal Barve, *Jâgirdâr*, possesses a set of 3 copperplates.

3. **Bhojapur**, 10 miles south of Sinnar, temple of Khaṇḍobâ cut in the rock in the hill fort.

IV.—Niphâd Tâlukâ.

1. **Nandur**, 20 miles east from Nâsik at the junction of the Kaḍvâ and Godâvarî Temple of Madhyamêśvara Mahâdêva, on a small rocky islet; said to be about 200 years old.

2. **Shivra**, 3 miles south-east of Niphâd, a group of memorial stones, but of little interest and of comparatively no antiquity.

V.—Chândor Tâlukâ.

1. **Châ'ndor.**—Here there are the temple of Reṇukâ Devi, a Jaina cave, some inscriptions, and a gallery of caves away up in Indrâi Fort adjoining.

III. (1) The temple of Reṇukâ is a comparatively modern construction of no particular architectural interest, save that it has a fine broad flight of steps leading up to it, and which appears to be its chief feature. At the foot of this flight of stairs are offerings in the shape of from twenty to thirty miniature flights of stairs (five steps in each) carved on small squared blocks of stones. Pilgrims bring these and leave them there. But the most interesting things at this temple are two images in wood lying in the inner courtyard of the temple and much bedaubed with red paint. They have been exceedingly well carved, but are much weather-worn. They are both Roman Catholic images—one representing the Annunciation and the other St. Anna with the infant Virgin on her knee. In the first, the Virgin Mary stands upon the crescent moon with a crown upon her head, and is robed in flowing garments, while all around her, forming an oval framo about her person, is a garland of flowers. The first image is a bas-relief, whereas the second is a statuette, both of wood. When or how they were brought here no one seems to know. They have now the names of Hindu goddesses and serve as such.

III. (2) The Jaina Cave which is excavated in one of the lower cliffs of the Chândor Fort hill, just above the town to the east, is a roughly cut small room, entered by one doorway, and supported within by two central, heavy, and clumsily cut square columns. Around the four sides of the cave in bas-relief are scores of figures, large and small, mostly images of the *tîrthankaras.* On the back or west wall is the principal figure, that of Chandraprabha, with the crescent moon beneath him. This was originally the principal object of worship in the cave. Upon the south wall of the cave are figures of Gaṇapati and a four-armed *devi* which are red-leaded and worshipped, the latter as Kâlîkâ Mâtâ, after whom the cave is now called.

III. (3) In the top of Indrâi Fort, above the upper cliffs, towards the north end, and facing east, is a row of thirteen caves varying from 12 to 20 feet square. They are in a continuous row, only separated from each other by thin partition walls. There is nothing about these caves to indicate to what religion they were dedicated, or whether they were excavated to afford shelter to a garrison in ancient days. Near the top of the steps leading up the cliff is a large Persian inscription. **(Surveyed.)**

2. **Dhodambe**, curious old temple of Mahâdêva with carved figures.

VI.—Yeolâ Tâlukâ.

IIa. **Anka'i**, 6 miles south from Manmâḍ station. Above the village are 7 or 8 Jaina caves of some interest, though small: the carved doorways are specially rich. In the fort of Ankâi are some Brahmanical caves of late date, and in the sister fort of Tankâi are some old temples (see *Archæological Survey Reports*, Vol. V.; *B. B. R. A. S.* Pt. XIII. p. 69; *Cave Temples of India*). **(Surveyed.)**

Inscription in old Devanâgarî on a pilaster in the Jaina caves.

VII.—Nândgâon Tâlukâ.

III. 1. **Bangaon**, 6 miles south of Nândgâon. An old Hemâdpanti temple of Baneśvara, but of no particular account. **(Surveyed.)**

III. 2. **Na'ga'pur**, 12 miles west by south from Nândgâon and 2½ miles east of Manmâd. Old Hemâdpanti temple of no special interest. **(Surveyed.)**

VIII.—Mâlegâon Tâlukâ.

IIb. 1. **Jhodga'**, 15 miles north-east of Mâlegâon. At Jhodgâ is the well finished temple of Mâṇikeśvara situated at the foot of a small hill to the west of the town. It consists of a central hall with its porch and three shrines, and the main *śikhara* is practically complete. The whole is richly wrought and decorated, and the temple looks exceedingly well as it stands out in the open without any surroundings. The main shrine, hall, and porch are of original construction, the two side shrines are of later and inferior workmanship, and no attempt has been made on these to preserve the lines of mouldings running round the older work. The interior of the temple is comparatively simple and plain. One large domical ceiling covers in the *maṇḍapa* without any intermediate free-standing pillars. In the middle of the floor of the shrine, which is rather lower than that of the hall, is a *liṅga*, while in the back-wall is a large empty niche. The shrine door is fairly well, but a trifle coarsely carved. Out in front of the porch, upon a roughly raised platform, is a large mutilated Nandi looking towards the shrine. Upon one of the pillars, inserted in the entrance under a broken beam, is a short inscription of a few letters only. About a hundred yards west of this temple are the ruined shrine and antechamber of a smaller temple of much plainer design. **(Surveyed.)**

III. 2. **Chikalvohol**, 10 miles north-east of Mâlegâon. At Chikhalvohol there are the remains of an old temple. Little of the original work, however, now remains, and the temple consists principally of mud.

IX.—Bâglan Tâlukâ.

III. **Devala'na'**, 9 miles east by north of Satâna. Here there is an old three-shrined temple dedicated to Jâgeśvara, but the three shrines have been rebuilt in a very plain manner. A few courses of the basement of the original building remain below the later work, and show that that part, like the porch, was originally highly carved. The porch is elaborately decorated though much damaged. Within, it has a central panel to a ceiling representing Kṛishṇa and the *gopis*, similar to the ceiling at Vâghli. **(Surveyed.)**

X.—Kalvan Tâlukâ.

III. 1. **Saptas'ringa**, in the Chândoḍ range of hills, with masonry tanks, and the temple of Siddhês'vara, now mostly in ruins, but with the dome standing, and having some rather elaborate stone carving. It was built of large blocks of stone without mortar. Near a *dharmaśâlâ* stands the *samâdhi* or tomb of a Râjâ of Dharmapur. Near by is a fine old *bastí*. The cave of Dêvî Mahishamardani or Saptaśṛinga Nivâsinî is at the base of a perpendicular scarp near the summit of the hill (*Ind. Ant.* Vol. II. pp. 161-164).

III. 2. **Dhodap**...... Hill fort with an inscription on the gate.

XI.—Dindori Tâlukâ.

III. 1. **Ra'masej**, 6 miles north from Nâsik. A hill fort in which is a large well with a flight of steps descending into it. There is also said to be an underground passage leading from it.

III. 2. **Jambutke**, 4 miles south-west from Dindori. A plain Hemâḍpanti well, 45 feet square.

III. 3. **Ambegaon**, 13 miles west from Dindori. Hemâḍpanti temple of Mahâdêva, 40 feet by 36,—the roof and portions of the walls fallen, but richly covered with sculptures.

III. 4. **Vani**, 12 miles north from Dindori and 26 miles from Nâsik. A plain temple of Mahâdêva, partially ruined. Copperplate grant, *Ind. Ant.* XI. 156.

III. 5. **Chandika'pur**, 15 miles north from Dindori. The ascent to Saptaśṛingi.

Inscription, stating that the steps were made by Konhar Girmâji, Krishna Girmâj, and Rudrâji Girmâji in *Śaka* 1692.

VI.—KHÂNDESH ZILLA.

I.—Dhulia Tâlukâ.

III. 1. **Amboda**, 12 miles from Dhulia. A small temple said to be Hemâdpanti, of the 17th century.

III. 2. **La'ling**, 7 miles south of Dhulia. At Lâling there is a small Hemâḍpanti temple on the south of the village by the roadside, but it is of no interest. Above the village rises the old fort, the extent of which is very limited. Within the walls, which are now partly in ruins, are a few large rock-cut water cisterns, and on the highest point is a ruined European bungalow, built, report says, by a former Collector, as a hot weather retreat from Dhulia. A few old iron guns lie about, and two or three with their breaches knocked off have been used as a waste water-pipe to one of the bath-rooms of the bungalow.

III. 3. **Vinchur Bk.**, 14 miles from Dhulia. Well, said to have been built during the times of the Gavali Râjâs.

III. 4. **Nandala**, 20 miles from Dhulia. Temple of Mahâdeva.

III. 5. **Dhadre**, 14 miles from Dhulia. Hemâdpanti temple of Mahâdeva.

III. 6. **Sirud**, 14 miles south-east of Dhulia. Hemâḍpanti temple of Devi and a well.

II.—Pimpalner Tâlukâ.

1. **Pimpalner**, copper-plate grant, *Ind. Ant.* IX. 293.

2. **Balsa'ne**, a small village, some twenty-five miles to the north-west of Dhulia, where there are the remains of some nine separate temples and buildings—three in a field belonging to Lakshman Gangâdhar just above the bank of the Burâi river on the south-east of the village; four on high ground to the east of the village; one, a *matha*, a short distance to the north-east of the last; and a small one in the fields, across the river, some distance to the south of the village. Of these the finest examples are one in the first group
I *b*. and one in the second. The former is now the most complete and highly wrought of all at Balsâne, though, judging from the amount of work lavished upon the great fallen blocks of the other temples, they were not much behind it, if at all. It is a Śaiva temple, with three shrines arranged around a central hall, and having a porch upon the fourth side, the west, which is the front of the temple. It is now very much shattered and weather-worn. Portions of the *śikharas* of the main (east) and south shrines remain, but the north shrine with its *śikhara* has almost entirely fallen, and those parts of it still standing threaten to topple over with the least shake. The exterior walls of the temple are much in the style of the temple of Lakshmi-Nârâyaṇa at Pedgâon in the Ahmadnagar District. The lower basement mouldings are highly decorated, while above them rises the main section of the walls, covered with figure sculpture of gods and goddesses, dancing figures, *jogis*, &c., while above all the *śikharas* rose, thickly adorned with delicate

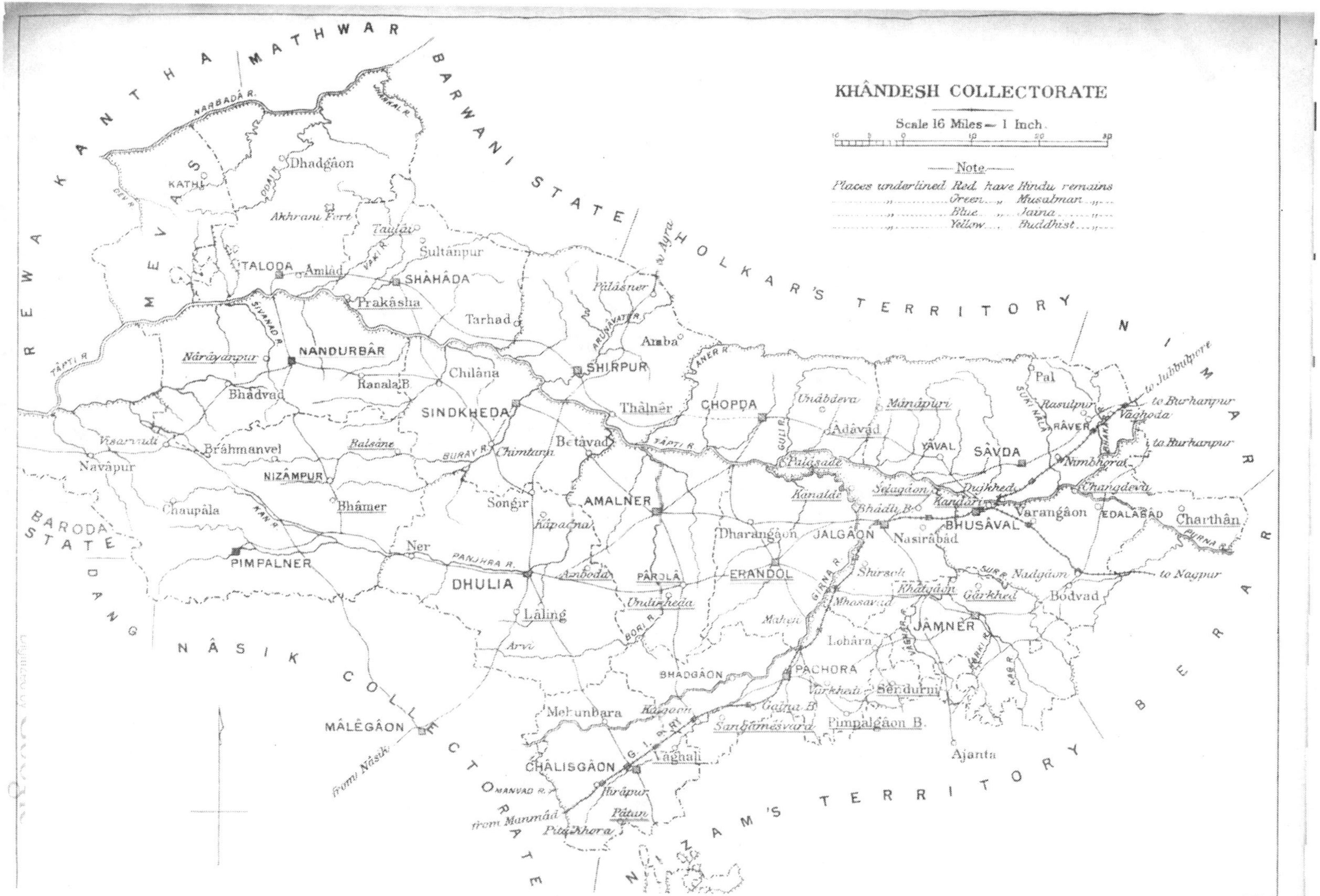
KHÂNDESH COLLECTORATE
Scale 16 Miles — 1 Inch.
Note
Places underlined Red have Hindu remains
Green Musalman
Blue Jaina
Yellow Buddhist
REWA KANTHA
MATHWAR
BARWANI STATE
HOLKAR'S TERRITORY
NIMAR
BERAR
NIZAM'S TERRITORY
NÂSIK COLLECTORATE
DANG
BARODA STATE
MEVAS
NARBADA R.
TÂPTI R.
GIRNA R.
PURNA R.
PANJHRA R.
KHÂNDESH
TALODA
SHÂHÂDA
NANDURBÂR
SHIRPUR
SINDKHEDA
CHOPDA
AMALNER
DHULIA
PIMPALNER
NIZÂMPUR
JALGÂON
ERANDOL
PÂROLÂ
BHUSÂVAL
SÂVDA
YÂVAL
RÂVER
EDALABAD
JÂMNER
PACHORA
BHADGAON
CHÂLISGÂON
MÂLÊGÂON
Dhadgâon
Akhrani Fort
Sultânpur
Prakâsha
Tarhad
Amba
Thâlnêr
Chilâna
Betâvad
Songir
Bhâmer
Navâpur
Chaupâla
Brâhmanvel
Ner
Lâling
Dharangâon
Nasirâbâd
Varangâon
Charthân
Bodvad
Lohâra
Sendurni
Pimpalgâon B.
Ajanta
Vâghali
Mehunbara
to Burhanpur
to Nagpur
to Jubbulpore
from Nâsik
from Manmâd

ornamental detail. The interior of the building is in no wise behind its exterior in the matter of decoration, its pillars, ceilings, shrine and entrance doorways being very richly wrought.

IIb. The second temple mentioned above has been no less highly finished than the first, but the whole of its shrine has fallen. Its plan differs from the first in that it had but one shrine and three porches in place of the three shrines and one porch. The interior of this temple is in a very dirty state, and, as no worship is carried on within it, it is entirely neglected. The figure sculpture, which is thick upon its exterior, is almost completely ruined, either by vandals or by both them and the weather. The stone being of rather a soft nature seems to have weathered to the condition of *murum*, and now crumbles away with the least touch. The broken walls of the fallen shrine give a good idea of how the structure was built up. Here we find an outer and an inner face of block masonry, set up more or less on edge, not bedded on the broad or flat sides of the blocks, and the interior space between them filled up with huge rough blocks thrown in in no particular order, and without the very least attempt anywhere at bonding. In fact the outer shells just keep the inner "filling in" from rolling out altogether, and the shells themselves are only prevented from bulging out and falling asunder by the weight of the blocks. Here and there, more especially at the corners, a clamp or two of iron is used, but very seldom.

IIb. Among the other temples at Balsâne, the one on the south-east of this last, with a single entrance and many small shrines within, is in a very filthy state. This is due to the front having been built up with brick and mud masonry at some time, thus keeping out light and air. The bats have taken possession of the interior, and the village cattle find it a very comfortable retreat from the hot rays of a midday sun.* (**Surveyed**.)

Upon the *matha* is a Sanskrit Inscription, dated *Śaka* 1106.

III. 3. **Bha'mer,** 4 miles south of Nizâmpur. This seems once to have been a large place, the whole area being covered with ruins. On the west is a gate flanked by round towers, with two pillars about 9 feet high for gate posts. There is also a finer gateway in better preservation, near which is a characteristic Hemâḍpanti or Gavali Râjâ's well. The fort on the hill above the village contains many rooms excavated in the rock. The caves of most importance face the south-west and are nearly all on the same level. The first group consists of three openings into each other; the roof of the central and largest room is supported by pillars. On the face of the hill facing Nizâmpur is a range of caves said to be inaccessible (*Ind. Ant.*, Vol. II. p. 128; Vol. IV. p. 339). (**Surveyed**.)

III. 4. **Niza'mpur,** 17 miles north-east from Pimpalner. A Jaina temple dedicated to Pârśvanâtha.

In addition to the above there are numberless fragments of ruins apparently of the same class of building as the Hemâḍpanti temples scattered about in many of the villages, which lie at the foot of the hills south of the Pânjrâ in the Pimpalner *tâlukâ*. These fragments are generally single pillars curiously carved, evidently very old and often built into other buildings. The most conspicuous is in a village due south of Pimpalner

* These temples are now being repaired where necessary and cleaned out.

III. about 5 miles from it. There is also a Hemâdpanti tank at the village of Indwa, 6 miles north-west of Dusâna, but it is of no account.

III.—NANDURBÂR TÂLUKÂ.

III. 1. **Nandurba'r,** 19 miles north from Nizâmpur, contains many mosques. The house of the Sar-Desâi is said to be about 400 years old.

Inscription in Persian on a ruined tower.

2. **Na'ra'yanpur,** 5 miles west of Nandurbâr. An old fort close to a stone dam on the S'ivanad river, and a little way up the stream are fragments of a curiously carved temple built into a well, and others lying near.

III. 3. **Watada,** 5 miles east from Nandurbâr. Old and large temple of Viṭhoba.

IV.—TALODA TÂLUKÂ,

III. 1. **Amlad,** 2 miles from Taloda. Temples of Chaṅkêśvara and Rokḍêśvara.

2. **Karda** copper-plate grant, *Ind Ant.* XII. 263.

V.—SHÂHÂDA TÂLUKÂ.

III. 1. **Praka'sha** on the Tâptî, 10 miles south-west from Shâhâda. A number of temples and tombs built on rocks, some five of them, *viz.* the temples of Gautama, Sangam-eśvara Mahâdêva, Kedârêśvara, Mansâpurî, and a temple of Mahâdêva, are fine handsome imposing buildings, but they are all more or less modern and of little interest. (**Surveyed.**)

Inscriptions.—Two Sanskṛit inscriptions over the door of the temple of Sangamêśvara Mahâdêva; one in a large *sâbhâ maṇḍapa*; and one partially effaced on the south side of the gate of Mahâdêva's temple.

III. 2. **Taula'i,** 2 miles north of Sultânpur. There is here an old step-well built in the Muhammadan style. It first descends a certain distance, then turns at right angles and continues down to the main shaft. Cross beams at the different levels, supported upon the pilasters in the walls, divide the depth into storeys, increasing in number as the passage descends. There are no free-standing pillars. (**Surveyed.**)

VI.—SINDKHEDA TÂLUKÂ.

III. **Dura'na,** 3 miles south of Chimtânâ. About two miles south-east of Chimtânâ, and on the east of the main road are the ruins of an old Hemâdpanti temple, standing upon rocky ground in the midst of the fields. (**Surveyed.**)

VII.—Shirpur Tâlukâ.

II *a*. **Thalner**, 10 miles from Shirpur. Ten Muhammadan tombs, of which eight are built with dressed black stone and two of burnt brick. One is octagonal with carved black stones and the others square and plain. Parts of the domes are destroyed but they are in good condition inside. Three of them are occasionally used by Europeans on tour. The largest three are 11 feet square each. The octagonal one is 10 feet wide. Two are 8 feet square, one 6, two are 4 feet square and one 3½ feet square.

Inscriptions.—On the octagonal tomb are some Arabic inscriptions, but they yield no date. The Musalmâns of the place say they were built about 500 years ago by one Shâh Ajam Mule Shârâni, whom they call their Pîr, and whose tomb is the 6 feet square one. One inscription reads :—

هو الشافي

بنوح مفاينت قل يا الله و يا خذمت مكتوفي حكمت بقفاک يا الله ساقد دقي وقات
بسلطان الد عظم اد حد الد سلطان فرمان جهلاے دادے خوقاتلا لد وعطلم في لا لللي
لساحم معلي الله وفا حولاف و اطايفا الديان واحطا الوجهر او مشرقي و حدا حب بيته
و سلب اوراحد واصعد الله جود مايها الا ادلي محشاين الله كل حطو مسلماني قايمه

VIII.—Amalner Tâlukâ.

III. 1. **Parola**, 22 miles east of Dhulia. Imâm Bâdshâh's *dargâh* on the east of the fort; *chattri* of Girdhar Śeṭh Bâlâji Vâlak; Svâmi temple about 24 feet square of stone, with brick spire ornamented in plaster; and temple of Japâtâ Bhâva about 58 feet by 56.

III. 2. **Undikheda**, 3 miles south-west of Pârolâ. Large temple of Śri Nâgeśvara Mahâdeva on an island in the Bori river. The outer walls of the spire have many angles and are carved: it is ascribed to Trimbakrâv Mâmâ Pethe. It is, however, modern and of no particular interest.

IX.—Chopda Tâlukâ.

III. 1. **Chopada**, 21 miles north-west from Amalner. Jami Masjid said to have been built by Miran Muhammadkhân, one of the Farukhi kings; Kâli Masjid, and other mosques; Sâtkothadyâ well, 37 feet square.

III. 2. **Adavad**, 10 miles east of Chopaḍa. A fine old well 30 feet by 12, with steps, but ruined; and a *masjid*.

Inscription.—On one of the stones at the steps of a well at the mosque is a short Persian inscription.

III. 3. **Unabdeva**, 3 miles north of Adâvad. A hot spring with some buildings.

III. 4. **Changaon**, a fort north-west of Chopda, supposed to be 500 years old. It is estimated to have cost Rs. 2,00,000, and its dimensions are 500′ long and 500′ broad. It is situated about a mile and a half to the north of the village on the top of rising ground in Survey No. 168. The plateau of the fort is reached by steps as in the fort of Lâling in Dhulia *tâlukâ*. There are tanks on the side, as in Lâling. Some of them are of carved stones. Inside the gate of the fort is a *pîr's* tomb and a tank. Remains of a wall are visible. The fort is said to have been built in the Gavali Râj.

III. 5. **La'sur**, north-west of Chopda, a temple of Nateśvara, said to be 300 years old. It is estimated to have cost Rs. 2,000, and its dimensions are 46′ long and 38′ broad. It is situated in the hills to the north of Lâsur, and is surrounded by a wall on the outside; on one of the wells inside the temple is an inscription.

X.—Erandol Tâlukâ.

II *b*. 1. **Erandol.** In the middle of the town is a large strongly built old quadrangle known as the Pândava's Vâdâ. It is the remains of one of those strongly built and enclosed mosques which were erected in the early days of Muhammadan rule, partly mosque partly fort, and is of the same style of building that the great Adina Masjid at Anhilvâd-Pattan must have been. Like the latter, the greater part of the mosque at the west end of the court-yard seems to have been built of the remains of older Hindu temples. The court-yard and the mosque is enclosed by a high strongly built black stone wall, with high arched recesses all around the inner side, in each of which is a barred or grated window. There appears to have been a fine porch before the entrance to the court-yard on the east, but it is now represented by a huge pile of fallen masonry over which the visitor has to climb to reach the interior. The mosque which, as usual, occupied the whole width of the west end of the enclosure, has almost entirely disappeared; the central bay only remains, and this has been enclosed by mud walls and is still in use as a mosque. Of the rest, all, except a few solitary blocks, has disappeared, leaving some beautifully carved *mehrâbs* in the back wall, which are partly buried in accumulated débris.

The Hindus claim the place as a Hindu building subsequently appropriated by the Muhammadans. But this is not quite correct. The building as it now stands is purely Muhammadan, but, as just said, it has in great part been built, as all the earlier mosques were, of pilfered material. Judging from the few columns that now remain, the whole of the pillars of the mosque were probably taken from some Hindu temple or temples, and where the court-yard wall is broken down in places, carved stones and broken images may
I *b*. be seen built into the interior. The beautiful *mehrâbs*, with their Persian inscriptions above them, now much obliterated, are purely Musalmân work. A Hindu temple possibly once existed here, and perhaps on the site of the mosque—nothing more probable—but the Hindus have now not the shadow of a claim to the place. (**Surveyed**.)

III. 2. **Pharkande**, 6 miles from Erandol, southwards along the Aujani *nâlâ*, has a *masjid* about 150 years old, built by a man named Chand Momin. The building is distinguished by two minarets, which are said to sympathize, so that if you ascend and shake the one, the other also shakes. The building has also fine chunam work, but is not otherwise remarkable.

III. 3. **Mukhpa't** is a village 3 miles south-east of Erandol. To its south-east is an irregular plateau, on which is a tank named Padmâlaya.

On the bank of the tank are temples of Mahâdeva, Mâruti and Gaṇapati. Inscription.

XI.—Nasirâbâd Tâlukâ.

III. 1. **Kana'lde,** to the north-west of Nasirâbâd. There is a quaint-looking temple of carved black stone, below the village on the banks of the Girṇâ. Close to it is the house of the *gosâvi;* in the middle of it is a flight of steps leading to a door beyond which are more steps and then a big hole, climbing through which we enter a small cell about 5 feet by 10; from this a door leads to a second 7 feet by 4; beyond it is a third measuring 4 feet by 3½, and then a fourth 3½ feet by 3. There is nothing remarkable about them, however, as they are dug out of the clay.

III. 2. **Selgaon,** north of Jalgâon. A *maṭha* or monastery said to have been built by Masangir Gosâvi about 200 years ago. It stands on high ground near the junction of the Tâptî and Wâghar rivers opposite Borawal, is built of stone and lime, and is about 80 feet long, 60 wide and 30 high. The east wall is falling. The temple is approached by steps.

III. 3. **Kanda'ri,** south of Jalgâon. Temple of Mahâdeva of small dimensions, said to be in the Hemâdpantî style and going to decay.

III. 4. **Palasade,** north-west from Jalgâon. Temple of Râmeśvara built on a raised podium (*óṭá*) upon a small hill near the junction of the Girṇâ with the Tâptî. The temple is about 17 feet long, 14 wide, 21 high, and is said to be 300 years old.

XII.—Sâvda Tâlukâ.

III. 1. **Rasulpur,** 2 miles from Râver. An old fort and palace.

III. 2. **Bhokaridigar,** on the Bhâkar river, west from Râver. Temple of Oṁkâreśvara, and a *dharmaśâlâ* said to have been built by Ahalyâbâi Hoḷkar.

Inscription on the temple reads :—

चरणरज विठ्ठल बल्लाळ दाल्ये मौजे धाकोली परगणे राजापूर तालुक्े विजयदुर्गकर निरंतर ११९९.

3. **Pa'l,** on the Suki *nâlâ,* north of Râver. A mosque of black stone, with three bays, and of considerable architectural merit.

III. 4. **Ma'na'puri,** north-west of Yâval. About a mile from the village is an old temple ascribed to the Gavali Râjâs.

III. 5. **Kalmadu,** north-east of Nhâvi. Well, supposed to be 400 years old, in a ruined state, situated on the old high road from Chopda to Burhânpur, and said to have been built by a Gavali Râjâ. The Nimbâlkar carried off some of the stones of this well to repair his fort at Yâval about 80 years ago. Since then it has fallen out of repair and dried up.

XIII.—Bhusâval Tâlukâ.

1. **Chângadeva,** situated at the junction of the Pûrṇâ with the Tâptî. Here there are two temples, *viz.*, the temple of Chângadeva near the village and the temple of
II *b.* Ahalyâbâi in the bed of the river. The temple of Chângadeva has been a very large and fine temple, but it is now mostly rebuilt in the most outrageous fashion. It was a Vaishṇava temple. The walls around the shrine, up to the cornice, are intact and highly wrought with ornament. Portions only of the lower parts of the walls of the hall remain, upon which mud and brick continuations have been carried up to supply the missing portions. As at Sangameśvara, near Nâgardevla, there is, in the antechamber to the shrine of this temple, a small oval dome. Within the shrine there is now an image said to be that of Chângadeva. At the entrance to the temple are some very much effaced inscriptions. **(Surveyed.)**

III. The temple in the river bed, built by Ahalyâbâi of Indor, is a modern construction. The whole of the upper part of the temple has tumbled over into the bed of the river *en bloc*, and now lies partly buried in the sand, while the lofty platform upon which it was built has nothing on it but the lower courses of the temple plinth.

III. 2. **Chârthân,** twelve miles east of Edalâbâd. A Hemâḍpantî temple, but of no particular interest. **(Surveyed.)**

III. 3. **Kandâri,** 2 miles north-east of Bhusâval. Old temple partially in ruins.

III. 4. **Ghodankhed,** *petâ* Edalâbâd, a ruined well situated 6 miles north-east of Edalâbâd.

III. 5. **Mehune,** 5 miles north-west of Edalâbâd. Temple of Mahâdeva in the Hemâḍpantî style.

III. 6. **Vadgaon,** 10 miles east of Edalâbâd. Temple of Mahâdeva in the Hemâḍpantî style.

III. 7. **Hartale,** 4 miles south-west of Edalâbâd, Two Hemâḍpantî temples and a ruined mosque.

III. 8. **Edalâbâd,** old fort in ruins.

III. 9. **Vaibhale,** 6 miles south of Bhusâval. Temple of Mahâdeva in the Hemâḍpantî style, 37 feet by 28 feet, having a dome and being supported upon pillars.

III. 10. **Ravad Chincholi,** 12 miles west of Bhusâval. Old stone Hemâḍpantî temples to Mahâdeva.

In many villages of this *tâlukâ* are temples described as Hemâḍpantî, but no satisfactory details are given of their characteristics.

XIV.—Jâmner Tâlukâ.

III. 1. **Kha'tgaon,** 3 miles north of Jâmner. At Khâtgâon there are the ruins of an old temple, now of no account.

III. 2. **Ga'rkhed,** north of Jâmner. There are the ruins of what was once a very fine temple of the best style of work. Portions only of the plinth and walls of the back of the shrine now remain, showing the mouldings of the basement, and portions of the richly carved wall above it. For the rest, the addition of mud walls has preserved the place as the habitation of the god now worshipped. **(Surveyed.)**

III. 3. **Shendurni,** a small ruined temple of Viśveśvara or Viśdevali. It has an inscription, which probably covered about 3 feet by 2 feet of wall surface on the outer wall on the south side, but now too much defaced to make anything of. **(Surveyed.)**

XV.—Pâchora Tâlukâ.

II *b*. 1. **Sangames'vara,** 4 miles east of Kajgâon Station. On the south side of the village, and near the junction of the two streams, perched upon the high bank, is the old temple of Mahâdeva. The temple consists of the usual shrine, a hall whose roof has disappeared, and a very prolonged porch. The exterior of the temple is perfectly devoid of figure sculpture, its place being taken by three bands of geometric ornament. These are exceedingly chaste and effective, and run round, in unbroken lines, the three sides of the exterior walls of the hall and shrine. The ceiling of the antechamber is peculiar in that the mouldings assume an oval in plan, a very unusual shape for a ceiling. In the shrine is the *liṅga*, and the temple would seem to have been originally dedicated to Śiva. **(Surveyed.)**

III. 2. **Pimpalgaon Budruk,** 6 miles south-east of Warkhed. At the village of Pimpalgâon is the temple of Hari-Hareśvara standing in the junction of the Bâvulâ and Dabbâ streams, about a mile south of the village. It faces the west. Though originally an old temple it has been almost entirely rebuilt with brick, rubble, and plaster masonry, and is now of no account architecturally. **(Surveyed.)**

III. 3. **Kurha'd Khurd,** 7 miles from the Mâiji Station. The temple at Kurhâd Khurd is small and in ruins, and is of no particular interest. The shrine walls and part of the west walls of the hall remain. **(Surveyed.)**

III. 4. **Loha'ra.**—The remains of an old temple, with very plainly moulded walls, on the Sonai stream, about a mile south of the village, called Tapeśvara. **(Surveyed.)**

III. 5. **Na'ndre,** near Mâiji, a plain old step-well of not much interest. It is square in plan and devoid of all the ornamental adjuncts which are generally found about these wells. **(Surveyed.)**

B 1169—16

XVI.—Châlisgâon Tâlukâ.

1. **Pa'tan** is the site of a deserted town, now overgrown with jungle, in the hills to the south, or, more correctly, south-south-west of Châlisgâon. Scattered among the ruins are the remains of several old temples. The hills here are recessed, forming a horse-shoe-shaped valley, the two horns of the former, which project northwards, being about a mile apart at their ends, while the glen between them runs back about a mile and a half. At the upper end of the valley, above the temple of Âi Bhavâni, on the east side, a mountain path winds up the lonely glen, the Pitalkhora, in which are situated the well known Pitalkhora caves. A stream, fed by the numerous mountain torrents from the hills around, winds down the Pâtan valley, and in one of its curves sweeps by the foot of the shrine of Âi Bhavâni, at which there is still kept up a yearly *jatrâ* or fair. The stream inclines, throughout its meanderings, towards the eastern hills, leaving a considerable area between it and the western cliffs in which, high up above, are the caves known as Nâgârjuna's *kotri*, Sita's *Nhâni*, and Sringâr *Châvadi*, a space ample enough for the old town of Pâtna whose ruins now occupy this ground. The whole of the valley is thickly wooded, being quite uninhabited, save by the owl, the jackal, the wild pig, the panther, and an occasional tiger. The ruins of the old town are thickly scattered about, and with difficulty maintain their ground against the encroachments of the jungle, which, when unable to displace them, just grows over them and casts its creeper entanglements firmly around their mouldering walls.

Beyond the few ruined temples, tanks, and wells, there is now nothing above ground to represent the more ancient city. The ruins that now exist, composed of mud and rubble stone walls and Musalmân graves, are of a comparatively recent town, and that a town of no great size. It appears to have been walled in with strong high mud walls and high bastions, within which was a citadel similarly fortified. The crumbling walls of these enclosures, with the foundations of mud and rubble built houses, still exist. One of the walls runs along east and west by the side of the principal temple, that of Maheśvara, and is built on to it on either side, thus making the temple itself, which is upon high ground, part of the wall, the north face being within, while the south face is without, the fort. Opposite this on the south, and separated from it by a broad passage, is another small fortified enclosure in which is a small ruined temple with an **inscription** over its doorway. Beside these there are two other small ruined shrines which, like them, have been included in the fort wall on its east side. These are a few hundred yards to the east and north-east, respectively, of the first temple, one being Brahmanical, while the other is Jaina. With the temple of Âi Bhavâni up the glen, these are all the remains above ground of the more ancient city of Pâtan. (**Surveyed**.)

I a. (1). The temple of Maheśvara, the largest and most important, is built on the usual plan of shrine, *maṇḍapa*, and porch, and faces east. Its *śikhara*, or tower, has gone. The exterior of the temple is profusely sculptured, and the pillars and doorway of the shrine have also been well chiselled. In the shrine, in the middle of the floor, is the *liṅga*, while in the middle of the back wall is a niche to hold a figure, with an ornamental frame around it. There are several figures lying about which may originally have been placed in the various niches among which are Śiva, Pârvati, Lakhsmi-Nârâyaṇa, Sûrya, &c. The most important thing, however, in the temple is a very fine and well preserved **inscription** slab built flush into the south wall of the antechamber before the shrine, and midway between the floor and the beam. The slab, which bears a Sanskrit inscription, has been slightly corroded on the left hand side by the action of rain-water. It is an inscription of Govana III. of the Nikumbhavaṁśa and records the grant of a village named Devasangama at the consecration of the temple of Śiva (Madanadahana) which was built, or perhaps commenced by his father Indrarâja in *Śaka* 1075 or A.D. 1153-54. (*Epig. Ind.* Vol. I. Part VII. p. 338).

III. (2). The temple on the south of this one, in the other enclosure, which is now in ruins, seems to have been part of the belongings of this larger temple. Its axis, passing through the entrance doorway and the doorway of its enclosure, passes through the centre of the shrine of the large temple; and this smaller temple faces the larger. Its interior is much like the interior of the hall on the south side of the enclosure round the temple of Gondeśvara at Sinnar. It has no cell shrine, the interior being a long plain hall. It was probably a *maṭha* or rest-house attached to the large temple. Over its entrance doorway is a much-worn and damaged **inscription**, just as occurs over the door of the *maṭha* at Balsâne.

III. (3). Straight in front of the large temple, at short distance from it, is the small ruined Brahmanical shrine already mentioned, facing north.

III. (4). And in front of this (north), at about a hundred yards distant, is another small ruined shrine dedicated originally to a *jina*, having a seated *jina* over the entrance doorway and the empty throne well carved, in the shrine.

III. (5). At the upper end of the glen, on the east side of the stream, is the insignificant temple of Âi Bhavâni. Very little of the original building now remains intact, most of what is seen being rebuilt from the material of an older temple. From what little does remain, the temple would appear to have been a cluster of small shrines, with one or two small halls. At present the place is in a very ruinous and dirty condition. In the outside
I *b*. of the courtyard wall, built into the wall, is a much-abraded **inscription** slab, but as this wall has been built partly of old temple materials the inscription may not be, and probably is not, *in situ*. It records the grant of land and money by Sonhadadeva to the college established for the study of the *Siddhántaśiromaṇi* and other works of the astronomer Bhâskarâchârya.

II *a*. (6). Śringâr Châvadi is the name applied to a cave about half a mile up the hill north-west from the temple of Âi Bhavâni on the way to the Kanhara fort. To the right of the entrance the excavation is continued forward at right angles with a low screen wall and pillars closing it in. This part is about 25 feet in length by 7½ deep, while the principal hall of the cave is about 18 feet by 15. Outside is a rock-cut cistern.

II *a*. (7). Nâgârjuna is a third cave just above the village, consisting of a *padasâli* or verandah and an inner cave. It is a Jaina excavation and contains several figures of the Digambara sect.

III. (8). Sita's Nhâni, near the preceding, is a plain Brahmanical excavation.

I *a*. 2. **Pitalkhora**, a glen not far from Pâtan to the south-east, contains a ruined *chaitya* and *vihâra*, very early Bauddha works, with some fragments of **inscriptions** in the Maurya character,—probably dating two centuries B.C. (see *J. B. B. R. A. S.* Part XVI.; *Arch. Survey Report*, Vol. IV. and V. *Cave Temples of India*.) (**Surveyed**.)

III. 3. **Va'ghli**, a village about seven miles to the north-east of Châlisgâon. The remains at Vâghli are the temple of Mudhâidevi, a mile to the south-west of the village, and the temple of Kṛishṇa in the village. The former is situated upon an artificial mound upon the bank of the river, and is now partly in ruins. Smaller shrines which surrounded it, and stood upon the margins of the platform, have disappeared save the ruins of one which stood on the south of the temple. Although passing now under the name of Mudhâidevi's temple, it would appear to have been originally dedicated to Sûrya, for, of the only three figures sculptured upon the walls of the shrine, the one upon the principal face, the west or back wall, is that of Sûrya with his seven horses. Lying within the temple, and also outside are large blocks, portions of the temple, upon which are carved full length figures of Sûrya, three on each. There are some very neat decorated ceilings in this temple. The *śikhara* or tower of the temple has disappeared.

III. I *b*. 40. In the village is the temple of Kṛishṇa, which, as it now stands, is of no interest save for three very fine inscription slabs built into the inner wall of the hall. There is no separate shrine, and what little of the original temple now remains has been so encased in mud walls that not even its plan can be guessed at. One of the ceilings is sculptured in bold relief representing Kṛishṇa and the *gopis*. Within the hall on a raised platform is an arrangement made up with a brass mask, and which is now worshipped as Kṛishṇa. The inscription slabs are rather corroded, but all three belong to one inscription and record the erection of a temple of Siddheśanâtha or Siddheśvara by Govindarâja with a well attached and a *sattra* or dispensary. The last few lines record a grant to this temple by Govindarâja and his superior, king Seuna, in *Samvat* 991 (A.D. 1069). Seuna is the Devagirirâja Seunachandra II. This temple was thus built some two hundred years before Hemâdpant lived, who is the traditional founder of these temples. This inscription is also very important as it gives a dynasty of petty kings ruling for about four hundred years previously who are said to have come from Dwârkâ. The well mentioned in it still exists beside the temple, but there is no sign of the dispensary. (*Epig. Ind.* Vol. II. Part XII. page 221. (**Surveyed**.)

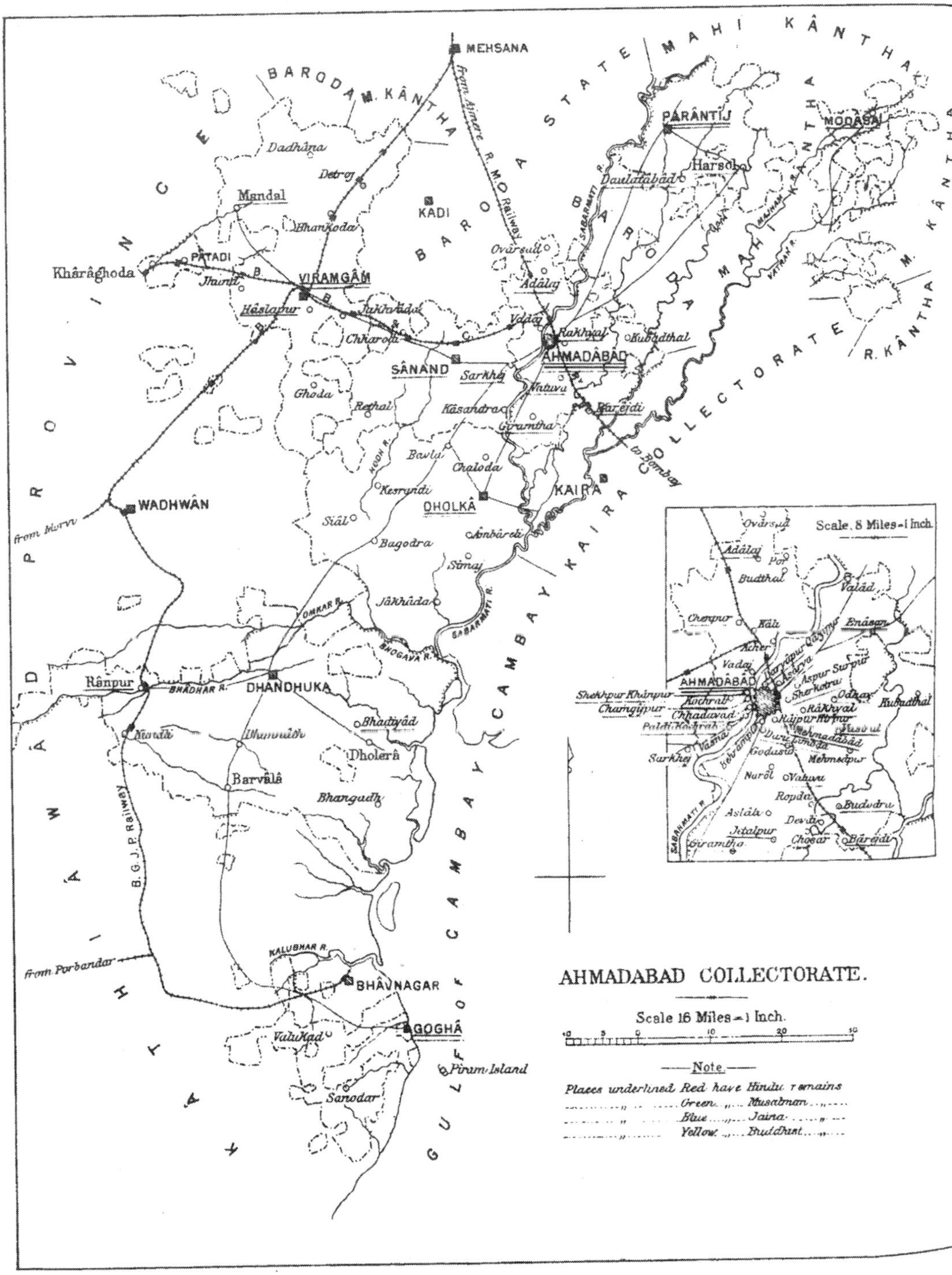
AHMADABAD COLLECTORATE.
Scale 16 Miles = 1 Inch.
Note.
Places underlined Red have Hindu remains
Green Musalman
Blue Jaina
Yellow Buddhist
Scale 8 Miles = 1 Inch.
MEHSANA
KADI
VIRAMGAM
SANAND
AHMADABAD
PARANTIJ
MODASA
DHOLKA
KAIRA
WADHWAN
DHANDHUKA
BHAVNAGAR
GOGHA
PATADI
Kharaghoda
Mandal
Ranpur
Dholera
Barvala
Harsol
Pirum Island
BARODA STATE
MAHI KANTHA
KAIRA COLLECTORATE
GULF OF CAMBAY
KATHIAWAD PROVINCE
B.G.J.P. Railway
from Porbandar
from Morvi
to Bombay
SABARMATI R.
BHADHAR R.
OMKAR R.
BHOGAVA R.
KALUBHAR R.

II.—NORTHERN DIVISION.

I.—AHMADÂBÂD ZILLA.

I.—Daskroi Tâlukâ.*

1. The city of Ahmadâbâd lies along the east bank of the Sâbarmatî river about 60 miles from its source. It is completely enclosed by high lofty walls which were first built by Sultân Aḥmad in 1412, strengthened by Sultân Muhammad Bîgarah in 1486, and were finally restored in 1832. The western wall is in nearly a straight line from north to south, its bastions looking down upon the river. The continuation of the walls round the north, east, and south of the city forms an irregular fan-shaped enclosure. Situated in the middle of the western side of the city, with the city walls forming its western defence, is the square enclosure called the 'Bhadr' (Cir. 1412). This was the citadel and contained the palaces of the Sultân and his nobles, and later the head-quarters of the Peśvâ when the combined Marâṭhâ forces held the city. The great bastion to the south-west corner of the 'Bhadr' is said to contain the foundation stone of the city.

The principal entrance to the Bhadr is on the east through a large massive gateway flanked and surmounted by bastions. To the south of this gateway, built on to it, and
I *a*. forming the south-east corner of the Bhadr, is Âzam Khân's palace, now used as public offices and one of the largest buildings in the city. About 500 yards in front of this
I *b*. gateway is the Tîn Darwâja, or triple gateway, which spans the main street.

II *a*. Between the Bhadr and the south-west corner of the city is another enclosure, now let for private use but originally the seat of the Gâikvâd's Government when the Peśvâ occupied the Bhadr. It is known as the Gâikvâd's Haveli (Cir. 1738).

The rest of the city traversed by a net-work of roads, streets, and lanes, remarkable for their narrowness and awkward turns, is thickly occupied and built upon. Amongst the dwellings and shops is a good sprinkling of mosques, tombs, and temples.

Although Ahmadâbâd takes its name from its reputed founder Aḥmad Shâh I., it was probably in existence as a city long before his time. Râjâ Karan of the Solanki race of Anhilvâda, in his excursions against the predatory tribes of this part, is said to have built the town of Karṇavati in the 11th century, which most probably was the town that Aḥmad Shâh took possession of as his capital and adorned with many of its mosques and tombs. That this locality was an important one before the Muhammadan annexation is sufficiently attested by the many remains of Hindu architecture in the city and suburbs. All the pillars in Aḥmad Shâh's mosque, the oldest in the city, are pillaged from a Hindu temple, and on one is an inscription in *Devanâgari* dated *Samvat* 1307, which seems to have escaped the hands of the Moslem iconoclasts. Many Hindu images have been found and are still turning up. The well of Mâtâ Bhavânî to the north-east of the city is far

---

* For fuller information see *Scheme for the Protection and Conservation of Ancient Buildings in and around the City of Ahmadâbâd*, by A. W. Crawley-Boevy, Esq., Bombay Civil Service, 1886.

older than the Muhammadan period, and in all probability served as a model for the far more advanced specimens of Dâdâ Harir's, Adâlaj, and others through the province.

But whatever the city was before the Muhammadan period, its chief interest lies in these subsequent times. The greatest part of the architectural work of that time has been swept away and its material used to raise the mosques and tombs, walls and bastions of the conquerors.

Ahmad Khân, or Ahmad Shâh, was the grandson of Muzaffar Shâh, who from being viceroy of the province under the imperial court of Delhi assumed regal power. Ahmad Shâh is said to have founded the city of Ahmadâbâd on or near the site of the village of Asâval in A.D. 1412. During his reign were raised some of the finest buildings in the city,—his own mosque in the Bhadr; the Jumâ mosque, the most extensive in the city; Râni Sipri's mosque and tomb, the most complete in all its parts; Haibat Khân's mosque; Sayyid Âlam's mosque; the Tîn Darwâja; Sîdi Sayyid's mosque, in which are two specimens of about the best window tracery in Gujarât, perhaps in India; and his own tomb and that of his queens. In the suburbs was constructed, during his reign, Malik Âlam's mosque, two miles to the south of the city.

Ahmad Shâh reigned until A.D. 1443, when he was succeeded by his son Muhammad Shâh, who reigned from A.D. 1443 to 1451. He does not appear to have done much to the city in his short reign, which was chiefly passed in foreign wars. In A.D. 1459 he was succeeded by his son Qutb Shâh. The mosque and tomb of Shêkh Ahmad Khuttu Ganj Bakhsh at Sarkej, with the adjoining tank, were completed during his reign. He built his own mosque in Mirzâpur during his father's lifetime. Kankaria's Tank was completed, Dharyâ Khân's tomb, and the Batwâ and Usmânpur mosques were finished in his time.

Dying in 1459 A.D. he was followed in the kingdom by his younger brother, Mahmud Bîgarah, the most celebrated of the kings of Ahmadâbâd. His was a long reign from 1459 A.D. to 1511 A.D. "His personal strength, courage, and military skill are as conspicuous as his religious bigotry and his stern but far-sighted statesmanship. His love for architecture is attested by the cities of Mustâfâbâd and Mahmudâbâd, which he founded at Junâgaḍ and Champanir, and another Mahmudâbâd (or Mehmadâbâd) near Kheḍa, as also by the numerous and elaborate additions which his nobles, following his taste, made to Ahmadâbâd and its environs."

During his reign were built the mosque and tomb of Sayyid Usmân on the west bank of the Sâbarmatî, Miyan Khân Chisti's mosque, Muhâfiz Khân's mosque, Achyut Bibi's mosque and tomb, Dastur Khân's mosque, Dâdâ Harir's well, and the Shâh Âlam group three miles to the south of the city. Mahmud Bîgarah was succeeded by his son Muzaffar II. (A.D. 1511—1526), and he by Bahâdur Shâh, Mahmud II., Ahmad Shâh II., Muzaffar III., in order down to A.D. 1572, when Akbar marched into Gujarât, captured Muzaffar, reduced the province, and left a governor to carry on its affairs.

"For about one hundred and fifty years subsequent to its invasion by Akbar, Gujarât was governed by the viceroys of the emperors of Delhi, among whom were Shâh Jahân and Aurangzib before they themselves ascended the imperial throne. During the first half at least of this period, Ahmadâbâd appears to have been in the zenith of its prosperity. Under Muzaffar Shâh III., indeed almost the last, and not the least beautiful,

MAP
OF THE
CITY
OF
AHMEDABAD
SCALE

of the stone mosques had been erected; and subsequent buildings are mostly in the plainer and more massive style of the Pathâns."

The Marâṭhâs appeared on the scene about the beginning of the eighteenth century. They carried their plundering raids into Gujarât, and the viceroys, at this time much enfeebled by the absence of aid from either Delhi or surrounding chiefs, could not cope with these new enemies and "in A.D. 1755 the Muhammadan power in Gujarât was finally extinguished, and the Marâṭhâs, though divided among themselves, took their place. They burnt and plundered the property of friend and foe with almost equal energy and spared neither mosque nor temple which it suited them to destroy. Innumerable are the architectural monuments which have thus suffered from their wantonness and malice, and the interesting ruins of which the very materials have been carried away for building purposes. Ahmadâbâd, in particular, felt so heavily the effects of their internal feuds and grinding rule, combined with the natural decay of the Muhammadan population, that its suburbs almost disappeared, large quarters within the walls became desolate, many splendid buildings were destroyed.......... Fortunately the tide of anarchy was arrested ere it had wrought even more disastrous results by the supervention of the British power."

An army under General Goddard advanced upon Ahmadâbâd "and on the 10th of February (1780 A.D.) displayed, for the first time, the British colours before the Moslem capital of Gujarât. The Marâṭhâ governor declining to surrender, a battery was opened on the 12th, and on the morning of the 15th a forlorn hope, followed by the Grenadiers of the Bombay division, rushed up the breach, which the garrison, after a determined stand, and when three hundred of their number had fallen, at length relinquished," Since then Ahmadâbâd has remained in the hands of the British.

Buildings in the City:—

I *a*. (1) The Mosque of Ahmad Shâh (A.D. 1414).—In the south of the Bhadr or citadel is the oldest Muhammadan building in the city. Architecturally it is unique; the external screened stair and the ladies' gallery being the most curious mixture possible of Muslim and Hindu styles. The pillars throughout the mosque are taken from old Hindu temples; on one of them there is a *Dêvanâgari* inscription dated *Saṁvat* 1307. The domes are richly carved. Over the principal *mehrâb* is an Arabic inscription. The minarets were taken down eleven years ago, being badly shaken, and the stones were marked and laid on the roof, but no attempt has since been made to rebuild them. The mosque has been deserted and neglected for many years, and is now in possession of Government. No income or land is attached to it. (*Ind. Ant.* IV. 289, 367.)

I *a*. (2) The Jami Masjid (A.D. 1424) in a court 382 feet by 228 feet, the mosque itself being 210 feet by 95 feet and 49 feet high. Within it are 252 pillars and 76 pilasters supporting 15 domes arranged symmetrically, the centre three being somewhat larger and considerably higher than the others. The minarets, once famous as "the shaking minarets of Ahmadâbâd," were thrown down by the earthquake of 1819. Mr. Fergusson says, this *masjid*, "though not remarkable for its size, is one of the most beautiful mosques in the East." The *mehrâbs* or *kiblâs* are inlaid with coloured marbles. Until 1871-72 it was in charge of several people, including the Qâzi of Ahmadâbâd. Now it is in charge of the Collector and is managed by the City Magistrate.

I *b*. (3) The Queen's or Râni Rupwanti's Mosque in Mîrzâpur quarter, near the travellers' bungalow, 105 feet by 46 feet and 32 feet high, consists of three domes standing on 12 pillars each with the central part so raised as to admit light to the interior. The minarets fell in 1819, but the bases of them are filled with exquisite patterns of tracery. In the adjoining tomb, which is in better style than Râṇi Asni's, the large central and two side domes are adorned with some pretty carved work in geometric patterns and arabesque. It is in charge of the *Mehellâ Panch*, and used by the Muhammadan butchers who live about the place.

I *b*. (4) Râni Sipri's or Râni Asni's mosque and tomb (A.D. 1514) not far from the Âstodia gate. The minarets of the mosque are 53 feet high and perhaps the most beautiful of their class. "Indeed that mosque is the most exquisite gem at Ahmadâbâd, both in plan and detail. It is without arches" (except a small one over a side doorway) "and every part is such as only a Hindu queen could order, and only Hindu artists could carve." The windows in the end are elaborately wrought, and the *mehrâbs* inside are of marble and carved with much care, though not so elaborately as in some other mosques. The walls of the tomb are filled with well carved lattice work and have been recently repaired. About a hundred yards north-west from this is a mound said to be the site of the Hindu village of Asâval, and where a mosque was built, but long since ruined. These buildings are in the charge of Sayyid Fâzalmiâ Sayyid Muhammad *alias* Sayyidmia.

II *b*. (5) Shâh Khupai, Shâh Khub-ki or Hazrat Shahab Shekh's Masjid (A.D. 1538) in Khâs Bâzâr, a small mosque in the city, with 32 pillars and two slender minarets, much in the style of the preceding, only inferior in details.

I *b*. (6) Tin Darwâzâ, a fine triple gateway in the middle of the city in front of the Bhadr, where was a large enclosure 1,600 feet by 800, into which it led. It is said to have been built by Ahmad I. The arches are 25 feet high, and the central one is 20 feet wide. The roof of the terrace on the top was removed in 1877.

I *a*. (7) Âzam Khân's Palace (A.D. 1636) now used as public offices. An elegant dome crowns the entrance.

I *b*. (8) Muhâfiz Khân's mosque in the north of the city, near Kutb Shâh's (No. 18), built by Jamâlu'd-din Muhâfiz Khân, Governor of Ahmadâbâd under Sultân Muhammad Bîgarah (A.D. 1465), distinguished for the exquisite character of its details; its minarets, the lower portions of which are of pure Hindu architecture, have recently been taken down and rebuilt; above the roof they "are round towers slightly tapering, relieved by galleries displaying great richness in the brackets which support them as well as in the balustrades which protect them." The *mehrâbs* in this mosque are about the finest in Ahmadâbâd. They are minutely and elaborately carved (Fergusson, *Ind. and East Arch.*, pp. 533-34). The *rauza* is a plain structure. There are ten tombs, only one of which is of marble. The mosque is in the custody of the Musalmân *Panch*.

I b. (9) Ahmad Shâh's tomb to the east of the Jami Masjid, a massive domed mausoleum with tracery windows of beautiful design, and with marble tombs inside, viz. of Ahmad Shâh, his son Muhammad Shâh, his grandsons Jalâl Khân, Kutbu'd-dîn Shâh, and Ahmad Shâh II. It is managed by a Muhammadan *Panch*. There is a *langarkhânâ* or alms-house attached where cooked food is daily doled out to the poor. Government allow Rs. 2,601 a year. In the enclosure, among the many graves, is one containing some children of the late General Ballantyne.

I b. (10) Tombs of the queens of Ahmad Shâh in an adjoining enclosure surrounded by a screen of tracery of great variety of pattern. The marble tombs are elaborately wrought in bands of sculpture, and that of Murkhî Bîbî is partly inlaid with black marble and mother-of-pearl. The principal tomb is known as Moghlâi Bîbî's, in white marble with a Persian inscription round it.

I a. (11) Sidi Sayyid's Masjid (A.D. 1412) in the north-east of the Bhadr and outside the Lâl Darwâzâ, with two remarkably richly carved sandstone windows measuring 10 feet by 7 high (see Fergusson, *I. and E. Arch.*, p. 533), is now used as the Mâmlatdâr's office. One of these windows was slightly injured at the apex when taking down the platform which was put up by Mr. Purdon Clarke for the purpose of paper casts being taken about thirteen years ago. The damage has grown since. Mr. DeForest, an American gentleman, had facsimiles made of these windows in wood. One of them is now in the Indian Section of the South Kensington Museum, and the other is in New York.

I b. (12) Haibat Khân's Masjid in the south of the city near the Jamâlpur gate, built of the pillars of Hindu temples, and one of the earliest examples here. The minarets are simply short thin cylinders. The porch on the east looks as if it were Hindu in its original position. The carvings are poor, and the floor of the mosque is of marble throughout. Haibat Khân was not buried here. His remains lie in a *rauza* outside the Kâlâpur Gate. The west or back wall of the mosque, which is faced with cut-stone and has handsome carved buttresses, is almost hidden from view by two huts. Haibat Khân was one of Sultân Ahmad Shâh's nobles.

I b. (13) Dastur Khân's Masjid in the southern part of the city close to Rânî Asni's (No. 4), was built by one of the ministers of Mahmûd Bîgarah (Cir. 1486 A.D.). It is a fine building, and is surrounded by a colonnade covered by small domes. The perforated screen enclosing a cloister round the courtyard is very varied and beautiful in design. To the south is a graveyard in which is the marble tomb of Dastur Khân, one of Sultân Muhammad Bîgarah's ministers, on a raised masonry platform. Neither the *masjid* nor graveyard are kept in order.

I b. (14) Sayyid Alam or Sayyid A'alamu'd-din's Masjid in the north-west of the city, near Wajihu'd-dîn's, built in the time of Ahmad Shâh, is an early and plain example of the Gujarât Muhammadan style. The façade strikingly resembles that of Ahmad Shâh's mosque. The details inside are exceedingly rich. The inscription over the central *mehrâb* bears the name of Sayyid A'alam Abu Bakr Husaini as its builder and A. H. 915 (A.D. 1509) is stated as the year of construction.

I b. (15) The Shâhpur or Qâzi Muhamad Chisti's Masjid built in 1565 by Shekh Husain Muhammad Chishti, but never finished, is in the north of the city close to the Shâhpur gate. The shafts of the *minârs* are very ornamental—the tracery in the niches being perhaps the finest in Ahmadâbâd, the pattern being small like those of Bâbâ Luluî's mosque. The façade is filled in with pointed arches, and a second storey is added on over the central three round the central stilted dome. The minarets are incomplete, the tops having fallen. It is owned by the descendants of Shekh Husain Muhammad Chisti, one of whom, Mehmud Miyaṅ, is the present hereditary Qâzi of the Shâhpur division of the city, and who is the Pirzâda of several nobles in the Nizâm's and Gâikvâd's territories. The mosque is neglected. It is also known as Kutb Olia's Masjid.

III. (16) Sîdî Basîr's Masjid and tomb, near the railway station. The archway and elegant *minârs* are all that are now left of the mosque. The style somewhat resembles that of Miyaṅ Khân Chishti's, and it probably belongs to about the same period. It was ruined about 1754 during the contest between the Marâṭhâs and the Muhammadan Viceroy. The tomb is in a very dirty state. Malik Sârang, who built the mosque within the Sârangpur Gate, lies buried in it. Sîdî Basir has his tomb in a walled enclosure below the *masjid* platform to the north-east.

I *b*. (17) The Queen's mosque in Sârangpur, near to the preceding, closely resembles Achyut Bîbî's. The tops of both *minârs* have fallen. This mosque was built by Mâlik Sârang, one of Mahmud Bîgarah's nobles, who had the title of Kiwâm-ul-Mûlk. The south minaret is said to have been taken down by a *mujâwar* several years ago and the stones carried off, and the north one by Government at a later date, both having been much shattered, but neither has ever been rebuilt. The pillars under the north dome have been enclosed by brick and mud walls for a dwelling. The tomb is an elegant structure on 140 slender but graceful pillars. The dressed ashlar of the outer walls has been torn off and carried away, and nearly all the perforated screen-work round the central chamber and the clerestory, also the marble top of one of the graves. This building is used as a wood store and is in a disgraceful condition.

I *b*. (18) Kutb Shâh's mosque near the Delhi gate (A.D. 1446). The central *mehrâb* is of white and grey marble but plain. (Briggs' *Gujarâshtra*, pp. 221, 223.) This is the mosque regarding which Sir T. C. Hope, in his book, says that "recently it narrowly escaped mutilation, a proposal having been gravely brought forward in the Municipality for cutting off the corner of it to straighten the road." The interior contains 60 pillars. At the southern end of the mosque two places have been enclosed, one of the rooms so partitioned off being occupied as a private residence. The *rauza* does not contain the remains of Kutb Shâh. It is now used as a place for storing cotton bales. There has been correspondence with Government regarding this mosque, *vide* Government Resolution No. 1044, dated 19th March 1886.

III. (19) Nawâb Shujât Khân's Masjid in Mirzâpur (with an inscription of A.D. 1695) 2 furlongs north-east from the Lâl Darwâza with two slender minarets three bays apart in a façade of five bays. The walls are lined with marble to a height of 6 feet. The adjoining tomb of Shujât Khân is of brick much destroyed (*Arch. Sur. Rep.*, vol. II). This is in a different style from the other mosques in the city, being more in the style of Northern India. The floor is of marble. The place is in possession of the Muhammadan *Panch*. To the north of the *masjid* is the *rauza* of Shujât Khân. Behind this *rauza* is a small *rauza*, much dilapidated, in which lie the remains of a daughter of Shujât Khân. To the south of the mosque is a *madrasa* and an open courtyard with open rooms on all sides. These rooms have been converted into small residences by the Muhammadan *Panch* with a view to raising an income, and they have been let to low people, including Goanese cooks, who keep the place in a filthy condition.

II *b*. (20) Sakar Khân's Masjid is a very large stone building with 5 domes and *mehrâbs*. It is next in size to the Jami Masjid. The pillars in front are in threes and of Hindu type; the front is open in three sections, separated by short portions of solid walling. The end sections have three spaces each, separated by pillars, and the central section is of 9 spaces. The northern and southern wings have been converted into rooms by the spaces between the arches being filled up with brick and mud. Entrance to the mosque is now possible only by a side door, the original front door being inaccessible except through a very narrow alley. Sakar Khân's Rauza stands by itself in a small open space in Hajira *pol*. The domed roof stands on 32 pillars. Under the central dome are three tombs of marble close to one another in a line.

II *b*. (21). Phuti Masjid is between the Dehli and Daryâpur gates, near the city wall. This is a large stone mosque with 5 domes and *mehrâbs*, the central *mehrâb* is of stone richly carved; the others are very plain. The domes have small pendentives but are otherwise plain. The pillars have partly at least been reft from Hindu or Jaina temples. The front is open and has 22 pillars. The end domes rise from the pilasters of the walls. It has two short slender minarets with very plain bases at the corners. There is a small *rauza* in front with Hindu pillars. The place is quite deserted and used only by weavers in the preparation of their webs. The original name of the mosque appears to have been "Fath."

III. (22). Shâh Wajihu'd-dîn's tomb built by Sayyid Murtaza Khân Bokhâri (1606-9), in the west of the city, 150 yards north of the Bhadr and as far south of Sayyid Alam's (No. 14), with a lofty dome, and windows of delicate trellis work. It is said to have been built by Amir Sadâ't Khân in Akbar's time; he also built a *madrasa* at the same place. The *chhatri* or wooden canopy was put up by Murtaza Khân about the same time. These buildings were completed in A.H. 1011 (A.D. 1602). Wajihu'd-dîn died in A.H. 999 (A.D. 1590). Mr. Hope gives a different account.

III. (23). Darvish Ali's mosque between Pankora Nâkâ and the Civil Hospital south of the Qâzi's mosque and of Pîr Muhammad Shâh's. The minarets are leaning away from the wall and in a very dangerous condition. The *rauza* is a very neat one, the walls being filled with perforated stone work. To the east of it, in the same enclosure, is Darvîsh Ali's *taka* or cistern, of considerable size and depth, covered in by vaults and with various openings above by which to draw up the water. A stair leads down to platforms above the water.

III. (24). Mahmûd Ghaus' mosque, 300 yards south of the Queen's mosque in Sârangpur, "looks like a bad transcription of the Jaunpur mosques, and though not deficient in a certain amount of grandeur, is painfully wanting in elegance." It was built in 1562, and bears some resemblance to the Jaunpur mosques of the 15th century. It is also known as Dolat Khân's Masjid and Ek-Todâ Masjid. To the north is an open space with a *rauza* still standing which contains the remains of two sons and a wife of Mahmûd Ghaus. Mahmûd Ghaus himself died at Gwalior, where he lies buried. The main entrance to the mosque was formerly surmounted by two minarets connected with each other by a carved arch. One of the minarets gave way during the earthquake of 1818-19. The other was taken down by the Public Works Department as it was in a dangerous condition, and the façade was repaired.

III. (25). **The Qâzi's or Chhotâ Idrus mosque** on the Ghi Kântha road, built by Qâzi Abu'l-Farah Khân in the reign of Aurangzib, is a small one of three bays and three aisles (4 pillars on the floor) and arched. It has one *mehrâb* neatly carved. There is a carved niche in the south end and two in the north. The roof is flat. In front is a neat *rauza* of 9 small domes, and to the north-east is another *rauza* with a large dome enclosed by lattice-work screens. All are in a very dirty and dilapidated condition. The northern half of this mosque was pulled down some years ago by the late Qâzi Husainu'd-din of Ahmadâbâd. On the ground so cleared he set up a range of shops and small houses, the rents of which are enjoyed by his successor, but nothing from the income is applied to repairs. The entrance gate of elaborate workmanship is in complete ruin.

III. (26). **Svâmi Nârâyaṇa's temple** (1850), with an octagonal dome supported by twelve pillars.

III. (27). **Mirâ Masjid** in Lunsavâdâ near Mirâ *chauki*.

III. (28). **Abdur Razzak's Masjid**, on the way from Dabhgarvâdâ to Popatiya road. A small stone mosque with marble flooring and of very plain architecture. The *rauza* is octagonal and domed, and the walls consist of perforated stone slabs all white-washed, Abdur-Razzak lies within. A handsome wooden canopy covers it. Close by is an arched *divânkhânâ*, The present holder derives an income of Rs. 200 to 250 per annum from the lands and houses belonging to the mosque.

III. (29). **Hazira Masjid** in Hazira's *pol* in Kâlupur.

III. (30). **Âlam Khân's Rauza in Danapith.** Âlam Khân was a Wazir of Sultân Ahmad Shâh's. The *rauza*, all of stone, with some pretensions to architecture, is in the grain market. It is full of rubbish and badly cared for by the *faqirs* in charge.

III. (31). **Hasti Bîbî's tombs**,—one of marble, the other of ordinary stone in Mânik Chauk in Râni Hajira.

III. (32). **Râni Hajira** in Mânik Chauk.

III. (33). **Abdullah Shâh's Rauza** in Mânik Chauk in Bâdshâh Hajira.

III. (34). **Qutbu'd-din's Rauza** in Danivâdâ in Jamâlpur. The *rauza* belongs to the time of Ahmad Shâh. There are three tombs in it but the place is now used as a dwelling-house by a *faqir*.

III. (35). **Mukhtam Sâheb's Rauza and Masjid** in Jamâlpur near Dâtâ Pathar. The original mosque has disappeared and a brick and mud structure now occupies its place. It is in a dilapidated condition. The *rauza*, which is of stone, has lost its outer verandah on the southern, eastern, and northern sides. The tomb inside is of marble under an ornamented canopy. Attached to the *rauza* is a graveyard called the Râni's Hazira.

III. (36) Mustafâ Shâhid's Masjid and Rauza near Sîdi Salem's Haveli in Jamâlpur. The *masjid* is very small now, all stone and whitewashed. Not far away, on a hillock in a graveyard, are to be seen ruins of what apparently was a mosque.

III. (37) Shâh-Alîji Ahmad's Masjid and Rauza in Rohilvâḍâ in Râyakhâḍ. The roof and all the pillars except one of this small mosque have been removed; two slender minarets and the back wall with three *mehrâbs*, each with an inscription over it, are all that remain. It is now inhabited by a *faqir*.

III. (38) Bâbi Masjid in Rohilvâdâ in Râyakhâd. Also called Shâh Ganj Masjid. Of stone, built about A.D. 1552. The three walls with the minarets are all that remain.

III. (39) Mardhawad Masjid in Mardhawad near the Lâl Darwâzâ. It is in complete ruin, the walls alone existing.

III. (40) Abdu'l Wahhâb Shâh's Rauza, between Khânpur gate and Mirzâpur, is trabeate in style, with a double colonnade all round and a high central dome. To the west of it are the back and north end walls of a brick mosque, in which are inserted a number of marble slabs bearing inscriptions. To the north-west of it is the *rauza* of Abdu'l Wahhâb's son Shâh Ghiâsu'd-din and of his grandson Sayyid Abdu'l Jalil. It is occupied by his descendant Sayyid Bâkir Miyâṅ the Pîr of the Râdhanpur Nawâb.

III. (41) Nawâb Sardâr Khân's Mosque and Tomb in Jamâlpur Chakla. The mosque to the west of the tomb is of brick, has two pillars in front supporting arches and three pointed domes with gilt tops and crescents. The *minârs* are octagonal and of four storeys. The *rauza* is inside a court with large gates. The corner spaces, and also round the four doors, are filled with good open work in simple but varied geometrical patterns. The floor is of marble inlaid and there is a loose inscription in the entrance. It has a high and egg-shaped pointed dome with eight smaller ones round it. The central dome bears a sort of brass *triśûla*, being a crescent with a cross bar. The court is filled with weeds, &c., and surrounded by a high crenellated wall. The entrance gateway is rather imposing.

III. (42) Miyân Khân Jahân's Masjid close to the Khanja gate is of brick with seven bays and three aisles. It is roofed with small domes and has three *mehrâbs*; the inscription from the central one has been removed. The *mimbar* has 7 steps. Of the tomb in front only two of the original nine domes are left. This mosque occupies the south-western angle of the city walls on the river side, and it was at this point of the city that the walls were breached at the storming of Ahmadâbâd by General Goddard in 1780.

III. (43) The Dargâh of Pirân Pîr, near this is a small dome surrounded by perforated work of no merit, and contains 3 tombs, with many others outside. The entrance porch to the court has been decorated in modern Muhammadan style. Pirân Pîr is the greatest *pîr* known in the Muhammadan world. Shâh Abdul Khalak Sayyid Abdul Kadar, one of his progeny in a direct line, came and settled here upwards of 275 years ago. He lies buried in a *rauza* with perforated walls. The tomb is of marble. The *masjid* and *rauza* are known as Pirân Pîr's. The *masjid* was built before the *rauza* but fell into complete decay. It has been rebuilt lately. The present holder is a descendant of Shâh Abdul Khalak.

III. (44) Shâh Gazni near Alîji Ahmad Shâh's tomb in Rohilvâḍâ dates from 922 A.H.

(45) Navvi Maholat in Kâlupur is a Borah *masjid* and contains two inscriptions. This *masjid* was built by Ashraf Khân, a Wazir under Shâh Kutbudin. There is nothing left of the original mosque. The Borahs have built a new one on the old site.

III. (46) The Herâti Masjid to the left of the Delhi gate is a very small tile-roofed mosque containing an inscription of 4 lines.

III. (47) Inâyat Shâh's Masjid in Shâhpur was a very large brick one, of which the three walls alone remain. It has 5 brick *mehrâbs* with a marble inscription over the central one.

III. (48) The City Qâzi's Masjid in Astodia is a very small stone one built A.H. 1271. The *mehrâb* and probably the windows have been taken from older buildings. Two windows in each end wall and two in front—each to the floor; two in the back are of 4 squares each. It has an inscription.

III. (49) The Madrasa of Hidâyat Bakhsh Muhammad Akram-u'd-din is said to have been built at a cost of Rs. 1,24,000; the mosque has 5 bays and 3 aisles, is very lofty with arches between the pillars, and roofed with domes and coved ceilings. It has perforated windows high up in the end and back walls: 5 plain *mehrâbs* and 2 slender octagonal *minârs*. It stands in a very large court surrounded with the buildings of the *madrasa*—now occupied by dyers and much dilapidated. Outside the *madrasa* is a small wooden mausoleum over the tombs of Maulâna Nuru'd-dîn Sîdî and Qâzi Muḥammad Nizâmu'd-dîn Khân; and to the west of it the tombs of Qâzi Muḥammad Rukhnu'l Hak (having an inscription) and Qâzi Muhammad Sâleh.

III. (50) Ibrâhîm Sayyid's tomb and Muhammad Âmin Khân's Masjid and Rauza, converted into Executive Engineer's Office in the Bhadr. There are three *rauzas* close to one another and they form the residence and office of the Executive Engineer of Ahmadâbâd. One of these is oval in plan and on that account is quite an exceptional structure. The old survey shews that there was a mosque attached to these *rauzas*, but it does not now seem to exist.

III. (51) Mâlik Sâbân or Hajurishâh's Masjid near the Khâs Bâzâr. A stone structure of plain construction with marble floor built upwards of 400 years ago. The minarets have disappeared and the ground all round and inside has been appropriated for dwelling houses. The mosque is now the private residence of an old man of the name of Jamâl Shâh and his family. A large tank, not unlike the Kankria tank, bearing the name of Malek Sâbân, exists in the lands of the village of Rakhial about three miles from Ahmadâbâd, where he lies buried in a stone *rauza*.

III. (52) Oja Bîbî's Masjid and Rauza near Pirmad Shâh's Rauza. A pretty little mosque all of stone built about A.D. 1504-5. The real name of the lady in whose memory this mosque was built is Khonja Bîbî. It is beautifully carved, the minarets and *kiblas* especially. In front of the mosque is a *rauza* with carved panelled walls of stone. The interior of the mosque has been whitewashed. Within the *rauza* are three tombs. It is in a dirty state. There is also a very large underground reservoir, the upper portion being beautifully terraced. The present holder of the property is the Pirzâda of Junâgad, who lives in Ahmadâbâd.

III. (53) Shâh Fâzil's Masjid in the Arsenal enclosure. It was built in A.D. 1437-88. It is a good stone structure in a very fair state of preservation. Under the *masjid* there is a sort of crypt holding a tomb.

III. (54) Ali Akbar Sayyid Jalali Masjid and Rauza in Dânâpith. These were held by a *faqir* who not many years ago sold them to a Bania. The mosque has disappeared and the *rauza* is used for storing grain.

III. (55) Nawâb Shâhjân Khân and Momin Khân's Masjid and Rastam Alikhân's Masjid in Mirzâpur. These buildings occupied a large area of ground, portion of which came to be subsequently used as a cemetery. Nearly all has been at various times sold and made away with.

III. (56) A small *rauza* near the Râekhad gate and the Arsenal. A very fine structure. The *rauza* and land are now in the possession of a Pârsi family.

III. (57) Edrus Shâh's Rauza in Jhaverivâdâ near Panjra Pol. A fine stone *rauza* domed, with walls done up with perforated slabs, belonging to the family of Sayyid Edrus. There are three large and two small tombs in it. Over the central tomb, under which lie the remains of the first Edrus who came to India, stands a canopy all inlaid with mother-o'-pearl. The building is all whitewashed and is now held by the present Sayyid Edrus who lives at Surat.

III. (58) A *masjid* called Galiara Masjid on the road leading from Khâdia *chauki* to Nawâ Darawâzâ. A fine small mosque. The entrance door of the mosque is surmounted by a stone arch of exquisite carving.

III. (59) Pîr Kamâl's Graveyard opposite the Khadiâ Police Station.

III. (60) Rauzas of Sayyid Muhammad Jâffar and Saraji Sâheb at "Norris' Bungalow." One of the *rauzas* is of stone with perforated panelled windows all around. The other is of brick and chunam.

III. (61) Qâzi Sâheb's Masjid in Râepur. A small mosque in ruins originally known as Nasar Sayyid's Mosque.

III. (62) Nasar Sayyid's tomb in Gundivâdâ in Âstodia. A fine marble tomb.

III. (63) Shekh Muhammad Jâhir Masjid and Rauza opposite Seth Jesingbhai's residence, Ghi Kântâ road. The mosque has fallen in, a portion of the back wall containing the principal *kibla* is all that remains.

III. (64) Muhammad Ali Sâheb's Masjid near Sidi Sâlem's Haveli. Stone and brick and chunam masonry, partly modern. Of no account.

III. (65) Qutb Sayyid's Rauza in Jamâlpur, Medanivâdâ. The *rauza* belongs to the time of Ahmad Shah and is now used as a dwelling by a *faqir*.

III. (66) Muhammad Sayyid's Masjid called also the Ghi Kântâ Masjid opposite the Ghi Kântâ Police Station.

III. (67) Pîr Dastgir's Masjid and Rauza near Dâyâ Bhâi's Wâdi, Ghi Kântâ road. The *masjid* has completely gone and the ground on which it stood is now occupied by a range of low buildings.

III. (68) **Rauzas of Shâh Ali and Ijat Khân and tomb of Shâh Gazon** on the road leading from Khâmâshâh's Chakla to Jamâlpur. The mosque has now disappeared. The tank is the only trace left of it. The *rauza* is in ruins, but the tomb in it is still standing.

III. (69) **Sayyid Jâffar's Masjid** near Sayyid Vâdâ in Âstodia. Well, built of brick and chunam. At present the *masjid* and its grounds are used by Afghân travellers.

III. (70) **Padshâhi Masjid** also called Dhâlgar Vâdâ's Masjid near Hope Market. The name of the mosque is properly "Khams Salât" (five *nimâzes* or services).

III. (71) **Âlef Masjid** in Khâs Bazâr near Karanj. A small structure on a very high plinth. The *masjid* was originally built about the time the Jami Masjid was completed.

III. (72) **Hâji Sâheb's Masjid** at Lâl Bâwâ's Tekrâ in Dariâpur. A mosque about 250 years old.

III. (73) **Miyan Muhammad Husen's Masjid** also called Dâdâmiyan's Masjid near Chandan Talavdi. A fine mosque and *rauza* but not very old.

III. (74) **Sayyid Ali Masjid** in Râepur opposite Makeriwâdâ. This mosque is of recent construction. The *rauza* is a plain domed building with a tomb of marble within.

III. (75) **Ambli Masjid** in Râepur, opposite Pakhâli *pol*. The present mosque is small and plain. The *rauza* has been cleared of the tomb it contained and is now used as a warehouse.

III. (76) **Husain Sayyid's Masjid** in Pânchpati road in Mogal's *pol*. The Masjid now goes by the name of the Qâzi Ali's Masjid and is used as a school.

III. (77) **Bâwâ Latif Masjid** in Khâs Bâzâr. The mosque is entirely gone and the site is occupied by a shed in which *faqirs* live.

III. (78) **Shâh Fath's Masjid and Graveyard** to the south of the Mills in Shâhpur, a small but massive mosque of brick and chunam, perfectly plain.

III. (79) **Minina Chhullani Masjid** otherwise Mirâ's Masjid near the Mira Police Station in Lunâsvâdâ. It is in ruins. Built by one Mira Sayyid Ali who is buried at Unav in Gâikvad's territory, about 3 miles distant from the Unjha Station. It is a place of pilgrimage among the Muhammadans.

III. (80) **Pîr Vazir Shâh's Masjid** opposite the travellers' bungalow.

III. (81) **Pirmadshâni Masjid** on the road from Pankornâkâ to Ghi Kântâ. A modern structure.

III. (82) **Badâ Sâheb's Masjid** behind Pirmadshâh's *rauza*.

III. (83) **Shekh Muhammad Chisti's Rauza** north of Rangrej *pol* in Patwasheri, Khâs Bazâr. A fine domed building of brick and chunam.

III. (84) **Asa Sâheb's Masjid** or Yâsinmiyan's Masjid in Râekhad, Handia's *mehalla*. A small insignificant mosque of brick and chunam.

III. (85) **Badshâh Sayyid's Masjid** or Naginâ *pol's* Masjid in Naginâ *pol* in Dariâpur. A small mosque of brick and chunam, well kept.

III. (86) Muhammad Masjid or Mâlik Ahmad's Masjid, near Topivâlâ *pol* in Kâlupur.

III. (87) Bâwâ Ahmad's Masjid on the Salapos Road behind Âlef Masjid in Khâs Bazâr.

III. (88) Tomb of Khân Jahân or Râv Manlik the last Râv of Sorath, who was defeated by Mahmud Bîgarah in 1470 or 1472 and became a convert to Muhammadanism.

III. (89) Ubramji Kuli Khân's Tomb included in the compound of the Collector's bungalow and office.

III. (90) Mosque of Shâh Jallel near Bhatiavâda in Râchhad.

(91) There are some beautifully carved wooden pigeon-houses and house-fronts well worth attention and delineation.

Buildings without the city walls—

II *b*. (92) The tomb of Daryâ Khân north of the city near Achyut Bîbî's Masjid (No. 96) erected in 1453 A.D., is imposing and notable for its constructional peculiarities. It is entirely of brick, the walls being very thick. It is the most massive building in or around Ahmadâbâd. It has a very large and lofty brick dome. It has five arches in each face of the verandah. Daryâ Khân was one of Mahmud Bîgarah's nobles who founded the quarter of Daryâpur in Ahmadâbâd. The structure is purely Muhammadan in style and is interesting as a fine specimen of brick-work on a large scale. Its proportions are fine, the walls are massive and form fitting supports to its large and lofty dome. Some of the arches and smaller domes of the outer corridors are cracked, and the brick-work of the piers near the ground is considerably worn away in places.

II *b*. (93) Achyut Bîbî's Masjid and Tomb, ¾ mile north of the city and on the east side of the river, partly ruined by the earthquake of 1819. The *masjid* was built by Hâji Malik Behâu'd-dîn Imâdu'l-mulk, brother of Malik Makhsud Vazir, in 1469, for his wife Bîbî Achyut Kuki. It has a fine façade and there is much tracery on the bases of the minarets. It is almost a copy of the Mîrzâpur Queen's mosque and has three marble *mehrâbs* with an inscription over the central one. The *mimbâr* is of marble and has a canopy over it. The central one of the three domes is raised and neatly carved inside. The tomb in the enclosure is small and neat. The upper portion of the wall surrounding the inner enclosure is perforated between small pilasters; and the entrance to it has been carved with much taste, but will soon be a total ruin unless cared for.

II *a*. (94) Tomb of Mîr Abu Turâb outside the city to the south,—an octagonal dome supported on twelve pillars, with a corridor round it forming a square of 41 feet, with six pillars on each face. Here the arch is used as a constructive feature throughout the building, the pillars becoming the piers that support it.

I *b*. (95) Mosque and tomb of Sayyid Usmân, a mile north-west from the city, and on the west of the river, built by Muhammad Bîgarah in 1460 in the style of the Sarkhêj mosque. In the tomb "a very considerable amount of variety is obtained by grouping the pillars in twos and fours and by the different spacing. In elevation the dome looks heavy for the substructure, but not so in perspective; and when the screens were added to enclose the central square, it was altogether the most successful sepulchral design carried out in the pillared style at Ahmadâbâd" (Fergusson). It is 78 feet square and has a dome 38 feet in diameter, supported on twelve pillars.

B 1169—20

III. (96) Miyan Khân Chisti's Masjid near the river, about 2 miles north of the city, between Achyut Bîbî's mosque and Shâhi Bâgh, built in A.D. 1465 by Mâlik Makhsud Vazîr, has been turned into a dwelling-house by the railway officials. This desecration took place about twenty years ago. It has two fine minarets with rounded or domed tops. The land is personal *inâm* land in the name of Mehmud Miâ Khub Miâ to whom a *sanad* has been issued by the Collector.

I *b*. (97) Shâh Âlam, about 3 miles south of the city. The tomb (cir. 1476) is surrounded by a screen of perforated trellis work, as is also the corridor round it. The interior of the dome is inlaid with mother-of-pearl and prettily painted. Beside it is the tomb of Mai Âlam, a somewhat plainer building, and the large *masjid* built by Muhammad Sâlah Badakshi with two lofty and elegant *minârs* built by Nisâbat Khân and Saif Khân; also just within the gate an assembly hall built by Muzaffar Shâh II. (1561-72) and several other buildings. At present there are there villages attached to these buildings for their up-keep, *viz.*, Sarsa in Mehmudâbâd *tâlukâ* of Kheda, and Isanpur and Vasna Maktampur in Daskroi *tâlukâ* of Ahmadâbâd: and an amount in cash of Rs. 143-8-8 is paid to the *Inâmdâr* annually from the Daskroi Mâmlatdâr's treasury. The edifices were totally neglected formerly just as the other large mosques and *rauzas* in and around Ahmadâbâd have been. Sir Barrow H. Ellis, K.C.S.I., in his official visit to the Ahmadâbâd district during his tour of 1862-63, as Revenue Commissioner, N. D., took advantage of the opportunity of the settlement of the rights of the *Inâmdâr* to stipulate for a portion of the revenues of the villages being taken over by the local authorities for the repair of the buildings and the arrangement received the sanction of Government. This portion amounts to upwards of Rs. 2,000 every year, more or less according to the season. The work of repair commenced in 1866 or 1867.

II *b*. (98) Mâlik Âlam's mosque, built by Mâlik Âlam *bin* Nur Kabir, styled Wazîru'l Mamâlik, son-in-law of Ahmad Shâh, in 1422 A.D., which is a little to the north of Shâh Âlam, and west of the Khedâ road, has richly ornamented niches on the bases of the minarets.

II *b*. (99) Bâbâ Lului's Masjid near Abu Turâb's tomb (No. 97), 69 feet by 37, resembles the Shâhpur mosque and must belong to the same period. It was built about 1560 by Bâbâ Lului or Bâbâ Muhammad, a pearl dealer. It was damaged in the great flood of 1875. The minarets are not now in existence, but their bases are beautifully carved. The mosque is remarkable for one peculiarity, which is that the frontage is open throughout with an arrangement of pillars standing about four feet from each other all along. The central dome stands on arches, and the arches are likewise open, so that there is a flood of light thrown into the *masjid* at all hours of the day. There are three *kiblas*, all of marble, beautifully carved. There is an oriel window in each of the side-walls well carved. The *rauza* is to the south-east of the mosque. It is a very low building, domed and walled, with one entrance. The principal tomb in it is of stone and there are other tombs also. The interior is dark.

III. (100) Rauza of Âzam Khân and Mozam Khân, 2 miles south-east from the city on the road to Sarkhêj:—a massive brick mausoleum like that of Daryâ Khân (No. 95,) built perhaps about 1457.

III. (101) Îbrâhîm Sayyid's Masjid outside the Âstodia Gate.

I *b*. (102) Bîbî Jî's Masjid at Râjpur Hirpur is a very fine mosque, very well proportioned and elegant, and deserves to be preserved as a good specimen of the Ahmad Shâhi style of architecture. Bîbî Jî was the daughter of Sayyid Khun Mir, and wife of Sayyid Buda Sâheb. The mosque has a gallery in the northern end like that of Ahmad Shâh. In the interior are 108 pillars. There are five *kiblas*, all of marble, with fine carvings. The *mimbâr* is all of stone with twelve steps and no canopy. There are five domes in the roof. The minarets are very fine, one of them is in fair condition but has lost its finial; the other has lost a great deal more of its top. These were shattered by lightning a number of years ago. The *rauza* is domed and walled with an arched opening on each side, done up with lattice work. The main tomb, which is of stone, is said to cover the remains of Bîbî Jî.

II *b*. (103) Mâlik Îsan-ul-Mulk's mosque at Îsanpur, 3 miles south of Ahmadâbâd. This is a very neat though small *masjid* with a corridor enclosing the court in front and in the middle of which stands a neat domed tomb. The central *mehrâb* of the mosque has been torn out and the outer wall of the corridor partly destroyed. The court is filled with weeds and shrubs. Mâlik Îsan entitled Nizâm-ul-Mûlk was a noble of Gujarât of the time of Mahmud Bîgarah.

III. (104) A furlong or so to the south is a small stone mosque somewhat of the style of Darvîsh'Ali's with central and side bays, separated by narrower ones. It has three richly carved *mehrâbs* and two windows in the back wall; a window and arched door in each end; and *minârs* sculptured in patterns differing from those prevalent in Ahmadâbâd.

III. (105) Between this mosque and the road is a neat stone stepwell known as Jethâbhâi's, with a domed *chhatri* on 12 pillars at the head of the steps, and has Hindu sculptures in the niches. A stair on the north side leads down to the platform in the middle. It was built with stones obtained from mosques, &c., at Dâni Limbḍi.

III. (106) At the entrance to the village is Jiji Bâbâ Râṇi's stone stepwell, and elsewhere are two other brick stepwells.

III. (107) Mâlik Âlim, called also Khudâvand Khân, father-in-law of Sulṭân Muḥammad the son of Sulṭân Aḥmad, built a stone mosque and tomb at Âlimpur, now Dâni Limbḍi. It has five large domes, without ornament except pendents in their centres; the central one is raised above the level of the roof like that of Kuṭbu'd-dîn. The five *mehrâbs* have all been torn out. In the roof just over the entrance, as also in front of the central *mehrâb*, are slabs beautifully carved in lozenge-shaped sunk areas. The tomb of Shekh Kamâl Mâlvi is close behind. It is utterly neglected and dirty and in a very dilapidated condition. The minarets were taken down about 12 years ago owing to their being shaky. The *rauza* which was in front of the mosque was sold some 35 years ago by the late holder, the *Inâmdâr* of Shâh Âlam, to the late Jethâbhâi Mulji who used the stones and other materials taken from it in the construction of the stepwell between Îsanpur and Dâni Limdâ. There is not a vestige left of this *rauza*.

I *a*. (108) The Moti Shâhi Bâgh (1455 A.D.), the palace built in the reign of Shâh Jahân is now the residence of the Commissioner N. D. The subsidiary building known as the "Chhotâ Shâhi Bâgh" was the *zenâna* or ladies' palace. It is now the residence of the Superintendent of Police.

III. (109) Ruined mosque at the railway station, of which only the *minârs* remain, and are the highest in Ahmadâbâd. It probably belongs to the early part of the 16th century.

I *a*. (110) Dâdâ Harir's well at Asârvâ, on the north-east outskirts of the City, built in A.D. 1499, is one of the finest in Gujârât. The entrance to this stepwell, all of stone, by a domed platform, the roof of which rests on 12 pillars. The flight of steps leading to the water is broken by landings surmounted by flat stone terraces standing on pillars. The first landing has one terrace, the second two, the third three, and so on. At the further end is the well from which water is brought up by *kos*. There is a winding staircase down each side to the lowest landing. It has an inscription.

II *a*. (111) Dâdâ Harir's mosque and tomb are situated behind the well which once formed part of the same property. The mosque is a fine building, well carved, but its interior is whitewashed. There is a good deal of carved work about the *kiblas*, *minârs*, and screens. The upper portions of the minarets were taken down some 25 years ago as they were very shaky. The *rauza* is on the north-eastern side and but a few feet from the mosque. The premises are in the charge of a Government *paggi* or watchman who lives in a small room to the south-east of the mosque. An inscription.

II *b*. (112) Mâtâ Bhavâni's well to the north of that of Dâdâ Harir. This well is supposed to be the only remnant of the old city of Asârvâ. It is popularly ascribed to the Pâṇḍavas. It is perhaps contemporaneous with the Mân Sarovar tank at Viramgâm and the Mulav tank at Dholka, both of which belong to the dynasty of Siddharâja.

III. (113) Kâch Masjid in Tâjpur, was so named from the tiles with which it was roofed being covered with a bluish green glaze. The two pillars in front and the walls are of stone. It has three *mehrâbs*, and a *mimbâr* of 5 steps. On the walls are numerous inscriptions, among which are six copies of the *Kâlima*, but from over the central and left *mehrâb* the inscription slabs have been taken out. The bases of the *minârs* are plainly carved. The court has a porch on the north side, and has been enclosed with a high wall having balcony windows. In this small court is a tank of water.

III. (114) Sâhâ Badâ Kasum's Rauza in Tâjpur near the Kâch Masjid. A fine stone building, the outer domes resting on 20 columns. The walls of the *rauza* consist of carved stone slabs rising from about 3 feet from the base. There are four tombs in the *rauza*, the main tomb having a plain canopy over it.

III. (115) Mithapur Masjid near the Nikol gate in Saraspur.

III. (116) Hamsa Salât Mashur's Masjid in Dhalgarvâdâ is a small brick mosque with wooden pillars and roof. The central *mehrâb* is carved and over it is an inscription; the two side *mehrâbs* are plain.

III. (117) The Jaina temple of Hatesingh (1848). The external porch is of great magnificence and most elaborately ornamented. In the court are sixteen shrines on each side and others at the back. The temple in the middle of the court is of two storeys and very richly ornamented.

III. (118) The Kânkaria tank or Hauz-i-Kutb, ¾ mile south-east from the Râepur gate, A.D. 1451, one of the largest of its kind in India, being a polygon of 34 sides each 190 feet long. The supply sluice is exquisitely carved. In the centre of the tank is an island connected with the bank by a causeway. On the island was the Naginâ garden and Ghattâmandal palace.

I*a*. (119) The Dutch tombs near the Kânkaria tank, to the south-east of the city, 1641 to 1699. (Briggs' *Cities of Gujarâshtra*, pp. 264-266).

III. (120) Jaina temple of Chintâman in Saraspur, 1½ mile east from the city, built by Sântidâs, a Bânia, in 1638, at a cost of nine *lâkhs*, was defiled by Aurangzib and is now neglected.

2. **Sarkhej**, 5 miles south-east from Ahmadâbâd. An important cluster of Muhammadan buildings of the 15th century, among which are:—

I*b*. (1) The tomb of Shekh Ahmad Khattu Ganj Bakhsh of Anhilvâḍâ, begun in A.D. 1445 by Muhammad Shâh and completed in 1451. In this "an attempt has been made to get a larger dome than the usual octagonal arrangement would admit of, but not quite successfully." The tomb is surrounded by an inner trellis screen of metal perforated in beautiful patterns. The exterior walls are filled with windows of perforated stone. To light the interior of the tomb four tracery windows are introduced into the dome.

I*b*. (2) In front of the tomb is a pavilion of sixteen pillars roofed with nine small domes, "forming as pleasing a mode of roofing as ever was applied to such a small detached building of this class."

I*b*. (3) A mosque with ten domes, "the perfection of elegant simplicity and an improvement on the plan of the Jami Masjid. Except the Motî Masjid at Agrâ there is no mosque in India more remarkable for simple elegance than this" (Fergusson, *I. and E. Arch.*, p. 532). It was completed by Mahmûd Bîgarah in 1451 A.D.

I*b*. (4) Tomb of Mahmûd Bîgarah and his son Muzaffar II., on the east.

I*b*. (5) Tomb of Bîbî Râjbâi, the queen of Mahmûd, to the west. Also a covered gateway leading into the front of the latter two tombs, a covered hall overlooking the great tank and other buildings.

II*b*. (6) The great tank with its sluices, &c.

II*b*. (7) The Palace and Harem, a large building on the west side of the tank.

II*a*. 3. **Batwa**, 5 miles south of Ahmadâbâd. Tomb of Burhânu'd-dîn Qutbu'l Alam, the father of Shâh Alam, who died A.D. 1452, erected by Mahmûd Bîgarah, similar to the one near Kaira. The outer arches have fallen down and all the perforated work has disappeared. "The monument itself is of most elaborate workmanship" (Hope), but was perhaps never finished. Near it is another tomb over the son of the saint, built without arches. The *Mirat-i-Ahmadi* describes this as the mosque and tomb of Hazrat Qutbu'l-Aktâb Sayyid Bûshanû'd-dîn Abû Muhammad Abdullah Bûkhârî, commonly called Qutbu'l-Alam, who died A.H. 850 (A.D. 1446). **(Surveyed.)**

I*a*. 4. **Ada'laj**, 12 miles north of Ahmadâbâd, a very fine well, built in A.D. 1499, in several storeys, with flights of steps and platforms alternately. **Inscription.** **(Surveyed.)**

III. 5. **Jetalpur,** 10 miles south of Ahmadâbâd. A building called the Rânî's palace. A public step-well of brick and stone, to the west of the village. A public *mahâl* on the village tank.

III. 6. **Vastral,** about 6 miles east of Ahmadâbâd. Temple of Śivarâya Mahâdeva. A public step-well of brick and stone near the village *talâv*. A public step-well of brick near the tank outside Sukhrâi Mahâdeva's temple.

III. 7. **Barejri,** south of the railway station, a public step-well of brick near the village *talâv*.

III. 8. **Ra'khyal,** 2 miles east of Ahmadâbâd. (1) Malik Shabân's *rauza* built of stone on the village outskirts. (2) Two brick step-wells. (3) A brick tomb on the way to Malik Shabân's tank. (4) Another tomb on the path to Râkhyal and other villages near Saras-pur. (5) The Recha mosque of stone on the right side of the way to Nikol. (6) A brick tomb behind the garden of Malik Shabân. (7) Three brick tombs behind Malik Shabân's *rauza*. (8) Malik Shabân's tank. (9) A stone step-well on the right side of the Ahmadâbâd road. (10) Another dilapidated public step-well on the right side of the Sakarkoi on the Ahmadâbâd road. (11) A brick mosque with a minaret. (12) A public step-well of stone on the Odhav road. (13) Another public step-well of brick on the left side of the way to Shim *talâv*. (14) Another public step-well on the left of the way to Nikol.

III. 9. **Giramtha,** 10 miles E.S.E. from Ahmadâbâd and 3 miles E.S.E. from Jetalpur. (1) Brick *rauza* of Bakr Ali on the west. It was repaired by Bakr Ali Sâheb 80 or 90 years ago. To the south of the *rauza* the mosque of Bakr Ali. (2) On the west side of Bakr Ali's house in Pirâna is a large *rauza* of Hazrat Imâm Shâh. (3) To the east of this is another called Sayyid Khân's *rauza*, built by Shâji Imâm, father of Bâla Muhammad Shâh. (4) To the south of this *rauza* is another called Shâji Imâm's, built by Muhammad Shâh. (5) Near the above is Dadimiyân's *gumti* opposite to Hazrat Imâm Shâh's *rauza* in Nagina *gumti*. (6) To the west of this is Nûrsai's *rauza*. (7) To the west again is Valam Shâh's *rauza*. (8) Near this is an open dome. (9) To the west is Dhaba's mosque. (10) To the west of the north wall outside Hazrat Imâm Shâh's *rauza* are Raje Târa Bîbî's buildings. (11) To the north of this building is Bâla Muhammad Shâh Bâwâ's *rauza*. All these buildings are of brick. The income of the *sadâvarta* is about Rs. 10,000.

III. 10. **Aslali,** 8 miles south of Ahmadâbâd on the road to Jeṭalpur. A public step-well of brick and stone, to the east of the village on the road to Jeṭalpur.

III. 11. **Budthal,** 2½ miles south-east from Adâlaj. A public step-well of stone on the west.

III. 12. **Valad,** 10 miles north-east of Ahmadâbâd. A stone step-well on the east.

III. 13. **Khoraj,** ½ mile south-east of railway station. A step-well of brick and stone on the north. An inscription on it says that it was built by a Brâhmaṇ in *Samvat* 1582 (A.D. 1526).

III. 14. **Kubadthal,** 11 miles east of Ahmadâbâd. A public step-well built of stone to the north.

III. 15. **Budedra,** 8 miles south-east from Ahmadâbâd and 2 miles north of Bârejri. A public brick and stone step-well named Mâtâ Khodiyâr's.

III. 16. **Enasan,** 8½ miles E.N.E. of Ahmadâbâd. A public step-well of brick and stone, called Totla Mâtâ's, on the north near the road to Degâon.

III. 17. **Mehmadpur,** 6 miles south-east from Ahmadâbâd. (1) A public brick step-well near the village. (2) Another on the north of the village near the road from Ahmadâbâd to Gatrad.

III. 18. **Narol,** 5 miles south of Ahmadâbâd. A brick step-well on the west.

III. 19. **Ropda,** 6 miles south-east of Ahmadâbâd. A brick step-well.

III. 20. **Mehmada'ba'd,** 2½ miles south-east of Ahmadâbâd. (1) A brick step-well on the west of the road to Ramôl. (2) Siddhavji Mâtâ's well situated in Survey No. 180.

III. 21. **Godasur,** 3½ miles E.S.E. of Ahmadâbâd. A brick step-well on the bounds of Vatuva on Batwâ.

III. 22. **Paldi Kochrab,** on the other side of the Sâbarmati opposite to Ahmadâbâd. (1) A neat stone mosque on the south of the village. (2) A public brick and stone step-well on the south of the road from Ahmadâbâd to Thaltej. (3) A brick and chunam mosque.

III. 23. **Chenpur,** 5½ miles N.N.W. of Ahmadâbâd. Soji Pîr's mosque on the west.

III. 24. **Chosar,** 8 miles south-east of Ahmadâbâd. (1) Dhoḷi step-well (public) on the west near the road to Batwâ. (2) A public stone well built of brick on the north of the village.

III. 26. **Chhadavad,** near Kochrab. (1) Two brick tombs on the south and west. (2) Two brick tombs on the west near the road to Vasna and on the main road to Sarkhej. (3) Chhâtan Shâh's mosque of brick and stone on the east near the river. (4) Mosque near the Dhulia Kot jail.

III. 27. **Chamgijpur,** near Chhadavaḍ opposite Ahmadâbâd. (1) Brick tomb on the north near the road to Navarangpur. (2) Another brick tomb on the south in survey No. 111 near the road to the Central Jail.

III. 28. **Ovarsad,** 3 miles north of Adâlaj. A public step-well of brick and stone.

III. 29. **Odhav,** 5 miles east of Ahmadâbâd. A brick mosque at the village tank.

III. 30. **Devdi,** 9 miles S.S.E. from Ahmadâbâd. (1) A public step-well built of brick and stone near the Bârejri road. (2) Another step-well of brick and stone near Garijpur road.

III. 31. **Por,** 2 miles east of Adâlaj. A public step-well of brick and stone on the east of the village.

III. 32. **Vasna,** 3½ miles W.S.W. from Ahmadâbâd. (1) A brick step-well named Malâv Vâv. (2) Another brick step-well on the Sarkhej road.

III. 33. **Acher,** 4 miles north of Ahmadâbâd on the river. A public step-well called Targala's Vâv near the Ovarsad road.

III. 34. **Kali**, 6 miles W.N.W. of Ahmadâbâd. A fort of brick and stone.

III. 35. **Harniav.** A public brick step-well on the north of the village.

III. 36. **Sherkotra**, or railway suburb, 2 miles east of Ahmadâbâd. (1) Abdul Khân's brick mosque outside the Sârangpur gate on the right side of the road to Râepur gate. (2) Tran *gumti*—three brick domes built near Harsadrâi's temple on the way from Sârangpur to Gomtipur. (3) Sattakâvali mosque with dome on the left side of the way from Sârangpur gate to Gomtipur. (4) The Kasbân's tomb of brick and stone near Bakr Shâh's *rauza* on the left of the road to Gomtipur outside the Sârangpur gate. (5) Borah's dome with 4 minarets near Bakr Shâh's *rauza* on the right side of the old road to Saraspur outside the Sârangpur gate. (6) Kâgdi's dome near the last. (7) Kâsim Shâh Pîr's *rauza* built of stone on the right side of the old road to Saraspur outside the Sârangpur gate. (8) Bahâdur Shâh Pîr's brick *rauza* near the last. (9) Pîr Muhammad Shâh's brick *rauza* opposite to Bakr Shâh's *rauza* on the left side of the road to Saraspur through the railway crossing outside the Sârangpur gate. (10) Shâhbân's brick *rauza* on the right side of the road to Saraspur outside the Sârangpur gate. (11) Haibat Khân Pîr's brick *rauza* near railway crossing outside the Kâlupur gate. (12) Abdur Razzak's mosque of brick and stone on the way to Mansukh Khân's Gujarât Spinning and Weaving Mills outside the Kâlupur gate. (13) Shâhbhâi's brick dome with 4 minarets near Bakr Shâh's *rauza* on the right side of the old road to Saraspur. (14) Mahmud Shâh Pîr's brick mosque on the right outside the Kâlupur gate. (15) Sîdî's mosque with stone minarets near the salt store opposite the *châvadi* on the road to Saraspur outside the Sârangpur gate. (16) Brick and stone dome and minarets in the railway compound opposite the Pânch Kuvâ gate.

III. 37. **Behrampur**, ½ mile S.S.W. of Ahmadâbâd. (1) Brick tomb in the field on the north of the road from Râepur gate towards Dholka. (2) Hâji Karmani's brick *rauza* on the east of the road to Dâni Limbdi. (3) Step-well of brick and stone on the east of the road to Dâni Limbdi. (4) Bâbâ Laulvi's *rauza* and mosque. (5) Dome with stone pillars on the north of the Saptaṛishi temple. (6) *Masjid* of brick and stone on the south side of the road to the Saptaṛishi temple. (7) Kachni *masjid* of brick and stone on the west side of the Dholka road. (8) Two brick *rauzas* on the east and south side of the Dâni Limbdi road. (9) Jhaliani brick *masjid* on the west of the Dholka road. (10) Brick *rauza* on the east of Shâhvâdi road. (11) Step-well of brick and stone on the road near to the boundary of Dâni Limbdi village.

III. 38. **Ra'jpur Hirpur**, one mile south of Ahmadâbâd. (1) Kalolia step-well of brick and stone on the east side of the Kânkaria road outside the Râepur gate. (2) Lotia Bohra's *rauza* of brick and stone on the right side of the Kânkaria road outside the Râepur gate. (3) Ibrâhîm Sayyid's masjid of stone outside the Âstodia gate on the west of the Kangalpuri road to Batwâ road. (4) Mamani Vâdi step-well of brick and stone on the west side of Dâni Limbḍi village outside the Âstodia gate. (5) A public step-well of brick and stone near the above. (6) *Idgâh* on the west side of Bhairavanâtha road near the Kânkaria tank. (7) A stone *rauza* on the west side of the Godâsar road near the Kânkaria tank. (8) A brick *masjid* in the street of Tai people. (9) A stone *masjid* on the road to Jagannâtha Mahâdeva south of Râjpur. (10) Sulṭân Shâh Pîr's *masjid* of brick in the narrow path north-east of Kaṅgalpuri. (11) Brick tomb to the west of this. (12) Other two tombs near the last.

III. 39. **Darya'pur Qa'zipur,** one mile north of Ahmadâbâd. (1) Mitha Sayyid's brick *rauza* near the Shâhpur ford. (2) Tomb of stone close to the city walls in the field of Hargowin Morâr. (3) A stone *masjid* near the paper manufactories. Another *masjid* near the Midi Kuva in Shâhpur village. (4) Brick tomb in the field of the Nagori community. (5) Domes and *rauzas* near the Lunatic Asylum. (6) Brick *rauza* and *masjid* with dome near Nâgadevatâ's step-well on the Dûdheśvar road. (7) Another brick *rauza* and dome adjacent to the last. (8) Another brick *rauza* and dome near Daryâkhân. (9) Another *rauza* and dome in the field of Râmchandra Gaṅgârâm. (10) Three domes near the Shâhibâgh road and near a large *vad* tree. (11) A *masjid* and a temple of brick. (12) *Rauza* and dome near the burning ground of the Dûdheśvar ford. (13) Another *rauza* and dome of brick on the road to Dûdheśvar. (14) Râjâ Sayyid's brick building on the north of the police line 3. (15) Two brick *masjids*, one belonging to Government in Seṭh Dalpatbhâi's garden. (16) Mûsâ Sowahag's brick *rauza* on the right side of the road to the camp, with an inscription in the mosque. (17) On the left side of the same road are three *rauzas* and *masjids*. (18) A brick *masjid* on the north side of Seṭh Hemâbhâi's garden. (19) A brick *masjid* in Narmavâla's garden. (20) A stone *masjid* on the south side of the Mâdhavpura road.

III. 40. **Asarwa,** 2 miles north-east of Ahmadâbâd. (1) Suliman's brick *masjid* on the south side of the village. (2) Karalia's *masjid* near the Svâmi Nârâyaṇa's garden. (3) Husain Miyân *rauza* on the left side of the village. (4) Kaneh Shâh's brick *rauza* on the north side of the Sarada road. (5) Shekh Mûsâ's step-well and *rauza* built of stone on the south of Kunîp Shâh's *rauza*. (6) Jalâludîn Sâheb's brick *rauza* east of the last. (7) Suliman's Sathia's *rauza* of brick adjacent to the last. (8) "Gundhatee" step-well near the east gate of Saraspur.

III. 41. **Aspur Surpur,** 3 miles north-east of Ahmadâbâd. (1) Khodiyar Mâtâ's public stone step-well on the left side of Shahijpur road from Saraspur. (2) Aspur step-well on the right side of the same road.

III. 42. **Shekhpur Kha'npur,** 2½ miles west of Ahmadâbâd. (1) Idlasa Pîr's *masjid* of stone near a well to the south of the village. (2) A brick *masjid* with *rauza* and three domes on the east side of the Disâ road. (3) A brick public step-well on the north side of Thultej road. (4) Dâdâ Sâheb's Pugla step-well.

III. 43. **Vadaj,** 4 miles north-west of Ahmadâbâd. A public step-well of brick and stone on the right of the village from the Kari road.

III. 44. **Barejdi,** 11 miles south of Ahmadâbâd. A public brick step-well.

III. 45. **Da'ni Limbda,** or Sondal Khamodar, 3 miles south-west of Ahmadâbâd. (1) A stone *masjid* called Pîr Kamal Shâh's, on the west side of the old road. (2) A public brick step-well in Pocha Nathu's field on the west side of the Isanpur road. (3) Two public step-wells of brick on the west and east side of the Chandola tank. (4) A public stone step-well on the road. (5) A public brick step-well on the old road. (6) On the north of Chandola tank and south of Shâh Alam is a public place for prayer (*namâz*). (7) On the west, south and east sides of Shâh Alam there are 8, 2, and 2 *rauzas* respectively—all public—and built of brick.

II.—PARÂNTÎJ TÂLUKÂ.

III. 1. **Para'ntij.** (1) Jami Masjid. (2) Banch Wâv. (3) Randal Wâv. (4) Temple of Malakeśvara Mahâdeva on the Bokhâ.

III. 2. **Daulata'ba'd.** Ruined fort.

III. 3. **Harsol.** Ruined fort.

III. 4. **Modasa,** 28 miles east of Parântîj. An old town with several *inscriptions*.

III.—SÂNAND TÂLUKÂ.

II *b*. **Sa'nand.** The *rauzas* of Bâvâ Alisâr and Bâvâ Ganj Bakhsh, very old and admirably built, containing much perforated lattice-work. The village of Okâj is an *inâm* for their maintenance.

IV.—VIRAMGÂM TÂLUKÂ.

II *b*. 1. **Viramga'm.** (1) Monsar Talâv with a number of small temples round it; and temples of Kṛishṇa and Mahâdeva, near by—very old. (2) A *masjid*.

II *b*. 2. **Ma'ndal.** (1) Vâveśvar Talâv (III). (2) Jami Masjid. (3) Sayyid Masjid. (4) Qâzi Masjid. (5) Ganjni or Ganga Masjid. (6) Râjgarhi Fort (III).

III. 3. **Haslapur.** A temple of Mahâdeva.

V.—DHOLKA TÂLUKÂ.

I *b*. **Dholka,** 22 miles south-west from Ahmadâbâd. (1) Mosque of Balol Khân Qâzi with a fountain and well.

II *a*. (2) Khân Masjid with *minârs*, partly ruined.

I *b*. (3) Jami Masjid with two unfinished *minârs* and dome, beautifully ornamented inside with sculpture. Two of the Dholkâ *masjids* are very beautiful, and "almost identical in size and plan, being each of them squares of about 150 feet and the mosque-front covered with five domes and the screen wall with three arches each" (Fergusson's *I. and E. Arch.*, p. 538.)

II *b*. (4) Tanka Masjid, built in the time of Firuz Shâh.

II *b*. (5) Multâv Talâv made by the mother of Siddharâja Jayasinha.

VI.—DHANDHUKA TÂLUKÂ.

1. **Ra'npur** derives its name from Rânâji Gôhel, its founder, and as Mokhrâji, the son of Rânâji, fought with the army of Muhammad Tughlak near Gogho and was killed in battle, it may be presumed that Rânâji flourished in the beginning of the fourteenth century. Rânpur is said to have been a large and flourishing town in former days. The debris of old houses is found to a distance of about two miles from the present village site. It appears to have suffered greatly in the time of Mahmûd Bîgarah of Ahmadâbâd.

III. On the south side of the village at the junction of the Bhâdar and Gomâ rivers stands an old fort, now much dilapidated, built in A.H. 1048 (A.D. 1638) by Âzam Khân, the Subedâr of Gujarât, during the reign of Shâh Jahân.

The inscription on the gate of the fort runs thus:

> "He is the Creator and the Omniscient. The great Lord Âzam Khân, the lord of his time, the like of whom was never given birth to by this bride of the world.
>
> "The intrepid lion, the bravest of the brave, and the lord of the earth.
>
> "The Khân of exalted rank, may his life be long, desired me to find out [*in verse*] the date of this castle.
>
> "From which be for aye removed the influence of the evil eye.
>
> "Plunging into the ocean of thought I impressed with the seal of my heart [the date derived from the numerical value of the letters composing the words]:
>
> "Azamu'l Bilad" (corresponding with the sacred month of Muharram 1048 A.H.)

It appears that at this time a chief named Shâhuji was reigning at Rânpur. The Kâthis living in the neighbourhood committed great mischief and plundered the villages. Shâhuji asked for assistance from Âzam Khân, the Subâ of Gujarât, to put down these marauders. He consented and was about to send one of his Sardârs for the purpose. At this time the Kâthis carried their excursions up to the gates of Ahmadâbâd, carrying off men and cattle. Âzam Khân went out in person to chastise them and hunted them to Botâd and Pâlyad. A battle was fought in which the Kâthi chief was taken prisoner and beheaded. Âzam Khân then intended to establish a *thânâ* at Botâd, but Shâhuji persuaded him to do so at Rânpur, telling him that the water-supply at the latter place was better than at Botâd. Âzam Khân acceded to this and built the fort at the junction of the Bhâdar and Gomâ rivers. Entering from the east corner of the fort we arrive at a gate which faces the south. Proceeding inside we come to another gate which faces the east. This last gate is the main entrance to the buildings. A little further on we find a *masjid* facing the east. Near the *masjid* is the grave of Râjushâh Pîr. An inscription in Persian is on the wall of the *masjid*, which is translated thus:—

> "God is great. In the reign of the king, magnificent as Jamshed, the just and the generous, Shâhbu'd-dîn Muhammad II., the lord of the time, Shâh Jahân, the valiant warrior,—may the Almighty perpetuate his dominion—in the month of Zil Haj in the year 1050 A.H., the humble slave of the Almighty, Âzam Khân, during the term of his Subâship of Gujarât, laid the foundation of this sacred mosque in this castle of Shâhpur and completed it that the servants of the true God may worship him."

There is a reservoir in the *masjid*, which was originally filled with the water from a well in the inner part of the fort. Chunam drains are still to be seen to carry the water of this well to all parts of the fort. On the west side of the well is a *hammâmkhânâ* or bath-room, and a terrace is built above. There is a cellar underneath this bath-room, which is said to proceed to a great distance underground. On the west of this subterranean passage is Mahâdeva and Râjbâi Mâtâ, which are said to have been put in after the fall of the Muhammadan dynasty and the assumption of the country by the Marâṭhâs.

There is an *inscription* on a stone in the wall facing the river with regard to the bath-room. It reads thus :—

> "God is great. The slave of God, Âzam Khân, during the tenure of his office of the Subâship of Gujarât, commenced the construction of this bath on the 1st of the month of Jumad-el-âkhar 1051 A.H., and completed it at the end of the month Muharram 1052 A.H. Ye who see this place remember him kindly."

On the south side of the spot where the Mahâdeva and Mâtâ are placed is another building, which was apparently used for *kacheri* purposes. Traces of a garden near this are still visible. Simultaneously with the erection of the fort and the buildings therein, a well was constructed on the bank of the river and on the east side of the village. There is a stone in this well bearing a Persian *inscription*, which reads :—

> "God is great. Âzam Khân, the servant of God, in the month of Shawwal in the year 1051 A.H. during his Subâship of Gujarât having constructed this well, bequeathed it to the garden that the public may be profited.
>
> "And Peace!"

A little further on are the ruins of an old fort. It is said that this fort was built of stone and mud by Rânâji who had fought with the Musalmâns, and on his death his seven widows committed suicide by throwing themselves into one of the wells in the fort. It is said to have been demolished by Mahmûd Bîgarah of Ahmadâbâd.

The ancestors of Rânâji Gohel claimed to be the descendants of Śâlivâhan. They lived in Khedgaḍ about 10 miles from Balotra in Mârwâr on the Lunâ river. The Gohels had conquered this country from a Bhill named Kheḍwa. The country remained in possession of the Gohels for about twenty generations. The last chief of the clan was Sejakji, the son of Janjarsi. The Râthors drove out the Gohels from the country, and Sejakji with his followers came to Junâgaḍ and entered the service of Râjâ Kalat Chuḍâsamâ. Sejakji was entrusted by the Râjâ and his son Khengar with the protection of Shâhpur and other 11 villages from the inroads of the Bhills. Sejakji remained for a long time at Junâgaḍ, when one day Khengar, the only son of Kalat, had gone out on a hunting excursion near Shâhpur and started a hare. The animal entered the camp of the Gohels, and Khengar demanded it. The brother of Sejakji and his other followers declined to give it up, stating that it was their principle to protect those who surrendered themselves. Upon this a fight ensued between the Gohels and the retainers of Khengar. The latter were all killed with one exception, and Khengar was taken prisoner. The man who escaped went and informed the Râjâ of what had happened, and said that he was not certain whether young Khengar was dead or alive. Sejakji, who was then in the presence of the Râjâ expressed his regret, and said that as the Râjâ's only son was killed by his men he could not now remain in his territory. The Râjâ's affection for Sejakji was, however, so great that instead of ill-treating him he soothed his mind and told him that he cared more for his friendship than for the life of his son. Sejakji then went to Shâhpur and there to his great delight found that Khengar was living; he saluted him and gave him his own daughter in marriage and sent him to Junâgaḍ. Subsequently under the orders of the Râjâ, Sejakji founded a village near Shâhpur, which he named after himself as Sejakpur.

Rânâji was the son of Sejakji and founded Rânpur. Rânâji was married to the daughter of Dhan Mer, and had a son by her who acquired the village of Khâs and settled there. The present holders of this village, known by the name of Khâsya Kolis, are descendants of Dhan Mer's grandson.

After Rânâji's death his son Mokharâji established his head-quarters at Piram near Gogha and was a renowned pirate. He was killed near Gogha in a battle which took place between him and the army of Muhammad Tughlak, the son of Giyâsu'd-dîn.

When Mahmûd Bîgarah was ruler of Gujarât, one of the Bhâyads or cousins of this Mokhrâji, who was also named Rânâji, was in the enjoyment of the Rânpur estate, and held it as an independent chief. The Râjâ of Mârwâr had married his two daughters, the eldest to Mahmûd Bîgarah and the younger to this Rânâji. It so happened that both the sisters one day met at their father's house. The Begam asked her younger sister to come and dine with her. Out of respect for her elder sister, without giving out the true cause, she refused to dine. When further pressed on the matter, Rânâji's wife plainly told her that as she had married a Musalmân, she could not now take her meals with her. The elder sister took this to heart and went and informed her husband about the insult that was offered to her. Mahmûd tried to effect an amicable settlement by converting Rânâji and his wife, but failed in his attempt to do so. Rânâji then fell under the displeasure of the chief. An army was sent to Rânpur under the command of Bhauderikhân. Rânâji was killed and the country came under the direct control of Mahmûd Bîgarah, who subsequently bestowed it on Hâloji Parmâr, the ancestor of the present Molesatam Parmârs in Rânpur.

A Jaṭ Sardâr residing in Sind had a beautiful daughter named Sumribâi. The king of Sind wanted to marry her, but his overtures were rejected and the Jaṭ left the country and came to Muli, where Lagdharji and Hâloji of Parmâr descent were reigning. They kept the Jaṭs under their protection and promised to assist them against the forces of the chief of Sind. The latter, however, followed and laid siege to Muli. Through the treachery of an officer the single well from which the Parmârs derived their water-supply was polluted by the head of a cow being thrown into it. The Parmârs then surrendered. Sumribâi, the daughter of the Jaṭ Sardâr, was, however, sent away to some secure place and Hâloji was delivered over to the enemy as a hostage. Sumribâi retired towards Vanod, where she died and where her grave is still pointed out. On the other side, Lagdharji sought the protection of Mahmûd Bîgarah, who thereupon sent an army against Sind and defeated him. Haloji was delivered, but only to fall into the hands of Mahmûd Bîgarah. He was converted to Muhammadanism, and Rânpur together with the surrounding villages which were recently conquered from Rânâji Gohel were bestowed on him. Thus the Gohel dynasty became extinct at Rânpur, and Haloji established himself at that place. Lagdharji, however, remained a Hindu, and his descendants are still at Muli. Haloji was killed near Dhandhuka in an engagement between him and the Kâṭhis, and his grave is still to be seen there and is known as Halusâ Pîr.

Hâloji was succeeded by Hasuji, who was succeeded by his son Kubanji, on whose death his son Shâhuji came to the throne. It was during the time of the latter that Âzam Khân, the Subhedâr of Gujarât, built the fort at Rânpur. Dâduji was the eldest son of Shâhujî and he succeeded his father. His son Tâjoji subdued the Kâṭhis. The succession remained in a direct line for three generations. Togâji succeeded his father Tâjoji. Hâmoji succeeded him at his death, then Sâhebji and Ahimbhâi ascended the throne in succession.

During the time of the last-mentioned, in A.D. 1736, Râjâ Sabalsing of Wadhwân and the son of the Dhrângadhrâ Râjâ had gone on a visit of condolence to the Râjâ of Bhâvnagar. On their way back they remained for one night at Rânpur. These two princes went to see the fort. They were so delighted with it that they did not wish to leave it, but resolved to occupy it by force if necessary. A fight ensued between the followers of Ahimbhâi and those of the two princes. The Râjâ of Dhrângadhrâ reprimanded his son and called him back with his men. Sabalsing also went away to Wadhwân, but returned with reinforcements and laid siege to the fort and reduced the garrison to great distress. At this time Dâmâji Gâikvâḍ of Barodâ had come to Dholkâ to levy tribute. Ahimbhâi secretly went to him and hired his assistance. On the arrival of the Gâikvâd's forces, Sabalsing raised the siege and proceeded towards Nâgesh. Dâmâji followed him, and in an engagement Sabalsing was defeated and taken prisoner. Owing to the intervention of Ahimbhâi, Sabalsing was spared an ignominious death, but kept in prison at Songaḍ, from which he returned after paying a large ransom. Ahimbhâi bestowed the lands and revenue of Rânpur on Dâmâji in consideration of the assistance thus afforded to him. The Gâikvâḍ then established his own *thânâ* in the village. Subsequent to this the country passed into the hands of the Peśvâ, and when the British Goverument came into possession after the battle of Khaḍki (Kirkee), the village of Rânpur was treated as *khâlsâ*, while the rest of the villages enjoyed by Ahimbhâi's descendants are held under the *Tâlukdâri* tenure.

III. 2. **Bhimna'th**. According to tradition the place where the present *mandira* of Bhîmnâtha stands was the abode of the giant Hidimbâ. The Pâṇḍavas came thither. Arjuna was in the habit of not taking his food till he had performed the *pûjâ* of Mahâdeva. In this jungle they could not find any *mandira* of Mahâdeva, so he could not take his regular meals. His brother Bhîma, thinking that he would have to fast long, went out in search of a *mandira*. He came to a place where some *jala* trees were. (Those now standing are said to have existed since that time.) He dug a hole in the ground, put a stone therein, and covered the same with a heap of earth and rubbish. Bhîma performed an imitation *pûjâ* and placed wild flowers on the heap. He returned to camp and informed his brother Arjuna that he had found out a Śiva station, and pointed to the *jala* trees. Arjuna went to the spot, made his devotions, returned, and took his meals. Bhîma then ridiculed his brother, and told him that the place where he had worshipped was not a Śiva station, but that he himself had put a piece of stone underground and promised to point it out if he wished. Arjuna replied that for himself he was sincere in his devotions, and had believed that it was a Śiva station. All the five brothers and their mother Kuntâji went to the spot. Bhîma removed the heap of dust and rubbish as well as the wild flowers, and struck his stick on the stone, which fractured it and to their astonishment milk began to flow from it. The fracture made with Bhîma's stick in the stone is still shown to the devotees. As the god thus showed himself by a stroke of Bhîma's stick, it was named after him as Bhîmnâtha Mahâdeva.

An ancestor of the present Mahanta who was at that time wandering round the place as an ascetic dreamed one night that he was directed to make *pûjâ* to this Mahâdeva. This story was thus circulated and the place grew famous. In *Samvat* 1535 Mahanta Mâdhavgiri built an *ôṭâ* round the Mahâdeva, which is not covered by any building. The branches of the *jala* trees have extended all along the place, and it is said to be the orders of Mahâdeva not to cut any portion of the wood of these trees. The wall round the *linga* was built in *Samvat* 1834, with several outhouses. In the time of the present

Mahanta Iśvargiri Budhgiri, the place has been greatly improved. The *ôṭâ* round the Mahâdeva is paved with marble, and one bullock and two elephants of the same material are placed in front.

There are about 150 houses in the village, surrounded by a wall, built by the present Mahanta at a cost of Rs. 80,000 in A.D. 1863. It has two principal gates, and two windows overlooking the river Zilkâ. The "Dehli" near the Mahâdeva *ôṭâ* was built in the time of Mahanta Asangiri in *Samvat* 1828. Most of the other buildings and the new houses were built in the time of the present Mahanta. The other buildings in the compound were also built in the time of Asangiri in *Samvat* 1847.

The revenue of nine villages is enjoyed by the Mahanta. All the expenses of the *mandira* and *Sadâvarta* are defrayed therefrom. The following are the villages:—(1) Bhîmnâth: The lands round about were all waste. Râghavgiri improved the same by cultivation, and built huts for the shepherds, and settled them in the village. (2) Polârpur: In *Samvat* 1816 the Pesvâ's government gave this in *inâm* for the expenses of the *Devasthâna*. After the grant the village was peopled. In A.D. 1863 the Tâlukdâri Settlement Officer, Mr. Peile, decided that the Thâkor of Gampha had a share in this village, and the revenue is now divided between the Mahanta and the Thâkor. (3) Jarvalâ: Was granted in *inâm* by the Pesvâ's government. Owing to failure of crops, &c., the people deserted it, but were induced by the Mahantas to come and reside in Bhîmnâth, and the people of Bhîmnâth now cultivate the lands of Jarvalâ. (4) Khaṣalyu was also granted in *inâm* by the Peśvâ's government in *Samvat* 1815. There was no population in the village at that time, but owing to the exertions of the Mahanta the cultivation is now prosperous. (5) Bhojpurâ: Granted by the Bhâvnagar *Darbâr* in *Samvat* 1872 during the time of Mahanta Khimgiri. (6) Khamisna: Was acquired by Mahanta Asangiri from the Wadhwân *Darbâr* in *Samvat* 1841. (7, 8) Bhalgamḍi and Shâhpur: Were held in *inâm* prior to the acquisition of the country by the British Government. It is unknown in what Mahanta's time it was acquired or who granted it. (9) Sagasar: Was acquired during the time of former governments. In A.D. 1863, however, Mr. Peile, the then Tâlukdâri Settlement Officer, decided that the Thâkor of Gampha had a share in the village, and now the revenue is divided between the Thâkor and the Mahanta of Bhîmnâtha.

Besides the above there are lands in isolated villages the revenue of which is enjoyed by the Mahanta. These lands were from time to time granted by the Kâṭhis and Grâsias of neighbouring villages. The total revenue of Bhîmnâth from landed property is estimated at about Rs. 30,000 per annum. Hundreds of people daily resort to this *mandira* for worship. Many come to perform their vows, and it is customary to pay in cash or to give a horse, cow, buffalo or bullock to the *mandira* after the fulfilment of the vows. In the month of Śrâvaṇa every year about 300 Brâhmaṇs daily resort to the *mandira* for *pûjâ*. On Śrâvaṇa *Śud.* 12th, Brâhmaṇs of all denominations are fed in memory of one Gehlaśâ, an inhabitant of Bârvâḷa, and *Kârbhâri* of the Limḍi *Darbâr*. He set apart about 200 *bighas* of land in the village of Mogalpur for this purpose, and it is now in the possession and management of the Mahanta. On Śrâvaṇa *Śuddha* 15th, the Balev or Cocoa-nut day, every Brâhmaṇ who is present at the *mandira* is fed and paid 4 annas. Owing to this inducement about 10,000 Brâhmaṇs assemble. Many other travellers and Sâdhus resort to the place, who are also all provided for. On Śrâvaṇa *Vad.* 6th another feast is given to the Brâhmaṇs of all denominations in memory of one Mulji Revâdâs of Dhandhukâ, who set apart about 200 *bighas* of land in the village of Vejalka for this purpose. On the last day of Śrâvaṇa, *Vad.* 30th, a fair is held at Bhîmnâth, which lasts for three days. Hindus think when visiting Dwârkâ that they *must* also visit and pay their devotion to Bhîmnâtha, hence there is a constant influx of pilgrims. Every morning and evening there is a general call for dinner. Those who can partake of the meals without objection to their caste feelings do so; those who cannot are provided with raw grain and cook their own food.

The Mahantas are not allowed to marry. They adopt a *Chêlâ*. They must make the selection of a *Chêlâ* from particular castes, such as Atit, Gosâvi, Bairâgi and Rabâri. As far as can be ascertained, the following is a list of the successive Mahantas who have had the management of Bhîmnâth *mandira* of Mahâdeva:—

1. Râghavgiri.	6. Khimgiri.
2. Amritgiri.	7. Bhagwângiri.
3. Bhâvgiri.	8. Jamnâgiri.
4. Asangiri.	9. Budhgiri.
5. Gumângiri.	10. Iśvargiri.

III. 3. **Bhadiya'd,** 2 miles north-west from Dholerâ. The *rauza* of Pîr Bhaḍiyâdra is a plain square-domed building held sacred by the Musalmâns and some lower castes of Hindus in Gujarât, as the tomb of Sayyid Bokhâri Mahmûdshâh Walid Sayyid Abdula Rahman. He was a native of Uchh in the Punjâb, and about 600 years ago left home at the age of 15 on pilgrimage. At that time a Râjput Râjâ ruled at Chokri, formerly known as Chakravartî, 7 *kos* south of Dhandhukâ. This Râjâ, it is said, was a bitter enemy to the Musalmâns and never broke his fast till he had killed one of them and made a mark on his forehead with the blood of the slain. This practice he continued till it reached the ears of Mahmûdshâh through a woman whose son had fallen a victim. Mahmûdshâh led an army to Chokri and killed the Râjâ. The son of the latter killed Mahmûdshâh in revenge for his father's death. When Mahmûdshâh was at the point of death, he requested the Musalmâns about him to be buried at the side of Gajbanshâh, and in compliance with this request he was buried where the *rauza* at Bhaḍiyâd stands now. This *rauza* was built some 200 years after his death at the expense of the Nawâb of Cambay, who also assigned to it an annual allowance of Rs. 350. The visits which Shâh Âlam of Ahmadâbâd and other Musalmâns of note paid to the *rauza* rendered it attractive to others. Thousands of people, chiefly Musalmâns from all parts of Gujarât, annually come to pay their homage to the Bhaḍiyâdra Pîr. A blind Brâhmaṇ is said to have had his eye-sight restored on his embracing the Muhammadan faith. There was an iron chain in the *dargâh* weighing a *maṇ* and a quarter. By means of this chain the innocence or otherwise of a person accused of a crime used to be tested. He was made to wear it and to walk with it to a distance of seven steps. If the chain broke into two pieces of itself after this the innocence of the party was proved beyond a doubt, otherwise he was held guilty and punished for his crime.

VII.—Gogha Tâlukâ.

III. **Gogha.** (1) The celebrated *makâm* of Pirân Pîr.

(2) The Sonâriya Tank attributed to Siddharâja Jayasinha.

(3) Some caves in the neighbourhood.

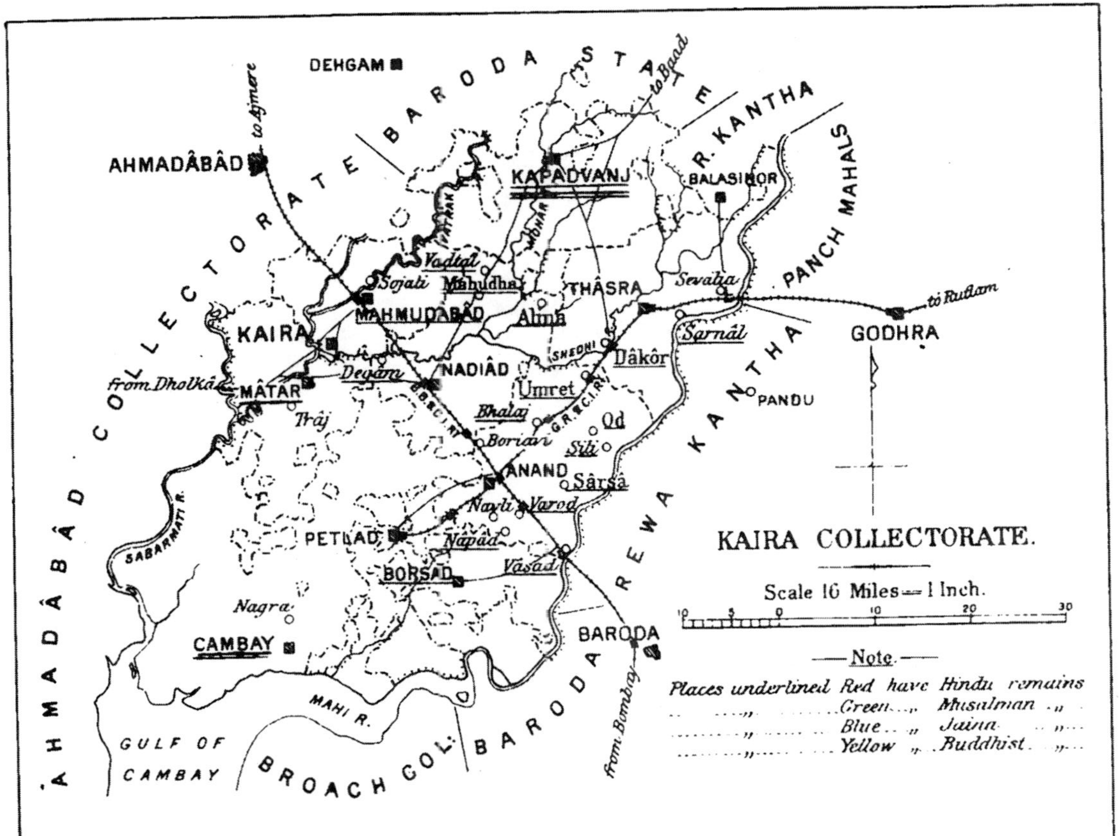

Drawn and Photozincographed Govt Photozinco Office, Poona 1896.

II.—KHEDÂ OR KAIRA ZILLA.

I.—KAIRA TÂLUKÂ.

I*b*. 1. **Mahmudâbâd.** (1) *Rauza* of Mubârak Sayyid, prime minister of Mahmûd Bîgârah (died 966 A.H.), at Sojâli, 3 miles north-east from Mahmudâbâd, one of the finest Muhammadan remains in Gujarât. "There is a simplicity about its plan, a solidity and balance of parts in the design, which is not always found in these tombs, and has rarely, if ever, been surpassed in any tomb in India. The details, too, are all elegant and appropriate, so that it only wants somewhat increased dimensions to rank among the very first of its class. Its constructive arrangements, too, are so perfect that no alteration in them would be required, if the scale had been very much increased. The tomb itself is surrounded by a screen of perforated stone-work, of the very finest tracery, and, with its double verandah, aids in giving the sepulchral chamber that seclusion and repose so indispensable in a mausoleum" (Fergusson's *Architecture*, p. 539). It contains two central tombs—of Mubârak Sayyid and his son Mirân Sayyid, and three later tombs, on the east side; also one enclosed at a later date in the east verandah. There are several recent tombs also in the verandahs.

The tomb stands in the corner of a small irregular fort, the lower portion of the walls of which are of stone—apparently Hindu work,—and the upper part of brick and probably much more modern. The north-east corner of the *rauza* has been restored with brick, and alterations have been made in the screens. It has been sadly injured by the villagers within the last 20 years, and is greatly in need of some care being taken of it. (**Surveyed.**)

Inscriptions:—Three of quotations from the Qurân, on the walls, and two short ones on the marble tombs.

II*b*. To the east of this *dargâh* are two low brick ones containing the tombs of Saifu'd-dîn and Nizâmu'd-din, brothers of Mirân Sayyid's mother, and of the architect of the large *dargâh*. To the west of them are the *minârs* of an *idgâh*. The larger of these small *dargâhs* has been built with small *chhatris* at the corners of the dome in imitation of the large one. Down the river a little are the *minârs* of a mosque, one of which is partly undermined by the river and leans over a good deal. It must soon fall in.

II*b*. (2) The Phir or Bhamaria well, a mile south, is a curious stone structure of the time of Mahmûd Shâh (15th century). It differs from those of Borsad and Umret in being octagonal, and having four stairs leading down to a range of galleries in a very poor state of repair.

III. (3) In the town of Mahmudâbâd is also a good *vâv* or step-well, of the time of the founder of the city.

For copperplates found in this district see *Jour. A. S. Beng.*, vol. VII. pp. 348, 908, 966, 978; Prinsep's *Essays*, vol. I. pp. 257, 262; vol. II. p. 70; *Jour. R. A. Soc.*, vol. I. p. 247; *Jour. Bom. B. R. As. Soc.*, vol. II. p. 22; vol. III. pt. ii. p. 101; *Ind. Ant.* VII. 241; XIII. 81.

II.—Kapadvanj Tâlukâ.

I.b. III. 1. **Kapadvanj** contains some very old buildings. A beautiful arch described by K. Forbes in his *Râs Mâlâ* and a *kuṇḍa* and well; also an underground temple of Śiva and a fine Jaina temple. **(Surveyed.)**

Inscriptions:—At the entrance to the Mâmlatdâr's *kacheri* is one of the beginning of the 13th century A.D., and on a mosque are three in Arabic.

(Copperplate grants, purchased by the Archæol: Survey, *Epig. Ind.*, vol. I. part i. p. 52).

III.—Nadiâd Tâlukâ.

III. 1. **Dega'm** or Devtî, 7 miles south-east from Mahmudâbâd and 4½ or 5 miles north-west of Naḍiâd, on the left bank of the Sherî river, the site of an ancient capital; old *lingas*, Nandis, and broken statues lie about, and coins are sometimes found bearing the legend—*Parama bhaṭṭâraka*. **(Surveyed.)**

III. 2. **Pati Harji**. A temple built by Santarâm Bâvâ, who came to Naḍiâd in 1810 A.D. and died in 1830. It is under his disciple Chaturdâs.

III. 3. **Wadtal**. Temple and monastery of Svâmi Nârâyaṇa, and seat of the southern *ḡâdi* of the sect.

III. 4. **Mahudha**. Tank of Patel Talandi, built in 1758 A.D. by Kusalji Bhukhan.

III. 5. **Alina**. Mosque built about 150 years ago.

IV.—Thâsra Tâlukâ.

IIb. 1. **Sarnal**, 5 miles east from Thâsra, said to be on the site of an old city Kuntalpura, where Râjâ Chandrasen ruled 300 years ago. A temple of Galeśvara Mahâdeva, on the banks of the Mâhî and Gultî built of stone and said to have been desecrated and the dome destroyed by Alau'd-dîn Khilji; it is much ruined, but has been a very large one: the *sabhâ maṇḍapa* is supported by 35 well carved pillars. The *gosâvi* in charge has an income from Government. **(Surveyed.)**

Close to Sarnâl are Bhadrasa and Aklâcha also said to be on the site of part of the city of Kuntalpura, and ancient foundations may still be traced.

III. 2. **Da'kor**. Temple of Ranchhôḍji, built A.D. 1772 by Gopâl Jagannâth Tâmbekar, a Sâtâṛâ banker to the Peśvâ, and is said to have cost a *lâkh* of rupees. The image was brought from Dwârkâ by Bodânâ, a Râjput. The temple is 168 feet from east to west by 151 feet from north to south and has 8 domes and 24 *śikharas* of which the highest is about 90 feet.

V.—Ânand Tâlukâ.

III. 1. **Umret,** 12 miles N.N.E. from Ânand, on the Dâkor branch railway. Another *bâvadi* or step-well, perhaps 400 or 500 years old, and by some ascribed to Siddharâja. It is built below of stone, and above of brick. It is between Umret and Dâkor, is of five storeys and is descended by 109 steps. In the upper storey is a seat and a niche dedicated to Bhadrakâlî. It bears no inscription.

III. 2. **Od,** about 8 miles to the north-east has another *bâvadi*, seven storeys deep, arched over, very plain, with external coating of chunam. (**Surveyed.**)

3. **Varod,** 4 miles south-east from Ânand, has a very old *bâvadi* said to have been built by Siddharâja Jayasinha. It was repaired and cleaned about a century ago by Jaysinghbhârati Malbhârati, a *gosâvi*.

III. 4. **Sarsa,** 8 miles east from Ânand. Another *bâvadi* said to have been built 500 years ago by a Khirawal Brâhman. It was repaired in 1820 and in 1866.

III. 5. **Wasad,** on the railway, 9 miles south-east from Ânand, is a *phîrnal* or well with a spiral stair leading down to the water. Over the well are terraces on two sides, that on a third has fallen, and the well is out of repair.

III. 6. **Sili,** 12 miles east from Ânand. A splendid tank 73 yards square with temple, &c., constructed by Bâi Bâlibâi, daughter of Râjaśrî Mehral (or Malhâr) Nârâyaṇa of Barodâ about 1826 A.D., known as the Hiri Tank, for the repair of which the rent of 821½ acres of land are set apart, assessed at Rs. 113.

III. 7. **Bhalaj,** 7 miles N.N.E. from Ânand on the Dâkor line. A *bâvadi* of six storeys with 70 steps down to the water,—attributed to Siddharâja, and in fair preservation. It has a seat at the foot of the first descent of 9 steps.

III. 8. **Napad,** 14 miles west of Wasad, a handsome octagon pond, with a causeway on twenty-four arches to the middle of it, where are the remains of a *chhattra*. Also some stone trellis work at the inlet. A *vâv* of the same age (about 400 years old) is to the east of the village.

VI.—Borsad Tâlukâ.

III. 1. **Borsad.** The step-well near the *kachêri*, built in 1497 by one Vasu Soma and his family, is of 7 storeys and has 13 arches, the surface of the water being reached by flights of steps. It was cleaned out in 1872-73.

Inscription :—On this well in Sanskrit, dated *Saṁvat* 1553, 13th Śrâvaṇa *Vad*.

III. (1) Napa Wanto tank ascribed to Mahmûd Bîgârah, with a house in the middle of it.

III. (2) There is a temple dedicated to Mahânkâleśvara Mahâdeva, about half a mile from Borsad,—not remarkable in any way but contains an enormous *Śiva liṅga*. (**Surveyed.**)

VII.—Mâtar Tâlukâ.

1. **Ma'tar**, 4 miles south-west from Khedâ. A Śrâvaka or Jaina temple, built about 80 years ago at a cost of 4 *lâkhs* of rupees.

2. **Traj**, 3 miles S.S.W. from Mâtar. A tumulus apparently artificial. (**Surveyed.**)

Khambâyat or Cambay State.

Khamba'yat or Cambay. (1) The Jami Masjid is a fine mosque with 44 large and 68 small domes and numerous pillars and pilasters. It was built "in the reign of Muhammad Shâh *bin* Toghlak Shâh in the month of Muharram 725 A.H. (A.D. 1325) by 'Umar *bin* Ahmad il Kâzaruni." It measures over all 200 feet by 210 feet and its internal court 120 feet by 135 feet. "Except in being somewhat smaller in scale, its plan and arrangements are almost identical with those of the Altamsh mosque at Ajmere." The pillars are all borrowed from Jaina temples, and it has two galleries similar to those in Ahmad Shâh's mosque in Ahmadâbâd. The *mehrâbs* are beautifully carved. (2) At the south end of the building are two marble tombs bearing beautiful Arabic **inscriptions**—one being that of 'Umar *bin* Ahmad il Kâzaruni, the builder of the mosque, who died Wednesday 9th, Safar 734 A.H., and the other that of his wife Fatima, daughter of Haja Husain il Ghilâni, who died after her husband. Over them is a fine mausoleum. "It is wholly composed of Hindu remains and is two storeys in height and was crowned with a dome 28 feet in diameter, but it fell in and is now a ruin." (**Surveyed.**)

Inscriptions:—One on the north entrance to the *masjid*; one on each tomb; one on a well in the court stating that it was made by Ali *bin* Abdu'n-nabi il Baghdâdi in A.H. 1030; on a marble shaft lying in the north corridor of the court is one in *Devanâgarî* dated *Samvat* 1468.

III. (3) A *masjid* near the Tin-darwâzâ bears an **inscription** of A.H. 1056 [or 1067 ?], (A.D. 1646). It has a marble arch and is supported on 32 wooden pillars.

III. (4) A Jaina temple called Chintâmaṇi Pârśvanâtha or Mehal Sagotapâdô in Dantarvâdâ dedicated to Pârśvanâtha, originally built in A.D. 1588 but rebuilt at a much later date. It has **inscriptions** on the images both in the underground storey and the main floor. (5) The temple of Âdîśvara is another Śrâvaka temple, said to have been built by Tejahpâla in 1605 A.D. (!!), has also a sunken storey and image. (6) The temple of Neminâtha in the Jeralâpâdâ; all three are built without spires, like common houses.

III. (7) About a mile from Cambay is a Muhammadan building erected in A.H. 771 (A.D. 1369-70), and dedicated to a Pîr named Khâja Khezir. It has four **inscriptions**.

III. (8) Outside the Pania gate on the east of the town is a *bâvadi* of considerable age. Nareśvara Tank outside the city on the north is a large reservoir cased with brick, with gardens and a summer house. Near it is a mosque built by one Imâmshâh of Brana near Ahmadâbâd, in memory of his two children Bala and Balî, who were said to have been turned into two small heaps of flowers here.

III. (9) At Nâgara, 3 miles out, are the vestiges of the old city.

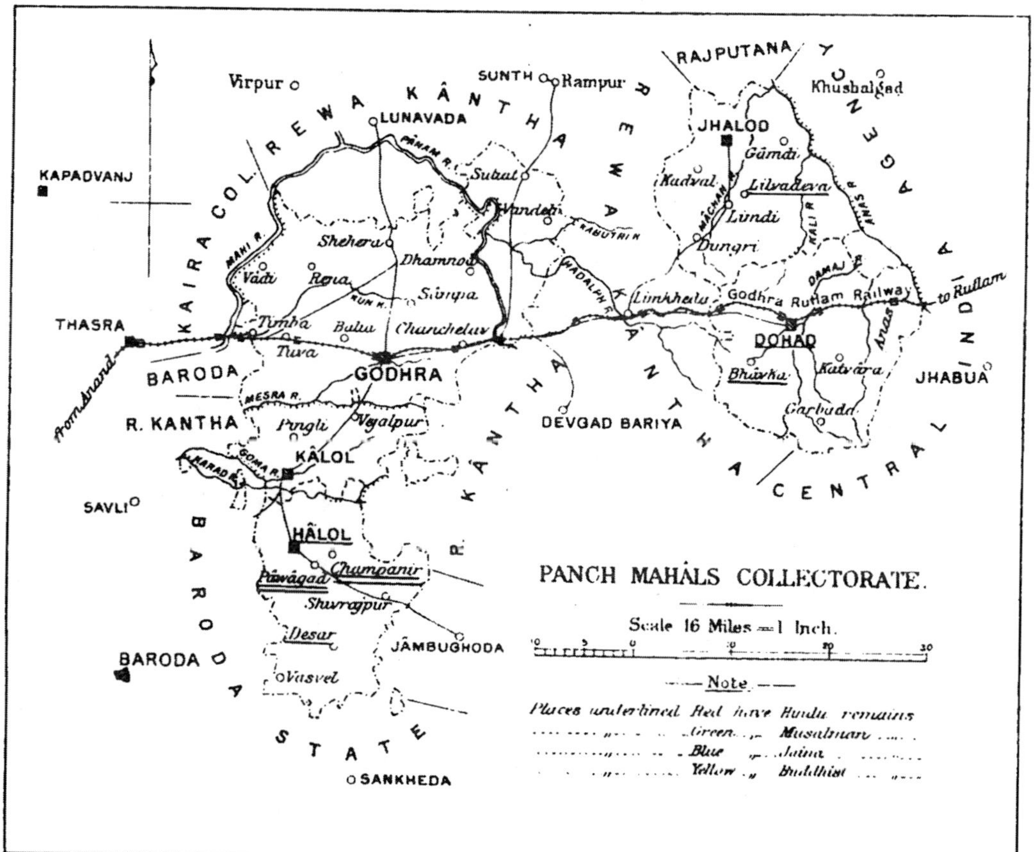
PANCH MAHÂLS COLLECTORATE.
Scale 16 Miles = 1 Inch.
Note
Places underlined Red have Hindu remains
Green Musalman
Blue Jaina
Yellow Buddhist
RAJPUTANA
REWA KÂNTHA
KAIRA COL.
BARODA
R. KANTHA
BARODA STATE
CENTRAL INDIA AGENCY
KAPADVANJ
THASRA
SAVLI
BARODA
SANKHEDA
JHABUA
Virpur
SUNTH
Rampur
LUNAVADA
Khushalgad
JHALOD
Gâmdi
Kadval
Lilvadeva
Lindi
Dungri
Subal
Vandeli
Shehera
Dhamnod
Vadi
Rena
Simpia
Timba
Balu
Chanchelav
Tuva
GODHRA
Limkheda
Godhra Rutlam Railway
to Rutlam
DOHAD
Bhâvka
Katvara
Garbada
DEVGAD BARIYA
Pingli
Vejalpur
KÂLOL
HÂLOL
Champanir
Pâwâgad
Shivrajpur
Desar
JÂMBUGHODA
Vasvel
From Anand
MAHI R.
PANAM R.
MESRA R.
GOMA R.
KARAD R.
KABUTRI R.
HADAPH R.
MACHAN R.
KALI R.
ANAS R.
DAMAJ R.

III.—PANCH MAHÂLS.

I.—HÂLOL TÂLUKÂ.

Ia. 1. **Champa'nir,** 30 miles north-east from Baroda. (1) The Jami Masjid, said to have been built by Muhammad Shâh in 1484,—but see Briggs's *Ferishtah*, IV. 70. The words خطبه و منبر give the date 914 A.H. (1508 A.D.). It is of white sandstone beautifully cut and has minarets in front, perfect in design and taste and beautifully ornamented and said to surpass even the Jami Masjid at Ahmadâbâd. "By the ravages of time the building has been injured in many places, but it has not yet lost its beauty." It is now quite disused. (**Surveyed**.)

Inscriptions :—Three were on the back wall, of which the middle and most important one has been carried off.

IIb. (2) Sakar Khân's *dargâh* near the Kasbin *talâv*, with handsome dome and fine pierced stone windows.

III. (3) Shahr-ka Masjid, in the Bhadr or citadel, a rather clumsy, low-roofed mosque, in a fair state of preservation.

III. (4) The *Mândvi* or custom-house, in the same, a well proportioned large portico.

III. (5) The east and south Bhadr gates have both **inscriptions** in Persian.

Ia. (6) The Nagina Masjid, about 600 yards north of the Bhadr, is a fine mosque of beautiful white stone, with the remains of an elegant domed mausoleum in front of it.

III. (7) Bâwâ Mân's mosque, south of the Bhadr, is a small plain mosque without minarets, and the façade of which is pierced by three equal sized arched doorways.

III. (8) Ruins of a small building and a mosque about 1½ miles east of the Bhadr on the bank of the Badâ *talâv*.

III. (9) The Kajuri Masjid west of the Nagina mosque is of brick and much dilapidated.

Ia. (10) Kevadâ Masjid, N.N.W. from the Nagina mosque, has the remains of an exquisitely carved mausoleum beside it.

III. (11) The Lili Gumbaz-ki Masjid, N.N.E. from the Jami Masjid.

III. (12) Some ruined Jaina temples, &c., in the old Hindu town of Champânir, south of the road near the foot of the hill.

III. (13) The Jepure, at a small lake considerably to the north of the Nagina Masjid. (*Ind. Ant.*, VI., 1.)

IIa. 2. **Pa'va'gad,** a mile to the south-west of Champânir—the remains of an old fortress; on the north-east spur of the hill (2,727 feet high) are the remains of the old Hindu town of Champânir. At the foot of the south cliff are some caves. The first gate is the Atak, the second is the Budiâ or great gate, a very strong work. The Sât Mahâl or seven-storeyed palace is on the edge of a cliff within the Sadan Shâh gateway. There are also other remains such as the Mâchi Haveli, Makai Kothâr, and Nava Lâkha Kothâr, several ruined Jaina and Brahmanical temples of about the 12th century, on the plateau; the

IIa. Gangâ Jamunâ *kuṇḍa* and Sûraj *kuṇḍa*, within the walls; and at the top the shrine of Kâlikâ Mâtâ, and a small group of Jaina temples just below it, of considerable age, but recently renewed and modified by the Jainas who are re-occupying them. (*Ind. Ant.* VI. 1; IX. 221.) (**Surveyed.**)

IIb. 3. **Ha'lol.** (1) A one-storeyed sandstone mausoleum of Sikandar Shâh (1526 A.D.) which had formerly two large and five small domes (Forbes' *Or. Mem.*, III. 476), but all of the domes are now fallen. It was built by Bahâdur Shâh. It contains also the tombs of Nâsir Khân and Latif Khân, brothers of Bahâdur Shâh (*Ferishtah*, IV. 108).

III. (2) Ek Minâr-ki Masjid, about 1½ miles west from Champânir on the Hâlol and Jâmbughoda road.

III. (3) Half a mile further south, close to Pâvâgaḍ, the Pânch Mâhudâ-ki Masjid.

III. (4) Half a mile south-west of Hâlol is a well—Chandrakalâ *vâv*—similar to the Bhamaria well at Mahmudâbâd; beside it is another called Sûryakalâ.

III. (5) A mile south are the eight *kûvas* and 9 *dâvra* (three-cornered small wells).

IIb. 4. **Desar** near Sonipur, 20 miles south from Hâlol. The Rudra Mâlâ, an old stone temple of Śiva, of small size, but its walls are richly carved, perhaps of the 14th century.

IIb. 5. **Bhavka,** 5 miles south-west of Dohad. An old ruined temple (15th century) of Mahâdeva, originally octagonal, with three belts of sculpture on the outside.

II.—Dohad Tâlukâ.

III. **Dohad.** Caravansarai built by Shâh Jahân in honour of Aurangzib's birth, 1619 A.D. **Inscription**, *Ind. Ant.*, X. 158.

III.—Jhâlod Tâlukâ.

III. **Lilvadeva.** This village with Lilva-pokhar and Lilva-thâkur are said to be on the site of an ancient city Lilâvati. There are several Śiva temples with well cut sculptures.

IV.—Godhrâ Tâlukâ.

III. 1. **Rattanpur,** between Godhrâ and Pâli station: an old temple containing a sculptured screen.

III. 2. **Tua,** 3 miles south of Rattanpur: remarkable hot springs and some old temples.

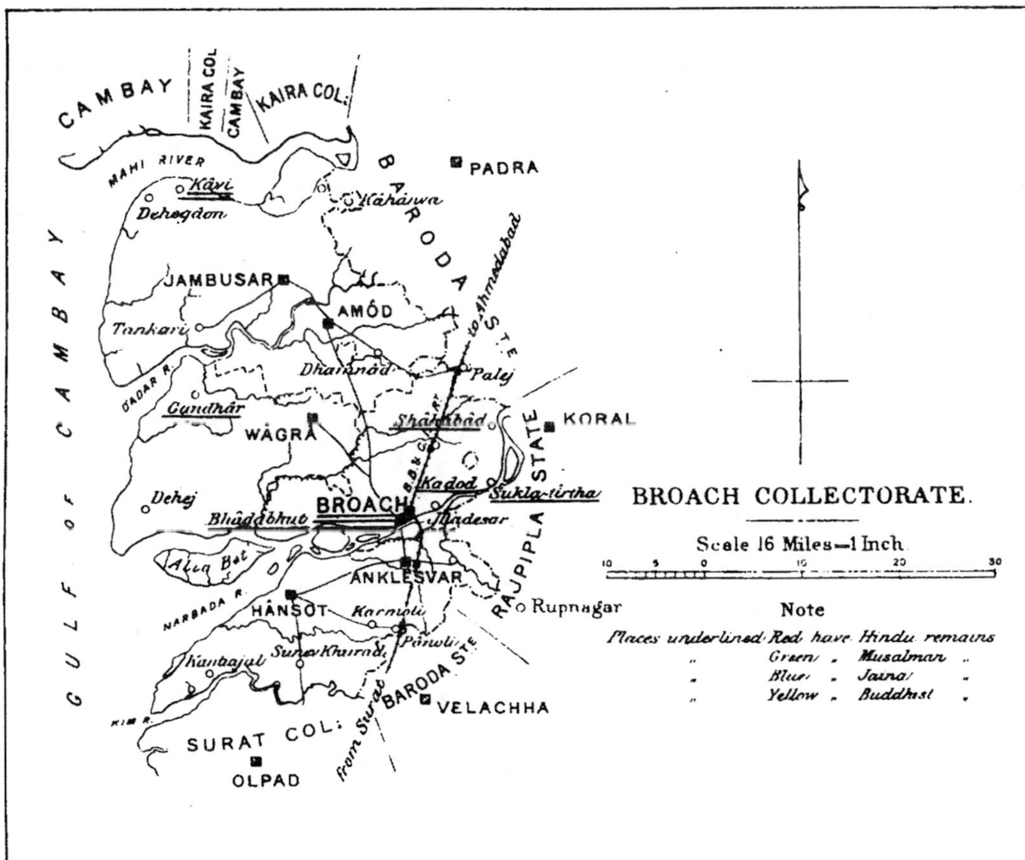
BROACH COLLECTORATE.
Scale 16 Miles—1 Inch.
10 5 0 10 20 30
Note
Places underlined Red have Hindu remains
" Green " Musalman "
" Blue " Jaina "
" Yellow " Buddhist "
CAMBAY
KAIRA COL
CAMBAY
KAIRA COL:
MAHI RIVER
Kâvi
Dehegâon
Kahânwa
PADRA
BARODA STE
to Ahmedabad
GULF OF CAMBAY
JAMBUSAR
AMÔD
Tankari
Dhamnâd
Palej
DADAR R.
Gandhâr
WÂGRA
Shâhbâd
KORAL
RAJPIPLA STATE
Dehej
Kadod
Sukla-tirtha
BROACH
Bhâdabhut
Nâdesar
Aliâ Bet
ANKLESVAR
NARBADA R.
HÂNSOT
Karmoli
o Rupnagar
Panoli
Kantajal
Suna Khairad
BARODA STE
VELACHHA
KIM R.
SURAT COL:
from Surat
OLPAD

IV.—BROACH ZILLA.

I.—Broach Tâlukâ.

I b. 1. **Broach.**—(1) Jami Masjid in the south of the city, perhaps constructed previously to the reign of Ahmad Shâh, but formed almost entirely of pillars taken from earlier Hindu or Jaina temples on the site of one of which it stands. It is 135 feet from north to south, and some of its details are very beautiful. The 72 pillars are carved, and the stone ceilings at the sides of the domes as well as the domes themselves are very elaborately sculptured in the Jaina style,—more so than usually the case in mosques. It is used mostly as travellers' quarters by Muhammadan mendicants. Though a very fine specimen of an early mosque with domes, it is falling into a very dilapidated condition (*Jour. Bom. B. R. As. Soc.*, vol. X. p. 19). Over the *mehrâb* on the west wall is a modern Arabic **inscription** containing extracts from the *Qurân*. (**Surveyed.**)

III. (2) Bâwâ Rahan Sâheb's *dargâh* in the Dungri suburb to the north of the city, said to have been built about the end of the 11th century, but now falling into decay. Forbes, *Oriental Memoirs*, vol. II. p. 252, describes it as a "grand mausoleum," "where columns and arches form corridors, and support several large domes, and smaller cupolas richly ornamented, which cover the marble tomb."

III. (3) The Idrûs Mosque, built as a tomb in A.H. 1022, for Sayyid Idrus, near the northern wall of the town. In the south of the large area belonging to it are the tombs of some of the Nawâbs of Broach. To the east of the mosque is a shed in which are tombs of several of the family of the late *Faujdâr* of Broach. A fair is annually held here on the 3rd of the Shab-i-barât holidays and Musalmâns visiting the fair and passing the night in the precincts are next morning feasted by Sayyid Husain el Idrûs, C.S.I., who pays the expenses from the revenues of the village of Umrâj in Broach *tâlukâ* which he holds in *inâm*.

III. (4) The Seth's Haveli in Lallubhâi Chakla in the east of the city, built in 1791, with a front of carved wood very richly designed.

III. (5) The tomb of Chattar Pîr, east of Bâwâ Rahan and 1½ miles north-east of the city, an old Muhammadan tomb formerly famous for its cistern which it is said could not be emptied.

III. (6) The *Madressa* Mosque near the Civil Hospital, built by Nawâb Murtaza Khân in A.H. 1018. The floor is of marble, as are also the bases of the pillars which are of teak: they are 30 in six rows of five each; and to the front is a verandah with a tiled roof. In the enclosure is a *hauj* or fountain and several tombs.

Inscriptions:—On two wooden boards fixed over a latticed window on each side of the east door are the following Persian inscriptions:—

تاريخ تعمير نواب مرتضي انتساب مرتضي خان

مونسي دوش درسراي خيال تا دل دردمند وسينه ريش

سال تاريخ اين خجسته مكان گفت آنسر عقل دور انديش

گفت بگذر ز مسجد قاضي   كه ازو مهرسي بمقصد خويش
كرد تعمير اين خجسته مكان   مرتضي خان مظفر غازي
سال تعمير از خرد جستم   گفت تاريع مسجد قاضي

III. Other buildings are:—(7) The *Sthâna* of Bhṛigu Ṛishi in Kalmi-wagâ, outside the Jhaḍeśvar gate: a plain domed temple containing 17 *lingas*. It is built of brick and lime with teak beams and has several *dharmaśâlâs* in the court.

III. (8) The *Sthâna* of Kabîrjî in Kabîrpura. The image is in a small underground cellar having a plain domed brick temple over it. It is used by the Kabir-panṭhis.

III. (9) Temple of Gaṅgânâtha Mahâdeva in Khâtrivâḍâ, has also a *linga* in an underground cell. It is of brick and is said to be old, but is being rapidly destroyed by the encroachments of the Narmadâ River upon it.

III. (10) The temple of Ambâjî Mâtâ in Kalmi-wagâ built of brick and not at all old, but in decay. It has a large court containing the tombs of *gosâvis*.

III. (11) The temple of Pingaleśvara Mahâdeva in Daśâśvamedha Tîrtha, is a plain brick and lime temple not a century old.

III. (12) Lallubhâi's *vâv* in Dândiâ Bazâr, has 10 arches and 75 stone steps, with a cell in each side wall, built of brick in the end of last century, but going to ruin.

III. (13) Kheru'd-dîn's *vâv* in Vejalpor, a suburb on the west of Broach, is said to be about 250 years old. The steps and cross lintels are of stone and the side walls of brick with stone pilasters and lintels to strengthen them. A passage on each side leads to a gallery below. The part nearest the well is of three storeys.

III. (14) The Phâtâ-talâv *vâv* has nine arches, and is said to have been built by Lallubhâi Mujûmdâr, and repaired about 1850 by Paraśrâm Tuiram, a *sâhukâr*. It is of brick and the steps of Porbandar stone.

IIa. (15) The Dutch tombs, a mile west of Vejalpor, are massive structures over the remains of members of the Dutch Factory and date from 1654 to 1770.

III. (16) Âdîśvara Bhagavân's temple in Vejalpor Paṭṭi, erected in 1869-70,—a Jaina temple of the Lâdvâ Srîmâlis, built of brick, with marble floor and carved pillars.

III. (17) Temple of Bahucharâjî Mâtâ in Vejalpor, a plain temple, nearly washed away by the river. It contains an image of Ambâjî.

III. (18) Nathu Thôban's *dharmaśâla*, between the Jhadeśvar gate and Dândiâ Bazâr, was built in 1875 by a member of the Kadavâ Kunbi caste, of Porbandar stone, and is three storeys high in front and richly carved.

III. (19) Svâmi Nârâyaṇa's temple on the Jhadeśvar gate slope built on a raised platform ascended by 45 steps of Porbandar stone. It was built in 1833, and is of brick and plaster. It is under the Wadtal high priest of the sect. It is surrounded by other buildings connected with it.

III. (20) Temple of Somanâtha Mahâdeva near the Jhadesari gate in what is called Old Broach, contains a *linga* in an underground cell over which is a plain, domed, brick temple.

IIa. (21) Temple of Bhrigu Bhâskareśvara in the Nâvâ Dehrâ, is built of brick and teak-wood by Bhâskar Râv, a *Kâmdâr* of Broach in the time of the Peśvâs.

IIa. (22) The temple of Bhûtanâtha Mahâdeva in Bhûtanâtha Phalia, contains a *liṅga* in an underground cell, said to be of great age, but the temple was enlarged and partly rebuilt in 1857. It is quite a plain building.

III. (23) Kâśî Viśvambhara Mahâdeva or Mugat Gor's temple at the Bhâgâkot, built in 1848 by Mugatrâm Vallabhrâm of the Bhitrâ Khedâvâl caste. It is a brick erection, and has a *dharmaśâlâ* in the court. The *liṅga* is of a greenish stone.

III. (24) Munisuvrata Svâmi's temple in Undi-vakhâr is of stone, carved and painted; the floor is of white and black marble in alternate squares. It is a Śrâvaka or Jaina temple and was built on the site of an earlier one in 1872 by the Śrîmâli Banyâs.

III. (25) Derâsar, also in Undi-vakhâr, a Jaina temple with an undergound shrine and a two-storeyed brick temple above it.

III. (26) Chovivatto temple in the Srîmâli Pol, contains a Jaina image bearing the date *Samvat* 1664 (A.D. 1608). Behind the image is a recess in the wall about 3 feet by 2, containing several rows of the twenty-four Tîrthankaras from which the temple takes its name.

III. (27) Temple of Pârśvanâtha in Śrîmâli *pol*: a plain temple of the Sâgaragachha Jains with an underground cell containing 11 white marble images. The middle image bears the inscription "*Vijayasimha Suryâchârya pratishthâ.*" Just over the cell, on the ground floor, are seven images one of which bears the inscription "*Phâlguna Śuddha* 5, *Samvat* 1849, *Chandragachha Nathu Kiksi Bimba bharâvit.*" There are also several metal images on one of which is the date "*Śrâvaṇa Samvat* 1085." The upper room contains ten images, the earliest date on them being *Samvat* 1844. The temple is of brick with wooden pillars.

III. (28) The temple of Âdîśvara Bhagavân in Śrîmâli *pol*, an unpretending temple of the Sâgaragachha, paved with white and black marble: the pillars are of teak and painted vermillion. The images are marble or brass, on the backs of the latter are the dates of their consecration, the earliest being 1499 or A.D., *Samvat* 1443. One of the marble images bears the date "*Phâlguna Śuddha* 5, *Samvat* 1849" (A.D. 1793).

III. (29) The Kothî or Dutch Factory near Kansârvâd is a large building and has been a fine one. On a sun-dial on the upper portion of the northern wall is the date Anno 1700. The west side is two-storeyed.

III. (30) Bhîdabhanjan well in Ali, a suburb on the north of Broach, belongs to the *dargâh* of Navâb Sultân Yâr close by. In a niche in the eastern wall is an image of Hanumân which has for its *pujâri* the Muhammadan *mujâvar* of the *dargâh*, who receives all the gifts made to the god.

III. (31) Temple of Nîlakantha Mahâdeva in Ali, contains the *liṅga* of the tutelary god of the Darzi or tailor caste: it possesses a revenue from a land grant.

III. (32) Sindhavâî Mâtâ's temple in Kalmwagâ is of brick and has a cash allowance of Rs. 37.

Copperplate grant, *Epig. Ind.*, vol. II. part IX. page 19.

III. 2. **Bhadabhut,** 9 miles west of Broach, a place of pilgrimage during the intercalary month of Bhâdrapada, with a temple of Bhâdabhut or Bhâdeśvara Mahâdeva, noways remarkable.

III. 3. **Kadod,** about 6 miles east of Broach.—Temple of Koteśvara or Navareśvara, a place of pilgrimage during the intercalary month of Vaiśâkha.

III. 4. **Sukla-tirtha,** 10 miles E.N.E. from Broach, a sacred place near to which are also Humkâreśvara-tîrtha and Ravi-tîrtha. It has a temple of Omkâreśvara Mahâdeva, noways remarkable.

III. 5. **Shaha'bad,** 13 miles north-east from Broach, has a Jaina Apâsarâ of Pârśvanâtha, of no special interest.

II.—Anklesvar Tâlukâ.

(*No Returns.*)

Ilav, copperplate grant, *Ind. Ant.* XIII. 115.

III.—Vâgrâ Tâlukâ.

III. **Gandha'r,** 26 miles north-west of Broach: a Jaina temple built in 1619 with a sunk storey containing the image, and some carved work. About the town are mounds of brick and stone scattered over an area 3 miles in circumference. Splendid tanks at the neighbouring village of Kesvân; and an old stone bridge and fine tombs at Chanchvâl.

IV.—Âmod Tâlukâ.

(*No Returns.*)

V.—Jambusar Tâlukâ.

III. **Ka'vi** on the Mâhi River (*Sans. Kâpika*); an old Jaina *tîrtha* with two temples known as Sâsu and Vahu-nu-deheru. There is also a temple of Rûpeśvara Mahâdeva of some pretensions (*Ind. Ant.* V. 109, 144.)

Inscriptions:—One in each of the Jaina temples. Some Brâhmaṇs in the village have some old copperplate grants.

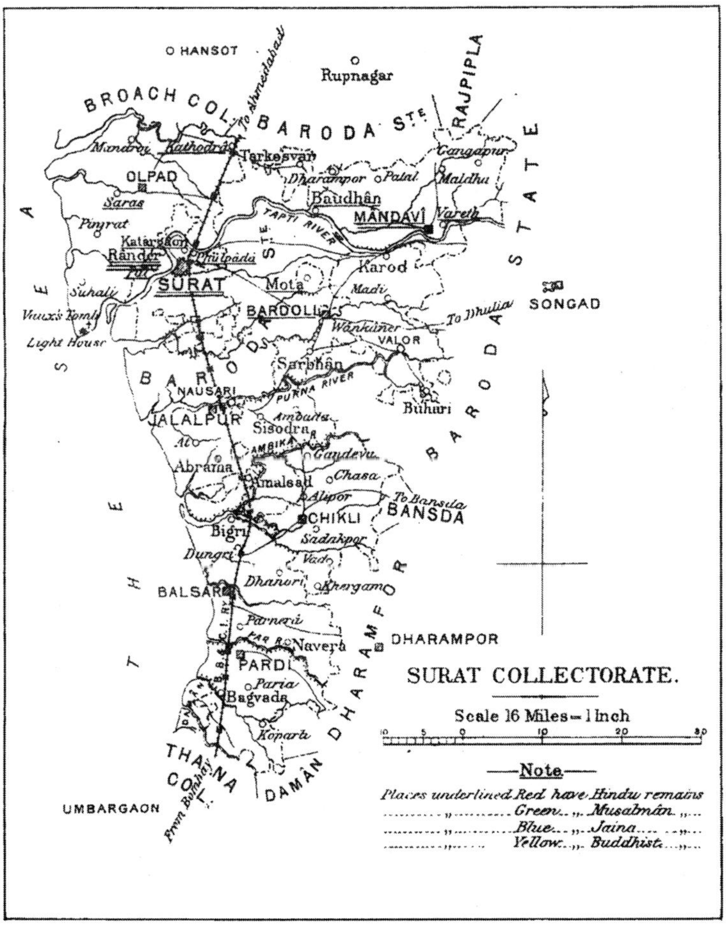
SURAT COLLECTORATE.
Scale 16 Miles = 1 Inch
Note
Places underlined Red have Hindu remains
" Green " Musalmân "
" Blue " Jaina "
" Yellow " Buddhist "
HANSOT
Rupnagar
BROACH COL.
BARODA STE
RAJPIPLA
BARODA STATE
OLPAD
SURAT
Rânder
BARDOLI
MANDAVI
TAPTI RIVER
SONGAD
NAUSARI
JALALPUR
PURNA RIVER
BANSDA
CHIKLI
BALSAR
PARDI
DHARAMPOR
THANA COL.
DAMAN
UMBARGAON
THE SEA

V.—SURAT ZILLA.

I.—Chorâsi Tâlukâ.

III. 1. **Surat.** The Mirza Sâmi *rauza*, said to have been built about 1540 by Khudâwand Khân, the architect of the Surat Castle; it is in the style of the later Muhammadan tombs at Ahmadâbâd. The windows are of perforated stone and the reticulated interiors of the cupolas are of rare beauty. At present it is in a dilapidated state. The wooden mosque in the enclosure is said to have been erected of the materials of a Jaina temple in the Shâhâpur ward.

III. (2) Mosque of Qàzi Diwân Sâheb, who is said to have come from Janok near Bukhârâ and died at the age of 116 Muhammadan (about 112) years. The mosque is said to date from A.D. 1530; other accounts make it two centuries later.

III. (3) The Nau Sayyids' *masjid* on the banks of the old Gôpî lake, in honour of the nine warriors whom Qâzi Diwân asserted were buried there.

III. (4) Mulla Muhammadu'd-dîn's *masjid*, near Mulla Khaḍki, built in A.H. 1136 (A.D. 1724.)

III. (5) Sayyid Idrus' *masjid* in Sayyidpura, Variàvi Bhâgal, with a lofty *minâr*; built in A.H. 1019 by Mirza Sayyid Beg in honour of the ancestor of the Idrus family, who is said to have come to Surat in 972 and died 1032 A.H. (?)

III. (6) Dariâ Mehel Masjid in Bakshi's Dariâ Mehel, built by the Bakshi Mir Azimu'd-dîn in A.H. 1196 (A.D. 1782).

III. (7) The Castle of Surat, now occupied by public offices.

II*a*. (8) The Old English tombs outside the Katârgâon gate and the Dutch tombs deserve attention (*Jour. Bom. B. R. As. Soc.* vol. VI. p. 146; vol. VIII. pp. cxlii. cxlv.; *Calcutta Rev.* vol. IX. pp. 125-ff; *Thevenot's Voyages*, vol. V. p. 71).

III. (9) The two *rauzas* of the Bohorah high priests, in Jhâmpa, with the palace of the Mulla and a large wooden mosque (see Mr. Bellasis' account). Also the *rauza* of the Momens in Rustampura, built by Sayyid Kâsim Ali about 1835, and the Musalmân *rauza* in Navsârī Bhâgal, built about the middle of the 16th century.

The following temples are also enumerated:—

III. (10) Bâlâjî Mahâdeva Hâṭakeśvara, and Jagannâtha, a group of three, in Rahiâsoni, built by Travâḍi Srîkṛishṇa Arjunji Nâthji, a Nâgar Brâhmaṇ, about the beginning of the present century.

III (11) Kâśî Viśvanâtha's in Rahiâsoni ward, a small one with an underground shrine.

III. (12) Ambâjî's, also built by Travâḍi Arjunji in the last quarter of last century.

III. (13) Kâḷikâ, built by the Kâsâra (coppersmith) Mahâjans.

III. (14) Mahâdeva in Raghunâthpura built by Dulachand and Multâni Kshatri about the end of last century.

III. (15) Moholeśvara or Muleśvara, in Gopîpura, by Abherâm Mehtâ, a Nâgar Brâhmaṇ, about 1775: it has an underground shrine.

III. (16 Svâmi Nârâyaṇa in Sayyidpura, a cluster of three temples built by the sect about 22 years ago.

III. (17) Bhavânî Mâtâ in Haripura street about 200 years old.

III. (18) Bahucherâ Mâtâ about a mile north of the city, built about the middle of the 17th century.

III. (19) Jaina temples of Chintâmaṇi Pârśvanâtha in Shâhâpur; (20) in Haripura street; (21) in Sayyidpura street; and (22) in Gopîpura street.

III. (23) Choramoḍhâṅ *vâv* in Gopitalâv, built in 1717 by Mîr Alam Shâh.

III. (24) The Nawâb's palaces: two in the city and one at Anjna, one mile south of Surat.

III. (25) Well or *vâv* of Bahucherâ Mâtâ, 3 miles north of Surat, with an **inscription**, built by Lakshmidâs Tuljarâm.

Specimens of very excellent wood-carving are to be found on many of the older houses.

Copperplate grant, *Ind. Ant.* XII. 196.

III. 2. **Varatia-devadi**, north of Surat near Katârgâon,—a cluster of more than a hundred small monuments, the tombs of Jaina priests, with **inscriptions**.

III. 3. **Rander**, 2 miles above Surat. The Jami mosque is constructed out of a Jaina temple, as is also the walls of the *hauj* in the court. The niches in the walls remain unaltered. In the Kharwa mosque also the wooden pillars are said to be Jaina. The Mîyan mosque is said to have been originally a Jaina *apâsarâ*. Mosque of Valîjî, also said to have been a Jaina temple. Munshi's mosque also said to have been a Jaina temple. Mosque in Chunarvâda street said to date from the 15th century. Tomb of Sayyid Sapula in the Khângâ, A.H. 1106.

III. Temples:—(1). Bhavânîśaṅkara Mahâdeva on the banks of the river, with a *ghâṭ* quite modern. (2) Śântinâtha built by Vimal Keśar in 1818. (3) Âdinâtha, built by Ghelâbhâi of Surat about 1750, (4) Neminâtha, built by Premchand Modi about the same time. (5) Âdîśvara, built by Lakshmidâs about 1730. (6) Pârśvanâtha, of about the same age.

III. 4. **Pal**, 3 miles from Surat; a considerable temple of Pârśvanâtha.

III. 5. **Asvini-kumar**, 4 miles east of Surat: Temple of Vaijanâtha Mahâdeva with *ghâṭ* to the river. Temple of Nîlakaṇṭha Mahâdeva and *ovaro* (flight of steps). Temple of Somanâtha Mahâdeva built in 1852 by Harkor, wife of Dayârâm Sâlvi of Surat with an

inscription on the entrance. Temple of Râmanâtha Mahâdeva built by Râjagir Bâvâ, a disciple of Râmanâtha in 1744: has an **inscription** on the entrance.

III. 6. **Katargaon**: Temple of Kantâreśvara with a *kuṇḍa* 105 feet long and 53 broad, built of white stone.

III. 7. **Phulpa'da** near Katârgâon: Temple of Gupteśvara.

II.—Olpâd Tâlukâ.

III. 1. **Saras**, 10 miles north of Surat: Temple of Siddhanâtha, built by Dâmâji Gâikvâḍ in 1736, with the Bâṇagaṅgâ Kuṇḍa in front. It enjoys rent-free lands assessed at Rs. 91-12-0; and cash allowances from Government of Rs. 656.

III. 2. **Suha'li**: At the hamlet of Râjgari is a tomb which is probably Tom Coryat's.

II *a*. 3. **Vaux's tomb** is at the mouth of the river. Vaux was book-keeper to Sir Josiah Child who rose to be Deputy Governor of Bombay, and was drowned in the Tâptî in 1697 (Anderson's *Western India*, pp. 256ff). Close to it is an old temple of Sikotrâ Mâtâ.

III. 4. **Kathodra**: remains of a *sarâi* erected by one Surâju'd-din in A.H. 1133, with an **inscription** over the door.

III.—Mândvi Tâlukâ.

III. 1. **Vareth**: Temple of Râmeśvara built of brick by one Jagannâtha in 1604, with the following **inscription**:—

श्रीगणेशायनमः शारदाईनमः संवत १६६१ वरषे श्रावण सुदी ४ सुके तापीनदिक्षणत्राटि
कडोद वास्तव्य वीसल्लनगरा नागर नाती पंड्य जनादननास प्रणवीत्र पंड्य जगन्नाथ तथा
पंड्या हरजी ईणि श्रीरामनाथनुप्रशाद कीधु श्री सीवप्रशाद सीवहशि कल्याणहशितापीत्तराणे
यत्र रामसरोवस यत्र सेनासरिदुरा ॥ तत्र कोनदिव्यं याति मकरस्थे दिवाकरे ? । रामकुंडस्य
सामीप्य मृतश्वक्तमयो मृगाः । मुच्यंते तेन संदेहो दुस्तरात् गर्भसंकटात् ॥ २ ॥

रामेश्वरस्य सान्निध्ये जगन्नाथाम्रयासुद्धॉ ॥ वछानुजोह्गिोविंदश्चकारश्रममान्मनः ॥ १ ॥

खरी नकल.

करनार पे. आ. दयालजी लालभाई. कस्बे मांडवी ता. स्कुल.

III. 2. **Ma'ndvi**: Temple of Nîlakaṇṭha Mahâdeva built by Dâdâbâvâ in 1762. **Inscription** as follows:—

॥ श्रीगणेशायनमः ॥ स्वस्ति श्रीनृपविक्रमार्कसमयान्यदावाति दुर्भिर्मिये श्रीवृषवत्सरे दीनमणे
याम्यायनं प्रस्थिते ॥ मासश्चाश्विनसंज्ञक स्वधवले पक्षे दशम्यां गुरो श्रीदादामहीडाभिधेन रचितो
देवालयो भिष्टदः ॥ १ ॥ श्रीमदुर्जनसिंहस्य भर्ता श्रीमंडपीपुरे ॥ भाई बाजी सुतो धीमान्
दादाबावा भिदो करोत् ॥ २ ॥

संवत १८१७ ना अश्विन शुदि १० गुरूवासरे संपूर्णः ॥ श्री ॥

III. Temple of Dayâleśvara Mahâdeva built of black stone by Dayâśaṅkar Bhâlodiâ. **Inscription**: illegible.

III. Temple of Durgeśvara Mahâdeva built by Durgan-singhjî, Râjâ of Mândvî, of brick and stone. Temple of Râmchandra built of marble and stone called Bâsâheb. Palace of the Râjâ of Mândvî built of stone in 1764. The town walls have 24 towers and 4 gates.

III. Sukhânand Vazir's temple contains his *pâdukâ*. He was killed on this spot by the Bohoras of Baudhân during an insurrection. The inscription on it is as follows :—

॥ श्रीगणेशायनमः ॥ मुनिविधुसतद्वित्रैशके वैतपसिसीतगणवेदी नेच सोमे यवनजनसमुही-
नाशकरता भ्रगुतिल्का किमुवोमहा अब्रु ध ॥ १ ॥ सोयं सुखानंद इति भ्राता जगति विश्रुतः ॥
वीरस्यां समाहत्यशिवलोके गताः ॥ किल ॥ २ ॥ सं १८६७ पौषशुदी ४ साम ॥ श्री ॥

III. Two Jaina temples containing the following inscription :—

(1) in Âdinâtha's temple.

॥ संवत १८९७ वर्षे वैशाखमासे कृष्णपक्षे दश्यांतिप्रेशनौ श्री मुत्त संवत्सर स्वतिगछे बलात्कार गणे कुंदकुंदाआचार्यल्ये भटारक श्रीसकल्कीर्ति तदनुक्रमेण मुप श्रीतीजबकीर्ति तत्पदे भ० श्रीनेमीचंद देवातत्पदे भ० श्रीचंद्रकीर्ति वासत्पदे भ० श्री रामकीर्ति देवातत्पदे भटारक श्रीयशकीर्ति पुरूष देशात् ममउशाक्षी वकंपुएम्दयं श्रीमांडवीग्रामे समस्त श्रीक्षीस श्रीमूल्नायक श्रीआदिनाथ नित्यं प्रणम्पति ॥ श्री ॥ श्री शुभं भवतु ॥

(2) in a Jaina *apâsarâ*.

॥ संवत १८४९ वर्षशाके १९ । १९ प्रवर्त्तमाने माघ सुदि ७ सोमवासरे श्री मांडविनगरे बास्तव्य समहासंघन श्रीशबक पुज्यं जिननिंबं नरापितं श्रीतपाटा च्मे जदारना श्री श्री विजय

जिनेंद्रसूरिजि प्रतिष्ठितं श्री व्याहारानगरे श्री

(3.) ॥ सं ॥ १८४९ वर्षे शाके १७१० प्रवर्त्तमाने माघशुदि ७ चंद्रे
श्रीमांडवीनगरवास्तव्य समस्तसंघेन श्रीनाडिन । ध बिंबंशा श्रीतपागछेगव्व । धिराजता श्री श्री
विजयजी नेप्रसूरितिः प्रतिष्ठितायं श्री व्यारानगरे श्रीयंभवः

(4.) ॥ संवत १८४९ ना वर्षे शाके १७१० प्रवेशमा नेमाघशुदि ७
सोमवासरे श्रीमांडविनगरे वास्तव्य श्रीसमस्त संघेन श्री कुंथुनाथ बींबंतरापिंतं
तपागछेभ श्रीविजयजिनेंद्रसूरि.

III. 3. **Baudhan,** 18 miles north-east of Surat; a place of pilgrimage and *mêla*, when Jupiter enters Simha: Temple of Gautameśvara Mahâdeva, of black stone and brick built in 1806 by Vajir Sukhânand. Inscription as follows :—

॥ श्रीगणेशायनमः ॥ स्वस्तिश्रीविक्रमशकाग्रुणाजवसुचंदकेवत्सरे प्रभवमाश्री ग्रीष्मार्तो माधवेशीते ॥ १ ॥ द्वादश्यां शशिवारे च वषेर्के चोत्तरस्छिते ॥ कार्मे सिद्धी योगेषु प्रासादः सेखरीकृतः ॥ २ ॥ बौधान्ये सुभेक्षेत्रे तापिन्या गौतमीतटे ॥ श्रीमदुर्जनसिंहस्य भूपतेरधिका-शिणः ॥ ३ ॥ आत्मारामाप्रवार्दोज द्विजभार्गवजातिना प्रधानेन सुपुण्येन सुखानंदेन धीमता ॥ ४ ॥ श्रीगौतमेशक्रपयानुतनंमंदिरंकृतं ॥ मंडपीपत्तनेस्छित्वा शिवसायुज्यलब्धये ॥ ५ ॥ संवत् १८९८ वर्षे शाके १७२३ प्र० वैसाख सुदी १२ चंद्रेमांडवीकर राजादुर्जनसिंहजी-नावजीर सुखानंदे बंधाव्युं छे.

III. Temples of Jñâneśvara and Gaḷateśvara; and the Râja *ovâro*, built about 90 years ago.

IV.—Bârdoli Tâlukâ.

III. 1. **Ba'rdoli**: Temple of Kedâreśvara east of the town and to the south of the river Mindholâ. The *liṅga* is 8 feet below the ground level, and is said to have been discovered by a cow losing her milk on the spot, according to the legend reported of so many others. This *liṅga* has four 'brothers' in the district.

III. 2. **Mota**: Temple of Râmanâtha, with a Râmakuṇḍa made by Râma with his arrow.

III. 3. **Balpur** in the Visampur division of the Navsâri Gâikvâḍi *parganâ*: Temple of Kardameśvara built of black stone in 1625 by Sundara Dâyâ. A *kuṇḍa* of black stone. A *vâv* 50 feet long and 25 feet wide, of black stone; also other remains of a large town.

4. **Anavat**: Temple of Śukleśvara of black stone.

V.—Jalâlpur Tâlukâ.

(*No Returns.*)

VI.—Chikhli Tâlukâ.

III. **Miya'gaon**: temple of Mallikârjuna Mahâdeva, has a dome 28 feet in diameter supported by eight pillars, and is said to have been built about 300 years ago.

VII.—Balsâr Tâlukâ.

III. **Pa'rner**: a hill fort, and a temple of Chaṇḍikâmâtâ, built in the Peśvâ times and in the custody of Government.

VIII.—Pârdi Tâlukâ.

III. 1. **Ba'gwa'da'**: a Muhammadan mosque, and temples of Bâlakṛishṇa, Ambâmâtâ, Lakshmî-Nârâyaṇa, Gaṇapati, Kedâreśvara, Siddheśvara, Someśvara, &c.

III. 2. **Tigra**: temple of Athuri Mâtâ.

III. 3. **Pa'rdi**; temple of Vaidyanâtha Mahâdeva and a *dharmaśâlâ*.

III. 4. **Palsana**: temple of Râmeśvara Mahâdeva.

III. 5. **Vatav**: temple of Kotîśvara Mahâdeva.

III. 6. **Kunta**: temple of Kulanâtha Mahâdeva.

THANA ZILLA.

I.—Sâlsette Tâlukâ.

III. **1. Tha'na.** Of old Hindu or Musalmân Thâna there is almost no trace. The temples and mosques, praised by early travellers, were pulled down by the Portuguese (1530—1560) and their stones used for churches and other religious buildings; and most of these Christian churches and buildings were in turn destroyed by the Marâṭhâs (1737—1740). Almost the only remains of Thâna before the Portuguese are the four reservoirs or ponds, Massunda, Devâla, Gosâla, and Haryâla, all of unknown date. There are also several finely carved broken images and sculptured stones, which have been gathered in the Jail Garden, and at the Executive Engineer's Work-shops. These belonged to some old Brahmanical temple. They were found in 1881, while clearing the Massunda lake of silt. There are some inscription stones in the Collector's garden. See "Mândir."

The chief Portuguese building is the fort which is now used as a jail. It was begun by the Portuguese in 1730. There are also remains of some of their forts along the creek, and one of their churches remains, that of St. John the Baptist. It is said that in order to build the church, Antonio do Porto pulled down twelve pagodas and built his church with the stones of the Hindu temples.

II *a.* In the English churchyard are the graves of two of the Chiefs of Sâlsette, *viz.* John Halsey who died in 1785 and George Page who died in 1794.

III. **2. Ghodbandar.**—Old church dedicated to St. John, monasteries, and fort. The church is now a bungalow. Owing to the influence of a *pîr* buried close by, all the efforts of the builders to construct a tower or spire are said to have failed and a Muhammadan dome was the result of their labours. A party of Sivâji's troops tried to surprise Ghoḍbandar when in the hands of the Portuguese in 1672, but were repulsed.

II *b.* 3. **Borivli** station on the Bombay, Baroda, and Central India Railway:—at Montpezir (Maṇḍapeśvara), old churches, watch-tower, convent and caves, which have been turned into a crypt for the church dedicated to N. S. da Conceição. College for the education of orphans. Duperron speaks of the Marâṭhâs after destroying the church carrying the timber to Thâna. Over the college door is an inscription with arms of Portugal to the effect that the edifice was built in 1623 by order of Infant Dom John III. of Portugal.
I *b.* In the *patel's* garden are some very curiously carved memorial stones, with sea-fights sculptured upon them. These are set up in a row. There are 6, five large and one small. Two represent a battle upon land in which mail-clad elephants take part. Three are sculptured with the representation of a sea-fight shewing the vessels approaching one another in long well ordered lines and also mixed up together in the fight itself. (**Surveyed.**)

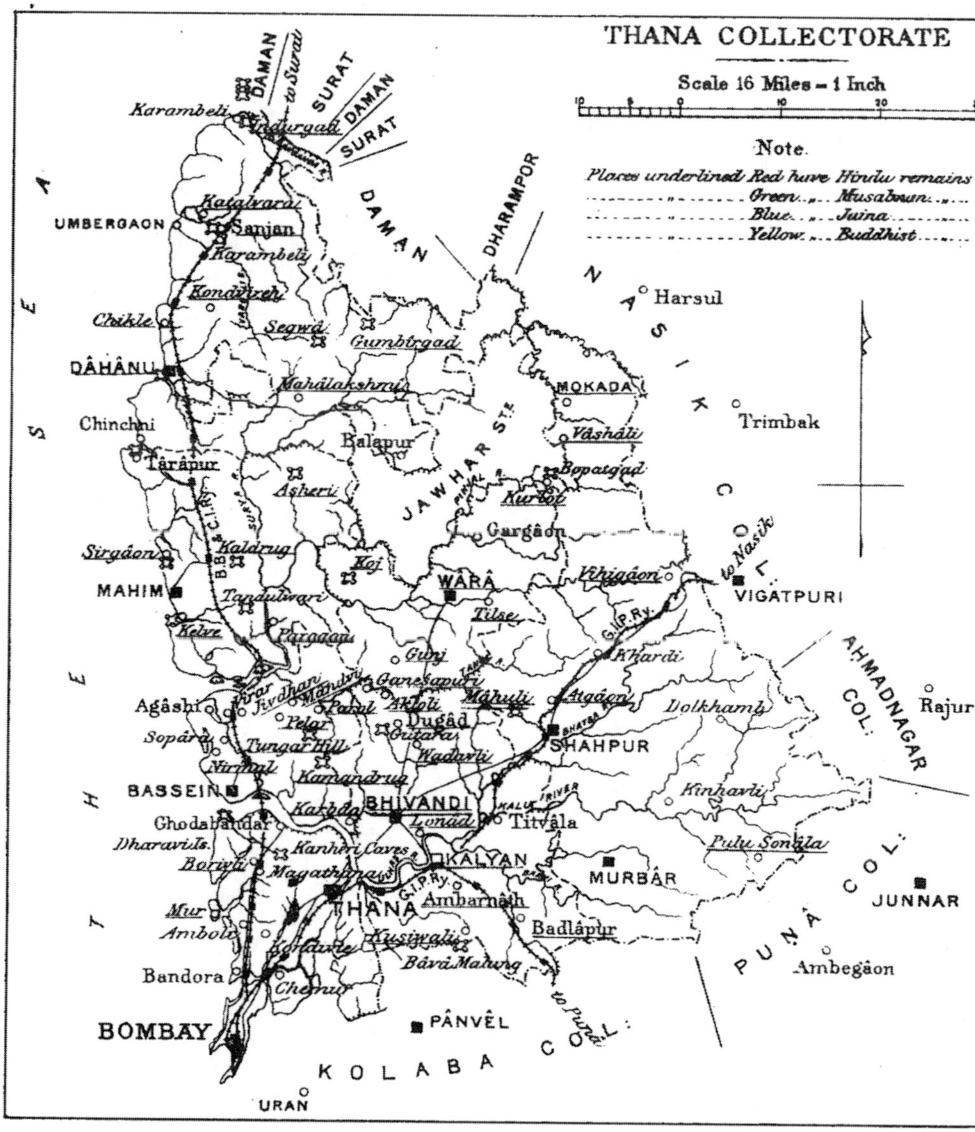
THANA COLLECTORATE
Scale 16 Miles = 1 Inch
Note.
Places underlined Red have Hindu remains
Green Musalman
Blue Jaina
Yellow Buddhist
THE SEA
DAMAN
SURAT
to Surat
DHARAMPOR
NASIK COL.
JAWHAR STE
AHMADNAGAR COL.
PUNA COL.
KOLABA COL.
Karambeli
Indargad
Katalvara
UMBERGAON
Sanjan
Karambeli
Konavireh
Chikle
Segwa
Gumbirgad
DÂHÂNU
Mahâlakshmi
MOKADA
Harsul
Trimbak
Chinchni
Balapur
Vâshâli
Târâpur
Bopatgad
Asheri
Kurlod
Gargâon
Sirgâon
Kaldrug
Koj
MAHIM
WÂRÂ
Vihigâon
to Nasik
VIGATPURI
Tandulwari
Tilse
Kelve
Pargaon
Guni
Khardi
Agâshi
Jivdhan
Mândvi
Ganesapuri
Atgâon
Dolkhamb
Rajur
Sopâra
Pelar
Akloli
Mâhuli
Dugâd
Tungar Hill
Wadavli
SHAHPUR
Nirmal
Kamandrug
BASSEIN
BHIVANDI
Kinhavli
Ghodabandar
Lonad
Titvâla
Dharavi Is.
Kanheri Caves
Pulu Sonâla
Borivli
KALYAN
Magathan
MURBÂR
JUNNAR
THANA
G.I.P.Ry.
Ambarnâth
Mur
Ambolo
Badlâpur
Kusiwali
Bandora
Bâvâ Malang
Ambegâon
Chembur
to Puna
BOMBAY
PÂNVÊL
URAN

I *a*. 4. **Kanheri Caves.** They are about 6 miles from Thâna, and two north of the Tulsi lake, and are excavated in a great knoll of a hill, situated in the midst of a large tract of forest country. There are upwards of one hundred excavations, almost entirely monastic dwellings (for full description see *Cave Temples of India*; also *J. B. B. R. A. S.*, part I. p. 34. Inscriptions, *Ind. Ant.* XII. 215; IX. 265; XIII. 133; *J. B. B. R. A. S.*, part XIII. p. 39; part XXI. pp. 1 and 116; part XVI. p. 1. *Arch. Survey Report*, Vols. IV. and V.) **(Surveyed.)**

III. 5. **Ma'ga'tha'na,** about half a mile east of the Borivli station on the Bombay-Baroda Railway, is the site of the deserted village of Mâgâthâna. At the foot of a mound, a little to the east, is a hole or quarry, apparently old. A little further, in a black round topped rock, are cut the Mâgâthâna or Poinsar Caves, including a chapel-cave on the south and a monastery cave on the north. Across the rice fields, about 300 yards to the east, a flat surface of trap, about two feet above the level of the ground, has been hollowed into an underground cistern. On the west bank of a double pond, about 200 yards north of the cistern, are two old Musalmân tomb stones, rather finely carved with hanging chains. About 300 yards to the east, on a low mound covered with grass and bushes are lying two *dâghobas.* To the west is a rough bush-covered mound of undressed stone. A yard or two to the north, hidden in thorn bushes and partly buried in the ground, stands another *dâghoba* similar to the former. About forty yards east is a small burial mound about four feet round and one foot high. Two hundred yards to the south-east, at the edge of the rice land, lying on the grass, is a big slab of trap, seven feet high by one
II *b*. foot six inches broad. At the top it is carved into a big funeral urn, while below are three belts of figures. The country round here shews distinct traces of Buddhist structural temples or monasteries. (For further information see *Thâna Gazetteer*; and *J. B. B. R. A. S.*, part XIII. p. 41). **(Surveyed.)**

II *b*. 6. **Amboli,** a small village in Sâlsette, about two miles north-west of Andheri station. The Brâhmanical caves of Jogeśvari or Amboli (A.D. 600—700) lie in the woodlands about two miles south-east of Goregâon railway station. (*J. B. B. R. A. S.* part XIII. p. 40; *Arch. Sur. Report*, vol. V.; *Cave Temples of India*). **(Surveyed.)**

II *a*. 7. **Kondivte** or Mahâkâla caves form two rows, one of fifteen caves on the south-east face, and one of four caves on the north-west face of a low flat-topped range of trap breccia, about four miles north-east of the Andheri station. The caves are Buddhist, probably between the second and sixth centuries of the Christian era. (*J. B. B. R. A. S.*, part XIII. p. 40; *Arch. Sur. Report*, IV.; *Cave Temples of India.*) **(Surveyed.)**

II *b*. 8. **Mandapes'vara** in Sâlsette, called Montpezier or Monpacer by the Portuguese, is about eight miles south of Bassein and two miles north of Borivli station. For miles around, it is easily known by a high whitewashed watch tower that crowns a wooded knoll. About 100 yards to the north of the watch tower, upon what was apparently a great isolated block of trap rock are the remains of a Portuguese Cathedral and College. The east face of the great mass of rock on which the buildings stand, has been cut into several Brâhmanical caves. The caye has been fitted as a Portuguese Church, with a plain altar and seated wooden image of the Virgin Mary. (*J.B.B.R.A.S.*, part XIII. p. 41). **(Surveyed.)**

III. 9. **Dharavi Island**, on the west of Sâlsette, at the mouth of the Bassein Creek, has, on a ridge of hill, the ruins of a large Portuguese church and the remains of a fort with a tank.

III. 10. **Versova** is a small village and port on the west coast of Sâlsette, twelve miles north of Bombay. Close to it is the island of Madh with an old fort that was rebuilt by the Marâṭhâs.

III. 11. **Bandora.**—An old *aguada* or fort at the Point, with the following inscription:—

ESTE. BALVAR
TE. SEFESEM
LOVOR. DONO
ME. DEIESVS
EM. 1640.

According to Da Cunha, the Portuguese fleets supplied themselves with water here. There are a number of old Roman Catholic churches about Sâlsette, many of which were destroyed when the Marâṭhâs conquered the island in 1738.

12. **Chembur** or Chemur, on the north-west of Bombay Island, is believed to be the Saimur of the Arab writers, the Sibor of Kosmas Indikopleustes, the Chamula of the Kanheri cave inscriptions, the Symulla of the author of the Periplus of the Erythræan Sea, the Symulla or Timulla of Ptolemy, and perhaps the Perimula of Pliny.

13. **Bha'ndup**: copper-plate grant, *Ind. Ant.* V. 276.

II.—KALYÂN TÂLUKÂ.

III. 1. **Kalya'n.** There are, at Kalyân, the Shenâle lake, said to have been built in 1505, the tomb of Mohatabar Khân, the minister of Shâh Jahân, who was sent in disgrace to Kalyân when Aurangzib usurped his father's throne, and twelve mosques of which seven are in use and five in ruins. Of these buildings the most interesting are Mohatabar Khân's

II *b*. tomb on the east bank of the Shenâle lake, and the graceful Kâli Masjid at the south-west corner of the same lake. A life-sized image of Vishṇu set up on the left side of the road leading from the station to the town.

III. 2. **Ba'wa' Malang**, near Kusiwali village; old fort, and two plain cells. Hill fort, Muhammadan shrine, and another called Pâlki. Information scanty.

I *b*. 3. **Ambarna'th** Village.—Temple of Ambarnâtha, a fine temple of the style of the 11th century (A.D. 1060). Though small it is richly carved and of great interest as a good type of its age. Festival held on the Śivarâtri in Mâgha (*Ind. Ant.* III. 316). (**Surveyed.**)

Inscription of the Śilâhâra dynasty in the temple, dated *Śaka* 982, A.D. 1060. (*J.B.B.R.A.S.* vol. IX. p. 219).

III.—Murbâd Tâlukâ.

III. Pulu Sonala, at the foot of the Nânâghât, about twenty miles east of Murbâd, has several plain Brâhmaṇical caves. They are situated on a scarp a little way up the hill-side and have a westerly aspect. They are very recent and very poorly cut, only one having any pretentions to rank as a cave, the remainder being rough cells much broken and dilapidated. There are a few figures in bas-relief, but no good architectural details. (**Surveyed.**)

IV.—Bassein Tâlukâ.

II *a*. 1. **Bassein or Wasai.**—Fine fort and old Portuguese churches with inscriptions: well-known. Copper-plate grant, *Ind. Ant.* XII. 119.

III. 2. **Nirmal.**—Temples and tanks. Pilgrimage here in the cold weather, in the month of Kârtika. *Jatrâ* on 11th Kârtika. The Portuguese or rather the Inquisition pulled down the temple and desecrated the *tîrtha* and caused the *liṅga* of Śiva to disappear. On the Marâṭhâs taking possession of Bassein, Nirmal was again purified, a tank constructed, and temples built.

III. 3. **Jivdhan' Hill**, about a mile east of the Virâr station on the Bombay-Baroda Railway, has on its top ruins of fortifications visible from the railway, and within the fortifications some very old-looking caves and cisterns said to be the work of the Pâṇḍavas, Throughout the fair season people, especially barren women from the surrounding villages, go to the caves to make offerings to an invisible deity, who is believed to have fled from a niche in one of the caves at the touch of a Mahâr.

III. 4. **Tunga'r Hill.**—Tanks, Tongeśvara. Temple half way up the hill with carved stones.

II *b*. 5. **Pelar.**—Temple and two large stones, with long inscriptions.

III. 6. **Pa'rol**, a village on the east base of Tungâr Hill, lies about eight miles east of Virâr Station on the Baroda Railway. It has the remains of four old Hindu temples. At none of these four temples is worship now performed. The two Pârol temples, called the temples of the Big and Little Pools, *Mothâ Tânkya* and *Lahân Tânkya*, stand on the southern and northern banks of a stream which runs down the steep side of Tungâr. The *Lahân Tânkya* temple is about half a mile west of Pârol village. It is levelled to the ground which is strewn with carved stones. The Big Pool or *Mothâ Tânkya* temple, about half a mile further up the stream bed, is better preserved. Of the two in the limits of the village of Majavli, one, not more than a few hundred yards south-west of the village site of Pârol, seems to have been the largest of the group. Its superstructure is gone, only the plinth and some of the steps remain. The stones and large blocks that lie about are finely cut, though not so well chiselled as the Ambarnâtha stones.

III. 7. **Ma'ndvi**, below the northern spur of Tungâr hill, and fifteen miles north-east of Bassein, lies on the old trade route from Sopâra up the Tânsa valley to the Tal pass. It has a picturesque ruined convent and a Portuguese fort. Among the inscribed stones in the Collector's garden at Thânâ there is one from Mândvi. It records a grant by a Śilâhâra king but is much worn and hard to read.

III. 8. **Ta'nsa River.**—Along the banks here and there are carved stones.

III. 9. **Kamandurg,** in Kâman village, about 10 miles east of Mânikpur: an old hill fort.

III. 10. **Aga'shi** is a town and port about 10 miles north of Bassein. Though now of little consequence Agâshi is probably an old timber trade and ship-building centre. In 1530, though poor in buildings, it had a rich timber trade, and built ships as good as Portuguese ships able to make the voyage to Europe.

III. 11. **Arnala,** an island fort off the coast opposite Agâshi, also called Janjira or the island. Among North Konkan coast-forts it ranked next to Bassein in size and strength. It was taken from the Gujarât Musalmâns by the Portuguese about 1530, and was taken by the Marâṭhâs about 1737, and, according to a Marâṭhi inscription over the northern gateway, was rebuilt in the reign of Bâjirâv I. in 1737, by an architect named Bâji Tulâji.

12. **Sopa'ra,** a village about 37 miles north of Bombay and three and a half miles south-west of Virâr Station. The Soupâra of Ptolemy, the Sopâra of the *Periplus* Subâra of the early Arab voyagers, and the Surpâraka of the Cave inscriptions. There is a village close by in Mâhim bearing a very similar name, Saphala, but it never seems to have been a place of note. For a full account of the discovery of a Buddhist *stûpa* here with its excavation and finding of relics see a paper by the late Pandit Bagvânlâl Indraji in the *Journal of the Bombay Branch of the Royal Asiatic Society*, 1882. (**Surveyed.**)

III. 13. **Karbao.** Old Portuguese Fort.

V.—Bhivandi Tâlukâ.

III. 1. **Gutara** (Dugâḍ Village).—Fort and tanks.

III. 2. **Vadavli.**—There is a celebrated modern temple here of Vajrâbâi with six *inâm* villages granted by Government for its support, where a pilgrimage is held in Chaitra.

III. 3. **Lonad.**—A small old temple of Mahâdeva of the style of Ambarnâtha. Also a cave with some sculptures, but it is doubtful whether they are Hindu or Buddhist. (*Ind. Ant.* IV. 65; *Arch. Sur. Report*, vol. V.) (**Surveyed.**)

III. 4. **Bhivandi.**—A beautiful tomb of Husain Shâh (*Ind. Ant.* IV. 65).

III. 5. **Ganes'apuri.**—Some sculptures of an old temple (*Ind. Ant.* IV. 67). Temple of Bhîmeśvara Mahâdeva with five or six hot springs.

III. 6. **Bhivandi.**—Varala Tank. The legend runs that the tank was dug to a certain depth but would not hold water. It occurred to a man in a dream that the tank awaited the sacrifice of a man and his wife within its area, that the said man having proceeded with his wife to the site of the tank during the night touched a large boulder in it. The tank was instantaneously filled with water and they were drowned in it. Latterly it has been enlarged by the Municipality of the town and the Bhivandi water-supply is obtained from it.

III. 7. **Akloli.**—Fine temple of Mahâdeva and five hot springs much resorted to.

VI.—Shâhâpur Tâlukâ.

III. 1. **Atgaon.**—Remains of an old temple.

III. 2. **Vihigaon.**—Old fort close to Reversing Station and past Kasâra Station, Great Indian Peninsula Railway.

III. 3. **Mahuli.**—On the summit of a most striking mountain are the remains of a fine old fort: in two of the gate bastions are caves with some Hindu and Muhammadan remains, and inscriptions. The only Hindu inscription is on a *Saṭi* stone; first line illegible; 2nd. "Śrî Padmâvati Satî." Two Musalmân inscriptions on the *idgâh*, one fallen and the other *in situ*. Four more picked up lying about are now in charge of Mulna Shâhpur. When Jîjîbâi, Sivâji's mother, was flying from the Muhammadan troops from 1633 to 1636, she with her young son frequently took refuge in this fort. In 1670 Moro Tirmal, the Peśvâ or Prime Minister of Śivâji, sustained a repulse at this fort from the Moghal troops with reported loss of 1,000 men. After a siege of two months, the fort, however, surrendered to him.

III. 4. **Mokhada Peta**, Bhopatgaḍ.—Kurlot village, old fort, and tanks.

III. 5. **Vashali** in Mokhâda, a rock-cut temple called Vâse, situated on the north slope of a small hill. It was blocked up for about 3 to 4 feet with earth which has been excavated at the expense of the late Mr. Gibson, in the hope of a *kuṇḍa* being found. The inner space is nearly square, about 12′ × 12′. The height about 6′ 6″. In the rock facing the door on either side of a niche, are two images each about 3′ high. They appear to have very large ears, and with their arms and hands by their sides are in the attitude of "attention." One has his sign of sex clearly shown, the other not. Over the lintel is a small broken image. There is a porch roofed with stone slabs held up on two pillars, squared, and having the angles cut off in portions. There is in front of these pillars a small enclosure, perhaps 3 feet or 4 feet from them, with walls of rock on either side, and a doorway through two little parapet-like walls 3 or 4 feet high. It is not much of a temple or cave in itself, but its locality makes it important. It appears to be Jaina.

VII.—Mâhim Tâlukâ.

III. 1. **Kelve and Sirgâon.**—Old forts.

III. 2. **Asheri.**—Asheri Fort described by Gemelli Careri. Besides being seated on the top of a hill, where there is no higher ground to command it, a crooked path cut out of the mountain, along which two men cannot go abreast, leads up to it and is defended by several guards who might withstand an army, by only rolling down stones placed there for the purpose. Dickinson described it after the Marâṭhâs had held it 80 years as accessible only at one point and of such natural strength that with a handful of men to defend it, it might justly be considered impregnable. The latter part of the ascent is up an almost perpendicular staircase (with a precipice of several hundred feet immediately below it) hewn out of the solid rock, forty feet higher. (Da Cunha's *Bassein*, page 206.)

III. 3. **Kaldrug,** Tândulvâdi and Tak Mak.—Old forts.

III. 4. **Ta'ra'pur.**—Old fort repaired by the Marâṭhâs in European style.

III. 5. **Pa'rgaon.**—A *gadda karao* or curious boundary mark with donkey and woman.

VIII.—Vâda Tâlukâ.

III. 1. **Koj.**—Fine hill fort and tanks.

III. 2. **Gunj.**—A temple of Śrî Bhârgavarâma, tank and ruins.

III. 3. **Tilse.**—Temple and sacred pool in islet in Vaitarnâ river. Pilgrimage in hot weather.

III. 4. **Va'da.**—Remains of temples and tanks; an inscription discovered here, of the Śilâhâra dynasty, is in the Bombay Asiatic Society's Museum.

IX.—Dâhânu Tâlukâ.

III. 1. **Maha'lakshmi.**—Very peculiar and conspicuously shaped hill. Shrine very holy and a pilgrimage to it in March.

III. 2. **Gumbirgad.**—Vihâli village, a very large hill fort.

III. 3. **Segva'.**—Shishne village, an old hill fort.

III. 4. **Chikle.**—Fort. Anquetil Duperron, 1760, says this was repaired to protect inhabitants from pirates.

III. 5. **Da'ha'nu and Umbargaon.**—Old forts.

III. 6. **Barat Hill.**—Kondvireh village,—fort and tanks.

III. 7. **Sanjan.**—Fort; this place is that to which Pârsi fire was originally brought by Pârsis.

III. 8. **Indurgad.**—Karambeli village, fort.

III. 9. **Katalwa'ra.**—An old fort.

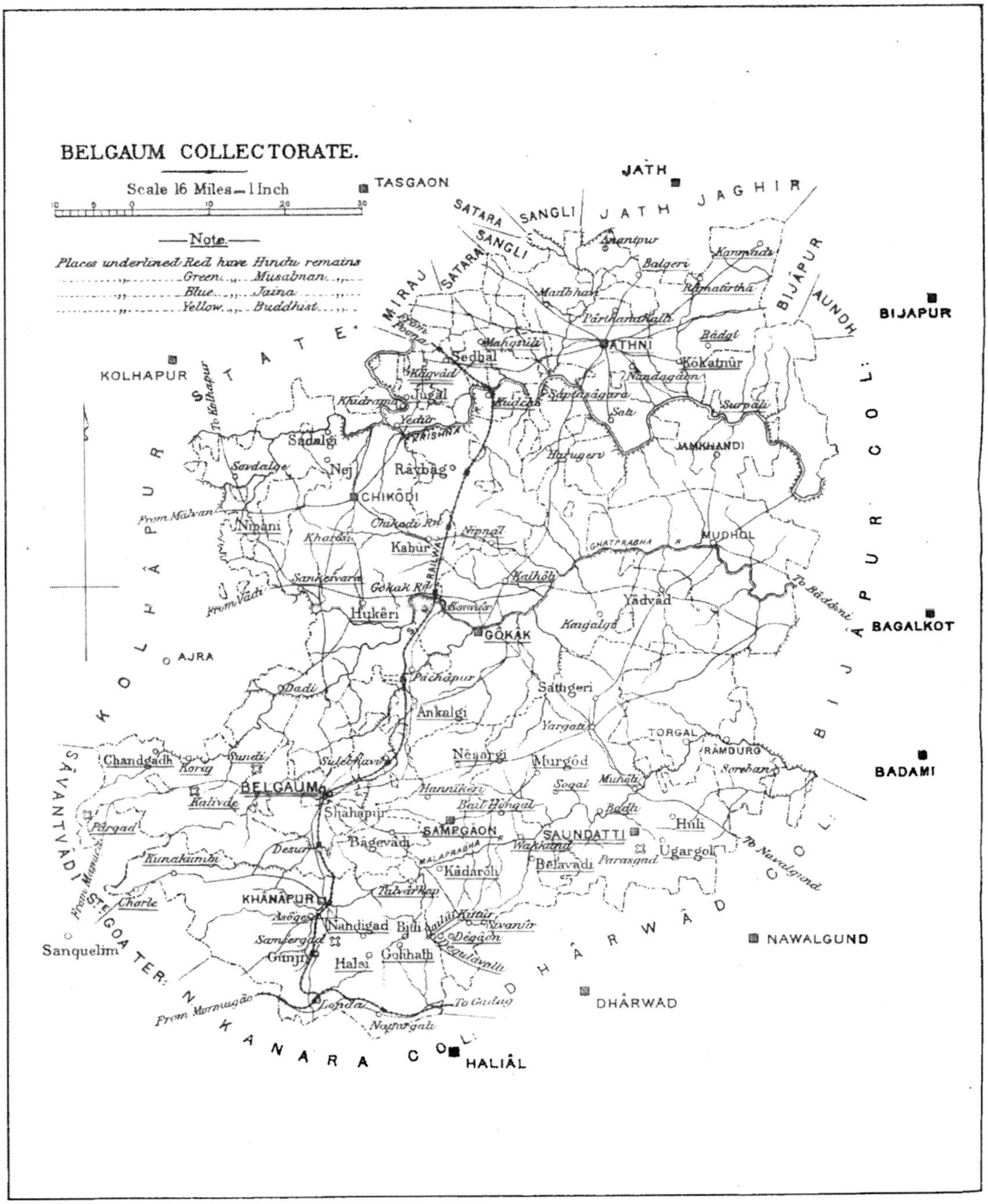

DRAWN & PHOTOZINCOGRAPHED, GOVT. PHOTOZINCO OFFICE, POONA 1896.

III.—SOUTHERN DIVISION.

I.—BELGAUM ZILLA.

I.—Belgaum Tâlukâ.

IIa. 1. **Belgaum.**—(15° 51'; 74° 35'). The fort to the east of the town is said to have been built in A.D. 1519. In it are Asad Khân's *dargâh* or *Masjid Safâ*, no longer used, and two Jaina temples of the 12th or 13th century, described in the first *Archæological Report*. (*Ind. Ant.* IV. 138.) (**Surveyed.**)

IIa. **Inscriptions**:—One, in Persian, in a recess to the north of the main gate, is dated A.H. 937 (A.D. 1530); another is over the entrance of the *Masjid Safâ*—"in the time of Adil Ayam......who utterly uprooted the unbelievers from the country of the Dakhan;" an inscription in the south-east part of the fort relates to the rebuilding of a portion of the wall in A.H. 1043 (A.D. 1633-34); a fourth (of A.D. 1648) is built into the front wall of the library, which was formerly the *Killedâr's* house; and a fifth, much effaced, is on the right side of the west gate. (See *First Archæological Survey Report.*) Also there were formerly, somewhere in the fort, two Raṭṭa tablets dated *Śaka* 1126 or 1127, but they have been removed from Belgaum, and it is not known where they are now (*Elliot MS. Coll.* vol. II. pp. 571 and 576; *Jour. Bom. B. R. A. S.* vol. X. p. 184; *Ind. Ant.* IV. 6.)

III. 2. **Sundi**, 9 miles W.N.W. from Belgaum; hill-fort of Mahîpatgaḍ.

III. 3. **Kalivde**, 17 miles west from Belgaum; hill-fort of Kalânidhigaḍ.

III. 4. **Koraji**, 19 miles W.N.W. from Belgaum; hill-fort of Gandharvagaḍ.

III. 5. **Pa'rgad**, hill-fort, 32 miles west by south from Belgaum.

III. 6. **Chandgad**, 22 miles west from Belgaum (15° 56'; 74° 15'). A temple of Revalanâtha, about 100 feet long by 38 wide.

Inscription:—A Persian one.

II.—Bidi Tâlukâ.

III. 1. **Talwarkop**, on the Malaprabhâ, 4 miles west of Kâdaroḷi and 3 miles south-west of Hubli. A small but very old temple of Śaṁkaraliṅgadeva in the bed of the river, ascribed to Jakhaṇâchârya.

III. 2. **Nandigad**,—20 miles south from Belgaum (15° 33'; 74° 36'). 1½ miles west of the town on a hill called Samśergaḍ is an old plain temple of Taṭeśvara, ascribed to
IIb. Jakhaṇâchârya. An old and typical Jaina temple in the jungle with fine carving.

III. 3. **Asoge**, 7 miles W.N.W. from Nandigaḍ. A small plain old temple of Râmaliṅgadeva, with many monumental, *satî*, and *nâga* stones.

III. 4. **Golihalli**, 1 mile south from Biḍi: A small plain ruinous old Jakhaṇâchârya temple of Râmaliṅgadeva; also similar temples of Siddhaliṅgadeva and Kalmeśvara.

I *b*. **Inscriptions**:—Two Kâdamba grants, one dated *Śaka* 1032 (*J. B.B. R. A. S.* vol. IX. pp. 263, 296), and the other Kaliyuga 4283.

III. 5. **Halsi**, or Halasige, 23 miles south from Belgaum (15° 32′; 74° 40′). A Vaishṇava temple of Varâha-Narasiṁha, about 90 feet long by 54 wide, ascribed to Jakhaṇâchârya. Another good-sized temple of Suvarṇeśvara, out of repair. On a hill about 2 miles west from Halsi is a temple of Râmeśvara and a sacred pool (*Bom. Sel.* CXV. p. 2).

I *b*. **Inscriptions**:—Two Kâdamba inscriptions, dated Kaliyuga 4270 and 4272, (*J. B. B. R. A. S.* vol. IX. pp. 262, 278; see also *P. S. & O. C. Insc.*, Nos. 2 and 5 to 10. Copper-plate grant, *Ind. Ant.* VI. 22.)

III. 6. **Kunakumbi**, 19 miles west by north from Khânâpur: A temple of Mâhulidevî, about 97 feet by 54; a somewhat modern shrine, but of considerable sanctity as being at the source of the Malaprabhâ.

III 7. **Chorle**, 24 miles west by north from Khânâpur. A small temple of Râmeśvara.

III.—Sampgâon Tâlukâ.

II *b*. 1. **Sampgaon**, 18 miles E.S.E. from Belgaum (15° 47′; 74° 50′). A small but beautiful mosque. (See *First Archæological Report*. *Ind. Ant.* IV. 6, 155.)

III. 2. **Belavadi**, 12 miles south-east from Sampgâon (15° 43′; 74° 59′). A very old temple of Vîrabhadradeva, in what is locally known as the Jakhaṇâchârya style; restored in the time of Kittûr Desâî.

II *b*. **Inscription**:—A fragment of a Western Châlukya one, dated *Śaka* 992.

III. 3. **Nesargi**, 7 miles north from Sampgâon: A fine old Śaiva temple of Basava partly in ruins.

I *b*. **Inscription**:—One dated *Śaka* 1141, of the time of the Raṭṭa chieftain Kârtavîrya IV. (*Jour. B. B. R. A. S.* vol. X. pp. 175, 240).

II *b*. 4. **Wakkund**, 10 miles south-east from Sampgâon: A large and fine old (Jaina) temple of Mukteśvara, with a spacious *pradakshiṇâ* and fine carvings and ornamentation.
III. Also smaller temples of Mallikârjuna and Rêṇukâ or Yellammâ, old and in ruins.

III. 5. **Sivanur**, 2 miles east from Kittûr. A very old temple and monumental stones.

I *b*. 6. **Degaon,** 3 miles south-west from Kittûr. A small but very old temple, elaborately ornamented. Close to it is Degalavaḷḷi which has another interesting temple.

I *b*. **Inscriptions**:—Four Kâdamba incriptions: two of them dated Kaliyuga 4275 (A.D. 1174) (*Jour. B. B. R. A. S.*, vol. IX. pp. 262, 266, 294, 310).

III. 7. **Degulavalli,** 1 mile north-west from Degâon: An old temple of Îśvara, probably originally Jaina, partly ruined.

II *b*. **Inscription**:—In Kânarese or Telugu of about the 15th century.

III. 8. **Kittur,** 14 miles south from Sampgâon (15° 36′; 74° 51′). A small temple, not very old.

I *b*. **Inscription**:—A Kâdamba grant, dated Kaliyuga 4289 (*J. B. B. R. A. S.*, vol. XI. pp. 263, 304).

9. **Bailur,** 4 miles south-west from Kittûr.

I *b* **Inscription**:—A Kâdamba grant, dated Kaliyuga 4282 (*idem*, p. 263).

III. 10. **Bail Hongal,** 6 miles east from Sampgâon. An old Śaiva temple partly ruined (**Surveyed.**)

I *b*. **Inscriptions**:—Two of the Raṭṭa chieftains, one dated *Śaka* 1086 (*Ind. Ant.*, vol. IV. p. 116, and *Archæological Report* for 1874).

III. 11. **Kadaroli,** on the Malaprabhâ, 6 miles south from Sampgâon. An old plain temple of Saṁkaradeva in the bed of the river (*Arch. Rep.*, 1874, p. 9). (**Surveyed.**)

I *b*. **Inscriptions**:—A Western Châlukya inscription of the time of Someśvaradeva II., *Saka* 997 (First and third *Arch. Rep.* and *Ind. Ant.*, vol. I. p. 141). A large fragment of another, but undecipherable one, lies uncared for in the village.

III. 12. **Hannikeri,** 4 miles north-west from Sampgâon: An old plain Jaina temple, now known as the Śivâlaya and also as the temple of Brahmadeva.

I *b*. **Inscription**:—A Raṭṭa tablet dated *Śaka* 1130 and 1178.

I *b*. 13. **Hunasikatti, inscription** (*Ind. Ant.*, X. 131).

IV.—Parasgad Tâlukâ.

III. 1. **Saundatti,** 40 miles east from Belgaum (15° 46′; 75° 11′). Temples of Ankuśeśvara, Purandareśvara, and Śaṁkaraliṅgadeva; also a Jaina temple; all plain and noways remarkable (see *Arch. Rep.*, 1874). (**Surveyed.**)

I *b*. **Inscriptions**:—(1) A Raṭṭa inscription at the temple of Ankuśeśvara, dated *Śaka* 971 and 1010 (*J. B. B. R. A. S.*, vol. X. pp. 172, 173); (2) another Raṭṭa tablet, a fragment in the same temple, dated *Śaka* 970; at the left side of the Jaina temple, of the Râshṭrakûṭa king Kṛishṇa and his Raṭṭa feudatory Prithvîrâma, *Śaka* 797; also the West. Châlukya king Vikramâditya Tribhuvanmalla and his feudatory the Raṭṭa great chieftain Kârtavîrya II. in the Dhâtu *Saṁvatsara*, *Śaka* 1018 (published *J. B. B. R. A. S.*, vol. X. pp. 170,

194; *P. S. and O. C. Ins.* No. 88); (4) an inscription of the Raṭṭa great chieftain Lakshmideva II., *Śaka* 1151. This stood in a street in the market, and has been placed for the sake of security against the outside wall of the Mâmlatdâr's *kacheri* (*Arch. Rep.*, vol. II. pl. lxxiii p. 223, and vol. III. 107; *P. S. and O. C. Ins.* No. 89; *J. B. B. R. A. S.*, vol. X. pp. 176, 260). (5) Another Raṭṭa inscription, now also in the *kacheri*, was found by Mr. J. F. Fleet, C. S., half-buried in the courtyard of the Jaina temple; it gives the genealogy of the family down to Kârtavîrya II., the feudatory of Someśvaradeva II.; the date and details of the grant are broken away (*Arch. Rep.*, vol. III., p. 114; and *J. B. B. R. A. S.*, vol. X. p. 223). (6) There is another Raṭṭa inscription at the Jaina temple, dated *Śaka* 902 (*J. B. B. R. A. S.*, vol. X.; *Ind. Ant.*, IV. 279; *J. B. B. R. A. S.*, vol. IX. p. 324).

III. 2. **Ugargol,** 3 miles E.S.E. from Saundatti. Large temple of Yellammâ, in a quadrangular enclosure (*Arch. Rep.*, 1874, p. 12). **(Surveyed.)**

II *b.* **Inscriptions**:—A Vijayanagar inscription of Kṛishṇarâya (*Śaka* 1430-1451), dated *Śaka* 1436 (*Arch. Rep.*, vol. III. p. 115).

II *b.* **Huli,** 5 miles east of Saundatti. A fine old temple of Pañchaliṅgadeva and several others, beautifully carved but in ruins, outside the village (*Arch. Rep.*, 1874). **(Surveyed.)**

I *b.* **Inscriptions**:—On two pillars in the temple of Panchaliṅgadeva are short ones. Among the ruined temples are at least two others. One of them(?) is of Vikramâditya Tribhuvanmalla and the Kâdaṁba chief Kâma, dated *Śaka* 1011 (*P. S. and. O. C. Ins.*, No. 90). Others dated *Śaka* 1067 to 1449.

III. 4. **Manoli,** 6 miles north of Saundatti. A fine group of temples in a court (*Arch. Rep.*, 1874, p. 14). **(Surveyed.)**

I *b.* **Inscriptions**:—(1) Against the wall of the temple of Pañchaliṅgadeva is an inscription of the Yâdava king Siṅghaṇa of Devagiri, *Śaka* 1145 (*Arch. Rep.*, vol. II. pl. lxxiv. and p. 233; vol. III. p. 116; and *J. B. B. R. A. S.*, vol. XII. pp. 2, 11). (2) In the fort, at the temple of Uḍachavva, another Yâdava inscription of Kandhara or Kṛishṇa dated *Śaka* 1174.

III. 5. **Sogal,** 15 miles north-west from Saundatti: Temple of Someśvara.

I *b.* **Inscription**:—One at the water-fall; a Raṭṭa inscription dated *Śaka* 902.

III. 6. **Murgod,** 15 miles north-west from Saundatti. A temple of Mallikârjuna.

II *b.* **Inscription**:—Sadâśivadevarâya of Vijayanagara.

III. 7. **Badli,** 5 miles north-west from Saundatti. A temple of Nârâyaṇadeva.

II *b.* **Inscription**:—A fragment of a Raṭṭa tablet, dated *Śaka* 1168.

III. 8. ....?. An old temple of Banaśaṁkarî and Vîrabhadra, half buried under ground.

I *b.* **Inscription**:—At the temple of Banaśaṁkarî a Western Châlukya inscription dated *Saka* 1015.

III. 9. **Sirsangi,** Temple of Kallamadevi, ascribed to Śṛiṅga Ṛishi.

V.—GOKÂK TÂLUKÂ.

III. 1. **Gokák,** 30 miles north-east from Belgaum (16° 10′; 74° 53′). Two mosques and a *ganjkhâna*—plain Muhammadan buildings.

II *b*. 2. **Konnur,** 5 miles up the river from Gokâk. A mile from the village is a group of old temples on each side the falls (see *Arch. Rep.*, 1874, p. 6). Near the village are
I *a*. three groups of dolmens, and in the village is a ruined but very pretty old temple, of
III. perhaps the 11th century. (*Ind. Ant.*, III. 306.) (**Surveyed.**)

b. **Inscriptions**:—(1) An inscription, much effaced, is in the temple of Mahâlingeśvara, at the falls. It is a Raṭṭa inscription of about *Śaka* 1075 (*Arch. Rep.*, vol. III. p. 103.) (2) In the outskirts of the village is an inscription on a carved stone in a ruinous temple. (3) In a Jaina temple in the village is another Raṭṭa inscription dated *Śaka* 1009 and 1048 (*J. B. B. R. A. S.*, vol. X. pp. 179, 287; *P. S. and O. C. Ins.* No. 93).

III. 3. **Kalholi,** 7 miles N.N.E. from Gokâk (16° 17′; 74° 56′). An old Jaina *basti* with mouldings.

I *b*. **Inscription**:—A Raṭṭa one, dated *Śaka* 1127 (*J. B. B. R. A. S.*, vol. X. pp. 178, 220; *P. S. and O. C. Ins.* No. 95).

III. 4. **Ankalgi,** 13 miles south-west from Gokâk. A *maṭha* or monastery of Adavyappa Svâmi and a temple of Lakshmîdevî. On the temple is a short **inscription** in Marâṭhî.

VI.—CHIKODI TÂLUKÂ.

III. 1. **Nipani,** 38 miles north from Belgaum (16° 24′; 74° 26′). Fort built about the year 1210 *Fasli*.

III. 2. **Kharosi,** 6 miles south from Chikoḍi: 1½ miles north of the village is the old temple of Ghatagi Basaveśvara.

Inscription:—On an arch.

III. 3. **Nipnal,** 24 miles south-east from Chikoḍi. On a small hill to the west of the village is an old Vaishṇava temple, of moderate dimensions, dedicated to Śri Govindarâja.

III. 4. **Kabur,** 12 miles south-east of Chikoḍi (16° 20′; 74° 47′). A very old temple of Îśvaradeva, about 120 feet long by 48 wide.

Inscriptions:—There is one, said to be illegible.

III. 5. **Yadur,** an *inâm* village on the Kṛishṇâ, 3 miles south-west from Khedrâpur (see Kolhâpur). A temple of Vîrabhadra, about 145 feet square. It is a modern temple on an old foundation (*Bom. Sel.* CXV., p. 69).

Inscriptions:—Two dated, respectively, *Śaka* 1752 and 1758.

III. 6. **Hukeri,** 25 miles north from Belgaum (16° 13′; 74° 40′). Three old *dargâhs*, the largest said to have been built about A.D. 1509, the second between 1547 and 1568, and the smallest about 1515. They are plain buildings of the sort, and now used as rest-houses (*Bom. Sel.* CXV. ii., pp. 23, 39, 41, 50).

III. 7. **Sankes'vara,** 8 miles north-west from Hukeri. On the banks of the Hiraṇyakeśî is an old temple of Śaṁkaraliṅga, about 82 feet by 48, built in the 'Jakhaṇâchârya' style.

Inscriptions:—There are three, but they are said to be illegible.

VII.—Athṇî Tâlukâ.

III. 1. **Athni,** 45 miles west from Bijâpur (16° 44′; 75° 8′). Temples of Amṛiteśvara and Siddheśvara,—plain buildings,—and a mosque, all in one enclosure.

III. 2. **Kokatnur,** 10 miles E.S.E. from Athṇî (16° 42′; 75° 17′). An old plain Jaina temple.

III. 3. **Na'ndgâon,** 6 miles south-east from Athṇî. A fine old temple in ruins.

III. 4. **Badgi,** 13 miles east from Athṇî. An old Jaina temple, not used and out of repair.

III. 5. **Ka'gva'd,** 22 miles west from Athṇi (16° 41′; 74° 47′). A rock excavation and a Jaina temple: a fine image in a cellar (*Bom. Sel.* CXV. p. 8).

III. 6. **Sedba'l,** 2½ miles east of Kâgvâd. Temples of Viśveśvara and Kalomeśvara.

I *b*. **Inscription**:—A Śilahâra inscription, dated *Śaka* 1078.

III. 7. **Jugal,** 5 miles south of Kâgvâd, and opposite Khedrâpur (see Kolhâpur). Temple of Masabati.

III. 8. **Kanamadi,** 26 miles north-east from Athṇî. Temples of Mallikârjuna and Harideva, the latter said to be worth photographing.

III. 9. **Balgeri,** 11 miles north by west from Athṇî. Temple of Basaveśvara, built of black stone, out of repair.

III. 10. **Mangrul,** 15 miles west of Athṇî (16° 44′; 74° 54′). A temple of Mârtaṇḍa.

III. 11. **Parthanahalli,** 4 miles N.N.E. from Athṇî. A temple of Pârtheśvara, built of black stone, out of repair.

III. 12. **Ra'matirtha,** 20 miles north-east from Athṇî. A temple of Râmeśvara, built of black stone, said to be worth photographing.

III. 13. **Kudchi,** 20 miles south-west from Athṇî. Two mosques or *dargâhs* on the banks of the Krishṇâ, built of black stone.

III. 14. **Saptasa'gara,** 10 miles south-west from Athṇî, (16° 38′; 75° 1′). A temple of Kâśiliṅga, built of black stone.

III. 15. **Surpali,** 17 miles south-east from Athṇî. An old Vaishṇava temple of Narasinha.

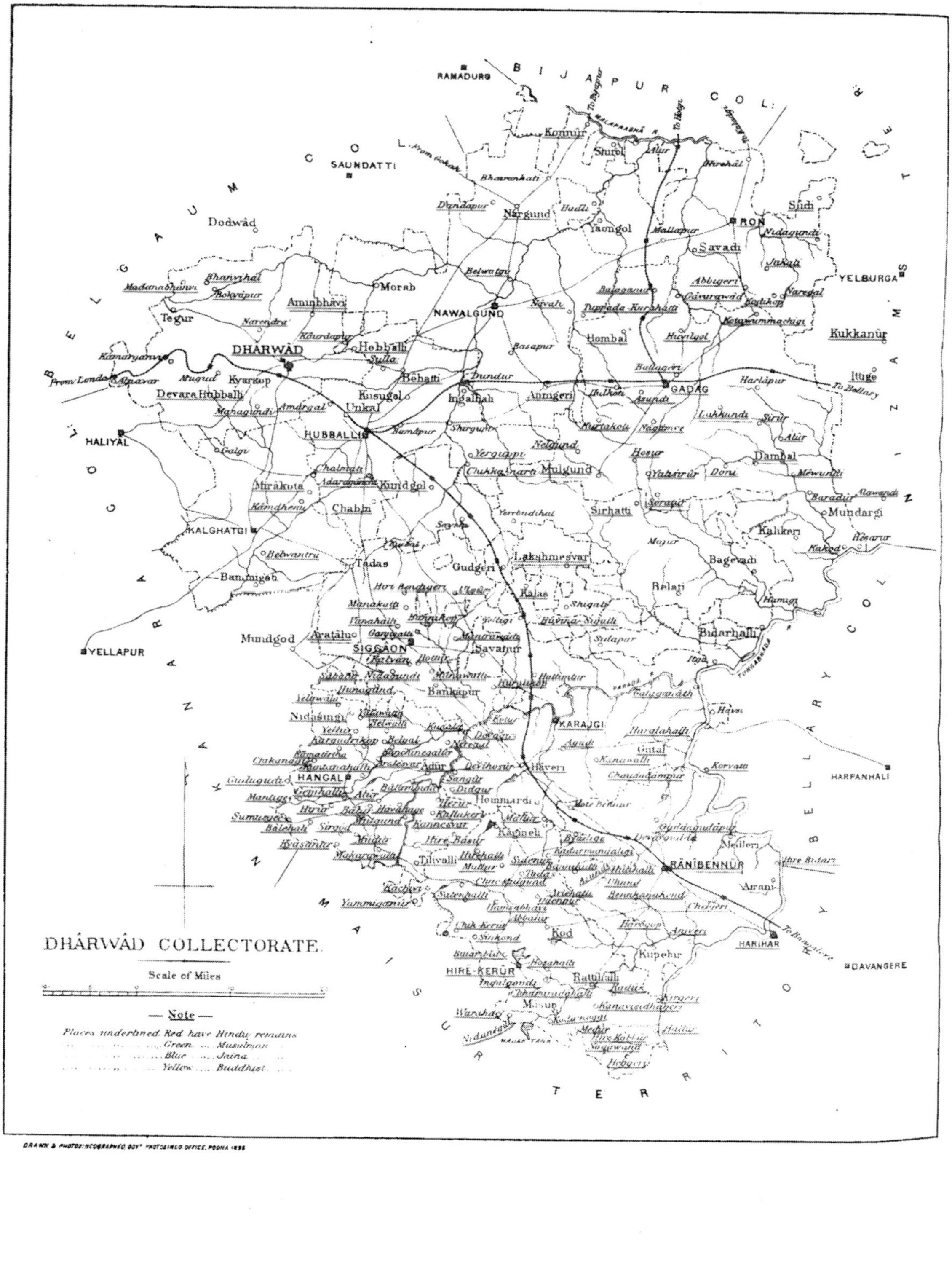

DRAWN & PHOTOZINCOGRAPHED GOVT PHOTOZINCO OFFICE, POONA 1895

II.—DHÂRWÂR ZILLA.

I.—DHÂRWÂR TÂLUKÂ.

II *b*. 1. **Dha'rwa'r**: 4 large massive slabs bearing sculptures of Śiva (2 slabs), Brahmâ and Vishṇu on Śesha. In 1885 they were found lying in the garden of Mr. Fletcher's house. On enquiries being made in February 1893, it was found they had been built into the porch and verandah of the house then in the occupancy of Mr. J. Campbell, Agent, Southern Marâṭhâ Railway. The slabs are supposed to have been brought from Bâdâmi some 25 years ago by Mr. William Frere, formerly District Judge of Dhârwâr, who then occupied the house. (**Surveyed**.)

III 2. **Managundi**:—Temples of Siddhaliṅga, partly in ruins, and of Kalmeśvaradeva, a small temple; both of black stone.

II *b*. **Inscriptions**.—One in each temple.

III. 3. **Narendra**, 4½ miles north-west of Dhârwâr (latitude 15° 30′, longitude 75° 3′). Temple of Śankaraliṅgadeva, rebuilt by the villagers.

I *b*. **Inscription**.—A Kâdamba stone tablet, on a mound between the road and the village.

III. 4. **Madanabha'nvi**, 14 miles from Dhârwâr (latitude 15° 35′, longitude 74° 55′). Temples of Râmaliṅgadeva in ruins, and of Kallapadeva, small.

II *b*. **Inscriptions**.—One in each temple.

III. 5. **Bhanviha'l**, a deserted village, 3 miles east from Madanbhâṅvi near Garag. Old temple of Siddheśvara, built of black stone, with 22 square pillars. It has *inâm* lands.

II *b*. **Inscription**.—One.

III. 6. **Bokya'pur**, 1 mile south-east from Bhaṅvihâḷ. Temple of Vîrabhadradeva built of black stone.

II *b*. **Inscription**.—One.

III. 7. **Aminbha'vi**, 7 miles north-east from Dhârwâr. Old Jaina *basti* of Neminâtha to the north of the village is of very considerable size—above 40 yards in length,—with numerous pillars. Temple of Mallikârjunadeva, of black stone, is mostly in ruins. Temple of Kalmeśvaradeva. Both small.

I *b*. **Inscriptions**.—Three, one in each temple; also (4) near an old well on the south of the Desâyi's *Wâḍâ*, *Śaka* 488 and 1035; (5) near the house of a barber, *Śaka* 1469 (II *b*.).

III. 8. **Kaurda'pur**, 7 miles W.N.W. of Dhârwâr, near Hubbaḷḷi. A Liṅgâyat temple dedicated to Vîrabhadra, Someśvara, and Siddhaliṅga, of black stone, with a central *maṇḍapa* and three shrines on different sides of it. The roof is supported by 12 pillars.

III. 9. **Hebballi**, 8 miles east by north from Dhârwâr and 5 miles from Byahaṭṭi (latitude 15° 28′, longitude 75° 12′). Temple of Śaṁbhuliṅga to the south of the village in the Jaina style of architecture, about 57 feet long. Temple of Changalovadevî in ruins

I b. **Inscription.**—In the temple of Śambhuliṅga is an inscription dated *Śaka* 1166, Krodhana *Saṁvatsara*, Bhâdrapada *Śuddha* 8th.

III. 10. **Devara Hubballi,** a Jakhaṇâchârya temple.

II.—Kalghatgi Tâlukâ.

1. **Belwantra,** 3 miles south of Kalghaṭgi.

II b. **Inscriptions.**—There are two inscriptions, one to the north of the village and between it and the tank; the other is to the west of the village.

III. 2. **Ka'mdhenu,** 6 miles north-east of Kalghatgi. Temple of Kalmeśvara, an old building, of black granite. The outsides of the walls ornamented with mythological carvings.

Inscriptions.—There are two near the temple, said to be much obliterated.

III. 3. **Misrikota,** 7 miles north-east of Kalghaṭgi (latitude 15° 14′, longitude 75° 7′). Old temple of Râmeśvara, built of black stone.

II b. **Inscriptions.**—There is one stone in the temple.

III. 4. **Chalmati,** 2 miles north of Miśrîkoṭa. Temple of Budangudda Bassappa outside the village. "About 1¼ miles from the village is a den called Ajavankatti, much visited."

II b. 5. **Tambur.** In the court-yard of the temple at this village there are several carved and inscribed slabs, and just outside the gateway are two very well preserved slabs with carved panels.

III.—Hubballi Tâlukâ.

III. 1. **Chikka-narti,** 19 miles east of Śirhaṭṭi (latitude 15° 17′, longitude 75° 22′) (on the Bennihaḷḷâ). Temple of Kalameśvara, in which is a stone **inscription** (II *b*.).

III. 2. **Yergruppi,** 1 mile north of Chikka-narti. Temple of Nârâyaṇa, in which is an
II b. **inscription** similar to that at Chikka-narti.

III. 3. **Chabbi,** 8 miles south of Hubbaḷḷi (latitude 15° 13′, longitude 75° 13′). The old name of the village is said to have been Sobhanpur, and it is said to have been in early times the capital of a Jaina prince, when it had seven *bastis*, of which only one is now left in the middle of the village. The Vijayanagar kings are said to have improved the place and Kṛishṇarâya (A.D. 1509-1529) is said to have resided here and built the fort as well as that at Hubbaḷḷi. The Muhammadans ceded it to the Navâb of Sâvanur. In later times it was an arsenal of the Peśvâ. On the south side of the tank is a small but very old temple of Mallikârjuna; and in the north-east of the village is a plain temple of Nettagalla Basavâṇṇa.

II b. **Inscriptions.**—In the middle of the fort is an old well bearing an inscription and there is another near the temple of Kâlikâdevi.

III. 4. **Adaragunchi**, a large Jaina image and **inscription** (I *b.*) (*Ind. Ant.* XII. 255.)

III. 5. **Hubballi**, (latitude 15° 20′, longitude 75° 12′). In Râyara-Hubbaḷḷi or old town is the temple of Bhavânîśaṅkara, and in the same area are three others to Nârâyaṇa, Bhavânîśaṅkara and Gaṇapati, with carved figures on the walls. A fine broken image of Sûrya lies outside, and an inscription. The temple of Hanumân bears a close resemblance in style to that of Bhavânîśaṅkara, with 24 columns. A photograph (ph. 53) of a ruined Jaina temple is given in *Architecture of Dhârwâr and Mysore.* (**Surveyed**.)

I *b.* **Inscriptions**.—One in front of the temple of Bhavânîśaṅkara.

I *b.* 6. **Unkal**, 3 miles north-west from Hubbaḷḷi. A very fine old temple of Chandramaulîśvara to the south of the village is built of black granite; the walls are carved with mythological figures, but it is almost deserted. Originally a temple of Brahmadeva (**Surveyed**.)

III. The temple of Kalmeśvara is in the modern style.

II *b.* **Inscriptions**.—One stands in front of the temple of Chandrakaleśvara and about 100 yards from the school-house. Near Bahiredevarkop, by the side of the main road, on the *band* of a tank, is another.

II *b.* 7. **Amargal**, 2 miles north-west of Uṇkal. Temple of Śaṅkaraliṅga in the middle of the village, built of black and light-coloured granite; partly in ruins. The walls and pillars are carved with figures of gods, &c. The expenses are defrayed from *inâm* lands. (**Surveyed**.)

III. **Inscription**.—In front of the temple is a broken and defaced inscription slab.

III. 8. **Behatti**, 8 miles north-east from Hubbaḷḷi (latitude 15° 27′, longitude 75° 16′). Temple of Vîrabhadra about 200 years old, of hewn stone.

II *b.* **Inscriptions**.—One at the temple of Râmaliṅga; one in the Kambhalli *maṭha*; one near the well of Dhumakava; and a fourth near the Charanti *maṭha*. One Bengeri Basappâ possesses a copper-plate grant. (*Ind. Ant.* IV. 274.)

III. 9. **Sulla**.—Temple of Kalmeśvara is a large building.

II *b.* **Inscriptions**.—One on the Hubbaḷḷi road is partly buried in the ground; another stands in front of the house of Rudrappâ Gaudâ; and there is a third.

IV.—Navalgund Tâlukâ and Râmadurg Jâghir.

III. 1. **Belwatgi**, 3 miles north-east of Navalgund. Ruinous temple of Râmaliṅgadeva

II *b.* and **inscriptions**.

II *b.* 2. **Annigeri**, 10 miles S.S.E. from Navalgund (latitude 15° 25′, longitude 75° 29′). The celebrated temple of Amṛiteśa is in the middle of the town, built of black stone, of considerable size, and the roof supported by about 76 pillars. The walls are carved with mythological sculptures said to be of some interest. Nothing is known by the natives of its age: they ascribe it to Jakhaṇâchârya. There is a great festival in Mârgaśîrsha. (**Surveyed**.)

I *b*. **Inscriptions.**—(1) In the *basti*, *Śaka* 993; (2) near a well close to the south wall of the temple of Mailâra, *Śaka* 1019; (3) near the temple of Puradappâ on the east of the village, *Śaka* 1106; (4) in the temple of Amṛiteśvara, *Śaka* 1079; (5) in the temple of Amṛiteśvara, *Śaka* 1122; (6) in the temple of Amṛiteśvara, *Śaka* 1124: this inscription is very long; (7) on a pillar in the door or gateway on the south of the temple of Amṛiteśvara, *Śaka* 1129; (8) on the east of the same gateway of the same temple, *Śaka* 1130; (9) on the west of the same gateway of the same temple, *Śaka* 1111: this is rather a long inscription; (10) in the yard in front of the temple of Banada-Śaṁkarî, *Śaka* 1108; (11) in front of the door of the temple of Banada-Śaṁkarî, *Śaka* 1084; (12) on the left hand in the gate of the temple of Hiri-Hanumanta, *Śaka* 1079; (13) in front of the temple of Basappa on the south of the Hubli Gate, *Śaka* 1094; (15) on a pillar in the temple of Gachchina-Basappa, *Śaka* 1119; (16) on the south of the temple of Gachchina-Basappa near the Kotwâl's *châvadi*, *Śaka* 1461.

3. **Tuppada-Kurahatti,** 9 miles north-east from Aṇṇigerî (lat. 15° 32′, long. 75° 33½′).

III. 4. **Navali,** 8 miles east from Navalgund and 1 mile west from Tuppada-Kurahaṭṭi. Temple of Kalmeśvaradeva.

II *b*. **Inscription.**—One.

III. 5. **Nargund,** 11 miles north from Navalgund (lat. 15° 33′, long. 75° 25′). Large temple of Sankaraliṅga, and smaller one of Mahâbaleśvara, built of black stone; and

II *b*. **inscriptions.**

III. 6. **Danda'pur,** 2 miles west of Nargund. Temple of Venkaṭeśa, built by Râmarâv, chief of Nargund, in A.D. 1706, in imitation, it is said, of the temple at Tirupati. It is a large temple with five spires, and is built of granite and brick. On the south side is a corridor 338 feet long, built by Dâdâji Râv Appâ Sâheb of Nargund about 50 years ago. A great festival is held in the month of Aśvina. Temple of Daṇḍeśvara, an old temple of considerable size, attributed to Jakhaṇâchârya; built of black stone and with figures of

I *b*. the *devas* on the outer walls. **Inscriptions** (*Ind. Ant.* XII. 222.)

III. 7. **Konnur,** on the Malaprabhâ, 12 miles from Nargund (lat. 15° 51½′, long. 75° 34′). Temples of Parameśvaradeva and of Râmeśvara, the latter a very large one, both built of black stone. More information desirable.

I *b*. 8. **Sirur, inscription** (*Ind. Ant.* XII. 216.)

V.—Ron Tâlukâ.

III. 1. **Abbigeri,** 3 miles north from Umachigi, and 7 miles south from Roṇ. Temples of Îśvaradeva and Jyotirliṅgadeva, of black stone. (**Surveyed.**)

II *b*. **Inscriptions**:—One in each of the temples.

II *b*. 2. **Naregal,** 4 miles east from Abbigeri (lat. 15° 34′, long. 75° 52′). The temples of Tripurântakeśvara, Someśvaradeva, Kalmeśvaradeva, and Chandramaulîśvaradeva, are all built of black stone, but the last is a ruin. In the hamlet of Kaḍikop is also a temple of Mûla Brahmadeva of black stone. (**Surveyed.**)

I *b*. **Inscriptions**:—(1) Built into the wall of the portico of the temple of Kalmeśvaradeva is an inscription in 58 lines of Permâdideva I. of the Sindavaṁśa family subordinate to Vikramâditya V. (A.D. 1076-1127), but commemorating a grant of *Saka* 872 (A.D. 950) (*J. B. B. R. A. S.*, vol. X. pp. 224); (2) another inscription in 47½ lines, built into the wall inside the temple of Tripurântakadeva; it belongs to the same chief under king Jagadekamalladeva II. (A.D. 1138-1150) and also commemorates a grant made in *Śaka* 872 (*ibid*, pp. 239); (3) in front of the temple of Hanumanta to the west of the fort, *Śaka* 966; (4) near a well with a flight of steps, *Śaka* 1022; (5) lying on a dunghill in the yard of the Taḍâḷavaru, *Śaka* 1026; (6) a *viragal* near the preceding, *Śàka* 1119; (7) a broken *viragal* near the village gateway, *Śaka* 1212.

III. 3. **Jakali,** 3 miles N.N.W. from Nâregal. Temple of Kalmeśvara of black stone, and temple of Siddheśvaradeva, in ruins.

II *b*. **Inscriptions**:—One in each temple.

III. 4. **Nidagundi,** 6 miles N.N.E. from Nâregal, and 9 miles E.S.E. from Roṇ. Temples of Râmaliṅgadeva, Dâseśvara, Kalmathadeva, and Nârâyaṇadeva of black stone, but small sized.

I *b*. **Inscriptions**:—One in the temple of Dâseśvara; another in that of Kalmatha, dated *Śaka* 1096; and a third in that of Nârâyaṇa.

III. 5. **Ron,** 20 miles N.N.E. from Gadag (lat. 15° 41½', long. 755° 48'). Some seven small temples of blackstone. (**Surveyed.**)

I *b*. **Inscription**:—One in the temple of Chameśvaradeva in front of the house of the Gireḍḍi, dated *Śaka* 1102.

III. 6. **Savadi,** 5 miles south-west from Roṇ. The temple of Brahmadeva is a large one built of stone, said to have been brought from Bâdâmi. The roof is supported by numerous carved pillars, and there are sculptures on the outer walls.

II *b*. **Inscriptions**:—One in the temple of Brahmadeva and another in that of Nâyâraṇadeva.

III. 7. **Kodikop,** 1 mile west of Nâregal. (**Surveyed.**)

I *b*. **Inscriptions**:—(1) Built into the wall on the right of the door of the temple of Molle Brahmadeva at Koḍikop, of which 29 lines are legible and the rest effaced; it is of the time of Âchugideva II., the father of Permâḍideva I., who was subordinate to king Vikramadeva V., and records a grant made in the 45th year of that king's reign, *Śaka* 1044 (No. 3 of Mr. Fleet's Sinda inscriptions in *J. B. B. R. A. S.*, vol. X.); (2) another on the left of the same door, in 37 lines, of Permâḍideva I., made in the seventh year of king Jagadekamalladeva II., *Śaka* 1066 (No. 4 of ditto, *ibid*, pp. 247-258).

III. 8. **Sudi,** 9 miles east by north from Roṇ. Several temples at this village.

I *b*. **Inscriptions**:—(1) On the left of the god in the temple of the two spires or *kalaśas* (*Joḍa kalaśada guḍi*), *Śaka* 932; this is very short but important; (2) again on the left of the god in the same temple, *Śaka* 1052; (3) on the right of the god in the same temple; this is a long inscription, *Śaka* 981; (4) in front of the temple of Mallikârjuna, about 990; (5) in a field outside the village, *Śaka* 991; (7) again in a field outside the village, *Śaka* 1006; (8) in the temple of Basavâṇṇâ in the village, *Śaka* 1006; (9) in the cowshed of Saṅkanur-Akivarra in the fort, *Śaka* 1102.

VI.—Gadag Tâlukâ.

II b. 1. **Nilgund,** 4 miles south-east from Bentur, and 12 miles south-west from Gadag. Temple of Nârâyaṇa, built of polished stone, with a large *maṇḍapa* in front. The 22 pillars supporting the roof are round and highly carved, and mythological sculptures adorn the walls.

I b. **Inscription** :—On the east of the north gate of the village, *Śaka* 966.

II b. 2. **Mulgund,** 2½ miles south-east of Nîlgund (lat. 15° 16′, long. 75° 35′). (1) Large Liṅgâyat temple of Siddheśvara, built of black stone, with figures carved on the
III. wall-bases of the front portion. (2) Temple of Nagareśvara, a very plain building. (3) Jaina *Basti* of Chandranâtha,—the shrine walls outside only worth attention. (4) *Basti* of Pârśvanâtha—both small.

I b. **Inscriptions** :—Two in the temple of Nagareśvara, of which one is a grant by Bappadeva, ruling at Mulgund, to the god. (1) In front of the door of the temple of Nagareśvara, *Śaka* 984 ; (2) in the wall outside on the left of the same temple, *Śaka*... ; (3) a third at the temple of Chandranâtha is dated *Śaka* 1197, Yuva *Saṁvatsara*, records the death of Bhamaṭṭi, wife of Madarasa ruling at Mulgund ; (4) a fourth on a pillar in the same temple, dated *Śaka* 1597 ; (5) another, dated *Śaka* 825, belonging to the Râshṭrakûṭa king Kṛishṇa Vallabha, is given in *J. B. B. R. A. S.*, vol. X. p. 190. Behind this temple is a very large rock on which is an unfinished carving of a figure 25 feet long, and an inscription partially effaced ; also a slab with a short inscription ; (6) in the wall of a Jaina *basti*, *Śaka* 824, see *J. B. B. R. A. S.*, vol. X. page 167 ; (7) in the Jaina *basti*, *Śaka* 975 ; (8) in the *Hiri-basti*, *Śaka* 1197 ; (9) on a pillar in the same *Hiri-basti*, *Śaka*...... ; (10) in the wall of the house of Gaṇâchârya, *Śaka* 1092 ; (11) two (effaced) at the temple of Peṭi-Basâppâ, *Śaka* 1129 ; (12) on a pillar in the *maṭha* of Ândanasvâmi, *Śaka* 1146 ; (13) on another pillar in the same *maṭha*, *Śaka* 1146 ; (14) at the door of Kâla Bhairava's temple is a stone with 7½ lines of inscription, and another carved one, a huge Bhairava inside ; (15) at the temple of Kumbheśvara is a stone sunk in the earth and inscription on it ; (16) in the court of the temple of Siddheśvara to the left of the entrance on a narrow stone, rudely cut ; (17) at the descent to a dry *talâv* is part of an old, distinctly cut, inscription half-buried.

3. **Soratur,** 2 miles E.N.E. from Śirhaṭṭi, and 6 miles E.S.E. from Mulgund.

I b. **Inscriptions** :—(1) On the left of the god in the temple of Vîrabhadra, *Śaka* 873 ; (2) in the Jaina *basti*, *Śaka* 993 ; (3) in the temple of Îśvara, *Śaka* 1013 ; (4) at the temple of Malleśvara, *Śaka* 1029 : (*Ind. Ant.* XII. 256.)

III. 4. **Hosur,** 4 miles E.N.E. from Mulgund. Temple of Kallavasaveśu is old, with sculptures on its walls. There are also three other old temples in the village rapidly falling into decay.

I b. **Inscriptions** :—One, dated *Śaka* 1129, Prabhava *Saṁvatsara*, records a grant by Yâdava Ballâḷa Nârâyaṇadeva. There are also others.

5. **Yalisirur,** 13 miles south from Gadag and north by west from Sôrâtur.

I b. **Inscriptions** :—(1) At the temple of Îśvara on the east of the village, *Śaka* 1031 ; (2) in the north wall of the temple of Îśvara, *Śaka* 1039 ; (3) at the temple of Îśvara, *Śaka* 1066 ; (4) near the temple of Hanumanta at the gate of the village, *Śaka* 1037.

6. **Kurtakoti**, 6 miles north of Mulgund and 10 miles west by south from Gadag.

I b. **Inscriptions** :—(1) In front of the temple of Kerî-Basappâ, *Śaka* 1004 ; (2) in the temple of Virûpâksha, *Śaka* 1009 ; (3) on the right of the temple of Śaṁkaraliṅga, *Śaka* 1054 ; (4) on the left of the temple of Śaṁkaraliṅga on the bank of the tank, *Śaka* 1060 ; (5) near the temple of Gavareśvara in front of the house of Râyanagauda, *Śaka* 1166.

7. **Na'gaon**, 5 miles south by east of Gadag.

I b. **Inscriptions** :—(1) On a pillar in the temple of Mahâbaleśvara, *Śaka* 1129 ; (2) on another pillar in the same temple, *Śaka* 1133 and 1136 ; (3) on another pillar in the same temple, *Śaka* 1177 ; (4) on another pillar in the same temple, *Śaka*.......

8. **Gadag** or **Gaddak**, anciently Kratuka, a junction station on the Southern Marâṭhâ Railway (latitude 15° 25′, longitude 75° 41′). Here there are several old temples, chief among them being those of Trikûṭeśvaradeva, Sarasvati, Someśvara, and Vîra-Nârâyaṇa.
II b. The temple of Trikûṭeśvaradeva, situated in the fort, is a triple-shrined temple but rather clumsily designed. It has two close halls or *maṇḍapas* in line with a shrine at each end in prolongation of these, while a small shrine has been built off the north side between the two halls. The workmanship is of the best but has been dreadfully overlaid with successive coats of whitewash. Some of the perforated screen work around the halls is very good. The original tower has been replaced by a modern brick and chunam monstrosity.
I b. Beside this temple, upon its south side, almost touching it, and set at right angles to it, is the little unused temple of Sarasvati—a little gem. The pillars of the hall are most minutely and delicately carved with a profusion of ornament. The ceilings, parapet wall and shrine doorway are all equally well decorated. Within the shrine, seated upon a *sinhásana*, is a mutilated life-sized image of Sarasvati wearing an abundance of jewelry,
I b. all beautifully carved in black polished stone. The temple of Someśvara in the middle of the town, now used as a school room, is a typical example of a fully decorated Châlukyan temple at its best. With the exception of the finial of the *śikhara*, the roof of the hall, and the front or east porch, it is entire in all its parts. The exterior is lavishly carved with ornament from base to summit. The plan of the shrine is star-shaped externally.

III. The large temple of Vîra-Nârâyaṇa is in the middle of the town of Gadag. It is also of black hornblende,—probably not of great age, perhaps of the 13th or 14th century,—and is chiefly remarkable for a large and lofty gateway or *gopura* in the eastern wall of the courtyard, built in the style of Southern India. It is over 100 feet high (upper part of brick) and richly decorated, some curious carvings, supposed to be remains of some previous structure, having been built into it. Temple of Îśvara, close by that of Someśvara, is plain below but richly carved above. It is at the temple of Trikûṭeśvara that Vîra Ballâḷa "commemorated by an inscription the victory obtained by his general Bomma over Ballamadeva Yâdava of Devagirî, capturing sixty elephants and destroying 'the ships of the southern country.' Another inscription on the temple records its restoration, in *Śaka* 900 (A.D. 978), by a prince of the Châlukyas; but the Brâhmaṇs claim for it a far greater antiquity extending back into the silver age, the edifice having, as they allege, been originally constructed of precious metals." (**Surveyed.**)

I b. **Inscriptions** :—(1.) In the *kacheri* are some copper-plate grants. (2.) At the temple of Trikûṭeśvara are nine inscriptions: (1) except in one or two places is in good preservation and consists of 50 lines ; it is dated *Śaka* 1135, Âṅgirasa *Saṁvatsara*, under the Yâdava Singhaṇadeva ; (2) is of the Hoysaḷa king Vîraballâḷa reigning at Lokkiguṇḍi, now Lakkuṇḍi and dated *Śaka* 1115. It is in 56 lines, extremely well preserved, and has been copied and translated by J. F. Fleet, Esq., C.S. (*Ind. Ant.*, vol. II. pp. 298-ff); (3) contains 32 lines, chipped in places, but fairly well preserved. It is a grant of the great chieftain Sâbhana or Sobhana under Âhavamalladeva in *Śaka* 984; (4) consists of 45 lines, with many flaws in the tablet; it is dated in the 25th year of king Tribhuvanamalladeva, *i.e.* *Śaka* 1023. These four inscriptions (and 3 others) stand up against the back wall of the temple; (5) was found by Mr. Fleet lying on the edge of a small tank outside the temple enclosure, and placed against the outer side of the north wall of the temple court. It consists of 57 lines, and records a grant in *Śaka* 1121, the Siddhârthî *Saṁvatsara* by the chieftain Râyadeva under the Hoysaḷa king Vîraballâḷadeva; (6) is half-buried in the back wall of a house adjoining the southern or back wall of the temple court; it is in tolerably good preservation, and belongs to the time of Sankamadeva of the Kaḷachûri family (*Śaka* 1098 to 1104); (7) against the back wall of the temple is in *Nâgarî* characters, but is broken about the 20th line. The top of another lies on the ground; (8) also in the same place, is of the time of Tribhuvanamalladeva. These inscriptions are worth removing, cleaning, and translating; (9) stands just inside the western gateway of the temple court. It consists of 14 lines, and is dated *Śaka* 1461, in the reign of Achyutamahârâya (A.D. 1529-1542); (10) is a *very* short one, which perhaps has the name of the builder, on the outside of the *garbhagṛiha* or shrine, in an angle; (11) leans against the western wall of the courtyard of the temple of Nârâyaṇadeva, and is a very long one of 72 or 78 lines each of about 63 letters, much worn away; (12) stands against the eastern wall; has Kṛishṇa and the *gopîs* at the top; and consists of 69 lines each of about 42 letters, partly worn in the centre; (13) on a stone built into the lower part of the compound wall behind the temple of Vîra-Nârâyaṇa, *Śaka* 959; (14) on another stone in the same wall, higher up and further to the south, short, and partially effaced; (15) on the roof of a room in or at the same temple, *Śaka* 1020; (16) at the same temple, *Śaka* 1461; (17) in the enclosure to the north of the same temple, *Śaka* 1022; (18) at the temple of Narasiṁha, on the south of the temple of Vîra-Nârâyaṇa, *Śaka* 1461; (19) at the small *dharmaśâlâ* east of the southern gateway behind the temple of Narasiṁha, on the bases of two pillars (some lines have been hewn out), *Śaka* 1046; (20) four lines on a pilaster in the old gateway between the temple of Trikûṭeśvara and the street; (21) one in *Devanâgarî* lying on its face on the margin of the *talâv*. (*Ind. Ant.* II. 298; *B.B.R.A.S. Jour.* XXVII. 321.)

9. Betgeri, 2 miles north-east from Gadag. (Surveyed.)

I *b*. **Inscriptions**:—A *vîragal* on the land of Haṭagâra Mallarâya. Kîlaka *Saṁvatsara*; also inscriptions upon several memorial stones which with others are clustered together in a walled enclosure in the village. These are elaborately carved.

10. Sirur, 4 miles south-east from Gadag.

I *b*. **Inscriptions**:—(1) Near the south gate of the temple of Toraṇagalla-Brahmadeva, *Śaka* 962; (2) on a pillar in the same temple, *Śaka* 964; (3) at the gate called Kuruvagalagasi, *Śaka* 970; (4) in front of the door or gate of the temple of Maḷigi-Îśvasar, *Śaka* 1195.

11. Hombal, 7 miles north-west from Gadag.

I *b*. **Inscriptions**:—(1) In the temple of Îśvara, *Śaka* 971; (2) on the south of the well near the temple of Bhogeśalinga, *Śaka* 1037.

12. **Huyilgol, 6 miles north from Gadag.**

I *b.* **Inscriptions** :—There are seven in the village : one in the temple of Râmaliṅga, one in that of Kalameśvara, four in that of Mâruti, and one near the *chauki*.

13. **Lakkundi,** 7 miles E.S.E. from Gadag (lat. 15° 23′, long. 75° 47′). Lakkuṇḍi is noted
not only for its beautiful temples, of which there are upwards of fifty of various degrees of
size and beauty, but also for its wells such as that of Chabbir-bhâṅvi in the Jakhaṇâchârya
or Hemâdpanti style, and other architectural remains. The principal temples are those
I *b.* of (1) Kâśiviśveśvara, a double temple—the smaller one facing the other, partially ruined,
but exquisitely rich in carving, the north door, north side, and back of the shrine, and a
sort of attached polygonal pillar between the shrine and *maṇḍapa* on the outside are
II *b.* pretty entire, and a fine specimen of Hindu decorative work ; (2) Mallikârjuna ; (3)
Halagund Basavanna ; (4) Śrî Virûpâksha, now the principal village temple, plain and half
ruined ; (5) Lakshmî-Nârâyaṇa,—the spire only entire, but interesting ; (6) Śrî Mânikeś-
vara at the Musukina-bhâṅvi, has three shrines, of which only one is occupied ; the upper
parts of the building are destroyed ; (7) Vîrabhadra,—with two doors in front, and sloping
I *b.* eaves ; (8) Nanneśvara has four pillars in the *madhyaranga* with square bases, neatly
carved ; in the *maṇḍapa* are 16 pillars of four distinct patterns—one being formed of eight
II *b.* slender round shafts clubbed together ; (9) Someśvara, a small, neat, deserted temple,
west from the fort ; (10) Nîlakaṇṭheśvara, in ruins, the outer walls of the shrine sculp-
tured ; (11) Kumbhârgiri-Îśvara or Nâdayadeva is now built all round ; it has three
shrines with carved doors, and four pillars with curiously sculptured bracket capitals ; (12)
Nâgadevara has lost the spire and upper portions ; it has been finished with great care
and elaboration of detail, but not overloaded with ornament ; inside the shrine is a curious
image of a Nâga, which appears to have formed the back of a Jina's throne ; like almost
I *b.* all the others, however, it has Gaja-Lakshmî on the door lintel ; (13) a Jaina *basti* of
which the *śikhara* is entire, preserving round the top of the walls from where it rises
the old forms found at the "Seven Pagodas" and other buildings of the 8th century, and
III. interesting on this account ; (14) beside it is another of which the spire is destroyed.
There are also many smaller temples. "These temples at Lakkuṇḍi," says Meadows
Taylor, "suffered severely in the invasion of the Choḷa king about A.D. 1000, when those
at Lakshmeśvar, the Châlukya capital, were destroyed, but afterwards rebuilt ; and the
feuds between the Brâhmaṇs and Liṅgâyats contributed to their injury."

"Our knowledge of the early Jaina architecture of the Dekkhan," Mr. Fergusson remarks, "is far too limited to enable us to pronounce a competent opinion as to the age of the temple in Lakkuṇḍi (Kâśiviśveśvara). The building also presents a curious mixture of the southern and northern styles of architecture, which may either arise from its being a very early example, when the Jaina architects were feeling their way in building in this country, or from its being a recent specimen, when the two styles were being amalgamated. From the style, as well as from what is known of history, I should feel inclined to place the building after the Choḷa incursion (A.D. 1000). My impression is that it belongs to the eleventh century.

"The doorway leading into the porch with its straight-lined cornices, and the windows in the Vimâna, or tower, with its trefoil canopy and the *śikhara* inside it, are clearly modern features, either just imported, or adhered to through long years of severance. These, however, are cunningly mixed with southern details in the upper part of the building.

"The sculpture and architectural details of this temple are of much more minute delicacy of finish than those of the temples of" Dambal and Chaudadámpur, "but are neither so rich nor so freely drawn as in those of the temples of Halabid and Belur. On the other hand, something may be owing to the temple having been originally erected by the Jainas* for their own religion, and its style may consequently be imported, while those dedicated to Śiva may be more indigenous. These, however, are questions which can only be settled on the spot by those who will take the trouble to learn all the variations through which the style passed during the time it was practised in that country."

All the temples here are being rapidly destroyed by trees on the roofs, and by the materials and sculptures being carried off for building purposes. (**Surveyed.**)

I *b*. **Inscriptions**:—These are numerous: (1) one near Kanner Bhânvi, dated *Śaka* 790, is used by *dhobis* to beat their clothes upon; (2) on the left of the god in the door of the Jaina *basti*, *Śaka* 1094; (3) one in a field belonging to Madivalaya Patri; (4) in the temple of Someśvara in the garden land of the Patriyavaru on the west of the fort, *Śaka* 1040; (5, 6) a little to the south are two Jaina slabs the inscriptions on which are nearly obliterated; (7) on the north of the same temple of Someśvara, *Śaka* 1097; (8) in the temple of Viśvanâtha, dated *Śaka* 790; (9) four lines on a beam in the *madhyaranga* of the temple of Nanneśvara near Hire-Maṭha, *Śaka* 1108; (10) on the base of a pillar in the same—one line on three sides; (11) sunk in the earth, north of the same temple, a slab with an apparently legible inscription—(should be removed to a place of safety); (12) in field No. 13, Revenue Survey; (13-15) three in the temple of Mallikârjuna; (16) near the temple of Hanumân in the bazâr,—much defaced; (17) on a beam in the east part of the *madhyaranga* in the temple of Chandramauliśvara in the fort, *Śaka* 1106; (18, 19); on two more beams in the same place, *Śaka* 1106; (20) lying under a tamarind tree on the north of the fort, *Śaka* 1038; (21) in the temple of Nâgadeva in the village, *Śaka* 1042; (22) under a *nim* tree on the spot on which a potter attending on the god Mâṇikeśvara lived, *Śaka* 1045; (23) on a beam in the *madhyaranga* of the temple of......*Śaka* 1096; (24) at the temple of Mâṇikeśvara near the well called "Musukina-bhânvi" near some garden land outside the village, 21 lines on the bases of two pillars in the porch, *Śaka* 1163; (25) on a stone called "Samádhikallu" at Kâśiviśveśvara, *Śaka* 1120; (26, 27) two large slabs built into the left wall in the temple of Vîrabhadra; (28) built, face downwards into a wall facing the well in the fort; (29) on the porch of the same well; (30) near the temple of Îśvara in the fort; (31) near the Vṛindâvana of Amanna Pautra Govindappa; (32) one in the temple of Gaṇeśa near the school-house; (33) to the east of the fort under a tamarind tree in Rev. Sur. No. 275; (34) two lines on a stone outside the temple of Vîrabhadra; (35) at the door of the temple of Gokarṇeśvara—partly peeled off.

II *b*. 14. **Doni**, 7 miles south of Lakkuṇḍi and 3½ miles west from Dambal; **inscriptions.**

15. **Dambal**, 13 miles S.E. from Gadag and 16 south-west from Ittagi (lat. 15° 18′,
I *b*. long. 75° 50′). Temples of Someśvara and Dodda Basappà are outside the town, and both much injured. The latter "has the merit," Mr. Fergusson notes, "of presenting us with the form of one of the *vimânas* of the style in a very complete state of preservation.

* The temple has always been Brahmanical, not Jaina.—EDITOR.

It never, however, was entirely finished, all the smaller string courses of the roof being still left in block, though the effect of this is as sparkling as if they had been finished to the extent originally intended. Assuming it to be finished it would not be easy to point to a more graceful form of roof for the cellar of a temple...... At first sight it may, of course, appear somewhat strange and *outre*, but with a little familiarity its form gains rapidly on the judgment of the architectural critic." (**Surveyed**.)

III. Totadasvâmi Maṭha is a large modern building of black stone, outside the town, on the Gadag-Mundargi road. Over the tomb of Totadasvâmi is a stone lotus, a specimen of good workmanship of its kind. The pillars are hewn in imitation of the turned ones of older times, and the door is carved with a pattern in very low relief. A door into a side cloister was brought from Lakkuṇḍi about 20 years ago and inserted here, the Lakshmî being hewn into a *linga* and the elephants left! The head of the *maṭha* is Ândanasvâmi, and under it are *maṭhas* in most of the villages near Dambal, all possessed of lands (*B. B. R. A. S. Journ.*, part XXVII., p. 321.)

I *b*. **Inscriptions** :—(1) At the temple of Doḍḍa Basavaṇṇa, outside the village, is an inscription of Someśvara Tribhuvanamalla dated *Saka* 1106, Krodhi *Saṁvatsara* (*P. S. and O. C. Insc.* No. 102); (2) on the left the small *basti* in the fort, in excellent preservation, 45½ lines, *Śaka* 1017; (3) two on the pillars at the entrance of the temple of Kâleśvara; (4) a fine one has been built into the wall of the well close by and nearly buried (*Ind. Ant.*, X. 185.)

16. **Alawandi,** 8 miles east by north from Mundargi.

I *b*. **Inscriptions**:—(1) On the right of the image in the temple of Îśvara, dated *Śaka* 960; (2) on the same position, *Śaka* 1124; (3) near the *hāḍe* belonging to Veṅkaṇaguṇḍa, *Śaka* 983.

I *b*. 17. **Ittagi,** in Nizam's territory; the temple referred to above (No. 157) with an **inscription** in the temple of Mâdeśa Niṅga in the fort, dated *Śaka* 1034. (**Surveyed**.)

18. **Kukkanur,** 4 miles north by east from Iṭṭagi. Here there are several old temples of the style of the temple of Virûpâksha at Pattadakal, the principal among them being

I *b*. those of Kalleśvara and Navalinga. Lying outside the town on the west are the remains of a lofty column with a short **inscription** round its shaft. The remains in and around the town show evidence of great antiquity. (**Surveyed**.)

I *b*. **Inscriptions** :—(1) In the temple of Nava-Siddha, within the western wall of the enclosure of the temple of Mahâmâyi, *Śaka* 92—(third numeral obliterated); (2) in the same temple of Nava-Siddha; this is a much longer inscription than No. 1; bottom of stone containing the date is said to be broken away; (3) in the temple of Mahâmâyi, *Śaka* 1071; (4) on the left of the god in the temple of Mahâmâyi, *Śaka* 1100; (5) on the right hand, outside the gate of the temple of Mahâmâyi, *Śaka* 1078; (6) on the right hand of the god in the temple of Kalleśvara on the west of the village, *Śaka* 1049; (7) on the left of the god in the temple of Mallikârjuna, *Śaka* 1085; (8) on the right of the god in the same temple, *Śaka* 1092.

19. **Kotavummachigi,** 15 miles north-east from Gadag (lat. 15° 32′, long. 75° 50′).

I *b*. **Inscriptions** :—(1) On the left of the god in the temple of Somappa, *Śaka* 1034; (2) in the same temple, *Śaka* 1064.

20. **A'lur**, 14 miles north-east from Gadag.

I *b*. **Inscriptions**:—(1) At the temple of Îśvara in which a potter lives, *Śaka* 932; (2) at the same temple of Îśvara, *Śaka* 1044. This is much longer than No. 1; (3) on the right of the god in the temple of Virabhadra, *Śaka* 1013 and 1043 (see *Indian Antiquary*, vol. VIII. page 21); (4) on the right hand in entering the door of the fort, *Śaka* 989.

21. **Asundi**, 3 miles west by south from Gadag.

I *b*. **Inscriptions**:—(1) At the temple of Bommappa, outside the village, *Śaka* 949; (2) at the temple of Hanumanta, outside the village, *Śaka* 975.

22. **Balaganur**, 14 miles north from Gadag.

I *b*. **Inscription**:—Behind the wall of the temple of Vîrabhadra, *Śaka* 1014.

23. **Baradur**, 2 miles south-east from Gadag.

I *b*. **Inscription**:—In the temple of Bharateśvara, *Śaka* 954.

24. **Ga'varava'd**, 12 miles north from Gadag.

I *b*. **Inscription**:—In front of the temple of Nârâyaṇa on the south of the village gateway, *Śaka* 994.

25. **Mewundi**, 18 miles south-east from Gadag.

I *b*. **Inscription**:—On the right of the image in the door of the temple of Venkaṭaramaṇa, *Śaka* 1188.

26. **Kakod**, on the Tungabhadrá, 1½ miles from Hesarûr.

II *b*. **Inscription**:—In the court of the temple of Mâruti, of 32½ lines, mostly in good preservation.

VII.—Bankâpur Tâlukâ.

III. 1. **Sa'balur**, (?) 8 miles west of Baṅkâpur and 7 miles east of Mundagoḍ (lat. 14° 57′ N., long. 75° 12′). Temple of Îśvara.

I *b*. **Inscriptions**:—(1) At the temple of Îśvara on the north of the village, *Śaka* 1033; (2) at the same temple, *Śaka* 1037.

III. 2. **Hungund**, 3 miles S.S.E. from Śâbal. **A broken inscription.**

3. **Nidgundi**, 5 miles west of Baṅkâpur.

I *b*. **Inscriptions**:—(1) In the court of the house Andânîgauda, 2 ft. by 2 ft.; (2) in the field Survey No. 57, 3′ by 1′ 9″; (3) in Survey No. 58, 4′ 9″ by 2′; (4) in the same, 4 ft. by 1½ ft.; (5) in Survey No. 84, 2 ft. by 1½ ft.

4. **Banka'pur**, (lat. 14° 55′, long. 75° 20′). Fine, large old temple of Raṅgasvâmi,

I *a*. usually called Arvattukhambada-basti or temple of the sixty columns, partially ruined, and a good deal buried in rubbish. It is built of polished stone, and the walls are carved with figures. The roof has an octagonal dome in the centre. "The form of the pillars, and more so the encircling wall which surrounds them, are simple and uniform to a degree very seldom found in buildings of this class in this part of the country. Except the form of the cornice, the whole looks exceptional, and partakes more of the northern style than of the wild exuberance of the South." * "It may be remembered, perhaps, that when king Firuz Shâh Bâhmani invaded the Vijayanagar dominions in 1406, he demanded

* Fergusson, *Arch. Dhar. and Mys.*, Ph. 47.

the daughter of the Râjâ of that kingdom in marriage, with the fort of Bankâpur as dowry; and eventually, when Vijayanagar had been reduced to sore straits obtained both. Bankâpur had previously belonged exclusively to the Hindus, and on account of the rich districts dependent upon it, and its valuable local produce, was a much desired possession. It was, therefore, surrendered only under circumstances of great distress. Henceforward, it continued subject to the Muhammadans, and was dependent upon Belgaum." The greatest damage to this temple was done by the Muhammadans when they defaced the sculpture and turned the great hall into a *masjid*.

III. The temple of Siddheśvara is smaller and not so old. It is built of black stone with three doors on the east side, and has some carved figures on the walls. The roof is supported by eight pillars. *Inâm* lands belong to the temple, and the Desâi of Handiganur supports the priest and executes the repairs. (**Surveyed**.)

I a. **Inscriptions.**—(1) Leaning against a wall to the right of the east entrance to the fort is a large *śilâśâsana* of 59 lines, each of about 37 letters, in old Kânarese. For the most part it is in fine order; but the 4th line has been deliberately cut out and almost entirely obliterated, and there are fissures in the tablet, which would probably result in its falling to pieces if an attempt were made to remove it to a safer place of custody. The emblems at the top of the tablet have been wilfully defaced; but traces of them can be made out. The inscription is dated *Śaka* 977 (A.D. 1055-56), while the Châlukya king Gangapermanadi Vikramâdityadeva,—the son of Trailokyamalladeva, the supreme lord of the city of Kuvalâlapura, the lord of Nandagiri, he whose crest was an infuriated elephant,—was ruling the Gangavâdi ninety-six thousand and the Banavâsi twelve thousand, and while the great chieftain, the glory of the family of the Kâdamba emperor Mayûravarmâ was governing the Banavâsi twelve thousand as his subordinate. It records a grant of land to a Jaina temple by Harikesarideva, his wife Sachchaladevî, the assemblage of the five religious colleges of Bankâpur, the guild of the Nagara, *mahâjana* and 'The Sixteen.'

(2, 3) On the wall to the left of the south entrance to the shrine of the Arvattukhambada-basti of Nagareśvara are short and very well preserved old Kânarese inscriptions: the one apparently a repetition of part of No. 1; the other is not dated and "consists of six lines of poetry, each line containing about 23 letters, and 2 letters over in the 7th line. The verses are in praise of a certain Simha or Singa."

(4-7) In the interior of the same temple there are three inscriptions let into the wall on the right of the shrine door, and one on the left. No. 4, the uppermost on the right, contains 39 lines of about 12 letters each, recording a grant to the god Narakeśvaradeva in the 12th year of the Châlukya king Bhûlokamalla or Someśvaradeva II. (*Śaka* 1060). No. 5, under it, is of 16 lines of about 23 letters each, and records another grant made the same year by a private person. No. 6, the lowest, has 12 lines of about 23 letters each, and records a grant made by an official in the reign of Tribhuvanamalla (Vikramâditya II., *Śaka* 1013). No. 7, on the left, has 37 lines of about 16 letters each, and records a grant to the Jaina temple of Kiriya-Bankâpur in the 45th year of king Vikrama (*Śaka* 1042) (*Ind. Ant.*, IV. 203 and V. 203-5).

5. **Munawalli**, 1 mile north-west from Bankâpur.

I b. **Inscriptions**:—Two in the village, and a third in a field near by.

6. **Huralikop,** 6 miles east of Bankâpur.

I *b*. **Inscriptions**:—(1) In front of the temple of Îśvara, 5′ by 1′ 4″; (2) in the land of the Desâi, 2 ft. by 1½; (3) between the boundary marks of Nos. 73 and 74, 2 ft. by 2; (4) in Survey No. 127, 2½ ft. by 1.

III. 7. **Shiggaon** (latitude 14° 59′ N., longitude 75° 17′ E.). Temple of Basappa.

I *b*. **Inscriptions**:—(1) In front of the door of the temple of Basappa, near the tank, dated *Śaka* 1043; (2-5) in front of the temple of Kalmeśvara are four slabs all in *Devanâgarî* characters and measuring respectively 4 ft. by 2, 2½′ by 1½′, 3′ 9″ by 2′, and 2′ 9″ by 2′; (6) near Baskankatli Honda, one 5′ by 2′; (7) to the north of the fence round the Jogi Ḥonda, 2½′ by 1′; (8, 9) to the south of the Hirikeri tank in the land of Hire Maṭha are two, 2½ ft. square, and 1 ft. square, in effaced *Devanâgarî* characters; (10) on the Ravattinkaṭṭi Honda is another in the same characters, also effaced.

8. **Hottur,** 2½ miles east of Nidgundi.

I *b*. **Inscriptions**:—(1) In Survey No. 1, 4 ft. by 2; (2-4) three more slabs in the same place, 3½′ by 1½′, 9½″ by 3′ and 7½′ by 3½′; (5) in Survey No. 55, 2½ ft. by 1; (6) in Survey No. 53, 7 ft. by 2.

III. 9. **Aratalu,** 6 miles west of Shiggâon. A Jaina *basti* built about 1120 A.D.

I *b*. **Inscriptions**:—(1) In the Jaina *basti*, *Śaka* 1044; (2) on the tank near the temple of Konteśvara, *Śaka* 1046; (3) in front of the temple of Vîrabhadra, 5′ 8″ by 2′ 4″; (4-6) in the house of Parvateva *kom* Solabangauda are three slabs, 5′ by 2½′, 5′ by 1′ and 5′ by 1½′; (7, 8) in front of the temple of Kalmeśvara two slabs 5′ 3″ by 2′ 8″ and 3′ 3″ by 2; (9) in the temple, 5′ 4″ by 3′.

10. **Vanahalli,** 2 miles north-west of Shiggâon.

I *b*, **Inscriptions**:—One, 5′ by 2′ 4″ in front of the temple of Îśvara.

III. 11. **Manakatti,** 4 miles north of Shiggâon. Temple of Solabeśvara.

Inscriptions:—Three on the pillars of the temple.

III. 12. **Hiri-Bendigeri,** 6 miles north of Shiggâon. Temple of Kalappa.

I *b*. **Inscriptions**:—(1) In front of the temple of Kalappa, 5′ 6″ by 2′ 3″, much obliterated; (2) in Hire-Maṭha, 6½ ft. by 1½; (3) in Koranya Maṭha, 6½ ft. by 1.

13. **Ulgur,** 7 miles north-east of Shiggâon (latitude 15° 4′ N., longitude 75° 21′ E.)

I *b*. **Inscriptions**:—(1) Near the well called Kapilabâvi, *Śaka* 1044: (2, 9) in the temple of Siddhalingadeva, eight legible inscriptions in old Kânarese characters, measuring 2 by 1′ 3″, 4′ by 2′, 2′ by 2′, 2′ by 2′, 2′ 6″ by 2′, 3′ by 3′, 2′ 6″ by 2′ and 3′ by 2′ 6″ respectively.

14. **Bannikop,** 2 miles north-east of Shiggâon. Temple of Dharvarâya.

I *b*. **Inscriptions**:—(1) On the wall of the temple, 2′ by 1′; (2) in front of the temple 2′ 6″ by 1′ 9″.

15. **Mantrava'di,** 4 miles east of Shiggâon.

I *b*. **Inscriptions**:—(1) In front of the temple of Hanumân, 5 ft. by 3′; (2) near the east gate of the village, 4′ 9″ by 2′; (3) in the court of the house of Râmana Bhanḍâri, 1½ ft. by 1′—mostly illegible.

16. **Huvina-Sigalli,** 14 miles east of Shiggâon (latitude 15° 2′ N., longitude 75° 30′ E.)

I *b*. **Inscriptions**:—In front of the temple of Hanumân are two.

17. **Kalas**, 5 miles W.S.W. of Lakshmeśvar, (lat. 15° 5′ N., long. 75° 28′ E.)

I *b*. **Inscriptions**:—(1) In front of the temple of Nârâyaṇadeva, 4′ 6″ by 2′ 2″; (2) in front of the house of Ayyanagauda *bin* Siddhangauda, 4′ 6″ by 2′ 1″; (3) at the house of Koneri-râv Bâgal, 7′ by 3′ 1″; (4) at the same place, 4 ft. by 2¼; (5) near a house used by Râmanna *bin* Koteppa Malali, for cotton ginning, 2′ by 2′ 4″,—all legible.

18. **Kalya'n**, 4 miles south from Shiggâon.

I *b*. **Inscriptions** on a stone on the south step of the tomb of Pîr Pâdshâh, *Saka* 947.

I *b*. 19. **Gundur**, 5 miles from Shiggâon, **inscriptions**, *Ind. Ant.* XII. 270.

I *b*. 20. **Ganjigatti**, near Shiggâon, a very fine, large, carved ceiling panel, lying in the village, portraying the eight regents of the points of the compass. (**Surveyed**.)

VIII.—Hângal Tâlukâ.

I *b*. 1. **Ha'ngal**, (lat. 14° 45′ N., long. 75° 11′ E.), the ancient Pânungal. Temple of Târakeśvara belonging to the Smârtas: a very large and elegant one built of black granite, and the walls carved with mythological sculptures. Tradition ascribes it to Vîra Ballâḷa (about A.D. 1192-1211). "The roof of the temple has been thoroughly church-wardened in modern times, and so covered with plaster that it is impossible to say what its original form may have been; but, as Colonel M. Taylor remarks, 'it serves to protect the interior, which is in perfect preservation. In one part of the temple (the *sabhâ manḍapa*) is the celebrated *Padma* or lotus of Hângal, a solid octagonal stone* nearly thirty feet in diameter, carved in the form of a lotus flower, and supported by eight neatly sculptured columns. It seems impossible to account for the manner in which this great mass of rock was lifted up and placed in its present position.' The roof of the porch is supported by pillars, with the lotus dome in the centre. The doorway of the detached temple, though similar in design to those of the temple at Lakkuṇḍi, shows a strong tendency towards the border style of decoration which was employed by the Ballâḷa architects at Halabid and elsewhere." For plan and elevation of the temple see *Ind. Ant.* IV. 205; V. 179 (*J. B. B. R. A. S.* IX. 325.) (**Surveyed**.)

III. The temple of Bileśvara, half a mile to the south of Hângal, said to be 500 years old, contains some carving.

II *b*. There is also the old fort and within it several old ruined Jaina temples. (**Surveyed**.)

I *b*. **Inscriptions**.—There are several inscriptions and memorial stones about Hângal. Among the latter is one of the western Châlukya king Vikramâditya Tribhuvanamalla dated *Śaka* 1035; two of king Nûrmaḍi-Taila; one in the temple of Târakeśvara of the time of the Hoysala king Ballâla and the Kâdamba Kâmadeva, *Śaka* 1118; also another of Kâma (*P. S. and O. C. Insc.* Nos. 103-107; see also *Ind. Ant.*, vol. IV. p. 205). (1) On a dunghill in front of the temple of Mailâradeva, Khara; (2) *vîragal* in the temple of Târakeśvara, Nala; (3) on the left hand in the door of the temple of Târakeśvara, *Śaka* 1101; (4) in the temple of Îśvara inside the fort, *Śaka* 1111; (5) at the Budimaṭha, *Śaka* 1097.

At the temple of Hanumândeva at Hâlekoṭi (close to Hângal on the west side) is an **inscription** 3 feet by 2 feet, that would repay examination. Near this is a small temple with some curious and interesting sculptures of Nâga men and women, &c. (*Ind. Ant.* vol. IV. p. 205).

* This is a mistake; it is a built dome.—Editor.

2. **Balehalli**, 6 miles south-west of Hângal, close to Śiragôḍ.

I *b*. **Inscriptions** :—(1) In front of the temple of Mailâradeva, *Śaka* 1066; (2) in front of the temple of Mallikârjuna, *Śaka* 1070; (3) a *vîragal* at the same place, *Śaka* 998. There are altogether eleven inscriptions in the village and one in Survey No. 136.

III. 3. **Kallukeri**, 6 miles north by east of Tilivalli (lat. 14° 42′ N., long. 75° 19′ E.). (1) Temple of Basaveśvara, a Lingâyat shrine 69 feet by 48 in the Jaina style, with images and walls ornamented with carving. (2) Temples of Lakshmi, Someśvara and Sarasvatî, ascribed to Jakhaṇâchârya, but plain. Some carving on detached stones near the temple of Basaveśvara.

I *b*. **Inscriptions** :—Seven outside to the east of the temple of Basaveśvara, varying in size from 6′ by 3′ to 3′ by 1½′.

I *b*. 4. **Herur**, 7 miles north by east from Tiḷivalli :—A *vîragal* at the temple of Basappa near the tank, *Śaka* 1079.

III. 5. **Hire Basur**, 4 miles south-east of Kallukeri. There is a cave in a rising ground near the village and said to go a fabulous distance underground.

I *b*. **Inscriptions** :—One in front of the temple of Viśveśvara, 4½ feet by 1½ feet; another standing in front of the temple of Hanumân, 3 feet by 1½ feet.

II *b*. 6. **Tilivalli**, 12 miles south-east from Hângal (lat. 14° 37′ N., long. 75° 18 E.) The temple of Śânteśvara in the middle of the village, about 75 feet long by 57 in breadth. It has comparatively little figure sculpture about it, but it is fully decorated with other ornament. The outer side of the parapet wall of the hall is very effectively decorated with an endless repetition of miniature *śikharas*. The three porches of the hall have rather pretty ceilings with very chaste-looking rosette centres. (**Surveyed**.)

I *b*. **Inscriptions**:—(1) One on a pillar inside the temple of Śânteśvara of 13 lines; (2) one, 7 feet by 3½, outside the temple, on the south, of the Yâdava king Simhaṇa, dated *Śaka* 1860, Thursday, 3rd Phâlguna *Śuddha* (*P. S. and O. C. Inscriptions* No. 112); (3) one *vîragal* near the south door; (4) at the temple of Basaveśvara in front of the Churachi *maṭha*, *Śaka* 975; (5—7) three—each 5 feet high—at the west wall of Churachi Ayya's *maṭha*, two of them illegible and the third damaged; (8) one, much obliterated, at the east gate of the town, 5 feet by 2½ feet; (9) one behind the Kalyâṇa *maṭha*, 2′ 6″ by 1′ 10″; (10, 11) an inscription and a *vîragal* behind the Kalla *maṭha*—one 4′ 2″ by 1′ 8″ and one 3′ by 1′ 10″; (12) a *vîragal* on the right of the temple of Îśvara, *Śaka* 1160; (13) one on the four sides of a *dipamâla* lying at the foot of the *pippala* tree; (14) one built into the coping of the wall of the new sluice in the *band*; (15, 16) at the temple of Basavaṇṇa are two *vîragals*. (*J. B. B. R. A. S.*, Vol. IX. p. 326).

I *b*. 7. **Kya'sanur**, 7 miles S.S.W. from Hângal.

Inscriptions:—(1) On the road, on the north of the village, *Śaka* 1054; (2) a *vîragal* on a mound on the same road, *Śaka* 1163; (3) a *vîragal* among a row of stones on the same road, *Śaka* 1098; (4) in a row of stones (? at the same place) *Śaka* 867 in words:—this is an important inscription. There is also one inscription in the village 1½ feet square, and two others outside.

8. **Havanage**, 7½ miles south-east from Hângal and 1 mile south of Bâlambîda.

I *a*. **Inscriptions** :—(1) On the south side of the temple of Râmeśvara, *Śaka* 948; (2) at the same place, *Śaka* 1039; (3) at the same place, *Śaka* 1053: and four others.

III. 9. **Chikanagi,** 2½ miles west of Hângal. Temple of Amṛitaliṅga belonging to the Smârtas said to be 500 years old. The pillars and walls of the temple are carved.

I b. **Inscriptions**:—Four outside the temple.

10. **Ra'mati'rtha,** 3 miles north of Hângal.

I b. **Inscriptions**:—There are four near the temple of Râmaliṅga.

III. 11. **Yalavatti,** ½ mile south from Nidaśingi. Temple of Râmeśvara, with carvings on each side the door. Old Jaina temple with carvings on the walls and an unfinished image.

I b. **Inscriptions**:—(1) One on the south side outside the temple of Râmeśvara, *Śaka* 1057; (2) on the right of the god in the temple of Râmalinga (?=Râmeśvara), *Śaka* 1070; (3) in the yard of the house of Yelegár Karibasappa, *Śaka* 1010; (4) a *vîragal* in the same yard, *Śaka* 1057; (5) near the temple of Mâleśvara, *Śaka* 1035; (6) a *vîragal* in the Desâi's field, outside the village, *Śaka* 1065; (7) a *vîragal* in a field on the east of the village, *Śaka* 1065; (8) on a stone at the place called Suladamaṭṭi on the east of the village, Rudhirodgâri,

12. **Yelavala,** 9 miles north from Hângal.

I b. **Inscriptions**:—On the east of the temple of Dyámavva, *Śaka* 1326.

III. 13. **Belvatti,** 8 miles N.N.E. of Hàngal (lat. 14° 51′ N., long. 75° 15′ E.) said to be the site of an old city, Lîlâvatî. Temple of Gokaleśvara-Śiva is a large one built of black stone, the walls covered with sculpture.

I b. **Inscriptions**:—Four to the west of the temple and one to the north; one in Revenue Survey field No. 23, and two, in No. 14, covered with prickly pear.

III. 14. **Kudala,** 12 miles north east of Hángal, at junction of the Darmà and Varadâ Rivers (lat. 14° 50′ N., long. 75° 22′ E.) Old temple of Saṅgameśvara, where a large annual fair is held.

I b. **Inscription**:—One to the east of the temple.

III. 15. **Neregal,** 2 miles south-west of Kudala, and 14 miles north-east from Hàngal. A very old temple of Sarveśvara, the roof supported by 24 round polished pillars. **(Surveyed.)**

I b. **Inscriptions**:—(1) On the south side of the temple of Sarveśvara, *Śaka* 999; (2) on a beam (?) in the western side of the *madhyaraṅga* of the same temple, *Śaka* 1047; (3) on another beam (?) in the same place, *Śaka* 1052; (4) another outside the temple; (5) on a broken stone on the wall of the sluice of the tank, *Śaka* 1108; (6) at the temple of Basappa, *Śaka* 1195; (7) a *vîragal* below a *nim* tree on the bank of the tank, *Śaka* 1021; (8) a *vîragal* on the shrine of the tank, *Śaka* 1072.

II b. 16. **Balambida,** 8 miles east of Hàngal (lat. 14° 46′ N., long. 75° 17′ E.) Temples of Râmeśvara and Kallameśvara, the latter with sculptures both inside and out and measuring 30 feet by 22 feet. **(Surveyed.)**

I b. **Inscriptions**:—(1) On the south of the temple of Râmeśvara on the north of the village, *Śaka* 1039; (2) on the north of the same temple; (3) in front of the temple of Kalleśvara, *Śaka* 1044; (4) in front of the same temple, *Śaka* 1087.

17. **Yellur,** 6 miles north by east from Hàngal and 2 miles east of Husanâbâd.

I b. **Inscription**:— (1) In the temple of Kallapa on the tank, *Śaka*.....; (2) an inscription in the village, dated Vikrama *Śaka* 250 (A.D. 1248).

I b. 18. **Belgal,** 2 miles south of Belwaṭṭi. On the dam of the large tank to the east of the village are two **inscriptions**, and a third is near the waste-weir.

19. **Kargudrikop,** 5 miles north-east from Hângal.

I *b*. **Inscriptions** :—(1) On the south of the temple of Nârâyaṇa on the west of the village, a well-preserved Kâdamba inscription, giving the whole genealogy, dated *Saka* 1030; (2) on a stone with the image of Bramhadeva on it, in front of the *basti*, *Śaka* 1198.

Kargudari inscription, *Ind. Ant.* X. 249.

20. **Adur,** 10 miles east from Hângal.

I *b*. **Inscriptions** :—(1) In the field of Mulla, on the south of the village, *Śaka* 956; (2) on the south side of the temple of Kalleśvara on the east of the village, *Śaka* 966.

III. 21. **Alur,** 5 miles south-east from Hângal;—a stone temple.

I *b*. **Inscriptions** :—(1) On the right of the god, in the temple of Kalleśvara, *Śaka* 1069; (2) in the temple of Kallameśvara (?= Kalleśvara), *Śaka* 1191; (3) in the temple of Kalmeśvara (?= Kalleśvara), on the side of a stone, Durmukha; (4) *vîragal* in the chief gateway of the temple of Kallameśvara, Vilambi; (5) a stone lying in the corner of the tank, *Śaka* 1037.

III. 22. **Aralesvar,** 5 miles north-east from Hângal;—a stone temple.

I *b*. **Inscriptions** :—(1) On a pillar on the south side of the god in the temple of Kadambeśvara, *Śaka* 998; (2) on the *makaratorana* of the same temple, *Śaka* 1010; on a pillar in front of the principal gate of the same temple, Khara *Saṁvatsara*.

23. **Balur,** 3 miles south-east from Hângal.

I *b*. **Inscriptions** :—(1) On the south of the temple of Râmalinga on the east of the village, *Śaka* 1047; (2) a *vîragal* near the tank on the south of the village, *Śaka* 1164.

24. **Gejjihalli,** 2 miles south from Hàngal.

I *b*. **Inscriptions** :—(1) In the temple of Basaveśvara on the right of the god, *Śaka* 1025; (2) in the same temple, on the left of the god, *Śaka* 1025.

25. **Gudugudi,** 5 miles north-west from Hângal.

I *b*. **Inscriptions** :—(1) On the south side of the temple of Kallapa, *Śaka* 960; (2) in the same place, *Śaka* 994.

26. **Hirur** appears to be 3 miles south-west from Hàngal close to "Seewully."

II *b*. **Inscription** :—In the temple of Saṅgana Basaveśvara, on the left of the god, *Śaka* 940.

27. **Kanchinegalur,** 7 miles north-east from Hângal.

I *b*. **Inscription** :—On a mound of earth, *Śaka* 1027.

28. **Kannesvar,** 10 miles south-east from Hângal, and 5 miles north of Tilivalli.

I *b*. **Inscriptions** :—(1) In front of the temple of Kannapa. *Śaka* 927; (2) at the same place, *Śaka* 1067.

29. **Kuntanahalli,** 2 miles north-east from Hàngal.

I *b*. **Inscription** :—In front of the temple of Basappa, *Śaka* 1069.

30. **Makarawalli,** 11 miles south by east from Hângal.

I *b*. **Inscription** :—On a pillar called Garuda-*khamba* at the tank, *Śaka* 1321.

31. **Mantige,** 6 miles south-east from Hângal.

I *b*. **Inscription** :—At.... ....*Śaka* 1087.

82. **Mudur**, 8 miles south from Hângal.

I *b*. **Inscriptions**:—(1) In the temple of Mallikârjuna outside the village, *Śaka* 1059; (2) a *vîragal* in front of the temple of Brahmâ, *Śaka* 1043.

83. **Nidasingi**, 10 miles north from Hângal.

I *b*. **Inscriptions**:—(1) At the Hiri *maṭha* on the west of the village, *Śaka* 1031; (2) at the same place, *Śaka* 1032.

84. **Sangur**, 14 miles east by north from Hângal.

I *b*. **Inscriptions**:—(1) On the right of the temple of Vîrabhadra, *Śaka* 1086; (2) on the left hand, in front of the temple of Vîrabhadra, *Śaka* 1334; (3) a *vîragal* on the bank of the ditch of the fort, *Śaka* 1156; (4) in the same locality, *Śaka* 1186; (5) in the same place, only a fragment.

85. **Sasangi**, probably "Sumusgi," 10 miles south-west from Hângal;—or perhaps "Sawásgi," 4 miles north-east from Hângal.

I *b*. **Inscription**:—On the south side of the temple of Kalleśvara, *Śaka* 1046.

86. **Sirgod**, 7 miles north by west from Hângal.

I *b*. **Inscriptions**:—(1) A *vîragal* in front of the temple of Kalleśvara, *Śaka* 1065; (2) at the temple of Îśvara, *Śaka* 1109.

87. **Mulgund**, 8 miles south-east from Hângal.

I *b*. **Inscription**:—On the south of the temple of Kalleśvara, *Śaka* 1037.

I *b*. 88. Village uncertain:—Hirur? ; **Inscriptions**:—In the *inâm* land of Kari-Mohadin, *Śaka* 946; and in the temple of Hâvali-Hanumanta, *Śaka* 1043 and *Śaka* 1071.

IX.—Karajgi Tâluka.

1. **Haralahalli** on the Tungabhadrâ, 3 miles east of Guttal (lat. 14° 50′ N., long.
II *b*. 75° 44′ E.) Temples of Someśvara of black stone and of Kaleśvara, and three **inscriptions**
I *b*. of 94, 110, and 76 lines respectively. (**Surveyed.**)

III. 2. **Gutal** (lat. 14° 50′ N., long. 75° 41½′ E.) Temple of Chûḍaśekhara of black stone,
I *b*. and two **inscriptions**, one of 95 lines, the other of 24.

II *b*. 3. **Galagana'th**, 6 miles north of Haralahalli, and 20 east by north from Karajgi, on the Tungabhadrâ. The temple of Gargeśvara to the north of the village is of black granite, about 80 feet by 40, with 4 pillars supporting the roof, the walls carved with mythological figures (**Surveyed.**)

I *b*. **Inscriptions**:—(1) A *vîragal* standing on the right of the god in the temple of Hanumanta in the village, *Śaka* 933; (2) in the temple of Galageśvara, *Śaka* 1069; (3) in the enclosure of the temple of Gargeśvara (?=Galageśvara), *Śaka* 1002.

III. 4. **Kanavalli**, 8 miles west by south from Gutal (lat. 14° 48′ N., long. 75° 35′ E.) Old temple of Parameśvara, built of stone and brick, the spire destroyed, contains also images of other *devas*. It is considered as very old and is about 50 feet by 17, with 4 pillars Temple of Bhogeśa is a similar structure.

I *b*. **Inscriptions**:—Three of 24, 16 and 70 lines respectively.

I b. III. 5. **Haveri**, 6 miles south-west of Karajgi (lat. 14° 47′ N., long. 75° 27′ E.). Temple of Siddheśvara, highly sculptured. *Maṭha* (or monastery) of Râghavendra Svâmi, and old temple of Kalappa. Four inscriptions—one, broken, of 63 lines, and the others of 58, 18 and 48 lines respectively. (**Surveyed**.)

I b. **Inscriptions**:—(1) Near the *maṇḍapa* on the north of the temple of Halevura Basavaṇṇa, *Śaka* 1056; (2) near the same temple, *Śaka* 1079; and others.

III. I b. 6. **Kotur**, 3 miles west from Karajgi;—Temple of Basavaṇṇa in the Jakhaṇâchârya style with 12 pillars. Two **inscriptions**.

III. 7. **Devagiri**, 6 miles west by south of Karajgi and 4 miles north-west from Hâveri (lat. 14° 51′ N., long. 75° 26′ N.). Temples of Hanumân, Basavaṇṇa, and Ellavvâ or Yellammâ, one attributed to Jakhaṇâchârya. In the last is an **inscription** dated "*Śaka* 1460, Vilambi *Saṁvatsara*, Âshâdha *Śuddha*, Monday." Three sets of copper-plates found here are published in the *Indian Antiquary*, vol. VII., pp. 33, 35, 37 (see also *Pâli, Sanskrit and Old Canarese Insc.* Nos. 1, 3, and 4).

8. **Devihosur**, 4½ miles south-west of Devagiri (lat. 14° 48′ N., long. 75° 24′ E.)

I b. **Inscriptions**:—An ordinary village temple of Bânaśaṅkara to the north of the village contains four inscription slabs. In the temple of Bhogeśvara are two, one of about 20 lines and the other of 11. In the temple of Basavaṇṇa is one. An eighth inscription is on the *band* of the tank to the east of the village. A ninth is in a field. And two inscriptions are by "the dunghill in the compound of one Kajanivali."

I b. 9. **Didgur**, 4 miles south-west of Devihosur. Six **inscriptions** in the temple of Hanumân, one in *Pujâri* Bandiya's compound, and an eighth on the waste-weir of the *talâv*.

III. 10. **Saugur**, 2 miles north of Didgur, on the Varadâ. A small temple of Îśvara with a roof supported by 2 octagonal columns; the outer walls carved with mythological subjects.

I b. **Inscriptions**:—Four in the village.

III. 11. **Karajgi**:—Stone temple of the Jakhaṇâchârya style.

III. 12. **"Agadi,"** 4 miles north-east from Haveri:—Old temple of the Jakhaṇâchârya class.

III. I b. 13. **Mallur**, 12 miles south of Karajgi:—Temple of Vîrabhadra in the Jakhaṇâchârya style, and three **inscriptions**.

14. **Hatti-Mattur**, *Ind. Ant.* XII. 224.

X.—Rânebennur Tâlukâ.

III. 1. **Kadarmandaligi**, 9 miles west of Râṇebennur (lat. 14° 38′ N., long. 75° 35′ E.). There is a temple of Mâruti Kanteśa in the village. The image is said to have been established by Janamejaya.

III. **Inscriptions**:—(1) On the *dhvajastambha* of the temple of Hanumanta, *Saka* 1498 and (2) another weather-worn in a field.

2. **Asundi**, 5 miles west of Rânebennur.

Ib. **Inscriptions** :—(1) At the temple of Kalleśvar, outside the village, dated *Śaka* 1034; (2) near the same temple, *Śaka* 1065; (3) another much obliterated.

Ib. 3. **Ukund**, 3 miles south of Kadarmandalgi. At the temple of Kâleśvara is an old Kânarese **inscription** slab 5 feet high by 2½ broad. Śaṅkara Niṅgapa Bâjar has a copper-plate grant.

III. 4. **Harogop**, 8 miles from Rânebennur (lat. 14° 29' N., long. 75° 38′ E.) **Inscription** of 12 lines, much effaced, near the temple of Hanumân.

III. 5. **Benakanakond**, 3 miles north of Hârogop, and 5 miles S.S.W. of Rânebennur. Temple of Kalmeśvara.

Ib. **Inscriptions** :—(1) On the south of the temple of Kalleśvara *Śaka* 955; (2) again on the south of the same temple, *Śaka* 1124; (3) on the lamp-pillar (*dipada khamba*) at the same temple, *Śaka* 1031; (4) a *viragal* below the tank, *Śaka* 1206.

III. 6. **Ra'nebennur**, (lat. 14° 37' N., long. 75° 42' E.). The *dargâh* of Hazrat Jamal Shâh Wali was rebuilt about 30 years ago by Amin Shâh Husaini *alias* Kamalshâh Husain at a cost, it is said, of only Rs. 5,000. The roof is supported by 40 stone pillars and numerous wooden ones. Jamal Shâh is said to have led in one halter a mouse, a cat, a dog, a stag, a snake, and a mungoose, one not molesting another; and he wore bangles up to his elbows. These were among his titles to sanctity. There is a great scene at the *dargâh* during Muharram. Three miles north-east is a circle of upright stones, in the jungle. **(Surveyed.)**

Ib. **Inscriptions** :—One near the *dipamâla* pillar at the temple of Siddheśvara is dated *Śaka* 1411 Sâdhâraṇa Jyeshtha *Vadya 5th*, and contains the names of some of the Vijayanagar kings.

Ib. 7. **Harihar** is 14 miles south-east from Rânebennur. There is here a large black stone temple of Hari-Hara with numerous **inscription** slabs. **(Surveyed.)** (See *P. S. and O. C. Inscriptions* Nos. 17, 22, 116-135; *Ind. Ant.*, IV. 327, 329; V. 362; Copper-plate Grant, VII. 168, 301; *J. B. B. R. A. S.*, Vol. IX. p. 327.)

Ib. 8. **Hire Bidari**, 8 miles north of Harihar on the Tungabhadrâ, has an old temple and three **inscriptions**, one dated *Śaka* 1205, in 50 lines.

III. 9. **Guddaguda'pur** or Devargaḍ, 6 miles north of Rânebennur. Temple of Mailâra-liṅga or Khaṇḍobâ of great celebrity in all the surrounding districts. It is built of black stone, polished; the roof is supported by 20 pillars, of which 4 are round and the rest square. The outer walls are ornamented with carved figures, but the spire is of brick. There is a great annual fair on the 9th of Aśvina *Śuddha*, when self-torture is practised by devotees, &c., to the present time. The temple is supported by *inâm* lands. Near it is a temple to Khaṇḍobâ's wife Mâlasâbâi, or Gaṅgi Malavâ, and six (?) other minor temples.

Ib. 10. **Chanda'dampur**, or Pura, 13 miles north of Rânebennur (lat. 14° 47′ N., long. 76° 43′ N.) Temple of Mukteśvara of black stone. The temple here is "less graceful than that at Dambal, but it is a fine, bold temple of the same age and style, with all its details more completely finished than they are in that example. As a design, its principal defects are the form of its dome, and the insignificance of its crowning member (the *kalaśa*), which is much too small for its position. In these respects it forms a very marked contrast with the Ḍambal example, where these parts are in as perfect proportion to the other parts of the design as in any example" in the country. (*J. B. B. R. A. S.*, Vol. IX., p. 326). **(Surveyed.)**

I *b*. **Inscriptions**:—(1) In the temple of Mukteśvara is a very short but important inscription, dated *Śaka* 821, Siddhárthi; (2) an old Kánarese inscription of king Vikramâditya Tribhuvanamalla (A.D. 1076-1127); (3) in the same temple a stone slab with three inscriptions dated *Śaka* 1181, 1148 and 1184; (4) in the temple of Îśvara on the bank of the Tungabhadrâ an inscription of the great chieftain Vikramâditya of the lineage of Chandragupta, dated *Śaka* 1113, at the time of a solar eclipse at the new moon of Mârgaśîrsha; (5) a slab also bearing three Yâdava inscriptions dated *Śaka* 1185, 1185 and 1164; (6) one dated *Śaka* 1186 (at the back of No. 1?); (7) another, *Śaka* 1213; (8) behind the image of Vîrabhadra in the temple of Gopadevamuni, *Śaka* 1184.

11. **Heggeri**, 4 miles south-west from Hallur, which is 23 miles south from Râṇebennûr.

I *b*. **Inscription**:—In front of the temple of Kallapa in the field of Sivaṇṇa, about *Śaka* 1104.

12. **Hire Kabbar**, 3 miles west by north from Hallur.

I *b*. **Inscription**:—In the field of Baḍaguṇḍa, *Śaka* 1094.

13. **Aniveri**, 12 miles south by east from Râṇebennûr.

I *b*. **Inscription**:—In an open space in the temple of Kallapa, *Śaka* 1104.

14. **Bidarakundi**, (?) 10 miles south-west from Râṇebennûr.

I *b*. **Inscription**:—In the temple of Saṅgameśvara, *Śaka* 954.

15. **Bya'digi**, 12 miles north-west from Rânebennur.

I *b*. **Inscriptions**:—(1) In front of the temple of Râmeśvara in the fort, *Śaka* 1014; (2) on the left of the same temple, *Śaka* 1542.

16. **Hulihalli**, 3 miles west by north from Rânebennur.

I *b*. **Inscriptions**:—(1) On the south of the temple of Kalleśvara in the fort, *Śaka* 1065; (2) on the right of the temple of Râmeśvara outside the village, *Śaka* 1104.

III. 17. **Motibennur**, a large dolman in the village.

I *b*. 18. **Korvatti**, on the Tungabhadrâ in Bellari district, an old temple in good preservation and having some good carving. **(Surveyed.)**

I *b*. 19. **Honatti**, 14 miles north from Râṇebennur; some temples with many **inscriptions**.

XI—Kod Tâlukâ.

III. 1. **Medur**, 3 miles south-east from Mâsur, has a temple of the goddess Nîlammâ.

I *b*. **Inscriptions**:—(1) On the south of the shrine of Nîlammâ at the temple of Basappa, dated *Śaka* 967; (2) on the north of the same shrine, *Śaka* 969; (3) a ***vîragal*** in the temple of Billeśvara near the temple of Basappa, *Śaka* 1186.

2. **Kod**, the chief town of the *tâlukâ* (lat. 14° 32′ N., long. 75° 30′ E.).

II *b*. **Inscription** :—In the temple of Hanumân is an old Kânarese one.

III. 3. **Nidanegal**, 3½ miles north-west from Madak and 11 miles south from Koḍ (lat. 14° 28′ N., long. 75° 27′ E.). The temple of Kâleśvara here is regarded as 500 or 600 years old, and is like those ascribed to Jakhaṇâchârya. It contains two images of Basava and one of Kâleśvara.

II *b*. **Inscriptions** :—Near the temple are 15 carved stones, some (?) with inscriptions.

III. 4. **Kodamoggi**, 1 mile south-west from Mâsur. Temples of Siddharâmeśvara and Bayala.

I *b*. **Inscriptions** :—(1) In the temple of Siddharâmeśvara, *Śaka* 1012; (2) in front of the same temple, *Śaka*......... ; (3) in front of (the god, or temple of) Bayala Basappa, *Śaka* 1080.

III. 5. **Waraha**, 2 miles W.N.W. of Niḍanegal, and 7 miles west from Mâsur, has a temple of Kalleśvara.

I *b*. **Inscriptions** :—*A vîragal* at the temple of Kalleśvara, *Śako* 1210; (2) a *mâstika* in the land belonging to Mallârappa Desâi, *Śaka* 1368.

III. 6. **Chhaparadahalli**, 2 miles south-west of Raṭṭihaḷḷi; has a temple of Hanumân, said to be very old.

II *b*. There is an **inscription** slab outside the village to the north.

III. 7. **Kanavisidhageri**, or Pura, (?) 2½ miles south of Raṭṭihaḷḷi; temple of Kanavi Siddheśvara.

I *b*. **Inscriptions** :—(1) On one of a row of stones on the south of the temple of Siddhappa, *Śaka* 1030; (2) in the temple of Siddhappa, *Śaka* 1074; (3) on a pillar in the temple of Siddhappa, *Śaka* 1191; (4) on a pillar in the temple of Siddhappa, *Śaka* 1187.

II *b*. 8. **Rattihalli**, 10 miles S.S.E. from Koḍ on the Choardi River (lat. 14° 25′ N., long. 75° 30′ E.). Temple of Kadambeśvara in the Jakhaṇâchârya style, built about 700 years ago. It is built of sculptured slabs, and has three domes supported by 36 pillars; also a temple of Vîrabhadra. (**Surveyed**.)

I *b*. **Inscriptions** :—(1) In the temple of Kadambeśvara, on the right of the god, *Śaka* 1096; (2) in the same temple, on the left of the god, *Śaka* 1160; (3) in the same temple, on a pillar in the *madhyaraṅga*, *Śaka* 1160; (4) in the same temple, on another pillar

II *b*. *Śaka* 1220; (5) on the right hand as you enter the gate of the fort, *Śaka* 1469; (6) another on the right hand as you enter the gate of the fort, *Śaka* 1479; (7) on the left hand as you enter the village gateway, *Śaka* 1472.

9. **Hire-Kerur**, 7 miles S.S.W. of Koḍ (lat. 14° 28′ N., long. 74° 27′ E.), has a large tank ascribed to Janamejaya (whom the return places in the 10th century A.D.). An inscribed slab near the temple of Vishapariharesvara is said to give some account of its construction. There is a copper-plate with one Chandi-Sivabasapa. The temples of Vishaparihareśvara (who is reputed to cure snake-bites), of Varâhakâleśvara, and of Durgâ are returned as of no antiquarian note.

I *b*. **Inscriptions**:—(1) In the burial ground, *Śaka* 984; (2) at the temple of Toṭada Vîrabhadra, *Śaka* 987; (3) at the same temple, *Śaka* 1021; (4) in front of the door of the same temple, *Śaka* 1094; (5) standing near the eastern wall of the same temple, Rudhirodgâri; (6) standing to the west of the Gaja-Lakshmi stone on the north of the garden-land of Kâlappa-Sânbhoga on the bank of the tank, *Śaka* 1031 or 1053; (7) on a stone to the east of a Gaja-Lakshmi stone on the bank of the tank, *Śaka* 1018; (8) on a stone to the south of the said Gaja-Lakshmi stone, *Śaka* 1025; (9) on a stone lying on the bank of the tank, *Śaka* 1023; (10) near the house of Aṅgḍi-Niṅgaṇṇa on the east of the mosque near the village gate, *Śaka* 1065; (11) on a stone in the burning ground near the tank near the house of Sarâyadava in the street, *Śaka* 997 to 1045.

10. **Hosahalli**, 2 miles east from Hire-Kerur.

I *b*. **Inscriptions**:—(1) In the *pâvuli* or open place in the temple of Mallappa, *Śaka* 1164, (2) on the south wall in the temple of Mallamma on the road, on the west of the village, Prabhava.

II *b*. 11. **Balambid**, 1½ miles north-west of Hire-Kerûr, has a temple of Vishaparihareśvara and Basava, in the Jakhaṇâchârya style, said to be 300 years old; but part of the stones have been used to build the Hire-Kerûr tank.

I *b*. **Inscriptions**:—(1) On the left of the god in the temple of Vishaparihareśvara, *Śaka* 979; (2) in the same temple, *Śaka* 1001; (3) on the south of the door of the same temple, *Śaka* 1009; (4) at the same temple, *Śaka* 1040; (5) at the same temple, *Śaka* 1150.

12. **Chik-Kerur**, 12½ miles west from Kôḍ.

I *b*. **Inscriptions**:—(1) On the bank of the tank called Hirikere, *Śaka* 1016; (2) at the temple of Someśvara on the bank of the tank, *Śaka* 1023; (3) on the bank of the tank *Saka* 1085; (4) at the temple of Hanumanta, *Śaka* 1023; (5) in front of the temple of Banaśamkari, *Śaka* 975; (6) a *vîragal* in the village gateway, *Śaka* 1144; (7) a *vîragal* near the village gate, *Śaka* 999; (8) lying on an anthill in the field of Kânibadiya Yagareru, *Śaka* 1047; (9) on one of a row of stones in a ditch at the end of the *agalapañavu*, *Śaka* 1051.

13. **Sitikond**, 2 miles south-east from Chik-Kerûr,

I *b*. **Inscription** on the edge of a paddy field to the east of the tank, dated *Śaka* 970; and a *vîragal* or a *satî* stone just below the preceding.

III. 14. **Chin-Mulgund**, 6 miles N.N.W. from Kod, To the north-east of this village is a temple to Chikeśvara, 'in the Jaina style' of black granite. The walls are carved with figures and the roof supported on 44 columns. On a small hillock to the east of the village is a *svayaṁbhu linga* called Siddheśvara. At some distance to the left of it is a cave, which is said to lead underground to a fabulous distance. The village is said to have been the hermitage of Machhakandarâya, from whom the village was called Mulgund (!); also that gold-dust is found in the neighbouring hills, and therefore it is called Chin-Mulgund.

I *b*. **Inscriptions**:—(1) On the left side of the central door of the temple of Chikeśvara is an inscription in 18 lines, each containing about 25 letters in old Kânarese characters; (2) lying outside the temple of Îśvara outside the village, *Śaka* 1165.

15. **Abbalur,** 2 miles west from Koḍ. Temple of Basappa.

I *b*. **Inscriptions**:—(1) In the temple of Basappa, *Śaka* 1022; (2) in the same temple, *Śaka* 1066; (3) a *vîragal* in the same temple, *Śaka* 1141; (4) in the temple of Somanâtha, on the right of the god, about *Śaka* 1090.

II *b*. 16. **Arlekatti,** 5 miles north of Koḍ. There are three **inscriptions** in the village in old Kânarese characters.

II *b*. 17. **Sidenur,** 4 miles north of Arlekaṭṭi; temple and **inscription** slab.

18. **Tadas,** 3 miles north-west of Arlekaṭṭi (lat. 14° 37′ N., long. 75° 28′ E.). There
II *b*. are four **inscription** slabs in this village on the *band* of the tank, two of them very much weather-worn.

II *b*. 19. **Bannihatti,** 9 miles north-east from Koḍ; an **inscription** in the field of Kallideva, dated *Śaka* 1236.

I *b*. 20. **Hamsabhavi,** 7 miles north-west from Koḍ; a *vîragal* on the bank of the tank, *Śaka* 1128.

II *b*. 21. **Odenpur** (Vadenpur), 2 miles east from Chin-Mulgund;—to the north of the village is a *śilâśâsana* dated *Śaka* 1422 Dundubhi *Samvatsara*, Kârtika *Śuddha* 12th, Somavâra, granting Maypur to the Liṅgâyats as an atonement made by Liṅga-Kunteyavadar Kenidsamnaknayak (?) for the murder of a woman named Kapite.

III. 22. **Muttur,** 3 miles west of Taḍas: a temple of Śiva 'in the Jaina style,' about 30 feet long by 15 wide, with a small shrine. It is of black granite, and the walls are carved with numerous figures; but it has been repaired with brick. The roof is supported by 32 pillars. The Guravas are supported by *inâm* lands.

I *b*. In front of the temple are 11 stones, one of which bears an **inscription** dated *Śaka* 1304. It is a *vîragal*.

III. 23. **Hirehalli,** 4 miles north-west of Muttur and 5 miles south-west of Kâginelli;— Old temple and an **inscription** slab.

III. 24. **Kaginelli,** 13 miles N.N.W. from Koḍ and 11 miles north-east from Tilivaḷḷi (lat. 14° 41′ N., long. 75° 25′ E.) In the same enclosure are two very plain stone temples dedicated to Âdikeśava and Lakshmî-Narasiṁha. The former measures 66 feet long by 23 wide, with 12 columns in the outer open *maṇḍapa*. That of Narasinha has a wooden-pillared front *maṇḍapa*. The temples are said to have been built by two persons named Kondapa and Venkapa. Kanakdâs, the Kânarese poet, is said to have brought the image of Âdikeśava from the village of Bad near Baṅkâpur. He was a devotee who obtained the village of Dasanakop and much land in adjoining villages as an *inâm* from the Vijayanagar kings. The priests are both Liṅgâyats and Brâhmaṇs, and have an allowance of Rs. 494 for the celebration of the car festival. In the court is a shrine of Bhaṇḍârigiri Svâmi into which are built four finely carved old pillars; other fragments lie about with excellent carving on them. There is a slab at the temple of Kalahasteśvara carved with figures of Śiva and Pârvatî and small ones of Gaṇapati and Kârtikasvâmi, in entire relief: in the same temple the pillars are carved with figures and festoons, the outer wall of the *maṇḍapa* is of mud and small stones, the *śikhara* however is old.

I *b*. **Inscriptions**:—(1) On the east of the temple of Kalahasteśvara on the north of the village, sunk in the earth, 6' 10" above ground by 3' 9½", *Śaka* 1042; (2) a *vîragal* at the same temple, *Śaka* 1204; (3) on the *dhvajastambha* at the same place; (4) one nearly quite covered, in front of the same; (5) on the north side of the temple of Vîrabhadra at the same place are three stones sunk deep in the earth; (6) about twenty yards south-east from Someśvara's temple, one over 6' high by 3' 2" broad, in good preservation except where the villagers have been sharpening their knives, &c., on the edge of it; (7) between this and the temple is another entirely sunk in the earth: it shoud be removed and preserved; (8) west from the same a *vîragal*, 2' 1" broad, an inscription deeply sunk in the earth; (9) at Sangameśvara's shrine is an inscription sunk in a mud platform—not very legible; (10) on three finely carved old pillars in the shrine of Bhandârigiri Svâmi at Lakshmî-Nârâyaṇa's temple are five short inscriptions.

I *b*. 25. **Ingalgondi**, 8 miles south from Koḍ (?). **Inscription** at the temple of Kalleśvara on the bank of the tank, dated *Śaka* 971; and a *mâstikal* on the edge of a small tank in the temple, Bahudhânya.

I *b*. 26. **Nagawand**, 9 miles south by east from Raṭṭihaḷḷi; **inscription** on the bank of the tank, *Śaka* 1042.

II *b*. 27. **Hallur** on the Tungabhadrâ, 10 miles south-east of Raṭṭihaḷḷi (lat. 14° 21′ N., long. 75° 41′ E.), has a temple and an **inscription**.

III. 28. **Bhairavanpad**. This village was the northern limit of Hailûr, formerly called Sindhunagara, the capital of the Sindhu Ballâḷa dynasty, whose *kuladevatâ* is said to have been Bhairava. The great temple was ruined by Tipu Sultân; and the present one built by the Svâmi of Kuḍalgi, to whom the village was granted by Hanmant Gauda, Paligar of Havanur.

Hallur, Harihar, Hampi and Sri Śaila are considered holy places, and the scenery on the Tungabhadrâ at them is said to be fine.

To the west of the village is an **inscription** of the Sindhu Ballâḷa kings.

III. 29. **Kukigeri** or Kirgeri, 9 miles east of Raṭṭihaḷḷi;—temple of Hanumân built by one Konappa Sunkad, a Collector of Customs, who grew rich, about 300 years ago. The roof is supported by 16 pillars.

III. 30. **Sa'tenhalli**, 10 miles W.N.W. of Koḍ and 8 miles south-east from Tiḷivaḷḷi (lat. 14° 35′ N., long. 75° 23′ E.) Temple of Râmaliṅga.

I *b*. **Inscriptions**:—(1) On the south of the temple of Râmaliṅga, *Śaka* 1036: (2) on one of a row of stones on the south of the temple of Râmaliṅga, *Śaka* 1125; (3) a *vîragal* at the temple of Râmaliṅga, *Śaka* 1125; (4) in front of the temple Kallappa on the bank of the Chikkoṇati tank, half a mile from the village, *Śaka* 1064; (5) near the temple of Hari-Hara, *Śaka* 1125; (6) a *vîragal* in a row of stones outside the village, *Śaka* 1125; (7) in the temple of Nârâyaṇa, *Śaka* 1162; (8) standing against the wall on the east of
II *b*. the temple of Hanumanta, *Śaka* 1502.

III. 31. **Kachivi**, 5 miles south by east from Tiḷivaḷḷi.

I *b*. **Inscriptions**:—(1) A *vîragal* in front of the temple of Râmeśvara, *Śaka* 1176;
III. (2) on the south front of the temple of Gaṇappa, *Śaka* 1673.

32. **Yammiganur**, 7 miles south from Tiḷivaḷḷi.

I *b*. **Inscriptions**:—(1) At the temple of Paramesvara, *Śaka* 1070; (2) a *vîragal* lying on the left of the temple of Paramesvara outside the village, *Śaka* 1095; (3) a *vîragal* at the temple of Basavaṇṇa outside the village, *Śaka* 1098.

III. 33. **Kadur**, 3 miles east of Raṭṭhaḷḷi:—temple and **inscription**.

III. 34. **Madak**, 12 miles south from Koḍ (lat. 14° 22′ N., long. 75° 29′ E.) on the borders of Maisur, has a large artificial tank, of which the following account was supplied by Lieutenant-Colonel Playfair, R.E.:—

"The so-called Madak Tank is a legacy to us from the ancient rulers of that part of the country. It was probably a work of the Anagundi kings, who appear to have been great tank-builders; at any rate, they have the credit of most of the fine tanks with which the southern part of the Dhârwâr Collectorate is dotted. In this particular case they failed from errors of construction. The site selected was, apparently, a very favourable one: a considerable river, after passing through an extensive plain, entered a gorge in the hills of no great breadth, which it was comparatively easy to close. This they did, and on a magnificent scale, by an earthen dam, about 800 feet thick at the base and 100 feet in height.. The hills in the neighbourhood still present clear traces of the vast excavations for material, and of the roads by which it was brought to the site, while a fort of considerable pretension on a hill commanding the tank is stated by tradition to have been erected for the protection of the work-people. Not content with the mass of earth thrown up, as an additional precaution they faced it, particularly at the point where it crossed the river, with enormous blocks of stone. The sluices were conceived on a similar magnificent scale. The same principle was adopted as is general throughout the Collectorate, viz., a rectangular masonry channel through the dam, closed with a perforated stone fitted with a wooden stopper; but the tank being large these sluices were in proportion, and where in ordinary practice small stone pillars would carry the platform over the stopper, here the supports, formed of a single stone, weighed about 20 tons each. To the upper sluice a tradition of human sacrifice is attached; it runs as follows: Being the crowning point or finishing touch to this great work, the king and all his courtiers had assembled to witness the erection of the first of the above mentioned monolith pillars, but all the efforts of the workmen were in vain. Day after day passed, still the pillar was obdurate. A rumour became current that the goddess was angry, and that nothing save a human sacrifice would appease her. The beautiful Lakshmi the virgin daughter of the chief Vaddar (or tank-digger) then stepped forward and offered herself, which the brutes accepted, and she was buried alive below the site of the stone, which was then erected without further trouble. I mention this anecdote as curious, and because I believe it founded on fact. The sluice is now a temple and I have been informed that it became so in consequence of this sacrifice.

"The tank was finished and gradually filled, when to the utter discomfiture of its constructors it burst, not through the valley they had so carefully closed, but through the hill-side itself. It is difficult now to ascertain the exact cause. Tradition says that there was a third sluice on the hill where the breach now is; if so, it must have been the waste weir, and utterly insufficient for its purpose as the native weirs generally are. The river in flood, of course, after filling the tank sought an outlet and found it here, but being too small blew it up, and a vast body of water passed over the saddle of the hill in a deep groove with a fall down to the old bed of the river of nearly 100 feet. The result was a chasm which looks as fresh now almost as the day it was made, with sides nearly perpendicular and as if cut with a knife. As the water decreased in volume and fall, and the strata to be cut through became harder, the erosion ceased and a certain quantity of water remained in the tank. Its surplus escapes now over the point where the cutting of the water ceased, and forms a pretty little water-fall. Such is the state we found it in, still, in comparison with the other tanks in the Collectorate, a very large one. The original builders appear, however, to have been thoroughly disheartened, and to have taken no steps to utilize the smaller quantity of stored up water yet left them. They abandoned the whole undertaking, and to our day the unfinished channels and the dam with all its appendages remained overgrown with jungle, the haunt of various wild animals, the main sluice on account of its vast monoliths being still a show place, and the upper one as before mentioned a temple.

"As may be supposed, after the English gained possession of the country, and the value of the irrigation from other tanks became known, the large area of water still held up by this ruined work was looked at covetously, and various schemes were suggested for its utilization; there were difficulties in the way, however, viz:—(1) The lowest of the old native sluices which offered the only channel for drawing water through the enormously thick dam was left, when the breach occurred, just too high above the surface of the tank to be of any value. (2) Any proposition to dam up the chasm where the outlet now is, and so raise the level of the tank sufficiently to use the old sluices, was met not only by the great expense inherent to it, but by the opposition of the Mysore villagers, whose lands lay on the margin of the tank, and would be swamped by any rise in its level; for I omitted to state that the boundary between the Bombay Presidency and Mysore runs along the top of the old dam, so that the tank itself is in Mysore, while the lands below it are in Bombay.

"Owing to the abovenamed difficulties nothing was done until I took the matter in hand when Executive Engineer, Dhârwâr. After long consideration, and abandoning, owing to its difficulty, the plan I first entertained of drawing the water off by a channel through the breach, it occurred to me that if a culvert could be laid below the old sluice the tank could be successfully tapped. This was done under my own immediate supervision, and was a very interesting piece of work, not unattended with danger. The old native sluice had first to be cleared out, as it was filled up with dirt, the accumulation of centuries. Clearing was commenced on both sides not without the opposition of the Mysore people, who at first drove the workmen off and objected to anything being done on their side. When the two parties of workmen had approached each other to within 100 feet, all progress was stopped owing to the stones that supported the roof being found to have fallen in. The sluice appears to have been originally laid on the rocky surface of the valley, then roofed with enormous stones, and the dam built over it. The weight of the 100 feet of earth above had, however, been too great for the covering to bear. The further clearing, then, became a matter of a great danger. The air was almost unbreathable as I have many times myself experienced. When trying to devise a plan for getting on, and in the absence of any miners or men at all skilled in tunnelling, the only plan appeared to be to gently dig over the broken stones and trust to find sounder ones beyond, and thus again get a roof over our heads. This turned out to be the case. Only a few of the covering stones had fallen in, and the earth above them was sufficiently consolidated by time to allow of a passage being dug over. In this way the two parties at length joined, and the old subterranean gallery was opened from end to end (800 feet in all), and the draught through them made the air pleasant enough.

"The culvert below the floor of the old work was then proceeded with, the latter acting as a ventilator as well as roof till the new tunnel was arched in. All went on well enough till towards the centre, where rock of the very hardest nature was met with, which could, as it were, be only scraped away by our tools. Blasting was out of the question with such a ricketty mass of old masonry above, and the remaining work was literally taken out in powder.

"The *rayats*, who had watched our efforts with interest not unmixed with grave doubts as to the water-goddess who had frustrated the original builder, ever allowing any one else to succeed, are now contentedly irrigating their lands with the plentiful stream issuing from the new culvert. A considerable length of canal has been made and more is making, and a very fine expanse of garden land is in course of creation. The sketches annexed (Plates I. and II.) sufficiently illustrate the work without requiring further description. The key to the whole was the tapping the long imprisoned water by the low level tunnel, which, though an insignificant work in England, was not so in that far-off corner of the Bombay Presidency, with no means or appliances but the unskilled cooly with his *pawrah*."

About four hundred years ago the *Pátil* of Mâsur, whose family lived at Pura Tarkeri in the Śimoga *tâlukâ*, had a beautiful daughter called Kenchavâ, whom the king of Anagundi wished to marry; but she objected to him as a Kshatriya, and fled. The Tungabhadrâ River made way for her. Her parents wished to marry her to the *Pâtil* of Isûr, Śikharpur *tâlukâ*, and set out to celebrate the marriage; but passing a temple which stood where now the Madak tank is, she entered it and devoted herself to the god. Her sister was married to the Isûr *Pâtil*, and the Anagundi king made the tank, when the temple was submerged. The rain-fall was so abundant the year that the tank was built, that it was watched lest it should burst. The *talavar* on guard became possessed of Kenchavâ, who told him to inform Mallangauda of Mâsur, that she would not remain any longer where she was, unless a woman in the ninth month of pregnancy were sacrificed to her. The *talavar* said he was afraid to leave the tank, for if it burst while he was away the *Pâtil* would punish him. Kenchavâ, however, promised that the embankment should not break, but if he were long in returning, the water would burst through the hills but not through the *bând*. The *Pâtil*, annoyed at the man leaving his post, had him tied up and punished, and did not offer the sacrifice. Kenchavâ consequently broke through the hill and the embankment as well.

Legend further says that poor people used to go to the tank and beg for a loan of nose and ear-rings to use at marriage ceremonies, and found them on the bank. Once, a man without returning the ornaments went and called Kenchavâ by name, to which she answered. He exclaimed, "Why, they say you are dead, and yet here you answer me." Since then she has been mute.

Twelve years ago a fisherman's tackle got entangled in the roof of the submerged temple. Diving down to disentangle it, he entered the temple and saw a golden image of Kenchavâ. She warned him that if he revealed to any one that she was alive, he would burst a blood-vessel and die. He asked her how he would get away, whereon she pushed him up to the surface. Two years after he went to Harihar and divulged the secret, but died from the bursting of a blood-vessel.

In times of drought the heads of the temples in Śikharpur *tâlukâ*, Maisur, come to this tank with a *tali* or round piece of gold and a nose-ring, which they obtain from the *Pâtil* of Mâsur. They place food on a small raft, and pushing it off into the tank pray to Kenchavâ for rain.

XII.—Jâghirs of Sîrhatti, Lakshmeśvar, Savanur and Jamkhandi.

1. **Lakshmes'var,** 21 miles north-east of Shiggâon and 20 miles north of Karajgi (lat. 15° 7', long. 75° 21'), the ancient Pulikeri, contains a group of extremely interesting tem-
II *b.* ples but "so completely ruined that it is almost impossible to make out their history with anything like certainty." One of them "is of great age, contemporary with the temples of Haralhaḷḷi and Kiruwaṭṭi (Korvatti) and belonging, therefore, most probably, to the thirteenth century."—Fergusson, *Arch.*, *Dharwar and Mysore*, Ph., 48, 49. The principal temples are—(1) that of Someśvaradeva in the south of the town, built of black granite and white stone, and is of very considerable size. Instead of the invariable *liṅga* it contains an image of Śiva riding on Nandî, with Pârvatî behind him. The walls inside and out are decorated with numerous figures,—much of the carving is regarded as illustrative of the *Mahâbhârata*. In the *maṇḍapa* are four lines of columns supporting the roof, the central compartment of which is beautifully carved. It measures about 80′ by 42′. To the west of the temple is a beautiful stone well with an inscription in a small room belonging to it. (2) The temple of Śrî Lakshmîliṅga in the west of the town is also a large one, and
I *b.* the walls are sculptured with mythological figures; near it is a tank. (3) Śaṅkhabasti, an old Jaina temple in the middle of the town, recently repaired with brick. The roof is supported by 36 pillars. (4) Hala-basti, a smaller Jaina temple. (5) The temple of Kodiyellamâ. Beautifully carved stones abound in walls, drains, &c. The *Mâmlatdâr* has saved such as attracted his attention, and built them up in the court of the *kacheri*. (**Surveyed.**)

I *b.* The Kâli Masjid 65′ by 35′ is noted for its chains cut out of stone and beautiful traceries, which are copied as excellent patterns by silversmiths, &c. It is one of the prettiest mosques in the Presidency. It was built in 1617 A.D.

Inscriptions.—These are numerous. Twenty-nine have been collected by the *Mâmlatdâr* in front of the *kacheri*. Two are at the temple of Lakshmîliṅga; three in that of Someśvara; one near the Desâî's well; six at the Saṇkhabasti; two near the Agarkatti Agaśi have been removed to the *kacheri*; one near the Saṇkhatîrtha; one near the Sahasraliṅga temple; and three Persian and Arabic ones are in the mosques. The dates read on some of them are *Śaka* 1354, "Châlukya Vikrama *Saṁvatsara* Sarvajita;" *Śaka* 1168 (a Yâdava inscription); the tenth year of Jagadekamalla, Prabhava *Saṁvatsara*

Thursday, 12th Âshâḍha *Śuddha* (*P. S. and O. C. Ins.* No. 97); two in *Śaka* 890 Vibhava *Saṁvatsara*; two of Sadâśivarâya of Vijayanagar (A.D. 1542-1564); one dated *Śaka* 1469, Plavaṅga *Saṁvatsara*; a *viragal* of *Śaka* 1000, Kaliyukta *Saṁvatsara* Śobhakritu *Saṁvatsara*, *Śaka* 48; in the reign of Tribhuvanamalla, Bhânu *Saṁvatsara*, *Śaka* 27; in the reign of the Yâdava king of Siṁhaṇa (A.D. 1132-1169); Vilambi *Saṁvatsara*, 1460; and one contains the Châlukya genealogy to Jagadekamalla, "the elder brother (?) of Bijala." (*Ind. Ant.*, VII. 101, 111; XI. 156. *J. B. B. R. A. S.*, Vol. IX. p. 329.)

II *b*. 2. **Sirhatti**, 10 miles north-east of Lakshmeśvar (lat. 15° 14′, long. 75° 39′). "The palace at Sirhaṭṭi is, though less magnificent (than that at Vijayanagar), a much more favourable specimen of the style. It is built in stone, and both artistically and constructively is well proportioned and elegant. Though the windows are pointed there are probably no real arches in the building; and the sculptures, though sufficient to authenticate its Hindu origin, are kept so subdued as not to interfere with its Muhammadan outline. It is easy to see that the building is a direct copy of one of the palaces of Bijâpûr, most probably the Ashar Mubârak, of which it is, in fact, little more than a reduced repetition; but it is copied with a degree of taste seldom found in such examples, and therefore more than usually pleasing."—Fergusson, *Arch.*, *Dhar. and Mys.*, Ph. 87, p. 72.

II *b*. 3. **Kundgol**, Jamkhandi, 20 miles south-east from Dhârwâr (lat. 15° 15′, long. 75° 19′). There is a fine old temple, more within the limits of the village of Par than Kundgol; it is built without lime, of highly polished stones, which are dovetailed into one another. The carvings and images on the pillars and roof are well cut, but have been injured by Muhammadans. It was repaired by a former chief in 1808-9, and dedicated to Śiva and Pârvatî. (**Surveyed**.)

III.—BIJÂPUR ZILLA.

I.—Bijâpur Tâlukâ.

Bija'pur, at one time the capital of the Dakhan, is situated about two hundred and forty miles, as the crow flies, to the south-east of Bombay. It is now reached by the Southern Marâtha Railway from its junction with the Great Indian Peninsula Railway at Hotgi, and is fifty-eight and a half miles south of this junction.

Bijâpur suddenly sprung into existence as an important factor in the affairs of the Dakhan, rapidly attained the highest rank among its states, and just as suddenly collapsed. It enjoyed the dignity of a capital, the seat of the 'Adil Shâhis, for two hundred years, and then surrendered its liberty to the overwhelming power of Delhi, and was thenceforth compelled to take the secondary rank of one of its numerous dependencies.

Yûsuf, son of Amurath II., of Antolia, Sultân of Turkey, would have shared the fate his brothers met with on the death of his father had he not been secretly sent away to Persia by his mother. Here he grew up, but, becoming known, was obliged to fly the country. He eventually reached India and found his way to Bidar, where he took service under the minister Mahmud Gavan, who appointed him to the body-guard of the king, Muhammad Shâh. He soon rose in the service and estimation of the latter and was eventually given the command of the guard, afterwards being created Master of the Horse with the title of 'Adil Khân. When the Bidar kingdom became too unwieldy to be governed direct from the capital it was divided into districts with local governors in charge. Yûsuf was so placed in charge of Bijâpur. The power thus put into the hands of these governors soon turned their heads from loyalty to their sovereign to thoughts of self-aggrandisement, and, collecting round them troops and followers who were promised rewards and distinction in the new régime, they soon threw over their allegiance to Bidar and started petty kingships on their own account. Yûsuf was not long in following suit, and established himself King of Bijâpur under the title of Yûsuf 'Adil Shâh in A.D. 1489. He and his descendants continued to hold their own, until, in the reign of Sikandar, Bijâpur was attacked by the Mughal army under Aurangzib, captured, and attached as a new district under the all-absorbing power of Dehli. During this period many stirring and romantic scenes occurred both within and without its walls and in the battlefield. In the city so many hostile elements were thrown together, Shiahs and Sunis, Hindus, Abyssinians, Dakhanis, Turks, Persians, Arabs and other mercenaries, troublesome and restless spirits, ever upon the alert for adventures by which to gain their own respective ends, that it is not surprising that the very streets were often the scenes of bloody conflicts, that the palaces harboured conspirators and assassins, and that at critical times these internal dissensions left them open to the mercy of their enemies, who, like vultures around them, ever sat watching their opportunity of swooping down upon the unfortunate city.

The real building period of Bijâpur did not commence until 'Ali (I.) 'Adil Shâh ascended the *masnad*. He was a great patron of the arts, and welcomed artists and learned men to his capital. One of the first buildings undertaken was the Jami Masjid, which, for simplicity of design, impressive grandeur, and the solemn stillness of its corridors, stands

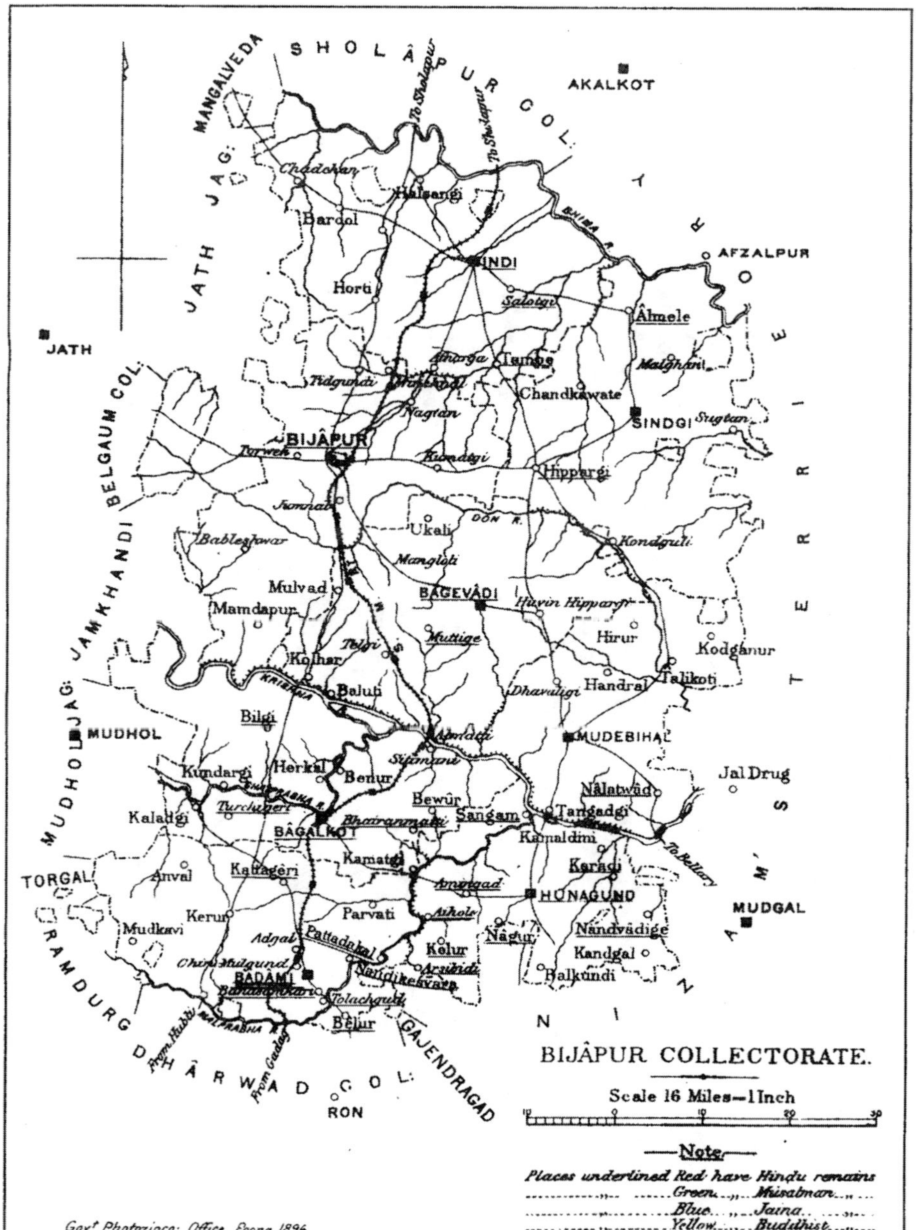
BIJÂPUR COLLECTORATE.
Scale 16 Miles—1 Inch
Note
Places underlined Red have Hindu remains
Green Musalman
Blue Jaina
Yellow Buddhist
Gov! Photozinco: Office, Poona 1896.
SHOLÂPUR COL.
AKALKOT
AFZALPUR
MANGALVEDA
JATH JAG:
JATH
BELGAUM COL:
JAMKHANDI
MUDHOL JAG:
MUDHOL
TORGAL
RAMDURG
DHÂRWAD COL:
RON
GAJENDRAGAD
NIZAM'S TERRITORY
MUDGAL
INDI
SINDGI
BIJÂPUR
BAGEVÂDI
MUDEBIHAL
BÂGALKOT
HUNAGUND
BADÂMI
Halsangi
Bardol
Horti
Almele
Tambe
Chandkawate
Hippargi
Ukali
Mulvad
Mamdapur
Kolhar
Baluti
Bilgi
Hirur
Kodganur
Handral
Talikoti
Jal Drug
Kundargi
Herkal
Benur
Bewûr
Sangam
Tangadgi
Nâlatwâd
Kaladgi
Kamatgi
Anval
Katagêri
Kerur
Parvati
Mudkavi
Karadi
Nandvâdige
Kandgal
Balkundi
Kelur
Pattadakal
Belur
Tolachgud
Nandikesvara
Krishna R.
Bhima R.
Don R.
Malprabha R.
Ghatprabha R.
To Sholapur
To Bellary
From Hubli
From Gadag

unrivalled. It is, too, the best proportioned building in the city. It was after 'Ali 'Adil Shâh, laden with spoils, returned from the great battle of Tâlikot and destruction of
Ia. Vijayanagar, that the walls and fortifications of the city were taken in hand and completed. Portions were allotted to each of his generals and hence the various styles and degrees of finish of the different sections of the same. The 'Adâlat Mahâl, the Sonahri Mahâl, and the first attempts to lead water into the town are ascribed to him.

Ibrâhîm (II.) followed up the good example of his father and continued to adorn the city with some of its most ornate buildings. He raised the elaborate pile of the Ibrâhîm Rauza, the most picturesque group at Bijâpur.

Muhammad, who succeeded him, has left one of the greatest and most wonderful domes the world has seen, over his own tomb, the Gol Gumbaz.

'Ali (II.), who followed, being determined to outdo them all, commenced his own mausoleum on so grand a scale that he had not time to complete it ere his death dispersed the workmen, and it remains a splendid ruin and a lasting monument to his ambition. With this tomb ended, virtually, the building age of Bijâpur. It flourished from the laying of the foundation stone of the Jami Masjid, about 1537, to the death of 'Ali (II.) in 1672, a hundred and thirty-five years. (*Ind. Ant.* VI. 230, VII. 121; *J. B. B. R. A. S.*, part VII. p. 367.) **(Surveyed.)***

For the sake of easy reference the buildings of Bijâpur are here described in classes, *viz.* Mosques, Palaces, Tombs, Tanks, &c. The numbers after each are the numbers by which they are indicated on the accompanying general plan of the city, and the dates in brackets indicate definitely or approximately the time of their erection.

Buildings in the City :—

Ia. (1). The Jami Masjid, 196 (*Cir.* 1537).—This building, the principal mosque in the city, is situated in the middle of the south-east quarter of the town, and stands upon the south side of the road leading from the Allâhpur gate to the citadel. Including the great open courtyard, embraced between its two wings, it occupies the greatest area of any building in Bijâpur—about 54,250 square feet to the bases of the towers at the ends of the wings, beyond which there is a further extension up to the eastern gateway. The main building, the mosque proper, is built across the west end of the great court. The massive square piers, which support the roof, divide the length of the façade into nine bays, and the depth into five, which would give a total of forty-five bays in the body of the mosque; but nine in the centre are taken up by the open space under the great dome, *i. e.*, the four central piers being absent a great square open area is enclosed by the surrounding twelve piers. Over this space, and towering above the flat roof, rises the dome.

IIa. (2). Batula Khân's Masjid, 149.—About three hundred yards further along to the westward of the Jami Masjid, and abutting upon the roadway, stands the gateway to this mosque, but it is now in disuse and is blocked up, and the entrance to the mosque, which stands back behind it to one side, is by a gap on the west side of the gateway. It is now occupied by a small Kânarese school, and the better to convert the building to this purpose, the three front arches have been closed up, a door and two ugly barred windows have been inserted, and the whole façade, save the cornice and parapet, white-washed.

* For a fuller account with translations of inscriptions see *Notes on the Buildings and other Antiquarian Remains of Bijâpur*, Government of Bombay Selection No. CCXLV.—New Series.

III. (3). Kanâthi Masjid, 145.—Still further west of this last, and standing out into the road, is a little mosque called the Kanâthi Masjid. There is nothing remarkable about it, but the story of its origin shows what sanctity, in Muhammadan eyes, surrounds their mosques. Tradition records that a certain man wished to build a mosque here, but the authorities objected as the site was in the main road. The man, under pretence of performing a marriage ceremony, enclosed the space with *kanâths* or screens, and under cover of these erected the mosque. The mosque once built could not be destroyed, not even by the king, and it has so remained under the name of the Kanâthi Masjid. There are some curious patterns in raised stucco along the parapet of the wall, and on the outside walls of the buildings is some very flat arching.

III. (4). The Haidariah Masjid, 146 (1583).—This mosque stands on the north side of the road close to the last, in a little enclosure which is entered through a small porch and doorway. The mosque was built, we are told, by an inscription over the entrance doorway, by Haidar Khân *bin* Jamil in the year A.H. 991 (A.D. 1583), during the reign of Ibrâhîm II. Haidar Khân was one of Ibrâhîm's generals who also built the Haidar or Upli Burj, and who took sides in the quarrel and subsequent tumult between the adherents of Hamid Khân and Ikhlâs Khân. Save for its connection, through the inscription, with a noted character in Bijâpur story, the mosque has nothing to make it worthy of attention; it was probably Haidar Khân's own household chapel and was possibly attached to his own dwelling which may have stood near here. It is a small plain plastered and white-washed mosque, with a three-arched façade, and surmounted with a plain dome.

IIa. (5). Yûsuf's Old Jami Masjid, 124 (1512).—This is the oldest building in the city, and is for that reason interesting, although, at present, one of the most insignificant structures within the walls. An inscription over the entrance doorway to the courtyard tells us it was built by one Asen Beg in A.H. 918 (A.D. 1512) during the time of Sultân Mahmud Shâh of Bidar.

Ia. (6). 'Ali Shâhid Pir's Masjid, 128.—This is a small but very peculiar mosque in the fields to the south of the Mihtari Mahâl. Its peculiarity lies in its singular wagon-vaulted roof which covers the whole building, and which, with the exception of a smaller and more rudely constructed mosque a short distance to the west of this one, and, perhaps the Chhotâ 'Asâr, is not found elsewhere in Bijâpur.

This mosque is most deserving of special attention and conservation.

III. Beside the mosque is the insignificant-looking tomb of Hazarat Sayyid 'Ali Shâhid, after whom the mosque is named. He was killed in battle fighting against infidels, and hence became a *shâhid* or martyr, and the mosque is said to have been built in his honour by 'Ali II.

IIa. (7). Mustafâ Khân's Mosque, 137 (*Cir.* 1600).—About five hundred yards to the east of the citadel, in the fields, are the mosque and palace of Mustafâ Khân. The mosque is a very lofty substantially built edifice. The front has three tall arches, the central one being very much wider than the side ones, and, being almost devoid of ornament, the façade has rather a bald appearance. A deep heavy cornice overhangs the front, and the octagonal buttresses, which were to carry the minarets, flank the front of the building. The minarets have never been built. The large dome is stilted by the introduction between it and the flat roof, as in the Jami mosque, of a second storey with a row of arched recesses on each face.

II *b*(?). (8). Nâu Gumbaz, 138.—The Nâu Gumbaz or Khawâs Khân ki Masjid is a very neat and compact little building situated in what was once the grounds of Khawas Khân's palace, about two hundred yards to the north-east of Mustafâ Khân's mosque. The peculiarity of this mosque is its roofing which is carried out more on the lines of the Ahmadâbâd and Gujarât buildings than on those of the rest of the edifices at Bijâpur. This multiple doming, so common in Gujarât, is quite a foreign feature at Bijâpur, and so much so that this unusual circumstance has given it the name by which it is best known, the Nâu Gumbaz, or "nine-domed" mosque.

I*a*. (9). The Andu Masjid, 92 (1608).—The mosque known by the name of the Andu Masjid stands on the east side of the road running from the citadel to the Lânda Qasâb bastion, and not far from the former. It is a two-storeyed building, but not a two-storeyed mosque, as the latter occupies the upper floor only, the lower or ground floor being a hall or rest-house.

I*a*. (10). The Zanjiri, or Malika Jahân Begam's Mosque, 34 (1587.)—The building known as the Zanjiri Masjid or Malika Jahân Begam's Mosque is situated among the trees immediately to the west of the Sât Manzli, just outside the citadel walls. It is an exceedingly neat mosque, with a well proportioned cornice and a particularly rich façade.

II*b*. (11). The Bukhâri Masjid, 293.—This small mosque, standing upon the roadside to the north of the citadel, had been converted into a general post and telegraph office for Bijâpur but is now vacated a new office having been built. Little is known about the origin of the name given to it, but it is possibly so called after some Bukhâran subject who sojourned in the city and built the mosque. It is a very neat, carefully finished little building, and has a well designed cornice whose brackets are beautifully carved. There is some pretty stucco work about the arches within. The mosque has been, or was intended to be, enclosed within a courtyard, part of which, with its outer arcade and gateway, still stands before it.

I*a*. (12.) The Zamrud Masjid, 6.—About sixty or seventy yards to the north of the Bukhâri Masjid, and between it and Mâlik Sandal's mosque and tomb, stands, upon a high platform, a miniature mosque, only twelve feet square. It is well built and quite unique in being the smallest mosque in Bijâpur.

II*a*. (13). Karîm-ud-din's Mosque in the Citadel, 281 (1320).—In the citadel, not far from the south-east corner of the Chini Mahâl, now Government offices, is one of the earliest mosques in Bijâpur. It is wholly made up of pillars, beams, and cornices taken from older Hindu shrines, the entrance porch being, in fact, part of a Hindu temple *in situ*—it is the hall or *maṇḍapa*, with its pillars and niches, but wanting part of its roof. The shrine, which was built on to this hall, on the west, has been entirely cleared away, and a through passage thus gained to the courtyard within. The inner doorway, with perforated screen panels on either side of it, has been inserted by the Muhammadans, and the space between it and the next opening was the antechamber to the shrine of the original temple. An examination of the ends of the walls here will show how the shrine has been broken away.

Across the west side of the courtyard is the mosque, made up of pillars of all patterns and heights, brought to one uniform level with superimposed pieces of others, and over these are laid the cross-beams and slabs forming the roof. The central portion of the mosque has been raised by pillars perched upon the lower ones, thus admitting more light and air into the body of the building. This construction is similar to that carried out in the Ahmadâbâd and Gujarát mosques, and, with the exception of another old converted mosque like this near the 'Adâlat Mahâl, it is the only example of that style in Bijâpur. In the courtyard is a mound which is said to be the place of burial of several Muhammadans who, in a *mêlée* with the Hindus, fell fighting for their faith, when the former first settled here.

II *a*. (14). **Old Mosque**, 294 (*Cir.* 1300).—This mosque, like the last, is a composition of rifled pillars, beams, cornices, &c., from Hindu temples. It is situated close to the road which runs through the Arg-qil'a, or citadel, from north to south, and on the west side of the 'Adâlat Mahâl. The arrangement is very simple and it is very much smaller than Karîm-ud-din's mosque.

I *a*. (15). **The Makkâ Masjid**, 285 (*Cir.* 1669).—In the south-east corner of the Arg-qil'a, shut in between high walls, is an exceedingly neat little mosque known as the Makkâ Masjid. The great heavy-looking towers or minarets, standing out before it, and from which the call to prayer was cried, are, without doubt, the only remaining portions of a very early mosque. On the east side of the enclosure is buried a *pîr* or saint, who is said to have built a mosque here about the end of the thirteenth century. It is possible that this was so, and that the towers are the remnants of it, the mosque itself, having become a ruin, being rebuilt upon the same site in later times as we have it now.

II *a*. (16). **The Chinch Diddi Masjid**, 288.—This is perched upon a bastion at the south-east corner of the citadel, and overlooks the 'Asâr Mahâl and the town between it and the Jami Masjid. It is a very plain building with little about it of interest save the remains of some wall painting within, which in itself is very poor and weak, and has more the appearance of the designs of common wall-paper.

III. (17). **The Anand Mahâl Mosque**, 276.—This is a very small plain building now forming part of the out-houses at the back of the Ânand Mahâl and fitted with doors and windows to suit its new character.

II *a*. (18). **Ibrâhîm's (I.) Jami Masjid**, 72 (*Cir.* 1551).—This mosque, also called the Dâtri ki Masjid, is known, too, as 'Ali's (I.) old Jami Masjid, probably so called when it was abandoned for the great Jami Masjid commenced by that king. It is situated in the fields about three hundred yards to the south-west of the Andu Masjid. It is one of the old-fashioned early mosques, of which there are a few other examples in Bijâpur, with brick and mortar minarets, not only over the corners of the building, but also over the central piers. A curious feature connected with this mosque is that it has no dome, nor has it ever had one, the roof being chunamed over in one flat terrace.

IIa. (19). Ikhlâs Khân's Mosque, 253 (*Cir.* 1560).—This mosque is situated about three hundred yards west of the Fath Gate. It is now very much dilapidated, but what is left shows us at a glance that, though small, it was originally a very ornate building. It is constructed upon the old lines before Ibrâhîm II. inaugurated the more elaborate style of well dressed and decorated cut-stone building.

IIa. (20). The Chhotâ 'Asâr Mosque, 14.—This is a small mosque about two hundred and fifty yards to the east of the Dakhani Idgâh, remarkable for the abundance of rich ornament in stucco which covers the walls, ceiling, and part of the façade; otherwise there is little worth note about the mosque. It has a very flat wagon-vaulted ceiling, a kind often met with in Bijâpur, but nothing like that in 'Ali Shâhid Pir's mosque.

III. (21). The Dakhani Idgâh, 12 (1538).—This building being, as all *idgâhs* are, practically a short length of walling flanked by *minârs* or bastions, is one of the ugliest buildings in the city. It is placed upon high ground in the west of the city not far from the last mosque.

IIa. (22). The Rangi Masjid, 216.—About three hundred yards east of the hamlet of Shâhapet, amongst ruined buildings, thickly overgrown with prickly pear and the wild custard apple, is a small mosque known as the 'Rangi Masjid,' and so called on account of the traces of some painted decoration which embellished its walls and ceiling.

III. (23). Mosque, 2.—This is a small, rough, and coarsely built mosque behind (north of) the 'Ali (II.) Rauza, and of no consequence. It has a wagon-vaulted roof. Before it was a tomb (?), but this has been broken down of late, and the stones removed by the owner of the field in which it is.

III. (24). Mosque, 3.—A small mosque about eighteen feet square, with a one-arched front, standing a little way to the north-west of the last. It has two *minârs*, is very plain, but fairly perfect; and out in front of it stands, on a high basement, a cut-stone tomb which has been split in two by a *nim* tree that has grown through it.

III. (25) Mosque, 4.—This mosque is not now of very much account, though what remains of its plaster decoration both inside and out shows that it was a very neatly finished building. It is now in a very dirty state, having been used for living in, and for this object rubble partition walls have been built up within. It is not far from the last two buildings, being about a hundred yards north-west of the 'Ali (II.) Rauza.

III. (26) Mosque, 7.—This small mosque, in the northern part of the new bazâr, has been converted into a Hindu temple in which is placed the *linga* and Nandi with a snake stone. Round the whole has been built an enclosing wall. This building is of no account.

III. (27) Mosque, 11.—This is a small strongly built mosque close under the west side of the Haidar bastion or Upari (or Upli) Burj. It is in fair preservation but of little architectural merit. It is now used by a family who have taken up their quarters in one corner of it.

III. (28) Mosque, 13.—A small substantially built mosque in good condition situated in a hollow, a little way to the south of the Dakhani Idgâh. Its parapet and cornice have been damaged, only the brackets of the latter remaining. Of no particular interest.

III. (29) Mosque, 15.—A small mosque, fairly well built, but of no merit, about one hundred and fifty yards east of the Chhotâ 'Asâr. The design of the bracketting under the cornice is slightly different from the usual patterns.

III. (30) Mosque, 17.—A small mosque near the tomb of Sikandar 'Adil Shâh with its north-east corner broken down. Of no account.

III. (31) Mosque, 18.—A small stone mosque of no particular merit with six brick and plaster *minârs.* It is known as the Fath Masjid.

III. (32) Mosque, 19.—Known as the Ghâs Mandi Masjid, and an insignificant little place.

II *b*. (33) Mosque, 21.—A small mosque at the back of the Chând Bâori and so called the Chând Bâorî ki Masjid. It has two large corner *minârs* and six smaller ones. The building is in good repair, is a fair specimen of its class, and should be cared for.

III. (34) Mosque, 54.—A small mosque of little account. There is an inscription in plaster over the *mehrâb* and there are some good plaster discs on the front of the mosque, and on the face of the *minâr* buttresses.

III. (35) Mosque, 60.—A small mosque of no account: now used as a stable.

III. (36) Mosque, 62.—A small mosque with one *minâr*, of no merit, used as a stable.

III. (37) Mosque, 66.—A small mosque of no consequence.

III. (38) Mosque, 68.—A very small mosque of no account.

III. (39) Mosque, 70.—Another very small mosque of little interest, with four *minârs* standing.

III. (40) Mosque, 73.—A small white-washed *masjid* having a complete cornice, with geometric patterns carved in low relief on the under sides of the cornice slabs, but much obscured by frequent application of white-wash. Nothing of particular interest about the mosque.

III. (41) Mosque, 74.—A small plain mosque of little account occupied by some Muhammadans as a dwelling. In the *mehrâb* is an inscription, the upper part of which tells us the mosque was built by Malik Ṣandal.

III. (42) Mosque, 84.—A small partly damaged stone mosque of no account.

III. (43) Mosque, 85.—A small mosque converted into a police *chauki*.

III. (44) Mosque, 88.—A small *masjid* with one broad low arch in front: of no account.

III. (45) Mosque, 90.—A small plain mosque with short brick *minârs*: of no interest.

III. (46) Mosque, 95.—Ruins of a small insignificant mosque.

III. (47) Mosque, 96.—A small mosque of no account; used to store grass in.

III. (48) Mosque, 97.—A small mosque of no consequence, and used like the last to store grass and hay in.

III. (49) M o s q u e, 99.—A small mosque of not much account and greatly damaged. It has a three-arched façade, and most of the plaster with which it was coated, both inside and out, has fallen away.

III. (50) M o s q u e, 101.—This is a small clean-looking plastered mosque with one large arch in the façade. It has brick and plaster *minârs* and *kanguras.*

III. (51) M o s q u e, 102.—A small mosque of no account.

III. (52) M o s q u e, 103.—A small mosque with four small blackstone tombs of females in front of it. The building is of no interest.

III. (53) M o s q u e, 107.—Of no importance.

III. (54) M o s q u e, 109.—An ordinary mosque with a three-arched façade, plastered within, and with little ornament. It has a deep cornice, but much damaged, and a row of plastered *kanguras* along the roof line.

III. (55) M o s q u e, 111.—A small damaged mosque of no account.

III. (56) M o s q u e, 112.—A small *masjid* of little account called Shâh Shâhid ki Masjid.

III. (57) M o s q u e, 113.—This mosque is situated in the corner between the roads leading to the Jami Masjid and 'Asâr Mahâl from the citadel gate. It is not of very much account, but from its position might be cleaned out and kept so. The vaulting of the roof is peculiar and looks antiquated, and is carried out in the same style as that of the tomb of 'Ali I. in the south-west corner of the city. The *minârs* are short ball-topped pillars rising but little above the roof.

III. (58) M o s q u e, 117.—This mosque, which was originally a fairly well finished building, stands close behind the Mihtari Mahâl mosque with so little space between the two that it is very evident it was built before the latter, as it would never, otherwise, have been built so close up behind another mosque. The masonry, which has been plastered, is not nearly so good as that of the Mihtari Mahâl buildings adjacent to it.

III. (59) M o s q u e, 119.—This is called Nazir Husain Sâheb ki Masjid. It is a small mosque with two short round chimney-like *minârs* of brick and plaster-work connected by a row of *kanguras.* One large single arch spans the front, over which projects a deep but much damaged cornice. The only ornament is a little plaster decoration around the little niches inside the *mehrâb.*

III. (60) M o s q u e, 112.—A small mosque of no account.

III. (61) M o s q u e, 126.—A small mosque very like No. 113 and vaulted in the same manner. The cornice is very plain and shallow and hardly dips at all. The central ceiling is worked in plaster into radiating spiral ribs. The *mehrâb* appears to have had painted letters upon the front of it.

III. (62) M o s q u e, 129.—A small mosque of little interest, with a much broken cornice, and plastered within and without.

III. (63) Mosque, 130.—A small mosque behind 'Ali Shâhid Pîr's mosque and, like it, wagon-vaulted, but it is very much smaller and more roughly built; in fact it looks like an experimental structure where the peculiar vaulting introduced into 'Ali Shâhid Pîr's mosque was first tried. It is of no account.

III. (64) Mosque, 131.—Hamza Husaini ki Masjid. This is a very plain-looking building with its central arch similar in outline to those of Yûsuf's old Jami Masjid, and on the roof, straight above its apex, and breaking the continuity of the *kanguras*, is a small *chhattri* with a dome similar to those of the corner ones above Yûsuf's old Jami Masjid.

III. (65) Mosque, 132.—Called Shâhzâdi Sâheb ki Masjid. This is a small stone building with two plain little thin octagonal *minârs*, surmounted with ball tops, above the forward corners of the roof, and smaller ones over the two back corners. The façade arches, which have a distinct turn-up at the crowns after the ogee type, have some very good plaster-work round their crowns. The interior of the mosque is vaulted like No. 113 and the tomb of 'Ali I. The arch springings and those of the *mehrâb* arch are on the same level.

III. (66) Out in front of this mosque are the ruins of a *mahâl*, and before this again is a laid-out garden and graveyard, in the centre of which is a high square masonry platform. Upon this an octagonal pavilion was to have been raised over three graves, but only the beginning of the basement and piers was accomplished.

III. (67) Mosque, 135.—An old rubble built mosque of not much account. The arches are of the very straight-lined style used in Yûsuf's old Jami Masjid and in mosque 131.

III. (68) Mosque, 144.—A small mosque of no account.

III. (69) Mosque, 153.—Munshi Âmin Sâheb ki Masjid, of no particular interest.

III. (70) Mosque, 154.—Nâgar Bâorî Wâllâ ki Masjid. This is a well built mosque of cut-stone, with the courses of the masonry, as a rule, level and regular. The *minârs* have octagonal shafts; the cornice slabs have been removed but the brackets, which are fine heavy substantial ones, remain. Along under the cornice, between each pair of brackets, is a shallow niche or panel holding a censer and chain. There are two end arches in the building, one each in the south and north end walls; the interior is vaulted like the tomb of 'Ali I. Close beside it is the Nâgar Bâorî which is used to irrigate the surrounding gardens.

III. (71) Mosque, 155.—A badly built mosque, in ruins. In front of it, on the east, is a partly built twelve-sided tomb, the piers being carried up as far as the springing line of the arches. Within this are two ruined graves.

III. (72) Mosque, 161.—The Kâli Masjid is a well built plain mosque standing on the north side of the main road running past the Jami Masjid and not far from the latter. There is nothing of interest about the mosque itself, but in a room attached to it is kept a *panjâ* called "Husain Alam" which is set up at the *Muharram*. It is said to be of old workmanship; it certainly is a splendid piece of perforated metal-work, the perforations leaving an interlaced Persian inscription. It is said to be made of an alloy composed of five metals with gold and silver among them.

III. (73) Mosque, 162.—Small ruined mosque of no account.

III. (74) Mosque, 165.—An old mosque converted into a dwelling.

III. (75) Mosque, 166.—Ibrâhîm Bodâd Masjid. A small whitewashed insignificant mosque.

III. (76) Mosque, 169.—A very small mosque of no account.

III. (77) Mosque, 175.—Called the Gatch Mahâl Masjid. This is a plain substantially built mosque in very fair condition. The *minârs* and *kanguras* are very plain; a neat string course, carrying a row of little balls or drops, runs round the sides and back.

III. (78) Pâr Khân's Masjid, 181.—A neat little mosque with two slender *minârs* and a good but damaged cornice. Of the three arches of the façade the central one is cusped and between the brackets under the cornice, as in Malika Jahân's mosque, are niches with the censer and chain. A gateway with two *minârs*, facing the road and at right angles to the mosque, likens the buildings in arrangement to the Mihtari Mahâl and Bâtula Khân's mosque, and the corbelling of the roof inside this gateway is on the same principle as in the former. The mosque is said to have been built by Pâr Khân, a Pathân.

II *b*. (79) Dhâi Wâdi Masjid, 182.—This mosque is situated between Pâr Khân's mosque and the Allâhpur Gate. Its minarets, only one of which now rises above the roof, are of a different style to any others in the city. Their plan is what might be called an octofoil, that is, it is bounded by eight convex curves, so that in elevation the minaret has something the appearance of a clustered column with narrow horizontal fillets binding it at intervals. The pendentives inside are rather well designed, and those in the central bay are prettily ornamented. On the façade are some good plaster medallions containing interwoven Persian or Arabic letters, and other ornament decorates the crowns of the arches. The cornice is in fair preservation but the slabs are damaged.

III. (80) Mosque, 187.—Small mosque whose façade is spanned by a single arch, but of no account.

III. (81) Mosque, 199.—A small mosque of no account.

III. (82) Mosque, 203.—This is an ordinary looking mosque built on a high plinth and standing out before the 'Adâlat Mahâl or Collector's residence. Instead of the regular *minârs* it had little ornamental finials above the corners of the roof, some of the back ones alone remaining. The building appears to be of very late workmanship.

III. (83) Mosque, 206.—A small mosque partly ruined beside the first milestone on the new road, but of no interest.

III. (84) Mosque, 207.—This small mosque was, in its day, a very ornamental one, but it is now sadly dilapidated. The façade, *kanguras*, and *minârs*, have been covered with delicate stucco ornament, the *kanguras*, themselves, being of a more ornamental style than elsewhere. There is not the usual sunk *mehrâb*, but two small niches, with gable tops, in the central panel of the back wall. The forward central dome of the ceiling, which is fluted, has its ribs decorated with ornament in each flute. There appears to be an inscription above the *mehrâb* buried beneath the plaster.

III. (85) Ali Razza's Masjid, 210.—This is a neat-looking mosque, the body of which is built of good cut-stone, with its surface well dressed. The central arch of the three in the façade is slightly wider than the side ones. Although the stone-work is so well dressed, yet there is the usual disregard of all rules for laying the masonry in level courses and the patch-work way in which even the arch rings are built up by corbelling forward, and the dressing of the stones to the nearest straight-sided figure, is remarkable.

The building, beyond the cornice, seems not to have been finished, but a square block with a very high stilted dome of brick masonry would appear to have been added at some subsequent time. The mosque has a neat good cornice with the censer and chain ornament between the brackets, and beneath these runs a band of panelling with various designs in surface carving. The manner in which the top of the flanking buttresses are corbelled out to give a greater area for the base of the *minârs* is peculiar.

III. (86) Mosque, 212—This is a small mosque with a three-arched façade, but of not much account. The interior is like that of 207. Wings have been built forward apparently with the intention of extending the front, before which is an enclosed courtyard with a gateway in the north wall.

III. (87) Mosque, 213.—This a plain-looking mosque but it has some very prettily designed pendentives between the arches within. These spread out fanlike, deeply fluted between the radiating ribs, and scolloped round the upper edge where they meet the overhanging octagon, under the corner of which they arch forward from the pier as supports. All the arches are of the *ogee* type, while the piers are all octagonal. The spandrils of the arches are everywhere decorated with plaster medallions containing interlaced Arabic letters.

III. (88) Mosque, 217.—A small ruined mosque of no account.

III. (89) Mosque, 218.—A small mosque of not much interest and vaulted within like No. 113. There is a well built tank beside this.

III. (90) Mosque, 221.—A small mosque with a good solid-looking cornice in fair condition. The front arches are rather small and low. Beside the usual corner *minârs* there were others, though smaller, over the central piers of the façade arches. In front of the mosque is a square masonry tank.

III. (91) Mosque, 229.—This is a well built stone mosque, with a plain cornice and *minârs* similar in style to those of No. 207, but the façade is much damaged. The *kanguras* are rather ornamental and the central arch is cusped or feathered. Above the mosque rise four *minârs*, one at each corner, and two over the *mehrâb*.

III. (92) Mosque, 230.—A small mosque of no particular interest domed in the same manner as No. 113.

III. (93) Mosque, 231.—This is a substantial mosque vaulted in the same manner as Bâtula Khân's mosque, No. 149, the central dome being decorated with spiral ribbing. The *minâr* arches are slightly ogee in outline. Its cornice, which was rather pretty, is greatly damaged, and the whole of the north *minârs*, with portion of the end wall, has gone. Ornamented medallions occupy the spandrils of the arches.

III. (94) Mosque, 234.—A small ruined mosque of no account, like No. 113.

III. (95) Mosque, 235.—A small mosque of no particular interest.

III. (96) Mosque, 236.—A small plain mosque of no interest with a vaulted roof similar in style to that of the Chhotâ Asâr, No. 14.

III. (97) Mosque, 237.—This is but part of a mosque—the façade and forward bays—the back wall not having been built above its plinth. It goes by the name of the "Kâbuta-khâna." Out before it was a small square tank, and the whole was enclosed by a low well built wall.

III. (98) Mosque, 238.—A small mosque with a single arch façade, with a *minâr* rising above each of its four corners and two above the *mehrâb*.

III. (99) Mosque, 240.—A ruined mosque of no account.

III. (100) Mosque, 241.—A small mosque with a three-arched façade, the central arch being larger than the side ones, but of no interest.

III. (101) Mosque, 242.—A small mosque of little account, arranged inside like No. 113.

III. (102) Bashir Bâori ki Masjid, 243.—A mosque with a three-arched façade, of no account.

III. (103) Mosque, 248.—Ruins of a mosque.

III. (104) Mosque, 250.—A small mosque with a single-arched front, of no interest.

III. (105) Mosque, 252.—A small mosque of no interest.

I*a*. (106) Mosque, 257.—This is described with the Gol Gumbaz, to which it is attached.

III. (107) Mosque, 261.—This is a neat little mosque vaulted like No. 113. There are slender *minârs* above the corners and two over the central arch piers. The cornice is plain but perfect. Over the *mehrâb* was originally an inscription stone, but it has been taken out.

III. (108) Mosque, 262.—A very small mosque with a one-arched front, and four small *minârs* over the corners; of two that rose above the *mehrâb* recess one remains.

III. (109) Mosque, 263.—This is a curious little mosque situated between the Bari Khudan and New Bazârs. The façade is pierced with three very low small arches. The walls in the south end of the mosque, with the *mehrâb* recess, are covered with little niches.

A doorway leads out through the north bay of the back wall, and there are two cisterns in the north end with a small one-and-a-quarter inch pipe leading into them from the north-east corner.

III. (110) Mosque, 265.—A plain-looking mosque, not far from the Sunda Burj, with the front arches built up and a door inserted, thus converting it into a store for field produce.

III. (111) Mosque, 267.—This is a very primitive-looking mosque. Two heavy-looking wings, each pierced with a single pointed window, flank the one single central arched entrance, above which is a rough cornice. The masonry façade rises considerably above the cornice and is brought to the same level as the tops of the wings. Inside, these two wings have been partitioned off so as to convert the mosque into a dwelling, and as such it is now used. There is no *mehrâb* recess in the back wall, but a little niche, about three feet off the ground, was probably used as such. On either side of this, staircases lead up through the thickness of the back wall to the roof. Before this building is a tank with a platform beside it on which are the tombs of two *pîrs*, another *pîr's* tomb being near the south-east corner of the tank.

III. (112) Mosque, 269.—A small mosque with a plastered façade much like those round abount the Rangi Masjid, No. 216, but of no account.

III. (113) The Ânand Mahâl, 273 (A.D. 1589).—This, the most conspicuous palace in the citadel, with a particularly fine large open hall, has been converted into a residence for the Judge and First Assistant Collector of the district. Its very imposing façade was never finished, it having been the intention of the builders to continue the arching further along on both sides of the present three arches. The appearance of the building has suffered very considerably from the new additions, and its former comeliness has been improved away. It is said to have been built by Ibrâhîm II. in A.D. 1589. It is difficult to say which was the finer palace of the two, this, or the Gagan Mahâl beside it. When in use the latter had the advantage of displaying a great amount of painted and gilded wood-work, of which the first floor and the balconies were constructed. The Ânand Mahâl, or Palace of Delight, was probably the king's residence, containing his private apartments, whilst the Gagan Mâhal was the great Darbâr or Audience Hall where public business was transacted. Immediately behind the Ânand Mahâl, and connected with it by a flying arch, constructed by the Public Works Department, are some small buildings, the nearest being a plain little mosque with two inscriptions in its *mehrâb*. This was no doubt a kind of private chapel. In the next room to this is the station library.

Ia. (114) The Gagan Mahâl, 274 (A.D. 1561).—The Gagan Mahâl, or Hall of Assembly, a little to the west of the last, is notable for the immense arch which, with two tall narrow ones flanking it, forms its façade. Its construction is ascribed to 'Ali (I.) 'Adil Shâh, when it was originally intended to serve the twofold purpose of a royal residence and a council chamber. The private apartments were above the great Hall of Assembly on the first floor which was supported in front by two massive wooden pillars. Projecting above were probably balconies from which the ladies of the royal household could see, through the suspended screens, all that was going on below. Staircases ascend to these upper apartments through the thickness of the back wall, and one stairway descends to the out-houses and kitchens on the west of the palace.

The façade now stands out alone from the rest of the building, the cross arches and vaulted roofing, which connected it with the main block, having fallen. This was probably due to the sinking of the back wall, and consequent canting over of the building, when the façade arches refusing to yield, the two parted company, with the result that the intermediate ceiling and transverse arches fell. In the Sangat Mahâl at Torweh, four miles west of Bijâpur, we have a duplicate of this building, though not quite so large, the roof of which is in great part remaining, and here may be studied the manner in which the Gagan Mahâl was roofed over. All the timber work, which must have been very valuable, was cleared away by the Marâṭhâs, the beams and brackets being ruthlessly torn from the walls.

The main feature of this palace is its great central arch which has a span of 60 feet 9 inches. It was desirable, of course, to have a clear open front before the Darbâr Hall, unobstructed by piers or masonry of any kind, so that the king and his nobles could have an uninterrupted view of the assemblage without, and also witness tournaments and duels that appear to have frequently taken place on the sward before the hall. To accomplish this the architect made his span equal to the length of the front of the hall, but, unfortunately, the result is not pleasing. He seems to have forgotten the height of the building. when he determined upon this great span, and the consequence is an unwieldy arch, out of all good proportion, and much too low for its width. It should have been at least one-third, or better, half as high again, in which case the narrow side arches would have been divided each into two arches one over the other, the second starting from the first floor. Many a stirring scene took place here, and it was on the green sward before the palace that Colonel Meadows Taylor in his delightful story "A Noble Queen" makes the deadly encounter take place between the Abyssinian and the Dakhani. It was within this hall that the glory of the 'Adil Shâhis departed for ever, when Aurangzib, after his capture of the city, commanded its unfortunate king, Sikandar, the last of his line, to appear before him in silver chains, while at the same time he received the submission of its nobles.

Ia. (115) The Sât Manzli, 278 (A.D. 1583).—The pile of apartments known as the Sât Manzli, or seven storeys, stands a little way to the south-west of the Gagan Mahâl, at the corner of a range of buildings enclosing a quadrangle, and called the Granary. At present it rises to a height of five storeys, 97 feet over all, but a narrow stair ascends from the fifth to a sixth which does not now exist. It is probable there was one still higher than this again, or perhaps a roof terrace, but it must have been very small, for the different storeys diminish in area as they ascend. It is said to have been built by Ibrâhîm II. in 1583 as a palace, but, if it was even used as such, it must have been far more extensive than it is now, for its accommodation is very restricted. It certainly extended a little way further on the south side and still further along the walls on the north. One peculiar feature of this class of buildings is the number of water pipes and cisterns about them, such as are found at Mubârak Khân's Mahâl in the south-east of the city, and the water pavilions at Kumatgi. Here we have cisterns on the different floors, and like those the walls were subsequently painted with figures and other ornament. Traces of two of the figures still remain on the north wall of the first floor, in which a lively imagination has detected the outlines of the portrait of Rambhâ, the favourite of Muhammad, and the Sultân himself. The walls are said to have been beautifully gilded, until the Râjâ of Sâtârâ ordered the precious veneer to be scraped off, thinking thereby to reap a veritable golden harvest, but, the Muhammadans resentfully remark that he got naught but dust for his pains. As with the Gagan Mahâl all the wood-work has been carried away. It is certainly by no means a handsome-looking building now, but there can be no doubt that the richly carved window-frames, brackets, screens, and weather boards, when they existed, added greatly to enhance its general effect.

I*a*. Immediately in front of the Sât Manzli, on the north, is a neat little structure, standing alone, the use of which is not very apparent. It was not unlikely a fountain or water pavilion standing in the middle of a reservoir, since filled up, and thus similar to those at Kumatgi and Mubârak Khân's Mahâl, but more ornate. Its finish and general workmanship are much like that of the little ruined pavilion in front of the 'Arash Mahâl. The Hindus have a belief among them that it is a *ratha* having its wheels buried in the ground below; but it is only a slight resemblance to such that has started this idea. There is a very similar edifice, though not quite so fine or so large, in the fields, a short distance to the north-east of Mustafâ Khân's mosque.

III. (116) The 'Adâlat Mahâl, 295.—The 'Adâlat Mahâl or Hall of Justice is now the residence of the Collector. There is nothing about it worth notice. It has been extensively rebuilt and added to, so that little of the original walls of the old ruin can be distinguished from the new work. Beside it, serving now as out-houses, is what was once the Suraj Mahâl, and beneath these are extensive under-ground vaults.

III. (117) The 'Arash Mahâl, 272.—Like the last, this is also a converted building, and is now the Civil Surgeon's residence. It is on the east of the 'Adâlat Mahâl
II*a*. Standing out before it, on one of the bastions of the old citadel wall, are the remains of a small pavilion. This was originally a little garden house, or pleasure resort, and beneath it ran the moat which divided it from the plain without the walls.

III. (118) The Chini Mahâl, and Granary, 279.—The great quadrangle, together with the Chini Mahâl at its south end, of which the Sât Manzli forms the north-west corner, has been known as the Granary, which is altogether a misnomer. The Chini Mahâl, called so from the amount of broken china found about there, was at one time a very fine building. It had a great lofty open verandah or hall in front between its two wings, and in this respect was somewhat similar to the Gagan Mahâl. Within is a splendid hall 128 feet long by 29 feet broad, rising to the roof of the building, and flanked with suites of rooms on different levels. Here again the staircases are built in the thickness of the back wall. It is difficult to say what the building was originally intended for, most probably a palace; but it has been turned to account of late years and is now the location of the public offices of the collectorate. All round the quadrangle was an arcade, which has also been converted, and is now used as record rooms, &c.

I*a*. (119) The 'Asâr Mahâl, 396 (*Cir.* 1646).—Upon the outer edge of the citadel moat, towards the east, and facing in that direction, is one of the ugliest buildings, yet the most sacred, in Bijâpur, the 'Asâr Mahâl, or Palace of the Relic. In one of the rooms within is supposed to have been enshrined a hair of the Prophet's beard.

III. Beside the 'Asâr Mahâl, on the north, are the remains of a contiguous building called the Jahâz Mahâl, from, as some say, its fancied resemblance to a ship, but it certainly has nothing about it now which would remind one of a ship. Others say it was so called because the offices of the Bijâpur Admiralty were established here, and we know Bijâpur possessed a considerable fleet at one time. With bare walls and hollow gaping doors and windows, from which all its old woodwork has gone, it is certainly now a wreck.

III. On the east side of the enclosure of the 'Asâr Mahâl are the ruins of a smaller building called the Pâni Mahâl.

Ia. (120) The Mihtari Mahâl, 118 (*Cir.* 1260).—On the south side of the road between the Jami Masjid and the citadel gate, and nearer the latter, stands one of the prettiest little buildings in Bijápur. Though called a *mahâl* or palace, it is really a gateway to the inner courtyard of a mosque, with upper rooms and balconies where men might assemble and converse and from its windows enjoy the different views of the city. The principal object of the group, the mosque within, is a neat little building and would have attracted more notice than it now does had it not been so completely thrown into the background by the more pretentious design—the gateway.

III. (121) The Fath Mahâl, 8.—This is a picturesque group of ruins situated on the north of the new Bazâr and to the left of the road leading down to the Bâhmani gate. The fallen walls of the palace with the dry cistern in front of it is surrounded by a high wall with its entrance gateway on the north.

III. (122) Mustafâ Khân's Mahâl, 80.—A short distance to the south-east of the 'Asâr Mahâl, in the fields, is a group of buildings composed of Mustafâ Khân's mosque and palace with its surroundings. A new road running north and south, under the Bari Kamân, now separates the former building from the latter. As in all the other palaces, this one faces the north. It is now in ruins, and several families have taken possession of nooks and corners within its crumbling walls.

III. (123) The Nakta Mahâl, 81.—This is now an insignificant ruin in the field on the other side of the road, opposite the Chhotâ Chini Mahâl, or residence of the Superintendent of Police. It is being knocked down and carried away. It has two segmental arches (nearly semi-circles), a rare form at Bijâpur.

III. (124) Bakshi ki Haveli, 82.—A little distance south-west of the last, forming part of the hamlet Haveli, are the ruins of this building. It is of no consequence. It had some very good carved wood-work about it which was bought by one of the Muhammadan families living in front of the Jami Masjid.

III. (125) The Chhotâ Chini Mahâl, 93.—Once one of the old Bijâpur palaces, this building has been converted into a residence for the Superintendent of Police.

III. (126) Khwâja Shâh ki Haveli, 108.—The ruins of a small residence. Has some very neat pigeon-hole niches in one of the walls.

III. (127) The Pailu Mahâl, 110.—This octagonal building, now converted into a modern dwelling which stands at the corner of the two roads from the Jami Masjid and Fath Gate, forms part of a long range extending from the corner down to the Mihtari Mahâl. This consists of a row of more or less ruined arches, facing the road, above which rise portions of the walls of an upper floor. Towards the east end the building extends further back, and the ruins of rooms and vaulted chambers exist, partly buried in their own debris. This place is said to have been the site of the old mint, and the garden adjoining it, which is still cultivated, is yet called the *Taksâl-kâ-bagichâ*, or mint garden.

III. (128) **Rassulbi-ka-ghar**, 116.—Of no consequence.

III. (129) **Mahâl**, 120.—Ruins of a *mahâl* of no consequence.

III. (130) **Mahâl**, 133.—Ruins of a *mahâl* out in front of which, in a laid out garden, is an octagonal basement upon a square plinth, where it was evidently intended to raise an octagonal pavilion over three graves which are upon the basement. Of no interest.

III. (131) **Khawâs Khân's Mahâl**, 141.—Of this building but a few vaulted chambers remain in ruins, with the entrance gateway, which stands alone, at some little distance away. This is said to have been the residence of Khawâs Khân, Vazir to Sikandar, and son of the traitor Khân Muhammad, who lies buried with his father in the tomb, one of the "Two Sisters," which is used as a residence by the Executive Engineer.

III. (132) **The Daulat Koti**, 164.—The Daulat Koti, or 'House of Happiness,' is a very complete little residence in very good preservation, situated on the right of the road leading north from the Jami Masjid. It was for some time used as a distillery until the new distillery was built, after which it was rented by Ralli Brothers. It faces north as usual, is a solid-looking building, and is constructed of fairly good masonry. The general plan of the rooms is I-shaped, a large open hall on both the north and south sides being separated from one another by a central line of rooms, and flanked by suites of rooms which lay at right angles to the direction of the middle ones. Ornamental niches decorate the walls. The building is said to have been erected during the time of Sultân Muhammad.

III. (133) **The Gatch Mahâl**, 178.—This is an old building still used as a private residence. Being almost wholly plastered it is called the Gatch Mahâl, *i.e.* the 'plastered residence.' Within is some very neat wooden ceilings in geometric tracery picked out with gold, and the carved wood-work which surrounds the court is very good.

IIa. (134) **Mubârak Khân's Mahâl**, 197 and 198.—Mubârak Khân's Mahâl is situated near the city walls to the south of the Jami Masjid. The principal feature about it is the water pavilion or fountain which stood in the centre of a tank as at Kumatgi. It was but a pleasure-house, possibly a hot weather resort, and does not appear from its scanty accommodation to have been used as a permanent residence. The walls of the *mahâl* have been plastered and painted, but most of this has now gone. The reservoir or tank, in which the fountain stands, has been filled in, and a great deal of the stone-work of this has been dug out. As this is an interesting little building it ought to be conserved.

III. (135) **Mahâl**, 224.—Ruins of a dwelling of some sort, of no account.

Ia. (136) **The Gol Gumbaz**, 256 (A.D. 1656).—By far the largest and most conspicuous building in Bijâpur. It is the mausoleum of Muhammad (or Mâhmûd as he is sometimes called) 'Adil Shâh.

Roughly speaking the building is a great hollowed-out cube of masonry, surmounted by a huge hemispherical dome, with an octagonal tower at each of its four corners, each crowned by a small dome. The only prominent feature on the faces of the building is the great deep overhanging cornice which, at a high level, runs round all four sides. The doorways, small lancet windows, and sparse surface decoration by no means assert themselves, and, from a short distance off, are hardly noticed on the bare-looking walls. The monotony of this, however, is broken by the towers which are pigeon-holed with windows from base to summit—seven in each of the seven storeys into which the tower is divided. The crest of the walls, above the cornice, is crenellated. A winding staircase ascends in each of the corners of the building, just where the towers abut on to it, and, communicating with each storey of the tower, at last leads out on to the flat roof, between the corners and the dome, whence passages lead, through the thickness of the dome, into the whispering gallery round the interior of the same.

The dome is practically a hemisphere of 124 feet 5 inches interior diameter, and is rather less than the breadth of the building. The thickness of the shell at the springing is 10 feet, whilst near the crown it is 9 feet. Thus the total external diameter at the springing is 144 feet. The curves of the surface are nowhere perfect, so that the measurements taken across different diameters vary several inches. The great compartment below, which is covered by the dome, is 135 feet 5 inches square at the floor level, and this gives an area of 18,337·7 square feet, from which if we take 228·3 square feet for the projecting angles of the piers carrying the cross arches, which stand out from the walls into the floor, two on each face, we get a total covered area, uninterrupted by supports of any kind, of 18,109 square feet, which is the largest space covered by any dome in the world, the next largest being that of the Pantheon at Rome of 15,833 square feet.

The total exterior height of the building above the platform on which it stands is 198 feet 6 inches exclusive of the wooden pole at the top. But this, when it held the gilt finial, formed part of the building, and another 8 feet must be allowed for it, and this would give an extreme height of 206 feet 6 inches. The interior height, from the level of the floor around the tomb platform to the top of the dome, is 173 feet. The drop from the gallery to the floor below is 109 feet 6 inches.

I*a*. (137) 'Ali (I.) Rauza, 55 (A.D. 1580).—This tomb is situated in the fields in the south-west quarter of the city. We have nothing but tradition to fix upon this as the last resting-place of 'Ali (I.) 'Adil Shâh, and if this be true—we have no evidence to the contrary—he was the first king of Bijâpur who was buried within the walls of his own city, Yûsuf, Ismâ'il, and Ibrâhîm I. having been interred in an old family graveyard at the village of Gogi, an *inâm* village given to Yûsuf by Sultân Muhammad of Bidar.

This is an exceedingly plain building. In plan it is a plain rectangular room surrounded by a corridor. The roofing of this room is a good example of a style of vaulting carried out in several early buildings in Bijâpur. In the inner room are four graves—two of adults, male and female, and two of children.

II*a*. (138) Tomb, 56.—Off the south-east corner of this building is a well built, high, square platform, upon the middle of which stands a tombstone of highly finished greenstone.

IIa. (139) 'Ali (II.) Rauza, 1 (1672).—The unfinished tomb of 'Ali (II.) 'Adil Shâh lies a short distance to the north of the citadel and the Gagan Mahâl. The great high basement upon which the building stands is 215 feet square.

The most peculiar characteristic of the building is its arches: they are quite Gothic in outline, being struck from two centres with the curves carried up to the crown.

Ia. (140) Tombs of Khân Muhammad and 'Abdul Razaq Qâdir, &c., 35 to 39.—The tombs of Khân Muhammad (36) and 'Abdul Razaq Qâdir (35), the domes of which are very conspicuous from afar, are known to European residents as the "Two Sisters," and to natives as the Jod Gumbaz, or 'pair of domes,' on account of their close proximity and likeness, in size and shape, to one another. The octagonal building on the south is the resting-place of the traitor Khân Muhammad, or Khân Khânan as his sovereign called him, and of his son Khawâs Khân, Vazir to Sikandar.

The larger square tomb (35), north of this, is that of 'Abdul Razaq Qâdir, Khawâs Khân's religious preceptor or domestic chaplain, and was, no doubt, built at the same time as the other.

Ib. (141) Tomb of Pîr Shaikh Hamid Qâdir, 45.—This building, which stands close to the walls in the south-west corner of the city, nearly four hundred yards west of 'Ali (I.) 'Adil Shâh's tomb, covers the remains of the saints Shaikh Hamid Qâdir and his brother Shaikh Lâtîf Ulla Qâdir, who lived in Bijâpur during the reign of Ibrâhîm II.

III. (142) Tombs of Karim Muhammad Qâdir and Sayyid 'Abdul Rahman Qâdir, 156 and 158.—These two tombs are situated near the south-east corner of the courtyard of the Jami Masjid. They both have ceilings which are said to have been coated with a wash of pulverised mother-of-pearl, which gives them a silvery sheen. The tomb of Sayyid 'Abdul Rahman has also some very pretty raised stucco work in the ceiling.

IIa. (143) Malik Sandal's Tomb, 5.—About one hundred and fifty yards to the north-west of the Post Office and Bukhâri Masjid is a group of buildings known as Malik Sandal's tomb and mosque, with its surrounding arcades and walls.

Ia. (144) The Kamrakhi Gumbaz, 9.—The small canopy covering a tomb, and seen at a little distance to the north of the last, with a ribbed egg-shaped dome, is called the Kamrakhi Gumbaz.

III. (145) Tombs, 16.—Two tombs, of no account.

IIa. (146) Sikandar Shâh's Tomb, 18 (1689).—Not far from the south-east corner of the Chhotâ 'Asâr, and three hundred and thirty yards due east of the Dakhani Idgâh, is a small walled enclosure containing within it a plain white-washed and chunamed grave, which is pointed out as that of Sikandar 'Adil Shâh, the last king of Bijâpur. There is, however, no inscription, or apparently any evidence, to support this tradition.

III. (147) Chând Bâori ki Gumbaz, 22.—This is a small square building upon the west margin of the Chând Bâori close by the Shâhapur gate.

Ib. (148) Tomb, 47.—This is a small well built tomb, close beside that of Pîr Shaikh Hamid Qâdir already described, and having within it the grave of a man.

I *b*. (149) Tomb, 48.—Close beside the last is another plain well built tomb, with two graves (of males) within it. Up in the dome are two bands of writing in stucco.

III. (150) Tomb, 50.—In the next field, to the north-east of the last, stands a solitary, small and damaged tomb with some curious pot and flower ornament in stucco under the dome.

III. (151) Jâffar Sakhâb ki Rauza, 51 (1647).—To the east of the last is a small *masjid* with a graveyard before it, in which are a number of graves in the open air, in some of which marble has been freely used. The principal grave is that of Jâffar Sakhâb, a saint, who is said to have come from Arabia to Bijâpur, and to have died there in A.D. 1647.

III. (152) Tomb, 52.—This is a small unfinished tomb, of no particular account, which, with Nos. 53, 57, 58 and 59, cluster around that of 'Ali (I.) 'Adil Shâh.

III. (153) Tomb, 53.—This is another small unfinished tomb of no interest.

III. (154) Tombs, 57, 58 and 59.—Small open four-piered canopies over tombs, but of no interest.

III. (155) Tombs, 63 and 69.—Small tombs of no account.

II*a*. (156) Kishwar Khân's Tomb, 75.—This tomb is situated close to the south-east corner of the Nau Bâgh, and not far south-east of the "Two Sisters." It is unfinished, its brick dome not having been carried up beyond the ring of leaves around its neck.

III. (157) Tombs, 76, 77 and 78.—These buildings are close beside the last, and are of no particular interest.

III. (158) Tomb, 79.—This is situated in a large garden, or what was once a garden in the Nau Bâgh. The garden is surrounded by a high wall. In the east side is the entrance gateway, in the north and south walls are small rooms, while in the west wall is a small *masjid* with a little room built on to either end of it. Around the four sides of the enclosure runs a broad raised path, and two other raised paths cross the whole area at right angles, dividing the garden into four quarters. At the intersection of these, *i. e.* in the centre of the garden, is a raised square platform around which is a broad masonry channel for water. Upon this is an octagonal plinth, in the middle of which is a single grave; but both the grave and the platform have been rifled of their marble (?) casing, and it is not possible, from external evidence, to say now whether it be the grave of a man or a woman. It is, however, said to be the grave of the wife of Aurangzib, who died here of the plague soon after he took possession of the city. The ground within this enclosure is now all waste land.

III. (159) Tombs, 87 and 89.—No. 87 is a small building used as a dwelling but evidently built for a tomb. Number 89 is a small plain domed tomb in a hollow. Neither of any account.

III. (160) Tomb, 98.—A small domed canopy upon four piers, with a very good stone tomb within. The rest of the building is of no account.

III. (161) Ganja 'Ilim Sâheb ki Rauza, 106.—This is situated on the road leading from the citadel to the Fath Gate, and not far from the former. It is known as Ganja 'Ilim Sâheb ki Rauza. The walls within the tomb have been painted a dark red picked out with black and yellow lines around the arches, and around the octagonal string course above the arches is a painted inscription. The dome has been painted to represent black, white, and red clouds. The grave is a plain whitewashed one of stone. The walls that enclosed the small court, in which this tomb is, has bands of perforated plaster-work in plain patterns. At the south-west corner is a small ruined mosque (107). Number 105 is a gateway. On the other side of the road, and belonging to this group, is a small mosque, of little account, called Ganja 'Ilim Sâheb ki Masjid (104). It has four circular-shafted Hindu-looking pillars.

III. (162) Shaikh Mera Mutwâlli ki Rauza, 121.—A small square chunamed tomb, standing beside the Mihtari Mahâl, of little account.

III. (163) Hamza Husaini's Tomb, 134.—A very plain little square-domed building like No. 106, and like it, too, in having been painted within. The second grave is that of Hamza Husaini's son.

III. (164) Tomb, 139.—A small domed building of no importance.

III. (165) Tomb, 150.—Commencement of a small masonry tomb with some graves.

III. (166) Manur Badi Sâheb ki Gumbaz, 160.—A small plain domed building of no account.

III. (167) Shamsa Zaha ki Gumbaz, 163.—A small domed tomb of no account.

III. (168) Shâh Qâsim Qâdir Tarfari ki Dargâh, 168.—A fine black stone tomb under a small canopy, upon a large square platform. Upon the platform are a number of graves.

III. (169) Tomb, 170.—This is a whitewashed stone tomb with four bands of inscription round it. The tomb was buried until recently when it was uncovered by persons who were building close by. The inscription contains the *Bismillah* formula, the profession of faith, and part of v. 256. ch. II. of the Qurân.

III. (170) Qâsim Qâdir's Tomb, 176.—Within this courtyard are two tombs and a mosque. Qâsim Qâdir's tomb is a plain square whitewashed building surmounted by a dome, with little ball ornaments along the edge of the roof, four on a side.

III. (171) Shâh Abu Tarab Qâdir's Tomb, 177.—This tomb is close beside the last, and is a small plain building. It has but four walls—a *chaukandi*—without roof, surrounding the grave.

II*a*. (172) Hâji Hasan Sâheb's Tomb, 179.—This is a square tomb in the south of the road, about midway between the Jami Masjid and the Allâhpur Gate and near the junction of that road with the cross road leading to the Gol Gumbaz. Around the four sides are rows of little windows with wooden shutters, and the doorway is, as usual, on the south.

III. (173) Tomb, 180.—A small domed tomb of no account.

III. (174) Tomb, 183.—Small building in three bays, domed above the central one, in which are three graves. To the west of it is an *idgâh* wall, and beyond this again is the platform of a building of no interest.

III. (175) Tombs, 184 and 185.—Small tombs of no particular interest.

III. (176) Tomb, 188.—Two well built but ruined platforms for tombs. Of no account.

III. (177) Husain Pâdshâh ki Gumbaz, 192.—Of no importance.

III. (178) Tomb, 208.—Three bays of arcade with a high stilted dome over the centre. Very poorly built. Of no particular interest.

III. (179) Tomb, 211.—This is a raised platform with ruined gravestones upon it. A high wall is built on the west margin of the platform, with a gateway through it and steps leading down from it.

III. (180) Tomb, 214.—A small well built tomb in ruins.

III. (181) Allâh Bâbu's Tomb and Mosque, 223.—These buildings stand upon a very high basement and are thus a very conspicuous and rather picturesque group. They are remarkable for their very high stilted domes which are mere ornamental adjuncts, since they are not the outer shells of domical ceilings. They are poorly built and are of no particular interest, save for the peculiarity just noted. Beneath the high platform on which these buildings stand are vaults for graves.

III. (182) Tomb, 226.—A substantial-looking small-domed pavilion with the grave of a female within it. There are some pretty plaster medallions in the spandrels of the arch in the north face.

III. (183) Tomb, 232.—A small ruined tomb of no account. It has a grave within covered with a white cloth.

III. (184) Tomb, 233.—A small tomb with a pyramidal roof, and on that account said to be that of a Shiah or Rabzi. Of no interest.

III. (185) Tomb, 239.—A walled enclosure, octagonal in plan, apparently intended to be a tomb. The walls are very thick. Of no account.

III. (186) Tombs, 246.—A fallen tombstone with an inscription in two lines round the top giving a part of the throne verse, Qurân chapter II. v. 256.

III. (187) Sakinâ Bibi's Tomb, 249.—A small square-domed tomb. Near it, upon a platform in the open, is a dark green, well polished tombstone.

III. (188) Shâh Alangi Majzub's Rauza, 251 (A.D. 1575).—Four walls enclose a small square court in which there is a grave said to be that of Shâh Alangi Majzûb.

III. (189) Tomb, 255.—A small Shiah tomb of no interest.

III. (190) Hashim Pîr ki Gumbaz, 259.—Of no particular interest archæologically, but of great sanctity in the eyes of Muhammadans as being the tomb of a celebrated saint.

III. (191) Tomb, 264.—In the north-west quarter of the city, of no account.

III. (192) Tomb, 268.—A small building of two bays, much ruined, with a man's grave in the north bay.

III. (193) Sayyid Shâh Abu Tarab ki Chaukandi, 294.—This is but the commencement of a building, being the four walls only. Good masonry.

I a. (194) The Chând Bâori, 92.—This tank, whose name is sometimes converted into Chandâ Bâori, and which is next in importance to the Tâj Bâori, is situated in the north-west corner of the town, not far from the Shâhâpur Gate. This was the model upon which the Tâj Bâori was constructed, and in general arrangement it is like the latter, though not so grand.

I a. (195) The Tâj Bâori, 42.—This tank stands alone as the most important reservoir of the most ambitious design, in the city. It is nearly square in plan—223 feet each way—and is enclosed within high walls on the east, south, and west, and a range of apartments on the north. The entrance is through the middle of this last side by a broad flight of steps over which is thrown a lofty arch, 35 feet in span, flanked by octagonal towers. The apartments on the east and west of this entrance were intended for the temporary accommodation of travellers. Descending the broad flight of steps between the towers and passing under the great arch, we come upon a landing which juts out into the water of the tank, from which flights of steps on both sides lead down to the water's edge. Around the inner side of the high wall that encloses it, runs a narrow gallery or terrace with a low parapet wall on the inner side. This communicates with sets of rooms in the middle of each of the three sides which overlook the tank, those on the south side being appropriated and converted into a Hindu shrine dedicated to Bâladeva. Above the sides of the tank are arrangements for raising water, those on the south being still used to irrigate the gardens behind.

III. (196) Bibi Bandi ki Bâori.—A tank close to the walls on the west of the Tâj Bâori, now all filled in.

II b. (197) The Gumat Bâori, 49 (A.D. 1562.—This is a small well close by the tomb of Pîr Shaikh Hamid Qâdir in the south-west corner of the city. Inscription.

III. (198) Bâori, 94.—An old well behind the Chhotâ Chini Mahâl, of no account.

III. (199) Bâori, 136.—To the north of Mustafâ Khân's palace is an old well, upon the south side of which is a stairway leading down to the water. This well appears to have supplied Mustafâ Khân's reservoir and gardens with water, and several earthen pipes may be seen leading from it.

III. (200) Bâori, 140.—This is an old underground well of very clear water on the premises of Khawâs Khân's palace. It seems to extend some distance under ground, and the temperature below is deliciously cool.

III. (201) Pâdshâh ki Bâori, 157.—A small well to the south-east of the Jami Masjid, partly underground and vaulted over. In use.

III. (202) Raffia ki Bâori, 167.—A large square well; of no interest.

III. (203) Peti Bâori, 171.—An old well with steps leading down to it; of no account.

III. (204) The Hal Bâori, 189.—A partly ruined well, being, like most of them, a converted quarry hole. The lower part of the descent is very dangerous, the steps having fallen away. A rumour says that at a certain time of the year it is covered and surrounded by myriads of little lights (fire-flies?) and no one knows how they come there. Dame Rumour also has it that three men are drowned in it every twelve years. With the very unsafe state of the descent this is not very extraordinary.

III. (205) The Bari Bâori, 200.—This is to the south of the Jami Masjid and not far from the walls of the town. It was one of the largest, but is now silted up.

III. (206) Mubârak Khân ki Bâori, 201.—This is near the last and was intended to supply water to the water pavilion of Mubârak Khân, which is close by.

III. (207) Jami Masjid ki Bâori, 202.—This is a large tank immediately on the south of the Jami Masjid, and evidently built in connection with that building. This was supplied from the Bari Bâori through earthenware pipes, and from this water passed on under the south wing of the *masjid* into the reservoir in the quadrangle within. The line of pipes may be traced by the narrow-shaft wells, or *usvâses*, along its course.

III. (208) Bashir Bâori, 245.—An old well of no account.

III. (209) Nagar Bâori, 247.—This is a short distance north of Kamâl Khâr Bazâr, in the fields. It is now used for irrigation purposes. Down below, near the surface of the water is a deep arcade running round the four sides of the well with three arches in each face.

III. (210) Bâori, 254.—A ruined well out in front of Ikhlâs Khân's mosque with arched rooms in it. Of no particular interest.

III. (211) Masa Bâori, 258.—An ordinary well north of the Gol Gumbaz, with a broad arch over the flight of steps which lead down to the water's edge on the west side.

III. (212) The Nim Bâori, 260.—A small square tank with a flight of steps on the south side, and an inscription in *Devanâgarî* in the north wall.

II*a*. (213) Water Towers, 61, 67, 91, and 115 are all on the line of the Begam Talâv conduit, and have been built at intervals along its course to relieve the pressure in the earthen pipes. The pipe enters the city, passing under the walls, close to water tower No. 61 and passes on to 67, thence to 91, and on to 115, after which it enters the Asâr Mahâl reservoir, where it mixes with the Torweh water which flows in from water tower No. 114. From the inscriptions upon Nos. 67, 91, and 115 we learn that this work was carried out by Afzal Khân during the time of Sultân Muhammad.

II*a*. (214) Water Tower, 114.—This is supposed to be on the Torweh conduit, which enters the city by the Makkâ Gate, passes the front of the Tâj Bâori, and continues thence by the "Two Sisters" to the 'Asâr Mahâl.

II*a*. (215) Water Tower, 142.—This is said to have been supplied from the 'Asâr Mahâl.

II*a*. (216) Water Tower, 147.—Said to be on the Begam Talâv water-course. It is situated opposite the Bari Kamân.

III. (217) Water Tower, 209.—Water tower broken down, apparently of late; of no particular interest.

III. (218) Water Tower, 225.—Of no account.

III. (219) Water Tower, 229.—This is a badly built octagonal tower of no account.

IIa. (220) Water Towers, 286 and 289.—These are two large towers within the citadel, the former being a principal distributary tower with upwards of seventy pipes leading off it to various parts of the citadel.

III. (221) 64.—A small gateway to a mosque.

III. (222) 56.—A large gateway, with its upper rooms in ruins. It has had two spiral ceilings in the lower floor worked in chunam.

III. (223) 71.—A long arcade of thirteen and a half arches, partly damaged. Two arches in the middle are broken down.

III. (224) 83.—A small ruin of no account.

III. (225) 100.—Ruins of a deep arcade or vault, of no account.

III. (226) 105.—A gateway of no interest.

III. (227) 123.—Small vaulted chambers which appear to have been part of a *hammâm* or bath. In one corner, within, low partition walls seem to form the bathing cisterns. Beside it is a deep narrow-shafted well.

III. (228) 125.—Portion of a row of vaults or arcade, much ruined, and used as dwellings. Of no account.

IIa. (229) 127.—A lonely ruined gateway with a large slab bearing the inscription already given in connection with the account of Yûsûf's old Jami Masjid.

III. (230) 139.—The remains of a lofty gateway; apparently the main entrance to Khawâs Khân's palace.

II a. (231) 148.—The Bari Kamân.—This great archway, which stands upon the side of the main road leading from the Jami Masjid to the Mihtari Mahâl, was originally the main entrance to the grounds of the palace and mosque of Mustafâ Khân. It is, from its size, an imposing entrance and it now forms the exit of a cross road which has recently been made connecting the two principal roads in Bijâpur. It is much damaged and requires repair.

III. (232) 151.—A gateway very much ruined. The upper storey had a very fine carved wood front with oriel windows, but the whole is falling in.

III. (233) 152.—A solid masonry arched gateway.

III. (234) 159.—Range of old W. Cs. behind the Jami Masjid.

II b. (235) 172 and 173.—*Ambar-khâna* or store-houses for grain. These two blocks of buildings are situated by the roadside a little distance east of the Jami Masjid. They are divided into rooms, each provided with a circular hole in the roof, a doorway with shutters fitting in grooves, and air vents in the roof. Staircases ascend to the roof up which grain was carried and tilted through the apertures above, into the rooms.

III. (236) 186.—Three bays of ruined arcade of no account.

III. (237) 190.—A small *ambar-khâna* or store-house, of no interest.

III. (238) 191.—A small ruin of no account.

III. (239) 215.—Gateway to No. 216.

III. (240) 219.—A ruined fountain.

III. (241) 220.—Three bays of arcade which appear to have been the gateway to some building or grounds to the south of the roadway; possibly another entrance to Khawâs Khân's grounds.

III. (242) 222.—A small ruined gateway, flanked by two thin octagonal *minârs.* It faces south, and is upon the north side of one of the old streets.

III. (243) 227.—Ruins of some building, with a broken water-pipe high up in the wall.

II *b*. There are now remaining but thirteen of the old guns of Bijâpur, or rather eleven, for two seem to have been left here by Aurangzib. Their positions in November 1888 were as follows :—

(244) The largest gun in Bijâpur, *viz.*, that on the Lânda Qasâb bastion, in the south of the town, 21 ft. 7 in. long; diameter at breech 4 ft. 4 in., at muzzle 4 ft. 5 in.; calibre 1 ft. 7½ in.; estimated weight 47 tons.

(245) An iron mortar beside the last on the same bastion, which Moore, in his narrative of Captain Little's Detachment, calls the "Cutcha-butcha."

(246) The Malik-i-Maidan, of cast gun-metal, the most notable gun in Bijâpur placed beside the Sherza Burj, about the middle of the western ramparts of the town. It is 14 ft. 3 in. long; 4 ft. 10 in. diameter of muzzle, 5 ft. 6 in. at breech; diameter of bore at muzzle 2 ft. 4 in.

(247) An iron gun on the Farangshâhi bastion, above the Makkâ gateway with a ring of small circles of inscription engraved on the muzzle.

(248) An iron gun on the seventh bastion south of the Makkâ gate.

(249) A small iron gun on the fifth bastion south of the Allâhpur gate, with a face on the muzzle.

(250) An iron gun, the Mustafâbâd gun, on the first bastion south of the Allâhpur gate, with an inscription on the muzzle. Sent to Bijâpur in A.H. 1042.

(251) An iron gun on the 'Ali Burj north of the Gol Gumbaz.

(252) An iron gun on the Sunda Burj, the second bastion north of the Shâhâpur gate.

(253) The long iron gun, the Lamchari, on the Haidar Burj, the longest gun in Bijâpur. It is 30 feet 8 inches long and has a bore of 1 foot in diameter.

(254) The shorter iron gun on the Haidar Burj, 19 feet 10 inches long.

(255) A well finished iron gun temporarily mounted on the platform of Khawâs Khân's tomb (the Executive Engineer's office); and

(256) A small mortar in gun-metal beside the last.

Several of these guns have been taken from their bastions and have been set up as a trophy collection in the citadel.

In addition to these there is a collection of small iron pieces called *janjâls* at the Museum. These are small iron tubes having a universal joint about the middle, which carried a ball from an inch to an inch and a half in diameter, being fixed on masonry blocks on the curtain walls, one opposite each embrasure, and were probably worked by one man each.

Buildings outside the City walls :—

III. (257) Mosque, 23.—Tâjam Tarak ki Gumbâz. Of no account.

III. (258) Mosque, 24.—This mosque is situated in Khudanpur suburb, without the Shâhâpur gate, and is called Satu Sayyid's mosque. It has two brick and plaster *minârs* which were originally very ornamental, but are now very much damaged.

II *b*. (259) The Mulla Mosque, 25.—This is also called Malik Rahân's masjid, and is situated within the suburb of Shâhâpur or Khudanpur.

III. (260) Mosque, 303.—This is on the north side of the road leading from the Shâhâpur gate to the Jail, and not far from the crossing of the Sholâpur road with it. It is of not much account. The coping stones of the cornice are gone, leaving the brackets bare and the plaster work within is much damaged.

III. (261) Mosque, 305.—A little mosque of no account, close to Shâh Navâz Khân's Tomb, and called Sayyid Shâh ki Masjid.

I *b*. (262) The Sonahri Masjid, 311.—This is a good-looking mosque with dome and *minârs*. Before it, in the high platform upon which it is built, are rows of vaults.

III. (263) Mosque, 313.—This mosque is in the corner of a large graveyard, within which are two high platforms with well cut tombstones upon them. Mosque of not much account.

III. (264) Mosque, 314.—This is a very good building surmounted by a dome. The *mehrâb* front is built in with well finished blackstone masonry. The *mimbâr* steps and the flagstones of the platform without have been carried off for the sake of the stone. The plaster patterns within have all been incised as in the Chhotâ 'Asâr mosque, and have been backed with black colour as in the Gol Gumbâz.

III. (265) Mosque, 315.—This is a small mosque with three *minârs* standing.

III. (266) Mosque, 316.—A mosque with dome and *minârs*.

III. (267) Mosque, 319.—An old mosque on the northern outskirts of Dargâhpur, much of the style of Ikhlâs Khân's mosque, having large brick *minârs* rising above the central piers of the façade as well as smaller ones over the corners. It is called the

Elephant Slayer's Mosque.' A story is told to the effect that a feud existed between the *mâlik* of this mosque and that of the Sonahri Masjid, about three-quarters of a mile to the east of it, and the *mâlik* of this mosque one day killed, with his sword, an elephant belonging to the *mâlik* of the other.

III. (268) Mosque, 324.—A mosque situated near the west corner of the Jail.

III. (269) Mosque, 329.—A mosque with a small tomb before it, in the fields, with a very pretty façade, and good cornice and brackets. It is very badly used, by the owner of the field, as a dwelling in which fires are lighted and rubbish heaped up.

III. (270) Mosque, 330.—This is a plain mosque, plastered within, with a long platform before it upon which are a number of tombstones.

III. (271) Mosque, 331.—A group consisting of a mosque, three tombs, and a gateway of not much account.

III. (272) Mosque, 332.—An old ruined mosque.

III. (273) Mosque, 333.—A small mosque, with two *minârs*, but no dome; of little account.

III. (274) Mosque, 334.—Mosque and tomb.

III. (275) Mosque, 344.—A mosque by the side of the road which leads from Bijâpur to Torweh, near the fourth mile-stone.

III. (276) Mosque, 345.—Another mosque, a little further on than the last, and near the point where an old aqueduct crosses the road.

II*b* (277) The Khidaki Masjid, 349.—This mosque stands in the midst of a thicket of prickly pear bush, a little way to the north of the Sangat Mahâl enclosure at Torweh, and takes its name from the windows in the end walls of the building. It is in a very dirty state, and almost inaccessible.

III. (278) Mosque, 350.—Another mosque on high ground, above the stream, to the north of the last.

III. (279) Mosques, 352 and 353.—Of no particular interest.

III. (280) Mosques, 354 and 355.—Mosques in the village of Torweh.

III. (281) Mosque, 356.—A mosque on the western outskirts of the village of Torweh.

III. (282) Mosques, 360 and 361.—Two mosques a little distance to the northeast of the Sangat Mahâl.

III. (283) Mosque, 362.—A small mosque on high ground to the west of the tombs of Afzal Khân's wives.

II*b*. (284) The Ibrâhîmpur Masjid, 364.—This is a good substantial looking mosque close beside the village of Ibrâhîmpur, not far from the railway crossing to the south of the city; said to have been built by Ibrâhîm I. in 1526.

IIb. (285) Mosque, 366.—This mosque stands on the northern edge of the hamlet of 'Ainâpur, two miles east of the Bijâpur Railway Station. It was, perhaps, built when the great tomb of Jahân Begam was commenced close by.

IIb. The principal palaces or *mahâls* without the walls are the (286) Sangat and (287)
Ib. Nari Mahâls at Torweh and the (288) 'Ainâpur Mahâl. There is another—the palace of
III. the (289) Navâbs of Sâvanur—312—near the Sonahri Masjid.

III. (290) Mâsâb ki Gumbaz, 28.—This is a plain tomb of no special interest outside the city on the west, in which are the graves of four males and one female. Behind the tomb is a neat little stone *masjid*—29—with rather graceful corner *minârs*. The various surface designs in geometric tracery, occupying the panels under the cornice, are very good.

III. (291) Tomb, 31.—An unfinished square cut-stone tomb within a large square mud-walled enclosure. Within the building are the graves of a male and female, and without in the open, are several graves.

Ia. (292) The Ibrâhîm Rauza, 33 (A.D. 1627).—The group of buildings collectively known as the "Ibrâhîm Rauza" is situated a short distance to the west of the city beyond the Makkâ Gate. Upon a high platform, within a great square enclosure are two large buildings facing one another with a reservoir and fountain between them, and between this platform and the surrounding walls, upon three sides, is a level greensward where, at one time, there were royal gardens. The building on the east side of the platform is the tomb of Ibrâhîm (II.) 'Adil Shâh, his queen Tâj Sultânâ, and four other members of his family. In order from east to west the graves are those of Tâj Sultânâ, wife of Ibrâhîm, Hâji Badi Sâheb his mother, Ibrâhîm Jagat-Gir himself, Zohrâ Sultânâ his daughter, Darvesh Padshâh his son, and Sultân Salaman another son. The sepulchral chamber, which is 39 ft. 10 in. square, contains the six tombs in a row from east to west, the tombs themselves, of course, lying north and south. In the middle of each of its four sides is a doorway, and on either side of these is a fanlight window. These are beautiful specimens of perforated stone-work. Each window is filled with interlaced Arabic writing, the perforations being the blank spaces in and around the letters. These let in a subdued light to the interior which, with that of the open doors, is just sufficient to reveal a most remarkable flat stone ceiling.

III. (293) The Moti Dargâh, 342.—This tomb, which is not far to the west of the Ibrâhîm Rauza, is conspicuous by its white-washed dome. In it rest the remains of Hazrat Molâna Habid Ulla, disciple of Shâh Sabgat Ulla, who died in A.H. 1041 (A.D. 1631).

Ib. (294) Haidar Khân's Tomb, 343.—A short distance away at the back of the Ibrâhîm Rauza is the square massive-looking tomb of Haidar Khân, one of the generals of Ibrâhîm II., built much after the style of that of 'Ain-ul-Mulk's, on the east of the town.

III. (295) Shâh Navâz Khân's Tomb, 304.—Scattered over the site of the old Shâhâpur suburb are a great number of tombs, great and small, among which those of Shâh Navâz Khân and Khwâjah 'Amin-ud-din are the more important. Shâh Navâz

Khân's tomb is situated off the left of the road leading from the Shâhâpur gate to the Jail, and near the latter. It is locally known as the Bâra Pâu-ki Dargâh, on account of the twelve piers which support the whole of the superstructure.

III. (296) Hazrat Khwâjah 'Aminu'd-din's Tomb, 320 (1675).—This is the whitewashed dome, perched upon the hill at Dargâhpur, which is so conspicuous an object from a distance. Khwâjah 'Aminu'd-din, the son of Shâh Burhânu'd-din, died in A.H. 1075 (A.D. 1664). Afzal Khân, Vazir, is said to have erected the tomb over the grave in 1675. There is nothing of much architectural merit about the building.

III. (297) Tombs, 298—302, 306—310, 316, 321—323, 326, and 328 are minor tombs scattered about among the ruins to the east, north, and west of Dargâhpur.

(298) Afzal Khân's Cenotaph, 337 (1658).—About a mile south-west of Shâhâpur and the 'Amin Dargâh is the village of Afzalpur or Takki, in which, on the highest ground, is the tomb of Chindgi Shâh, and half a mile west of this again is the
Ib. cenotaph of Afzal Khân. This is the Afzal Khân who commanded the Bijâpur troops which were sent against Śivâji, and who was killed by the latter on the slopes of Pratâpgaḍ.

IIb. (299) Afzal Khân's Wives' Tombs, 338.—Some distance to the south of the last, in a grove of trees, is a platform with the remains of a large tank before it, called the Muhammad Sarovar. Upon the platform are eleven rows of tombs, all of them being the tombs of females, amounting in all to sixty-three, with an unoccupied space which would have made the sixty-fourth.

About two hundred and fifty yards east of this is the Surang Bâori—339, from which the great tunnel starts which carried water into Bijâpur, and which can be traced as far as the Ibrâhîm Rauza by its air-shafts which rise to the surface at frequent intervals along its route. The mouth of the tunnel may be seen low down in the north side of the well and, when the water is low, a person may walk some distance into it.

IIb. (300) Jahân Begam's Tomb, 365.—Two miles east of the city may be seen the unfinished tomb of Jahân Begam. The plan of this building is exactly the same, both in size and design, as that of the great Gol Gumbaz. There are also the four corner towers as in the latter, but the four façades of the building were to have been left open, with three great arches in each face between the corner towers.

IIb. (301) 'Ain-ul-Mulk's Tomb, 368.—Standing some distance to the north-west of the last is the tomb of 'Ain-ul-Mulk. It is a square massive-looking building, surmounted by a very elegantly shaped dome. Within, upon the walls, is some very pretty stucco work, in the shape of great pendants hanging down upon the face of each. This is the burial place of 'Ain-ul-Mulk, one of the officers of Ibrâhîm I., who rebelled against him, and was killed near Bijâpur in 1556. Beside the tomb is the mosque—369.

III. (302) Tomb and Mosques, 370 to 377.—These are scattered over the plain between the last and the walls of Bijâpur.

Miscellaneous Buildings :—

IIb. (303) Among the miscellaneous buildings around the city are the *sardis*—317 and 318—in the Shâhâpur suburb ; the *band* and outlet sluice of the great Râmalinga tank to the north-west of it ; the dam, conduits, and air-shafts, from the Bhat Bâori to Torweh, and thence on to the Sârang Bâori ; the great tunnel thence to the walls of Bijâpur ; the Sandal Bâori ; the Begam Tank ; the walls of Nauraspur (III.), etc.

2. **Kumatgi** is now a small village, ten miles east of Bijâpur, on the Hippargi road. It was at one time a place frequented by the nobles, and, perhaps, the Court of Bijâpur as a pleasure resort, and on one side of the lake are the remains of many buildings, walls and gateways. Chief among these are several little pavilions with tanks and cisterns round

Ia. about them. On the walls of one of these are some very remarkable and interesting frescoes which must be over two hundred years old.

III. Here are extensive ruins of a small town or bâzâr, which appears to have been walled in, and there is a long broad road, down each side of which is a fine row of stabling arcade for the horses of masters and followers. From this a broad road led down, through a great gateway, along the margin of the lake and past the different pavilions. (**Surveyed.**)

3. **Tidgundi**, 12 miles north from Bijâpur ; a copper-plate **inscription** was found here (*Ind. Ant.*, vol. I. p. 80.)

II.—Indi Tâlukâ.

1. **Indi**, 30 miles N.N.E. from Bijâpur.

Ib. **Inscription** :—On a stone before the *châvaḍi*, 3 ft. 9 in. long, 16 inches broad and 8 inches thick, in old *Devanâgarî* characters on three sides, and in Kânarese on the fourth, —partly illegible.

III. 2. **Salotgi**, 6 miles south-east from Indi. Temple of Śiva Yogîśvara on the north of the village, with brick spires ; the shrine is said to contain a raised seat like a Musalmân tomb covered with a *châdar* said to cover a *liṅga*. At an annual fair Brâhmaṇs, Mângs, Musalmâns, &c., all mingle together and eat the same food.

Ib. **Inscriptions** :—(1) On a stone pillar, set up for cattle to rub themselves on, at the left side of the gate, 4 ft. 10 in. long, 1 ft. 9 in. broad, and 1 ft. 2 in. thick,—an inscription in old *Devanâgarî* characters, dated *Śaka* 867, of the Râshṭrakûṭa dynasty : *Ind. Ant.* vol. I., p. 205. (2) Below the preceding are some lines in *Haḷe Kannaḍa*. (3) On another stone lying inside the gate an inscription in *Devanâgarî*.

3. **Tambe**, 13 miles south of Indi.

Ib. **Inscriptions** :—(1) In front of the temple of Mâruti, 2 ft. 6 in. long, 1 ft. 6 in. broad, and 1 ft. thick, in Kânarese characters. Above are a *liṅga*, sun and moon, cow and calf and a sword. (2) Near the *châvaḍi*, 3½ ft. long, 15 in. broad and 1 ft. thick, in 31 lines, each of 13 or 14 letters.

III.—Sindgi Tâlukâ.

III. 1. **Almele**, 12 miles north from Sindgi. It is said there was a large Jaina temple at the tank on the west side of the village, and numerous rude figures are found in the neighbourhood ; the *dargâh* and the old large *vâḍâ* in the middle of the village.

I b. **Inscription** :—On a stone lying near the Government school-house, and said to have been brought from the *vâdâ* of Nâdgauda. It is 2 ft. long, 1 ft. square, with *Bâlabodha* character on one side and Kânarese on the other three, dated *Śaka* 1007. On the top are a *liṅga*, the sun and moon, a cow and calf, and a man standing with his hands folded.

III. 2. **Hippargi,** 14 miles south-west from Sindgi. Temple of Kalmeśvara in a large quadrangular courtyard; temple of Mallaya to the north-east of the village, also in a courtyard surrounded by *dharmaśâlâs* with numerous carved figures, and a *dîpamâlâ*. Across the stream is a third old temple with a lamp-pillar, and a well said to be worthy of note.

I b. **Inscription** :—In the north-east corner of the court of Kalmeśvara's temple is a stone about 4 feet long, 1 ft. 4 in. broad and 6 in. thick, with a Kânarese inscription in 55 lines, dated *Śaka* 1176, Paridhâvi *Saṁvatsara*.

IV.—Bâgevâdi Tâlukâ.

III. 1. **Ba'geva'di,** 25 miles south-east from Bijâpur. Basaveśvara temple is a large one, about 36 yards long by 15 wide, in a large court surrounded by a wall. It is built of carved stone and the roof of the *maṇḍapa* is carved with figures of the eight *dikpâlas*, &c. It contains two *liṅga* shrines of Mallikârjuna and of Sangameśvara with a large Basaveśvara. At Bâgevâdi, Basappa, the founder of the Liṅgâyat sect, is said to have been born in the 12th century.

Inscription :—A Kânarese one at the door of the temple, much effaced.

III. 2. **Muttige,** 7 miles W.S.W. from Bâgevâdi. Near the north gate of the village are three small temples of Mukteśvara; of Lakshmî-Narasiṁha, octagonal, with an image of black stone, and containing much sculpture; and of Kâśi-Viśveśvara.

V.—Muddebihal Tâlukâ.

1. **Nalatwad,** 12 miles south-east from Muddebihal.

II b. **Inscriptions** :—(1) Near the village gate dated *Śaka* 1422. The stone is $9\frac{3}{4}$ feet long, $2\frac{1}{2}$ ft. broad and 1 ft. thick; at the head are the Śaiva symbols of a *liṅga*, the sun and moon, a bull, &c. (2) In the temple of Mâruti, the stone is $2\frac{3}{4}$ ft. long, $1\frac{3}{4}$ ft. broad and 9 inches thick, and at the head are figures of Îśvara, the bull, sun and moon. (3) Near the *châvaḍî*, 3 ft. 4 in. long, 1 ft. 10 in. broad, and 9 inches thick, with Îśvara, Nandî, and a worshipper at the top. (4) At the Benkan well, 2 ft. 3 in. long, 1 ft. 10 in. broad and 10 in. thick, with cow and calf above.

VI.—Hungund Tâlukâ.

I b. 1. **Aihole,** 15 miles E.S.E. from Bâdâmi (16° 50′; 75° 57′). Near the village is a Brahmanical cave called Râvaṇaphadi, and to the east is a Jaina one known as Menâbasti. On the hill above this cave are many dolmens (*Ind. Ant.* III. 306); also, nearer the other cave the ruins of an old temple called Megutî, of the 7th century. In the village is an old Vaishṇava temple remarkable as "the only known example of its class as a structural building, though there are numerous instances at Kârle, Elurâ, Ajaṇṭâ, and elsewhere of similar edifices. These, however, are all cut in the rock, and, consequently, have no exterior except the façades. It has always, therefore, been a great problem to know how the structural prototypes of these rock-cut temples were formed, and what their interior arrangements may have been. The example at Aihoḷe does not answer all these problems, but it goes nearer to it than any other we know" (*Arch of Dhar. and Mys.*, p. 67). It has been described in the *Arch. Sur. Reports* I and V and *Cave Temples of India.* (**Surveyed.**)

At a short distance to the south-west of the village is a temple, small but highly interesting on account of the quaint and elaborate sculptures with which it is decorated. It is now disused, and is partly in ruins, the whole of the roof having been removed. It is of about the same age as the Durgâ temple. It appears to have been also originally a Vaishṇava temple, as there are figures of Garuḍa over the doors both of the *maṇḍapa* and of the shrine, and a figure of Lakshmî, with her elephants, over the entrance. But there is also a figure of Śiva dancing on the roof, with Pârvatî holding a child.

Further to the south-west of the village, on the right bank of the river, is a large group of ruined and disused temples. The largest and most interesting of them is the temple of the god Galiganâtha. On the front or east side of the courtyard is a handsomely sculptured gateway, still nearly entire, but only ten or twelve feet high. It is the only gateway of the kind in this part of the country.

In the same group of temples with that of Galiganâtha, and rather closer to the river, there is a temple of the god Nârâyaṇa. It contains three separate shrines, all leading out of the central hall.

I *b*. **Inscriptions**:—The Meguṭi temple inscription is of Pulikeśî II., *Śaka* 556, and one of the most interesting in the Kânarese country (see *Ind. Ant.*, vol. V., p. 67, and vol. VIII. *Third Arch. Rep.*, p. 129). One on the temple of Galiganâtha is of the Râshṭrakûṭa king Kannara, *Śaka* 831; and another is of Vikramâditya Tribhuvanamalla. There are at least nine others. (See *P. S. and O. C. Ins.* Nos. 73-84; *Ind. Ant.*, vol V. pp. 67 and 175, VIII, 237, 245, 284 and vol. IX. 74-96; *Third Arch. Rep.*, pp. 127—138. *B. B. R. A. S. Journ.* XXVII. 315.)

III. 2. **Hungund**, 12 miles east from Aihoḷe (16° 4′; 76° 7′). On a hill to the north are the ruins of a large Jaina temple. In the fort is a temple of Râmaliṅga.

Inscriptions:—There are inscriptions on two slabs on the roof of the verandah of Râmaliṅga.

II *b*. 3. **Nagar**, 5 miles south-west from Hungund. An **inscription** about 4½ feet long.

III. 4. **Kelur**, 3 miles south of Aihoḷe. On the south of the village on a hill are five old Śaiva temples. About 1½ miles to the west of Kelur is a *kol* or glen, in which is a temple of Siddheśvara with a rock excavation to the north and another to the south of it.

III. 5. **Arsibidi**, 8 miles south of Aihoḷe (15° 54′; 76° 0′) a ruined village. Several ancient Śaiva temples. (**Surveyed.**)

Inscriptions:—Many inscriptions are found here and in the neighbourhood.

II. 6. **Karadi**,? 9 miles east of Hungund. Temple of Basaveśvara on the north of the village, a small old temple, the roof supported by many pillars.

II. *b.* **Inscription** :—About half a mile from this village is an old temple of Mahâdeva, with a dated inscription in the Rudra *Saṁvatsara*. Another defaced inscription is near the gate of Karadi.

III. 7. **Sangam,** 10 miles north of Hungund at the junction of the Malaprabhâ and Krishṇâ. About 1 mile north-east from the village is the temple of Saṅgameśvara, about 75 feet by 40, surrounded by a large courtyard, in which are several houses and *dharmaśâlâs*. It is old and attributed to Jakhaṇâchârya, and is regarded as of great sanctity. In the bed of the river Malaprabhâ is a cave, the fabled abode of the *Ṛishis*, the mouth of which is stopped by a large stone.

Inscriptions :—In the temple of Saṅgameśvara are two inscriptions.

III. 8. **Amingad,** 7 miles west of Hungund. About a mile to the east of it is Rakhasgi, where is a temple of Kalleśvara ascribed to Jakhaṇâchârya.

III. 9. **Nandwadige,** 13 miles east from Hungund (16° 2′; 76° 20′). Temple of Mûkâdevî.

I *b.* **Inscription** :—Of the Râshṭrakûṭas, dated *Śaka* 722, over the door of the shrine (*P. S. and O. C. Ins.* No. 85 ; *Ind. Ant.* XII. 220).

VII.—Bâgalkot Tâlukâ.

1. **Bhairanmatti,** 3 miles south-west from Bewûr (16° 11′ ; 75° 55′).

I *b.* **Inscription** :—Of king Tailapa Âhavamalla, *Śaka* 911 ; and of the Sinda ciheftains Sevya and Nâgâditya : also of king Jayasiṃha Jagadekamalla, *Śaka* 955, 7 ft. 11½ in. by 2 ft. ½ in. (*P. S. and O. C. Ins.* No. 86).

III. 2. **Bewur,** 12 miles east from Bâgalkot (16° 12′; 75° 57′). Three old temples ascribed to Jakhaṇâchârya, dedicated to Râmeśvara, Nârâyaṇadeva, and Kâlikâbhavânî; the first is of moderate size and decorated with sculpture.

Inscription :—There is an inscription in Kânarese characters to the west of the village.

3. **Ba'galkot,** on the Ghataprabhâ (16° 17′ ; 75° 46′).

III. **Inscription** in *Devanâgarî* about 1½ miles from Bâgalkot on the left side of a temple of Mâruti.

III. 4. **Turchigiri,** about 4 miles east of Kalâdgi. Temple of Mârutideva of considerable celebrity, with an image of Mâruti about 6 feet high. The walls are about 4 feet thick.

III. 5. **Bilgi,** 12 miles north-west from Bâgalkot. About 200 yards from the north gate is a well called Arettinbhâvi (the well of 6 bullocks), 50 yards long by 25 wide, with galleries in the sides. It was built by Mâdhavji Visâji in *Śaka* 1630. There are **inscriptions** to this effect in Kânarese, Sanskrit, Marâṭhi, and Hindustâni. About 1½ miles north from Bilgi near the village of Badgandî is a well about 28 yards long by 14 wide ; according to an **inscription** on it, it was begun in *Śaka* 1509 and completed in 1511, by a servant of Ibrâhîm Adil Shâh.

VIII.—Bâdâmi Tâlukâ.

I *a*. 1. **Ba'da'mi,** 24 miles S.S.E. from Kalâdgi (15° 55'; 75° 45'). Three Brahmanical caves of the 6th century, and a Jaina one, with much sculpture and some fragments of painting, in good preservation. Also many old temples, a *dargâh*, mosques, &c. (see *Arch. Sur. Reports I and V*, and *Cave Temples*, 1880; *Ind. Ant. VI*. 354; *J. B.B. R. A. S.*, part XIII., p. 61. (**Surveyed.**)

Inscriptions :—(1) One in the largest cave, No. 3, of *Śaka* 500 ; (2) three in Kânarese on pillars in cave 3, one dated *Śaka* 1446 ; (3) an old Kânarese one of soon after *Śaka* 500 outside the cave, and some names of the 6th or 7th century ; (4) an inscription of the time of Sadâśivarâya of Vijayanagar (*Śaka* 1465) on the porch of a temple to the north of the town. (See *First Arch. Rep.*, pp. 22-27, and *Third*, pp. 119-121 ; *P. S. and O. C. Ins.* Nos. 38 to 49 ; and *Ind. Ant.* III. 305 ; VI. 139 ; VIII. 238 ; IX. 99 ; X. 57 *et seq.* ; *B. B. R. A. S. Journ.* XXVII. 317 ; XIII. 61.)

III. 2. **Nandikes'vara,** 4 miles east from Bâdâmi. Temple of Mahâkûṭeśvara among the hills in a quadrangular courtyard, in which are also several smaller ones.

I *b*. **Inscriptions** :—A large stone pillar lying in front of the temple inscribed on all four sides in old Kânarese characters: others in the porch and one inside dated *Śaka* 856 (*P. S. and O. C. Ins.* Nos 50, 51, 52).

III. 3. **Banas'amkari,** 3 miles south-east of Bâdâmi. An old temple and other remains (*Arch. of Dhar. and Mys.*, No. 88 and p. 72; *Ind. Ant.*, X. 66; *First Arch. Sur. Report*).

Inscription :—A Vijayanagar inscription of Achyutarâya, dated *Śaka* 1455 (*Ind. Ant.*, vol. V., p. 19); and others (*B. B. R. A. S. Jour.*, part XXVII. p. 321).

I *b*. 4. **Pattadakal,** 9 miles east from Bâdâmi (15° 57'; 75° 52'). Several old temples both Brahmanical and Jaina, dating from the 7th or 8th century (*Rep., Arch. Sur.*, 1874).

Several of the temples at Paṭṭadakal "are very pure examples of the Dravidian style of architecture : they are all square pyramids divided into distinct storeys, and each storey ornamented with cells alternately oblong and square. Their style of ornamentation is also very much coarser than that of the Châlukya style, and differs very much in character. The domical termination of the spires is also different, and much less graceful, and the overhanging cornices of double curvature are much more prominent and important."

These Dravidian temples "are wanting in all that elegance of form and detail which is so characteristic of the Châlukya style, but are not without a purpose-like boldness of form expressive of stability and a certain amount of grandeur; though this is, of course, more easily observed in the larger examples in the south of India than it is in those at Paṭṭadakal. If, on the other hand, we compare it with the more modern temples, such as those at Hampi and Maisur, it will be seen how much the form lost by the gradually growing steepness of outline and attenuation of details. The modern forms are not without a certain degree of elegance which is wanting in the more ancient; but in all the higher characteristics of design, the older are by far the finest examples."

Besides these the village of Paṭṭadakal possesses a group of temples, "not remarkable for their size or architectural beauty, but interesting because they exhibit the two principal styles of Indian architecture in absolute juxta-position" (*Arch. of Dhar. and Mys*, pp. 63, 64). The temple of Pâpanâtha is of the northern style, and is probably rather older than that of Virûpâksha, which dates from the early part of the 8th century. (**Surveyed.**)

Inscriptions :—Seventeen have been collected here, and there are probably more (*P. S. and O. C. Ins.* Nos. 53 to 69; *First Arch. Rep.*, pls. xli to xliv; *Second*, p. 241; *Third*, pp. 121—127; *Ind. Ant.*, vol. V. p. 174; XI. 24; *B. B. R.* A. *S. Journal* XXVII. 319, and XXXI. 222.)

III. 5. **Belur**, 7 miles S.S.E. from Bâdâmi (15° 51′; 75° 49′). Temple of Nârâyaṇa in the fort.

I *b*. **Inscription** :—Of Jayasimha Jagadekamalla and his elder sister Akkâdevî, *Śaka* 944, 5 ft. 1½ in. by 1 ft. 9½ in. (*P. S. and O. C. Ins.* No. 70).

III. 6. **Tolachgud**, 3 miles south-east from Bâdâmi (15° 53′; 75° 48′). Temple of Banaśaṁkarîdevî.

Inscription :—Of Achyutarâya of Vijayanagar, *Śaka* 1455 (*P. S. and O. C. Ins.* No. 72).

7. **Kattageri**, 11 miles north from Bâdâmi (16° 5′; 75° 43′).

I *b*. **Inscription** :—Of the 21st year of Vikramâditya Tribhuvanamalla (*Śaka* 1018), on a stone at the top of the steps at the north end of a small tank under the wall of the fort, 1 ft. 0½ in. by 1 ft. 4 in. (*P. S.* and *O. C. Ins.* No. 71; *Ind Ant.*, vol. VI., p. 187).

IV.—KÂRWÂR ZILLA OR NORTH KÂNARÂ.

I.—Kârwâr Tâlukâ.

II *a*. 1. **Ka'rwa'r**. Some old European graves in a small walled enclosure, about 6 miles from Kârwâr across the Kâlinadi.

II.—Haliyâl Tâlukâ with Supa Petâ.

III. 1. **Supa'**, (lat. 15° 16′ N., long. 74° 34′ E.), about 60 miles from Kârwâr, has a temple of Râmalinga built on an island at the confluence of the Kâlinadi and the Ujalî or Pâṇḍhrî. It is supposed to be about 700 years old, and is not in good repair though it enjoys an allowance of Rs. 600 per annum.

III. 2. **Ulavi**, Supâ Peṭâ (lat. 15° 0′ N., long 74° 34′ E.) The temple of Basaveśvara is built of laterite in a court surrounded by a high wall. It is of no architectural pretensions, but is of great repute among the Liṅgâyats, and the original building is said to be of great antiquity. In front of it is a tall handsome granite *dhvajastambha*, and outside, in a hollow beneath the outer wall, is a large cistern with a perennial supply of water. This was the principal place of devotion for the Liṅgâyat Râjâs of Sondâ, who were usually buried here. Traces of old buildings and caves, said to have been occupied by Liṅgâyat devotees, are still pointed out.

III.—Yellâpur Tâlukâ.

(*No returns.*)

IV.—Sirsi Tâlukâ.

1. **Banava'si**, about 15 miles east by south from it, (lat. 14° 32′ E., long. 75° 5′ N.,) on the river Varadâ, a very ancient place, mentioned in the Bauddha records as a place of note in the 3rd century B. C. and by Ptolemy, the geographer, in the 2nd
II *b*. century A.D. It had also the name of Jayantîpura. (1) The temple of Madhukeśvara is attributed to the mythic architect Jakhaṇâchârya. It is in a courtyard containing also smaller temples to Gaṇapati, Narasiṁha, Kadambeśvara, &c. The temple is of considerable size and ornamented with sculptures, with a short Dravidian spire. The large Nandî in front is under a canopy or outer *maṇḍapa* supported by four pillars. A king of Sondâ, about 250 years ago, is said to have found it surrounded by forest, and to have assigned lands for its maintenance and instituted the car ceremony. A fine stone *maṇḍapa* was presented, according to an inscription, by Raghurâja, king of Svâdi : the date is obliterated, but it was in the Vibhava *Saṁvatsara*,—probably *Śaka* 1550. An annual allowance of Rs. 4,000 is paid by Government. The place is one of great repute among the Smârta Brâhmaṇs. It was the old capital of the Kâdambas, whose power was restored, if not founded, by Mayûravarmâ who formed an alliance with the Châlukya kings, perhaps in the 5th century A.D. In the 11th and 12th centuries they were feudatories of the Kalyâṇa Châlukyas. The succession of the different chiefs, however, has not yet been clearly made out, and it is

NORTH KANARA

Scale 16 Miles = 1 Inch

10 5 0 10 20 30

Note

Places underlined Red have Hindu remains

„ „ Green „ Musalman „

„ „ Blue „ Jaina „

„ „ Yellow „ Buddhist „

possible there were two or three branches of the family. The examination of more of their inscriptions would probably clear this up and throw light on the history of the district. In 1075 the province was under Udayâditya, the general of Bhuvanaikamalla. He was displaced in 1076 by Vikramâditya, who gave the province to his brother Jayasiṁha, who soon after rebelled, and the district was bestowed on Barmadeva. When the Kalachuryas, in 1157, rose against the Châlukyas, the latter maintained himself at this place (*Ind. Ant.* IV. 205.) (**Surveyed.**)

I*b*. **Inscriptions**:—Four are on stones set upright in the ground right and left of the portico of the great temple, and four lean against the enclosing wall: (1) on the left is one of the Châlukya king Vibhu-Vikramadhavala-Permâḍideva, and a Kâdamba chieftain,—38 lines only are above ground; (2) of the time of Vîra-Bukkarâya of Ânegundi, *Śaka* 1290; this is also partly buried; (3) of the Kâdamba chieftain Kîrtivarmadeva, *Śaka* 990; (4) to the right of the temple an inscription of 37 lines of about 25 large but scarcely legible letters: (5) against the northern wall of the court an inscription of Sadâśivadevarâya of Vidyânagari, *Śaka* 1474: (6) against the same wall, another inscription of the same king; (7) near the east wall, one of 22 lines, each of about 23 letters, not easily read; (8) against the same wall, an inscription very much defaced; (9) in one of the smaller shrines in the court is a handsomely carved litter, or throne, and on it is an inscription of Raghunâtha Nâyaka of Sonḍâ *Śaka* 1550; (10) on a pillar in the Nandî *manḍapa*; (11) on a pilaster to the right of the entrance of the small temple of Trimalladeva in 49 lines. And (12) on a slab carved with a five-headed snake (Nâgendra) in a little modern shrine on the east side of the court of the great temple is a Pâli inscription. It begins at the top of the left side of the slab with the words *Siḍhaṁ Râno Hâritiputasa* and a line and a half are on the right side of the slab. This is an early Ândhra inscription, and is dated in the 12th year of the 'century' of Sâtâkarṇi Hâritiputa. (*Ind. Ant.*, IV. pp. 205-6.)

I*b*. 2. **Annavatti**, nine miles east from Banavâsi, and six south-west from Tilivalli (lat. 14° 35′ N., long. 75° 13′ E.) A fine temple of Kaiṭabheśvara with 16 pillars in the great *manḍapa* and 22 on the screen wall, and the following— (**Surveyed.**)

I*b*. **Inscriptions**:—(1) On the right of the god in the temple of Kaiṭabheśvara, dated *Śaka* 1152; (2) on a pillar in the *madhyaranga* of the same temple, *Śaka* 1163; (3) on another pillar in the same temple, *Śaka* 1163; (4) on another pillar, dated *Śaka* 1171; two of these cover two sides of the bases of the columns; (5, 6) two on the edge of the *madhyaranga*—one much effaced, *Śaka* 992; (7) another on the opposite side; (8) on the lintel of the antechamber of a small temple of Pârvatî. Outside to the south are two *vîragals*, the inscriptions much effaced.

II*b*. 3. **Kubtur**, a neighbouring village about a mile from Annavaṭṭi. **Inscriptions**, etc. (1) at the sluice of the *talâv*, four *vîragals* in front of a small ruined temple; behind the sluice two more and a long slab carved with mythological figures and worth preserving; built into the sluice itself is a *śilâśâsanam* in much older characters than usual. (2) on the way from the tank to the village *pippala* tree are a *satî* stone and another on the left side of the road nearly buried. (3) at the tree—a thick stone with an elephant on it and five lines of inscription; a *satî* stone with a short inscription, faintly cut; a *vîragal*, with three females, the middle one on a couch, below them four dancing or flying off with a man, and a man on horseback fighting with one on foot, one slain, and a fourth with hands clasped; another with *linga* above, next a *devî* and attendants, and below a fight, and 16 lines of inscription. (4) at an old Jaina *basti* are four stones all partially weathered and one of the two largest split; each has a Jina with two *chauris* and sun and moon at the top; the two large ones have long inscriptions; inside is a section of an inscription partially effaced by grinding *keśara* on it:—there are also four black stone Jinas, one with a short inscription on the base. (5) at Îśvaradeva's temple is a sort of double *vîragal*, there being two compartments across and three vertically with 11 lines of inscription; inside on the base of a pillar is one of 14 lines. The roof has an elaborately carved slab over the central area with Śiva in the *tâṇḍava* attitude in the centre and the 8 *dikpâlas* on the sides. In the left aisle of the *maṇḍapa*, on a long *vedî* are the *saptamâtṛis* with Gaṇapati and Śiva, also a spirited Mahishâsura-mardanî to the right of the shrine door, in which she has got the *asura* by the arm and has made a great gash in his side with a broad-pointed spear; outside to the right is a stone with a *kalaśa* on it and 4 lines of inscription; and a split *śilâśâsanam*. (6) at Mailâradeva's temple is a thick slab with an elephant and 5 lines of inscription.

III. 4. **Sonda** (lat. 14° 44′ N., long. 74° 52′ E.). (1) Three miles west of the Soṇḍâ station is the temple of Trivikrama said to be about 400 years old. It consists of one central room with surrounding verandahs. The central room is in the shape of a car with four wheels (two of which are broken), drawn by two elephants. It has a tall *dhvajastambha* in front. Tradition says that one of the eight monks of the Udapi *maṭha* in South Kânarâ, called Vaddirâja Svâmi, of great repute for his austerity, was aided by a spirit named Nârâyaṇa-Bhûta, who removed this temple entire from Bhadrikâśrama to Soṇḍâ, and the monk installed Trivikramadeva therein. A car festival is celebrated every year: the temple is also endowed. (2) At Huṇasehond, half a mile from the Soṇḍâ station, is Kâlmaṭha or Râjendramaṭha, a Lingâyat monastery, founded some three or four hundred years ago by the Soṇḍâ Râjâs. It is constructed with very large stone slabs.

V.—Kumta Tâlukâ.

III. 1. **Gokarna**, (lat. 14° 32′ N., long. 74° 23′ E.) on the coast about 10 miles north of Kumtâ. The most famous *tîrtha* or place of pilgrimage in this part of India. It contains several temples built probably about A.D. 1400. (1) The temple of Mahâbaleśvara. This has two courts, an outer and an inner, with corridors inside the walls for the accommodation of pilgrims and devotees. The temple itself consists of *maṇḍapa* and shrine, the latter surmounted by a low spire. Thousands of pilgrims flock to the annual fair held in the month of Mâgha, which concludes with the drawing of a huge idol car elaborately carved.

Legend accounts for the origin of this *tîrtha* in the following way: Śiva, pleased with the austerity of Râvaṇa, king of Laṅkâ, allowed him to ask a boon, and he asked his *Âtmaliṅga*, which was granted. Râvaṇa was told that if he worshipped it for three successive years, he would be equal with Mahâdeva, but he was not to set it down till he should reach his capital. Vishṇu, alarmed at this, resolved to outwit him. While Râvaṇa was passing Gokarṇa, Vishṇu hid the sun behind his weapon *sudarśana*, at which Râvaṇa, supposing it to be sunset, went to the shore to perform his devotions. Seeing a boy tending a herd of cows he asked him to hold the *liṅga* till he should return. The boy, who was Gaṇapati in disguise, promised to hold it as long as he was able, and then to call out his name three times before placing it on the ground. No sooner was he gone, however, than the boy called his name thrice and set down the *liṅga*. Returning, the giant saw the trick that had been played him, and applied his utmost strength to pull it up, but in vain; so he called it Mahâbaleśvara. He is said to have broken off four pieces and thrown them towards Murdeśvara, Gaṇavanteśvara, Dhâreśvara and Shajeśvara, where there are also temples (see Buchanan's *Mysore*, &c.) Annual allowances are paid to the temple.

III. (2) The temple of Bhadrakâlî in the east of the town is a small one in a courtyard, entered by a single doorway from the north. (3) Temple of Veṅkaṭaramaṇa of black stone. (4) Ahalyâbâi's temple built by the princess of Indor about a century ago. (5) Koṭi *tîrtha*, a large, dirty, oblong pond surrounded by a decaying flight of steps. (6) Ballâḷa *tîrtha* near the beach.

Śataśṛiṅga and Maṇinâga are two hills close to Gokarṇa, and the Tâmraparṇî is a small stream that falls into the sea here. In the vicinity there are some natural caverns in the laterite. There are no Jaina remains in Gokarṇa.

I*b*. **Inscriptions**:—There are said to be several inscriptions: (1) in Narasiṁha's temple; (2) in the house of Muliman Timana Adi; (3) in Hire Kuppa Bhat's house; (4) in the temple of Mâruti; (5) in Vighneśvara Bhat's house; (6) in temple of Śrî Tâmra Gaurî; (7) at the side of the door in the *maṇḍapa* of Mahâbaleśvara temple; (8) in Viṭṭhala temple.

Prasâd Nârâyaṇa Bhat has a copper-plate.

III. 2. **Dha'res'var,** about 4½ miles S.S.E. of it (lat. 14° 22′ N., long. 74° 29′ E.). A temple in a courtyard 105 feet by 69. The temple is of black stone with sculptures on the walls. An allowance of Rs. 1,440 is made to it annually by Government.

Inscriptions:—Four stone tablets, from one of which it appears that it was founded by Rudroji Paṇḍit, son of Nâgoji, and built by Sanappâ.

VI.—Siddâpur Tâlukâ.

III. 1. **Sidda'pur. Inscriptions**, &c.—A mile west from the town at Hosûr at a small rude temple near the wayside are two carved stones: two more stand about a dozen yards west of it, one of them very elaborately carved; at the bottom is a man carried in a litter, with traces of inscription, and a fifth stands close to the road leading to Jog. At the temple of Gaṇapati in Siddâpur is a Kânarese inscription, 5′ 6″ by 2′ 10″ in 43 lines, dated *Saka* 1574 Khara *Saṃvatsara*. And at Râmeśvara at the site of an old temple in the jungle 1¼ miles N.E. from the town are two carved slabs, one 4′ 7″ by 2′ 10″, with short inscriptions much obliterated.

2. **Bilgi,** about 8 miles from Siddâpur (lat. 14° 22′ N., long. 74° 52′ E.). It was formerly known by the name of Śvetapur, and is said to have been founded by a son of Narasiṁha, a Jaina prince, who ruled at Hosûr (near Sidddâpur) about
II*b*. *Saka* 1515. (1) The Jaina *basti* of Pârśvanâtha is said to have been built by the founder of the town and afterwards extended by a Jaina prince, Ghantevadia, the son of Râghapparâja in *Śaka* 1573, when images of Neminâtha, Pârśvanâtha and Vardhamâna were consecrated. It is in the Dravidian style: the shrine walls are formed of slabs the whole height of the walls, with square pillars at the corners and in the

middle to give them support. The upper part of the walls of the *maṇḍapa* are formed in the same way, set on a carved screen wall. The outer *maṇḍapa* has four round black stone pillars somewhat of the style of those at Belgaum; at each side of this *maṇḍapa* is a small shrine. From the two *śilâśâsanas* still standing it appears that a grant was made of the revenues of 9 villages amounting to Rs. 1,772-7-8, and lands yielding 300 *khaṇḍis* of rice were allotted to it. It has a flat roof supported by carved basalt pillars. (2)
III. There is also a temple of Virûpâksha and another near the town, very plain buildings. **(Surveyed.)**

II *b*. **Inscriptions**:—(1) At Virûpâksha temple to the right of the entrance is a slab 5′ 10″ by 3′ 1″ with a *liṅga* at the top attended by a female on the left with *damaru* and bell, and with cow and calf to the right, the usual figures of sun, moon, and *kaṭâr* above. The inscription is in 42 lines dated *Śaka* 1493 (in words) Promodi (? Pramodi) *Saṁvatsara*. (2) Inside the door of Pârśvanâtha *basti* are two large slabs with the usual Jaina symbol, and in excellent preservation, one measures 6′ 9″ by 2′ 6″ in 78½ lines, *Śaka* 1510, Sarvajit *Saṁvatsara*; (3) the other 6′ 10″ by 2′ 7″ in 84½ lines, *Śaka* 1550, Nandana *Saṁvatsara*. (4) On the other side of the road at a temple of Hanumân is a smaller inscription much defaced.

III. 3. **Baidarkanni** on the road from Bilgi to Siddâpur. A quarter of a mile east of the village, and a little south from the road, is a group of 16 carved stones (three of them broken), some of them very tall and covered with carving of worship, festivity, and war. Near a small *basti* a little to the south-east from these are two more; and in the mud wall of the *basti* are four with *liṅga* emblems at the top; a fifth is a little way off in front on a small platform, and a sixth at the foot of a tree close to the *basti*.

III. 4. **Ittige**, 3 miles west of Bilgi. Temple of Râmeśvara, a building of the usual modern construction, enjoys an annual cash allowance of Rs. 1,000. This is a place of considerable repute, and has a large annual fair attended by numerous devotees.

VII.—Honâvar Tâlukâ.

III. 1. **Hona'var** seems to have no remains of note. There is an old ruined fort, on the west side of which the Portuguese had their warehouses in early times. Basavarâjadurga to the north is said to have been built by the same king as built Chaṇḍâvar. The temple of Râmaliṅga, about 1½ miles north of the town, is said to be two or three centuries old. **(Surveyed.)**

When Honâvar belonged to Madras, before its transfer to Bombay, it was a place of much more importance than it is now, and it is to that time that the fine roads and long lines of splendid *banyan* trees belong. Other relics of that time are a very lofty column on one of the highest points, serving as a landmark to shipping, erected over the remains of Major-General Clement Hill, Commanding the Maisur Division, who died at Gersâppâ in 1848, and an old European grave-yard containing a few tombs, dating from 1778 to 1864. Of early Hindu remains there is little. Slabs, inscribed and otherwise sculptured, generally found built into some bridge or house, attest to the existence at the time of some temple or temples of no mean size. One culvert, near the *dhobie's talâv*, is almost entirely constructed of such material, and an inspection of the under sides of the slabs, as they have been thrown across to form the roadway, discloses three very large inscription slabs, covered with old Kânarese writing, and one sculptured *vîragal* of the style of the Murdeśvara ones, also bearing inscriptions upon the alternate bands. Besides these, there are several large sculptured slabs covered with ornament and figures in bas-relief. In the culvert over the *châmbâr-kâ-nâlâ* is built in another inscribed slab, and a fourth is inserted in the culvert called the *Gundi Bail* culvert.

At Bhatkal and Honâvar, and very commonly in the Konkan, are found odd looking groups of curious stones crowded together under a tree, upon a hill side, or in a garden. They are generally of two forms, one a small pillar or cylinder of various degrees of finish, round or octagonal, with or without a finial, and snake stones,—that is, small slabs with knotted or single snakes carved upon them in relief. Sometimes other carved stones are added bearing small human figures in relief. These stones are called *jetigâs* and are, in most cases, worshipped once a year by Brâhmaṇ *pujâris* attached to some neighbouring temple. It is difficult to find out what they mean, but it is certain they are connected with the worship or appeasing of the spirits of departed ancestors which are represented by these stones, and the setting up and occasional attention to them is by way of propitiating those restless spirits and keeping them in good temper, they being a particularly jealous and vindictive lot. The snake stones here do not seem to have any special connection, if any at all, with the annual snake worship at the *Nâgapanchamî* festival. Tree worship is also very prevalent in these parts, more especially the *pippala* and *tulasi*. They are cared for and protected from injury, around the trunks of the former being built square, octagonal or circular platforms upon which daily circumambulatory ceremonies are performed. The *tulasi*, being a small plant, is generally placed in a receptacle upon the top of a high altar or pedestal within the courtyards of temples and private houses.

III. 2. **Chandâvar,** about 5 miles south-east from Kumtâ (lat. 14° 24' N., long. 74° 33' E.), is a deserted city, said to have been built by a king Sarpanmalika by birth a cowherd, who rose to rank by magic. It passed from the possession of the Svâdî kings to that of the Muhammadans. The last Muhammadan prince dying without issue in A.D. 1686, it declined and is now deserted, and the stones are being carried away for building purposes.

III. 3. **Haigudna,** a village about 12 miles from Honâvar; near it, on an island in the Śarâvatî are some sacrificial *kuṇḍas*. The Haiga Brâhmaṇs are said to have come from the north at the invitation of a Berad king to perform a sacrifice for him here. *Haiga* in old Kânarese means 'sacrifice.'

III. 4. **Bailur,** 12 miles south of Honâvar, (lat. 16° 8' N., long. 74° 32' E.), has a very old temple of Mârkaṇḍeśvara. The Nâyars who ruled over Bârkur repaired the old temple and made grants of land for its support. Some documents relating to this grant are said to exist, dated *Śaka* 1356 (A.D. 1434).

5. **Murdesvar,** 3 miles south of Bailûr and 10 miles north of Bhatkal, has a temple on a promontory called Kandugiri, said to have been built by the Jaina Râjâs of Kaikuri (?). In *Fasli* 1221 Government arranged to grant an endowment of Rs. 1,440 annually. **(Surveyed.)**

I *b*. **Inscriptions** :—There are at least thirty well sculptured *vîragals* and inscriptions (one dated *Śaka* 1336, and another *Śaka* 1380) near this place. (1) About 150 yards west from the school is a Jaina one, of 54 or more lines, each of about 50 letters; (2) two miles north-east from the bangalow, at Basti-Maki, a ruined Jaina temple; (3) at the foot of a *kâju* tree east from the school is a *vîragal* with some lines of inscription; (4, 5) opposite the school in a small cell are two *vîragals*; (6) beside this at the foot of a tree is another; (7) at the left side of Areholle *basti* is a fine slab, 5' by 2' 3" in 64 lines; (8) another against the wall, 6' 3" by 2' 3½", with at least 61 lines; (9) near the bridge a slab, much effaced; (10—28) a collection of beautifully carved stones at the same place, some Jaina and others Śaiva—all with inscriptions; (29, 30) two *satt* stones at the same place.

6. **Bhatkal** or Susagadi, about 24 miles south of Honâvar (lat. 13° 58′ N., long. 74° 36′). Formerly it was called Maṇipur, and was an important place in old Jaina times, during which very fine *bastis* or temples were erected. They usually consist of an *agraśâlâ*, or hall, and a shrine with a *dhvajastambha*. (**Surveyed**.)

I *b*. (1.) Ketapai-Nârâyaṇa-Devasthâna is built of black stone, with a good deal of sculpture on its walls. On the door-lintel is a figure of Śrî. On the base of the temple, and on the inside of the court wall are numerous scenes, some quaint, some indecent, said to be illustrative of the *Râmâyaṇa*. The four pillars inside are short and clumsy. The temple contains an image of Nârâyaṇa of black basalt; it is partly in ruins: it measures about 34½ feet by 18 feet. The base of the wall enclosing the courtyard is pretty entire. Two brick *tulasi kuṇḍas* stand by the sides of the entrance. The *dhvajastambha*, a fine fluted column, is just outside the court, and is sculptured with effigies of the founder and his family. To the north-west of it is a *śilâśâsanam*. The temple enjoys an endowment from Government.

I *b*. (2.) Śâṅtappâ Nâyaka Tirumal Devasthâna is built entirely of black basalt, according to an inscription in it in *Śaka* 1477 by Śâṅtappâ. It measures about 32 feet by 16, is much after the plan of No. 1, with a sloping stone roof, but not so richly carved. The doors are elaborately sculptured, as is also the inner base round the court. The *dhvajastambha* is about 18 feet high, but has lost the top.

III. (3.) Narasiṁha Devasthâna, built about *Śaka* 1460, the date given in an inscription. It measures about 36½ feet by 19, and has a small *dhvajastambha* wanting the capital. It is supported by lands granted by the founder and by a Government allowance.

III. (4.) Jośî Śaṁkara-Nârâyaṇa Devasthâna is a plain temple built, according to an inscription, in A.D. 1554. It consists of a *saṅdhyâmaṇḍapa* in front; about 32 feet by 13 over all, and behind it an *agraśâlâ* about 12 feet by 10. The roofs are formed of slabs sloping down. The *dhvajastambha* is about 14 feet high but has lost the top. It enjoys private grants and a Government allowance.

III. (5.) Choḷeśvara-Devasthâna is also of black basalt, two storeys in height, the lower roofed with stone slabs, the upper with tiles. It has *dvârapâlas* at the door jambs standing on snakes and in front a canopy over the Nandî supported on four pillars. There is also a good *dhvajastambha* and a small temple of Gaṇeśa. Legend says, a king of Choḷa-maṇḍala lost all his children by snake-bite, and coming to the village of Hadili (? Hadavalli), his queen was delivered of a son, which a snake immediately bit; but a Brâhmaṇ of the place skilled in the *mantras* for curing snake-bite, forced the snake to suck back its own poison: whereupon the child revived and the king erected this temple to commemorate the event. On the jambs of the door are two short Tamiḷ inscriptions.

II *b*. (6.) Raghunâtha-Devasthâna is said to have been built by Balkini, son of Anantakini, about *Śaka* 1512, Virodhi *Saṁvatsara*. The *agraśâlâ* is separated from the shrine or temple proper by an open verandah or *sandhyâmaṇḍapa*. It is a small, ornate temple in the Dravidian style. It is supported by private donations and a Government endowment.

III. (7.) Lakars Kamati Nârâyaṇa Devasthâna built about 330 years ago, is a small stone temple out of repair. (8.) Aḍike Nârâyaṇa Devasthâna is similar to the last, but more ruined; the eight *dikpâlas* are represented on the roof, and Śrî on the lintel. The *dhvajastambha* is a small one. (9.) Virûpâksha-Nârâyaṇa Devasthâna is a small temple like the last two, built in *Śaka* 1487 by Jîvana Nâyaka. It is out of repair, but is said to enjoy a Government endowment. (10.) Veṅkaṭaramaṇa is said to be about 300 years old, and resembles No. 6 above, being ornamented by sculptures. It is surrounded by a verandah called *chandraśâlâ*. The *agraśâlâ* is of brick. The car ceremony is celebrated every year, and has a good endowment and considerable land. (11.) Śirâḷe Śambhuliṅga Devasthâna is a modern temple built on the site of an older one. Legend accounts for its origin as for that of many others by the story of a man who accused his herdboy for milking his cow. The boy protested his innocence, but watched the cow, who went into a thicket and poured her milk upon a burrow. The owner, being informed of this, dug up the place and found a *liṅga*, over which he built a temple.

I *b*. (12.) Jattapa Nâyakana Chandranâtheśvara-Basti is the largest Jaina temple here. It stands in an open space surrounded by an old wall, and consists of an *agraśâlâ*, *bhogamaṇḍapa* and *basti*; the latter is of two storeys, the lower being of larger area than the one above. Each storey has three rooms, which are said to have contained images of Ara, Malli, Munisuvrata, Nama, Nemi, and Pârśva, but only fragments of them are left. The walls of the *bhogamaṇḍapa* on the west of the *basti* are pierced with beautiful windows; the *agraśâlâ* or shrine is of two storeys, each of two rooms, which contained images of Rishabha, Ajakasaṁbhava, Abhinanda, and Chandranâtheśvara. There are also *dvârapâlas* at the door. The total length is about 112 feet and breadth of the shrine 40, of the *basti* 50 feet. The *dhvajastambha* is a very elegant pillar and stands on a platform about 14 feet square: the shaft is of a single block 21 feet 6 inches in height, and is surmounted by a quadrangular capital. Behind the *basti* is a smaller pillar called *Yakshabrahmakhamba*, the shaft of which is 19 feet in length. It stands on a platform with four smaller pillars at the corners, with lintels laid over them. Jaṭṭapa Nâyaka made over lands for the support of the temple, but they are said to have been confiscated by Tipu Sultân. This is the finest old temple at Bhatkal, and should be preserved: the villagers used to carry off the fine stone slabs at pleasure.

III. (13.) Pârśvanâtheśvara-Basti is 58 feet long by 18 wide. According to an inscription it was built in *Śaka* 1465. The *dhvajastambha* is a fine pillar on a lofty moulded base, and the small *maṇḍapa* atop contains a four-headed image.

III. (14.) Śânteśvara-Basti is somewhat like No. 12. Other remains of Jaina temples and inscriptions exist. (15.) The Jami Masjid is tile-roofed, but said to be very old. It enjoys a Government allowance of Rs. 400 a year. (16.) Sultân Palle Masjid is about 200 years old. The buildings here have all sloping roofs.

I *a*. There are three European graves situated on the north bank of the creek, part of the way between Bhatkal and the sea. The upper slabs of each, which are single stones, contain old English inscriptions deeply cut in large letters fairly well formed. They are as follows:—

(1) Here lieth the body of William Barton
Chyrvrgion : Dec : XXX : Novembr :
Anno Dni Nri Christi : Salv : Mvndi
MDCXXXIII :*
1638 : William Barton :

(2) Here lyeth the body of George Wye
Marchant : Dec : XXXI : March :
Ano : Dni : Nri : Christi : Salv : Mvndi
MDCXXXVII :
1637 : Geo : Wye :

(3) Here lieth the bodie of Ant : Vernworthy
Marcht. Dec : I : April. Ano. Dni : Nri :
Christi Salv : Mvndi : MDCXXXVII :
Anto. Verneworthy : 1637 :

There are several combination letters in the inscriptions formed much in the same manner as diphthongs are usually printed, H and E, V and E, and A and N. In the last combination they resemble a W upside down with a cross stroke in the first angle to form the A, the cross stroke of the N then becomes reversed. In 1637 the English started a factory at Bhatkal, and it is to this time that belong the three English tombs. There are many old European tombs scattered throughout the country, and a complete list of them with copies of any quaint inscription is a desideratum.

I *b*. **Inscriptions**:—(1) At Jaṭṭapa Nâyakana Chandranâtha Basti, on the east side, 7′ 0″ by 3′ 1½″, containing 70 lines; (2) beside the first, 7′ 11″ by 3′ 6″, in 79 lines; the back of this stone is also covered by an inscription in 63 lines, dated *Śaka* 1479, Nala *Śaṁvatsara*; (3) in the south-east corner of the court is another also bearing Jaina symbols, 6′ 0″ by 2′ 6½″; (4) at Pârśvanâtha *basti*, a slab 5′ 9″ by 2′ 5″, *Śaka* 1468, Viśvâvasu *Śaṁvatsara*; (5) another at the same place; (6) inside the porch 5′ 9″ by 2′ 4″, *Śaka* 1465, Plava *Śaṁvatsara*; (7, 8) behind the same temple sunk into the earth, one 1′ 10″ broad and the other 1′ 9″,—the inscriptions faintly traceable; (9) in the court of Śânteśvara temple a fine carved Vîrakshetrapâla, 6′ 1″ by 2′ 8″, with a good deal of inscription upon it, *Śaka* 1465; (10) a small damaged one beside it, 3′ 1″ by 1′ 10″; (11) near the same place deeply sunk in the earth are two large slabs, which should be preserved; (12) in the court of Khetapai Nârâyaṇa temple is one 6′ 6″ by 2′ 7½″, *Śaka* 1468, Viśvâvasu *Śaṁvatsara*; (13) behind the same is one of *Śaka* 1489, Kshaya *Śaṁvatsara;* (14) outside the court of Jośi Śaṃkara Nârâyaṇa's temple and sunk deep in the earth is a slab 3 feet wide, which should be cared for; (15) at Sântappâ Nâyaka's temple is a slab, with a *gṛihastha* bearing an umbrella in the centre, to the right a *râkshasa* or demon, and to the left a cow and calf, 4′ 9″ by 2′ 9″, *Śaka,* 1478, Raktâkshi *Śaṁvatsara*; (16) in Mûrgopinâtha Kṛishṇadeva's temple is an old slab with *liṅga* at the top; (17) another close by is broken and buried; (18) at Chaturmukha *basti* (now wholly carried away by the villagers) in a

* This should have been MDCXXXVIII; the V has been omitted on the stone.

jâmbul bush is a fine large *śâsanam* with Jaina symbols, 5′ 10″ by 2′ 8″; (19) another close beside it, 6′ 9″ by 2′ 4½″; (20) at Lakars Kamati Lakshmî-Nârâyaṇa temple, 6′ 9″ by 2′ 4½″, of which 1″ 9½″ is covered with inscription partially effaced; (21) on a pillar on the right side of the entrance to Raghunâtha's temple, 27 lines, *Śaka* 1512, Virodhi *Saṁvatsara*; (22) in a watercourse in the street 150 yards from the bangalow, a Jaina inscription, 4′ 11″ by 1′ 10″,—ought to be removed to a place of safety; (23) on the door-jambs of Choleśvara temple are two short Tamil inscriptions; (24) about a quarter of a mile behind the *dharmaśâlâ*, one with Śaiva emblems, 6′ 0″ by 2′ 5″, 61 lines. Copper-plates:—Four: belonging to (1) Virûpâkshadeva Jośi Śaṃkara Nârâyaṇa temple: (2) to Pâśupati Śambhu Liṅga temple; (3 and 4) not stated—in Bhatkal.

III. 7. **Sunkadagoli,** a mile east from Bhatkal: Râmaliṅga Vîrabhadradeva temple, with two inscription slabs.

III. 8. **Hadavalli,** 11 miles E.N.E. from Bhatkal, three old temples, two almost entire in the village and one in ruins on the top of the adjoining hill of Chandragiri, all of them being Jaina shrines. These are of the style of the Bhatkal ones, having the same sloping roofs which make them look like long thatched barns. (**Surveyed.**)

9. **Gersa'ppa'** is about 15 miles east of Honâvar (lat. 14° 12′ N., long. 74° 44′ E.). A mile and a half east of the village and of Nâgankûrâ are extensive ruins called

IIa. Nagarbastikeri. Among them is a Jaina temple called Chaturmukha-Basti, having four doors and a four-faced image in the centre. A small sum was expended by Government about 20 years ago in clearing away grass and bushes; the place is again overgrown. It has been a fine large cruciform temple, 63′ 8″ from door to door inside, the shrine is 22′ 9″ square inside and 24′ 11″ outside; the walls are all thin. There are four thick round pillars with square bases in each hall with the overhanging brackets of the southern style. The *dvârapâlas* cut on slabs on each side the doors both of the *maṇḍapa* and of the shrine have high *mukuṭas* and each holds a club and snake. The temple is built of grey granite, but the roof of the verandah, the stones of the *śikhara*, the slabs of the floor, &c., were carried off some 25 years ago, it is said, by a Mâmlatdâr at Honâvar who was building a temple there. Inscription slabs, &c., were also carried off by road contractors and others to make culverts, &c.

III. The other temples here are all of laterite, and are only of interest on account of the images and inscriptions which have still escaped the spoilers. The temple of Vardhamâna Svâmi, now deserted, still contains a fine black stone image of the *tîrthankara*, almost perfect. Across the foot-path from it is the temple of Nemi, also deserted, but with a fine large image on a circular *âsana*, the back of which is composed of three pieces neatly jointed and elaborately carved. Round the edge of the *âsana* are two *ślokas* in Kânarese letters. In Pârśvanâtha's temple many images have been collected from other shrines,—one of them is cast of an alloy of five metals. To the west of it is a large stone building with long stone beams, and in a corner of it are nearly a dozen neglected figures of standing Digambara Jinas huddled together. Kaḍe *basti* wants the roof and contains a neglected black stone figure of Pârśvanâtha 4′ 4½″ high, with the *śeshaphaṇâ* beautifully carved. And at Vîrabhadra *deval*, a large tree has grown up on what was once the back wall of the shrine, where is a fine image of Vîrabhadra with arrow, sword, shield, and bow,

Ia. and wearing high wooden sandals (*khaḍâvas*). Many of these images are well worth preserving and should be removed to a place of safety before they are destroyed. (**Surveyed.**)

I *a*. **Inscriptions**, &c. :—At Varddhamânsvâmi temple (1) a slab 6′ 3″ by 2′ 5″ with a Jina at the top, two worshippers, and cow and calf, under which is a long inscription; (2) another with a Jina and attendants above, in the second line two male worshippers on each side a cross-legged table, and in the third compartment below, two female worshippers on each side a similar table. The stone measures 4′ 8″ by 2′ 2½″; (3) a slab 5′ 2″ by 2′ 2″ with, first, a Jina in a temple, next, below a male seated, a table, two females squatting and one standing, and third, three females, a temple and female image, and three females, below which are 6½ lines of inscription; (4) behind the temple and sunk in the earth is a small stone about a foot broad and an inscription partially effaced. In the east corner of the area round Pârśvanâtha's temple are three carved stones similar to those described above but much weatherworn; (5) one 7′ 2″ by 2′ 3½″ with an inscription a good deal obliterated; (6) outside the wall of Kaḍe *basti* is an inscription slab 4′ 3″ above ground and 2′ 5″ broad; (7) in the south-west corner of Trimalla Devasthâna, a Vaishṇava temple, is a slab 5′ 6″ by 2′ 3″, with a man in a robe and carrying a vessel, and the cow and calf beside him. The inscription is covered with lichen but very distinct.

I *a*. 10. Between 5 and 6 miles up the Ghât from Gersâppâ there is an Old Kâṇarese **inscription** stone standing at a corner of the road.

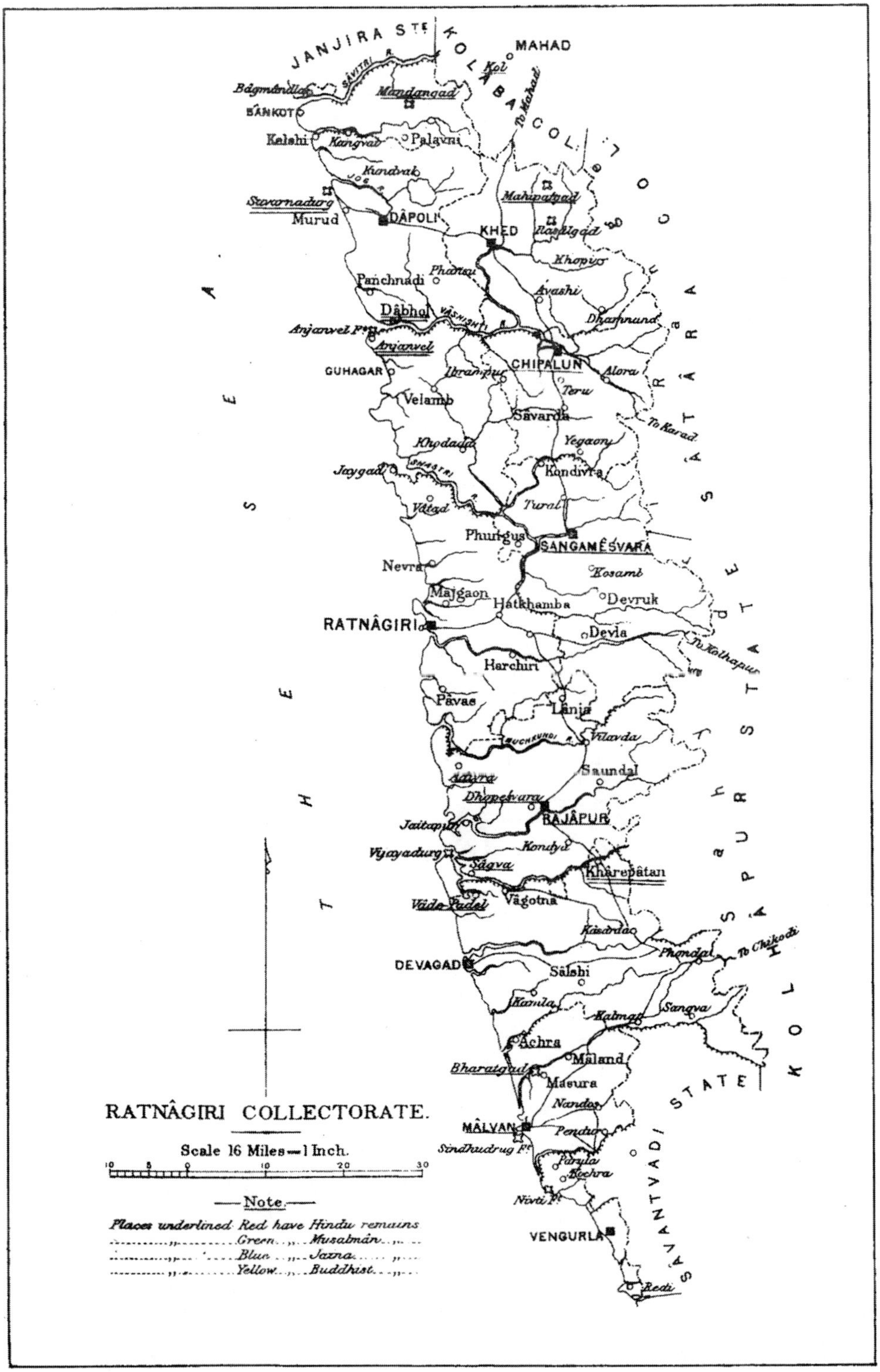

JANJIRA STE
KOLÂBA COL.
MAHAD
Kol
To Mahad
Bâgmândla
Mandangad
BÂNKOT
Kelshi
Kangvai
Palavni
Kundvali
Suvarnadurg
Murud
DÂPOLI
KHED
Mahipatgad
Rasalgad
Khopi
Phansu
Panchnadi
Avashi
Dâbhol
Anjanvel Ft.
Anjanvel
Dhamnund
CHIPALUN
GUHAGAR
Ibrampur
Alora
Teru
Velamb
Savarda
To Karad
Khodaula
Yegaon
Jaygad
Kondivra
Vâtad
Tural
Phungus
SANGAMÉSVARA
Nevra
Kosamb
Majgaon
Hatkhamba
Devruk
RATNÂGIRI
Devla
To Kolhapur
Harchiri
Pâvas
Lânja
Vilavda
Saundal
Dhopeśvara
Jaitapur
RÂJÂPUR
Vijayadurg
Kondye
Sâgva
Khârepâtan
Vâde Padel
Vâgotna
Kâsarda
DEVAGAD
Phonda
To Chikodi
Sâlshi
Kamla
Sangva
Kalmat
Âchra
Mâland
Bharatgad
Masura
Nandos
MÂLVAN
Sindhudrug Ft.
Pendur
Parula
Kochra
Nivti Ft.
VENGURLA
Redi
THE SEA
SÂTÂRA COLL.
KOLHAPUR STATE
SÂVANTVADI STATE
KOLHAPUR STATE
RATNÂGIRI COLLECTORATE.
Scale 16 Miles = 1 Inch.
10 5 0 10 20 30
Note.
Places underlined Red have Hindu remains
" " Green " Musalmân "
" " Blue " Jaina "
" " Yellow " Buddhist "

V.—RATNÂGIRI ZILLA.

I.—Ratnâgiri Tâlukâ.

III. Ratna'giri (*Ind. Ant.*, II. 317.)

II.—Dâpoli Tâlukâ.

III. 1. **Ba'gma'ndla**, a large coast fishing village in the Dâpoli Tâlukâ on the north bank of the Sâvitrî opposite Bânkoṭ. Bâgmândla and Kolmândla are probably the remains of Mândal, or Mândan, an old trading place of some consequence. Barbosa (1514) has a Mandabad at the mouth of the Bânkoṭ river, where many ships, especially from Malabâr, came taking stuffs and leaving cocoanuts, areca-nuts, a few spices, copper, and quicksilver. (Stanley's *Coasts of East Africa* and *Malabâr*, by D. Barbosa, p. 71). The name and position suggest that it may be the site of Ptolemy's Mandagora.

2. **Da'bhol**, N. lat. 17° 34' and E. long. 73° 16', lies 6 miles from the sea, on the north bank of the Anjanvel or Vâsishṭhî river, eighty-five miles south-east of Bombay. Large remains, several feet underground, seem to show that Dâbhoḷ was, in very early times, a place of consequence. An underground temple of Chaṇḍikâbâi is said to be of the same age as the Bâdâmi rock-temples (550-578 A.D. Mr. Crawford's MS). A local history, *bakhar*, states that in the eleventh century Dâbhol was the seat of a powerful Jaina ruler, and a stone inscription has been found bearing date 3rd Vaisâkha 1078 Sâlivâhana. According to a local saying, Dâbhoḷ once bore the name of Amarâvatî or the abode of the gods. The present name is said either to be a short form of Dâbhilâvatî, a name given to it from the still remaining temple of Śiva Dâbhileśvara, or to be a corrupt form of *Dábhya*, according to the *Purâṇas*, a god-inhabited forest. (*Ind. Ant.*, II. 278.)

Ia. Of Musalmân remains the chief, close to the sea and almost buried in cocoanut trees, is a handsome mosque sixty-three by fifty-four feet in its inner measurements, with minarets and a dome. The style is like that of the chief Bijâpur mosques. It is on all sides enclosed by a stone wall and approached by a broad flight of steps. In the centre of the stone terrace, in front of the mosque, is a well and a fountain. The mosque is said to have been built in 1659, by Âisha Bibi, popularly known as lady mother, *mâsâheba*, a princess of Bijâpur. The real date is probably much earlier. The local account is that the princess, with a retinue of 20,000 horse, arrived at Dâbhoḷ intending to go to Makka, but was kept back from fear of pirates. Determining to spend, on some religious work, the £150,000 (Rs. 15,00,000) she had with her, by the advice of the *maulvis* and *qâzis*, she began building this mosque and finished it in four years. The builder's name was Kâmil Khân. It is currently reported that the dome was richly gilded, and the crescent of pure gold. The gold and gilt have long since disappeared, but much of the beautiful carving and tracery remains. Eight villages, Bhopan, Saral, Isâpur, Bhostân, Chivili, Modpur, Bharveli and Pingâri, were granted for its maintenance. After the overthrow of the Bijâpur kingdom, the grant was renewed by Śivâji (1670). The mosque still bears the name of its founder Mâsâheba, but it is no longer used for worship. The local Musalmâns are too poor to keep it in repair. In 1873 a small sum was granted by Government to

III. carry out the most necessary repairs and it has again been taken in hand (Nairne in *Ind. Ant.*, vol. II. p. 280-81). Dâbhoḷ has also a Jâma mosque built in 1650 (1059 H.) in the beginning of Aurangzib's reign, by Pîr Mahammad Abdullâh, the chief officer, *subhedâr*, of the district. What of the inscription on this mosque has been read runs: 'In the name of God, the Just, the Merciful. Verily mosques belong to God, so be not co-sharers with Him. The rival of this mosque in colour does not exist in the world. The best of well born Governors Pîr Ahmad.................(built this mosque) in the year 1059 (1649 A.D.) of the *Hijra* of the Prophet, on whom be peace and blessing.' On the sea face of a third mosque an inscription has lately (1879) been found cut in wood. It begins with the usual Shiah blessing of the Prophet, his daughter, and the twelve Imâms, and ends 'May God help Saâdat Ali, king of kings, who raised this building in 1558 (967 H.)' (Bombay Asiatic Society's Meeting, September 1879). There is also a cenotaph, or *mukâm*, of Khâja Khizr, the Prophet Elias, bearing the date 1579 (987 H.), and a tomb of the Pîr Âzam Khân.

III. 3. **Kol, across the Sâvitrî river, south of Mahâd, to the south-east of the hill behind the village, has two small groups of caves. The first to the north-east of the village consists of a few broken cells of no pretension as to size or style. The other group to the south-east has one cell rather larger than any of the others. All are apparently unfinished and are much damaged. In the second group are three short inscriptions.**

III. 4. **Mandangad Fort**, on the high hill of the same name, about twelve miles inland from Bânkot, has two forts and a triple stockade with an area of about eight acres. Of the three fortifications Manḍangaḍ proper, with two reservoirs, lies to the south, Pârkoṭ is in the middle, and Jâmba, with a dry reservoir on the north. In 1862 the walls were in several places much ruined. The likeness of the name suggests Manḍangaḍ as the Mandagora of Ptolemy and the *Periplus*, a town of the Konkaṇ coast. But Mândla at the mouth of the Bânkoṭ creek is perhaps more likely. Though they are probably much older, local tradition ascribes the fort of Manḍangaḍ to Śivâji, Pârkoṭ to the Habshi, and Jâmba to Angria.

III.—Khed Tâlukâ.

III. **Mahipatgad Fort**, about twelve miles from Khed, facing the Hâtlot Pass and Makrângaḍ, the Mahâbaleśvara 'Saddleback,' stands at the head of a high spur, that, running parallel to the Sahyâdris, is crowned by the three forts of Mahipatgaḍ, Sumârgaḍ, and Rasâlgaḍ. Reached by a very narrow difficult pass six miles long, Mahipatgaḍ is a table-land 120 acres in area, with no surrounding wall, but with well-built battlements and gateways in six places where the approach is easy. These defences are in bad repair. The wood-work is gone, and in many places the stone work is in ruins. Of the doors the Kotvâl gate to the north is formed by two battlements one on each side and joined with parts of the ramparts; and from the Kheḍ door to the south are still traces of the path by which the garrison received their supplies.

IV.—Chiplun Tâlukâ.

III. 1. **Chiplun**, N. lat. 17° 30′ and E. long. 73° 36′, the chief town of the Chiplûn subdivision, and twenty-five miles from the sea, on the south bank of the Vâsishṭhî river. Chiplûn, the first home of the Konkanasthas or Chitpâvan Brâhmans, according to local tradition, was peopled with Brâhmaṇs and supplied with sixty ponds and sixty gardens by

Paraśurâma, the reclaimer of the Konkaṇ; it has for long been a place of consequence. A stone has lately been found at Chipḷûn bearing the date 1135 (S. 1078—*Jour. Bom. As. Soc.*, September 1879.) In the seventeenth century it was a great village, very populous and plentifully supplied with all kinds of provisions. (Ogilby's (1670) *Atlas*, V. 247.)

About a quarter of a mile south of the town is a series of rock-temples. Of these the chief is a tolerably large hall twenty-two feet long by fifteen broad and ten high, with, at its inner end, a Buddhist relic shrine or *dâgoba*. There are also two or three smaller caves and a deep pond thirteen feet square. Three stages on the road from Chipḷûn to Karâḍ in Sâtârâ is another series of Buddhist caves, consisting of a room with a small round relic shrine, six feet in diameter, and a hall, *śâlâ*, nineteen feet by eighteen, with a raised seat at one corner and three recesses at the inner end (*Jour. Bom. Br. Royal Asiatic Society*, vol. IV. p. 342; part. XIII. p. 47).

III. 2. **Anjanvel**, N. lat. 17° 31′ and E. long. 73° 15′, stands on the south shore of the entrance to the Vâsishṭhî or Dâbhoḷ river: Anjanvel fort, called Gopâlgaḍ, was built by the Bijâpur kings in the sixteenth century, strengthened by Śivâji about 1660, and improved by his son Sambhâji (1681-1689). It stands on a gently sloping point on the south shore of the creek entrance half a mile from Anjanvel. It covers seven acres, and is surrounded on three sides by the sea, and on the fourth by a deep ditch now partly filled. (Government List of Civil Forts, 1862.) There is no complete line of outworks, only one or two covered ways leading down to batteries. (Nairne's MS.) The fort walls built of stone and mortar are very strong, about twenty feet high and eight thick, with twelve bastions at some distance from each other, until very lately armed with cannon. South of the fort is a deep trench eighteen feet broad. There are two gates to the east and to the west. On either side of the west gate is a guardroom. The interior of the fort still has traces of small houses. There are also three wells, with a plentiful supply of water. Near the wells is a building said to have been the store-room, close to it a granary, and, at a little distance, the governor's palace. Some Persian verses on a flat oblong stone give the date 1707 and the builder's name Sidi Sayyid. The verses are: 'Whoever built a new mansion, when he was called away, did it not belong to another? God is immortal and all else subject to death. When the kind king, the light of the world, ordered, the fort was made which he could not live to see. Sidi Sayyid (built) the fort. Written on the 10th of Zil Hajj the first year of the reign, *Hijra* 1119 (1707 A.D.).'

V.—Sangameśvara Tâlukâ.

II *b*. **Sangameśvara**, N. lat. 17° 9′ and E. long. 73° 66′, a town on the Śâstrî river, about twenty miles from the coast,—the meeting of the Alaknandâ and Varuṇâ, is a place of some sanctity and of high antiquity. According to the *Sahyâdri Khaṇḍa* it was originally called Râmakshetra and had temples built by Paraśurâma or Bhârgava Râma. In later times, perhaps about the seventh century, a Châlukyaṇ king Karṇa, coming from Karavîra or Kolhâpur, made Saṅgameśvara his head-quarters, and, founding a city, built a fortress, temples, and palaces. The date of this Karṇa, who seems to be the same as the founder of the Mahâlakshmî temple at Kolhâpur (*J. B. B. R. A. S.*, vol. XI. p. 100), has not yet been fixed. The style of building is supposed (*J. B. R. R. A. S.*, vol. XI. p. 107) to point to some time about the 8th century A.D. At the same time, according to some verses in the Kolhâpur Mahâlakshmî temple, Karṇa flourished about 100 A.D. (30 *Śâlivâhan*) (*J. B.*

B. R. A. S., vol. XI. p. 104), and according to the Saṅgameśvara Mâhâtmya he became king in 178 (Ś. 100). (*J. B. B. R. A. S.*, vol. XI. p. 99.) Of the temples, one, called **Karṇeśvara** after its founder, remains. Saṅgameśvara continued for some time the head-quarters of a Châlukya chief. It is mentioned in a Châlukya grant probably of the eleventh or twelfth century. In the fourteenth century it was for long the residence of Basavâ, the founder of the Lingâyat sect. Two miles up the river, in old Saṅgameśvara, called the *kasbá* to distinguish it from the new town, *peth*, are several interesting temples. The chief of them is the temple of Karṇeśvara already referred to. But the shrine of the Saṅgameśvara temple is said to be older dating from as far back as Paraśurâma's time. (*J. B. B. R. A. S.*, 100.) According to Lieut. Dowell (1829) Karṇa repaired temples originally built by Paraśurâma. Mr. Dowell noticed that the chief temple was of the same age and style as the Kolhâpur temple. There were then (1829) the remains of over a hundred ruined shrines.—(*Bom. Rev. Rec.* 225 of 1851, 2730.) Karṇa is said to have built or repaired 360 temples and granted the revenues of many villages for their support. Every year on Mâgha *vadya* 30th (January-February) a fair is held attended by about 1,000 persons. At the meeting of the rivers are several sacred places, *tîrthas*, among them one known as the cleanser of sins, *dhûtapâpa*. There are also some rock excavations here. (*Ind. Ant.* II. 317; *J. B. B. R. A. S.*, Part XXXI. p. 99.)

VI.—Râjâpur Tâlukâ.

III. 1. **Adivra**, 12 miles west of Râjâpur, has a well-known temple dedicated to Mahâkâlî. In her honour a fair is held from the second to the tenth day of the first fortnight of Âśvina (September-October). Petty shops are opened and about 1,000 persons attend.

III. 2. **Ra'ja'pur**, N. lat. 16° 38′ and E. long. 73° 22′, the chief town of the Râjâpur sub-division, is built on a slope rising from the water's edge, at the head of a tidal creek, thirty miles south-east of Ratnâgiri and about fifteen miles from the sea. At the time of the first Musalmân conquest (1312), Râjâpur was the chief town of a district. (Jervis' *Konkan*, 81.) In 1638 it is said to have been one of the best Dakhan maritime towns (Mandelslo in Harris, Vol. II. p. 130).

III. 3. **Va'de-Pa'del** and Sâgva, both near Vâgotna, some ruined cells probably Brahmanical (*J. B. B. R. A. S.*, Part XX. pp. 611-12).

III. 4. **Dhopes'vara**, a mile or so west of the town of Râjâpur. A noted temple; the village revenues are alienated for the support of the shrine, and every year a fair is held on Śivarâtri (February-March) attended by about 1,000 people. A procession is formed, and the idol, covered with a gold mask, is carried round the temple in a palanquin.

VII.—Devagad Tâlukâ.

III. **Kha'repa'tan**, about 25 miles up the Vijayadurg river. On a small hill overlooking the town is a fort about an acre in area. The walls and bastions were taken down in 1850, and used to make the Vâgotna landing place. (Government List of Civil Forts, 1862.) The sites of twelve or thirteen mosques are shown, and the remains of one, the Jumâ mosque, prove it to have been a building of large size. Outside of the limits of the present town is a very large brick reservoir, ruinous and nearly dry, with an inscription, stating that it was built by a Brâhman in 1659. Near the middle of the town is a half buried stone believed to have been the boundary between the Hindu and the Musalmân quarters. And in the middle of the town there is a colony of Karnâṭak Jains and a Jaina temple said to be the only one in the southern Koṅkaṇ. In the temple is a small black marble idol, found three or four years ago in the bed of the river. Copperplates of the Râshṭrakûṭa dynasty were found here (*Ind. Ant.*, vol. II. p. 321; IX., 33; *J. B. B. R. A. S.*, Part V. p. 209).

VIII.—Mâlvan Tâlukâ.

III. 1. **Achra,** about 10 miles north of Mâlvaṇ. Temple of Râmeśvara. The principal building, enclosed by a stone wall and surrounded by a paved courtyard, measures sixty-three feet by thirty-eight, and, besides the shrine, has a large rest-house with accommodation for all Hindu castes. A fair, held yearly on Râmanavamî in Chaitra (March-April) is attended by about 1,000 people from the neighbouring villages. The village revenues (Rs. 2,500 per annum) are, by a grant of Śambhu Mahârâja of Kolhâpur, dated 1674, set apart for the support of the temple.

III. 2. **Bharatgad Fort,** on the south shore of Bâlavali creek, on a hill commanding the Mâlvaṇ village of Masura, has an area of between five and six acres. The inside of the citadel is an oblong of 105 yards by 60. The citadel walls are about seventeen or eighteen feet high and five feet thick. At the opposite ends of a diagonal running north and south are outstanding round towers. Within the citadel, about a quarter of its whole length from the north end, is a square watch tower reached by steps. Close to the north tower is a small temple, and near it is a well, about 228 feet deep, cut through the solid rock. About seventeen yards from each side, and 100 yards from each end of this citadel, is an outer wall with nine or ten semicircular towers. The wall is ten or twelve feet thick with an outer ditch. It is not very strong and seems to have been built without mortar. In 1862 the walls were in fair order.

III. 3. **Suvarnadurg,** the 'golden fortress,' with an area of eight acres, on a low irregular island, about a quarter of a mile from the shore, surrounded by a very high wall, is perhaps the most striking of the Ratnâgiri coast forts. Great part of the fortifications are cut out of the solid rock and the rest is built of blocks of stone ten or twelve feet square. Relieved by bastions, and broken by one rough postern gate just above high tide mark, the walls are so overgrown with trees and bushes, that, except at low tide, it is impossible to walk round them. Within the fort are several reservoirs and a small step-well with water enough for a large garrison. On a stone at the threshold of the postern gate is a figure of a tortoise, and opposite it, on the wall towards the left, one of Mâruti, the monkey god. There are two guard-rooms to the right and left, and rooms also under the bastions. At a little distance is a stone building plastered with mortar, said to have been the magazine. Some very extensive foundations are probably the sites of old palaces. In 1862 the walls and bastions were in good repair, but the gateway was ruinous. There were fifty-six guns, all old and unserviceable.

Suvarndurg was built by the Bijâpur kings in the fifteenth century, in 1660 it was strengthened by Śivâji, in 1698 it was a station of Kânohji Angria's fleet, and in 1718 it was formally made over to him by Sâhu Râjâ. Under Kânhoji's successor Tulâji, Suvarṇadurg became one of the head centres of piracy.

III. 4. **Ma'lvan** (the name Mâlvaṇ is said to come from the great salt marshes, *mahâ, lavaṇa,* to the east of the town—(Mr. G. Vidal, C.S.)—N. lat. 16° 4′ and E. long. 73° 31′. In a bay, almost entirely blocked by rocky reefs, there were formerly three small islands, two of them about a quarter of a mile from the shore, and the third separated from the mainland by a narrow channel. On the larger of the two outer islands stands the famous fort of Sindhudurg, and, on the smaller, the ruined fort of Padamgaḍ, now, at low tide, connected with the mainland by a neck of sand. On what once was the inner island, and is now part of the mainland, lie, almost hid in palms, the old town of Mâlvaṇ. This inner island was called Medha, but the channel separating it from the mainland has been long dried up. This island stretched from a point about a quarter of a mile to the north of the old residency to the site of the custom house on the south, and in it stood the old fort of Râjkoṭ. The modern town of Mâlvaṇ has spread far beyond the limits of the former island.

About the middle of the seventeenth century, when Śivâji fortified Sindhudurg, the creek about a mile and a half north of Mâlvaṇ was navigable some miles up to Maland or Milandi, then a place of considerable trade. (Nairne MS. Dom João de Castro (1538) mentions that at low tide gallies could enter the river of Malundi. *Prim. Rot. da Costa India,* 22.) In 1750, under the name Molundi, it is mentioned as a fortified town belonging to Bhonsle. The similarity of the name Melizigeris, the island of Meli, and the fact that the chief export was pepper (Lassen Ind. Alt., I. 327) would seem to make it probable that Ptolemy's island of Melizigeris, and the mart of Melizeigara, mentioned in the *Periplus* and perhaps Pliny's Zîgerus, and Strabo's Sigerdis were the island-town of Milandi or Mâlvaṇ. Ibu Khurdâdba (Cir. A.D. 900) mentions Mâli, an island five days' south of Sanjân in the north of Thâna (Elliot's *History,* vol. I. p. 15) and Al Biruni (A.D. 130) has Mâlia south of Saimur, that is Chaul in Kolâba (Elliot, vol. I. p. 66). This may refer to Mâlvaṇ or Milandi, but they more likely belong to the Malabâr coast. Compare El Idrisi (A.D. 1150) in Elliot, vol. I. p. 85.

The chief object of interest is Śivâji's fortress and coast capital, Sindhudurg, or the ocean fort. On a low island, about a mile from the shore, although less striking than Suvarṇadurg, it is very extensive—little less than two miles round the ramparts. The figure of the fort is highly irregular with many projecting points and deep indentations. This arrangement has the advantage that not a single point outside of the rampart is not commanded from some other point inside. (*Report on the condition of Forts in South Konkan,* 1828.) The walls are low, ranging from twenty-nine to thirty feet. On the sea side so low are the walls that at one place they seem almost below high water level, and inside of the fort are masses of wave-worn rock and stretches of sand. (Nairne's MS.) They are on an average twelve feet thick, and have about thirty-two towers from forty to 130 yards apart. The towers are generally outstanding semicircles with five embrasures for cannon. The entrance is at the north-east corner. The area of the fort is forty-eight acres. Once full of buildings it is now a mere shell with nothing inside but a few small temples. To the Marâṭhâs Sindhudurg is Śivâji's cenotaph and in its chief shrine Śivâji's image is worshipped (Grant Duff in Nairne.) In 1862 the walls and bastions were with a few exceptions in a fair state of preservation. Within the walls were thirteen houses, three temples, and one *dharmaśâlâ*. There was, in one of these temples, an effigy of the Marâṭhâ monarch, Śivâji, held in the greatest veneration. (*Gov. List of Civil Forts*, 1862.) The image is of stone. The head is covered with a silver mask, or, on high days, with a gold one. In the stone of the walls prints of Śivâji's hands and feet are held in reverence and protected by small temples. (Nairne's MS.) But for their exceeding smallness these imprints are very accurate representations of a hand and foot. (Mr. R. B. Worthington, C. S.) Monday is the chief day for Śivâji's worship and the Kolhâpur chief sends turbans and other presents. The shrine is seldom visited by pilgrims and is not honoured by a fair.—(Mr. G. Vidal, C. S.)

III. 5. **Masura**, about half-way between Mâlvaṇ and Mâland or Milandi on the Khâlâvli creek, has been identified with the Muziris of Ptolemy and the *Periplus*, then one of the chief places of trade in Western India. (*Ind. Ant.*, vol. II. p. 298.) Muziris was probably further south on the Kânarâ or Malabâr coast. [Muziris by Forbes, 1783, *Or. Mem.* IV. 109, and by Rennel, 1783, *Map of Hindustan*, XXXVII. has been identified with Mirjân near Kumta in North Kânarâ. Dr. Caldwell's suggestion (*Dravidian Grammar*, Introd. p. 97) that Muziris is Muyir-kotta, the modern Kranganor in Cochin, though this is much further south than Ptolemy puts it, is now generally accepted (Balfour's *Cyclopœdia*, Muziris: McCrindle *Periplus*, 131). Yule (*Cathay*, II. 374) marks it doubtful.]

III. 6. **Nivti**, six and a half miles south of Mâlvaṇ and eight north of Vengurla. At the mouth of a small creek, in rather a striking bay, stands Nivti fort in the village of Kochra. If Rennell's suggestion, that it is Ptolemy's (150) Nitra and Pliny's (77) Nitrias 'where the pirates cruized for the Roman ships' is correct, Nivti is an old settlement. But as far as has been traced it has never been of importance as a centre of trade. (Rennell's *Memoir of a Map of Hindustan*, p. 31.) Nitra or Nitrias is more commonly identified with the *Periplus* (247) Naoura and so probably with Honâvar. (McCrindle's *Periplus*, p. 130.) In 1819 its trade was quite insignificant. (Mâlvaṇ Resident to Government, 31st May 1819; Rev. Dia. 141 of 1819, 2299.)

III, 7. **Kochra**, copper-plate grant. *Ind. Ant.*, VIII. 44.

VI.—KOLÂBÂ ZILLA.

I.—ALIBÂG TÂLUKÂ.

III. 1. **Aliba'g.**—The Hirakot, or old fort, now used as a sub-jail and treasury; and temple of Bâlâji.

III. 2. **Korle Fort**, on a rock about 400 feet high running half across the mouth of the river at Chaul. In plan and works it is different from any other on the west coast. It was taken by the Portuguese in 1594 and rebuilt by them between 1646 and 1680. It is about half a mile in length. There are several Portuguese **inscriptions** in it. The greater part of the works is still in good preservation. The promontory is fortified all round and crossed at the top by two lines of walls with gateways and bastions, and several of the gateways have the names of saints engraved upon them. At the point commanding the entrance to the harbour is a large battery, and the level space between this and the bottom of the hill apparently contained the quarters for the troops. The chapel, now roofless, is in the highest part of the fort and close to the magazine. (*Ind. Ant.*, vol. III. pp. 100, 181.)

III. 3. **Revadanda'.**—Ruins of large Portuguese buildings, principally churches, built between 1630 and 1700 A.D., also an old Fort.

Two miles north-east are two Buddhist caves.

III. 4. **Agarawa.**—Between Revadaṇḍâ and the seashore, on the south. Muhammadan mosque with an **inscription**;—also a *hammâmkhâna* in ruins, built by a courtezan.

III. 5. **Chaul.**—Many temples, tanks, &c. The temple of Śrî Hingalâja—in which are also images of Âśâpûrî and Chatuśśringî. The temple is said to be old, but is small and covered with whitewash. The temple of Dattâtreya has an **inscription** round the *pâdukâ*. (*Ind. Ant.* III. 100.)

III. 6. **Sagaon, 4 miles north-east of Alibâg, temple of Kanakeśvara on the hill.**

II *b*. 7. **Na'gaon.**—**Inscription** 2′ 4″ by 1′ 6″ in steps of temple of Bhîmeśvara. Also a mile east of Bhîmeśvara's temple an **inscription** 4′ 3″ by 1′ (*Bombay Gazetteer*, Vol. XI. p. 351.)

II *b*. 8. **Akshi.**—Twenty paces from Kâlkâbarva Devi's temple, to left of the house of one Râmâ Nâyak, an **inscription** 4′ 3″ by 1′. Also 10 feet to the left of the Someśvara temple an **inscription** 5′ 5″ by 1′ 3″. (*B. G.* XI. 253.)

II *b*. 9. **Khanda la'.**—At foot of Kârli pass an **inscription** 6′ 6″ by 2′ 9″. (*B. G.* XI. 324.)

III. 10. **Kha'nderi.**—A fort on a small island six miles north-west of Alibâg. (*B. G.* XI. 324.)

III. 11. **Ra'mdharan.**—Artificial caves five miles north-east of Alibâg. (*B. G.* XI. 377.)

III. 12. **Sa'gargad.**—A fort six miles east of Alibâg. (*B. G.* XI. 379.)

III. 13. **Underi.**—A fort on an island. (*B. G.* XI. 395.)

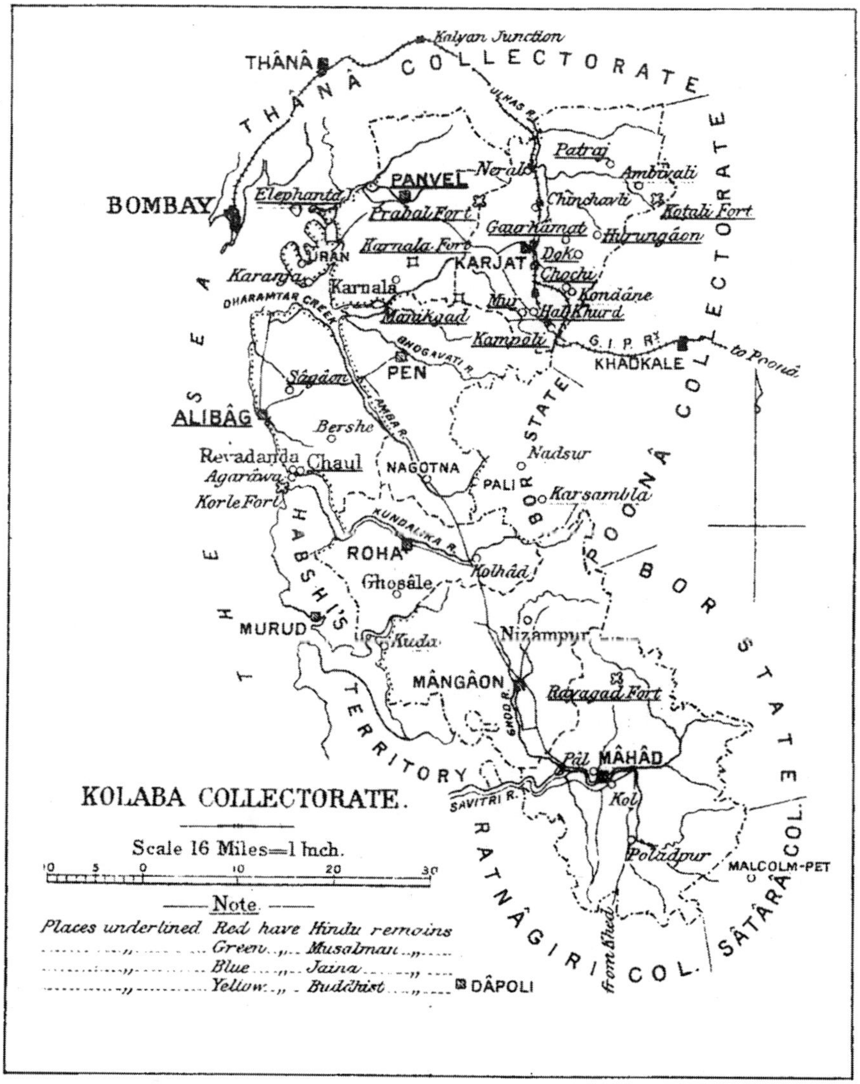
KOLABA COLLECTORATE.
Scale 16 Miles=1 Inch.
10 5 0 10 20 30
Note
Places underlined Red have Hindu remains
" Green " Musalman "
" Blue " Jaina "
" Yellow " Buddhist "
THÂNÂ COLLECTORATE
THÂNÂ
Kalyan Junction
ULHAS R.
BOMBAY
Elephanta I.
PANVEL
Prabal Fort
Neral
Patraj
Ambivali
Chinchavli
Kotali Fort
Gaur Kamat
Hurungâon
Karnala Fort
KARJAT
Doko
Chochi
Kondâne
URAN
Karanja
Karnala
DHARAMTAR CREEK
Manikgad
Mur
Hal Khurd
Kampoli
G. I. P. RY.
KHADKALE
to Poona
BHOGAVATI R.
PEN
Sâgâon
ALIBÂG
AMBA R.
Bersho
Revadanda
Chaul
Agarâwa
Korle Fort
NAGOTNA
PALI
Nadsur
Karsambla
BOR STATE
POONÂ COLLECTORATE
KUNDALIKA R.
ROHA
Kolhâd
Ghosâle
THE SEA
HABSHI'S TERRITORY
MURUD
Kuda
Nizampur
MÂNGÂON
Râyagad Fort
GHOD R.
Pâl
MÂHÂD
SAVITRI R.
Kol
Poladpur
MALCOLM-PET
SÂTÂRÂ COL.
RATNÂGIRI COL.
from Khed
DÂPOLI

II.—PANVEL TÂLUKÂ.

I *a*. 1. **Elephanta** or Ghârâpurî island in the Bombay harbour; the well-known Elephanta caves. (*J. B. B. R. A. Soc.*, Part I. p. 40, and Part XIII. p. 41.) **(Surveyed.)**

III. 2. **Karanja**, on the east side of the harbour; caves. (*J. B. B. R. A. S.*, XIII. 43.)

III.—PEN TÂLUKÂ.

III. 1. **Ratangad.**—Ruined fort with rock-cut cisterns. (*B. G.* XI. 378.)

III. 2. **Sa'nkshi.**—A fort five miles north-east of Pen. Musalmân tomb and rock-cut cisterns. (*B. G.* XI. 383.)

III. 3. **Songiri.**—A fort eight miles south-east of Pen with rock-cut cisterns. (*B. G.* XI. 388.)

II *b*. 4. **Na'gothana**—Old Musalmân bridge 480 feet long with **inscription**. (*B. G.* XI. 353.)

IV.—ROHÂ TÂLUKÂ.

III. 1. **Avachitgad.**—A fort with **inscriptions** in Marâthi. (*B. G.* XI. 265.)

III. 2. **Birwa'di Fort.**—A fort six miles south-west of Roho. (*B. G.* XI. 267.)

III. 3. **Shosalgad.**—A fort six miles south of Roho. (*B. G.* XI. 312.)

III. 4. **Surgad.** A fort 8 miles east of Roho with **inscriptions**. (*B. G.* XI. 390.)

V.—MÂNGÂON TÂLUKÂ.

III. 1. **Mashidva'di.**—A fort called Mângaḍ and 9 rock-cut cisterns. (*B. G.* XI. 350.)

III. 2. **Niza'mpur.**—Ruins of old temples. (*B. G.* XI. 358.)

III. 3. **Tale.**—An upright slab 5′ 6″ × 1′ 6″ in the middle of the village. (*B. G.* XI. 391.)

III. 4. **Talagad.**—A fort. (*B. G.* XI. 391.)

III. 5. **Vishra'mgad.**—A fort 13 miles north-east of Mângâon with rock-cut cisterns. (*B. G.* XI. 397.)

III. 6. **Bhaimad.**—Rock-cut cisterns in a hill called Bhorundurg.

I *a*. 7. **Kuda** in the Janjira creek, an extensive series of early Buddhist caves with numerous **inscriptions**. (*Ind. Ant.* vol. VII. p. 253; also *Cave Temples of India.*) **(Surveyed.)**

VI.—MAHÂD TÂLUKÂ.

III. 1. **Maha'd**, temple of Vîreśvara.

II *b*. 2. **Ra'yagad Fort**, 16 miles north from Mahâd. On the temple of **Mahâdeva**, inside it, is an **inscription** in honour of Śivâji.

II *a*. 3. **Pa'l**—about a mile north-west from Mahâd—has a group of caves excavated in the sides of a hill, with some inscriptions. (*J. B. B. R. A. S.*, Part XIII. p. 43; *Arch. Sur. Report*, IV.; *Cave Temples of India.*) (**Surveyed.**)

III. 4. **Kol**, two groups of unfinished caves. (*Arch. Sur. Report*, vol. IV. and *Cave Temples of India.*) (**Surveyed.**)

III. 5. **Chandragad.**—A fort in the village of Dhavali, 15 miles south-east of Mahâd. (*B. G.* XI. 269.)

III. 6. **Da'sga'on.**—A long creek from Ghodegâon to Mahâd; two old rock-cut cisterns. (*B. G.* XI. 311.)

III. 7. **Kangari.**—A fort 11 miles east by south of Mahâd. (*B. G.* XI. 323.)

III. 8. **Linga'na Fort.**—A fort on the Sahyâdris between Râyagaḍ and Tornâ. (*B. G.* XI. 343.)

III. 9. **Loha'ra.**—Old plinth and battle stones. (*B. G.* XI. 343.)

III. 10. **Ma'thera'n.**—Old plinth, battle-stones and sculpture. (*B. G.* XI. 351.)

III. 11. **Sov.**—Three cisterns of cut-stone. (*B. G.* XI. 388.)

VII.—Karjat Tâlukâ.

III. 1. **Chochi.** Gambhîranâthadeva and caves.

II *a*. 2. **Konda'ne.**—About eight miles from the Karjat Station on the Bombay-Poona Railway line, and in the base of the hill which is crowned by the old fort of Râjmâchî, is the Kondâne group of caves. They are in the face of a steep scarp, and quite hidden from view by the thick forest in front of them. They must be nearly, if not quite contemporary with those at Bhâja. (See *Cave Temples*, p. 220; and *Ind. Ant.*, V, 309; *J. B. B. R. A. S.*, Part XIII. p. 46; *Arch. Sur. Report*, IV.) (**Surveyed.**)

III. 3. **Dok.**—One cave and a Bhairavadeva and cistern.

II *a*. 4. **Ambivali.**—Ambivali cave is about half a mile from the village of Ambivali, near Jambrug, north from Karjat under Kotaligaḍ, and to the east of it. It is cut in a long low hill forming the concave side of a curve in the bank of the river. The cave overlooks the river, being about 20 feet above it, sloping rock leading up to it from the water. It consists of a large square hall, about 42 feet by 39 feet and 10 feet high, having four cells off each of three sides (12 cells in all). Around these same three sides runs a low bench similar to bench in Cave 35, at Kâṇheri. Two doorways, a central and a side one to the right, lead into a verandah, 31 feet long by about 5′ 10″ deep, the eaves of which are supported by 3′ 9″ of return of the wall at either end and by four pillars. Between each pair of pillars (except the central pair—the entrance) and the end pillars and pilasters is a low seat, with a parapet wall running along the outer side and forming a back to the seat. The outside of the parapet wall was ornamented in the same style as Cave III. at Nâsik, with festoons and rosettes, but is so damaged that little now remains. The pillars are of the same pattern as those of Nâsik—pot capitals with the flat tiles surmounting them, but roughly finished. The shafts springing from the seats have no bases. The central pair of pillars have octagonal shafts, the remaining two 16-sided. The doorways have had modern carved doors inserted, the cave has been converted into a Brahmanical temple. A *jogi*, recently dead, occupied the cave, the consequence being that the surface of the rock, in the hall and verandah, could not be much blacker.

On the second pillar of verandah, on the left of entrance, is a Pâli inscription in one vertical line, reading downwards. There are some remains of letters on each of the centre pair of pillars, though indistinct. (*Ind. Ant.*, V. 310; *J. B. B. R. A. S.*, Part XIII. p. 45; *Arch. Sur. Report*, IV.) (**Surveyed.**)

III. 5. **Kotali Fort.**—There are a few excavations of no pretensions or interest in the base of the cliffs of Koṭali Fort. In one is the ubiquitous red daubed stone converting it into the village shrine of Peṭh which lies at the foot of the fort. A spiral staircase leads up through the rock for about two-thirds of the way to the fort, and then emerges and continues the rest of the way up the precipitous surface of the rock. The fort on the top is about 150 yards long by 60 yards wide. There are one or two water cisterns, but nothing else.

II *a*. On the hill side, on the ascent to the fort, are two iron guns about 5 feet long and one small bronze mortar, the latter in good condition. In the excavations in the base of the cliffs are several iron cannon balls lying about. (**Surveyed.**)

III. 6. **Gaurkama'l**, four miles east of Karjat, has a small hill fort with several rock-cut water cisterns. The masonry of the fort and the ruins of an old temple below are in the pre-Musalman or "Hemâdpanti" style.

III. 7. **Halkhurd**, eight miles south of Karjat, has, in an overhanging scarp not far from the village, a plain monastery cave twelve feet by eleven, surrounded by cells. One cell on the left of the entrance has been turned into a shrine of Bhairava, and, within living memory, the front wall of the cave has been thrown down. It is said to have borne an inscription. (*Ind. Ant.*, V. 310.)

III. 8. **Ka'mpoli.**—A beautiful tank, the finest in the district, of clamped stones, and a fine temple built by Nânâ Phaḍnavis. There was also an *annachhatra* to feed all who came to the place. This has been pulled down, but the huge grinding stones for the grain are still lying close by.

III. 9. **Prabal-Moranjan.**—Varoshi village: an old hill fort.

III. 10. **Patraj.**—An old fort.

III. 11. **Hurungaon.**—Bhivapuri. Tank said to have been constructed by Pârvatîbâi, widow of Sadâśiva Chimnâji, a member of the Peśvâ's family, at a cost of Rs. 75,000. The tank is situated at the foot of the Kusur Ghâṭ on the road to Poona.

Janjira State.

III. 1. **Janjira.**—An island fort. (*B. G.* XI. 462.)

III. 2. **Padmadurg.**—A fort with cistern. (*B. G.* XI. 466.)

IV.—SINDH..

I.—KARÂCHI DISTRICT.

1. Thata or Tattâ, 60 miles east of Karâchi, an old city founded probably about the middle of the 15th century. The site of the older city of the Samma dynasty lies under the Makli hills, about 3 miles north-west of Thatâ upon the crest of the Makli hills. Running from north to south for some 4 or 5 miles, is one vast burial ground which has been in constant use for over five hundred years and is still the great burying ground for the Musalmân population of Thatâ. Among these thousands of graves are the more pretentious tombs of the rulers of Thatâ. Beginning at the northern end they trend southward approximately in order of time.

III. (1) The tomb of Sayyid Ali Shâh Shirâzi, the furthest to the north, is of brick on a masonry plinth, plastered and whitewashed. The tomb is oblong, 48½ feet by 33, and is roofed by a large and two small fluted domes. It was built by the Jokhias. Sayyid Ali Shirâzi died in 980 A.H. (1572 A.D.). There are inscriptions on some of the small tombs within the enclosure, but none on the Sayyid's.

II *a*. (2) At some distance south of Sayyid Ali Shâh's tomb is a group of old tombs, among which is a small domed brick building with some good coloured tile work within. It stands a little way from the north-west corner of No. (3). Within it are two graves, one of which is of a woman named Makli from whom the hill takes its name. The tomb is supposed to have been built about 813 A.H. (1410 A.D.). Close by are other very early brick tombs, very plain, and in ruins.

I *a*. (3) The tomb of Jâm Nizam-u-din (commonly called Jâm Nindo) is a great square solid stone structure without a dome which has been built in great part from the remains of some magnificent Hindu temple. This old carving is very fine. Pure Hindu elements in it are a band of the sacred geese, two miniature temple *śikharas*, and the Hindu *kalaśa* or finial which surmounts several eight-pillared *chhatris* which are close by. Under these latter graves have been dug and tombstones erected. It is not clear, however, whether the original temple stood here or at Samûi; more probably at the latter place. Date 914-15 A.H. (1508 A.D.). All the tombs in this group belong to the time of the Sammas.

III. (4) South of the last some little distance, and near the edge of the plateau, is the ruined brick-domed tomb known as "Juman Jati."

III. (5) Still further southward, and just below the edge of the tableland is the small insignificant whitewashed tomb of Sayyid Muhammad Baghdâdi.

III. (6) Next comes, on the hill, a square building with a curious arrangement of four half domes each set above a corner of the building. It is the tomb of Shekh Jiâ, the

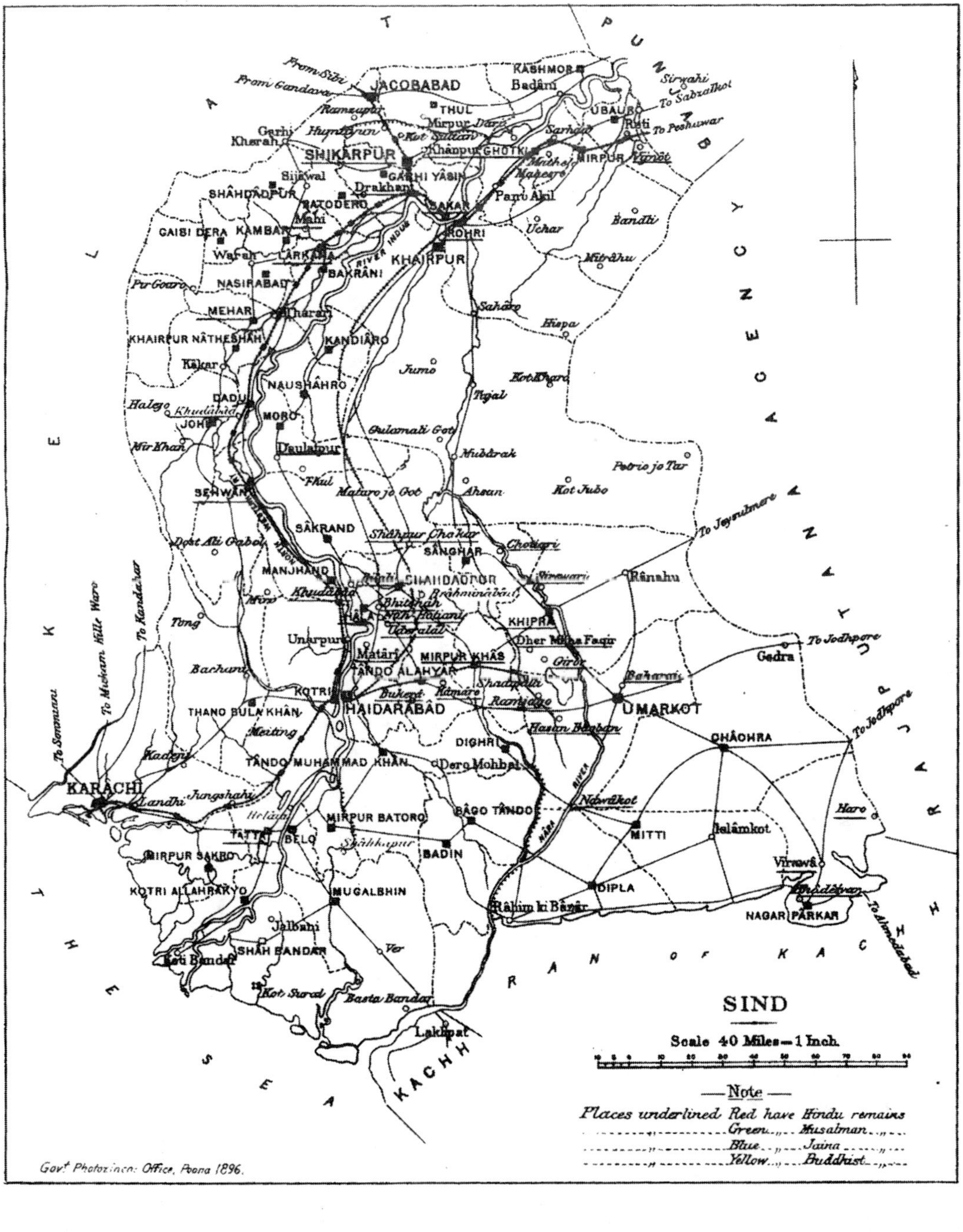
SIND
Scale 40 Miles — 1 Inch.
— Note —
Places underlined Red have Hindu remains
Green Musalman
Blue Jaina
Yellow Buddhist
Govt. Photozinco: Office, Poona 1896.
KALAT
PUNJAB
AGENCY
RAJPUTANA AGENCY
THE SEA
RAN OF KACHH
KACHH
JACOBABAD
SHIKARPUR
KASHMOR
THUL
UBAURO
GHOTKI
MIRPUR
ROHRI
SAKAR
KHAIRPUR
LARKANA
KAMBAR
SHAHDADPUR
MEHAR
NASIRABAD
KHAIRPUR NATHESHAH
KANDIARO
NAUSHAHRO
DADU
MORO
SEHWAN
SAKRAND
SANGHAR
SHAHDADPUR
MANJHAND
HALA
KHIPRA
MIRPUR KHAS
TANDO ALAHYAR
KOTRI
HAIDARABAD
UMARKOT
CHHAOHRA
THANO BULA KHAN
TANDO MUHAMMAD KHAN
DIGHRI
KARACHI
MIRPUR BATORO
BAGO TANDO
MITTI
Islamkot
TATTA
BELO
BADIN
MIRPUR SAKRO
DIPLA
KOTRI ALLAHRAKYO
MUGALBHIN
Rahim ki Bazar
NAGAR PARKAR
Virawa
Jati
SHAH BANDAR
Keti Bandar
Lakhpat
RIVER INDUS
NARA RIVER
To Jodhpore
To Jeysulmere
To Sabzalkot
To Peshawar
To Ahmedabad
To Kandahar
To Sonmiani
From Sibi
From Gandava

religious instructor of Bahâ-ud-din Multâni Koreshi, and is supposed to have been built about 900 A.H. (1494 A.D.).

III. (7) Further along below the crest of the hill is a group of stone-built enclosures. That on the north containing the grave of Sayyid Mâhmud Miraki, Shekh-ul-Islâm, from Kandâhâr. Date 927 A.H. (1520 A.D.).

III. (8) The next enclosure, which is separated from the last by an old *masjid*, contains the grave of Barâ Mîrza Isâ Khân Turkhân said to have been built in 981 A.H. (A.D.1573-74). It stands in a large court, within which are two minor courtyards. It is entirely of carved stone, with perforated slabs introduced in a few places. Mîrzâ Isâ Khân was the first of the Turkhâns who ruled in Lower Sindh, A.H. 962-980 (A.D. 1555-1572).

Inscriptions:—Arabic inscriptions are carved on the slabs above the doorways of the courtyard, and on several of the small tombs enclosed in it.

III. (9) Upon the hill, slightly further southward, is the small ruined tomb of Pîr Asâd with an inscription over the entrance door.

III. (10) The tomb of Sayyid Abdullâ Jilâna from Gujarât. A whitewashed tomb of no account architecturally.

II *a*. (11) The tomb of Nawâb Amîr Khalîl Khân is in ruins. It was built during the Amîr's lifetime, or between 980 and 993 A.H. (1572-1584 A.D.), during the period that Mîrza Muhammad Baki Khân governed Lower Sindh. Nawâb Amîr Khalîl Khân is said to have left directions not to bury his body inside the tomb near it; and seven Hâfizes or religious devotees were buried within it. It stands in the middle of a courtyard, 156 feet square, and has a stone foundation and plinth, but is built of glazed coloured bricks with a few perforated slabs introduced between them. It is octagonal outside but square inside and is covered by a dome. Each side of the outer octagon is 24 feet, and the sides of the square within are 21 feet each. Inside are four tombs.

Inscriptions:—On each of the four tombs inside is an Arabic inscription.. There are also inscriptions on the outer walls of the building, and in large letters in blue and white tiles over the entrances, but much damaged.

II *a*. (12) A short distance south of the last is a ruined enclosure, which contains the grave of Nawâb Amîr Mîr Abul Bakr. The dome of the *mihrâb* is partly demolished and the walls are in a very ruinous state. It has however the remains of some very good coloured tile work. Its date is 1037 A.H. (1627 A.D.).

II *a*. (13) Diwân Shurfa Khân's tomb is the best preserved of the brick buildings on the hill. It is a massive square structure with heavy round towers at the corners, and is constructed of fine brickwork pointed in the joints with strips of dark blue tiling. The dome has been covered with blue glazed tiles, a portion only of which remains. Within, the central grave stone is very elaborately carved. The *mihrâb* has been decorated with glazed blue and white tiles. The tomb was built in 1049 A.H. (1638 A.D.) in the lifetime of Shurfa Khân, the grandson of Mîr Alak Arghun, and was *Nawâb* or minister to Amîr Khân until A.H. 1054. It stands on a platform, and is 38½ feet square. The foundation and plinth are of stone, but the superstructure is of glazed coloured bricks.

Inscriptions:—One in Persian over the entrance, and others on several small tombs inside; also on two stones over the *mihrâb*.

I *a*. (14) Tomb of Nawâb Isâ Khân in good preservation. It was built in A.H. 1038-1054 (A.D. 1628-1644), while Nawâb Amir Khân, son of Nawâb Kâsim Khân, was governor of Sindh. It is built entirely of stone which is said to have been brought from Sorâth, and is richly decorated throughout in the Fathipur-Sikri style with surface tracery. It stands on a raised platform in the middle of a court, and is 70 feet square. It is surrounded by a verandah on carved pillars and an upper storey. The roof of the main building is a stone dome, and the verandahs are also roofed with stone, though in some places small domes have been inserted at a later date. Stairs on the east side lead up to the roof. This is the largest tomb on the hill.

Inscriptions:—In Arabic character, over the entrance to the court, on various parts of the building, and on the eleven tombs inside. Nawâb Isâ Khân died in A.H. 1054.

I *a*. (15) In front, that is to the east, of the last is an enclosure built in the same style, with a magnificently carved *mihrâb*. It is said to contain the remains of ladies of the *zanâna* of Isâ Khân. One of the graves, however, bears the date 964 A.H. (1557 A.D.). A pillared porch has been clumsily added as an after-thought before the entrance which abuts upon and covers up some of the best work on the building.

II *a*. (16) On the south side of Nawâb Isâ Khân's tomb is a ruined brick enclosure containing the grave of Mirzâ Baki Khân upon a platform in the centre.

II *a*. (17) Next comes a small stone twelve-pillared canopy containing the grave of Mîrzâ Tugral Beg, over which is a heap of small stones still added to regularly by small boys. The tomb bears the nickname of "Dukâria."

I *a*. (18) Tomb of Mîrzâ Jâni Beg *bin* Pâyind Beg and of Ghâzi Beg *bin* Jâni Beg Turkhân, like that of Diwân Shurfa Khân is of brick, the faces of which are glazed blue and blue green and the pointing is filled in with strips of white enamelled tile work. The basement and surrounding walls are of stone with some good surface-carving on the *mihrâb* and front door-way. The door frame of the tomb is of stone surmounted by a prettily perforated window, the other four sides are filled with geometric tracery windows. There was a deep dado around the outside of coloured tiles, but it has been wholly stripped off. Within is a corresponding dado, a part of which has also been damaged. Some fine panels of the same work adorn the walls. Inside are three graves. It was built in A.H. 1009 (A.D. 1599-1600). Mîrzâ Jâni Beg Turkhân was the last of the Turkhân rulers of Lower Sind (A.H. 993-1008). Ghâzi Beg was governor of Kandâhâr, where he died, A.H. 1020 (A.D. 1610-11), and was buried here in 1022.

Inscriptions:—An Arabic inscription over the door of the courtyard; another above the entrance to the *dargâh*; others on the walls, and on each of the three tombs within.

II *a*. (19) A twelve-pillared pavilion covering a grave with a ruined brick *mihrâb* beside it.

I *a*. (20) A quarter of a mile or less south-west of the last tombs is the grave of Edward Cooke, who seems to have been a merchant at Thatâ about the middle of last century. It is dated 1743, and is of stone with a long inscription upon the top in letters fully half an inch high and closely crowded together. (See account in the Sindh Gazetteer, p. 325).

I *a*. (21) Within the town of Thatâ is the great Jami Masjid which is still in use. Its general design and construction is simple, being constructed of brick with heavy square piers. It consists of the *masjid* proper with the counterpart of the same on the opposite side of a great square court and the two linked by side corridors. But the great feature of the building is its old coloured tile work. The patterns and soft harmonious combinations of colour are exquisite. This became badly damaged, and to a very great extent, but has been lately repaired, the missing tile work having been restored by tiles from Hâlâ and Multân. But the colours of the latter are crude compared with the older work. The mosque was repaired in 1855-58 when Government subscribed Rs. 5,000, and again in 1894 at a cost of Rs. 20,500, 18,000 of which was subscribed by the Muhammadan community of Sindh and 2,500 Government. The mosque was begun in 1054 A.H. and completed in 1057 (1644-1647 A.D.), but the floor was not laid till 1068 A.H.

Inscriptions :—Over the façade archways and near the south entrance to the courtyard.

II *a*. (22) Upon the outskirts of the town, on the south, is the oldest mosque at Thatâ. It is of brick and is now a ruin, but contains some remains of very good tile work. It is known as the "Dabgar Masjid" or Amîr Khusro Khân's *masjid* and was built in 997 A.H. (1509 A.D.). It is 93 feet long by 48 feet deep and has three bays surmounted by one large and two smaller domes. The central *mihrâb* is beautifully carved with fine surface tracery. *Kalar* has eaten into and rotted the brickwork of the walls for a considerable height from the ground.

Inscriptions :—Over the central *mihrâb* giving the date.

III. (23) Three miles south of the town of Thatâ, near the right bank of the Bhagiâr, is the interesting old ruin, the Kalân Koṭ or great fort. Its ruins cover about a square mile and consist chiefly of brick debris. The only standing building is an old ruined *masjid* (S. G., p. 324).

III. 2. **Shâhkapur**, 27 miles W.S.W. of Thatâ, ruins of ancient city (*B. B. R. A. S.* Vol. V. No. XX. pp. 424 and 541, 1857). In the delta of the Indus are several sites of old ruined cities such as Lâhori, Kakar Bukera, Samui, Fathbâgh, Kât Bâmbhan, Jûn, Thari, Badin, and Tûr.

II *b*. 3. **Sehwân**, a station on the North-Western Railway, 192 miles from Karâchi. The tomb of Lâl Shâh Bhâz in the south-east quarter of Sehwan, built of first rate brick, and profusely decorated with coloured tiles, built about A.D. 1340. Also the remains of the old fort said to have been built by Alexander (S. G., p. 724).

III. 4. **Bambura** is a ruined city near the town of Ghârs, in the Mirpur Sakro *tâlukâ* of the Jerrak district (S. G., p. 123.)

III. 5. **Helâ'i** in the Thatâ *tâlukâ*. Near this place is an ancient building in ruins, known as the Mâri, or house of Jâm Tumâchi, the fourth sovereign of the Samma dynasty in Sindh (S. G., p. 324).

III. 6. **Râni-ka-kot**, an old fort distant about 7 or 8 miles from the town of Sann, a station on the North-Western Railway.

II *a*. 7. **Khudâbâd** near Dâdu on the North-Western Railway. (1) The great *masjid* built in A.D. 1710 and decorated with coloured tiles is a conspicuous building, but it is now very dilapidated and dirty and the tile work is very greatly damaged. (2) About a mile from the ruins of Khudâbâd is the tomb of Yâr Muhammad Kalhorâ—a large square tomb decorated with coloured tiles and in a fair state of repair.

III. 8. **Kanheri**, about 14 miles south-west of Dâdu. Ruins of old Muhammadan (Kalhorâ) town.

III. 9. **Daro or Manik Taro**, about 7 miles north of Dâdu. Ruined city.

III. 10. **Lohan**, about 6 miles from Phulji, railway station. Ruins of old city.

III. 11. **Charlo Fort**, about 24 miles south-west of Sehwan. An old ruined fort.

III. 12. **Chakar Kot**, 17 miles west of Johi. An old hill fort in ruins.

III. 13. **Kot Drigh Mathi**, 13 miles west of Johi. An old fort.

III. 14. There are also old forts known as Koṭ Nurpur (8 miles north of Manjhand), Koṭ Dharanjo (5 miles north of Kotri) and Dilaniji Bhit. Also at Makân Dunichand, Kandi Tarâi, Makor Khadi, Damach, Thunwari, Goth Arab Khân, and Goth Sari.

III. 15. **Raniji Kot**, 22 miles west of Sann, a large old fort.

II.—HYDERÂBÂD DISTRICT.

1. **Hydera'ba'd.** Upon the plateau, to the north-west of the city, are two solitary tombs of the Kalhorâ kings, and two enclosed groups of the tombs of the Tâlpurs. They are profusely decorated with coloured tiles in geometric and floral patterns, but the colours are more crude and the designs poorer than the old work of that kind at Thatâ. The first two are in a more or less ruinous condition, the second having no separate *mujâvar* or
III. custodian, the Tâlpur tombs on the other hand being properly cared for by descendants of those families.

I *a*. The great square tomb, the furthest from the town, is that of Ghulâm Shâh Kalhorâ, the octagonal one being that of his son Sarafraz Khân. These are very dilapidated, the tile work having suffered very much from bad workmanship in the original building of the tombs. Within recent years the dome of the former collapsed, damaging the fine marble platform which covers the grave within.

III. To the south of the town and touching it is the old fort within which are still some of the apartments of the Mîrs, among which is one known to visitors as the painted chamber. A very well carved door upon the eastern side of these is a very good specimen of woodwork. Within the enclosure now used as a magazine are three tombs, two being those of British officers killed in the battle of Hyderâbâd and one that of a gunner of the enemy who was killed while bravely working his gun. The latter with the muzzle blown away has been placed on his tomb. At a short distance to the west of the fort is a smaller fortified enclosure said to have held the *haram* in former times.

I *a*. 2. **Daulatpur** in Moro *tâlukâ*, about 80 miles north from Hyderâbâd:—(1) Thul Rukhan, 9 miles east by south from Daulatpur on the east side of the Hyderâbâd and Rohri postal road. This is a large Bauddha *stûpa*, built of burnt brick and mud, and surrounded by a mound about 6 yards broad and 5 or 6 feet high. Above this the *stûpa* rises about 50 feet and has two bands of pilasters, 20 in each storey, round the upper portion of the drum, which diminishes from 51 to about 46 feet 8 inches in diameter. The pilasters have moulded capitals and a cornice runs over them, but the top of the work has been ruined. The bricks measure 16″ × 11″ by 3″. There is no tradition of its origin or
I*a*. date. (2) Seven miles north-east of Daulatpur is the tomb of Nûr Muhammad Kalhorâ decorated with coloured tiles.

III. 3. **Sha'hapur Chakar** in Sâkrand *tâlukâ*. Two and a half miles north from this are some tombs of the Mîrs of Khairpur.

III. 4. **Ma'o Muba'rak,** 10 miles north of Naushahro station. An ancient mound, the site of an early stronghold. (*Ind. Ant.*, vol. XI. p. 7.)

I *a*. 5. **Bumbra-ke-Thul** is the more modern name of Brâhmaṇâbâd, the site of an ancient and ruined city, situated about 11 miles east by south of Shâhdâdpur and about 21 from Hâlâ. It is one vast mass of ruins, forming irregular mounds, contained within a circumference of four miles. Beside Brâhmaṇâbâd is the ruined city of Dolora about a mile and a half distant, and six miles in another direction is the ruined city of Depur (*J. B. B. R. A. S.* Vol. V. No. XX. p. 413, 1857.)

6. **Old Badin**, 60 miles S.E. of Hyderâbâd; ruins of old city.

7. **Nasarpur**; remains of an old brick city, with three old Muhammadan tombs.

II *b*. 8. **Matia'ri**, 16 miles north of Hyderâbâd :—(1) Jami Masjid, built A.H. 1218, (A.D. 1803) of brick with stone cornices and ornamented with carved stone and coloured tiles, about 86 feet by 32.

Inscription over the archway at entrance of the main central dome giving the date.

III. (2) Dargâh of Pîr Rukanshâh, built in A.H. 1179 (A.D. 1764-65) of brick and floored with tiles set in lime, 27 feet square.

III. (3) Dargâh of Pîr Hashimshâh, built in A.H. 1175—similar to the preceding.

III. 9. **Bukera**, about 5 miles south-west of Tando Alahyar. (1) Tomb of Mîr Kaimshâh Koreshi, erected in A.H. 1216, of brick with coloured decoration.

Inscription on glazed tiles above doorway that Mîr Kaimshâh died in A.H. 1215.

(2) *Masjid* of Pîr Kaimshâh, 48 feet by 30, built in A.H. 1274.

(3) Tomb of Pîr Fazil Shâh, 30 feet square, erected in A.H. 1267.

Inscription stating that Makh'dum Fazlshâh Koreshi died on the 1st Zu'l-haj, 1266.

(4) Tomb of Shekh Bhanapotra, said to be 500 years old.

(5) Tomb of Pîr Firozshâh of comparatively recent date.

III. 10. **Mirpur Kha's**, 40 miles east from Hyderâbâd. About 1¼ mile north or north-west, the Honourable J. Gibbs, in January 1859, excavated the base of a brick *thul*. It is popularly known as "Kâhû jo Dâro" in which was found a vase of fine earthenware containing some pieces of crystal and amethyst. The vase is said to be now in the Karâchi Museum. A head in greenish stone was also found, and sent to the Museum by Sir Bartle Frere. Brick figures found in a Buddhist tower at Kâhû, near Mirpur Khâs. (*B. B. R. A. S.*, Vol. XIX. No. LI. p. 44, 1895,)

III. 11. **Nuh-Hotiani**, about 3 miles north-west from Uderalâl and 5 miles north-east of the village of Khebrâni, which is 8 miles north of Matiâri. *Dargâh* of Pîr Nuh Hotiani, built in A.H. 1092 (A.D. 1681) of brick, about 24 feet square.

III. 12. **Uderalal**, 10 miles E.N.E. of Matiâri. *Dargâh* of Uderalâl erected in A.H. 1044 (A.D. 1634) by Bedarang, son of Shâmdâs Thâkur, of brick on a stone foundation. The floor is of glazed tiles set in lime.

Inscription in Persian engraved on two stones imbedded in the wall on either side of the entrance to the antechamber of the *dargâh*, giving date, &c.

III. 13. **Ha'la',** 35 miles north of Hyderâbâd. The shrine of Makh'dum Nuh, built by Pîr Muhammad Zamân in A.H. 1205 (A.D. 1790-91), of brick with coloured ornamentation. The foundation is of stone and the floor of glazed tiles. It measures 33 feet by 30 feet.

Inscription over the entrance to the *dargâh* recording the names of the builder, mason, scribe, &c.

(2) Tomb of Makhadum Mîr Mahammad, built in A.H. 1210, of brick with coloured decorations on a stone foundation. It is about 25 feet square, and the floor is of glazed tiles.

Inscription over the entrance to the *dargâh* recording that Mîr Fateh Ali Khân Sulṭân desired that a splendid tomb be erected, and that a spirit informed the writer of the year in which it was built.

(3) Makhadum's Masjid 36½ feet by 20 feet, built in A.H. 1222, of brick also.

Inscription over the centre of the middle one of three archways at the entrance of the mosque stating that Mîr Karamali constructed this mosque, and that a spirit informed the writer of the date in the words "The mosque of God which resembles the Kâbâ."

III. 14. **Bhitsha'h,** 5 miles east of Hâlâ. (1) Tomb of Shâh Abdul Latif, built in A.H. 1167 (A.D. 1753-54), of burnt glazed brick on stone foundations, and about 36 feet square.

Inscription over the doorway at entrance to the *dargâh* stating that "when the tomb of Shâh Latif was erected by Sayyid Jamal he saw it splendidly adorned and called it 'the tomb of Latif, full of heavenly light.'"

(2) Tomb of Pîr Habîb Shâh, built A.H. 1221, is 29 feet 6 inches square.

Inscription over the doorway at the entrance to the *dargâh* "Death is a bridge that leads us to our friends."

(3) Tomb of Pîr Kaimdîn, and Latif Ali, erected in A.H. 1238.

Inscription over the doorway at the entrance to the *dargâh* stating that "it was erected by Abdu'l Rahîm, mason of Hyderâbâd and son of Haider, a resident of Nasarpur and Punu Faqir *wallad* Ishak, in 1238."

III. 15. **Bila'li,** 6 miles north of Hâlâ. Pîr Bilali built A.H. 1168 (A.D. 1754-55) of brick 32 feet 6 inches square.

Inscription in Arabic, painted round the doorway.

III. 16. **Khuda'ba'd,** 1½ miles west of Hâla. Tomb of Mîr Fateh Ali, about 26 feet by 27 feet, built of brick, on a stone foundation and ornamented on the inside with carved stone and outside with coloured tiles.

Inscription over the doorway at the entrance to the *dargâh* giving the date of its erection as A.H. 1210.

III. 17. **Kama'ra'v,** 6 or 7 miles east of Tando Alahyar, which is 24 miles east of Hyderâbâd. (1) Pak Sanghar Lorâo, 14 feet 3 inches square, built about A.H. 900 (A.D. 1495) of brick.

(2) Tomb of Pîr Ashrafshâh, 15½ feet by 14½ feet, built of brick with coloured tile facings, built A.H. 1234.

III. 18. **Moriahi,** 18 miles north-east of Tando Alahyar. Mashaik Hoti, 20 feet square, built A.H. 894 (1489 A.D.) of brick, with coloured decoration.

19. **Bra'hmana'ba'd** :—See Bumbra-ke-Thul.

III. 20. **Myo Vahio,** half way between Alahyar-jo-Tando and Tando Adam. A tomb built about 80 years ago, in good repair.

II *a*. 21. **Depur,** about 6 miles north-east of Brâhmanâbâd. An old brick *thul* or tower (*J. B. B. R. A. S.*, Vol. XIX. No. 51.)

II *a*. 22. **Tando,** a few miles from Tando Muhammad Khân. An old brick tower (*J. B. B. R. A. S.*, Vol. XIX. No. 51).

III.—SHIKÂRPUR DISTRICT.

II ? 1. **Mahi,** in Kambar *tâlukâ*, 6 miles north-east from Kambar and 6 miles north-west from Lârkhâna: the *kubâ* or tomb of Shâhu'l Muhammad Kalhorâ killed in A.H. 1030 (A.D. 1621), on the right bank of the Ghâr canal at the 39th mile. The *kubâ* was erected to his memory by Mîyân Ghulâm Shâh Kalhorâ, A.H. 1188 (A.D. 1774). It is 15½ feet square and 35½ (?) feet high covered by a dome plastered outside with *cheroli* (burnt mica) plaster. The walls are faced with the usual coloured tiles—mostly fallen off. Inside are the tombs of Shâhu'l Muhammad and his son Shâh Hassan.

II ? 2. **Lârkhâna** :—The *kubâ* of Shâh Bahâro on the bank of the Ghâr canal close to the town. Shâh Bahâro held a military command under Nûr Muhammad Kalhorâ and died in A.H. 1148 (1735-36 A.D.), and Ghulâm Shâh Kalhorâ, the son of Nûr Muhammad, erected this tomb to his memory in A.H. 1188 (A.D. 1774). It stands on a platform 75 feet square and is 39 feet square and 47 feet high to the crown of the dome. The dome is covered with bluish grey and green coloured tiles. The walls are faced outside with coloured tiles. It is in no one's charge and is uncared for. Also an old fort.

Inscription:—On white glazed tiles on the tomb is a bombastic Persian inscription containing the date 1188 A.H.

II *b*. 3. **Sakar** or **Sukkur**:—(1) Mîr Mâsum's *minâr*, begun in A.H. 1003 (A.D. 1594-95) and completed by Mîr Buzing Manwar, son of Mîr Mâsum Shâh, in 1027 (A.D. 1618). It is built of good brick, is 84 feet in circumference at the bottom, 100 feet high, and is surmounted by a dome.

Inscription:—Over the door on an oblong stone giving the date A.H. 1003 &c.

II *b*. (2) Beside it are the tombs of the Mâsumi Sayyids, descendants of Mîr Mâsum. That of Mîr Sâfai, the father of Mîr Mâsum, has several inscriptions, one of them bearing the date of his death, A.H. 991 (A.D. 1583).

II *b*. (3) Another near it, built in A.H. 1004, is octagonal with four arched entrances, those on the east and west having a cut-stone balcony over them. It is built of brick and decorated with coloured tiles. About 14 feet from the floor inside is a gallery running round, and above it is an **inscription** running all round but consisting of quotations from the *Qurân*, with a verse containing the date expressed in a phrase meaning "the abode of liberality"; there are also others over the small balconies.

II *b*. Mîr Mâsum Shâh's own tomb bears an **inscription** giving the year of his death, A.H. 1014 (A.D. 1605-6).

III. 4. **Old Sakar**.—The tomb of Shâh Khairu'd-din (said to have been born at Baghdâd A.H. 898, and died at Sakar 1027, *i.e.* A.D. 1492—1618, which is very improbable), built in 1758 A.D.

5. **Bakar**, or Bukkur, a fortified island in the river between Sakar and Rohri. On a smaller island is the tomb of Khwâja Khizr Ind Pîr, which has inscriptions in cameo.

III. 6. **Drakhan**, or Dakhan, 30 miles west from Sakar; about a mile west and close to the Drakhan and Ratodero road and 6 miles from the latter place are the Thahim Tombs, four large domed buildings built of brick and covered with glazed tiles built in 1781. They are in memory of Sâheb Khân Thahim, Dilâwar Khân Thahim, both killed in battle near Garhi Yasim, of Jelâl Khân much ruined, and of Jâr Shâh. These are all uncared for. Three miles from Ratodero, on the same road, is the tomb of Bhando, built in 1740, in fair condition.

III. 7. **Shika'rpur.**—Tomb of Makh'dum Abdul Rahman built about 150 years ago, but restored in A.D. 1837, and more recently by the municipality. It is of brick and is about 21 feet square and 30 feet high.

III. 8. **Kha'npur**, 8 miles E.N.E. from Shikârpur. The Jami Idgâh of Fakiru'd-dîn, said to have been built by Maghzal dîn Pathân some 400 or 500 years ago. It is of brick and mud, with four domes, but is now ruinous.

III. 9. **Mehar**, 72 miles south-west from Sakar. Tombs of Shâh Panjo (1730) and Saydi Musani (1750); the dome of the latter fell in and was rebuilt about 75 years ago.

III. 10. **Got Kariya Mithozangi**, Kâkar *tâlukâ*. About four miles from the village is the tomb of Mîyân Nasir Muhammad Kalhorâ, supposed to have been built in A.H. 1130 (A.D. 1718), with carved stone pillars, &c. The place is one of great sanctity and is surrounded by about 60 other *kubâs*.

III. 11. **Rohri.**—The principal buildings of note in Rohri are the Jami Masjid built in A.H. 992 (A.D. 1564) by Fath Khân, a massive pile of red brick adorned with coloured tiles; the *Idgâh* erected in A.H. 1002 (A.D. 1593); and the "War Mubârak," a building about 25 feet square, containing a hair from the beard of the prophet. (See *Sindh Gazetteer*, p. 679). Five miles south-east of Rohri is the site of the ancient city of Alor.

IIa. 12. **Vijnot**, 4 miles south of Reti railway station, Ubauro *tâlukâ*. A series of mounds marking the site of an old city, in which are found carved slabs, brick foundations, &c. Many of the mounds have been recently excavated for the building materials they contain (see *Ind. Ant.*, vol. X. pp. 1—9). In the vicinity are the old sites of "Ther," "Sarwahi," and Pattan Minâr.

III. 13. **Sirwahi** or Sivrai, 3 miles north-west from Walhar station, 5 miles north-east from Sabzalkot, and half a mile south from New Sanjarpur. The site of a deserted city. The bricks and materials have been largely carried off for the Indus Valley Railway. It contains the *rauza* of Hazrat Musa Nawâb.

III. 14. **Mathelo** or **Nagar Mathela**, about 6 or 7 miles S.E. from Ghotki railway station; sites of an old town and fort (*Ind. Int.*, XI. p. 8.).

---

* The original returns were full of erroneous dates and measurements: no supervision had been exercised. One placed a tomb 38½ feet square on a platform 19 feet 9 inches broad!

III. 15. **Ghotki**, a station on the North-West Railway. In the town is a *masjid* of some note known as Musan Shâh's *masjid* erected in 1732 A.D. It is constructed of brick, 113 by 65 feet, and is decorated with coloured tiles.

III. 16. **Fathpur**, about 6 miles from Lârkhâna. The tomb of Shahal Muhammad, plainly built, but decorated within with coloured tiles.

I*a*. 17. **Hakrah**, about 2½ miles from Rohri. The ruins of an ancient town. (See *Sindh Gazetteer*, p. 677).

III. 18. **Tajodero**, on the Jhâli *band* of the Ghâr Canal, at the 28th mile, the tomb of Tâjo Kalio, erected in 1742. It is in a very dilapidated condition.

IV.—THAR AND PÂRKAR DISTRICT.

III. 1. **Baharai**, 3 miles north-east from Umarkot. A temple of Mahâdeva, built of stone. In A.D. 1790 a certain Brâhmaṇ of Umarkot, who used to send out his cows to graze in the vicinity, observing that one of them gave no milk for some days continuously, accused the herd of dishonesty. The latter denied the charge, and next day reported that while driving the cows home in the evening he observed the cow stop at a certain place, and the milk to flow of itself. The owner went next day to the place himself and ascertained the truth of the statement. At night he said a spirit appeared to him in a dream and informed him that a *linga* was buried at the spot, and if he erected a temple there he would never come to want. This he did with the aid of the Sodas,—then influential here. The temple is annually visited by large numbers of Hindus from Umarkot: it is only about 12 feet square and is of no architectural merit whatsoever. The same story is told of many temples.

I *b*. 2. **Gori**, 14 miles north-west from Virâvâh and 27 due west of Haro, Nagar *tâlukâ*. A Jaina temple about 125 feet by 50 feet, built of marble. It is related that about five hundred years ago one Manga Oswâl of Pâri-Nagar went to Paṭṭan to make purchases, and was informed in a dream by a spirit that there was an image buried beneath the house of a certain Musalman, which he should try to secure. Having succeeded in this he brought it to Pâri-Ṇagar, where the spirit again appeared and ordered him to procure two calves and have a cart made of the wood of the *nimb* (Margosa) tree, and placing the image on it to move on without looking behind. On reaching the place where the temple now stands the cart broke down, and being fatigued he fell asleep, to be informed by the spirit that both marble and treasure were buried where this had occurred and that he should send for workmen and build a temple worthy of the idol, which is worshipped under the name of Gaurî. It was built in *Saṁvat* 1432 (A.D. 1375-16). In A.D. 1835 the image disappeared. The temple is visited by Jainas and others. It is a temple of great architectural interest. It is very similar, though superior, to the one at Bhodeśar. It has been much defaced at various times by the fanaticism of the Sindhi troops. It is also said to have suffered from fire, and from gunpowder which was used by Colonel Tyrwhitt, at the time of the Nagar outbreak, in order to secure a Sodha Chief who was supposed to be hiding himself in its passages.

Inscription :—Put up when the temple was repaired in 1715 A.D.

II*a*. 3. **Bhodesar**, 4 miles N.N.W. from Nagar Pârkar. The remains of three ancient Jaina structures. Two of these were used as stalls for cattle, and a third, the interior of which is both beautiful and interesting, has large holes in the back wall and is blackened with the filth which its abandonment to bats and wasps has created. Mr. R. Giles had the occupants of these buildings ousted, and a wall built from Local Funds to protect them. In future they will be preserved as Government buildings. A tank 400 feet by 200, said to have been excavated in the reign of Bhoda Parmâra, son of prince Jeso Parmâra, who was induced by the Brâhmaṇs to sacrifice his son to the goddess of the city in order that the tank might retain the water.

(2) A mosque with carved marble pillars about 20 feet by 12, said to be of the same age.

III. 4. **Sirewari,** 10 miles north from Khiprâ. A mosque about 40 feet by 12 feet, built of brick by Tâj Muhammad about a century ago.

III. 5. **Khipra,** 3 miles to the north-west of it, at Kubah, the Jami Masjid about 40 feet by 12 feet, built by wife of Ghulâm Shâh Kalhorâ, last century.

III. 6. **Chotiari,** 14 miles east from Sanghar. A mosque about 30 feet by 15 feet, of brick, about the same age as the last.

III. 7. **Dher Mitha Faqir,** 12 miles south-west from Khiprâ. Shrine of Mitha Faqir, erected about a century ago by his followers.

III. 8. **Giror,** 25 miles north-west from Umarkot. The shrine of Abdûl Rahim, erected of brick by Mîr Bijar Khân scarcely a century ago, is about 16 feet square.

III. 9. **Nawa'kot,** 40 miles south-west from Umarkot. (1) Shrine of Razi Shâh, 30 feet by 15 feet, built by his followers about 35 years ago.

(2) Fort erected by Mîr Murâd Ali, about 50 years ago.

III. 10. **Ramjago,** 24 miles west from Umarkot. Tomb of Mir Mubârak Khân Tâlpur, 20 feet square, built of grey stone and painted inside. It is about 150 years old.

III. 11. **Juariasar,** 25 miles W.S.W. from Umarkot. Tomb of Walidad Mari, 16 feet square, of brick, about the same age.

III. 12. **Hasan Bagban.** 26 miles west from Umarkot. Tomb of Hasan Bagban, 50 feet by 14 and 20 feet high, built of brick about 200 years ago.

13. **Vira'va'h,** lat. 24° 31′ N., long. 7° 50′ E. The ruins of Pâri-Nagar are close by. It is said to have been founded in A.D. 456 by one Jeso Parmâra of Bâlmir, and is supposed to have been destroyed by the Muhammadans. Among the ruins are the sites of many Jaina temples. Only one small temple, however, is now standing. Mr. Giles here found a magnificently carved block of marble which he got permission to remove to the Karâchi museum; with these exceptions Pâri-Nagar is a large brick heap. Carved stones are built into the Virâvâh temple, and other places.

II *b.* In the first there are some beautifully carved stones, but the second contains little of interest. The third was evidently a temple, and its outer walls, except for some stone carving by the door, are of plain ashlar work. The roof is flat, with the tops of the twenty-seven domes rising from it,—one large one in the centre, and twenty-six very small ones round. The interior is, in spite of dirt and decay, very striking. As you enter, you look down into a little cluster of beautifully shaped pillars with carved capitals. In the centre is a dome, the top of which has elaborate stone tracing on it such as I have only seen in the churches of the West. Round the rim of the dome, which measures 18′ in diameter, are massive carved stone bosses with figures on them, while between the dome and the walls is a narrow pillared colonnade and in the walls small domed recesses with carved seats, such as may be seen in old monastic buildings. The whole is, I have no doubt, a very ancient structure and of great interest.

II *b*. * In the village is another Jaina temple, built in the curious irregular pagoda-like pile which is apparently commonly used for such buildings. This is doubtless a much more modern structure than those under the rocks, but it is none the less, perhaps, several centuries old, and has traces of beautiful carving about it. You ascend to it by a large flight of steps which, like the temple itself, are considerably out of repair.

III. Very noticeable on the banks of the Bhodeśar tank and in other places in the neighbourhood are the *sati* stones with their rude knights in armour carved on them, and always opposite the knight the pathetically outstretched arm of the lady, who joined his funeral pyre, with the auspicious mark in the palm of her hand reminding one of the stigmata in medieval pictures. In one village, a *sati* stone tells of the fate of the present *Patel's* grandmother.

On the roadside near the tank is a mosque with carved marble pillars which may have been brought from Pâri-Nagar. Some of the carving has the same patterns as may be seen at Pâri-Nagar. Captain Raikes states that this mosque bears the inscription "If it may be injured, any one in power who will not repair it will be considered a sinner by God." This inscription, however, is not now to be seen, but there is an Arabic and Gujarâthi inscription. The latter is dated 1505 *Saṁvat*, *i.e.* A.D. 1449.*

* From a memorandum drawn up by Mr. R. Giles.

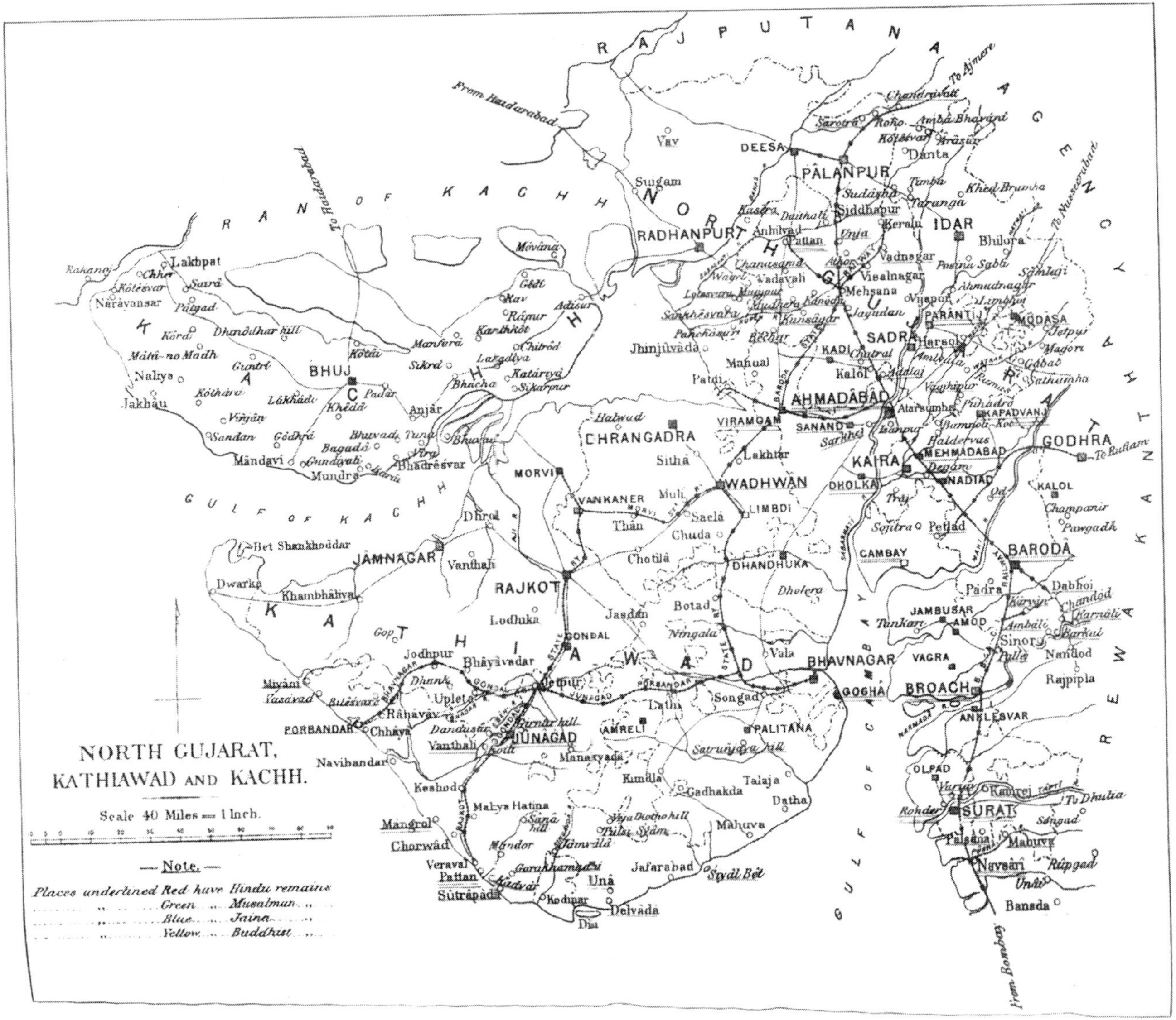
NORTH GUJARAT,
KATHIAWAD AND KACHH.
Scale 40 Miles = 1 Inch.
Note.
Places underlined Red have Hindu remains
Green Musalman
Blue Jaina
Yellow Buddhist
R A J P U T A N A
A G E N C Y
R E W A K A N T H A
R A N O F K A C H H
G U L F O F K A C H H
G U L F O F C A M B A Y
N O R T H G U J A R A T
K A T H I A W A D
K A C H H
From Haidarabad
To Haidarabad
To Ajmere
To Nusserabad
To Rutlam
To Dhulia
from Bombay
DEESA
PALANPUR
RADHANPUR
IDAR
SADRA
PARANTIJ
MODASA
KADI
AHMADABAD
VIRAMGAM
SANAND
KAPADVANJ
GODHRA
MEHMADABAD
KAIRA
NADIAD
DHOLKA
KALOL
BARODA
CAMBAY
JAMBUSAR
AMOD
VAGRA
BROACH
ANKLESVAR
OLPAD
SURAT
DHRANGADRA
WADHWAN
LIMBDI
MORVI
VANKANER
DHANDHUKA
JAMNAGAR
RAJKOT
GONDAL
BHAVNAGAR
GOGHA
PALITANA
AMRELI
JUNAGAD
PORBANDAR
BHUJ
Lakhpat
Narayansar
Jakhau
Mandavi
Mundra
Anjar
Bhadresvar
Sugam
Vav
Siddhapur
Mehsana
Visalnagar
Vadnagar
Danta
Patdi
Jhinjuvada
Halwud
Sitha
Than
Chotila
Lodhika
Dwarka
Bet Shankhoddar
Khambhaliya
Jodhpur
Bhayavadar
Jetpur
Upleta
Chhaya
Navibandar
Keshod
Mangrol
Chorwad
Veraval
Pattan
Sutrapada
Kodinar
Una
Delvada
Diu
Jafarabad
Mahuva
Talaja
Datha
Songad
Botad
Vala
Dholera
Padra
Dabhoi
Sinor
Nandod
Rajpipla
Navsari
Bansda

V.—BARODÂ, AND OTHER NATIVE STATES OF N. GUJARÂT.

1. **Baroda'**, the capital of the Gâikvâd's dominions.

III. (1) The Juni Koṭhi or old fort, probably the oldest building in the city. In digging the foundations for a new office, some gold and silver coins were found, probably the *gadhia paisâ* current in the 8th to the 10th centuries; but no satisfactory account of them has been published.

III. (2) In the Bhadr is a solid old palace of the Musalmans with a marble bow-window of singular beauty.

III. (3) The palace of His Highness Sayâji faced by a building erected by His Highness Khaṇḍerâv, a curious building with a labyrinth of little rooms, dark passages and deep yards.

III. (4) The Najar Bâg palace is a recent building.

III. (5) Temples where the bodies of each of the Gâikvâḍs were burned. (6) Temple of Viṭṭhal Bande. (7) Temple of Siddhanâtha. (8) Lakshmaṇ Bâvâ's Mandira. (9) Temple of Kâlikâ. (10) Temple of Bolâi. (11) Temple of Bhîmanâtha, where Brâhmaṇs are employed undergoing penance for the benefit of the Gâikvâd's house. (12) Gaṇapati's Mandira. (13) Kâśî Viśveśvara temple. (14) Svâmi Nârâyaṇa temple.

III. 2. **Petla'd.** *Dargâh* of Arjunshâh Pîr, who died A.H. 633; the Jami Masjid and another mosque.

III. 3. **Sojitra.** Two old wells of brick and stone of ancient date and some pretensions.

III. 4. **Pa'dra'.** Temple of Ambâmâtâ, and others.

II*b*. 5. **"Sevasee Contra".** Fine step-well with an inscription (Forbes' *Oriental Memoirs*, Vol. II. p. 102).

I *b*. 6. **Dabhoi,** in lat. 22° 8′ N. and long. 73° 28′ E., is an ancient fortress, the walls of which form an irregular four-sided figure approaching to a square. The north, east, south and west walls are respectively 1,025, 900, 1,100 and 1,025 yards long, and have a round tower at each angle. The remains of its fortifications, double gates and temples indicate great magnificence. The stones used are chiefly huge blocks of a very durable sandstone. Of the gates by far the finest was the eastern or Hirâ gate (Gate of Diamonds). It was covered with handsome carvings representing groups of warriors, animals, birds and serpents, some of which remain, but the gate has been, in most part, rebuilt in Musalman style. There is a quaint legend about a man having been built up alive in the masonry at the king's orders, but his protectress, the Râṇî, used to have him fed by a large quantity of *ghî* being poured down an opening, which is shown to this day. Adjoining the gateway is the temple of Kâlikâ Mâtâ covered with bands of rich moulding and sculpture. Upon the opposite side of the gate are the ruins of a smaller temple, and on the gate itself are the remains of two old inscriptions.

Within the walls is a large tank lined with hewn stone and having steps all around. The legend about the building of the city is interesting and may be found in Forbes' *Oriental Memoirs*, Vol. II. It is said to have been built by Siddharâja Jayasiṁha about A.D. 1100. Dabhoi was for a long time inhabited by Hindus only, no Musalman being permitted to reside within the walls or to wash in the tank. A young Muhammadan named Sayyid Bâlâ, on a pilgrimage with his mother Mâmâ Dukhri, in ignorance of the prohibition, ventured to bathe in the tank, and the Brâhmaṇs prevailed on the Râjâ to mutilate him, and he died. Mâmâ Dukhri at once returned home and sued to her sovereign for redress. He sent a large army under his Vazîr, which took Dabhoi after a long siege. The Vazîr had all the fortifications destroyed except the western face and the four double gates. When Mâmâ Dukhri died, she was revered as a saint and was buried in a grave near the Hirâ gate. By her tomb is a stone of ordeal, and the proof of innocence lies in being able to wriggle through the perforation in the stone. After this Dabhoi was for many years almost deserted. When the Musalmâns finally conquered Gujarât, Dabhoi became more populous, and was held by them for two centuries. The Marâṭhâs then obtained possession of it, and partly rebuilt the walls. During the campaign of 1775 it submitted to Râghobâ Peśvâ, who levied a contribution of three *lâkhs*, which the inhabitants were scarcely able to pay. In January 1780, General Goddard took the town on his way to attack Fatesingh Gâikvâd, who however gave in and concluded a treaty with the English. Mr. James Forbes, author of *Oriental Memoirs*, was left as Collector of Dabhoi till the 24th April 1783, when the *pargânâ* of Dabhoi was with others handed back to the Marâṭhâs according to treaty. Dabhoi is now the chief town of one of the *tâlukâs* of Barodâ territory, and has of late gained in importance by the State Railway joining it with Miyâgâm station of the Bombay Baroda and Central India line. (**Surveyed.**) (See *Archæological Report*, vol. II. and *Antiquities of Dabhoi* by Burgess and Cousens).

III. 7. **Ka'rva'n**, Dabhoi division, on the railway 5 miles east of Miyâgâm. One of the four oldest and most famous seats of the worship of Śiva, once had a large tank now broken up, with many ruinous old temples. Coins are occasionally found here. The tank called Kâyâvirohaṇa and the remains of a host of very old temples in ruins.

III. 8. **Karna'li** in Sinor division, on the Narmadâ near the junction of the Uri or Or—a sacred place containing the temples of Someśvara, Kubereśvara and Pâvakeśvara.

III. 9. **Amba'li**. Temple of Anasûyâ, the mother of Datta-Muni, a supposed incarnation of the Triad.

III. 10. **Barkal**, also on the Narmadâ. Temple of Vyâsa Muni.

III. 11. **Cha'ndod** on the Narmadâ, a famous sacred place. Temples of Śeshaśâyi, Kâśî-Viśveśvara Mahâdeva, Kapileśvara Mahâdeva and Chaṇḍikâ Mâtâ, mostly sculptured on the outer walls.

III. 12. **Navsa'ri**. A palace of the Gâikvâḍ; temple of Pârśvanâtha; temples of Âśâpûri-Mâtâ, Kṛishṇa, &c.; *dargâh* of Makhtam Shâh and Sayyid Saâdat, and an old Pârsi Fire-temple.

III. 13. **Palsa'na**, in the district of the same name, has two Hindu temples "of some interest" and a large tank.

III. 14. **Ka'mrej**, the chief town of a sub-division, 20 miles from Navsârî, on the south bank of the Tâptî. (1) Temple of Śrî Nârada Brahmâ with a fine image in a subterranean vault. (2) Temple of Śrî Koṭîśvara. (3) Temple of Mokshanâtha Mahâdeva visited by pilgrims to perform the *Nârâyaṇa Nâgabali* and *Tripiṇḍi* ceremonies. (4) Old temple of Śrî Kâlabhairava.

III. 15. **Varia'v**, 2 miles from Surat, has two Hindu temples and a large mosque.

III. 16. **Mahuva**, on the river Pûrṇâ. "A Jaina temple with a modest exterior, is an excellent piece of architecture inside."

III. 17. **Una'i** in the village of Khambhâliâ, Viâra *tâlukâ*,—a famous hot-spring (see *Ind. Ant.*, vol. I. p. 142).

III. 18. **Songad**, south of the Tâptî. Near it is what was once a very notable fortress and the town still contains the remains of several notable buildings and ruined temples. Near it, but just within Khândesh, is the renowned fortress of Sâlher.

III. 19. **Rupgad**, between Soṅgaḍ and Sâlher, is a ruined fort with a perennial spring on the highest point.

III. 20. **Atarsumba** on the Vatrak, in Dehgâm, Kaḍi *zillâ*, with a ruined but striking fort with a fine gateway.

III. 21. **Vagjhipur**, 4 miles north from Atarsumba on the Mesvâ. A temple of Utkaṇṭheśvara Mahâdeva.

III. 22. **Chatral**, 5 miles from Kalol, has a well of some pretensions built in the time of Maḥmud Bigarah, and repaired by Mahârâv (Malhârav) Gâikvâḍ, the Jâgirdâr.

III. 23. **Kadi**. The Rang Mahâl and Supra Mahâl and other remains of old buildings. Temple of Yudheśvara Mahâdeva. The *mandira* of Gosâvi Mahârâja containing some elaborate carving. Temple of the Khâkhi Bâva and others.

II *b*. 24. **Anhilva'd—Pattan**, the old capital of the Châvaḍa and Chaulukya kings, but destroyed by the Muhammadans in the 13th century and still further despoiled by the Marâṭhâs; said to have been built by Vanarâja in A.D. 746. It contains a few fragments only of its former greatness. Very little remains now in *situ*, and the dismantled materials of the scores of fine old temples that once adorned this old city are scattered far and wide. Mosques, tombs, tanks and wells, with the modern walls, have made a clean sweep of almost all, and it is sad to see the use to which some of these richly sculptured fragments have been degraded. The celebrated Râni Vâv, a step-well said to have been constructed by Udayamatî, the Queen of Bhîma Deva Solanki, King of Paṭṭan, in the eleventh century, is now represented by a small portion of its bracketted main shaft at one end and part of a single standing column at the other extremity, the intervening space being a vast pit from which pillars, beams, and step-slabs have been rifled, to build, it is said, some eighty years ago, Bahâdur Singh's step-well in the town. Not far from this is the great Sahasra Linga *talâv*, once one of the largest tanks in Gujarât, ascribed to Sidhharâja, but which tradition says never held water, through a curse pronounced upon the king and his work by a good-looking damsel, engaged on the excavation, with whom the king tried to trifle. It appears to have been finished, for fragments of the numerous little shrines (said to be a thousand in all), which encircled it and stood upon the steps leading down to it, lie about, but the whole of the stone lining of the banks has been carried off, leaving the brickwork core in huge heaps.

On the south side of the town is the Khân Sarovar, a fine large tank, constructed, like most of the buildings of the early Muhammadan period, chiefly of appropriated materials. The arrangement of the inlet and outlet sluices is worthy of note. Like most of these ancient buildings it has been allowed to fall into a ruinous state, although it is still used by the town; the accumulation of silt, which is gradually filling it, seems never to be cleared out. When these works were constructed, it would appear that no provision was made for their subsequent up-keep and repair. Without the walls, on this side of the town, are several *rauzas* or tombs constructed almost wholly of old temple materials—principally white marble columns and beams. On one of these pillars is a short **inscription**.

Within some of the more modern temples with which Pâṭṭan abounds, may be found
Ib. fragments and relics of older ones. In the temple of Panchâsara Pârśvanâtha is a marble image said to be that of Vanarâja, the founder of Anhilvâd or Paṭṭan. Beneath it is an **inscription** in which the name of Vanarâja occurs and the date *Saṁvat* 802, but, owing to the fineness of the letters and the wear of the surface, it is difficult to follow it. In another Jaina temple, that of Śrî Pârśvanâtha, is a beautifully carved wooden ceiling and an important **inscription** of the Khaḍataragachha Jainas. In another we have a most elaborately carved white marble throne upon which the image is seated. In a small in-
Ib. significant-looking Hindu shrine are two very old images dated *Saṁvat* 802, while in another is an old image of Gaṇapati, of the same age. There are some very fine specimens of old wood carving to be found in Paṭṭan, chiefly employed as decoration on the façades of houses.

Ib. But, perhaps, the best piece of ancient work remaining at Paṭṭan is the great ceiling scroll which was drawn and published in one of the numbers of the *Indian Art Journal*. The work is superb, but, unfortunately, the three great slabs bearing it received very much damage when the porch, in which it was placed, fell into the river. The scroll was recovered, and now lies upon the pavement near its original position, at Shekh Farîd's tomb in the river.

At Hâjipur, near Paṭṭan, is an old well with an **inscription**.

III. 25. **Cha'nasama** in Vadavali sub-division. The largest Jaina temple in the Barodâ territory, dedicated to Pârśvanâtha and built about fifty years ago at a cost of 7 *lâkhs* of rupees raised by subscription. It is built of Dhrângadhra stone and very richly carved, with numerous spires. The interior is rich and floored with marble.

III. 26. **Kunsagar**, 12 miles from Chânasama and not far south of Aṇhilvâḍ-Paṭṭan. The remains of an immense reservoir on the course of the Rupen, attributed to Karṇa, the father of Siddharâja Jayasiṁha. It was destroyed by a flood in 1814.

III. 27. **Bechar.** Becharâjî's temple is on the north-west border of the Kaḍi division, about 23 miles from the town of that name and 15 miles south of Chânasama, 1½ mile south-east of Saṅkhalpur and near the British frontier of Viramgâm. It has numerous surrounding buildings, and is enclosed in a fort, the south gateway of which rises to a height of 50 feet. The original temple was built by Sankhala Râjâ in A.D. 1152, the second or Madhyasthâna was built by a Marâṭhâ, and the third or largest by His Highness Mânâjirâv Gâikvâḍ in A.D. 1779—1791.

I *b*. 28. **Siddhapur,** in the Kaḍi District, on the Sarasvatî river, 64 miles north of Ahmadâbâd on the railway. (1) Some fragments of the great Rudramâlâ temple, built of stones of gigantic size and elaborately carved, by Siddharâja, and destroyed by Alau'd-dîn Khunî, still remain, and a beautiful *kîrttistambha*, from which, however, the *toraṇa* and sculptures in the pediment have been taken away since K. Forbes wrote his *Râs Mâlâ*. A portion of the Rudramâlâ building has been converted into a Jami Masjid. The city having been an old capital of the Chaulukya kings deserves examination. The *kîrttistambha* and other fragments should be conserved. (**Surveyed**.)

III. (2) On the opposite side of the river is a large square and very plain building, the *dharmaśâlâ* of the Kevalapuri Gosâvis built by Ahalyâbâî of Indor.

III. (3) Temples of Siddheśvara Mahâdeva and Nilakaṇṭha Mahâdeva, built by Bâbâji Divân about the beginning of the present century.

III. (4) A temple at the bend of the Sarasvatî to Bhûtanâtha Mahâdeva—the lord of demons—with a *pippala* tree, under the temple of Siddheśvara Mahâdeva, into which the evil spirits of deceased devotees are believed to pass.

III. (5) Below the preceding are two smaller temples marking the spots where ladies immolated themselves as *satîs*.

III. (6) Temple of Govinda Mahâdeva in the town, contains two images, both of Kṛishṇa.

III. The other chief temples are those of (7) Raṇachoḍji, (8) Sahasra Kâlî Mâtâ, (9) Syâmji Mandira, (10) Svâmi Nârâyaṇa, (11) Gosâvi Mahârâja, (12) Khardana Ṛishi, (13) Kapila Muni, (14) Lakshmî-Nârâyaṇa, (15) Gopînâthaji, (16) Govardhananâthaji, (17) Raghunâthaji, (18) Gaṇapati, (19) Brahmâṇḍeśvara Mahâdeva, (20) Arbudeśvara Mahâdeva, (21) Vâlkeśvara Mahâdeva, (22) Siddhanâtha Mahâdeva, (23) the Moksha Pippala tree, and (24) Khâk Chauk.

The chief tanks are: (25) the Bindu Sarovar, one of the fourmost sacred tanks in India, (26) the Jnâna Vâpikâ, and (27) the Alpa Sarovar.

III. 29. **Daithali** or **Dadhisthala,** on the Sarasvatî. Near it is Mandikeśvara—a sacred place.

III. 30. **Athor** 15 miles from Siddhapur. A celebrated temple of Gaṇapati, and the Gaṇapatîya *dharmaśâlâ*.

III. 31. **Unjha,** 8 miles south of Siddhapur. A large temple of the Kaḍavâ Kunbis, built about 1858 in the style of the Jaina temples.

II *b*. 32. **Akhaj,** about 18 miles from Mehsana railway station. Remains of a *kîrttistambha*.

I *b*. 33. **Vadnagar,** 9 miles north-west of Visalnagar. (1) A large and substantial *châvaḍi*, with arches ornamented with rich carving. (2) Two *kîrttistambhas* in a good state of
III. preservation. (3) Temple of Hatkeśvara Mahâdeva to the west of the town, the walls of

it covered with sculpture quaint and suggestive. (4) Two good Śrâvaka temples. (5) Several other Hindu temples. (**Surveyed.**)

I *b*. 34. **Mudhera'**, about 16 miles west from Jagudan railway station; called in the legends Modherapura and Modhabankpaṭṭaṇa. It gave name to the Modh Brâhmaṇs. It has a fine ancient temple of Sûrya, of the 12th century—a gem of the Chaulukya style, either the Karṇeśvara or Karṇanaru Prasâda of Gujarât history. In front of the temple is the fine Sîtâ's Chauri, and a tank, the Râma Kuṇḍa originally called the Sûrya Kuṇḍa. Part of the remains seems to have been recently carried away. The whole is pre-eminently worthy of preservation. (**Surveyed.**)

III. 35. **Pallej**. Near this are said to be some interesting old temples.

II *b*. 36. **Sarotri** or Sarotra, 5 miles from Sarotra station—an old Jaina temple with many short **inscriptions**—an interesting old white marble Jaina temple. The principal shrine stands within a closed rectangular court, around the four sides of which, and facing inwards were 52 small cell shrines; but the back or south corridor, with part of the eastern, has been demolished and cleared away. A portion also of the sculptured walls of the main shrine has also fallen, or has been removed, from the south-west corner. The temple has been thoroughly desecrated, and all its images, of which there must have been at least sixty, have been removed.

III. 37. **Roho**, 4 miles north-east of Sarotra, situated in the north of the Pâlanpur Agency on the river Bânas. Here is an old step-well, with a short Sanskṛit **inscription**, constructed entirely out of white marble, the material having been taken from the ruins of previous old temples. It is now in rather a ruinous condition and in disuse. Not far from it are the ruined remnants of a white marble Jaina temple, and close to this again are the crumbling walls of a very substantially built railway bungalow, in the outer gateway of which are used some old temple columns.

III. 38. **Rantoj**, near Pañchâsar. Some Jaina temples.

III. 39. **Vishroda** has vestiges of an ancient town similar to those found at Wallâ.

III. 40. **Munjpur**, 24 miles south-west of Paṭṭan. The only relic of former times in the town of Munjpur, of any consequence, is the old Jami Masjid. This, as is the case with most of the very early mosques of Gujarât, has been constructed chiefly from the material of old Hindu or Jaina temples, and the remnants of the porch on the north of the court-yard seem to point to that particular part having once been portion of an original temple undisturbed. In the mosque are two Persian and one Sanskṛit **inscription**. The latter is on a beam, and belonged to an older temple, but is now almost illegible.

III. 41. **Lotes'vara**. Two miles to the east of Munjpur. A curiously built well, in the plan of a Greek cross. In the centre is the circular shaft, the deepest portion, with its own containing wall, while on the north, south, east, and west of this there are branches. Steps descend the three sides of each to the water which communicates with that of the central shaft by openings in the circular wall. It is of recent construction. The place is a noted resort of pilgrims, and once a year a great *melâ* or fair is held here.

III. 42. **Sankes'vara**, an old seat of the Jains, 6 miles south-west of Munjpur. Here in the middle of the village is the courtyard, surrounded with cell shrines, built in old brick and plaster, of an old Jaina temple of Pârśvanâtha, which has itself entirely disappeared. The brick work is much of the same style as that of the old temple at Sarotra the bricks being carefully moulded to suit the different curves and recesses of the mouldings. This has been covered with fine plaster, cut whilst wet into the most delicate geometric patterns. But it has suffered greatly from the weather, the most part of it having peeled off. Over the shrine doors, upon the stone lintels, are numerous short inscriptions ranging in date between *Saṁvat* 1652 and 1686. It is said that the image of Pârśvanâtha which occupied the principal temple here, was carried to the new temple hard by, which was built very recently. The inscription upon the base of the image seems to corroborate this, since it is dated in *Saṁvat* 1666, whereas the only other inscription on the new temple recording the gift of five thousand rupees towards the building of it, is dated *Saṁvat* 1868. There is nothing of note about this new temple ; it is constructed in the style of the mordern Jaina temples.

III. 43. **Pancha'sur**, 6 miles south of Sankeśvara, is, according to tradition, one of the oldest towns in Gujarât. It was here that the famous Jaya Śekhara was besieged, eleven hundred years ago, by the invading army of the south under King Bhuvar, and where, on his fall, four queens with the ladies of his court, after they had made a desperate and sudden sally for the recovery of his body, threw themselves upon his funeral pyre and were consumed with him. Though once the seat of the oldest known dynasty of Gujarât it has absolutely nothing left upon the surface to commemorate those days. Some ancient bricks of larger size than usual are sometimes unearthed. Groups of *páliyás* and *sati* stones are found in the village and on the burning ground at some distance from it, but none of these seem to go back further in date than seven hundred years, and those of that age only number five, with much abraded inscriptions. It is recorded that over the spot where Jaya Śekhara's body was burnt, a temple was erected to the memory of Gujar Deva. A common little shrine, with nothing ancient-looking about it, upon the burning ground, is pointed out, with some hesitation and doubt, as the same, but to antiquity it has not the shadow of a claim. It is possible that the *linga* within it *may* have been the original " Gujar Deva ".

The town, or rather the village of Panchâsur, is a comparatively modern cluster of houses and huts, with a population of perhaps about four or five hundred souls. On the east of the village are some large mounds some twenty or thirty feet high, but these are said to consist entirely of village refuse and manure, and certainly what lies on the surface is such. A mile to the west of the village in a modern little shrine, are placed a few mutilated images which might have belonged to some temple or temples of the thirteenth century, while in the village is a small mound with a heap of carved stones about it, evidently the site of an old shrine.

I *b*. 44. **Jhinjuva'da'**, south of Panchâsur, is an old Hindu fortress with gateways profusely sculptured and a multilateral tank (see *Archæological Reports*, vol. II). **(Surveyed.)**

III. 45. **Va'gel**, 19 miles south-west of Paṭṭan. The *Râs Mâlâ* after describing the temple of Sûrya at Mudherâ, the finest extant in Gujarât, says : " At Waghel is a temple similar in style to those which have been described, but of smaller dimensions. It consists of a single open *maṇḍapa* one storey in height with pyramidal roof, three porticoes, and an adytum surmounted by a spire." Not a vestige of this temple now remains, and it is almost forgotten by the villagers themselves. Those that do remember it say it was carted away *in toto*, some 20 or 25 years ago, its material being used in the construction of a *talâv* at Râdhanpur! The very foundations were dug out and carried away. Near the village is a very large multilateral tank, but it has long ago fallen into disrepair, and most of its stone-work has disappeared.

II *b*. 46. Dilmâl, 10 miles north-west of Mudherâ and 19 miles south by west of Paṭṭan. Judging from the number of small shrines, now more or less ruined, which lie in the vicinity of the village, and extend for some distance from it on the south and south-east, Dilmâl must have been a place of considerably more importance than the present small village can claim for itself. Perched upon little knolls, at some distance apart are five partly ruined shrines, with many other mounds indicating the sites of so many more.

In the village, enclosed within a rectangular walled court, is the principal temple, that of the presiding deity of the village—the goddess Limboji Mâtâ—of comparatively recent construction. This temple occupies the site of a far older shrine, a portion of whose materials has been rebuilt into the new one. The surrounding minor shrines, which were appendages to this older central temple, still remain in very good preservation, and shew, by their careful finish and abundant detail, that they were constructed during that period when architectural construction had reached its highest point of excellence. The image of Limboji Mâtâ was originally in an old temple which now stands in ruins on the bank of the tank to the east of the village. The new temple has been built on precisely the same lines as the old one, in larger proportions, the figures around the walls of the latter being literally copied upon the former, but of far inferior workmanship. Like the old shrine the new one faces north, a direction reserved for temples dedicated to Vishṇu, goddesses, and minor deities.

A very curious sculpture occurs on the west face of the little shrine in the south-east corner of the courtyard of the temple. In one figure the four deities, Śiva, Vishṇu, Brahmâ, and Sûrya, are blended. The image has eight arms, three faces, and is seated upon Garuḍa. The three faces (the fourth not appearing, of course, in a bas-relief) with the two lower arms—in the hand of one being the water-pot and the other lying extended, palm outward—belong to Brahmâ; his vehicle, the goose, being represented below. Śiva is represented by the trident and serpent in the upper pair of hands, while the full-blown lotus in each of the next lower hands, the Hessian boots, and the horse below, denote Sûrya. Garuḍa, upon which the image rides, is Vishṇu's vehicle, and the pair of hands now broken off no doubt held his symbols, the conch shell and *chakra* or discus. This fourfold representation is rare.

III. Without the village, on the south, and built into a long platform are 26 *pâliyas* or memorial stones, commemorating the decease of certain individuals who died between the years *Saṁvat* 1513 and 1891 (A.D. 1457—1835). A panel on the upper part of each slab portrays the individual himself, arrayed in all his war-paint, sometimes mounted upon his horse, and sometimes standing beside his wife, while below the dated record is inscribed. These sculptures are exceedingly crude and coarse, the sculpture also being very shallow, thus forming a violent contrast with the infinitely better executed bas-reliefs on the old shrines. They are entirely void of expression, and lack the slightest animation of pose.

III. 47. **Kamboi**, 3 miles north-east of Dilmâl, an old temple in the village, still in use.

III. 48. **Itoda**, 2 miles south-east of Dilmâl, ruins of small shrines near the village.

III. 49. **Dhenuj**, 16 miles south-east of Paṭṭan. Here is the old temple of Vyâgheśvarî in most part rebuilt. The older work is of the very best class, and the carving of the *vedî* or parapet wall of the *maṇḍapa* is particularly good. In the porch is a well-carved ceiling. Close by are remains of an old tank sluice, and near the town are the ruins of a very old step-well.

IIb. 50. **Kanoda**, 3 miles south by west of Dhenuj. Remains of an old temple on the west of the village. The open *maṇḍapa* remains, while the shrine has been destroyed.

III. 51. **Mota'p**, 3 miles south of Dhenuj. A small shrine with sculptured walls.

III. 52. **Ghura'd**, 3 miles north-east of Dhenuj. A small sculptured temple.

III. 53. **Virta'**, near Ghurâd, old temple of Mahâdeva: An inscription on the base of an image at this temple.

III. 54. **Manoj**, about 5 miles north of Dhenuj. An old temple of Nârâyaṇa still in use. It has a curiously sculptured ceiling.

Ib. 55. **Sandera**, 10 miles east by south from Paṭṭan. Two old temples, one in the Solanki style and the other in the northern style. The first consists of an open *maṇḍapa* supported upon pillars and the shrine, while the latter, which stands beside it on the south, is merely a square shrine with antechamber surmounted by a spire of the northern or Orissan type. These temples are in disuse.

III. 56. **Rua'vi**, two miles east of Sandera. An old but small temple with a complete *śikhara* perched upon a high brick foundation near the village. The walls are sculptured.

Ib. 57. **Sunak**, 4 or 5 miles west of Unja Railway Station. Two old temples, one in ruins the other of Nîlakaṇṭha Mahâdeva in good preservation and richly decorated. On a pillar in the smaller ruined temple is a Sanskrit inscription dated *Saṁvat* 1356 recording the establishment of an image in the temple. A short while ago a set of two copper-plates was dug up here, and they are now in the possession of Mr. Nârâyan Bhârati, of Paṭṭan. They have since been translated by Dr. Hultzsch, and have appeared in the *Epigraphia*. They record a grant of land by King Karṇadeva at Sunak, and in giving the boundary of the same it mentions the villages of Laghu Dâbhi and Sandera, both of which still retain the same names and are situated a mile and four miles south-west, respectively, of Sunak.

III. 58. **Va'yad**, 15 miles north-west of Paṭṭan. An old step-well. An inscription on a pillar.

Ib. 59. **Kasera**, 15 miles west by north of Paṭṭan. A small, but very old, triple-shrined temple dedicated to Śiva, Brahmâ and Vishṇu. It is profusely covered with sculpture, but has been very badly battered and defaced, and that maliciously, probably by the Muhammadan iconoclasts, who, in the early days of their ascendancy in India, so frequently overran Gujarât and destroyed and desecrated its shrines. The temple is now in disuse. The carving and projecting portions of the work have suffered much from time, and vandalism, but the structure itself, except the upper portions of the *śikharas*, is well preserved, the temple being almost entire. The plan is that of a central *maṇḍapa* with three shrines, one at each side, as well as the usual one at the back. Its greatest length is about 30 feet.

It is dedicated to Vishṇu. The idol which it originally contained of Chaturbhuja was, it is said, carried away by the Emperor Alau'd-dîn. Tradition ascribes the temple to Gandharvasena. The present structure is evidently of a very old date, say 400 or 500 years. What is supposed to be the symbol of an ass's hoof occurring in the ornamentation of this temple, as in all those which are said to have been built by Gandharvasena, is perhaps connected with the origin of the legend of its age, which also states that he assumed the form of an ass during the day, resuming that of a man during the night. The symbol, however, is really the same as that occurring so frequently on most Bauddha and Hindu works of early date, and which is now known as the "Chaitya window" ornament. On the temple, inscribed upon the different parts of it, are names which are, with little doubt, those of the workmen who finished off these several portions. They are carefully inscribed and are in the old character. One of these names was Âjada. Curiously enough this same name is found inscribed on an old marble column at Paṭṭan in a tomb on the south of the town, where a short inscription records the setting up of the column by the wife of one Âjada in *Saṁvat* 1256, thus giving us the date of the Kasera temple, if we take it for granted that the two Âjadas are one and the same person, which I consider very probable.

III. 60. **Bhilri**, 24 miles north-west of Paṭṭan. Here, as well as at the adjoining villages of Mundeta and Kemâna, there was an old white marble temple, but it has been pulled down, and even the foundation has been dug out to get at the stone for conversion into lime.

III. 61. **Pa'lanpur.** There is nothing of any interest from an archæological point of view at Pâlanpur itself, save a few short inscriptions of no great age or interest.

III. 62. **Wa'v**, 4 miles or so north of this village is another ancient temple in a jungle far from any habitation. It is a Mahâdeva temple of the usual kind, which has been restored, all the upper part being comparatively modern and built over the old portion, which is of carved sandstone. It is surrounded by a low wall and its preservation is doubtless due to the fact of its having been restored and its sanctity preserved. There is, however, no custodian or indeed any one living in or near it.

III. 63. **Chandra'vati**, about fifteen miles to the north-east of Roho, and not far from the foot of Mount Abu. Colonel Tod, in his *Travels in Western India*, in speaking of this place, says: "The city, to judge from the fragments of marble and stone strewn over an extensive plain, must have been of considerable size, and its pretensions to great refinement and riches, may be admitted from the beautiful specimens still remaining of its marble edifices, of which twenty of different sizes were discovered when the spot was first visited by His Excellency Sir Charles Colville and his party in January 1824. The one here represented (in his volume) is Brahmanical and adorned with rich sculptured figures and ornaments in high relief, those of the human form being nearly statues and only attached to the building sufficiently for their own support. They are executed with a degree of excellence scarcely equalled in Indian sculpture, and which would not in some instances disgrace more cultivated artists. Of these images there are one hundred and thirty-eight. The smallest are two feet high and placed in niches of the most elegant workmanship. .... The interior of the temple and centre dome is highly finished; but the roof and exterior of the domes have lost their outer coating of marble. The pillars in the ground of the drawing appear to have been part of a colonnade, which once surrounded the temple; they are of marble, which material is strewn over the adjacent ground in great profusion, and columns, statues, cornices and slabs are tossed in heaps all around."

Save portions of the basement of one temple and a few blocks of the back wall of another, nothing remained in 1890 of these beautiful shrines, discovered in 1824, excepting one solitary column, which, by its loneliness, rather accentuates the desolation around it. A short walk from here discovers one of the chief causes of this, for there, under the railway bridge, upon either side of the stone piers, lie, in heaps in the river bed, upwards of a hundred cart-loads of sculptured fragments and images, the unused portion of the vast amount of marble carried there from those temples. The site of the old city, and its extent, is still indicated in great measure by the mounds of old brick work which formed the foundations of these old temples, and of which there are a great number; and, on the south side, by portions of the city walls which faced the river Śivâlan.

VI.—MAHI KÂNTHÂ.

1. **Idar**. (1) At the foot of the *gaḍ* or fort is the cave-temple of Khokanâtha Mahâdeva partly ruined, supposed to be upwards of 400 years old. It is an oblong apartment 30×20 feet and from 4 to 6 feet high, excavated in the rock and used as a place of worship. (2) In a rising ground south of the town, and close to the wall, is the cave-temple of Dhaneśvara Mahâdeva, a natural rock cavern 20×10 feet and from 5 to 7 feet high. (3) In a rising ground ¾ of a mile south-west of Îdar is the cave of Mankâleśvara Mahâdeva. It measures 20×12 feet and the height varies from 5 to 10 feet. (4) On the summit of the *gaḍ* to the north-east of the town the Ruṭhî Rani-nu-mâlium built of brick plastered with chunam. It is said to be upwards of 600 years old! It has a domed roof, in the Muhammadan style, with a courtyard in front, and measures 25×19 feet and 12 feet high. It is visited by pilgrims and travellers. The wife of a former chief of Îdar having some disagreement with her lord was ordered to live on the hill, where this palace is said to have been built for her and is thus called after her name. (5) In the *gaḍ* to the north of the town the Radmalaî Choki appears to be an unfinished Jaina temple, built of white sandstone. It measures 375×34 feet and 16 feet high, in the Jaina style. (6) On the *gaḍ* is the cave (a natural cavern) of Vajar Mâtâ with a wall and terraces in front. It is 22×18 feet and 7 feet high and contains an image of Vajar Mâtâ worshipped by all castes. It has a ruined *dharmaśâlâ* attached to it built of brick and plastered with chunam. (7) In the *gaḍ*, the temple of Śântinâtha of white sandstone, sculptured, and brick plastered; is upwards of 400 years old and entire, measuring 160×125 and 55 feet high.

2. **Limbhoi**, the temple of Kâlaṇâtha Mahâdeva with a *dharmaśâlâ* partly in ruins, is built of white sandstone and brick plastered. It measures 37×15 feet and 30 feet high.

3. **Ahmadnagar**. The Bhadr palace in ruins, upwards of 400 years old; built of white sandstone. The space within the surrounding fortified walls measures 700 by 500 feet. The palace is said to have been originally constructed in the reign of Ahmad Shâh, the founder of the town. It is also called Mohinâ-râṇi-nâ-mahâl. (2) A *kuṇḍa* or reservoir mostly in ruins, having a courtyard, is built of white sandstone plastered. It measures 100×50 feet. The reservoir is said to have been constructed during the reign of Ahmad Shâh as a bathing place for "Mohinâ-râṇi" who it is said used to visit it daily by an underground passage from the Bhadr palace.

4. **Khed Brahma**, the temple of Bramhâji surrounded by a wall measuring 57×30 feet and 36 feet high, is built of white sandstone and brick plastered. It has been recently put in repair by the Brâhmaṇ community of the town and has an image of Brahmâ which is worshipped. The temple is known by the name of "Bhṛigu Ṛishi." The river Harnav, on which the village stands, is considered sacred. A fair is held every year on Mâgha *Śud*. 14th.

5. **Desan**. The temple of Bhavanâtha Mahâdeva, upwards of 400 years old,* measures 50×25 feet and 36 feet high: is built of white sandstone and brick: partly in ruins: has a *dharmaśâlâ* attached to it. This temple is known by the name of Chuman (Chyavana?) Ṛishi, a great sage. A fair is held here annually in the month of Śrâvaṇa.

* This is the age of most objects in the return, which is an unsatisfactory one.

III. 6. **Bhilora.** The temple of Śrî Chandraprabhuji, of white sandstone sculptured and plastered. It measures 70 × 45 feet and 30 feet high. It has a tower four storeys or 75 feet high, and a *dharmaśâlâ* within the entrance gate. It has been recently put in repair by a Jaina merchant.

III. 7. **Posina Sabli.** The temples of Pârśvanâtha and Ñeminâtha measuring 150 × 140 feet and 26 feet high are built of white sandstone plastered with chunam.

III. 8. **Sa'mlaji.** The temple of Sâmlaji is built of white sandstone and brick and is surrounded by a wall with a gateway. It is of two storeys supported on pillars and a canopy with arches on each side. It is supposed to be upwards of 400 years old. It contains an image of Vishṇu. Some old **Inscriptions.** A city is said to have existed at this place in the time of Râjâ Harichandraji, signs of which still remain. A number of images of Brahmâ, Vishṇu and Śiva are found in several places which are now in ruins. A large fair is held here every year for fifteen days on Kârtika *Sud.* 13th.

III. 9. **Timba,** in the Gadwârâ *zillâ.* The Târangâ temples on the top of a hill surrounded by other peaks. They are seven storeys high and are temples of Ajitanâthaji and Sambhunâthaji built of white sandstone and brick. These temples are said to have been built in the reign of Kumârpâla of Paṭṭan 700 years ago (*vide* Forbes' *Râs Mâlâ*).

III. 10. **Suda'sna.** There is a cave temple of Moksheśvara Mahâdeva about 4½ miles north-west of Sudâsna on the bank of the river Sarasvatî with a monastery close by, built of sandstone and brick, now in ruins. This temple is held sacred by all castes from being on the river Sarasvatî (Kumârikâ) the waters of which are offered to the idol and to a *pippala* tree. A fair is held every year, Bhâdrapada *Sud.* 11th.

III. 11. **A'ra'sur,** 15 miles north-east of Dântâ. The temple of Ambâ Bhavânî, measuring 25 × 20 feet and 19 feet high is built of marble of inferior quality by Nâgar Brâhmaṇs. It has a *dharmaśâlâ.* The floor is paved with marble.

Inscriptions :—(1) on the edge of a reservoir near the principal shrine called the Manasarovar, of Mahârâṇâ Śrî Mâladeva, dated A.D. 1359. (2) Also at the door of the adytum of the temple of Ambâji is a tablet which records offerings made in A.D. 1545 by the Râṇî of Râv Barmal of Idar. (3) There are several other inscriptions on the pillars of the temple, principally of the 16th century, recording gifts of private individuals and one, dated A.D. 1723, when the "lord of the land Râjâdhirâja Râṇâji (one hundred and eight times repeated) Śrî Prati Singhji was ruling": states that a Vânia family built a *dharmaśâlâ* for the sake of a son, and adds "by the kindness of Ambâ, the hope was fulfilled" (*vide* Forbes' *Râs Mâlâ*). It is visited four times a year by large *saṅghas* in the months of Kârtika, Mârgaśîrsha, Śrâvaṇa and Bhâdrapada. The revenue of the temple is considerable (Forbes' *Râs Mâlâ*, Chapter IX. vol. I.).

III. 12. Four miles north-east of Ambâ Bhavânî, the temple of Koṭeśvara Mahâdeva, measuring 20 × 15 feet and 25 feet high. There is a *dharmaśâlâ* attached to it, partly ruined. The pilgrims who visit the Ambâ Bhavânî shrine visit this also, as without doing so their pilgrimage would not be considered complete. The sacred river Sarasvatî takes its rise from near this temple, and the pilgrims consider that by bathing at this spot in its water they are cleansed from all their sins.

Inscription :— On the jamb and threshold are two, of *Saṁvat* 1156 and 1159.

III. 13. **Kumbharia.** The temples of Neminâtha built of white marble were, according to tradition, 360 in number but were afterwards reduced to 5 by volcanic disturbance. They are much visited by pilgrims.

Inscriptions:—In the temple of Neminâtha there is an inscription dated A.D. 1249, recording additions to the edifice made by Bramhadeva, the son of Chahud, the minister of Kumârapâla Solankî. On one of a group of *pâliyâs* close by is an inscription dated A.D. 1200, which states that "Śrî Dharavarshadeva, the lord of Arbuda, the throne of all Mâṇḍalîkas on whom the sun shines, constructed a well in this city of Araṣanpur" (Forbes' *Râs Mâlâ*). There are also other inscription both in the temples and on the stones of this group.

These Jaina temples were constructed, it is said, by Vimalaśâh to the number of 360. They were dedicated to Pârśvanâtha. It is said that Ambâ Mâtâji gave great wealth to Vimalaśâh and asked him by whose aid he had built these temples; he replied, by the aid of his spiritual preceptor. The Mâtâji repeated the question thrice and each time received the same answer. She then said to him, escape as soon as you can. He fled into the crypt below one of the temples and emerged on Mount Abu. Then the Mâtâji consumed all the temples by fire with the exception of five (*vide* Forbes' *Râs Mâlâ*).

III. 14. **Haldervas** on the bank of the Vâtrak, half a mile south-east of the village in the Ghorasir *tâlukâ*, is the temple of Mahâdeva named Bhṛigu Ṛishi, measuring 20 × 14 feet. On the other side of the river opposite the preceding is a temple of Parâśara (?) Mahâdeva 36 feet by 18: repaired about 70 years ago.

III. 15. **Bamnoli Kot,** a ruined fort about half-way between the villages of Haldervas and Barmuara on the right bank of the Vâtrak river. It is said to have been built by Muḥammad Bigaṛah.

III. 16. **Jetpur,** 3 miles from Gabat. The Khânerâ Talâv, a large tank with masonry *band* on the north side. This fine tank and *band* are said to have been made by the orders of Siddharâja Jayasiṁha.

III. 17. **Prantvel,** about 4 miles from Gabat. ¾ of a mile east of the village is a raised platform on which there are three stones like *pâliyâs*, a large one in the centre and a smaller one on either side. Round the platform there are thirty or forty graves. The people of the neighbourhood say that these stones were erected and are now worshipped by a wandering tribe called "Chamathas."

III. 18. **Magori.** Three *pâliyâs*, on one of which is carved a man and a horse. There is an **inscription** on one of the *pâliyâs* which is illegible. Another *pâliyâ* is called Hathia. A black stone on which are carved 3 snakes is called by the natives "Gok Chuhân."

III. 19. **Punadra.** An old fort of the time of Muḥammad Bîgaṛah.

III. 20. **Telnal** on the Vâtrak. The very old temple of Kedâreśvara about a mile from the village. It has been recently repaired.

III. 21. **Ramas.** A step-well, said to have been built by the wife of the Nawâb of Kapadwanj, 500 years ago.

III. 22. **Sathamba.** A step-well and a *pâliyâ* with an **inscription** which runs as follows:—
सवंत १३२९ वरखे अषाड सुादि १४। शानिवार दिने सोता कविनी श्रीवंता।राजश्री सामजनळ सातसिंह राजश्रीडं. तकाजेतत्रडकरिमोपलप्रा।शैनश्राति.

III. 23. **Amlyala.** The temple of Nîlakaṇṭha Mahâdeva, an old Musalmân tomb and the ruins of old Amlyala.

VII.—KÂTHIAWÂD.

I.—JHÂLÂWÂD PRÂNT.

1. **Tha'n.** (1) Opposite the town on the west side of the tank, on the east, is the temple of Vâsukinâtha, supposed to have been built about 450 years ago. It measures 17 feet by 10 and is supported by 4 pillars. All classes of Hindus reverence Vâsukinâtha as a god. It belongs to a Mahant, Atit Revâgarji, who is the head of a monastery at Thân. Two villages and some more landed property yielding an annual revenue of about 4,000 rupees are granted for defraying the necessary expenses appertaining to this temple. Close to the temple there is a well (*vâv*) having two entrances, built about the same time. The whole town with its adjoining lands, and particularly this *vâv*, abound in serpents. In this town people have a firm belief in the sanctity of the "Vâsuki." They consider him as their deity, and would never run the risk of saying anything against him. This temple is said to have existed long prior to the time when the town was built. The local legend is as follows: Once Abherâj, the chief of Lakhtar, was wandering in search of bullocks in the jungle which is said to have then existed all about the site of Thân. He saw from a distance smoke arising from the place where the temple at present stands. The chief came up and saw the Mahant Sûkhdevagarji, who welcomed him greeting him by his name Abherâj, although they had never seen each other before. The Thâkor, astonished at this, bowed to the Mahant, who ordered him to re-populate the place, some old remains of an ancient village being visible there. The Thâkor asked for some boon or blessing, which the Mahant refused, but said that the serpent-deity would grant it. He encouraged the chief to hold his hand before the serpent, which he did. The cobra raised his hood to grant the asked-for boon, but the Thâkor losing his courage withdrew his hand so that the hood fell on the tip of one of his fingers. The Mahant Sûkhdevagarji then told him that every third ruler on the *gâdi* of Lakhtar should be a minor or child.

Before the temple was built there was only a "Râfadâ," or mound of earth in which the serpents hide themselves, which is still preserved in the temple. The present Mahant Revâgarji daily pours down a hole in the "Râfadâ" a *ser* of cow's milk. It is said that if the person who pours the milk be unclean, or if the milk be that of a cow not more than ten days after calving, it is thrown out by the serpent.

On some *sati pâliyâs* near the temple may be read the dates *Saṁvat* 1720, 1772, 1792, &c.

Thân is situated in the district of "Pâñchâla," belonging to the father of Draupadî, the common wife of the Pâṇḍavas.

(2) Sativâv is a *vâv* or well, hewn in the rock, at a little distance from the town to the north of the eastern gate. It is 38 by 17 feet. The descending flights of steps are also cut out of the same stone. People believe that if a woman who has too little milk in her breasts for her child goes to this *vâv*, sweeps its steps with her bodice, immerses it in the water, and puts it on dripping, her breasts will burst out in thin streams of milk as soon as she returns home. People from distant places resort to this *vâv* for the attainment of this object. About the *vâv* there are one or two *pâliyâs*, one of *Saṁvat* 1774.

III. (3) Hinglâj cave is situated near this Sativâv in the east. It is also hewn out of the rock and measures 18 by 15 by 7 feet. The entrance is sufficient for a man to enter in. There appear to have been two pillars to support the roof of the cave, and there are ten raised seats supposed to be those of ancient saints for sitting in meditation. In the cave there are five images, one that of Hinglâj and the other four of other goddeses.

III. (4) Bhiḍabhanjan cave is to the south at a little distance from Thân. It is cut in the rock and is 17 by 14 by 7 feet. It has also ten hewn seats outside the cave on the right. There is no image inside, but there are two seats on the south and east walls and a raised bench along the west side.

II *b*. (5) Muni Bâvâ's *deval* is two or three miles to the south of Thân on a hilly ridge forming the western bank of a large tank and close to the Mahânadî, and may have been built when the *band* was thrown across the river, perhaps in the 14th century. It is dedicated to Śiva and is partly ruined. It is built of red and white stone, richly sculptured inside in a spirited style resembling those on the Pâwâgaḍ hill in Gujarât. It has three domes supported by 16 pillars. It measures 36 by 25 feet. There is one broken *linga* about 2 feet high, together with some broken images of goddesses. They are said to have been broken by the Muhammadans.

According to a local tradition some horses belonging to Maghâbhâi of Junâgaḍ were taken away by the renowned thieves Khâprâ and Kodiyâ, who lived about this place. The return journey of over 100 miles with the stolen animals was accomplished in so short a time as passed between the setting of the sun and the rising of the moon in the same night, so that neither the sun nor the moon might be witnesses of their guilt. Maghâbhâi asked Khâprâ and Kodiyâ for the horses, but they would not admit having taken them. Maghâbhâi thereupon uttered a curse, "Should you have made off with the horses, this pond shall burst." The curse is said to have been realized by the instant bursting of the pond and giving rise to the river Mahânadî.

III. (6) Sûrya temple is a mile north of Thân on a hill which was originally the old fort of Kandolâ, and close to Songaḍ, the fort on the adjacent hill. It is said to have been originally built 1,000 years ago, but it was entirely destroyed by Kartalab Khân of Ahmadâbâd in 1692. The temple is said to have been erected by Lâkhâ Fulâni. The present temple is built of old materials, and plain. It is 80 by 28 feet and supported by 38 pillars, of which 8 are new. It contains two images of Sûrya and of his wife, here called Ranâde. This temple is enclosed in a compound having stone walls and other smaller temples. There is one inscription of *Saṁvat* 1432 (A.D. 1376), which is read thus :—

संवत् १४३२ वर्षे वैसाषसुादे ९ सो बूटडला । षीआ पुत्र सीह कासप तवुका उपइं
तो दंतकाढी डागरि पाला नाणा काडीबो संकर उदव नंडो भान माहाराज.

II *b*. (7) The temple of Mahâdeva at Trinetra, commonly called "Tarnetar," is 6 miles to the north of Thân in Ḍerâ Pânchâla. This temple is said to have been built by the king Mândhâtâ in the Satyayuga. The interior and exterior of the temple are highly sculptured all over with various forms and figures, but is weather-worn. It measures inside 40 by 30 feet. It probably dates from the 11th or 12th century. The original *linga* having been broken, it has been replaced by two others one after the other. There is a pool or reservoir of water in front forming three sides of an oblong, and having two descending flights of steps on both sides. The space containing water is 200 by 32 feet. The temple along with the reservoir is enclosed by a compound wall out of repair. A large fair is annually held here on the 5th and 6th of Bhâdarvâ *Sudh*, when 30,000 or 40,000 persons collect from the surrounding districts. Outside the compound in the east are some *pâliyâs* carved in high relief. The figures on them have their hands joined as if in prayer. On one the date *Saṁvat* 1282 can be read with difficulty.

III. 2. **Sitha'**, 10 miles north-west of Wadhwân under Dhrângadhrâ: on the east about a mile from the village is the fine tank of Chandrâsar built by Chandrasingji, a late chief of Halwad, *Saṁvat* 1665. It is multilateral in form, built of stone on all sides and measuring about 500 feet by 400. The style is quite plain. *Saṁvat* 1524 with the following *śloka* is found in an inscription on one of the stones :—

चंद्राहारं तडागं च कारितं दर्भगोत्रिणा ।

वृषाणां शान्नयेन्यूनं चंद्रराधनक्षत्रिणा ॥

There is a small temple on the bank of this pond. The words ગન્ધન આખુંઃ were inscribed on the upper part of the door frame. This led people to conjecture that some treasure was buried underneath, and hence the ruined state of the temple.

III. 3. **Sa'ela'**, about 15 miles south-west from Wadhwân: has an artificial lake about 700 yards long and 300 broad. It is very old and said to have been built by Siddharâja Jayasiṁha. The yearly collection of silt has considerably reduced its depth; yet if properly filled with water it suffices for the people of the place for the whole year.

III. 4. **Wadhwa'n.** (1) The temple of Rânik Devî is a simple *chhatri* at a little distance from the northern wall of the town. It is said to have been built by Siddharâja Jayasiṁha about 750 years ago to the memory of a *sati* and is about 20 feet high and 44 feet in circumference. It is sculptured. (See Forbes' *Râs Mâlâ*.)

III. (2) The Mâdhava *vâv* in the town of Wadhwân near the western gate, called Lakha Pol, is 188 feet 9 inches by 22 feet 2 inches and 80 feet deep. The style is bold and ornate. It has six arches, the lowest of which has six storeys above it. There is a flight of fourteen steps between each two arches. At the top near the Kotha there is a stone mortar or pot seven feet deep. An underground pipe goes to a well in the Darbârgad, so that water was easily taken through the pipe during the Holi holidays. It is styled Mâdhava *vâv* after Mâdhava, a Nâgar by caste and *Kârbhâri* to Karan Ghelâ, the last king of Gujarât, and who is said to have brought the Musalmâns to Paṭṭan in revenge for the seduction of his wife. In the side walls are mutilated images, one of Hanumân and the other of Bhairava, which are said to have been broken by Alau'd-din Khuni.

There is an inscription of *Saṁvat* 1350 (A.D. 1296) in a niche under the arch, which reads on one side—

संवत् १३५० वर्षे कार्तिक वदी ८ गुरु नागरज्ञातीय व श्रीसामसुतमीदसं श्रीसींपुं

and on the other—

नागरज्ञातीय महं श्रीसाढलसुतामहं श्रीतशमादीती.

III. (3) Gangâ Vâv, near the eastern gate, which is called the Śiani Pol. It is of six storeys and measures 150 by 70 feet and 62 feet deep. There are five arches in it having storeys above them. In the third arch is an inscription in which the date "*Saṁvat* 1225 Phâlguna *Sudi* 3rd" is legible.

III. (4) Mahâvîra Svâmî's temple on the bank of the river in the north-east of the town, dates probably from about the 11th century, and is built in the ordinary Jaina style.

III. (5) Half a mile from the south gate called the Kharva Pol is a *vâv* near the garden belonging to Dâjirâj. It measures 99 by 14 feet. It has three arches; the storeys above two of these arches have been ruined. There is an **inscription** some part of which, though almost illegible, can with difficulty be thus deciphered :—

संवत् १३०१ पोश शुद्ध १ चंद श्रीवर्धमानमंडले महाराज श्रीसेनपत्ती श्रीसिधराजदेव.

III. 5. Between Wadhwân and Khamisânâ, about a *kos* to the north-west of the latter, is the cave of Khamisânâ called Dholidhaj—a natural cavity about 18 inches square. All about here there was a thick grove, which was washed away by the heavy inundation of Bhogâvâ in *Saṁvat* 1922. It is a very old place, but no inscription is known to exist. Lately some rooms have been built near this cave by the Wadhwân Darbâr for ascetics to live in. The local legend is as follows: There were two white *rainchalis* (heavenly she-goats) which used to pour their milk on an ascetic who lived there. These *rainchalis* were seen by a shepherd, who disclosed the mystery to the public, and hence the name of the cave is Dholidhaj. Formerly the grove about was said to be the resort of lions and tigers, but now it having been washed away by the river it is not difficult of access. It is said that the cave has two subterranean passages, one leading to Abu and the other to Girnâr.

III. 6. **Halwad,** about 20 miles west of Dhrângadhrâ, dates from about A.D. 1446: it was the capital of the Jhâlâs after Kuhâ and before Dhrângadhrâ. There is a fine palace about 250 feet square, erected in 1709 A.D. by Rânâ Śrî Jasvantsinghji, and bears an **inscription** to that effect. There are said to be some fine carved wood screens in the interior. A large number of *sati pâliyâs* near the town date from A.D. 1633.

III. 7. **Dives'vara,** about 3 miles north from Chotilâ, has a small temple of Mahâdeva.

I *b*. 8. **Kodina'ra**; a stone tablet with a *Praśasti* **inscription** giving the name of Ânandapura.

II *b*. 9. **A'nandapura,** 64 miles north-west of Wala, has a fine temple attributed to Siddharâja. *Ind. Ant.*, VII. p. 7.

II.—Junâgad State.

III. 1. **Juna'gad.** (1) About a mile to the east is the Dâmodara Kuṇḍa; a very small spring that flows through it keeps it constantly full of water. As it is considered a place of great sanctity, the dead from the town are brought there to be burned, and pilgrims from different parts go to bathe in its holy water. It is 287 feet long and 54 feet broad. *Ghâts* are constructed on its south and north sides. Near the north *ghât* are small temples built where influential Nâgars were burnt. In connection with the south *ghât* is the temple of Dâmodaraji looking on the tank. It is ascended by a flight of 25 steps. The temple, though very old, is entire. It is said that it was built by Vajranâbha, fourth in descent from Kṛishṇa. The wall around the temple was built by the late Divân Amarji. The courtyard, which is 109 feet by 125, contains, besides the temple proper, a *dharmaśâlâ* and a temple, smaller in size, dedicated to Baladevaji, brother of Kṛishṇa. The temple proper consists of the vestibule and the idol chamber. A dome covers the vestibule and a *śikhara* is over the shrine decorated with niches and mythological carvings on its walls. The courtyard was also paved by the Divân Amarji.

(2) Revatikuṇḍa. The courtyard of the temple of Dâmodaraji communicates with the Revatîkunda which is 65 feet long and broad. It has two inscriptions. The *kuṇḍa* has niches filled with images. Its water is considered holy and pilgrims are required to bathe in this *kuṇḍa* prior to their bathing in the Dâmodarakuṇḍa.

Inscription :—

ॐ नमोविनायकाय । योगींद्रैर्मुनिपुंगवैरनिमिषैर्योभक्तिवश्यः परं न ध्यानेन न
चेज्यया न तपसा धर्तुं हृदाप्याप्यते । गोप्यासौ नवनीततस्करपरोबद्धोगवां दामभिः स्थाणुत्वं
निरमोचयद्द्रुव [रयो] दामोदरोव्याज्जगत् ॥ १ ॥ मंडलीकनृपतिर्यदुवंशे योबभूव युधि
मुद्गल्जेता ॥ श्रीकरो सहितभूपतिसेव्यस्तस्य सूनुरभवन्माहिपालः ॥ २ ॥ तत्तनयोवानिभर्त्ता
खंगारोनामवेदमुद्धर्त्ता ॥ द्वीपनवद्वयहर्ता सोमेशस्थापनाकर्त्ता ॥ ३ ॥ भूरुक्मदानपरितो-
षितभूमिदेवस्तन्नंदनः समभवज्जयसिंहदेवः ॥ वर्णाश्रमस्थितिकरोनृपमुक्तसिंहस्तस्मादरिद्विर-
दविक्रममुक्तसिंहः ॥ ४ ॥ मधुपनृपतिशुद्धेस्तीर्थराडन्यनार्यां जनितानिजजनित्रीतुल्यबुद्धिर्व-
दान्यः ॥ समितिसुभटमुख्योमंडलीकस्तदीयोजानि च तमनुजन्मा मेलिगः स्थूललक्षः ॥ ९ ॥
भीताभयदव्रतपरनृपमेलिगनंदनश्च जयसिंहः । अस्ति च तस्य तु राज्ये यदुसामंतसैन्यपे
समये ॥ ६ ॥ अभिषेणयितुमुपेतं शिखरकोटस्य परिसरे स [म] रे ॥ योहत्वा यवनबलं
मुमोच धर्माध्वना शेषं ॥ ७ ॥ संवद्रामतुरंगसागरमहीसंख्येय शाके सिते पंचम्यां भृगुवासरे
व्यरचयत् षट्कृष्णषट्कर्मकृत् ॥ पाटीश्रीनरसिंहदेवतनयोदामोदरः पूर्वजानुद्धर्तुं यतियात्रि-
कोपकृतये तिष्ठत्वखंडं मठं ॥ ८ ॥नागराभ्यंतराज्ञातिद्विजधांधलनंदनः ॥ मंत्रिसिंहस्तस्य सुतः
प्रशस्तेः शामलः कविः ॥ ९ ॥ इति सं ० १४७३ वर्षे सूत्रजाल्हासुतसूत्रकरणकेन ॥

III. (3) The temple of Muchakuṇḍa is very small and has a cell, which can only be entered from the shaft of a well.

III. (4) Near the monastery of Pyârâ Bâvâ are nine caves cut in the rock. These caves, once inhabited by Pyârâ Bâvâ and his disciples, are now overgrown with grass and very filthy. Besides these there are seven caves cut in the south side of the rock (see *Archæological Report*, Vol. II.)

(5) The Uparkot contains a large cave, the Jami Masjid, Adichadi *vâv* and Noghan well. The upper storey of the cave is 37 feet long and 31½ feet broad, and has six pillars on the capitals of which figures are carved, which are corroded. This storey leads to a small bath. The lower storey is 44 feet long and broad. Figures are carved on the capitals and three walls are also decorated with a belt of carving. A hole in the roof admits sufficient light. The whole depth of the cave is 29 feet. (See *Archæological Report*, Vol. II., and *Views of Somanâtha, Girnâr*, &c.)

III. (6) The Jami Masjid is 137½ feet long, 96 feet broad, and 19 feet high. Its roof is supported by 140 pillars. On the east is a *hoj* or bath, now disused. (See *Archæological Report*, Vol. II.)

III. (7) The Adichadi *vâv* and Noghan well. The former is cut through a thick stratum of stone, but the steps are entirely destroyed for the greater part of the descent. The water, though drinkable, is not used. The latter well, though sunk very deep, does not contain water and is entered by a flight of steps.

III. (8) The roof of the old gate Uparkot is supported by four arches carved after the Hindu fashion.

III. (9) Tombs of the Nawâbs of Junâgaḍ. The platform on which the *mûqarbâ* of Ahmadkhânji stands is 21¾ (?) feet long and broad. The whole building is decorated with Muhammadan sclupture, and the doors of the room containing the grave, with brass work. There are five domes with spires and small minarets not higher than the spires.

The *mûqarbâs* of Bahâdûrkhânji and Lâdadi Bibi are of the same description but differ in the kind of sculpture. The platform of the former is 32¾ feet and that of the latter is 26½ feet long and broad. The doors of the latter are ornamented with ivory work. The average height of these *mûqarbâs* is 43 feet. Besides these, there are nine *mûqarbâs* different in size but not larger than those described.

III. (10) Tank of Bhavanâtha or Mṛigikuṇḍa This tank is 23¼ feet by 31¼. It is shallow and in a dilapidated state. Beside it is the old temple of Bhavanâtha which is 56⅓ feet long, 26 feet broad, and 21½ feet high. It is built of stone and has nine small domes undecorated with sculptures. There is an **inscription** carved on the threshold of the shrine, which is illegible.

(11) Bordevî: There is a small temple at the foot of the Girnâr Hill dedicated to this goddess. In this valley was discovered and opened, in January and February 1889, the Boria or Lakha Medi *stûpa* by Mr. J. M. Campbell, I. C. S., which yielded relics. For an account of it see the Journal of the Asiatic Society of Bengal, Vol. LX. Part I. No. 2, 1891.

III. (12) Khengârvâv. About 6 miles west of Junâgaḍ is the Kengârvâv, which is 18¾ feet by 128. There are two storeys over the lower part of the steps. The upper storey is supported by nine round pillars and leads to the balconies looking over the water. The lower storey is also supported by the same number of pillars, which are decorated with images carved on them. This *vâv* is in a ruined condition.

I *b*. (13) Nearly half-way from Junâgaḍ to the tank of Dâmodarajî, is the famous rock bearing three **inscriptions** of Aśoka, Skandagupta, and Rudradâman.*

III. (14) Caves of Nava Durgâ. No caves are dedicated to these Mâtâs, but their images are carved in the side of a rock. The images are plastered with red stuff.

III. (15) Mâi Ghadhechi. Within the confines of the *sthâna* of Mâi Ghadhechi in the northern part of Junâgaḍ is the small cave of Dâtâr containing his tomb. Near this is a *masjid* 39 feet long and broad. From the sculpture on the door frame and the form of the pillars, which are thirty in number, it seems to have been formerly a Hindu temple dedicated to Mahâdeva. There is an Arabic **inscription** carved on the lintel. The *sthâna* of Mâi Ghadhechi is a large cave 54 feet long, 46½ broad, and 23½ high. Within the cave is a small temple dedicated to Mâi Ghadhechi. It has a small rough dome undecorated with sculpture. South of this temple is an oblong hall, the roof of which is supported by six pillars. The entrance of the cave is supported by four pillars.

---

* For identification by Khân Bahâdur Ardasir Jamsetji, late Naib Divân of Junâgaḍ, of the site of the Sudarasana lake and dams, mentioned in the As'oka rock inscription, see the paper read at the meeting of the Bombay Branch of the Royal Asiatic Society on 19th January 1891.

II *b*. (16) Near the *sthâna* of Mâi Ghadhechi are the five caves of Khâprâ Kodiâ, all communicating with one another and containing 59 pillars, in the capitals of which were carved the forms of animals, particularly of lions, parts of which are still visible. The caves are not looked after. There is a Persian inscription on a wall of the third cave (see *Archæological Report*, Vol. II).

II *b*. (17) Girnâr hill near Junâgad, the ancient Ujjayanta. At an elevation of about 2,700 feet is a large and fine group of Jaina temples, with numerous inscriptions, which will be found collected in the *Appendix*, with rough translations. On the summit of the hill is a temple of Ambâ Mâtâ, the foundation of which at least is probably of very early date. For an account of the Jaina temples on Girnâr, see *Archæological Survey Reports*, Vol. II.

2. **Vanthali.** (1) The Sûrajkunda is very old and considered a holy tank, in which the inhabitants of the surrounding villages bathe on holidays. It is 32 feet long and broad.

(2) The Jami Masjid stands in the west of Vanthali. It was a Hindu building and is still known as a court of Balirâja. It was converted into a *masjid*, and is 148 feet long and 52½ feet wide. The courtyard contains some tombs and a small *mûqarbâ*. In the interior is a long hall 33½ feet by 73½, the roof of which is supported with 72 pillars. It has 7 domes decorated with sculpture. The images carved in the capitals of the pillars and in the concave part of the largest dome were knocked off by the Musalmâns. There is a small dark room in the southern part containing six pillars, one of which bears the following inscription :—

संवत १४०८ वर्षे माघ शुदी १३ रवौ सू० चाहड सुता सू० भलमडा राजश्री रांसिक्नीं
भार्या दिवंगतोऽस्ति शुभंभूयात् ॥

An inscription in the Hârivâv near Dhandhûsar reads :—

॥ ९० ॥ ॐ नमः श्रीगेणशायं[1]: ॥ [2]कंनत्कनककं [क] णकणितभृंगझंकारितं
विचंद्रक [म] काल्याकरतलेन संवाहितं ॥ रसालसदृशोभृशं [3]श्चपदपद्मसत्पश्यतो जयाय
जलशालिनः शयनतः प्रबोधोदयः ॥ १ ॥ श्रीचंद्रचूडचूडाचंद्रं चूडासमानमधृतयतः ॥
जयति नृपहंसवंशोत्तंसः शंसत्प्रशंसितो वंशः ॥ २ ॥ श्री [षंगार] स्तकुले खड्गलक्ष्मक्षोणी
क्षुण्णाशेषविद्वेषिपक्षः ॥ यत्रामित्रक्षत्रनक्षत्रमात्रस्ताशिस्त्राशत्रय – शृक्सांध्यरागे ॥ ३ ॥
तस्याभवत्तानुभवः क्षितिमूर्तिमीशमं – – यात्रविजयी जयसिंहदेवः ॥ तीक्ष्णक्षुरप्रनखखं-
डितचंडचौरमुंडावली [कम] लकु [डूम] लमाल्यैव ॥ ४ ॥ तस्मा [द्यस्यक] ति [निं]
जेष्यविकृतिः पापे कृते निःकृतिर्योग्यायस्यमतिर्द्विजेष्वनुगतिर्दुष्टेषु नो संगतिः ॥ विद्यायां
निचितिर्गुरौ परिचितिर्यस्या [गमे] निष्टितिः संग्रामे विजितिर्महीपतिरिति ख्यातः क्षितौ
भूपतिः ॥ ५ ॥ जयसिंहदेवतनुजो ननु यो मनुजो नुजो ऽस्यदनुजारिगणे ॥ जलसीतलः
कुलिनिमोकलसील्यलसीभवन्मकल – [5]मंलसीतभनक ॥ ६ ॥ भूंभकोभोग तृतेन भैरवेनणं[6]
पुरद्विषा ॥ मुक्तामोकलसिंहेन कतसीकिल सीधुनः ॥ ७ ॥ भूभृत्पं[7]ह्लिरनीयतप्रतिभटैर्योजा-
तुकस्छेश्वरैः पात्राय प्रभुणापिसिंधु – – – प्यनेनानिन्येनवा. जु – मेवक (षा) कषेनपुरुषैस्तां

---

[1] य. [2] क. [3] स्त्र. [4] त. [5] The whole sentence is not clear. [6] वेणपुर. [7] स्पङ्क्ति.

[1]मूवलसिंहशून्यासत - स्कंदल्लसदिंदुसुंदरयशा[2] श्रीमोकलःक्ष्मापतिः ॥ ८ ॥ आदेशादिहदेश देशनमनुश्रीपातशाहिप्रभोः सद्यो निर्म्मितनव्यभव्यभवनप्रासादशालादिभिः ॥ वापीकूपसरोभिपानविविधोद्यानादिभिर्द्योतितं श्रीमद्वा[3]वंनधामनामनगरं यद्राजधानीं जगुः ॥ ९ ॥ बार्हस्पतीषौ[4]शंनशीष्वधीता चाणक्यमाणिक्यवचोविनीतः कामंदकी सुंदरमंदिरश्रीगदाधरो यस्य गृहेस्ति मंत्री ॥ १० ॥ तन्नंदनो नंदतिवैश्यनाथ - ना - देभ्रेत्यरुजामृजाक्रत् ॥ कुमारभावेपि च येन सारव्यापारभारो बिभरांबभूवे ॥ ११ ॥ हानीमिहानीयकृतार्थमानी स्थानी प्रधानीकृतराजधानी ॥ स्वंभासि संभावयति स्म रंभादंभान्न जंभारिपुरं चिरंभात् ॥ १२ ॥ धंधूसरस्सुत्तमलोकलाभलोभात्तयापीदृगकारिवापी ॥ अपीय पीयूषजलंनतापी तापं न पापं बुबुधे च पापी ॥ १३ ॥ राजति यशः प्रशस्तिर्मधुरास्यास्तां चकार कोपि कविः ॥ शरयुगमनुसंवत्सर १४४९ वर्षे फाल्गु शुदि पंचमी सोमे ॥ १४ ॥ प्रशस्तिकर्त्ता त्रिवाडि श्रीरामः सूत्र नारायण प्रशस्तिमुत्कीर्णा राजवाछाभार्या बाई रतनी सुता बाई हानी वापी कारापिता शुभं भवतु श्रीः ॥

III. 3. **Chorwa'd.** Two miles south is the small temple of Bhavânî.

III. 4. **Ma'ngrol.** The Jami Masjid stands in the western part of the town. According to the **inscription** it was metamorphosed into a *masjid* by Samaskhân, Vazîr to Firûzshâh, in 1364. It is said that Bhân Jethwâ, wishing to re-marry his divorced wife, referred to the Brâhmaṇs, who told him that he could only do so by marrying 1800 girls in one house at one time as atonement for the sin, and hence the origin of the building. It was built by him in *Saṁvat* 1208 (A.D. 1252). The Musalmâns have broken off the sculptures and images in the inner part of the dome and those carved in the capitals of the pillars. This mosque is 278 feet long and 256 broad, has 9 domes, and its roof is supported by 818 pillars. Râvali Masjid, according to an **inscription** in the interior, was metamorphosed in 1401 into a *masjid* by Jâfarkhân in the time of Muhammad Taghlakh. The sculpture is pure Hindu. The images carved in the concave side of the domes bear testimony to its formerly being a Hindu temple. These images are defaced or knocked off from the niches. This mosque is 109 feet long and 90 feet broad and its roof is supported by 155 pillars. It has three domes without spires.

Inscription :—

(१.) संवत् १४९२ वर्षे वैशाकवादि १९ रवौ श्रीयोगिनीपुरे पातशाहि श्री नसरयाविजयराज्ये तन्नियुक्तश्रीगुर्जरधरित्र्यां श्रीदफरखाने राज्यं कुर्वति इह सुराष्ट्रायां श्रीमंगलपुरे रायमूल्स्तालिराज वयरसिसुतथमीममल्किश्री आकुबे मुकती व्यापारं कुर्वति [नायब] कोटवाल मल्किश्री मुसिनाम्ना प्रतोलीद्वयेपि निविडलोहजटिता कपाटयुगली प्रत्येकं कारिता लोकरक्षार्थं ॥ तोरकी लिपिः कादीबदरदीनषोजा जहीरसुतेन लिखिता सुत्र राणिगसुत सूत्र वीरधवलेन उट्टंकिता ॥

(२.) ॐ नमः शिवाय ॥ मुकुटः स हरस्य पातु वः शशिपंकेरुहकंदकांक्षया ॥ गगनादचिरेण यत्र सा सुरहंसीव पपात जान्हवी ॥ कृत्वा राज्यमुपारमन्नरपतिः श्रीसिद्धराजो यदा दैवादुत्तमकीर्तिमंडितमहीपृष्ठो गरिष्टो गुणैः ॥ आचक्रामक्रागिन्य [झटित्य] चिंत्यमहिमातद्राज्यासिंहासनं श्रीमानेष कुमारपालनृपतिः पुण्यप्ररूढोदयः ॥ राज्येमुष्य

[1] These three letters (मूवल) do not agree with the metre. [2] शाः. [3] म. [4] ष्वौ.

महीभुजो भवदिह श्रीगुहिलाख्यान्वये श्रीसाहार इति प्रभूतगरिमाधारो धरामंडनं ॥ चौ-
लुक्यांगनिगूहकः सहजिगः ख्यातस्तनूजस्ततस्तत्पुत्रा बलिनो बभूवुरवनौ सौराष्ट्ररक्षाक्षमाः ॥
एषामेकतमो वीरः सोमराज इति क्षितौ ॥ विख्यातो विदधे देवं पितुर्नाम्ना महेश्वरं ॥ श्रीसो-
मनाथदेवस्य जगत्यां पुण्यवृद्धये ॥ इंदुकुंदयशाश्चक्रे कीर्तिमेरुसमाश्रितं ॥ पूजार्थमस्य देवस्य
भ्राता ज्येष्टोस्य मूलुकः ॥ सुराष्ट्रानायकः प्रादाच्छासनं कुलशासनं ॥ ठ० श्रीसहजिगपुत्रः
ठ० श्रीमूलुकेन श्रीसहजिगेश्वरदेवस्यानवरतपंचोपचारपूजाहेतोः श्रीमन्मंगलपुरशुल्कमंडपि-
कायां दिनं प्रति का १ तथा तलासभाव्यमध्यात् दिनं प्रति का १ तथा वलीवर्द्धछाट-
माणकाभाव्ये छाटां प्रति का १ कणभृतगडकं प्राति का ४ तथा रासभछाटाप्राति का० ॥
तथा समस्तलोकेन निःशेषवल्लीकारैश्चपत्रभरां । वीडहरा । केरी । वादुया । प्रभृतीनांप्रत्ये-
कका० ॥ तथा पत्रभृतउटधरकंप्रतिका ॥ २ ॥ तथा पत्रभृतगंत्रींप्रतिद्र १ क्षेत्रंप्रतिउच्च-
ताभाव्येका १ तथा आगरमध्ये खुटिंतखरालिहासाप्रतिका० । तथा अनयैव स्थित्या चोरु-
यावडेवलइजेव [च] ग्राह्यं । तथा लाठिवद्रापथकेवहंतशुल्कमंडपिकामध्यात् दिनंप्रति ठ०
श्रीमूलुकेन रूपकैकः प्रदत्तः ॥ तथा चोरुयावडेन्यसमस्तबृहत्पुरुषैरेकमतीभूय चतुराघाटन-
विशुद्धा यथा प्रसिद्धपरिभोगा सवृक्षमालाकुलावीसणवेलीग्राममार्गसमासक्तादिगुयावावीना-
मवापी राजानुमत्या श्रीसहजिगेश्वराय प्रदत्ता ॥ तथा श्रीवामनस्थल्यां शुल्कमंडपिकायां
दिनंप्रतिका १ तथा द्यूतमध्ये दिनं प्रातिका १ तथा पत्रकुट्टांभराप्राति पत्रप्रात १ तथा
वीडहरा । केरी । वादुया । प्रभृतीनां प्रत्येकं पत्र ९० तथा तलासभाव्यमध्यात् तांबूलिकहट्टं
प्राति प्रतिदिनं पत्र २ मडावापुग १ देवदायः समस्तोयं समस्तैर्भावि भूमिपैः ॥ पालनीयो-
नुमान्यश्च दानाच्छ्रेयोनुपालनं ॥ शिवः पात्रं जनो दाता पालकः पुण्यभाक्परं ॥ लोपकश्च
महापापी विचार्यैवं प्रपालयेत् ॥ यत उक्तं च ॥ बहुभिर्वसुधा भुक्ता राजभिः सगरादिभिः ॥
यस्य यस्य यदा भूमिस्तस्य तस्य तदा फलं ॥ श्रीमद्विक्रमसंवत् १२०२ तथा श्रीसिंहसंवत्
३२ आश्विनवदि १३ सोमे प्रशस्तिरियं निर्मिता ॥ कृतिरियं परमपाशुपताचार्यमहा-
पंडितश्रीप्रसर्वज्ञस्य

III. 5. **Delwa'da'.** The Jami Masjid stands near the western gate. It is 77 feet long and 60 feet broad and has two minarets 66 feet high. It is built of stone and its roof is supported by 20 pillars. Copy of an inscription on a grave is as follows:—

در جامع مسجد قصبه دلواره که از بنا و پادشاهان سابق از
احمدآباد است در ان تربتي اولياء الله است که نامش شاه مشهور
است بر مرقدش در سنگ سرخ آيتي کلام الله نوشته - انيست —
يبشرهم ربهم برحمة منه ورضوان وجنات لهم فيها نعيم مقيم خالدين
فيها ابدا - وبر بالينش همدران سنگ نبشته است - الملک لله
الواحد القهار

III. 6. **Gupta Praya'ga** is composed of three *kuṇḍas* or tanks connected with one another. Their names are Prayâganokuṇḍa, Sarasvatînokuṇḍa and Jamunâjinokuṇḍa. Their average length and breadth is 150 feet. The water of these tanks accumulates in the Prayâganokuṇḍa whence it flows into the sea. Besides these, there are three *kuṇḍas* more, viz. Brahmagayâ, Rudragayâ, and Vishṇugayâ to the north. The dead from Delwâḍâ and Unâ are brought there to be burned, it being considered a place of great sanctity.

III. **7. Vejalkotho** is the name given to a small hill about 15 miles north-east of Uná. It is now a barren hill, but was formerly the abode of Vejal Vâjo, chief of a predatory tribe who conquered Uná from Chandrabal Ojra.

III. 8. **Una'.** The Jami Masjid is said to have been a temple of Śiva and Máta when Chandrabal reigned at Uná. The building is purely Hindu. It was built of stone and its roof is supported by 80 pillars.

The *masjid* of Hazratsháh stands at a little distance north of Uná. It is 300 feet long and 120 feet broad.

III. **9. Tulsi Sya'm,** about 20 miles north of Uná. On entering the place there is a hall on the right where pilgrims, particularly mendicants, receive the stamp (or brand) of the *śankha* and *chakra* on their hands. The courtyard contains two small temples of Hanumán and Śiva. The vestibule is entered from the east and contains stone benches attached to the walls, and its dome is supported by 12 pillars. The chamber between the vestibule and the shrine has three store-rooms and 12 pillars that support its dome. Next to this is the chamber containing the idol of Śyâmji, 2½ feet high, placed on a small platform 4 feet high. At the distance of about 50 yards are the hot-springs, seven in number. The temple is very old and built of stone.

About two miles east of Tulśi Śyâm is a small ditch called Bhimchas, into which the river Zameri falls from a height of 12 feet. It is about 150 feet long, 7½ feet broad, and 10 feet deep. Near it is a small temple dedicated to Kuntîjî, mother of Bhîma. It is said that Bhîma struck a ploughshare against the ground and got water for his mother, and hence the name of the place.

III. 10. **Sutra'pa'da'.** The temple of Chyavaneśvara stands between the village and the beach with the Chyavankuṇḍa in front. This *kuṇḍa* or tank is 20 feet long and 18 feet broad. Its water is considered holy, and people from surrounding villages bathe in it on holidays.

There is an old temple of the sun near the beach at a little distance from the Chyavanakuṇḍa with the Surajkuṇḍa in front. The temple is in a decaying state and the inscription on the door frame is corroded. The words that are legible are संवत् १३९७ ना वरखे चैत्र वद. It is about 30 feet long, 13 feet wide, and 30 feet high.

III. **11. Dha'mlaj.** Chakra Tîrtha, otherwise called Vishṇu Gayâ, is a tank to the west. It is 40 feet long and broad. There is the following inscription in *Bâlabodha* character carved on a stone lying under a *pippala* tree :—

ॐ नमः श्रीगणेशाय ॥ पातु यातुकुकारातिर्विश्वं विश्वंभरो हरिः । जनान् पुनातु तत्तीर्थं जिष्णुविष्णुगयाख्यया ॥ १ ॥ आसीद्गुर्जरराजमुख्यसचिवश्रीतेजसूनुः पुरा श्रीराणः सुजनद्विजावनधनोम्लेच्छाकुले क्ष्मातले । तत्पुत्रः सचिवाग्रणीर्जयति सत्कर्म्माह्वयः प्रतया राजद्राजकराजकार्यचतुरः प्राग्वाटवंशांकुरः ॥ २ ॥ स्वस्ति श्रीमत्प्रभासाधिपतिशिवसदा-राधनावाप्तलक्ष्मीस्तुल्यः श्रीभर्म्मभूनोजयति जनमनःश्रांतिहृत्कल्पवृक्षः ॥ तन्मंत्रीकर्मसिंहः सचिवसुरागिरिः क्ष्मासुराधारउच्चैर्भात्येनंसाधुमार्गाचरणविनयतः सेवमानोऽसमानः ॥ ३ ॥ यन्नाम पामरमपीह पुनाति यत्र श्राद्धे प्रयांति पितरोऽक्षयतृप्तिमेव । तत्तीर्थमेतदमलो-पलबद्धमूलसोपानमुच्छ्रितनिपानमकारयद्यः ॥ ४ ॥ उद्धृत्य यः सगरभास्करसद्म मूलात्तन्मंडपं परिकरेण समं समंतात् । नव्यं सुभव्यमिह कारयति स्म पूजां माध्याह्निकीमनुदिनं ननु

सोमनाथे ॥ ५ ॥ स्वभ्रातृमेघनृपतेः परलोकयात्रासौख्याय नित्यजलधान्यनिधिं द्विजेभ्यः ।
श्रीभर्म्मभूपतिरदात्सचिवेन येन विज्ञापितोऽभिनवमेघपुराग्रहारं ॥ ६ ॥ आद्यावंघाःसुराशाः
प्रथितसुयशसस्तेंऽजनानंदनाद्या एकः श्रीकर्मसिंहः स्फुरति कलियुगे सेवकः सन्परोक्षे ।
ग्रामं यः स्वामिनामप्रथितमतनुत स्वःस्थितौ मेघराज्ञोविप्राणां स्थाण्णुवृत्तिं श्रुतिचयमिह च
स्थापयामास साक्षात् ॥ ७ ॥ अमृतं पाययन् गायः सुरपत्तनगोपुरे । आहावे कीर्तिसद्धर्मा-
वाप्तीमारममेकल्पत् ॥ ८ ॥ वंशवृद्धिकराः संतु रामाद्यास्तस्य नंदनाः । सुरवृक्षोपमाः श्रीम-
त्स्वपूर्वबयसा समाः ॥ ९ ॥ किं दुर्लभं महदुपासंनया यदस्मा काठिन्यगेहमपि विष्णुग-
घातटस्थः । लब्ध्वा सुदर्शनतनुं सुजनाय दत्ते स्नाने गदाधरनतौ च मतिं सुदृष्टः ॥ १० ॥
ज्ञानंददिर्भाति जनेषु भानुः सानंदमानंदपुराद्विजाग्र्यः । श्रितः श्रुती तत्सुतवासुदेवः सांगस्मृती
चक्र इमां प्रशस्तिं ॥ ११ ॥ लिखितेयं पंडितसर्वादित्येन ॥ सूत्रमधुसूदनेनोत्कीर्णा ॥ संवत्
१४३७ वर्षे आषाढ वदि ६ शनौ ॥ छ ॥ ॥ श्रीः ॥ शुभं भवत ॥ विष्णुः प्रीयतां ॥

North-west of this tank is a cave of ordinary size containing the *linga* of **Naṭeśvara Mahâdeva.**

III. 12. **Kadva'r,** a village between Sutrâpâḍâ and Paṭṭaṇ, has a very old temple of Varâhaji built after a peculiar fashion. It is said that this temple was built by the brother-in-law of a king called Nanda. The temple is about 40 feet long, 33 feet wide, and 20 feet high, and is very old. Its dome is supported by 12 square pillars. It is built of stone and its cross beams are made of sandal-wood. South-east of this temple is the Varâhakuṇḍa, which is 30 feet long and broad.

III. 13. **Gorakhamadhi** cave-temple is entered from the north and contains the images of Gorakhnâtha and Machhendranâtha. It is 30 foot long and broad. The head of the monastery has a grant of twelve villages for necessary expenses.

III. 14. **Vera'val Pattan.** (1) About 10 miles from Paṭṭan are the two tanks known as the Prâchikuṇḍas through which the river Sarasvatî flows. Near this tank is the old *pippala* tree called Prâchi-pippala. At a distance of about 25 yards north of these tanks is the image of Mâdhavarâiji placed in the Sarasvatî under the shade of the *jambu* tree. The place is considered holy and is visited by pilgrims and those who suffer from evil spirits.

I *b*. (2) The old temple of Somanâtha stands on the sea-shore. Most of it is destroyed and its materials are used by the people for building purposes. The standing part consists of two chambers covered with domes which are decorated with sculpture and niches filled with mythological images. The first dome is supported by 65 pillars and the second dome is a *śikhara*. What remains is 90½ feet long, 68 feet broad, and 43 feet high. It is said that this temple was built in the Valabhî year 850.

III. (3) The new temple of Somanâtha was built by Ahalyâbâi of Indor in *Saṁvat* 1839. The courtyard is 127 feet long and 82 feet broad, and the temple proper is 39 feet long and broad and 42 feet high. The court contains a *dharmaśâlâ* built by Viṭṭhal Devâji, late Divân to the Gâikvâḍ of Barodâ, and two small temples of Annapûrṇâ and Gaṇapati. The temple has three domes built after the Musalmân fashion. The shrine contains the *linga* of Saṅkleśvara and under it is a cell 12 feet long and broad containing the *linga* of Somanâtha. The domes are supported by 32 pillars. Paṭṭan is considered a place of great sanctity and people from different parts go there to visit the temple and bathe in the Triveṇî, *i. e.* the confluence of the three rivers, the Sarasvatî, Hiraṇyâ, and Kapilâ.

Ib. (4) The Jámi Masjid at Paṭṭan, formerly a Hindu temple dedicated to the sun, is very old and stands in the bâzâr. It is built of stone and decorated with fine sculpture, which is purely Hindu. It is 111 feet by 171 and its roof is supported by 251 pillars. The Sûrajakuṇḍa is turned into a *hoj* or bath.

III. (5) A Jaina temple, converted into a dwelling house by the Musalmâns, stands in the bâzâr near the Jami Masjid alluded to in the above para. Its domes and pillars are sculptured. Under the building is a cave 35 feet by 47½ divided into six chambers. It is built of stone, but contains no inscription.

III. (6) The temple of Bhidiâ, properly Bhidbhanjana Mahâdeva, stands on the beach between Paṭṭan and Verâval. It is about 40 feet high, 137 feet long and 22 feet wide. It is built of stone and its dome is supported by 20 pillars.

III. (7) Between Verâval and Paṭṭan is the tank of Bhâlkâ, which is 25 feet by 37. This tank derives its name from a Bhulu or Bhâlodâ, *i. e.* a shaft of an arrow. Kṛishṇa was killed here by a Bhill named Vâl (Jarâ?) with an arrow.

III. (8) The temple of Nâganâtha near Chorwâḍ is very small, but it contains an inscription, a copy of which is as follows :—

॥ ९० ॥ ॐ नमः [1]शवाय ॥ तापत्रयं त्रिभुवनस्य तनूकरोतु तेजस्ततिस्तरणिजा
तिमिरं तुदंती ॥ या पूर्वपर्वतशिरः पुनती प्रबोधं पंकेरुहेषु च सतां हृदयेषु दत्ते ॥ १ ॥
ये रेणुकेयेन रणांगणांतान्नीताः क्षयं क्षोणिभुजः क्षणेन ॥ ते क्षेत्रजा ब्रह्मकुलप्रसूतास्तदा-
न्वयया ख्यातिमुगु[2]ः क्षितीशाः ॥ २ ॥ नृहंससंसत्प्रथितप्रशंसस्तदंकभृन्मंकणकार्षिवंशः ॥
नृशंसविध्वंसकृदस्त्ययं सः षट्त्रिंशदंशक्षितिपावतंसः ॥ ३ ॥ मरुस्थलीमंडलमौकदेशे देशे
दशारोहिणिरोहिलादौ ॥ विशालभालः कलिकालकालस्तत्राभवल्लूणिगभूमिपालः ॥ ४ ॥
ससैन्यपालत्वधरः सुराष्ट्रां प्राप प्रतापैकनिधिर्बलेन ॥ तस्यांगजोभूद्भुवि भीमसिंहः समस्त-
शौर्यादिगुणै[3]रुपितः ॥ ५ ॥ तत्रापि पंचालककालिंजरादिग्रामावलिग्रासविलासवृत्तिः ॥
लावण्यपालस्तनयस्तदीयो. बभूव सूरः समरे करालः ॥ ६ ॥ निजप्रतापं तपनं त्रिलोक्यां
यशः शशांकं च पटुप्रकाश्य ॥ लावण्यपलः किल भूमिपालः सकालिजे कालमवाप
कालात् ॥ ७ ॥ बभूवुस्तस्य तनया विनयानतमस्तकाः ॥ लक्ष्मसिंहः सतां मुख्यो लक्षो
लषणपालकः ॥ ८ ॥ लक्ष्मसिंहोलसल्लीलललनाफलकामुकः ॥ जगाम जीर्णदुर्गे स
स[4]संरादमरावतीं ॥ ९ ॥ तस्य सुनूरनूजश्रीराजसिंहोभवद्भुवि ॥ बिभेद संदये शंखोके
धृतोमार्तंडमंडलं ॥ १० ॥ षट्त्रिंशक्षत्रवंशप्रथितगुणगणः शौर्यगर्ज्जद्विषस्त्रीविधव्यव्याधिदा-
नो[6]थूंतकरकमलः शस्त्रशास्त्रप्रवीणः ॥ प्रीणन्पात्राणि पृथ्वीद्रविणवितरणैर्विश्वविख्यातकी-
र्तिर्वाघेलावंशए[7] क्षितितलवलये तद्भुवां मातृपक्षे ॥ ११ ॥ भूमंडकस्य मरुमंडलमंडनं या सो-
दर्ककर्करपुरीति गरीयसी या ॥ श्रीक्षेमराज इह राजसमाजराजी विभ्राजमानगुणएष रराज
राजा ॥ १२ ॥ सोमभ्रमः क्रमत एव बभूव भूपसद्रूपकल्पणनिरूपितविश्वरूपः ॥ म्लेच्छायनोवि
बहुलेपि न देशसीमां तत्याज गोत्रिभिरपि प्रबलैः परीतः ॥ १३ ॥ वीरोगर्वः प्रवरवीरवृत-
स्ततोस्य सौराष्ट्रमंडलमवाप मपापतीर्थैः ॥ यो वीरवारनयसाराविचारवारुः खंगारगानगुण-
सौहृदमाचचार ॥ १४ ॥ स श्रीमहम्मदबृहन्मदपातसाहिक्रांतेपि रैवतगिरावपि जीर्णदुर्गे ॥

---

[1] शि. [2] मगुः. [3] पेतः. [4] सम. [5] वैधव्य. [6] त्थितः. [7] एष. [8] अत्र.

खंगारभूपमुपवाह्य सभीमदेवं भ्रातुः सुतं[1]सुभटशल्यमापि प्रमीतः ॥ १९ ॥ रत्नादेवी प्रथमदुहिता वीरजा राजसिंहान्मल्लं[2] मुख्यं तनुजमपरं मत्तराजं[3] लेभे ॥ मुंजं तस्याप्यवरजमहोमोहनं गोगृहेरी[4]न्नंघ्नन्प्राणांस्तृणमिव रणे यः खुरासे निवासे ॥ १६ ॥ मन्ये मल्लो मत्तराजश्च मुंजोव्यंजन्नंजः खंजने मोहनश्च ॥ चत्वारोमी सामपुख्या उपाया रत्नादेव्यां राजसिंहात्प्रसूताः ॥ १७ ॥ प्रवराजिविराजविक्रमो युवराजः श्री[5]शिवराजभूपतिः ॥ खुरवासकवासशासने न्यधुं[6]नमल्ल[7]मुतुल्यसद्गुणम् ॥ १८ ॥ दृष्ट्वा तत्र पुरा पुराणपठितं पाथोजपाणेः प्रियप्रासादं निजपूर्वपूरुषपरप्रीत्यै स्वपुण्याय च ॥ कालांते पतितं कृतार्थितमतिर्लक्ष्मीर्ध्यै[8]येर्नूतनं तत्कालाद्रचयांचकार नियतं तं मल्लदेवो[9]भिधः ॥ १९ ॥ तद्भार्या विमलादेवी सती सीतेव तावुभौ ॥ परमारकुलोद्भूता नारीगुणगणावता ॥ २० ॥ आनीय चातुश्चरणीयविप्रान्सा मल्लदेवेन विचित्रमंत्रैः ॥ सन्मंडपे मंडलकुंडवेदीनेदीयसाकारिरविप्रतिष्ठां ॥ २१ ॥ रोहेलामाल्देभार्या बिमलः[10] सूतदूदा लाषादेपा रामा सांगा लूणसी बई हांसी मल्लदेवभ्रात्त मातराभायबाई नामल्दे सुत ली बा हरराज बाघेलामूलराजः संबत १४४९ वर्षे फागणसुदी ९ सोमे तृवाडी वाछा कवि सूत्रसाल्हा सुत मधुसूदननारायणः आचार्य लंगसतपुरुष प्रतिष्टा ॥

III. (9) About 300 yards east of Paṭṭan is the cave of Hinglâj Mâtâ. It is 39½ feet long, 28 feet broad and 10 feet deep. The cave, though very old, is entire. It is divided into two chambers, one of which contains the image of Hinglâj.

The following is a copy of an inscription in the temple of Harasad at Verâval*:—

ॐ नमः श्रीविश्वनाथाय ॥ नमस्ते विश्वनाथाय विश्वरूप नमोस्तु ते ॥ नमस्ते शू[11]न्यरूपाय लक्षा[12]लक्ष नमोस्तु ते ॥ १ ॥ श्रीविश्वनाथ प्रतिबद्धतोजनानां बोधकरसुल्लमहमद संवत् ६६२ तथा श्रीनृपविक्रमसं० १३२० तथा श्रीमद्वल्लभी सं० ८४९ तथा श्रीसिंहसंवत् १५१ वर्षे आषाढ वदि १३ रवावद्येह श्रीमदणहिल्लपाटकाधिष्टितसमस्तराजावलीसमलंकृतपरमेश्वरपरमभट्टारकश्रीउमापतिवरलब्धप्रौढप्रताप निःशंकमल्ल अरिरायहृदयशल्य श्रीचौलुक्य चक्रवर्ती महाराजाधिराज श्रीमत्अर्जुनदेव प्रवर्धमान कल्याणविजयराज्ये तत्पादपद्मोपजीविनिमहामात्य राणक श्री माल्देवे श्रीश्रीकरणादिसमस्तमुद्राव्यापारानूपरिपंथयती-त्येवंकाले प्रवर्तमाने इह श्रीसोमना[13]त्तदेवपत्तने परमपाशुपताचार्य महापंडित महत्तरधर्म्ममूर्त्ति गंड श्री परवीरभद्र पारिमहं. श्रीअभयसिंहप्रभृति पंचकुल प्रतिपत्तौ तथा हुर्मुजवेलाकुले अमीर श्रीरुकतदीन राज्ये परिपंथयाति सति कार्यवशात् श्रीसोमनाथदेवनगरं समायात हर्मुजदेशीय खोजा नौ. अबूब्राहिमसुत नाखू. नोरदीनपिरोजेन श्रीसोमनाथदेवद्रोणीप्रतिबद्धमहायणांतःपातिप्रत्ययबृहत्पुरुष ठ. श्री पलुगिदेव बृहत्पुरुषराणक श्रीसोमेश्वरदेव बहत्पुरुष ठ. श्रीरामदेव बहत्पुरुष श्रीभीमसीह[14] बृहत्पुरुष राज श्री छाडाप्रभृतिसमस्तमहणलोकप्रत्यक्षं तथा समस्त जमाथ प्रत्यक्षं च राजश्रीनानसिंह सुत बृह० राज० श्रीछाडाप्रभृतीनां पार्श्वात् श्रीसोमनाथदेवनगरबाह्ये सीकोतर्यां महायणपाल्यां संतिष्ठमानभूषंडनवनिधानसहितं यथेष्टकामकरणीयत्वेन स्पर्शनन्यायेन समुपात्तं ॥ ततः नाखू० पीरोजेन स्वधर्म्मशास्त्राभिप्रायेण परमधार्मिकेण भूत्वा आचंद्रार्कस्थायिनी कीर्तिप्रसिद्ध्यर्थं आत्मनः श्रेयोर्थं उपर्यालापितभूषंडस्य स्थाने पूर्वाभिमखामोजिगीति धर्म्मस्थानं बृह० राज० श्री छाडास-

---

[1] तं. [2] ल्लं. [3] राजं च. [4] न्नि. [5] जः शिव. [6] न्मल्ल. [7] मतु. [8] ध्य. [9] वा. [10] विमला. [11] शू. [12] लक्ष्यालक्ष्य. [13] थ. [14] सिंह. [15] नव.

* See *Ind. Ant.*, XI. 241.

खायत्वेन धर्मबावेन कारितं नाखु० पीरोजेन अस्यमिजिगिति धर्मस्थानस्य वर्त्तापनार्थं प्रतिदिनं पूजा दीप तैल पानीय तथा मालिममोदिन मासपाठक तथा नौबित्तकानां समाधारेण बराति राति खतमराति विशेषपूजामंहोत्सवकारापनार्थं तथा प्रतिवर्षं छोह चूनाभग्नविशीर्णसमारचनार्थं च श्रीसर्वघनेश्वरदेवीय स्थानपाति श्री परत्रिपुरांतक [1]चिंसायक महारक पररतनेश्वरप्रभृतीनां पार्श्वात् उमापाति श्रीसोमनाथदेवनगरमध्ये श्री[2]घंठकेश्वरदेवीय समग्रपल्लुंडिका नानामुखवृणछाद्य कवेलुकाछादित गहेरूपेता तथा उत्तराभिमुखद्विभौममठसमेता परं अस्या मध्ये सूत्र०कान्हैआसक्तपूर्वाभिमुखगृहैकबाह्यं चतुराघाटेषु अन्यप्रप्राकारोपेता उत्तराभिमुखप्रतोलीप्रवेशानिर्गमोपेता यथावस्थितचतुराघाटनविशुद्धा यथा प्रसिद्धपरिभोगा तथा घाणी १ सक्तदानपलं तथा अस्यामिजिगिति अग्रतः प्रत्ययनिर्म्माल्य छडासोठल्सुत कील्हणदेव तथाठ. सोहणसुत छुणसींह धरणिमसूमा तथा बाल्यर्थकरेणाधिष्टितराण. आसधरप्रभृतीनां पार्श्वात् स्पर्शनेनोपात्तहट्टद्वयं एवमेतत् उदकेन प्रदत्तं अनेन आयपदेन आचंद्रभट्टतारकं यावत् नौ० पीरोजसक्त मिजिगिति धर्मस्थानमिदं नौ० पीरोजश्रेयोर्थं प्रतिपालनीयं वर्तापनीयं भग्नविशीर्णं समारचनीयं च ॥ अनेन आयपदेन धर्म्मस्थानमिदं वर्त्तापयतां प्रतिपालयतां तथा विशेषमहोत्सवपर्वव्यये कुर्वतां च यत्किंचित् शेषद्रव्यमुद्वराति तत्सर्वं द्रव्यं मषांमदीनाधर्म्मस्थाने प्रस्थापनीयं। अस्य धर्म्मस्थानस्य आयपदं सदैव जमाथमध्ये नाखुयानोरिकजमाथ तथा खतीबसहित समस्त आहडसक्तघंचिकानां जमाथ तथा चुणकरजमाथ तथा पात्रपतीनां मध्ये मुसलमानजमाथ प्रभृतिभिः समस्तैरपि मिलित्वा आयपदमिदं पालापनीयं धर्म्मस्थानमिदं वर्तापनीयं च ॥ दाता च प्रेरकश्चैव ये धर्म्मप्रतिपालकाः ॥ ते सर्वे पुण्यकर्माणो नियतं स्वर्गगामिनः ॥ यः कोऽपि धर्मस्थानमिदं तथा आयपदं च लोपयाति लोपापयति स पापात्मा पंचमहापातकदोषेण लिप्यते नरकगामी भवति ॥ छ ॥

गोवर्द्धनमूर्तिमध्ये.

श्रीमद्वल्लभी संवत् ९२७ वर्षे फाल्गुनसुदी २ सोमे ॥ अद्येह श्रीदेवपत्तने सकलराजावली पूर्वगल्लकजातीय श्रेष्ठि मूलजोगभार्या श्रे० मादि तथा सुतगंधिक जोजाभार्या घेवइ तथा पुत्र जयता द्वितीय पुत्र जसदेव तृतीयपुत्र जयपाल प्रभृतय श्रीगोवर्द्धनमूर्तिनमस्करणार्थं स्वश्रेयसे पूर्वजानां श्रेयोभिवृद्धये स्वभक्तया कारापिता सूत्र विसदेवपुत्र सूत्र राघवेन घटिता ॥

Inscription :—

संवत् १४४८ वर्षे ज्येष्ठ शुदि १३ दिने संगमेश्वर प्रस्थापितः ।

ॐ नमः शिवाय । अव्यक्तं व्यक्ततां यातमक्ष्यं लक्ष्यतां गतं । सोमशार्ङ्गिगाछकतः स्पष्टं ब्रह्म पुनातु वः ॥ १ ॥ या भारती शब्दमयी चतुर्विधा ततोधिका भाति जडा जलात्मिका ॥ क्षेत्रे प्रभासे शिवमाप्य संस्थिता पंचप्रवाहा जगतोस्तु शांतये ॥ २ ॥ शीर्षे विधृत्य वडवानलफालगोलं वाग्देवता कथयतीव हि दिव्यपूर्वं ॥ कस्माद्विवादमधियांति च दर्शनानि तत्व शिवात्परतरं न हि किंचिदस्ति ॥ ३ ॥ तत्पत्तनं यस्य मुखे सरस्वती गर्भे धृता येन हरिर्हराद्याः ॥ सामान्यजंतोरपि मुक्तिदं यत्केनोपमेयं नगरेण तत्स्यात् ॥ ४ ॥ भीतोहमेकेन हि वाडवेन दृष्ट्वा पुरे वाडवमुख्यलक्षं ॥ स्तुतिं वदत्यर्णव एष घोषैः करोर्मिभिस्तचरणौ

[1] विना. [2] धव. [3] तृण. [4] का.

नमस्यन् ॥ ९ ॥ महो प्रसिद्धः किल यादवानां वंशोवतंसोहि वसुंधरायाः ॥ तत्राभव-
द्धीमनृपोरिभीमः श्रीभीमचित्तो न जनेषु भीमः ॥ ६ ॥ एवंगुणं तं पतिमाप्य रम्यं
माणिक्यदेवी सुतरां चकास ॥ तयोश्च योगाद्यमुनाप्रवृत्ता किंस्यादयेयं नवमी च सिद्धिः ॥७॥
नाम्ना भवेद्या यमुना न निम्नगा राज्ञी भवेन्नोयमगर्भधारिणी ॥ भैमी भवेद्या न रुचिः
स्वयंवरे मदालसा या न भवेन्मदालसा ॥ ८ ॥ शीलेन गंगा भवतीति शुद्धा या
नामधेयाद्यमुना प्रसिद्धा ॥ सरस्वती तद्वदनान्न याति प्रयाग एषोभिनवो विभाति ॥ ९ ॥
वंशो प्रसिद्धो हि यथा रवींद्रो राष्ट्रोडवंशस्तु तथा तृतीयः ॥ तत्राभवद्धर्मनृपोतिधर्मस्तस्मा-
च्छिवं सा यमुना जगाम ॥ १० ॥ दत्तानि दानानि ययाखिलानि तपांसि तप्तान्यति-
निर्मलानि ॥ कृतानि पुण्यान्यतिनिश्चलानि प्राप्तानि सर्वाणि जनैः फलानि ॥ ११ ॥ या
कारयामास नवापि वापिकासरस्विदेवायतनप्रपाश्च ॥ तया प्रतोलीमुखमंडनोपमं निर्मापितं
चत्वरमत्र सुंदरं ॥ १२ ॥ संवत् १४४२ वर्षे आषाढ वदि ८ शनौ ॥

III. 15. **Mandor,** 6 miles north-east of Somnâtha Paṭṭaṇ, a ruined site, with six Buddhist caves, all with inner cells.

III. 16. **Ja'mva'la'.** There are also some solitary caves in the bank of the Singâvḍâ river. One at the ruined site of Vairâṭa, and one close to Jânwadlâ in the centre of the Gir forest, a few miles north of Chhelnâ.

III. 17. **Tarnetar.** Two miles west of Koili is the temple of Tarnetar or Trinetra, looking on the river Uben. It is divided into two chambers: one containing the *linga* is covered by a *śikhara* 26 feet high, and the other by a concave dome supported by 18 pillars. Besides this there are three small domes attached to the larger one, covering the images of Gaṇapati Śîtalâ. This temple has a courtyard 130 feet long and broad. It has a gateway on the north and contains storehouses, stables, and a building where the *Mahantas* are enthroned. The *Mahanta*, or head of the monastery, has a grant of three villages for defraying the expenses. A fine *ghâṭ* 125 feet long is built on the bank of the river Uben. This *ghâṭ* communicates with the temple.

III.—Bâbriâwâd.

III. 1. **S'a'na' Hill.** About 10 miles south-west of Dedân is the Śânâ Hill. It contains many Bauddha caves; most of them are overgrown with grass and there are tanks in the front of the caves containing fresh water. Most of them are in a dilapidated state (see *Archæological Reports*, Vol. II.)

III. 2 **S'iya'l Bet** abounds in ruined tanks and *vâvs*, most of which are buried. There are at present about 30 *vâvs* containing a little water and one old tank called Gangâ Talâv, which is 150 feet square. From the inscriptions and materials of the ruined houses and temples now used by the people for building purposes it appears that there once existed a flourishing town here. Four marble stones bearing **inscriptions** are in the fields of this island. Copies of these inscriptions are as follow:—

९०॥ सं० १३०० वर्षे वैशाख वदि ११ बुधे सहजिगपुरवास्तव्य पल्लीजातीय ठ०
देदा भार्या कडूदेविकुक्षिसंभूनपरी० महीपाल महीचंद्रतत्सुतरतनपालविजयपालैर्निजपू-
र्वजठ० शंकरभार्यालक्ष्मीकुक्षिसंभूतस्यसंघपतिमुंधिगदेवस्य निजपरिवारसहितस्य योग्यदे-

चकुलिकासहित श्रीमल्लिनाथबिंबं कारितं ॥ प्रतिष्ठितं श्रीचंद्रगछीय श्रीहरिप्रभसूरिशिष्यैः श्रीयशोभद्रसूरिभिः ॥ छ ॥ मंगलं भवतु ॥ छ ॥

संवत् १३१९ वर्षे फागुणवादि ७ शनौ अनुराधानक्षत्रेऽद्येह श्रीमधुमत्यां श्रीमहावीरदेवचैत्ये प्राग्वाटज्ञातीयश्रेष्ठि आसदेवसुत श्रीसपालसुतगंधिवीवीकेन आत्मनः श्रेयोर्थं श्रीपार्श्वनाथदेवबिंबं कारितं चंद्रगच्छे श्रीयशोभद्रसूरिभिः प्रतिष्ठितं ॥

९० ॥ संवत् १२७२ वर्षे ज्येष्ठ वादि २ रवौ अद्येह टिंबानके मेहरराजश्रीरणसिंहप्रतिपत्तौ समस्त संघेन श्रीमहावीरबिंबंकारितं प्रतिष्ठितं श्रीचंद्रगच्छीय श्रीशांतिप्रभसूरिशिष्यैः श्रीहरिप्रभसूरिभिः ॥ छ ॥

६० ॥ संवत् १३४३ माघशुदि १० गुरो गुर्जर प्राग्वाट ज्ञातीय ठ० पेथडश्रेयसे तत्सुत पाल्हणेन श्री । नेमिनाथबिंबं कारितं प्रतिष्ठितं श्रीनेमिचंद्रसूरिशिष्य श्रीनयचंद्रसूरिभिः ॥

IV.—Porbandar.

III. 1. **Porbandar.** (1) In the east of the town is the old temple of Kedâreśvara which is 54 feet long and 42 feet wide. It was repaired by Bâi Śrî Rûpâlibâi, mother to the late chief, in *Saṁvat* 1894. The temple is built of stone and the dome of the *maṇḍapa* is supported by 26 pillars. The shrine is small and has a *śikhara*. The courtyard is enclosed by a stone wall, having a gateway in the east, and is 141 feet by 144 containing a *dharmaśâlâ* and Kedârakuṇḍa, a small tank.

(2) The temples of Laṅkeśvara and Dudheśvara have one *maṇḍapa*, and are in the north of the town. They are very old and built of stone. The ground floor is 39 feet by 51 feet and the dome of the *maṇḍapa* is supported by 32 pillars and has some sculpture. The *śikharas* of the shrine are 37 feet high and conical in form.

(3) The Sûrya temple is the oldest and stands in the middle of the town. It appears from an inscription in the interior that it was rebuilt by Bhansâli Kalyâṇji Shavji in *Saṁvat* 1918 (1862 A.D.). It is about 81 feet long, 33 feet broad and 37 feet high. It is built of stone and the dome of the *maṇḍapa* is supported by 36 pillars. The *śikhara* is, as usual, conical in form.

(4) The temple of Siddhanâtha is very small.

III. 2. **Chha'ya',** about 2 miles from Porbandar, contains a castle where the Jethwâ princes are enthroned.

III. 3. **Miya'ni.** (1) Near this is the temple of Harsata Mâtâ. It is about 72 feet long, 57 feet wide and 60 feet high. The courtyard contains a *dharmaśâlâ* and a small room having in it four idols, which, it is said, were placed there in memory of Jaghadushâ and his family who built the temple. It is very old and its dome is supported by eight pillars, one of which bears the words—

संवत् १७१८ वना आसाढ सोद ८ सोमवार हाले जेठवात्र मारीबाकगो [पाक] सुसंवायो.

The former temple of this goddess stands on the Koilâ Hill. It is very old and out of repair. Its length and breadth is 24 feet.

III. (2) The temple of Khimeśvara Mahâdeva, 5 miles north of Porbandar, was built, as its name indicates, by Khimâji and afterwards repaired by Sultânji. Both these were chiefs of Porbandar. It is about 45 feet high, 51 feet long, and 45 feet broad. It is built of stone and its dome is supported by 6 pillars. A festival is held here on the 14th Mâgha *Vad*, to which the inhabitants of the surrounding villages go.

III. 4. **Bagavadar.** Half a mile from this is the temple of Somâditya. It is very old, decorated with sculpture, and contains the idols of Sûrya and Randel. It is 24 feet by 30. The roof is supported by 18 pillars. Some part of this temple was pulled down by the Râṇa in 1868 A.D. as it afforded shelter to the Vâgher mutineers.

III. 5. **Ma'dhavpur.** The only remaining part of the temple of Mâdhavarâj is a dome 45 feet high. Its lower part is buried under the ground. A new temple which was built by Bâi Śrî Bâdibâi in *Saṁvat* 1789 was afterwards extended and rebuilt by Bâi Śrî Rûpâlibâi in *Saṁvat* 1896. A festival, to which many people go, is held here in commemoration of the marriage of Kṛishṇa, with Rukhmiṇi.

III. 6. **Amardad,** near Rânâvâv. About 5 miles east is the temple of Jadeśvara, which is 36 feet long and broad and 15 feet high.

III. 7. **Barda' Hills.** The temple of Bileśvara stands in the eastern part of the Bardâ Hills. It is 51 feet long and 45 feet broad. It is said that this temple was built and dedicated to Bileśvara by Sûrajmall Hâdâ, king of Bundikoṭâ, and that the *liṅga* was broken by Alâu'd-dîn Khilji. It is built of stone and well sculptured, and is very old.

III. 8. **Vasa'vad.** A *masjid* 150 feet long and 120 feet deep. It looks on to the river Vasâvadî and contains a well, a bath, and a *bangalâ* of three storeys with wooden balconies decorated with carving. The south part of it is used by Muhammadan travellers as a halting place. There is a canopy supported by four pillars at each end of the ground floor. In the middle are three marble graves covered by a dome which is supported by 12 pillars. The greater part of the building is carved and it has 32 pillars. It is said that this *masjid* was built by Ghori Belum.

V.—Gohelwâd.

III. 1. **Tala'ja,** south of Bhâvnagar; for an account of the caves at this place see Volume II. of the Archæological Survey of Western India Reports. See also *Ind. Ant.*, XI. 337.

III. 2. **Satrunjaya.*** The most sacred spot of Jaina worship in Western India. The temples, which are counted by hundreds, crown the top of a high isolated hill, about a mile south of the town of Pâlitânâ in Kâthiâwâd. It rises gently from the plain to twin summits linked together by a saddle or valley. The temples occupy these two tops with the intervening depression and the whole temple city is surrounded by a high wall with strong bastions and gates. In olden times it was a well fortified stronghold defended by an armed force. Within the outer wall the area is subdivided into *ṭuks* or smaller enclo-

* For fuller accounts see Volumes II, XI. and XIII. of the *Indian Antiquary*.

sures, each with its own name, and each surrounded by high battlemented walls. The only protectors now of the great wealth stowed away within these walls are the guards at the various gates, who are the only human beings who are permitted to stay upon the hill after sunset when the great ponderous gates are swung to for the night.

Although very remote antiquity is claimed for many of the shrines, more especially that of Âdîśvara Bhagavân, the rebuilding and repairing of the older ones have left but little, if any, of the original work above the surface anywhere. There is nothing dated earlier that the 12th century A.D. Between that and the 15th century there are many dated inscriptions; of the 16th century there are but three; while from the earlier part of the 17th to the present time they abound in unbroken succession. Those of the earliest set are all found inscribed upon old marble seats or *sinhâsanas* more or less mutilated, stained by age, and now built in, in fragments, in modern cells and shrines. From these dates it follows that two hundred and fifty years ago there could have been but two small groups upon the hill—perhaps not a dozen shrines in all—*viz.*, that of the Chaumukha on the northern summit and that of Âdîśvara Bhagavân on the southern, with a few isolated old Hindu shrines, of earlier date, appropriated to Jaina worship. Among these latter were the Pâncha Pâṇḍava temple and one or two that stood on the site of the present Bhulavani temple, and, perhaps, Kumârpâla's in the Vimalavaśi *ṭuk*. The number of images upon the hill exceed 10,000, and they are yearly being added to, for, for every image a man sets up, he obtains credit for one-tenth of the merit that accrues to those whom it attracts to worship. They are mostly in marble—white, yellow, and black, and of all sizes from the colossal Ṛishabhadeva to others but one or two inches high. There are also a few brass images and symbols. The images in the principal temples possess quantities of jewelry in the shape of crowns, breastplates, armlets, necklaces &c., often of gold studded with precious stones. Ṛishabhadeva alone is said to possess four *lakhs* worth. It is all stowed away in strong rooms upon the hill, and only used upon great occasions.

Âdîśvara Bhagavân Tuk.

(1) The principal temple upon the hill is that of Ṛishabhadeva in this *ṭuk*, who is also called Âdîśvara Bhagavân. It is said to have been restored at different periods. The 13th restoration is attributed to Jâvadśâh in *Saṁvat* 1018; the 16th to Karmaśâh of Chitod in *Saṁvat* 1557. In the entrance are two long inscriptions.* The temple has two fine inlaid marble floors, one in the porch and the other in the main hall. The seated image of Ṛishabhadeva is in white marble of colossal proportions, and when adorned with its jewels the great brazen-barred shrine doors are securely fastened, the custodians remaining within. Upon the roof of the temple are built miniature *idgâhs* in order to prevent a repetition of Muhammadan aggression.

In the temple are 190 white marble images, 14 black marble, and 10 yellow marble = 214 in all.†

In the little cell-shrines which are clustered round the base of the temple, and attached to it, are 128 W, 4 B, and 5 Y = 137.

---

* The inscriptions upon Śatrunjaya are treated at length by Professor G. Bühler in the *Epigraphia Indica*, Vol. II. Parts IX. and X. (1892), Nos. I. II. IV. VI. VII. VIII. IX. X. XI. XII. XIII. XXII. and CXVIII. are in and about this temple.

† These numbers were counted when the hill was surveyed in January 1889.

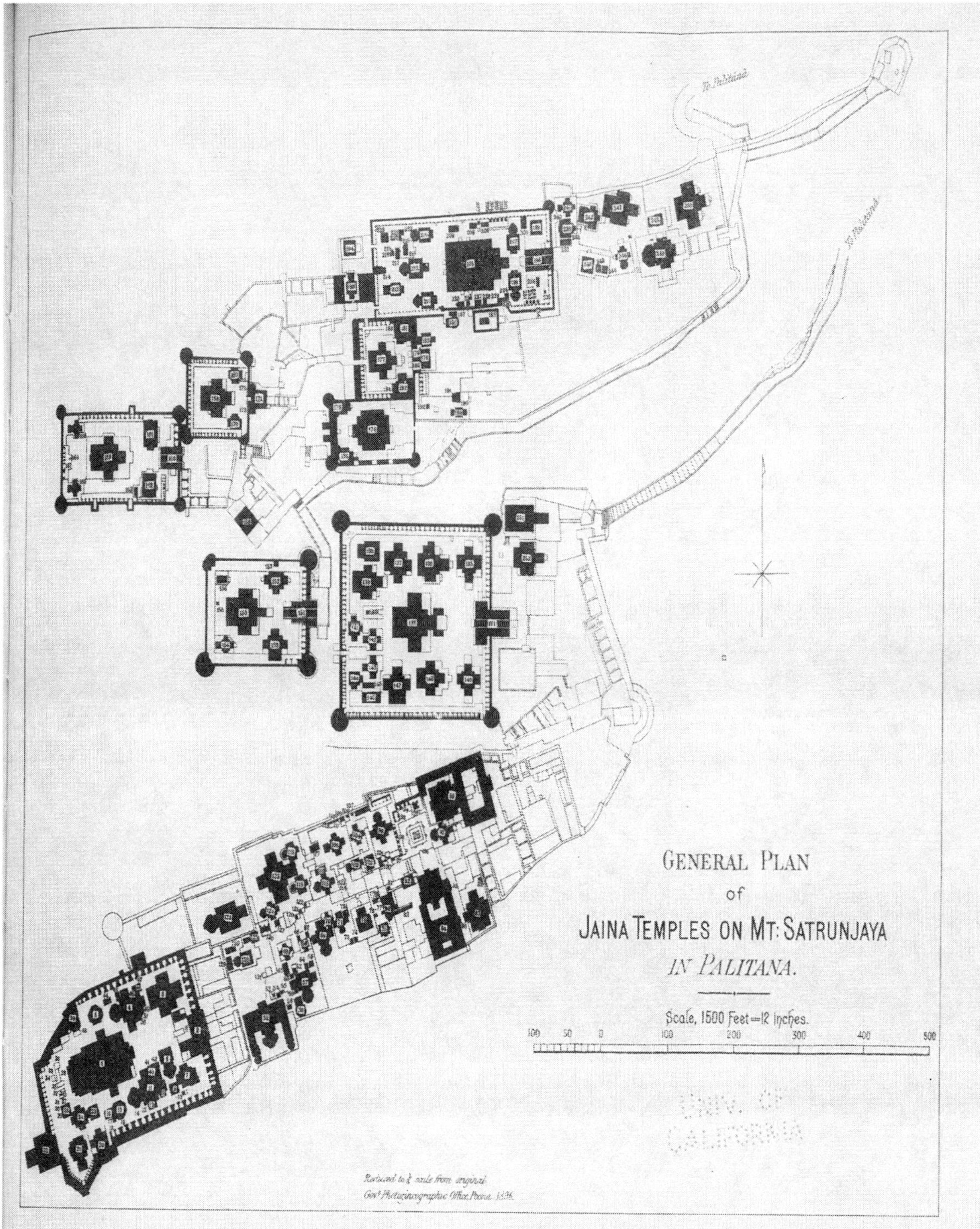
To Palitana
To Palitana
GENERAL PLAN
of
JAINA TEMPLES ON MT: SATRUNJAYA
IN PALITANA.
Scale, 1500 Feet = 12 inches.
100 50 0 100 200 300 400 500
Reduced to ¼ scale from original.
Govt. Photozincographic Office, Poona. 1896.

(2) The Puṇḍarîka (*puṇḍarîka*, a lotus) shrine is above the main or eastern gateway to the *ṭuk*. Each principal temple has its Puṇḍarîka shrine on the east and in front of it. Puṇḍarîka or Puṇḍarîka Svâmi is said to have been a leading disciple of Ṛishabhadeva. The image as set up is just a repetition of those of the *tîrthankaras* and has the sign—the lotus —of the 6th *tîrthankara*, Padma-prabha. An exception is the Puṇḍarîka shrine in front of No. 57 in the *ṭuk* of Sâkarchand Premachand, which from the symbol upon it is intended for Pârśvanâtha, an image of the same *tîrthankara* occupying the shrine of the principal temple. This image of Puṇḍarîka was, according to an inscription under it, set up by Kâmalde and his son Bhîśaji in *Saṁvat* 1587.*

Images,—148 W, 20 B, 16 Y, and 11 brass, = 195.

(3) This temple, in the north-east corner of the court, contains a large *chaumukha* in the lower shrine and another in the upper. An inscription† records that a man, whose name is not very distinct, with his family, built the shrine of Śântinâtha in *Saṁvat* 1620. In the south porch upstairs is a small iron gun, one of those which in days gone by helped to defend the place. On the west of the shrine is a store room.

Images,—4 W, and 7 Y, = 11.

(4) In this temple, which is on the west of the last, is set up Ṛishabhadeva. The interior of the dome is painted in outline representing processions of musicians and others. There are also red-leaded images of Mahishâsura-Mardanî and Chakreśvarî Mâtâ. Here are some very old seats built in under some of the images. Some of the rooms in this building are used as strong rooms for storing the jewels belonging to the image in the great temple.

Images,—41 W, 1 B, and 4 Y, = 46.

(5) This is a raised altar or temple containing a great number of *pâdukâs*, or pairs of foot-prints, 1,452 in all.

Images,—8 W.

(6) In the shrine is a fine large image of Âdîśvara Bhagavân with an elaborately carved *sinhâsana* and throne-back in cream coloured marble, about 10 feet high. The date upon the image is *Saṁvat* 1667. In the antechamber are images of Mahâkâla and Mahishâsura-Mardanî red-leaded as usual. It is only the Hindu images in these temples that are smeared with red paint.

Images in the temple and in small shrines round outside,—24 W, 3 Y, and 1 brass = 28.

(7) This temple occupies the south-east corner of the court. It is a plain hall with Neminâtha installed in the shrine.

Images in the temple and around it,—37 W, 1 B, and 1 Y, = 39.

(8) A small shrine adjoining the last, on the west.

Images,—5 W.

(9) A small *Meru-śikhara* behind (7) composed of two circular drums with a *chaumukha* above.

Images,—12 W.

* No. III. *Ep. Ind.*, Vol. II. Part IX. p. 48.

† No. V. *Epig. Ind.*, Vol. II. Part IX. p. 48.

(10) A small shrine behind No. (7) with an image of Mahâvîra.

Image,—1.

(11) At the south-east corner of the great temple. A plain white-washed hall with white and mottled marble floor. On either side of the antechamber stand colossal white marble images of Âdîśvara and Pârśvanâtha, the latter with a nine-hooded snake canopy. In the north-east corner of the hall are two gigantic foot-prints, about the largest on the hill. In the shrine is a colossal seated image of Âdîśvara. The temple is known as the Navâ Âdîśvarajî's temple, and was built by Saṅgvi Târâchand of Surat in *Saṁvat* 1821. In the upper shrine is a small *chaumukha,* and above this, on the projection before the tower, is built a miniature *idgâh.*

Images,—51 W, 1 B, and 2 Y, = 54.

(12) A small shrine built into the back or south side of No. (11).

Images,—2 W, and 2 Y, = 4.

(13) and (14) are two small *chaumukhas* close to the last.

Images,—8 W.

(15) *Sahasrakûṭa* shrine, containing a solid square block with pyramidal top covered with little Jinas in relief and standing straight before the south porch of the great temple. Two inscriptions of the same date refer to the *sahasrakûṭa.* One commemorates its erection and the other its consecration in *Saṁvat* 1710. A third inscription* records the erection of a shrine of Pârśvanâtha by one Govindaji of Divabandar and his family in *Saṁvat* 1696.

Images,—10 W, 1 Y, = 11.

(16) On the west of the last and attached to it is a small shrine with some niches on the north of it.

Images,—9 W.

(17) and (18) are two small *chaumukhas.*

Images,—8 W.

(19) Is a small shrine to Âdinâtha.

Images,—5 W.

(20) A temple built on to the south wall of the court-yard in the shrine of which is an image of Vâsupûjya.

Images,—18 W and 4 Y, = 22.

(21) Contains a plain whitewashed hall with Ṛishabhadeva in the shrine, seated upon an old *sinhâsana* which is dated *Saṁvat* 1318. The lower parts of the walls of the temple look old. Near the door is a red daubed Gaṇeśa.

Images,—35 W, 4 B, and 7 Y, = 46.

(22) *Ashtâpada* temple built off the western wall. Within is a great square massive plinth block on the top of four steps. Around the base of this is a row of female

---

* Nos. XXXI. XXXII. and XXXIII. *Epig. Ind.* Vol. II, Part X. p. 72.

musicians in plaster. Sitting above this on each face, with their backs to the marble block, are 23 images. Along the wall are others and still more images stand against the pillars.

Images,—48 W, 6 B, and 17 Y, = 71.

(23) A small *chaumukha* temple.
Images,—22.

(24) *Meru-śikhara* in an open pillared hall with a dome over it, all in plaster.
Images,—26 W.

(25) Is a *chaumukha* at the south-west corner of the great temple. On the temple is an inscription recording the setting up of an image of Chandraprabha at a cost of 3,500 rupees by Premaji of Cheula in *Saṁvat* 1788, Śaka 1653.*
Images,—24 W.

(26) A *chaumukha* in two storeys with an inscription recording the setting up of an image of Âdinâtha by Jasapâla of Paṭṭan in *Saṁvat* 1284. This inscription is upon the seat which is an old one used a second time.
Images,—8 W.

(27) A six-pillared canopy over seven pairs of foot-prints, and an open space with 47 pairs.

(28) A long canopy with 10 pairs of foot-prints.
Images,—7 W.

(29) A small *chaumukha*.
Images—4 W.

(30) Nine pairs of foot-prints in an octofoil, one pair being in the centre.

(31) A *chaumukha*.
Images,—4 W.

(32) Nine pairs of foot-prints.

(33) Twenty-six pairs of foot-prints or *pâdukâs*.

(34) Six pairs of *pâdukâs*.

(35) A slab with twenty-eight pairs of *pâdukâs*.

(36) A single image and four pairs of foot-prints.
Image,—1 W.

(37) Small *chaumukha*—also some feet under south-west edge of the *râyana* tree.
Images—4 W.

(38) A very pretty little marble shrine with porch, containing a large pair of Âdîśvara Bhagavân's foot-prints. Upon the back wall of the shrine, in relief, is sculptured a mythological scene.

---

* No. XXXVII. *Epig. Ind.* Vol. II. Part X. p. 77.

(39) A temple attached to the walls at the north-west corner, west of No. (5). A plain white-washed hall with very ornamental frames round the niches.

Images,—14 w.

(40) On the west of the porch of No. (6) are two little shrines in line facing north, Nos. (41) and (42). No. (40) stands behind No. (41). It is a small temple containing an image of Mahâvîra and others.

Images,—6w and 1 B = 7.

(41) and (42) Two little shrines with Pârśvanâtha and Mahâvîra respectively and other small images.

Images,—4 w and 2 B = 6.

(43) Is a very small *chaumukha*.

Images,—4 w.

(44) A small free standing temple facing west in which Âdîśvara Bhagavân is installed.

Images,—14 w.

(45) A small shrine attached to the north-west corner of the hall of No. (4), Padmaprabha presiding.

Images,—4 w.

(46) A small shrine attached to the east end of the north face of the hall of No. (4) to Pârśvanâtha.

Images,—7 w.

(47) A little shrine at the north-east corner of temple No. (4), to Pârśvanâtha.

Images,—16 w and 1 B=17.

(48) A small cell close beside the last on the south.

Images,—5 w.

(49), (50) and (51) Three small cells at the south-east corner of No. (4) containing Sântinâtha, Âdinâtha and Ajitanâtha.

Images,—12 w.

In addition to the foregoing there are rows of small cell shrines attached to the surrounding walls of the Âdîśvara Bhagavân *ṭuk*, with long corridors in front of them. In these are to be found great numbers of old images and fragments of old *sinhâsanas* built into the new work. These show signs of having been dreadfully smashed up at one time. The old figures have had the tops of their noses knocked off but new noses have been excavated from the face. These are, of course, very flat, the cheeks fall in on either side of them, and in many cases the mouths have also been flattened in the operation. They are consequently not very handsome faces, being exceedingly flat. The older marble has yellowed with great age and is in strong contrast with the newer bluish white material. These older images have carved seats, the *śrîvatsa* sign on the breast, and the nipples picked out with rings and dots of black and red paint which in many cases has partly worn off.

Many of the old yellow marble figures appear to have been carved from the same dull yellow stone from which the old door-frames in the temples of Kumârapâla and Sampriti Râjâ were fashioned. The folds of the waistcloth are distinctly shown emerging from below the folded legs in the centre. The old seats have been beautifully carved and the under-cutting, especially in the seat backs, is very delicate.

The most of these fragments are dated, among them being the following dates in the *Saṁvat* era—1131, 1185, 1187, 1280, 1281, 1310, 1314, 1341, 1370, 1371, 1391, 1418 and 1430—(Compare also old dates in the Chaumukha *ṭuk*).

Images, in corridors and round base of No. (3),—462 W, 31 B, 21 Y and 3 brass, = 517.

Total number of images in the Âdîśvara Bhagavân *ṭuk*, not including the hundreds of small ones in relief upon the *sahasrakûṭas* and slabs = 16,41.

Vimalvaśi Tuk.

(52) The oldest temple in this *ṭuk* is perhaps that of Kumârapâla's, close beside the Hattipol or Elephant gate leading to the court of Âdîśvara Bhagavân. The doorway of the shrine is of the same yellow sandstone as that of the temple No. (249) on the northern summit. It is intricately carved and looks old. This with the two pillars in the front porch, which are much of the pattern of those of the great temple at Mudherâ in North Gujarât, are, perhaps, the only remnants of antiquity left, the rest having been rebuilt. The main shrine stands in the middle of an inner court which is surrounded on three sides, front and wings, with corridors and niches filled with images. The temple is ascribed to Kumârapâla of Anhilwâd Paṭṭan; the original temple was probably built by him.

Images,—44 W, 4 B, 9 Y and 1 brass = 58.

(53), (54), (55) and (56) are four small shrines at the north-east corner of Kumârapâla's temple, dedicated to Padmaprabha, Ajitanâtha, Vâsupûjya, and Sîtala respectively.

Images,—20 W.

(57) To the east of the last is the larger temple dedicated to Śântinâtha, having a perfectly plain hemispherical dome.

Images,—9 W and 1 B = 10.

(58) To the south-west corner of the last is a smaller temple upon a high plinth with a brightly coloured porch, within which Śreyânsa presides.

Images,—8 W.

(59), (60), (61), (62), (63), (64), (65), (66), (67) and (68) are small separate shrines in front and to the west side of No. (57).

Images,—58 W, 1 B 1 Y, and 1 brass = 61.

(69) This temple has a large open pillared hall with three porches, the front porch having double pillars, the inner small ones carrying a pretty *toraṇa*. The throne upon which the image is placed is beautifully carved. The exterior of the temple is much like that of No. (2) with *ashṭadikpâlas* and other Hindu figures around it. This is generally

called Jagat Shet's temple, but an inscription* in it says that the image in the shrine, Sumatinâtha, was set up by the whole *Sangha* Kachara Kîkâ and the rest in *Saṁ.* 1810.

(70) To the north-east corner of the last is a smaller temple with carved pillars in front.

Images,—6 w (?).

(71) On the east of the last is another temple of about the same size dedicated to Chandraprabha, which contains a very nicely carved *Sinhâsana* and throne back. In the hall is an inscription† which tells us that "while Jahângîr was ruling over the whole of the earth" in *Saṁ.* 1682, Hirâbâi set up the image and in 1683 made other additions or alterations.

Images,—5 w.

(72), (73) and (74) are beside the last, on the east, and are dedicated to Dharmanâtha, Śambhava and Vimala.

Images,—8 w.

(75) A temple upon a high plinth with one long shrine and three doors and a pillared hall in front. An inscription‡ tells us that in *Saṁ.* 1815 an image of Pârśvanâtha was set up by Kuyarajî Lâdhâ, resident of Bhâvanagar. The image of Pârśvanâtha has a most elaborate multiple-hooded snake canopying him, the whole cockle-shell shaped with serrated edge.

Images,—25 w.

(76) A small square room: rather an unusual plan for a temple. It has a neatly domed ceiling and niches for images all around the four sides

Images,—3 w, and 1 Y = 4.

(77), (78) and (79) Small shrines in front of No. (76), containing images of Pârśvanâtha, Rishabhadeva and Ajitanâtha.

Images,—9 w, 1 B and 1 brass = 11.

(80) A small temple with three seated *jinas* in a line in the shrine, viz., Vidyanâtha, Vimala and Chandraprabha. In the hall is a very pretty ceiling with a central pendant.

Images,—3 w.

(81) A very small shrine by the side of the paved roadway, facing east.

Images, —5 w.

(82) East of the last is a room containing a half-life-sized model of a camel in plaster, mounted upon which is a male figure holding a festoon in his hands. Underneath him are several figures and one life-sized one behind. Under the middle of the camel, and helping to support it is a block, and between this and the forelegs is left a space which is used as a test of a man's righteousness. If he can squeeze himself through he has no sin. The bottom stone is black and polished by the passing of people through. A thin man might pass, but a fat *Bania* would stick.

* No. XL. *Epig. Ind.*, Vol. II. Part X. p. 78. † No. XXVII. *Epig. Ind.*, Vol. II. Part X. p. 68.
‡ No. XLII. *Epig. Ind.*, Vol. II. Part X. p. 78.

(83) Behind the last are small corridors containing cell-shrines.

Images,—26 w, 1 B and 4 Y=31.

(84) A very small shrine attached to No. (82) on its eastern side.

Images,—3 w.

(85) The Bhulavani or Labyrinth temple, the largest in this *ṭuk* and looked upon as one of the oldest. An inscription on the principal image within it gives the date *Saṁ.* 1675. A long rectangular enclosure, surrounded with colonnades, partly open to the sky and partly roofed in, contains within it several shrines built after various plans and curious designs. The main shrine, however, is towards the front end of the enclosure. The eastern portico of this shrine is covered with an exceedingly neat domical ceiling carved in a very friable looking sandstone and white-washed. In the portico on the west is another very elaborate ceiling absolutely overflowing with figures. They are arranged in concentric circles, representing groups, processions and single figures. This ceiling is much damaged. Behind the main shrine is a three-storeyed arrangement, containing images on its four sides, the lower storey of which is sunk in a pit, the second storey being on a level with the ground floor. This is what is called *Meru Śikhara.* Above it is a very elaborate ceiling with a pretty pendant. On the north wall of the west wing of the lower floor, round the base of *Meru Śikhara*, is a large marble slab with numbers of figures and mythological scenes in relief. Carved upon one of the beams here, and apparently old, is a bas-relief representing four female figures worshipping upon either side of two empty seats or thrones. This savours much of Buddhist design. Fragments of two very old female figures are one on either side of the entrance at the back of the *Meru Śikhara.* The mutilated bodies are built into the wall. All this lower part of the temple, together with the pillars to the south of this entrance, behind the *Meru Śikhara*, is without doubt part of an old Hindu temple. In a small blind porch outside the temple, on the west, is another fragment of the old original temple, namely, a beautiful, though small, scroll built into the ceiling. It is a miniature copy of the magnificent scroll lying at Paṭṭan.

Images,—111 w, 6 B, 20 Y and 6 pinkish-brown=143.

(86) and (87) are two small cells, in a low level passage on the east of the Bhulavani temple, built into the sides of the latter under the upper corridor. The first is a gaudily painted shrine of Chakreśvarî Mâtâ, the image being dressed in skirts of silk and gold cloth. The second has a four-armed marble image of Vâgheśvarî Mâtâ seated upon a tiger.

(88) To the east of the Bhulavani temple, and the last in this direction, is the temple of Hirâchand Râya Karana. It is dedicated to Śântinâtha who sits under a silver-gilt triple umbrella. The date on the base of the image is *Saṁ.* 1860, *Śaka* 1726. In the hall is a neat inlaid coloured marble floor. The hall is gaily coloured and is hung with mirrors and chandeliers.

Images,—44 w, 1 B and 13 brass=58.

(89) A small shrine in front of the last to Vimala.

Images,—8 w.

(89) Crossing the roadway we begin the northern half of this *ṭuk* with Keśavji Nâyak's temple, which is considered a small *ṭuk* in itself, compact and neat. Upon the western side of the enclosure or court and raised considerably above the latter, is the main temple. In the centre of the temple is an enclosed space in the shape of a Greek cross. Within this are five erections,—one in each wing and one in the centre. The central one is called Śatrunjaya, the northern is Meru-Śikhara, the southern Samat-Śikhara, the western Ashṭâpada, and the eastern or front one Samosarana. The clustered pillars in the hall are very neat. No colouring has been employed, all is pure white. Across the courtyard in front of the temple is the usual *Puṇḍarîka* shrine, and around the courtyard are rows of cells under long colonnades. Two little shrines are attached, the north-east and south-east corners containing images of Vâgheśvarî Mâtâ.

Images in the temple, corridor and store-room,—391 w, 16 B, 7 Y, 22 brass, 2 pinkish-brown and 1 brown=439.

(90) A small temple at the south-west corner of Keśavji Nâyak's temple.

Images,—10 w and 1 brass=11.

(91) West of the last is a small square temple surrounded by two high walls with passages between. In the centre is a *chaumukha.* A belt of panelling runs round the inside surfaces of these encircling walls and are filled with bas-reliefs of birds and beasts of kinds, chariots, palanquins, men, &c.

Images,—4 w.

(92) A little shrine on the north of the last.

Images,—5 w.

(93) A small oblong shrine with two entrances to the west of the last.

Images,—2 w and 3 Y=5.

(94) Between Nos. (92) and (93) is a corridor with small cells.

Images,—35 w and 2 Y=37.

(95). A range of shrines against the north wall of the *ṭuk*, north-west of last.

Images,—19 w.

(96) and (97) Two small shrines near the roadway. In (96) there is a small painted image of Indra.

Images,—4 w.

(98) A corridor with seven small cell shrines, running north and south.

Images,—22 w, 1 Y=23.

(99) A small temple with an open pillared hall. In the shrine is a very large black figure of Pârśvanâtha, with a standing one on either side.

Images,—4w and 1 B=5.

(100) and (101) are two small shrines in front of the last.

Images,—15 w.

(102) A curious little temple beside the last two, called the Nandidvîpa temple.

(103) A small temple dedicated to Chandraprabha.

Images,—9 w and 3 B=12.

(104) A small temple to Chandraprabha at right angles to the last.

Images,—5 w.

(105) In the north wing of the hall of this temple is a colossal image of Ṛishabhadeva, one of the largest on the hill. Kunthi installed in the shrine.

Images,—20 w and 1 Y=21.

(106) A range of three shrines against the wall.

Images,—17 w.

(107), (108), (109), (110), (111), and (112) Six small shrines in line with the last against the wall. In No. (107) is an inscription* which says that two images were dedicated by Parasottama Sûdarajî with his nephew and brothers, all of Meśânâ, in *Saṁ.* 1822.

Images,—20 w and 1 Y=21.

(113) and (114) are two small shrines close beside each other at the margin of the roadway.

Images,—8 w.

(115) A neat temple with an open pillared hall. The back of the throne of the principal image Śambhava is well carved in white marble. The exterior of the temple is very chaste in design. An inscription† upon this temple records the setting up of the image of Chintâmaṇi Pârśvanâtha in *Saṁ.* 1791 by *bhandâri* Ratnasiṃha, a *Mahâmantri*.

Images,—14 w, 2 B and 1 Y=17.

(116) On the north of the last, a small shrine of Ajitanâtha.

Images,—5 w.

(117) A small shrine similar to the last, to Pârśvanâtha.

Images,—5 w.

(118) and (119) A pair of temples of the same size and plan, both facing east, with open pillared halls, dedicated to Âdinâtha and Dharmanâtha respectively. An inscription ‡ in (119) states that in *Saṁ.* 1860 a temple was begun and finished in 1861 by Virachand of Ahmadâbâd.

Images,—20 w and 1 Y= 21.

(120), (121), and (122) Three small shrines standing in echelon by the side of the roadway dedicated to Neminâtha, Ṛishabhadeva and Mahâvîra respectively. An inscription§

* No. XLIII. *Epig. Ind.*, Vol. II. Part X. p. 78.
† No. XXXVIII, *Epig. Ind.*, Vol. II. Part X. p. 77.
‡ No. L. *Epig. Ind.*, Vol. II. Part X. p. 79.
§ No. XLI. *Epig. Ind.*, Vol. II. Part X. p. 78.

upon No. (120) records the building of a *prâsâda* or shrine to Neminâtha by Kâśarisangha in *Saṁ.* 1814.

Images,—8 w.

(123) This is usually called the 100-column temple, but it has rather less than 100 in all. The central shrine, whose walls are moulded after the fashion of the older temples, contains a *chaumukha* of Mahâvîra, Dharma, Âdinâtha, and Kunthi. In the north porch of this temple are lying three old iron guns, each about 5 feet long with their old and rotten low wooden carriages with wooden wheels, and a short distance from the porch to the north-east is a fourth.

Images,—4 w.

(124) At the south-west corner of the last is a small temple with an open hall upon tall columns, dedicated to Adinâtha.

Images,—14 w.

(125), (126), and (127) Three very small shrines to Śambhava, Chandraprabha and Ṛishabhadeva respectively.

No. (126) is a marble shrine.

Images,—13 w, 1 B, and 1 Y=15.

(128) A small temple upon a high basement at the end of the roadway. The hall is plain and neat. The back of the throne is made up of fragments of two old backs which are of different designs. The upper fragment is much mutilated, the front of the umbrella being broken off. In the hall is a long inscription* which begins by dispraising Śiva, Vishṇu, and Brahmâ, and declaring that none can do any good but the Jina. It records that Padmasiṃha and Vardhamâna built the temple and installed the images of the 24 Jinas, Śântinâtha being foremost, in *Saṁvat* 1675, and in the next year one Padmasi added other images. The inscription is a good sample of oriental hyperbole. The principal figure has a bird under him as his cognizance and therefore should be either Sumati or Ananta. A short inscription beside the bird calls the image that of Śreyânsa, whose cognizance should be a rhinoceros. There is thus a great confusion. The reason of this probably is that as the images come from the marble districts ready made with their symbols upon them, and as each man who sets one up generally prefers a particular Jina, if he cannot get the image of that one at the time, he sets up another and inscribes the name that pleases him most irrespective of any previously engraved symbol which it may be he is more or less ignorant of the meaning of.

Images,—16 (?)

(129) and (130) Behind the last are two small shrines.

* No. XXI. *Epig. Ind.*, Vol. II. Part X. p. 64.

In (129) are two fine brass images of Pârśvanâtha.

Images,—7 w, 2 B and 2 brass = 11.

(131) Just across the roadway stands a canopy covering 18 *pâdukâs* or foot-prints overshadowed by a large tamarind tree.

(132) Within a separate enclosure close by is a large temple, the only Digambara temple on the hill, the rest belonging to the Śvetambara sect. The Digambara sect have absolutely nude images, whereas the others represent their Jinas as wearing a waistcloth and sacred thread. The interior is painted as usual. The dome has been painted and gilded with considerable care. Two nude brass images stand on either side of the central seated one in the shrine. In a niche on the south side of the shrine is a figure of Mahâkâla with his dog below. It is a nude figure and has been well bedaubed with red paint. Within this temple is an inscription* dated *Saṁvat* 1686, stating that in that year the image of Śântinâtha was installed by one Ratnasi, of Aḥmadâbâd, and relatives, during the reign of Jahângîr.

Images,—14 w, 3 B and 6 brass = 23.

The total number of images in the Vimalvaśi *ṭuk* including Keśavji Nâyak's and the Digambara temple = 1,257.

The Motishâh Tuk.

(133) The Motishâh *ṭuk* is a compact, square walled enclosure occupying about the centre of the hill and the valley between the summits. The principal temple was built by Motishâh in *Saṁvat* 1893. In the main shrine is installed Âdinâtha, upon a beautifully carved white marble throne, adorned with a gilt crown and breast-plate. Inscriptions † also tell us that in *Saṁvat* 1893 Shet Shemachandra installed the images of Bâi Divâli and her husband Shet Motichand, and that Khemachand, with his wife, set up the image of Chakreśvarî Mâtâ. Another inscription ‡ records the setting up of the images of Shet Motichand and his wives Mâji Bâi and Rupabâi by Bhâi Keśavachand of Bombay in *Saṁvat* 1903. The hall of the temple is gaudily coloured, but it has a very good inlaid marble floor having the *nandyâvarta* symbol in the centre and the *svastika* on each of the four sides. In panels on either side of the side-doors are the sacred symbols of *Oṁkâra* and *Hrîṁkâra*. In a small marble shrine in the hall is an image of Śântinâtha. The exterior of the temple is most vulgarly painted. There are a second and third storey, in each of which a *chaumukha* is installed.

Images,—96 w and 3 brass = 99.

(134) The shrine of Puṇḍarîka in front of the last. An inscription § tells us that the image was installed by Khemachand, son of Divâli Bâi, in *Saṁvat* 1893. The hall has an inlaid marble pavement. The walls of this hall serve the purpose of a visitor's book and are pretty well decorated with scrawled autographs especially of Pârsi aspirants

* No. XXX. *Epig. Ind.*, Vol. II. Part X. p. 72.

† Nos. LXXXI. and LXXXIV. *Epig. Ind.*, Vol. II. Part X. p. 82.

‡ No. LXXXVIII. *Epig. Ind.*, Vol. II. Part X. p. 83.

§ No. LXXXV. *Epig. Ind.*, Vol. II. Part X. p. 82.

to immortality. The principal image wears a gilt crown and other decorations pertaining to his office.

Images,—40 w, 1 y, and 2 brass=43.

(135) Stands in the north-east corner of the court, and contains a *chaumukha* of Âdinâtha, Ajitanâtha, Chandraprabha, and Śambhava. In the upper storey is another *chaumukha*.

Images,—26 w.

(136) To the west of last. A temple to Dharmanâtha. Interior gaily painted and hung with mirrors. A very pretty tesselated marble floor in the hall. The image of Dharmanâtha was installed, as an inscription* tells us, by Sâ Sâhivisiṁgha of Ahmadâbâd in *Saṁvat* 1893.

Images,—36 w and 4 brass=40.

(137) A temple to the west of the last containing a *chaumukha* in both the lower and upper shrines.

Images,—21 w.

(138) In the north-west corner of the *ṭuk*, a temple to Ṛishabhadeva with an open hall.

Images,—17 w.

(139) To the south of the last. A temple to Padmaprabha.

Images,—32 w 1 b=33.

(140) This is a very pretty little shrine with perforated plaster sides in which is a large pair of foot-prints.

(141) Near the last, a *chaumukha* set in the middle of a plinth on which are over 2,000 pairs of *pâdukâs*.

Images,—12 w and 7 brass=19.

(142) A small new temple with a red coloured dome and decorated architraves. The shrine door is highly coloured in red, green, yellow, and blue, with the sacred symbols *Oṁkâra* and *Hrîṁkâra* on either side of it. An inscription† records the setting up of an image of Âdinâtha by Phulachand of Bombay in *Saṁvat* 1897. The principal image in the shrine is Pârśvanâtha.

Images,—16 w.

(143) A small temple like the last, dedicated to Śambhava.

Images,—9 w.

---

* No. LXXIX. *Epig. Ind.*, Vol. II. Part X. p. 82.

† No. LXXXVI. *Epig. Ind.*, Vol. II. Part X. p. 82.

(144) A temple containing a stand of figures, the *Sahasrakûṭa*, with 1,024 small *Jinas* in bas-relief. In the shrine in the upper storey is a *chaumukha*.

Images,—17 w, 1 B, and 5 brass=23.

(145) This is a plain little temple to Supârśva.

Images,—12 w.

(146) In the south-west corner of the *ṭuk*. A small temple with open hall dedicated to Mahâvîra.

Images,—25 w, 1 B, and 2 brass=28.

(147) This is a large temple with a plain white hall with *chunam* floor covered with imitation inlaid work, dedicated to Âdîśvara.

Images,—22 w.

(148) Temple on the south of the principal temple, with a very gaily painted interior and inlaid marble floor, and further embellished with large mirrors hung round, glass balls, and chandeliers. In the hall are the sacred symbols *Oṁkâra* and *Hṛîṁkâra*. Dharmanâtha presides in the shrine and wears a very elaborately worked gilt crown and other ornaments. He sits upon a very finely carved throne, the whole being of a delicate creamy white marble. An inscription* records the setting up of this image by one Amarachand and family, inhabitant of Bombay, *Saṁvat* 1893.

Images,—23 w, 2 Y and 11 brass=36.

(149) This is a *chaumukha* temple situated in the south-east corner of the *ṭuk*, built precisely like No. (135) in the opposite corner. In the second storey there is also a *chaumukha*.

Images,—33 w.

The corridors around the four walls are lined with cell-shrines, some of which are still empty and "to let." And in addition to these there are large rooms in the corner bastions where stores of images are kept for sale to those who wish to set them up.

Images,—749 w, 28 B, 11 Y and 11 brass=799.

Total number of images in the Motishâh *ṭuk*=1,276.

The Bâlâbhâi Tuk.

(150) The main temple of the *ṭuk*, with a gaudily painted interior, hung with chandeliers and *batti* glasses. Before the shrine door is a white marble elephant about 2½ feet high. Within the shrine sits Ṛishabhadeva in white marble, with the back of his throne elaborately worked. The shrine lit up by side windows. Upstairs is a second storey with three shrines each containing a *chaumukha*. This temple was built by Bâlâbhâi, the son of Kalyânji Kâhânji of Bombay in *Saṁ*. 1893.

Images,—77 w and 5 brass=82.

* No. LXXVIII. *Epig. Ind.*, Vol. II. Part X. p. 82.

(151) The shrine of Puṇḍarîka built at the same time by the same man.

Images,—27 w.

(152) Temple in the north-east corner of the *ṭuk*, built in *Saṁ.* 1903. Interior painted and hung with mirrors and chandeliers. The shrine contains a *chaumukha.*

Images,—15 w, 1 y and 1 brass = 17.

(153) Temple opposite the last, in the south-east corner with a very pretty inlaid marble floor. The interior is very gaily painted and decorated with mirrors above the arch rings. A marble slab with an inscription in a niche in the south end of the west wall of the hall. In the shrine is Vâsupûjya, dated *Saṁ.* 1903.

Images,—15 w.

(154) A newly built temple in the south-west corner of the court set up seven years ago.

Images,—3 w and 2 brass = 5.

(155) A large pair of *pâdukâs* dated *Saṁ.* 1893.

(156) A small temple which was to have been consecrated in 1889 A.D.

(157) A small shrine behind No. (152) dedicated to Ara.

Images,—3 w.

Cell-shrines are being built against the enclosing walls. They have been added along the east wall and a portion of the south wall.

Images,—116 w, and 6 B = 122.

Total number of images in the Bâlâbhâi *ṭuk* = 271.

(158) Between the Motishâh and Modi Premachand *ṭuks*, upon the hill side, is the isolated temple of Bhîmadeva. The image is a colossal one roughly cut in the rock. Upon the temple is an inscription* which records some restoration by Tukaji of Devagiri-nagara, in *Saṁ.* 1686.

MODI PREMACHAND TUK.

(159) The Modi Premachand *ṭuk* is the highest group on the hill, and overlooks all the others. From here on a clear day the outline of the famous Girnâr hill near Junâgaḍ may be seen. The interior of the hall of the principal temple of this *ṭuk* is elaborately painted and gilded with a quantity of inlaid mirrors. This has a very tawdry and vulgar look about it and is in execrable taste. An inlaid marble floor with the *nandyâvarta* symbol in the middle. In the shrine is, as usual, Âdinâtha with silver-gilt crown and other ornaments. Plaster images above the pillars of the hall represent the *ashṭadikpâlas.*

---

* No. XXIX. *Epig. Ind.*, Vol. II. Part X. p. 72.

The exterior of the temple has representations of the Hindu deities Brahmâ, Sûrya, Indra, Agni, Yama, Narasimba, Lakshmaṇa, Hanumân, Râma, Mahâkâlî, Gaṇapati, Vishṇu, Varuṇa, Vâyu, Mahishâsura-Mardanî, Kubera, Śiva, and Varâha, in addition to two filthily indecent figures (the only such things on the hill) accentuated with red paint. The temple was built by Modi Premachand in *Saṁ.* 1843.*

Images,—88 W, 3 B, 4 Y, and 1 brass=96.

(160) The temple of Puṇḍarîka opposite last. An **inscription**† records the installation of an image of Chandraprabha (it is not called Puṇḍarîka) in *Saṁ.* 1886, by a woman named Ichhâvahu on her husband's behalf.

Images,—24 W, 1 B, and 5 Y‡,=30.

(161) An open pillared temple with ten large white images of Pârśvanâtha. In the second storey is a *chaumukha.* An **inscription**§ records the building of the temple and installation of an image of Pârśvanâtha by Savâichand, son of Premachand Jhaverîchand of Surat in *Saṁ.* 1860.

Images,—11W and 2 brass = 13.

(162) Another two-storeyed temple in the south-east corner of the court. Within the hall, which has an open front, are two beautifully carved white marble niches, covered with the most delicate work, and occupied by images of Pârśvanâtha. The upper storey contains a little *chaumukha.* The whole of this temple is constructed of marble even to the spires. Upon a great slab built in across the wall above the heads of the three central *jinas* in the shrine, are a number of mythological scenes in panels carved in bas-relief. An **inscription**¶ records the installation of the image of Pârśvanâtha and building of the temple by Jhaverî Premachand of Surat in *Saṁ.* 1860.

Images,—24 W.

(163) and (164) are *pâdukâs* or pairs of foot-prints.

(165) A small temple in the south-west corner of the *ṭuk* dedicated to Ajitanâtha.

Images,—14 W.

(166) A temple in the north-west corner, exactly like the last, to Chandraprabha.

Images,—2 W.

(167) Small shrines against the western wall.

Images,—59 W, and 1 B=60.

Images in the corridors,—201W, 2 B, 3 Y, and 4 brass=210.

Total number of images in the Modi Premachand *ṭuk*=449.

---

* No. XLIV. *Epig. Ind.*, Vol. II. Part X. p. 78. This inscription has been wrongly located in the foot-note.

† No. LIX. *Epig. Ind.*, Vol. II. Part X. p. 80.

‡ These are rather a pink fleshy brown.

§ No. XLVI. *Epig. Ind.*, Vol. II. Part X. p. 78.

¶ No. XLVII. *Epig. Ind.*, Vol. II. Part X. p. 78.

HEMÂBHÂI VAKHATACHAND TUK.

(168) The principal temple is dedicated to Ajitanâtha, and its interior is painted and decorated with mirrors. The throne is very richly carved with fine delicate work, and certainly looks much older than the image. A long inscription* here gives the pedigree and record of benefactions of Shet Vakhatachand, his son Hemâbhâi, and his grandson the late Nagarshet Premâbhâi of Ahmadâbâd and is dated *Saṁ*. 1905. Within the temple tablets have been set up by various individuals containing the symbols *Oṁkâra* and *Hṛîṁkara* set with little images of the 24 *tîrthankaras*.

Images,—35 W, 5 B, and 6 brass=46.

(169) A small *chaumukha* temple in the north-east corner of the court. An inscription† says it was built for the welfare of Hemâbhâi by his whole family, in his own *ṭuk*, in *Saṁ*. 1889. The south image is dated, however, *Saṁ*. 1682, shewing it to have been an old image previously used elsewhere.

Images,—4 W.

(170) Another *chaumukha* temple in the south-east corner, corresponding to the last. Images, 4 W.

(171) Puṇḍarîka's temple. The principal image was set up in *Saṁ*. 1886, as recorded by an inscription‡.

Images,—16 W, and 4 Y,=20.

(172) A small shrine joining the north wing of the last. An inscription§ records the setting up of an image of Chandraprabha in 1886.

Images,—1 W, and 2 Y=3.

(173) A corresponding shrine to the last on the south. An inscription¶ says the image of Pârśvanâtha was set up in *Saṁ*. 1886.

Images,—2 W, and 1 B=3.

In the corridors around the walls are, including the store-room, 169 W, 6 B, and 1 brass=176.

Total number of images in this *ṭuk*=256.

THE NANDÎŚVARA DVÎPA-TUK.

(174) The principal temple in this *ṭuk* is more after the style, in its interior arrangement, of that of Keśavji Nâyak's, (No. 89). The centre of the hall is filled with *Meru* and

---

* No. XCI. *Epig. Ind.*, Vol. II. Part X. p. 83.
† No. LXV. *Epig. Ind.*, Vol. II. Part X. p. 80.
‡ No. LV. *Epig. Ind.*, Vol. II. Part X. p. 79.
§ No. LIX. *Epig. Ind.*, Vol. II. Part X. p. 80.
¶ No. LVI. *Epig. Ind.*, Vol. II. Part X. p. 79.

Samat-Sikharas and *chaumukhas*. Some of these are dated *Saṁ*. 1818, whilst one is *Saṁ*. 1897. This temple faces west and has no Puṇḍarîka shrine.

Images,—228 w.

(175) and (176) Two corner shrines and store-room. Most of the images in the store-rooms of these *ṭuks* are old ones with inscriptions upon them. These are sold for setting up in shrines upon the hill or they are sometimes taken away to Ahmadâbâd and other places. The pillars in the verandah between these shrines are very elaborately decorated in plaster surface ornament, the plaster being finished off to a fine creamy tinted polished surface like marble.

Images,—62 w, and 1 brass=63.

Total number of images in this *ṭuk*=291.

Sâkarchand Premchand's Tuk.

(177) This small *ṭuk* adjoins the last on the north. The principal temple is dedicated to Pârśvanâtha, a large brass image occupies the shrine. The hall is of the usual style and has an inlaid coloured marble floor with the *nandyâvarta* in the centre. Disreputable looking chandeliers, *batti* glasses, and mirrors are hung about. An inscription* gives the date of the installation of the image as *Saṁ*. 1893.

Images,—22 w, and 4 brass=26.

(178) The shrine of Puṇḍarîka in which we find not the usual Chandraprabha but an image of Pârśvanâtha. This was set up at the same time and by the same party as that in the main temple.†

Images,—12 w.

(179) and (180) Two shrines adjoining the north and south wings of the last, respectively.

Images,—4 w.

(181) Temple in the north-east corner of the *ṭuk*. Image of Padmaprabha set up in *Saṁ*. 1893.‡ Usual painted and decorated hall, with the *svastika* emblem in the middle of the shrine floor.

Images,—9 w.

(182) Corresponding temple in the south-east corner with a vulgarly and ugly coloured interior dedicated to Padmaprabha erected in *Saṁ*. 1900.§

Images,—17 w.

(183) and (184) Two small shrines adjoining Nos. (181) and (182) respectively.

Images,—8 w.

---

* No. LXXV. *Epig. Ind.*, Vol. II. Part X. p. 81. † No. LXXVI. *Epig. Ind.*, Vol. II. Pt. X. p. 81.

‡ No. LXXVII. *Epig. Ind.*, Vol. II. Part X. p. 82. § No. LXXXVII. *Epig. Ind.*, Vol. II. Part. X. p. 83.

The corridor surrounding the *ṭuk* is, as usual, lined with cell-shrines.

Images,—68 w.

Total number of images in this *ṭuk*=144.

THE CHHIPAVASI TUK.

(185) This *ṭuk* is the enclosure to the east of the last having no regular arrangement. The temple nearest the entrance is a very modern looking erection with much plaster work about it. There are two neat pillars with *toraṇa* in the porch.

Images,—3 w.

(186) A small temple to the north-east of the last.

Images,—1 w.

(187) A little shrine beside the last.

Images.—6 w.

(188) Further eastward still, and of a curious plan, the shrine being in the centre with a *pradakshiṇá* around it.

Images,—4 w, and 2 Y=6.

(189) A small temple upon the opposite side of the *ṭuk*, of little account.

Image,—1B.

(190) and (191) Two small shrines besides one another. Upon the image in (191) is an inscription dated *Saṁ.* 1330. The image is probably older than the shrine.

Images,—2 w.

(192) One pair of *pâdukâs* under a large *râyana* tree. Beside it is a row of empty shrines.

Total number of images in this *ṭuk*=19.

THE PANCHA PÂNDAVA TUK.

(193) This temple is without doubt an old Hindu shrine converted to Jaina use. The exterior, which remains in much of its original condition, has been beautifully carved, but has also been much mutilated. The proportions of the images which decorate the walls are much better than those of any other statues on the hill. Among them are the Hindu gods and goddesses Mahâkâlî, Varuṇa, Vâyu, Kubera, Îśa, Sarasvatî, etc. Two inscriptions* in this temple record the setting up of the images of Tîmamuti (not Bhîmamuni) and Yudhishṭhira in *Saṁ.* 1788.

(194) Behind the last is a small temple containing a *sahasrakûṭa, i. e.,* a central pedestal or block of marble having 1,008 little images of *jinas* carved upon its sides.

* Nos. XXXV. and XXXVI. *Epig. Ind.*, Vol. II. Part X. p. 77.

THE CHAUMUKHA TUK.

(195) This is the largest *ṭuk* on the northern summit, and the principal temple is, next to that of Âdîśvara Bhagavân, the largest on the hill. Within the shrine, which occupies the centre of the building, is the great *chaumukha* composed of four colossal images of Âdinâtha or Ṛishabhadeva. The floor of the hall is prettily inlaid with coloured marble with the *svastika* emblem in the centre. Great brass barred doors close the shrine. The images are adorned with massive gilt crowns, armlets, and breastplates. On the second storey is a shrine with canopy. A long inscription* records the setting up of the great *chaumukha* in *Saṁ.* 1675.

Images,—55 w, 1B and 2 brass=58.

(196) In front of the great temple is the shrine of Puṇḍarîka. Upon the shrine door is an inscription† which gives the date of the erection of this shrine as *Saṁ.* 1675.

Images,—14 w and 1Y=15.

(197) and (198) Two temples flanking the entrance to the great temple known as Shet Devarâjâ's and Sundardâs's temples respectively. Inscriptions‡ give the date of their erection as *Saṁ.* 1675.

Images,—17 w, 1B and 1Y=19.

(199) A *chaumukha* in the north-east corner of the enclosure with a 14th century inscription.

Images,—4 w.

(200) A little shrine near the last.

Images,—3 w.

(201) to (209) A row of small shrines along by the northern corridor.

Images,—38 w.

(210) Temple at the north-west corner of the great temple similar to Nos. (197) and (198).

Images,—18 w and 1B=19.

(211) Temple similar to the last at the south-west corner.

Images,—2 w, and 1B=3.

(212) Temple immediately behind the *chaumukha* temple with an open pillared hall with a painted ceiling. The exterior of this temple is richly carved.

Images,—14 w and 1B=15.

(213) A small temple behind the last with some very neat *toraṇas*, dedicated to Śântinâtha.

Image,—1 w.

---

* No. XVIII. *Epig. Ind.*, Vol. II. Part X. p. 62. See also Nos. XIX. and XX.
† No. XIV. *Epig. Ind.*, Vol. II. Part X. p. 60.
‡ Nos. XXIII. and XXIV. *Epig. Ind.*, Vol. II. Part X. p. 67.

(214) A neat little hall projecting from the middle of the west wall of the *ṭuk*.

Images,—3 w.

(215) and (216) Two little shrines beside each other, the former having a small *chaumukha* and the latter a figure of Âdinâtha.

Images,—5 w.

(217) A small shrine in front of the last two with a number of *pâdukâs*. An **inscription*** round them records that they were placed there by the same party who built the walls of the *ṭuk* in *Saṁ.* 1675.

(218) A small rectangular temple in front of the last, of white polished marble but very plain. The curved roof is also of white marble, the slabs of which are so thin that they are translucent. Outside, on the front wall, is an **inscription**† recording its erection in *Saṁ.* 1910.

Images,—10 w (?)

(219), (220), (221) and (222) are four small shrines beside the last, containing *pâdukâs* and *chaumukhas*.

Images,—7 w.

(223) A small canopy behind the last covering innumerable small *pâdukâs*.

(224) A small shrine to Pârśvanâtha.

Images,—6 w.

(225) to (230) A row of small shrines along the south wall of the *ṭuk*.

Images,—10 w.

(231) to (236) A cluster of small shrines in the south-east corner of the *ṭuk*. No. (236) are little canopies covering 2,503 *pâdukâs* or foot-prints.

Images,—18 w, 1B and 2 brass=21.

In the corridors of the *Chaumukha Tuk* are a number of old fragments and images with many of the *simhâsanas* dated in the 14th century *Saṁ.*, while these images are dated in the 17th century. One is dated *Saṁ.* 118, but there is evidently a numeral omitted here.

Images,—193 w, 6B and 3Y=202.

The following temples, though outside the principal enclosure round the great Chaumukha temple, are reckoned with it as being within the Khartaravasi Tuk.

(237), (238), (239), (240) and (241) Five shrines in a line outside the great Chaumukha enclosure on the east. Nos. (237) and (239) are dated *Saṁ.* 1892 and 1891, respectively, and No. (241) *Saṁ.* 1887.‡ No. (240) has an **inscription** dated *Saṁ.* 1960! (the present year being only 1952).

Images,—22 w; 2 Y and 2 brass=26.

(242) A temple standing in front of the last with an open pillared hall, and a long rectangular shrine with three doors.

Images,—13 w and 2 B=15.

* No. XV. *Epig. Ind.*, Vol. II. Part X. p. 60.
† No. XCVI. *Epig. Ind.*, Vol. II. Part X. p. 84.
‡ Nos. LXIX. LXVIII. and LX. *Epig. Ind.*, Vol. II. Part X. pp. 81, 80, and 61.

(243) and (244) Two small shrines on one platform, the former with plain and the latter with decorated walls. No. (243) has an inscription* which records its erection in *Saṁ.* 1885.

Images,—16 w.

(245) A square plain domed building containing a *chaumukha* with other figures seated on low benches round the walls and in niches.

Images,—62 w and 3B = 65.

(246) A small temple facing north with an open pillared hall. The exterior of the walls are very well carved, being of the same class of work as in the Ahmadâbâd buildings.

Images,—8 w.

(247) A larger temple to the north of the last upon a high basement, with three porches. Inlaid marble floor. The walls and pillars are all painted red, picked out with yellow and black. An inscription† gives its date as *Saṁ.* 1905.

Images,—34 w, 2 B and 3 brass = 39.

(248) Temple of Marudevî Mâtâ, a plain little square temple.

Images,—14 w.

(249) Sampriti Râjâ's temple with an open hall with three porches. The doorway to the shrine looks like an old frame from an older temple. It is carved in a yellow clay-stone. Round the basement of the temple are eleven *pâliyâs* which are said to mark the spots where some of the builders were killed by the scaffolding giving way.

Images,—15 w, 1B and 1 brass = 17.

(250) Temple of Narsi Keśavji Nâyak. Interior gaily painted and adorned with mirrors. A long inscription‡ records the building of this temple by Keśavji in *Saṁ.* 1921.

Images,—99 w, 6 B and 15 brass = 120.

Total number of images in the Khartaravasi or Chaumukha Tuk = 759.

(251) and (252) are two temples standing by themselves outside upon the eastern side of the Motishâh *ṭuk*, the former to Vimala and the latter to Ananta. The latter has an inscription recording its erection on the hill in *Saṁ.* 1893 by Devachand Kalyânchand of Bombay.

Images,—81 w, 1B and 1Y = 83.

The number, therefore, of free standing images upon the hill, as actually counted in 1889 were 6,446, which, with the innumerable small ones upon the *Sahasrakûṭas*, tablets and symbols, not detached, amount to more than 10,000; and these are being daily added to.

---

* No. LIV. *Epig. Ind.*, Vol. II. Part X. p. 79.
† No. XC. *Epig. Ind.*, Vol. II. Part X. p. 83.
‡ No. CV. *Epig. Ind.*, Vol. II. Part X. p. 74.

VIII.—KACHH.

III. 1. **Bhadres'var**, 12 miles E.N.E. from Mundra : (1) The large Jaina temple of Jagadusah, outside the village, has been largely rebuilt and repaired at different times : on the walls and pillars are some inscriptions, but only very partially legible (see *Archæol. Report, W. Ind.*, vol. II.). (2) Two old mosques, one much buried up in the sand, the other in tolerable repair. (3) Beside an old *kuṇḍa* is a temple of Mâtâ Âśâpûrâ ; and on a broken pillar is an inscription dated *Saṁvat* 1358 (A.D. 1302). (4) The *dargâh* of Pîr Lâl Shobhah has an old Arabic inscription along the upper course of the wall. The foundations of the old city of Bhadrâvatî extend over a large area close to the modern town (*Archæol. Report, W. Ind.*, vol. II.).

II*b*. 2. **Bhuvad**, 7 miles N.N.E. from Bhadreśvar : An early temple of Bhuvaneśvara Mahâdeva, of which the shrine has fallen, but the *maṇḍapa* still remains, and is a good example of the early Kachh style. It bears an inscription, very illegible, but dated *Saṁvat* 1246 (A.D. 1190).

III. 3. **Vira**, 6 miles east from Bhadreśvar : The *kubâ* or domed tomb of Pîr Jâdia, a Sayyid from Sindh, built by Nayi Punjâ, about 250 years ago. The temple of Yoginîdevî, rebuilt by Gurji Motichand of Anjär, about 30 years ago ; *śrâddha* ceremonies are performed at the *kuṇḍa* by the Hindus of surrounding villages.

III. 4. **Anjar**, 16 miles north-east from Bhadreśvar, and 22 south-east from Bhuj : No remains of much interest, most of the temples, &c., having been rebuilt after the earthquake of 1819. It contains the *sthânas* or sacred places (1) of Ajayapâla—said to have been a prince of Ajmir (Tod's *Râjasthân*, vol. I. p. 205n) : the head of the *maṭha* has a copper-plate grant of *Saṁvat* 1673, and two others : (2) of Jesal or Jesar Jîr, said to have been a notorious freebooter who was reclaimed by Turî, a Kâṭhî woman : (3) Temples of Wankal Mâtâ, Mahâdeva Baḍeśvara, Ambâ Mâtâ, and Mâhanrâi,—but of little interest.

III. 5. **Barai**, near Mundra : Temple of Mahâdeva Nîlakaṇṭha, built in 1668 A.D. The *liṅga* is said to have been brought from Bhadreśvar.

III. 6. **Gedi**, 13 miles north-east from Râpur (lat. 23° 44' N., long. 70° 45' E.) : said to be the ancient Vairâṭanagarî ; old coins are found about the locality. (1) Mâlan Vâv, of which the pillars are half buried in the ground and the well overgrown with trees ; an inscription said to have belonged to it, lies in the temple of Achaleśvara, and is dated in 1476 A.D. (2) Temple of Mahâdeva Achaleśvara, said to be about 300 years old, but built on an older site by a Sâchora Brâhman. (3) Temple of Lakshmî-Nârâyaṇa, built in 1841, on the site of one destroyed by the earthquake ; some of the old images remain ; and in a niche over a Gaṇapati is an inscription of *Saṁvat* 1675. (4) Temple of Mahâvîra, containing images of Âdîśvara dated *Saṁvat* 1534, and of Śântinâtha dated *Saṁvat* 1925. (5) On an image of a Kshetrapâla in the bazâr is the date *Saṁvat* 1268. The tomb of Ashaba Pîr is only a platform with tombs on it.

III. 7. **Rav**, 9 miles south-west from Geḍî : The temple of Ravechi Mâtâ, built by Sâmabâi Mâtâ, the priestess, in 1822 A.D., on the site of a very old one, and at a cost of 24,000 *koris* ;

the temple maintains about 500 cows and feeds all travellers. On a *pâliyâ* is the date *Saṁvat* 1328 "when Arjunadeva of Anahillapaṭṭan reigned through his viceroy Mâladeva." The temple stands on the verge of a fine *kuṇḍa*.

III. 8. **Movana**, 14 miles north-east from Gedî : The old site is to the north of the village, and there are two caverns in the hill.

III. 9. **Kanthkot**, 16 miles south-west from Rav and 36 north-east from Anjâr : (1) A Jaina temple of the 13th century, much ruined and having some abraded **inscriptions**, one dated *Saṁvat* 1340. (2) Temple of Sûrya, containing an image of that god. (3) Temple of Kanthaḍanâtha, a neat small shrine on the site of the old one destroyed by the earthquake ; it belongs to the Kânphâṭa sect.

III. 10. **Varnun**, 25 miles south-east from Geḍî and 24 E.N.E. from Chitroḍ : On the edge of the Raṇ is an old temple said to date from the time of Mûlarâja. It is small, with three porches. In repairs executed in 1851 an **inscription** is said to have been plastered over.

III. 11. **Chitrod**, 13 miles E.S.E. from Kanthkoṭ : Four old and much dilapidated temples at Mewâsâ, about a mile to the north, have been sculptured. The temple of Mahâdeva at the ruins of Betî, a mile east of Mewâsâ, has an **inscription** of *Saṁvat* 1559.

III. 12. **Lakadiya**, 11 miles south-east from Kanthkoṭ and 8 south-west from Chitroḍ : *minâr* built by Jâḍejâ Devaji in 1760, on a platform ; it is octagonal, and said to be about 10 ft. in diameter and 44 ft. high, with balconies and a dome.

III. 13. **Katariya**, 5 miles south-east from Lakaḍiya : A small temple of Mahâdeva Bhaḍeśvara on the west of the village, erected in 1683 by a Bhâtiya. *Pâliyâs* or *satis* on the bank of the *kuṇḍa* bear dates *Saṁvat* 1684, 1764, &c. The Jaina temple in the bazâr is deeply buried in the earth and dilapidated, but has been richly carved.

III. 14. **Sikarpur**, 4 miles south-east from Katâriyâ : The tombs of the *pîrs* Pâṭhâ, Gebanshâh, Multâni, and Ashâbah are of no interest.

III. 15. **Manfara**, 7 miles west from Kanthkoṭ : A temple and monastery.

III. 16. **Sikra**, 15 miles south-west from Kanthkoṭ and 3 W.N.W. from Bhachau : The ruined temple of Kageśvara ; two tombs of Momana Kunbis built in 1667, of good workmanship ; a *pîr's* tomb on the site of the old town ; and a fine Jaina temple of Vâsupûjya, built in 1717 ; also some old *pâliyâs*.

II. 17. **Kotai**, 13 miles north from Bhuj : A fine old temple attributed to Lâkhâ Phulâni, and well worth preserving ; also others more dilapidated, but all of considerable age, perhaps of about the 10th century (*Archæol. Reports*, vol. II.).

III. 18. **Bhuj**, the capital : (1) The tombs of the Râvs, much injured by the earthquake in 1819, but several of them are deserving of repair and preservation. In the tomb or *chhatri* of Bhârmalji is a *pâliyâ* bearing an **inscription** commemorating the *sati* of Bâi Śrî Lîlâvatî, daughter of Mânḍalîka of Jûnâgaḍ in *Saṁvat* 1688. The *chhatri* was erected in *Saṁvat* 1714. Another **inscription** in the *chhatri* of Prâgmalji gives the date of his death in *Saṁvat* 1772, *Śaka* 1637; and states that he married the daughter of Râv Râvalsiṅgh of Idar. (2) The old palace has some good architectural details. (3) The mosque inside the gate is of some interest. (4) There are temples of Suvarṇarâya, Kalyâṇeśvara, Svamaṇḍapa, &c.

IIb. 19. **Kheda**, 11 miles south from Bhuj and 18 north from Mundra: said to have been the capital of Lâkhâ Phulâni. The *vimâna* of a very fine temple of about the 10th century remains, and is well worth preservation; the *maṇḍapa* was thrown down by the earthquake (see *Archæol. Rep.*, vol. II). Near the town is a fine modern tomb and other buildings raised by Ghulâm Ali Shâh Kâdivâl since A.D. 1792; they belong to the Khojahs or Shîah-Imâmi-Ismaëli sects introduced into Gujarât by Sudru'd-dîn; they reverence Ali and Fatima, their sons Hasan and Husain, and Muḥammad, of whom they have representations but without faces.

III. 20. **Ma'ndavi**, 23 miles west from Mundra and 24 south-west from Kheda: (1) Temple of Sundaravara, belonging to the Vaishṇava sect, built by the *Darbâr* in *Saṁvat* 1631, but is going to decay; the *maṇḍapa* is domed and surrounded by parapet walls. (2) Râṇeśvara, built by Kamâbâi, the sister of Bhârmalji, in *Saṁvat* 1684; it is larger and finer than Sundaravara, the dome being supported by 16 pillars; it is a Śaiva shrine. (3) Lakshmî-Nârâyaṇa, built by Śâṭh Topan in *Saṁvat* 1664, and is larger than the others. (4) Rañchoḍji Mahârâja, of the Vallabhâchârya sect, is of two storeys. (5) Qâziwali Masjid, *Saṁvat* 1665, ruined by the earthquake. (6) Jami Masjid, *Saṁvat* 1660, built of materials from a Hindu temple, but also ruined; neither mosque was of much pretensions.

III 21. **Gundiylai**, 3 miles S.E. from Mâṇḍavî: Temple of Râval Pîr, built by two *Shets* in 1820, on the shore, and visited by Hindus and Musalmans at the annual fair.

III. 22. **Bagada**, 7 miles north-west from Bhadreśvar: between this village and Vâghorâ is a small temple of Phulseśvara, rebuilt about 1838; also the Selora step-well, restored in 1854.

III. 23. **Godhra**, 8 miles north-west from Mâṇḍavî: The town was built in 1609; the temple of Chaturbhujarâya *Saṁvat* 1776, and another smaller one *Saṁvat* 1751, are of little interest.

III. 24. **Vinja'n**, formerly Kâñchibâ-Pâṭṭan, 2 miles west from the present village, was a place of importance, and coins are sometimes found on the site, where also is a shrine of Kâlikâ Mâtâ. The temple of Rakheśvara Mahâdeva, at Viñjân, is 45 ft. by 35 ft., built of hard yellow stone, *Saṁvat* 1688.

III. 25. **Guntri**, 26 miles north from Viñjâṅ and 36 W.N.W. from Bhuj: The ruins of a deserted city, surrounded by walls with towers 2,250 yards in circuit. It was the capital of the Sândh Râjputs, perhaps about A.D. 1300, and deserves examination. (*Trans. R. As. Soc.*, vol. III. p. 586).

III. 26. **Lakhadi**, 16 miles south-east from Guntrî and 18 west from Bhuj: Near it and Mañjal another village to the south-west is Puvrâgaḍ or Paddhargaḍ, an ancient fort, said to have been built by Puṅvrâ Gahâni, the nephew of Lâkhâ Phulâni. The walls are 2,385 yards in circuit. The larger palace is about 55 ft. square and 20 high, built of large blocks of stone and with considerable taste; it is of two storeys, and the upper was supported by 84 round pillars, about 7 ft. high and mostly of single blocks of stone, having square capitals ornamented with the heads of men and animals. The porch and colonnade in front are carved. The area in the centre is open to the sky. The smaller palace, called Addhaṭâro, is about 40 ft. long by 23 wide, of one storey, with front and pillars carved, but inferior to the larger one. The Mint is a heap of ruins, but there is a small building in the enclosure which has perhaps been a temple. The gateway on the west is a very narrow one. Near it is a fine old Śaiva temple, similar to the one at Kheḍâ, with sculptures. To the west of the fort are two temples of the Meghavâlas or Dheḍs, now in ruins; one of them is on a platform, 70 ft. by 50; it has pillars 10 ft. high supporting a very fine dome; and the shrine door is richly sculptured. The other is quite a ruin. These ruins are probably of about the same age as the remains at Kheḍâ and at Bhumlî in Kâṭhiâwâḍ.

III. 27. **Kotha'ra'**, 9 miles north-west from Vinjâṇ: The great Jaina temple of Śântinâtha, built in 1852, at a cost of 16 *lâkhs* of *koris*, is similar to that of Hathisingh at Ahmadâbâd.

III. 28. **Dhinodhar,** 27 miles north-west from Bhuj and 12 E.N.E. from Guntri: The chief seat of the Kâṇphâṭas, with a small temple of Dharmanâtha the founder of the sect, and other buildings, on a hill 1,268 feet high.

III. 29. **Kora',** 24 miles W.N.W. from Guntri and 5 north-west from Maḍh: The ruins of the *medi* or house of Pîr Aliyâji, of little interest.

III. 30. **Ma'ta'-no Madh**: on a hill to the north-east is a small temple to Âśâpûrâ, built about 1745. At the top of a hill called Jâgorâ Dongar, 2 miles to the north, is a small cavern dedicated to Âśâpûrâ. The temple of Âśâpûrâ at Maḍh is said to have been founded in the 13th century, but was destroyed by the earthquake, and rebuilt in 1824; it has a *pradakshiṇâ* and is 58 feet long by 32 wide. The Kâpâdî sect of ascetics are devotees of Âśâpûrâ, who is the *Kuladevatâ* of the Jâḍejâ clan. The temple and *kuṇḍa* of Châcharâ are partly hewn out of the sandstone rock; the water is charged with sulphates and used in the manufacture of alum.

III. 31. **Pa'tgad** or Vâgham Châvaḍâ's *gaḍ*, 10 miles north of Korâ and near Sairâ and Araṭḍâ: the site of an ancient city extending about 2 miles along the banks of the stream, with two forts; much of the materials have been carried off to build the town of Lakhpat. To the west of the site is a cave with a hall 35 feet long by 30 wide, the roof supported by two 16-sided pillars with capitals, their shafts being 8 feet high; to the right is a room 12 feet square with a carved door, and beyond it is a third, while a fourth is in the back of the hall. The temple of Kateśvara was rebuilt in 1825; on the east of it is the *kuṇḍa* with stone steps. The temple of Kâlikâ Mâtâ was re-built in 1839 of old materials.

III. 32. **Lakhpat,** 6 miles west of Sairâ: The *kubâ* of Gosa Muhammad, begun in 1855, on a platform 54 feet square and 7 high, is octagonal and about 38 feet in diameter, of black stone and richly carved, with fine stone lattice work; it is floored with marble and has a marble canopy over the grave.

III. 33. **Chher,** 7 miles south-west from Lakhpat: The *kubâ* of Lâl-Chhattâ is of brick and not noteworthy.

III. 34. **Rakanoj**, 4 miles north-east of Amara, on the north bank of the river Kinnar and the south side of the Sanandhro: the ruins of an ancient town, extending for more than a mile, with heaps of ruined temples and other buildings. The tomb of Kara Kâsim is a mile west of Amârâ; he is worshipped by both Hindus and Muhammadans, and a legend is told of him, which would identify him with Muhammad *bin* Kâsim, 712 A.D.

III. 35. **Na'ra'yansa'r**, 18 miles south-west from Lakhpat and 26 west by north from Madh, a place of reputed sanctity, and a rival to Dwârakâ. The temples were erected by a Râṇî of Râv Desalji I. in *Saṁvat* 1780 (A.D. 1734), and are of considerable splendour. That of Trikamarâya is 72 feet long by 68 wide; it has three porches and a *maṇḍapa*, supported by pillars 12 feet high with capitals, and having cusped arches between; the domes are carved; the doors are plated with silver; the image is of black marble on a *siṅhâsana* of silver work, and over it are 40 gold and silver *chhatras*. In the same enclosure are temples to Kalyâṇarâya, Lakshmî, Dwârakânâtha or Rañchhodaji, Govardhananâtha, Âdinârâyaṇa and Lakshmî-Nârâyaṇa, with inscriptions of *Saṁvat* 1790 and 1797.

III. 36. **Kotes'var**, close to Nârâyansâr: On a mound to the north-west is a walled enclosure with a temple of Koṭeśvara Mahâdeva, built, or rather re-built, in 1820; beside it is a smaller one to Kalyâṇeśvara; at the pier is the Gayâkuṇḍa: also the temples of Nîlakaṇṭha, Kanakeśvara or Jag Dado, and Rûpeśvara.

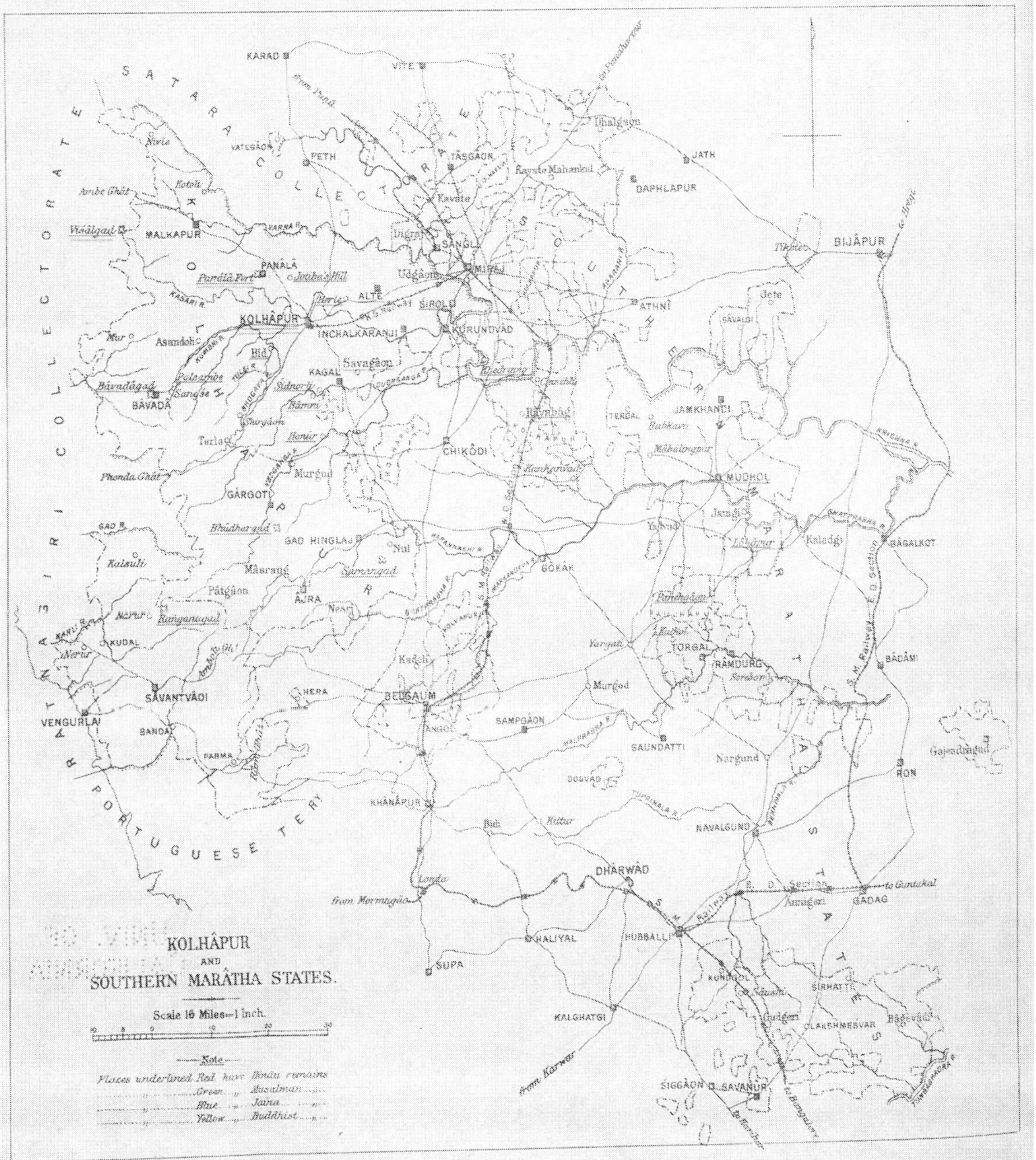
KOLHÂPUR
AND
SOUTHERN MARÂTHA STATES.
Scale 16 Miles=1 Inch.
Note
Places underlined Red have Hindu remains
Green Musalman
Blue Jaina
Yellow Buddhist
SATARA COLLECTORATE
RATNAGIRI COLLECTORATE
PORTUGUESE TERY
KARAD
VITE
PETH
TÂSGAON
JATH
DAPHLAPUR
BIJÂPUR
MALKAPUR
PANÂLÂ
SANGLI
MIRAJ
ATHNI
KOLHÂPUR
INCHALKARANJI
KURUNDVÂD
KAGAL
BÂVADA
JAMKHANDI
CHIKÔDI
MUDHOL
GÂRGOTI
GAD HINGLAJ
GOKAK
BÂGALKOT
ÂJRA
KUDAL
SAVANTVÂDI
VENGURLAI
BELGAUM
TORGAL
RAMDURG
BÂDÂMI
SAMPGÂON
SAUNDATTI
RON
KHÂNÂPUR
NAVALGUND
DHÂRWÂD
GADAG
HALIYAL
HUBBALLI
SUPA
KUNDGOL
SIRHATTI
KALGHATGI
LAKSHMESVAR
SIGGÂON
SAVANUR
Drawn and Photozincographed Govt. Photozinco Office, Poona 1896

IX.—SÂVANTVÂDI AND KOLHÂPUR.

SÂVANTVÂDI.

Nerur, 15 miles north of Sundarvâḍi.

Inscriptions:—A number of copper-plate grants were found here many years ago (see *J. B. B. R. A. S.*, vol. III. pt. ii. pp. 203, 212, 333; *Ind. Ant.*, vols. VIII. and IX.)

KOLHÂPUR.

In the valuable *Statistical Report on the Principality of Kolhâpur*, compiled by Major D. C. Graham in 1854, almost all the antiquities are noticed in some detail.

1. **Kolhâpur**, the capital, 68 miles south from Sâtârâ (16° 43′; 74° 17′).

II *b*. (1) The temple of Ambâbâî or Mahâlakshmî is in the middle of the town, about 100 yards north-west from the Râjâ's old palace. The main portion of the building is of two storeys, and is built of black stone from local quarries. The *śikharas* or spires are said to have been put up by a Śaṅkarâchârya of Saṅkeśvara: they in nowise harmonize with the carved stonework below, which is earlier work, but still much later than the better Châlukyan work of the Kânarese districts. The lower work is of the same age and style as that of the temple of Kopeśvara at Khedrâpur. The greater part of an older and smaller temple still exists with its own columns and sculpture embedded, as it were, within the larger building, and in the smaller subsidiary shrines in the courtyard we find still more of the old work. All this is genuine old Châlukyan masonry, but it is now so much encrusted with whitewash that the minute details of the carving are obliterated. The liberal coatings of crude whitewash with which the *śikharas* are covered throws them into violent and painful contrast with the well-finished black-stone work which they surmount. The walls are covered outside by a multiplicity of mouldings, and with figures in niches along the upper portion of the lower storey. The plan is cruciform, with three shrines—of Ambâbâî as the principal one, Mahâkâlî on the left, and of Mahâsarasvatî in a smaller one on the right. The length from east to west is 144 feet, and from north to south 157 feet, and the total height of the *śikhara* 82½ feet. The outer and principal *maṇḍapas* and the vestibule of the shrine are crowded with columns. In the court are many accessory buildings. The Navagraha and Śeshaśâyî temples, said to have formed parts of Jaina *bastis*, were removed from other parts of the town, and fitted up in the enclosure. The carving on them is very good.

I *b*. **Inscriptions**:—To the left of entrance on the left side of the porch or outer *maṇḍapa*, in *Devanâgarî* characters, dated *Śaka* 1140; (2) on a pillar on the left hand after entering the courtyard, also in *Devanâgarî*, *Śaka* 1158; (3) on a pillar of the small temple of the Navagraha, to the left of the main building, in *Devanâgarî*; (4) and a fourth is behind the temple, on the left hand when entering from the eastern gate (see Graham's *Kolhâpur*, pp. 330-ff. Nos. 11, 13, 17, 19, 20, 21, and 23); (5) gathered at the Town Hall are some inscribed stones in Kânarese and *Devanâgarî*; (6) on a beam in the *maṇḍapa* of the Śeshaśâyî temple.

III (2) The *Nagârkhâna* or Palace Gateway is the main entrance to the old palace, and stands about 40 yards north from it. It is built of black stone, and was erected between 1832 and 1837. It is in modern Musalmân style, with pieces of old carving from Jaina *bastis* inserted here and there. The Court-room on the upper floor is of highly polished stone, the walls being divided into reflecting panels of large dimensions, and the polished stone-ceiling is supported on massive pillars. The area covered by this building is 101 feet by 40, and the total height 64 feet.

III. (3) Memorial temples: These are on the Panchagangâ River, at the north-west corner of the town and close to the Brahmapuri hill. They are in memory of deceased members of the royal family,—Sambhâji, Śivâji II, and Abâ and Bâva Sâhebs. The second, built in 1815, is the largest and most elaborate, but it is an ill-assorted combination of a large Musalmân *maṇḍapa* and a lofty Hindu spire covered with plaster formed into mouldings and with a few ornaments. They are *liṅga* shrines. Near by are a number of small shrines on the fine *ghâts* that lead down to the river.

III. (4) Jaina *Basti*. This is an old Jaina temple in the Hemâḍpanti style, the outer contour of the shrine walls having obliquely-set angles. The walls are of black stone, but the spire is a copy of that on Ambâbâî's temple, and probably of the same age. It is 73 feet long by 38 wide; the walls with a multiplicity of horizontal mouldings, are 12 feet high, and the height of the spire above that is 34 feet. It has a porch, the width of the *maṇḍapa*, like the second temple at Belgaum; a *maṇḍapa* on four pillars of the "broken square" pattern, a very small ante-chamber, and square shrine.

I *b*. **Inscriptions**:—Close to this temple are two Śilâhâra legible inscriptions, dated respectively *Śaka* 1058 and 1064 (Graham's Nos. 3 and 4).

III. (5) Bâbu Jamal's *dargâh* is a small building with an ill-proportioned heavy dome re-built within the last hundred years.

(6) Brahmapuri hill is said to be the site of an old fort, and the foundations of walls, &c., have been discovered on it in making excavations within late years. A few years ago numerous lead and a few copper coins of the Ândhrabhṛitya dynasty were found, when making deep excavations. The foundations also of a Buddhist *stûpa* were dug up in the Kharala garden, in which was a stone-box, the lid of which bore an inscription in old Maurya or Aśoka characters (see *Arch. Sur. Mem.* No. 10 on Inscriptions). Within it was a crystal casket, which, no doubt, contained a relic; but it was overturned and broken before it was noticed. There was also found a brass model of a *stûpa*.

There are several underground temples in the town. Three temples dedicated to Temblâî are about 3 miles to the east of Kolhâpur: they were constructed about 70 years ago by Akarâm Bâbâ Yâdav. The temple of Mahâkâlî is in Budhavâr Street: goats are sacrificed to her. Temple of Pṛithiangirâ (Pratyangirâ?) is believed to be very ancient. Temple of Viṭhobâ near the Padmâlâ gate. Temple of Yellammâ is in the east of the city: women devote themselves to her and wear a necklace of white beads: they do not marry.

II *b*. 2. **Pana'la Fort,** 12 miles north-west from Kolhâpur. It is now dismantled, but contains a number of antiquities. The fort is ascribed to the Śilahâra Bhoja Râjâ in the 11th century, and the small quadrilateral citadel on the top goes by his name. Three entire rock-caves remain and portions of others. The gateways are the work of the Bâhmani dynasty of the 15th century. The Tîn Darwâjâ is still entire, and is a good specimen of work of the kind with a great deal of light tracery work on the jambs and architrave.

The Wâgh Darwâjâ is partially destroyed; the Châr Darwâjâ, destroyed after the disturbances of 1844, is roughly sketched in Graham's *Kolhâpur* (p. 120).

Within the citadel of Bhoja Râjâ are two large granaries or magazines (*ambarkhâna*) built by the Muhammadans. To this citadel the legend, told of so many other masonry works, is also attached—that a woman was buried alive under the foundation. The cave of Paraśurâma Ṛishi is near the east end of the fort.

Inscriptions:—Seven Persian inscriptions, given by Major Graham, pp. 481-489.

III. 3. **Pa'ndava Dara**, about 6 miles west from Panâlâ. At the head of a narrow ravine is a group of about half a dozen caves, apparently of the same plain type as the Śirwal, Kuḍâ, and other southern Buddhist excavations. Two of them have halls measuring about 28 feet square, with *dâgobas* in the cells.

III. 4. **Jotiba's hill**, 5 miles from Kolhâpur, and east from Panâlâ, is covered by "a labyrinth of temples and gateways." None of the present temples are of great age; the three principal ones are dedicated to Śiva or Kedâranâtha, and built of a fine blue basalt. The revenues of the establishment amount to Rs. 12,000, of which Sindhiâ pays Rs. 7,500. In the same hill are some old rock-cut cells.

III. 5. **Pa'wala Caves** near Jotibâ's hill consist of a large one about 34 feet square with 14 pillars, arranged as in the Koṇḍâṇe *vihâra* parallel to the three inner walls, in which have been 18 or 19 cells, several of them on the left side entirely destroyed,—and outside to the right are several other rooms or cells; to the left is a very irregular *chaitya*-cave, 31 feet deep and 16½ feet wide in front, with the remains of a *dâgoba*. The back of the room, however, is more nearly quadrantal than semi-circular. To the left of the entrance are other small apartments.

Eastwards near Alte is an old Jaina college, since occupied by the Brâhmaṇs. Alte also possesses some old temples (*Graham's Report*, p. 324).

III. 6. **Vis'algad**, 42 miles north-west from Kolhâpur and 12 west from Malkâpur (16° 55′ 73° 47′), formerly called Khelnâ. Whilst the Muhammadans held it, they added a gate and bastion called the Daulat Burj, which bears an **inscription**, about the date of which there is some doubt (*Graham's Kolhâpur*, p. 339; *Ind. Ant.*, vol. II. pp. 318, 372).

III. 7. **Ba'vada'gad**, about 36 miles south-west from Kolhâpur (16° 33′; 73° 53′), ascribed to Bhoja, son of Mârasiṁha Śilâhâra.

III. 8. **Palsambe**, 4 miles north-east from Bâvaḍâ (16° 34′; 73° 56′). In the bed of the river are three large blocks that have been hewn into little monolithic shrines. In the rock on the bank a larger shrine has been excavated for a *linga*, on which a spring pours its waters.

III. 9. **Sangse**, a mile south-west from Palsambe. In a hut temple of Śeshaśâyî is an image of a male recumbent figure, with a female seated at the feet.

III. 10. **Ranganagad**, about 18 miles north of Sâvantvâḍi, is also ascribed to Bhoja. It was a favourite resort of Śivâji's.

III. 11. **Bhudhargad**, about 42 miles south from Kolhâpur, dismantled after the revolt of 1844.

III. 12. **Samangad**, 14 miles east from Bhûdhargaḍ, was dismantled at the same time.

III. 13. **Ra'yaba'g**, about 50 miles south-east from Kolhâpur and about 14 miles north-east of Chikoḍi (16° 29′; 74° 50′). It is said to have been the capital of a Jaina principality in the 11th century, as were also Berud, Khelnâ and Sankeśvara. (1) The Jaina *basti* is said to be the oldest building in the place. It is of black stone, 76 ft. by 30 ft., with massive pillars supporting the roof (*Bom. Sel. CXV.*, p. 4). (2) Temple of Narasiṁha is an underground structure, 31 feet by 26 feet, with a modern *sabhâ-manḍapa* added above. The image is said to be very well carved. (3) Temple of Siddheśvara on the west side of the old village is 168 feet long by 136 wide; it is of black stone, much dilapidated, but now being repaired. (4) Temple of Someśvara is of *kurundi* or red stone richly worked, but falling to ruins. (5) The dome of Randullâ Khân is about 32 feet long, 20 wide, and 22 feet high. It is being destroyed by vegetation.

Inscriptions.—One on two slabs in the Jaina *basti*, dated *Śaka* 1124 (Graham's No. 9, pp. 330-415); a Persian one in Randullâ Khân's dome, stating that it was built by Abu Bakr Vazîr, and that it cost Rs. 10,300.

IIb. 14. **Khedra'pur** on the Krishṇâ, 30 miles east from Kolhâpur and 7 miles south-east of Kurundwâḍ (16° 37′; 74° 45′), held in *inâm* by the Svâmi of Saṅkeśvara. (1) The temple of Kopeśvara is a comparatively late structure of the style of the great temple in Kolhâpur city and that at Yeoat near Poona. Moreover, it has never been finished, save with rude brick and plaster in the most vulgar style. The workmanship, though elaborate and careful, lacks the finish, delicacy, and richness of design which are found in the older work. There is a clumsiness and stiffness in all the figure sculpture never found in the latter. Before the temple stands an unfinished open hall which would have been an imposing and ornate building had it been completed. It was intended that it should have had a magnificent domical ceiling, as a few lower courses of the moulding shew; but this unfinished top has been crowned, in later times, by a very ugly, low, crenelated, rough brick parapet in the very worst taste. The whole of the spire of the temple is of similar workmanship. This temple probably occupies the site of an older one, for fragments and pillars of a genuine old Châlukyan shrine lie about, and are built into the gateway to the temple enclosure and elsewhere. In the village at a short distance from this one is a small Jaina temple of about the same date, judging from the style. In the village of Jugal are some old pillars, but no sign whatever of any old temple having been built there.

Inscriptions:—By the south door of the great temple is a Devagiri Yâdava inscription of Siṁhadeva in *Devanâgarî* date *Śaka* 1135 (Graham's No. 10, pp. 418-424).

III. 15. **Bid** or Beraḍ on the Pañchgaṅgâ, 9 miles south-west from Kolhâpur (16° 39′; 74° 11′), is said to have been the capital of a chieftainship including Kolhâpur and Panâlâ. There are many ancient ruins about the place. An old stone temple exists in the village, the walls and columns with numerous mouldings in the style in vogue about A.D. 1200: small ancient gold coins are sometimes found about the old mud fort.

Inscriptions:—Under the image is a fragment of stone, bearing part of an old inscription. Another fragment is built into the wall. There are some inscriptions in a village 4 miles east of Kolhâpur close to the high road.

III. 16. **Herle**, about 7 miles north-east from Kholâpur on the road to Miraj.

I *b*. **Inscription**:—A Śilâhâra inscription on a stone in old Kânarese characters dated *Śaka* 1040, making a grant to a Jaina temple (Graham's No. 2, pp. 349-356).

III. 17. **Sirol,** 4 miles north of Kurundwâḍ (16° 44′; 74° 40′). "There are a few very sacred temples here in excellent preservation, and one especially called Bhojaputra and dedicated to Dattâtreya, an incarnation of Śiva" (*Graham's Report*, p. 324).

18. **Honur,** 8 miles south of Kâgal (16° 27′; 74° 20′).

III. **Inscription**:—Of Ballâḷadeva and Gandharâditya (Graham, No. 22).

19. **Savagaon,** 3 miles east of Kâgal.

III. **Inscription**:—On the *âsana* of the image of Pârśvanâtha in a Jaina temple (Graham, No. 18).

20. **Sidnorli,** 4 miles south-west from Kâgal. Temple of Siddheśvara.

III. **Inscription**:—Dated *Śaka* 1199, on a slab in the wall of the portico of the temple (Graham, No. 16).

21. **Bamni,** close to Śidnorli.

I *b*. **Inscription**:—In a Jaina temple, dated *Śaka* 1073 (Graham, No. 5).

"The territory throughout," says Graham, "teems with religious edifices, and every village is most amply supplied with temples, endowed with all the appliances in wood and stone requisite for the purposes of the grossest superstition."

MIRAJ,* &c.

III. 1. **Miraj,** 28 miles east from Kolhâpur (16° 50′; 74° 43′). *Dargâh* of Pîr Shamnamîr about 60 feet square, built of black stone and the dome of brick. The outer and inner courtyards are surrounded by corridors. Some verses from the Qurân are on the dome inside.

III. 2. **Mudhol,** 16 miles E.N.E. from Kalàdgi (16° 20′; 75° 21′). Two old granite temples in the Jaina style, dedicated to Śiva.

III. 3. **Loka'pur,** 8 miles E.S.E. from Kalàdgi. A temple of Lokanâtha of sandstone, of fair size but probably of no great age.

Inscription:—A short one.

III. 4. **Panchgaon,** 4 or 5 miles to the west of the village, on the high road from Belgaum to Kalâdgi, close to the roadside and apparently in Native States' territory, there is a small but typical temple, probably of Jaina origin, which will before long fall down if the sides, which are bulging out, are not repaired or propped up. At Pañchgâon itself there is a very small *liṅga* shrine of rather peculiar construction, and the remains of another like it beside it.

---

* Return of the Political Agent, Kolhâpur, No. 310, of 17th September 1879. For other remains in the Miraj territory, see under Dhârwâr Zilla, p. 150, "Lakshmeśvara".

APPENDIX.

INSCRIPTIONS FROM GUJARÂT.

The following inscriptions collected in Gujarât when these *Lists* were being printed originally, are here printed for future preservation. They have been transcribed from the facsimiles and translated by the late E. Rehatsek, Esq., M.C.E.

1. Inscriptions over the central *mihrâb* in Muḥâfiz Khân's mosque (*ante*, p. 68, No. (8)) :—

قال الله تبارک وتعالي ان المساجد الله فلا تدعوا مع الله احدا وفي الحديث من بنا لله
مسجدا بنا الله له قصرا في الجنة [بني] هذا العمارة في عهد السلطان السلاطين شمس الملوک
والحق ناصر الدنيا و الدين ابو الفتح محمود بن محمد شاه بن احمد شاه بن محمد شاه بن
المظفر السلطان لجمال الدين بن شيخ معين الدين بقريشي المخاطب من ذالک السطان
محافظ خان في الرابعه عشر من شهر رجب سنه سبع و تسعين وثمان مايه

Translation.

" Allâh, who be blessed and exalted, has said[1] and in the *Hadîth* [*the prophet has said*] :—' Who builds a mosque for Allâh, Allâh will build a castle for him in paradise.' This edifice [*was built*] in the reign of the Sulṭân of Sulṭâns, Shamsu'l-muluk wa'l-ḥaq Nâsiru'd-dunyâ wa'd-dîn Abu'l-Fatḥ Maḥmud, son of Muhammad Shâh, son of Aḥmad Shâh, son of Muhammad Shâh, son of Muzaffir the Sulṭân, for Jamâlu'd-dîn the son of Shaikh Mu'înu'd-din al- Quraishî, who received from the same Sulṭân the title of Muḥâfiz Khân; on the fourteenth of the month Rajab in the year eight hundred ninety-seven [13th May 1492]."

2. On the entrance to the court of Muḥâfiz Khân's mosque is the following :—

مسجد بهو دروازه را کشت باني • عجب مرد نيکو قطب خان ذو نامي
خدايا گناهش همه عفو کرده ان • نگه داريش از آفت آسماني

Translation.

" As the wonderfully good and renowned Quṭb Khân has become the architect of the mosque-gate, O God! pardon all his sins and preserve him from the calamity of heaven."

3. And on the other side of the entrance :—

تاريخ تا تکه که خير جاري
چون بمسجد از محافظ خان نيک • شد عجايب بر که شکر سرشت
سال تاريخش چو پرسيدم زغيب • گفت هاتف چشمۀ آب بهشت
۱۰۵۹

[1] Here follows *Qurân*, ch. LXXII. v. 18.

Translation.

"Chronogram of the auspiciously inaugurated *Tánkah*.
When in the mosque of the good Muḥâfiz Khân,
The wonderful reservoir of saccharine nature was completed,
I asked for the chronogram of the year from the invisible world.
A celestial herald replied:—'The fountain of paradise-water'
1059 [begun 15th January 1649]."

As some slight mistakes were made in Prof. Blochmann's decipherment of the inscriptions in Rânî Siprî's (p. 68, No. (4),) and Dastur Khân's (p. 69, No. (13),) mosques, when copied in 1874, the readings of these two inscriptions are here given afresh:—

4. From Dastur Khân's masjid[1]. :—

قال الله تبارك وتعالي وان المساجد الله فلا تدعوا مع الله احدا وقال النبي صلي الله عليه
وسلّم من بني مسجد الله بني الله مثله بيتا في الجنة عمرّ عمارة هذا المسجد الجامع في عهد سلطان
لسلاطين ناصر الدنيا والدين ابو الفتح محمود شاه بن محمّد شاه بن احمد شاه بن محمّد شاه
بن مظفر شاه السلطان العبد الراجي برحمة الله المالك الملك غني خاصه زاده المخاطب
من حضرة الاعلى والملجاء والمعلي بدستور الملك يديم الله معاليه ابتغاء لمرضات الله وطلبا
لجزيل ثوابه وكان العاشر من شهر شعبان سنه سابع وستين وثمانمايه من سنه النبي عمر

5. From Rânî Siprî's mosque :—

قال الله تبارك وتعالى وانّ المساجد الله فلا تدعوا مع الله احدا وقال النّبي صلّى الله عليه
وسلّم من بني مسجد اللّه تعالى بني اللّه له قصرا في الجنة بني المسجد في عصر السلطان
والاعظم المويد بتايئد الرحمن شمس الدنيا والدين ابو النصر مظفّر شاه بن محمود شاه بن
محمّد شاه بن احمد شاه بن محمّد شاه بن مظفر شاه السّلطان خلّد اللّه ملكه بانيه المسجد المذكور
والدة ابي بكر خان بن سلطان محمود شاه المسمّاة برانى سبرائني شهور سنه اربع خمسه
سنة العشرين وتسعمائه

6. Over the central *mihrâb* of Sayyid 'Alamu'd-dîn's masjid (p. 69, No. (14),) is the following inscription :—

كعبهٔ آسا ملم دولت دين مرب است * شهر ياري كه شهنشاه جهانش لقب است
لهٔ وقار وكرم ومكنتش اندرحست است * سيد عالم ابوبكر حسبى نيست است
[نه] صد و پانزده و غرهٔ ماه رجب است

[1] Copied by Shekh Ghulâm Ali bin Muhammad Ali Sâhib, the Nâ'ib Qâzi.

Translation.

"Like the *Ka'bah*, science is the glory of the Arab religion! The prince whose title is the Shahanshâh of the world. Whose dignity, generosity and power is under ground. Sayyid 'Alam Abu Bakr Hasbî is annihilated.

"It is the first of the month Rajab in [*nine*] hundred and fifteen" [26th October 1509].

7. On Quṭbu'd-dîn Shâh's Mosque[1] (*ante* p. 70, No. (18),) over the central *mihrâb*, is the following inscription, which however has been brought from elsewhere and inserted within the last few years :—

قال الله تبارک و تعالی ان المساجد لله فلا تدعوا مع الله احدا و قال النبي صلي الله
عليه وسلم من بني مسجد الله بني الله له بيتا في الجنة بني عمارة هذا المسجد في عهد
السلطان السلاطين غياث الدنيا والدين المجاهد محمد شاه ابن احمد شاه ابن محمد شاه بن المظفر
السلطان العبد المفتقر الي الله المستعان اعني نظام بن هلال السلطاني المخاطب بمختص الملک
ميمنة قرين ابتغاء لمرضات الله و طلباء لجزيل ثوابه وکان ذلک في التاريخ من هجرة النبو
سادس من شهر رمضان المبارک سنه ثلاثه و خمسين و ثمانمايه

Translation.

"Allâh, who be blessed and exalted, has said[2] :—'Verily the mosques belong to Allâh, therefore do ye not invoke any one with Allâh.' And the prophet, upon whom be the benediction of Allâh and peace, has said :—' Who builds a house for Allâh, Allâh will build a house for him in paradise.' The edifice of this mosque was constructed in the reign of the Sulṭân of Sulṭâns Ghiyâthu'd-dunyâ wa'd-din al-Muḥâmmad, Muḥammad Shâh, son of Ahmad Shâh, son of Muḥammad Shâh, son of Muzaffar the Sulṭân, by the slave who has need of the aid of Allâh. I mean by Nizâm the son of Halâllu's-Sulṭânî who bears the title of Mukhtisu'l-Mulk Maimanat-qarîn, desirous for the approbation of Allâh and hoping for his abundant reward. This was [indited] in the era from the exile of prophetship, on the the sixth of the blessed month Ramadân in the year eight hundred and fifty-three [24th October 1449]."

8. On Nawâb Shuja'at Khân's tomb (p. 70, No. (19),) is an inscription in which no name of the person buried is given ; it is as follows :—

بسم الله الرحمن الرحيم لا اله الا الله محمد رسول الله قل يا عبادي الذين سرفوا علي
انفسهم لا تقنطوا من رحمة الله ان الله يغفر الذنوب جميعا انه هو لغفور الرحيم تاريخ وفاته
الرابع عشر يوم الخميس في شهر صفر سنه الف و مايه الثلث عشر من الهجرة النبويه

---

[1] This has been taken from some other mosque and inserted over the central *mihrâb* within the last ten (now twenty) years. The original inscription had previously disappeared.—J. B.

[2] Here follows *Qurâ* , c. . LXII. v. 18.

Translation.

"In the name of Allâh, the merciful, the clement ! No God but Allâh, Muhammad the messenger of Allâh. Say, O my servants, who have transgressed against your own souls, despair not of the mercy of Allâh ; for Allâh pardons all sins, because he is forgiving and merciful.[1] Date of his decease, Thursday the fourteenth of the month of Safar, in the year one thousand one hundred and thirteen of the prophetic exile " [14th July 1701.]

9. The following inscription occurs over the central *mihrâb* of Bîbîjî's mosque at Râjâpur (*ante* p. 79, No. (102)) :—

قال الله تعالي و ان المساجد الله فلا تدعوا مع الله احدا و قال عليه السلام من بني
مسجد الله تعالي بني الله له بيتا في الجنة بني هذا المسجد الجامع الرفيع مخدومة جهان
ا من السطان الاعظم قطب الدنيا والدين ابو المظفر احمد شاه ابن محمد شاه ابن احمد شا
بن محمد شاه ابن مظفر السلطان وكان تاريخ بنا هذا مسجد من الهجرة ربيع الاخر سنه ثمانة
وخمسين و ثمانمايه

Translation.

"Allâh, who be exalted, said, 'Verily the mosques belong to Allâh, therefore do ye not invoke anyone with Allâh.'[2] And he to whom be salutation [*i. e.* Muḥammad] said :— 'Who builds a house for Allâh, be he exalted, Allâh will build a house for him in paradise'.[3] This noble Jami' mosque [*surnamed*] 'Mistress of the world' [*Makhdumat Jahân*] was built by the great Sultân Quṭbu'd-dunyâ wa'd-dîn Abu'l-Muzaffar Ahmad Shâh, son of Muḥammad Shâh, son of Aḥmad Shâh, son of Muhammad Shâh, son of Muzaffar the Sultân ; and the *Hijra* date of the building of the mosque is Rabî' II, in the year eight hundred fifty-eight " [April 1454].

10. On the east of the mosque is a *rauza*, with some good open lattice work, and containing a marble *qadr* or tomb on which are the following inscriptions round the base : (1) on the east side,—

قل اللهم مالک آلملک توتي الملک من تشاء وتنزع الملک ممن تشاء وتعا من تشاء
و تذل من تشاء بيدک الخير انک علي كل شي قدير [و] فاة ذوالقعد [ة] سنه احدي ستين
و ثمانمايه

Translation.

"Say, O Allâh, possessor of the kingdom ; thou givest the kingdom unto whom thou wilt, and thou takest away the kingdom from whom thou wilt ; thou exaltest whom thou wilt, and thou humblest whom thou wilt. In thy hand is good, for thou art almighty.[4]

---

[1] *Qurân*, ch. XXXIX. v. 54. [2] *Qurân*, ch. LXXII. v. 18. [3] In the *Hadith*. [4] *Qurân*, ch. III. v. 25.

Decease [*in the month of*] Dhu'l-Qa'dah in the year eight hundred and sixty-one." [October-November 1457.]

(2) On the west side,—

شهد الله انه لا اله الا هو والملايكه واولوا العلم قايما بالقسط لا اله الا هو لعزيز الحكيم
ان الدين عند الله الاسلام

Translation.

"Allâh hath borne witness that there is no God but he; and the angels and those who are endowed with knowledge [*profess the same*] dealing righteously. There is no God but he, the mighty, the wise. Verily the religion in the sight of Allâh is Islâm."[1]

(3) On the north end,—

الله لا اله الا هو الحي القيوم لا تاخذه سينة ولا نوم له ما في السموات وما في الارض
من ذالذي يشفع عنده الا باذنه يعلم ما بين ايديهم وما خلفهم ولا يحيطون بشي من علمه
الا بما شاء وسع كرسيه السموات والارض ولا يوده حفظهما وهو العلي العظيم

Translation.

"Allâh! there is no God but he; the living, the self-subsisting; neither slumber nor sleep seizeth him; to him belongeth whatever is in heaven and on earth. Who is he that can intercede with him except by his permission? He knoweth their present and their past, and they encompass nothing of his knowledge except so far as he pleaseth. His throne is extended over heaven and earth, and the preservation of both is no burden unto him. He is the high, the mighty."[2]

11. On the Queen Râjabâi's tomb at Sarkhej [*ante* p. 81, No. (5),] are the following inscriptions: (1) at the top,—

بسم الله الرحمن الرحيم نصر من الله وفتح قريب وبشر المومنين الله خير حافظا وهو
الرحم الراحمين يا حافظ لا اله الا الله محمد رسول الله

Translation.

"In the name of Allâh, the merciful, the clement! Assistance from Allâh and a speedy victory; and do thou bear glad tidings to the true believers.[3] Allâh is the best guardian; and is the most merciful of those that show mercy.[4] O guardian! no God but Allâh, Muhammad the messenger of Allâh!"

(2) At the bottom,—

تاريخ وفات راني رجباي سنه تسع وتسعين وتسعماية عرفه المشتهر با ببي سلطاني ۹۹۹

---

[1] *Qurân*, ch. III. v. 16 and beginning of v. 17.

[2] This is the whole of the celebrated Throne verse called *Ayyat-u'l-Kursi* of the *Qurân*, ch. II. v. 256, which is often also engraved on amulets and talismans worn on the person.

[3] *Qurân*, ch. LXI. v. 13.

[4] *Ibid*, ch. XII. v. 64.

Translation.

"Date of the decease of Rânî Râjabâi; year nine hundred ninety-nine (999). Her usually known name was Bibi Sultânî, A.H. 999" [began on the 30th October 1590.]

12. Inscription in the mosque in the Gâikwâd's Haveli. After the *Bismillâh* we have the usual LXXII. 18, from the *Qurân*, and the saying of the prophet about the house in paradise; then :—

بني المسجد في عصر سلطان الاعظم ناصر الدنيا والدين ابو الفتح محمود شاه بن احمد شاه
بن محمد شاه بن مظفر السلطان خلد الله ملكه قد مضي السادس عشر في شهر ذوالحجه سنه ٨٩٢

Translation.

"This mosque was built in the reign of the very great Sulṭân Nâsiru'd-dunyâ wa'd-din Abu'l Fatḥ Shâh, son of Muḥammad Shâh, son of Muzaffar the Sulṭân, may Allâh perpetuate his kingdom. Verily the sixteenth Dhu'l-Hijjah has elapsed. Year 892" [4th December 1487.]

13. Inscription in Bîbî Achut Kuki's mosque (p. 77, No. (93)). Exactly the same as the above, but after the words "may Allâh perpetuate," the conclusion "his kingdom" being omitted, we have :—

العبد الراجي لرحمة الله المالک الملک تهليجه سلطاني المخاطب من حضرت الاعلي
والملجاء المعلي بدستور الملک يديم الله معاليه ابتغاء لمرضات الله وطلباً الجزيل ثوابه وكان
ذلک في التاريخ من جمادي الخامس — سنه سته وسبعين وثمانمايه

Translation.

"By the worshipper hoping for the mercy of Allâh, the Mâlik Malik Tahlîjah[1] Sulṭâni, surnamed Dasturu'l-mulk by the exalted refuge [*i. e., the king*] may Allâh perpetuate his exaltation, desirous to obtain his abundant reward. And this was on the date of the fifth Jumâdâ......in the year eight hundred seventy-six" [19th October 1472.]

14. Inscription on Darvish 'Alî's mosque (p. 71, No. (23)) :—

No *Bismillâh*, but only LXXII. 18; then :—

هذا المسجد المبارک من شاه الاعظم بن محمود شاه بن محمد شاه بن احمد شاه بن
محمد شاه بن مظفر السلطان خلد الله ملكه و دولته — در ماه صفر و در سنه عشر و تسعمايه

Translation.

"This blessed mosque is of his majesty Shâh Maḥmud, son of Muḥammad Shâh, &c., [*as in the preceding two numbers*] may Allâh perpetuate his kingdom and prosperity...in the month Safar and in the year nine hundred and ten" [between 14th July and 12th August 1504.]

---

[1] No diacritical points, and therefore not certain.

15. Inscription in the court of Aḥmad Shâh's tomb (p. 147, No. (13)) :—

The following five Persian distiches, flanked by two vertical lines which contain the whole of the throne verse (II. 256) :—

در الف و شصت و شش بنهان کوتوالخان ٭ آمد برون و رفت خرامان سوی جنان
هفتم زماه شعبان بود است کان عزیز ٭ در زیر خاک کرد رخ سپر مه نهان
جز دانه نکوی اندر زمین نکشت ٭ آن حاتم زمانه بتوفیق مستعان
فیض عمیم او بهمه خلق چون رسید ٭ گویند ذکر خیرش تا شر انس و جان
ای خالق کریم برین تربت شریف ٭ باران لطف و رحمت از فضل بران

Translation.

"In one thousand sixty-six secretly Kutwâl Khân
Came out, and departed walking to the mansion of paradise.
It was the seventh of the month Sha'bân[1] when that beloved one
Concealed under ground his moon-like countenance ;
He sowed but good grain on the earth.
That Hâtim of the period, by the grace of the helpful [God]
As his universal bounty extended to all mankind ;
Even the wicked among men and genii praise him !
O gracious creator, upon this noble tomb
Pour the showers of mercy and reward."

16. Inscriptions on the tomb of Mr. Ballantyne's child, in the court of Aḥmad Shâh's tomb.

Superscription :—The *Kalimah*, then the following two Persian distiches,—

بتاریخ ششم بماه صیام ٭ بدار البقا کرد جوجس خرام
چنان گشته پر نور روضه بجانش ٭ کز مي برد رشک ماه تمام

Translation.

"On the sixth of the fasting month [Ramḍân]
To the mansion of eternity Jojes [Joseph ?] departed.
The *rauza* became so full with the light of his spirit
That the full moon bore him envy."

17. On a tomb in the court of Musâ Suhâgjî's mosque, between the city and camp :—

This is a double inscription ; the first part in English capital letters, thus,—

" To the memory of Subedâr Peer Khân. Order of merit XIV. Regiment, N. I., who died on the 19th July 1860, aged 55 years. This is erected as a token of respect by the officers of his regiment."

---

[1] Wednesday, 31st May 1656 A.D.

The second part is in Urdu but begins with the Arabic Kalimah, and corresponds to the English with the exception of the words "the Sâheb-loq of the regiment have given him much *abru*," which is not a happy rendering of "token of respect by the officers"; also the *Hijrah* date 1276 and 30th Dhu'l Hijah is added. The whole text is as follows:—

صوبیدار بهادر پیر خان چودوین رجمنت کے وفات پائي تاریع انیسوین ١٩ ماه
جولائي سنه ١٨٢٠ عیسوی عمر پنچاون برس کي تهي اور رجمنت کے صاحب لوگ انکو
نهایت آبرو بخشش کي تهي اور سنه ١٢٧٦ هجری تاریخ ان تیسبی ماه ذی الحج روز جمرات

18. Inscription in the Shâhpur mosque (p. 69, No. (15)):—

This consists of the following two Persian distiches, with the words حرره دوست محمد سکهر "written by Dust Muḥammad Sakhar" on the intersection of the bars which separate the lines in the shape of a cross surrounded by a frame:

قطب زمانه شیخ حسن ساخت مسجدی   کانجا کنند اهل عبادت دعای شیخ
چون شیخ این رفیع مکان را بنا نمود   تاریخ سال او شد رضا بنای شیخ

Translation.

"The axis of the period, Shaikh Hasan built a mosque,
That their religious people may pray for the Shaikh.
When the Shaikh built this exalted edifice
The date of it became *rfda bnay shaikh*."

19. Another inscription in the same mosque, in one long line, is broken in a few places, but contains *Qurân* IX. 18 complete, and nothing else.

20. Inscription in the Herâti mosque, near the Dehli gate (p. 160, No. (73)). This begins with *Qurân* LXXII. 18, followed by the usual saying of the prophet about the house in paradise; then we have:—

عمارت هذه المسجد الجامع في عهد السلطان الزمان ناصرالدنیا والدین ابوالفتح
محمود شاه بن محمد شاه بن احمد شاه بن محمد شاه بن مظفر شاه السلطان خلد الله ملکه
العبد الراجي الی رحمت الله المالک الملک غني — سلطاني المخاطب من الحضرة الاعلي
بملک البر و قوام الملک دام علوه ابتغا لمرضات الله و طالبا بجزیل ثوابه في التاریخ السادس
من ذو القعده سنة ثمانین و ثمانمایه

Translation.

"The construction of this blessed Jâmi' mosque [*took place*] in the reign of the reigning Sulṭân Nâsru'd-dunyâ wa'd-dîn Abu'l-Fatḥ Maḥmud Shâh, son of Muḥammad Shâh, &c.,... [2]May Allâh perpetuate his kingdom. By the worshipper hoping for the mercy

---

[1] The words in italics give 1254, which began on the 27th March 1838.

[2] Pedigree as in Dastur Khân's mosque, *Ind. Ant.* vol. IV. p. 291, in the mosque in the Gâikawad's Haveli, in Bibi Achut Kuki's mosque and in several others.

of Allâh, the Mâlik Malik Ghanî [*an illegible word*] Sulṭânî who received from his most exalted majesty the title of Maliku'l-barr and Qawwâmu'l-mulk, may his exaltation be permanent, desirous of the approbatiou of Allâh and craving for his abundant reward; on the sixth Dhu'l-Qa'dhah in the year eight hundred and eighty " [*4th March* 1476.]

21. Inscription in 'Inâyat Shâh's mosque,—a ruined brick *masjid* near the Shâhpur gate (p. 74, No. (47)).

It begins with *Qurân* LXXII. 18, like the above, but the usual saying of the prophet is omitted; then we have :—

الواثق بالله المنان ناصر الدنيا والدين ابو الفتح محمود شاه ابن لطيف شاه ابن مظفر شاه
ابن محمود شاه ابن محمد شاه ابن احمد شاه ابن مظفر شاه السلطان بهر طاعت ساخت مسجد
شمس خان بهر خدا بود نه صد و شش وجد تاريخ اين سال بنا كتبه عبد الحي بن علي

Translation.

" The confider in the gracious Allâh, Nâsiru'd-dunyâ wa'd-dîn Abu'l-Fath Mahmud Shâh, son of Latîf Shâh, son of Muzaffar Shâh, son of Muhammd Shâh, son of Ahmad Shâh, son of Muhammad Shâh, son of Muzaffar Shâh the Sulṭan. For the sake of worship Shams Khân built the mosque for God. The year nine hundred and six was found to be the date of the building [*Began 28th July* 1500]. Written by 'Abu'l-Haiy, the son of 'Alî."

22. An inscription over the central *mihrâb* of mosque behind Shâh Aliji's *Rauza* (p. 73, No. (37)) contains only *Qurân* LXXII. 18.

23. Over the left *mihrâb*, Shâh Aliji's mosque, Rohilwâḍa :—

This is a rather ugly specimen of writing, but appears to contain the pedigree of the prophet, and terminates with a date. As however in the trouble of decipherment *le jeu ne vaudrait pas la chandelle*, only the beginning is here given :—

محمد رسول الله صلى الله عليه وسلم بن عبد الله بن عبد المطلب بن هاشم بن عبد مناف
بن قصى بن—

Translation,

" Muhammad the messenger of Allâh, upon whom be the benediction of Allâh and peace, [*was the*] son of 'Abdu'llah [*who was the*] son of 'Abdu'l-Muṭallab [*who was the*] son of Hâshim [*who was the*] son of 'Abd Munâf [*who was the*] son of Qusaiy [*who was the*] son of..."

The first half of the last line is :—

سنه احدي و ستين و تسعمايه

" Year nine hundred and sixty " [*Began 18th December* 1552.]

24. Over the right *mihráb*, in the Sháh Aliji's mosque, Rohilwáda.

This contains nothing but the pedigree of the penultimate king Ahmad, thus :—

المعتصم بالله الرحمن غياث الدنيا والدين ابو المحامد احمد شاه ابن عم محمود شاه
بن لطيف شاه اخ بهادر شاه بن مظفر شاه بن محمود شاه ابن محمد شاه بن احمد بن محمد
بن مظفر السلطان خلد ملكه

Translation.

"The securely trustful in Alláh the merciful, defender of the world and of the religion, possessor of laudable qualities, Ahmad Sháh, cousin of Mahmud Sháh [III], son of Latif Sháh, the brother of Bahádur Sháh,[1] the son of Muzaffar Sháh [II], son of Mahmud [*surnamed Bigarah*] Sháh, son of Muhammad Sháh [II] son of Ahmad Sháh [I], son of Muhammad Sháh [I], son of Muzaffar Sháh [I] the Sultán, may his kingdom be perpetuated."

Then come two distiches in mixed language which I am not bold enough either to transcribe or to translate, but give only the chronogram embodied in the last distich :—

مسجد جامع كي بيچ بتهايا نبي نور

As Ahmad, the penultimate king of Gujarát, who began to reign A.H. 961 [began 7th December 1553] was only eight years on the throne, and the kingdom was finally annexed to the dominions of the Mughal emperor Akbar in 969 [began 11th September 1561], the inscription appears to have been made even after the reign of the last king of Gujarát, Muzaffar Sháh III.

25. In the small mosque of Musa Suhág on the right side of the road to the camp (see above No. 17) :—

بسم الله الرحمن الرحيم انما يعمر مساجد الله من آمن بالله واليوم الاخر واقام الصّلوة
واتي الذكوة ولم يخش الا الله فعسي اوليك ان يكونو امن المهتدين قال رسول الله
صلي الله عليه واله وسلم من بني لله مسجدا بني الله تعالي له بيتا في الجنة كتبه جلال
في سنه ١١٠٢

Translation.

The *Bismilláh*; then IX. 18 of *Qurán* complete; then the usual saying of the prophet that Alláh will build a house in paradise for him who builds a mosque for Alláh. Lastly:— "Written by Jalál, in the year 1102" [Began 5th October 1690.]

---

[1] Who was slain by the Portuguese in the island of Diu on the 14th February 1537, as described by me in my Article in the *Calcutta Review* (January 1882) "How the Portuguese obtained a footing in the island of Diu." —E. R.

Then the following two Persian distiches :—

چون بتوفیق یزدی جعفر * ساخت مسجد بزیب و زینت و ساز
گفت احمد برای تاریخش * کرد آراسته مکان نماز

1100 | 7 40 50   50 1 20 40   5 400 60 1 200 1   4 200 20

Translation.

" When by divine grace Ja'far
Built a mosque with elegant arrangements
Aḥmad said for the date of it:—
He adorned the place of prayer."

The last hemistich gives the number 1100, and beneath the inscription we read :—" Year 1100."

26. Arabic inscription on Dâdâ Harîr's Vâv or step-well (p. 80, No. (110)).

It will be seen from the inscription that this Vâv was constructed during the reign of the same King Maḥmud, surnamed Bigarah, under whose sway the Herâti mosque, that in the Gâikwâḍ's Haveli, Bîbî Achut Kuki's, Dastur Khân's, and others were built. The illegible portion of this inscription probably contained the name of this king's Vazîr, Mâlik Malîk Ghânî, which likewise occurs with variations in other inscriptions. What the figures 26 below may mean is unknown.

بني هذه العمارة الظريفه والبقعه الشريفه
والرواق الرفيعه والجدر الاربعته المصورة وغرس
الاشجار المثمرة بالفواكهته مع البير والبركه
لينفع الناس وخدمة في عهد سلطان سلاطين
الزمان الواثق بتايد الرحمن ناصر الدنيا والدين ابوالفتح
محمود شاه بن محمد شاه بن احمد شاه بن محمد شاه بن مظفر شاه
السلطان خلد الله ملكه [حرير سلطاني التي
جعلها الحضرة العلية خاوطته الباير الدار]
المحروسته في الثاني من جماد الاول سنه سته وتسعين وتسعمايه
٢٦

Translation.

" This elegant building with the noble arrangement, the lofty gallery, the four walls with pictorial ornaments, was constructed, and the productive fruit trees were planted, and the well with the reservoir provided, for the benefit and service of the people, in the reign of the Sulṭân of Sulṭâns of the period, who trusts in the aid of the merciful [*the Creator*], Nâsiru'd-dunyâ wa'd-din Abu'l-Fath Maḥmud Shâh, son of Muḥammad Shâh, son of Ahmad Shâh, son of Muhammad Shâh, son of Muzaffar the Sulṭân, may Allâh perpetuate his kingdom......[*some broken words*] the well guarded. On the second of the month Jumâdâ I, in the year eight hundred ninety-six " [13th March 1491.]

27. Sanskrit inscription on the left side of the same well :—

1. नमः सृष्टिकर्त्रे । नमोपांपतये तुभ्यं सर्वजीवनरू-
2. पिणे । वरुणाय नमस्तुभ्यं नमः सुकृतसाक्षिणे १
3. जयति जगत्रयजननी कुंडिलिनी नामतः परा श-
4. क्तिः । सुरनरवंदितचरणा वापीरूपात्मना सततं । २
5. नमामि विश्वकमर्णि (र्माणं) सकलाभीष्टदायकं । कृपातो
6. यस्य सर्वे स्युः कर्तुं कर्म्म कर्तें[1] क्षमा नराः ॥ ३ स्वस्तिश्री
7. गूर्ज्जरधरित्र्यां श्रीमदहिम्मदवादनगरे पातुसा-
8. ह श्री श्री श्रीमहमूदविजयराज्ये राज्ञोंऽतःपुरद्वारि स-
9. र्वाधिकारिणी बाई श्री हरीरनाम्नी श्रीनगरादीशान-
10. दिगाश्रितहरीरपुरमध्ये चतुर्दिगायातानेकतृषा ।
11. कुलमनुष्यपशुपक्षिवृक्षादिचतुरशीतिलक्षजी-
12. वोपभोगायपरमेश्वरप्रीत्यर्थं संवत १९१६ वर्षे शा-
13. कि[2] १४२१ प्रवर्तमाने पौषशुदि १३ सोमे वापीं कार-
14. यामास । यस्यामगाधामृतपानीयराशिमवलो-
15. क्य क्षीरोदधिर्निवासमकरोदिव । सा स्वेदजांड-
16. जोद्भिज्जजरायुजपोषणार्थमाचंद्रार्कं स्थिरा भू-
17. यात् । तत्र व्ययीकृतद्रव्यसंख्या ३१९००० सर्व
18. महमूद महीपालमंत्रिमुख्या प्रतापिनी । धर्म्मार्थिनी हरीरा-
19. ख्या वापीमिषमचीकरत् । चतुष्पथे चरच्चारुचतुर्दिग्ज-
20. नसंकुले आचंद्रार्कमियं वापी मधुरा पीयतां जनैः । २
21. दुर्गाणि पुण्यानारामान् शतशश्च जराशयान्[3] । पदे
22. पदे च सत्राणि धनिनः संति शोभनाः । ३ महाधनव्य-
23. यं कृत्वा विश्वोपकृतिहेतवे । बाई श्रीहरीरनाम्नी वा-
24. पीमियमचीकरत् । ४ वापीनिर्माणेऽधिकारी परमेश्वराज-
25. पालकमलक श्रीबिहामद तथा गजधरवैश्यसूत्र०वीरात-
26. थाज्ञाकर सू० देवा श्रीगिरणामहंसाया आतथामहंवीरा

Translation.

"Salutation to the Maker of creation![4] Salutation to thee, thou lord of the waters, Varuṇa! who art the cause of the forms of all living beings, who dost witness all deeds. (2) The supreme Śakti named Kuṇḍalinî, the mother of the three worlds, whose feet are worshipped by gods and men,—ever conquers in the world in the form of a well. (3) I adore Viśvakarman, the giver of all blessings, through whose compassion all men are able to perform their actions. Hail! in the holy Gurjjara, in the holy city of Aḥmadâbâd, the victorious kingdom of the Pâdshâh Śrî Śrî Śrî Muhammad—there the Bâî, named Harîra, the chief superintendent at the gate of the king's palace,—in the middle of Harîrapura, situated to the north-east of Śrînagara,—through (*pity for*) the thirst of the many coming from the four quarters, for the enjoyment of the eighty-four *lâkhs* of beings—of men, beasts, birds, trees, &c., and in honour of Parameśvara,—in the current *Saṁvat* year

---

[1] This word has no meaning here. [2] Should be शाके. [3] Should be जलाशयान्.

[4] *Srishṭikartrî* literally means the *maker of creation*, *i. e.* the Creator.

1556, and of *Śaka* 1421, on Monday the 13th of the bright half of Pausha, (*the Bâî*) caused a well to be made, wherein, seeing the deep volume of ambrosial water, the milky ocean, as it were, took up its abode.

"May it be established as long as the Sun and Moon endure for the sake of sustaining beings taking birth from sweat, eggs, the soil, and the womb. The money spent upon the well is 3,19,000.[1] The illustrious and charitable chief minister of the king Mahmûd, named Harîra, caused this well to be made. May this sweet well, pleasing to wayfarers coming from the four directions, be drunk by men, while the Sun and Moon endure. Forts, holy groves, tanks by the hundred, choultries at every step, are the pride of rich men; this Bâî, named Śrî Harîra, for the benefit of the whole world, having incurred an expenditure of much treasure, caused the well to be made. The manager in the making of the well (*was*) Bihâmad the executor of the orders of the great king......."[2]

28. Inscription on the north side of the corridor in the Jami' mosque (p. 145, No. (8)). This consists of the following six Persian distiches:—

ندیده دهر جز میرک حسن کسی • که ذاتش باعث هر مدح باشد
بکار خلق خلقش در رکا پوست • بملک خیر سعیش پیشوا شد
بسان حوض کوثر برکه ساخت • که کوثر دیدنش را رونما شد
مگر آینه اسکندرست این • که سر تا پا همه نور و صفا شد
اگر زمزم نشد در لطف و پاکی • درش چون کعبه حاجت روا شد
پی سال بنایش گفت فایض • صفا برکه میرک ز ما شد

1,020 | 4 300 1 40 7 20 200 10 40 5 20 200 2 1 80 90

Translation.

"This age has seen no one except Mîrak Hasan,
Whose character has become the occasion for every praise;
His whole nature is engrossed with the affairs of the people.
In the realm of beneficence his efforts have become exemplary;
He made this reservoir resembling the basin Kauthar [*in paradise*],
Which stands forth as the image thereof.
Is this perchance the [*wonderful*] speculum of Iskandar [*Alexander*]?
From top to bottom all light and purity.
If it has not become like the Zamzam in pleasantness and limpidity,
It is [*nevertheless*] accessible like the Ka'bah of necessity [*the throne of God to whom all the necessitous may apply*].
Of the year of its construction Fâ'id said:—
The purity of Mîrak's reservoir was effected by us."

[This last hemistich gives 1020, which year began 16th March 1611.]

---

1 The coin is not mentioned.

2 The last two lines contain some abbreviated words, and are incomplete; they are left untranslated.

29. On a doorway near Shâh Âliji's in Rohilwâd, Aḥmadâbâd (p. 78, No. (37)) :—

Above, some very large characters which may be read الله في محمد "Allâh fee Muḥammad." Below are a number of words indistinctly jumbled together in one mass.

30. Inscription in the gateway of the Bhadr :—

This inscription consists of six distiches, about 5 feet long and 1½ broad. Each hemistich stands in a separate compartment and was carved in *relievo* in large beautifully flowing Persian characters, but appears to have been purposely defaced by some Vandal. Whether accidentally or not, the most legible words are only two, which seem to read بيت ظلم *"house of tyranny."* Fortunately the date 1032 being on the margin, outside, was also left untouched ; that year began on the 5th November 1622 when the kingdom of Gujarât had lost its independence, and had been already 52 years annexed to the Mughal empire.

31. Inscription from the entrance to the jail at Aḥmadâbâd :—

همایون جاه سلطان ابن سلطان • یکی صاحب پرست از بندگانش
که هست از جان و دل منقاد فرمان • بهار عدل اعظم خان غازي
که تیغش کشت جسم ملک را جان • سرائی کرد در گجرات بنیاد
که مثلش را ندیده چشم دوران • زهي عالی بنا کزروی رفعت
گذشته پایه قدرش ز کیوان • بخوبي و لطافت چون بهشت است
بدرباني او شائسته رضوان • سرا و قیصریه یافت اتمام
بامر خان عادل نقد مردان • زهاتف سال تاریخش چو جستم
ندا آمد مکان خیر و احسان
۱۰۴۷

Translation.

"Humâyun jâh Sulṭân son of a Sulṭân
One of his servants, obeying companions,
Who with soul and heart is subject to command,
The spring of justice 'Azam' Khân Ghâzî,
Whose sword has become the soul of the body of the realm,
Has built a *sarâi* in Gujarât
The like of which the vision of the period has not beheld,
Bravo ! For the high edifice which in altitude
Has excelled Saturn by the basis of its excellence.
In beauty and gracefulness it is like paradise,
Riḍván [*the gate-keeper of paradise*] is worthy to be its porter.
The top of it has received a complete Qaisariyah
By order of Khân' Âdil the jewel of men.
When of the invisible herald I asked for the chronogram,
The exclamation came :—Place of goodness and beneficence."
1047 [Began 26th May 1637].

32. In the Borah mosque in Nova Mohallâh, on a marble slab (p. 74, No. (45)).

This inscription belongs to the reign of Ahmad, the founder of Ahmadâbâd and of Ahmadnagar; several mosques of Ahmadâbâd were also built during his reign, and it is not improbable that this was carried off from one of them and placed here.

The inscription begins with a Persian distich, and the whole of it is in that language as follows:—

یک ذرّه عنایت تو اي بنده نواز • بهتر ز هزار ساله خیرست و نماز
در ایام دولت و نوبت سلط خلیفه العهد و الزمان الواثق المستعان بالله ناصر الدنیا
والدین ابوالفتح احمد شاه بن محمد بن مظفر شاه السلطان خلد خلافته وبدّ رافته عمارت کرده
این بیت و بقعه شریف لطیف لله بندهٔ اُمیدوار برحمت افریدگار حقیر ضعیف عالمگیر
نوزدهم محرم الحرام سنه سته وعشرین وثمانمایه

Translation.

"One atom of Thy grace, O cherisher of [*thy*] servants,
Is better than a thousand years of gifts and prayers."

During the reign of the Khalîfah of the period who trusts in and asks help from Allâh Nâsiru'd-dunyâ wa'd-din Abu'l-Fath Ahmad, son of Muhammad Shâh, son of Muzaffar Shâh the Sulṭân, may his Khalîfate be perpetuated and his clemency spread, this house and noble, graceful locality was built for [*the worship of*] Allâh, by the mean, feeble adorer 'Âlamgir who hopes for the mercy of the Creator. The nineteenth of the sacred month Muharram, in the year eight hundred and twenty-six" [24th December 1423].

33. In the Nova Mohallâh mosque, right hand. It will be seen that this inscription belongs to the reign of Mahmûd [Bigarah] whose name occurs on so many others. There is no *Bismillâh*, but only *Qurân* LXXII. 18, with the usual saying of the prophet about the house in paradise. Then:—

عمل السلطان الاعظم ناصر الدنیا والدین ابوالفتح محمود بن محمد شاه بن احمد شاه
بن محمد شاه بن مظفر شاه السلطان خلد الله خلافته — ثمان عشر بتاریخ المحرم سنه سته
وتسعین وثمانمایه

Translation.

"The work of the great Sulṭân, defender of the world and of the religion, possessor of victory, Maḥmûd, son of Muḥammad Shâh, son of Aḥmad Shâh, son of Muḥammad Shâh, son of Muzaffar Shâh the Sulṭân, may Allâh perpetuate his Khalifate......[*illegible*]. Eighteenth of the month of Muḥarram in the year eight hundred and ninety-six" [2nd December 1490].

34. In Pîr Muḥammad Shâh's mosque:—

This is a distich with the *Kalimah* prefixed, and the name of a person with the date appended, thus :—

لا اله الا الله محمد رسول الله

چراغ و مسجد و محراب و منبر ٭ ابوبکر و عمر و عثمان و حیدر

Translation.

"No god but Allâh, Muhammad messenger of Allâh
Lamp and mosque and *mihrâb* and pulpit
Abu Bakr and 'Umar and 'Uthmân and Haidar [*i. e.* 'Ali]
Hadrat Mîr Maḥiu'd-din. Year 1135" [Begun 12th October 1722].

35. In Pîr Muḥammad Shâh's mosque. This consists of two Persian distiches between which the writer's name is inserted as well as the date, but for the sake of distinctness that line is given the last in the following transcript :—

خوشا مسجدي ساخت سيّد محمد ٭ كه مردي توانكرد ياد خليلي

سزد كر كعبه كني تو اماني ٭ كه تاريخ او كشته بيت خليلي

كاتبه عبد الرحمن سنه ۱۰۹۲

Translation.

"Sayyid Muḥammad built an elegant mosque
In which the most glorious [God] may be worshipped.
It is proper for thee to trust in the Ka'bah
The date whereof is :—*Bait Khalili.*
The writer of it was 'Abdu'r-raḥman, year 1092."

This date is also the numerical value of the two last words, and their meaning is :— *House of Khalîlî*, namely of *Abraham* in his capacity of the *Khalîlî*, namely *friend* of God.

36. Left of central *mihrâb*, Pîr Muḥammad's mosque ;—

لا اله الا الله محمد رسول الله بحق ابوبكر و عمر و عثمان على آلهي خير جاي باد

سنه ۱۰۷۷

Translation.

"No God but Allâh, Muḥammad the messenger of Allâh. May it be prosperously inaugurated O Allâh ! by the merits of Abu Bakr, and Umar, and Uthmân, and Alî. In the year 1077 [Began 4th July 1666]."

37. Over a window to the left of the central *mihrâb*, in Pîr Muḥammad's mosque :—

نماند بعصيان كسي در كرو ٭ كه دارد چنين سيدی پيش رو

نپندارم كه سعدی را بيازاری وبكذاري ٭ كه اوجز سايه لطفش ندارد درجهان جائے

Translation.

"No one remains plunged in sin who has such a Sayyid for his guide; I do not think you will injure and abandon Sa'dî, for he has in the world no other place, but the shadow of his favour."

38. At Shâh 'Alam, over the door of the tomb (p. 147, No. (24) :—

This is a wretched doggrel composition which contains no date nor information of any kind, and the beginning of it is quite sufficient for insertion in this place. It is as follows :—

بسم الله الرحمن الرحيم المنة چون جنة رسولاباد جاي للنسان قد تعالي انعم وفيها
علامات الجنان اي دار روي الجنة الفردوس ببين روضه بزيور شاه عالم ماهِ جهان

Translation.

After the *Bismillâh* :—"Beneficence is like paradise. Rasulâbâd is a place verily bestowed by the Most High (God) upon man; it contains characteristics of the garden, that is to say the abode of the face of the *jinnat* of paradise. Behold the adorned *rauza* of Shâh 'Alam, moon of the universe. [Then follows a description of the beauties of the garden, &c.]

39. Round a tomb in the second *rauza* at Shâh 'Alam :—
The follwing two Persian lines make together a distich ;—

صد شکر کہ شد خاک سرم درقدم دوست • این عیش کہ دارد کہ مرا درقدم اوست

Translation.

"A hundred thanks, that my head has become the dust at the feet of the friend [*i.e.*, at the feet of God].

"Who has this life like that which I have at his feet."

40. Round the railing of the great tomb at Shâh 'Alam :—

بسم الله الرحمن الرحيم شاه عالم ماه عالم نور عالم سرور عالم بادشاه عالم سخي عالم
مهربان عالم سيد عالم بخاری عالم خواجه عالم درويش عالم شيخ عالم مخدوم عالم
امير عالم ولي عالم عالم اوليا عالم عالم مير عالم كبير عالم عالم قطب اقطاب عالم
غوث عالم مغيث عالم هادي عالم خاص عالم شرف عالم اعظم عالم اكرم عالم نص عالم
اخص خواص عالم اول عالم آخر عالم ظاهر عالم باطن عالم حاضر عالم ناظر عالم واصل عالم
كامل عالم مكارم عالم عالم عالم عالم عالم قصد عالم مقصود عالم سجاد عالم
محب عالم محبوب عالم عالم عالم عالم عالم عالم عالم عالم عالم عالم عالم
عالم عالم عالم عالم صادر عالم عالم عالم عالم عالم عالم محمود عالم عالم
معز عالم معين عالم علامه عالم علو عالم محسن عالم حمت عالم خير عالم حسن عالم عالم

لازم جليل عالم حاج عالم لطيف عالم لطف عالم حامد عالم حميد عالم مقرب عالم مخ عالم
فرح عالم شوق عالم خليل عالم مجيب عالم معرب عالم عارف عالم پناه عالم برهان عالم
حجت عالم

Translation.

"In the name of Allâh, the merciful, the clement! Shâh of the world, moon of the world, light of the world, server of the world, Bâdshâh of the world, the liberal of the world, the benevolent of the world, the Sayyid of the world, the Bukhârî of the world, the Kh'âjâh of the world, the Darvîsh of the world, the Shekh of the world, the served by the world, the Amîr of the world, the Walî of the world, the Avliâ of the world, the chief of the world, the great one of the world, world, the axis of the axes of the world, the implored of the world, the aid of the world, the director of the world, the paragon of the world, the most noble of the world, the most great of the world, the most generous of the world, the beazle of the world, the most exquisite of the exquisites of the world, the first of the world, the last of the world, the extension of the world, the interior of the world, the present one of the world, the supervisor of the world, the arrived of the world, the perfect one of the world, the honour of the world, world, world, world, world, world, the intention of the world, the wished-for of the world, the prayer carpet of the world, the lover of the world, the beloved of the world [*the word* world *repeated* 17 *times*], the arising of the world [5 *times* world], the praised one of the world, world, the honour of the world, the assistance of the world, the 'Ullâmah of the world, the exalted benefactor of the world, the mercy of the world, the benefit of the world, the beauty of the world, world, world, the glorious one of the world, the Hâjj of the world, the gracious one of the world, the grace of the world, the praiser of the world, the praised of the world, the implored one of the world, the marrow of the world, the joy of the world, the ardent desire of the world, the friend of the world, the answerer of the world, the Arabiser of the world, the 'Arif of the world, the asylum of the world, the argument of the world, the evidence of the world."

41. Over the central *mihrâb* of the mosque at Batwâ (p. 81, (No. 3)) :—

This inscription is of the reign of Maḥmûd [Bîgarah]. Like so many others it has no *Bismillâh,* and begins with *Qurân* LXXI. 18, followed by the usual saying of the prophet about the house in paradise; then we have :—

امر عمارت هذه المسجد الجامع المبارک في عهد ناصر الدنيا والدين ابو الفتح محمود
بن محمد شاه بن احمد شاه بن محمد بن مظفر شاه السلطان بسعي العبد الراجي الي رحمت الله
بشير سلطاني خواجه المخاطب من الحضرة الا علي بخواص الملک — بني في عشر صفر سنه
اربع و سبعين و ثمانمايه

Translation.

"The edifice of this blessed Jâmi' mosque was renewed during the reign of the protector of the world and of the religion, the possessor of victory, Maḥmûd son of Muḥammad Shâh, son of Aḥmad Shâh, son of Muḥammad, son of Muzaffar Shâh the Sulṭân, by the efforts of the worshipper hopeful of the mercy of Allâh, Bashîr Sulṭânî Khâjah who obtained from his most exalted majesty the title of Khâsu'l-mulk [*one word is not clear*]. Built on the tenth Safar, year eight hundred and seventy-four " [10th August 1469].

42. Inscription inside Batwâ mosque :—

درین جاه سنگ هاي خاره مدفون است

Translation.

" In this well gravel is buried."

43. An inscription on a loose stone at Batwâ consists of the following three Persian distiches :—

بعهد دولت شایسته خاني * که زو کشته بناي دین موسس
بتوفیق الهي ناظر ادراک * نموده مسجد با حوض نفیس
پي سال بنایش گفت هادي * بگو مسجد شده بیت المقدس
سنه ۱۰۶۳

Translation.

" During the incumbency of governor Shâyistah Khân
Who laid the foundation of the edifice of religion,
By the divine grace the spectator has
Beheld the mosque with the exquisite reservoir.
Concerning the year of its construction the guide said,
Say :—*The mosque has become the holy house* [*i. e.* Jerusalem]
Year 1063."

The numerical value in the last hemistich gives 1064, whereas the figures sculptured are 1063, which latter year began on the 2nd December 1652.

44. On a loose stone No. 2 at Batwâ, after the *Bismillâh* we have *Qurân* LXXII. 18, and then the following Persian line, which makes a distich :—

منور شد جهان زین چهار گوهر * ابوبکر و عمر و عثمان حیدر

Translation.

" The universe was illuminated by these four jewels,
Abu Bakr and 'Umar and 'Uthmân, Haidar."

45. On a pillar of the porch of the great *rauza* at Batwâ :—

This consists of the following two Persian distiches with the name of their maker under them as follows :—

قطب عالم که هست شاه افلاک * از روضه فزود جاه افلاک
زین پیش کلاه آسمان بي سربود * شد گنبذ او سر کلاه افلاک
خانه زاد این درگاه جلال بن محمد بن جلال شاهي گفته

Translation.

"Quṭb 'Alam who is sovereign of the spheres
Has by the *rauza* augmented the glory of the spheres.
Ere this the vault of the sky had no crown;
His *Gunbad* [sepulchral cupola] became the crown of the spheres.
Composed by the born slave of the family Jalâl *bin* Muhammad *bin* Jalâl Shâhî."

The following four inscriptions (46—49) are from 'Abdu'l-Wahhâb's mosque (p. 73, No. (40)):—

46. Over the left *mihrâb* we have again the usual saying of the prophet about the house in paradise; but as it occurs here in a more elaborate form than hitherto, it may not be quite superfluous to insert the whole of the inscription:—

بسم الله الرحمن الرحيم قال النبي صلي الله عليه وسلم من بني لله تعالي بيتا بني
يعبد فيه الله من مال حلال الله تعالي له بيتا في الجنة من درّة و ياقوت

Translation.

"In the name of Allâh the merciful, the clement! The prophet, may Allâh bless and keep him! has said:—Who builds from lawfully acquired property, for Allâh, be He exalted! a house in which Allâh may be worshipped, Allâh, be He exalted! has built for him in paradise a house of pearls and rubies."

47. A Persian distich:—

مريد و معتقد حضرت محي الدين • بصدق خواجه شهباز تاكه دهر بود

Translation.

"A disciple and confidential of Hadrat Mahîu'd-dîn
In truth Khâjah Shâhbâz as the world will exist."

48. A Persian distich:—

بروضه فرح افزاي شاه غياث الدين • ملک سريرت سيد جليل فيض درود

Translation.

"To the joy augmenting *rauza* of Shâh Ghiyâthu'd-dîn
Malik Sarîrat Sayyid Jalîl abundance of greetings."

49. A Persian distich:—

برخصت و برضاي شد اماجد دين • از آنچه باشدن را طريق حق نمود

Translation.

"With permission and approval Amâjid Dîn departed
With what appeared the proper way of his departure."

The preceding three inscriptions, now on loose slabs, evidently constitute one piece, which is however not satisfactory either in meaning or in style, as must be evident also from the English translation.

50. Two Persian distiches :—

چو رکن الحق از دار دنیا برفت • بیک لحظه در ظل طوبا برفت
خبر داد هاتف ز سال وصال • از ینجا بفردوس اعلا برفت
سنه ۱۲۰۰

Translation.

" When Ruknul-haqq [*pillar of the truth*] from the mansion of the world went,
In a moment he into the shade of the Tabâ [*name of a tree in paradise*] went,
An invisible herald gave notice of the year of the arrival :—

Hence to the highest paradise he went. Year 1200" [4th Nov. 1785—3rd Oct. 1786.]

51. On a fallen stone in Bâbâ Lului's Rauza (p. 78, No. (99)) :—

بسم الله الرحمن الرحيم
لا اله الا الله محمد رسول الله • محمد علي فاطمه حسين حسن
خود کفت تاریخ آن بنت زهرا • مخیر که بس بود باخیر شد
سنه ۱۱۱۷
والدهٔ محمد جعفر ولد سید محمد علي بن سید محمود سادات باره ساکن کیهتوره ٥

Translation.

" In the name of Allâh, the merciful, the clement ! No God but Allâh, Muhammad the messenger of Allâh, Muhammad, 'Alî, Fâṭimah, Husain, Hasain. That daughter of Zuhrâ [*planet Venus*] has herself pronounced the chronogram; the option which was sufficient *was completed well*. Year 1117. The mother of Muḥammad Ja'far, son of Sayyid Muḥammad 'Alî, son of Sayyid Maḥmûd Sâdât Bârah, inhabitant of Kîhtûrah."

The above-named year 1117 began on the 25th April 1705, and the three last words با خير شد constitute the chronogram.

52. Two Persian distiches on a Qâdhi's tomb near the Madrassah give in the last hemistich a chronogram, but as the piece is rather obliterated, and requires guesses, I shall not attempt to translate it; it appears to be one of value.

53. In Quṭb Shâh Divân's masjid near the Kâch Masjid in Aḥmadâbâd :—

بسم الله الرحمن الرحيم ادخلوها بسلام امنين بعهد دولت قاهره و ايام مملكت به
خسرو تاجدا خديو نامدار سلطان
السلاطين زمان ماحي كفر و طغيان ناصر الدنيا والدين احمد شاه بن محمد شاه
بن مظفر شاه السلطان بن السلطان بن السطان خلد الله ملكه

زاید دولته و سلطنته بنا کرد این مقبره را بنده امیدوار برحمت پروردگار قطب بن خواجکی

اتمام این خیر مبرور برائي نیل سرور. در ماه محرم

Translation.

"In the name of Allâh, the merciful, the clement: 'Enter ye therein in peace and security.' [*Qurân, sûrah* XV. v. 46.] During the period of the conquering monarchy and in the days of the permanent reign of the crown-wearing celebrated **K**hidîv, the Sulṭân of the Sulṭâns of the age, the abolisher of unbelief and of rebellion, the protector of the world and of the religion, Aḥmad Shâh, son of Muhammad Shâh, son of Muzaffar Shâh the Sulṭân, son of Sulṭân [*twice*], may Allâh perpetuate his kingdom and augment his monarchy and his sulṭânship this sepulchre was built by the slave hoping for the mercy of the Nourisher [*God*] Quṭb *bin* Kh'âjagî. Completion of this pious good work for the sake of acquiring [*eternal*] joy, in the month of Muḥarram" [*year not given*].

54. Inscription at Adâlaj well (p. 81, (No. 4)):—

1 संवत् १५५५ वर्षे । माघ मासे । पंचमी दिने । पादसाह श्रीमहिमूदराजा

2 ओं नमो विनायकाय नमः ॥ यस्यान्वये मोकलसिंह आसीदंडाहिदेशाधिपतिर्नरेंद्रः । वाघेल आखंडल

3 तुल्यधामा । योद्धाहि यो भागवतप्रधातनं ॥ ? ॥ तस्याभव (त्) सूनुरतुल्यवीर्यः । कर्णो नृपः कणइव क्षितीशः ।

4 संग्रामभूमिं महतीं हि लब्ध्वा । हता विपक्षाश्च धनुष्मता ते ॥ २ ॥ उन्मूलयिता परेषां । मूलुराजावा नीश्वरः । तस्माद

5 जायते नृपा । द्रैणुकेयो यथा भगोः ॥ ३ ॥ महीपतीनां प्रवरो । महीप इति विश्रुतः । तस्य सूनुरभूत्पांडो । यु

6 धिष्टिर इवापरः ॥ ४ ॥ महीपतनयो ह्यासीद्वीरसिंहो धराधिपः । लीलागृहीतदेहोसौ । रामो दशरथादि-

7 व ॥ ५ ॥ अभूतां नृपती यौ तु भ्रातरौ रामलक्ष्मणौ । वरसिंहश्च जेत्रश्च महीपतनयावुभौ ॥ ६ ॥ दं-डाहिदे-

8 शाधिपति । वीरसिंहो धराधिपः । क ! स्यवल्लीसमासाद्य । स्वशोभत पुरंदरः ॥ ७ ॥ तस्य श्रीं-वीरसिंहस्य । राज्ञी राज्ञी

9 रमेव या । वापिकां शिल्पिमुख्यैश्च । रूडादेवी व्यचीकरत् ॥ ८ ॥ स्वस्तिश्रीनृपविक्रमार्कसमयातीते

10 काले सांप्रतं । संवत्पंचदशेतु पंचमिलिते वर्षे पंचा शति । वीरश्रीवरसिंहदेवनपतेरा-

11 ज्ञी हि रूडाभिधा । वापीं देवधुनीसमं सुतनया निर्म्मातिवणेशितुः ॥ ९ ॥ कौबेरीं दिशमा

12 श्रिते दिनपतौ मासे च माघाभिधे पक्षे शुक्लतमे तिथौ फणभृतो वारे बुधस्योत्तरा । न-

13 क्षत्रे भवसंज्ञके च करणे योगे व सिद्धोपरे । रूडाख्यापतिदेवता तु महतीं वापीमकार्षीच्छुभां ॥ १० ॥

14 मानसाख्यं सरो दिव्यं । किंवा स्वर्गापगा किमु । कैलाशो वेति सर्वेषां विभ्रमं विदधाति

15 या ॥ ११ ॥ या वापिकेति तनुते विशयं सुराणां । वातायनै सुरवधूसमधिष्ठितैश्च । स्वर्गो

16 असौ किमुत वा सुरसद्मभूः सा । सा किंनु जन्हुतनया अथवेयमुच्चैः ॥ १२ ॥ अपांशुलानां

17 प्रथमाभिधेया । या रूडराज्ञी कविकल्पवल्ली । श्लाघ्यैश्चरित्रैः स्वकुलं च पत्युः । विभासयंती

18 किल मैथिलीव ॥ १३ ॥ कोटिर्धनं तृणमिव प्रसृष्टं (!) ययातु । क्षिप्रं नृपेषु विबुधेषु तुलां तु तस्याः

19 का नाम राजदयिता न च कामधेनुर्नाप्योति कल्पलतिका किल रूडाराज्ञ्याः ॥ १४ ॥ टंककानां

20 तु लक्षाणि । पंचानीतानि कोशतः । वापीकृतेऽनया राज्ञ्या । रूडादेव्योति संश्रुतं ॥ १५ ॥ अडालिजे

21 वरग्रामे । वीरसिंहस्य वल्लभा । रूडाराज्ञी न्यधाद्वापीं । भूषिता वलभीशतैः ॥ १६ ॥ स्वस्तिश्री-

22 मन्नृपविक्रमसमयातीता आषाढादि संवत् १५५५ वर्षे शाके १४२० प्रवर्तमाने उत्तरायनगते
23 श्रीसूर्यशिशरुतौ माघमासे शुक्लपक्षे पंचम्यां तिथौ बुधवासरे उत्तराभद्रपदनक्षत्रे । सिद्धि
24 नाम्नि योगे बवकरणे मीनराशौ स्थिते चंद्रे । पातसाहश्रीमहमूदविजयराज्यं । दंडाहिदेशाधि
25 पतिनृपतिचक्रचूडामणिवाघेल श्री महींपतनयराजश्री वरसायीनी धर्मपत्नी राणी श्री रुडबा
26 इ भर्तारसपश्वरलोकार्थं बडालिजि वावि करावी । श्रीमालीज्ञाति । महंभीमा । सुतमराण
27 वाविनीपजावीटंकालाष १०००१११ अंकेपांचलीक्षयंथा । आचंद्रार्कस्थिरस्थावरत्वमस्तु ।

Translation.

"On the fifth day of the month of Mâgha in the *Samvat* year 1555 *(in the reign of)* the king Pâdasâha (Pâdshâh) Srî Mahimûd.

"(1) Om. Salutation to Vinâyaka: Salutation! In whose family was Mokalasimha the sovereign king of Daṇḍâhideśa, a Vâghela, equal to Indra in power, who protected the assembly of *Bhâgavatas*[1];

"(2) His son was prince Karṇa, an earth-ruler, of unequalled valour, like Karṇa, for having attained a great battlefield the enemies were slain by him, the archer.

"(3) An uprooter of enemies, Mûlarâjâ, lord of the earth, sprung from that king even as Raiṇukeya[2] from Bhṛigu.

"(4) The best of kings, famed as Mahîpa, was his unrivalled son, even as Yudhishṭhira was of Pâṇḍu.

"(5) The king Vîrasimha, most graceful in body, was Mahîpa's son, as Râma was of Daśaratha.

"(6) The two kings Vîrasimaha and Jetra were *(like)* the two brothers Râma and Lakshmaṇa, and were the sons of Mahîpa.

"(7) The king Vîrasimha, the lord of Daṇḍâhideśa, shone beautifully like Indra with his desire-fulfilling creeper.

"(8) This Vîrasimha had a queen named Ruḍâdevî, resembling queen Ramâ (Lakshmî), who caused this well (*vâp*) to be made by the best of masons.

"(9) Hail! After fifty-five years added to fifteen hundred of the era of the king Vikramârka have passed, Ruḍâdevî, the queen of the valorous Vîrasimha and a very good daughter of the ruler of Veṇa, (?) causes this well, which is like the Ganges, to be made.

"(10) The Sun standing in the region of Kubera (*north*) on Wednesday the fifth of the month of Mâgha, the *Śukla* fortnight, in the Uttarâ Nakshatra (*asterism*), in the *Karaṇa* called Bava and in the Siddhi-yoga, (*the lady*) called Ruḍâ who has her husband for her god, made this good and great well.

---

[1] The devotees of Vishṇu according to usage. [2] Paraśuráma the son of Reṇuka.

"(11) This well creates a doubt in the minds of all as to whether it is the divine lake Mânasa, or the celestial river Ganges, or Kailâsa itself.

"(12) This well by its niches adorned with the images of celestial damsels creates a doubt even in the minds of gods, whether it is heaven, or a celestial mansion, or the great daughter of Jahnu.

"(13) The queen Ruḍâ, the foremost of virtuous women, the poets' desire-fulfilling tree, like Sîtâ rendered her and her husband's family illustrious by her praiseworthy actions.

"(14) She was a queen by whom a *kror* of coins were at once bestowed as (if it were worthy as) a straw upon wise kings. (?) No other queen, nor the Kâmadhenu nor the Kalpavalli can be named as an equal to the queen Ruḍâ.

"(15) It is said that for this well 5 *lâkhs* of *ṭankas* were brought from the royal treasury by the queen Ruḍâdevî.

"(16) In the good village of Adâlaj Ruḍâdevî, the beloved queen of Vîrasimha, made a well adorned with hundreds of niches.

"(17) Hail! While the year 1555 of the era of the king Vikrama and 1420 of the *Śaka* was current, in the Âshâḍha month and *Śis'ira* season of the Uttarâyana, on Wednesday the fifth of the light fortnight of Mâgha in the *nakshatra* of Uttarâbhâdrapadâ in the Yoga called Siddhi and in the Karaṇa named Bava, the moon being in the Mînarâśî (Pisces), in the victorious reign of Pâdshâh Mahamûd, the queen Ruḍâbâî, the faithful wife of Vîrasimha—Mahîpa's son, the lord of the country of Daṇḍâhi, a Vâghêla, the crest-gem of all kings—made a well at Adâlij for the benefit of all. The overseer was Maham, the son of Bhîma of the Srîmâlî caste. The money spent in building the well was 500,111, or in round figures five *lâkhs* only. May this continue firm during the existence of the Sun and Moon!"

55. Inscription at Borsad step-well (p. 95, No. (1)[1]:))—

1 ऊँमृ संवत् १५९३ वर्षे श्रावणवदि १३ रवौ अद्येहश्रीस्तंभतीर्थवास्तव्य। ल्लाटज्ञातीय वसा। सोमा सुत। वसा षेता सुत

2 वसा परवत सुत वीरपाल ॥ वसा सोमा सुत् वसा हथरमसी सुत वसा नरस्युंग सुत वसा श्रीरंग भ्रात्रि

3 रूपा श्रीपाल ॥ वसा सोमा सुत वसा माणिक सुत वसाइ वीका सुतवसा सगर सुतसाइ ॥ सुतार वर देग. नरबद।

Translation.

In the *Samvat* year 1553 on the 13th day of the dark half of Śrâvaṇa, the day of the week being Sunday, on this day here, Vasâsomâ, resident of Stambhatîrtha (Cambay), Lalâṭa by race, his son Vasâ Khetâ, his son Vasâ Parabata, his son Vîrapâla.

---

[1] Transcribed and translated by Pandit Bhagwânlâl Indraji, Ph.D.

Vasâ Somâ, his son Vasâh Dharamsi, his son Vasâ Narasyanga, his son Vasâ Śriranga, his brothers Rûpâ and Śrîpâla (or sister and brother Rupâ and Śrîpâla).

Vasâ Somâ, his son Vasâ Mâṇik, his son Vasâh Vîkâ, his son Vasâ Sagara, his son Sâi.

Architect Varade, ga., Narabada.

56. Epitaph on the end of a tomb, among those known as the Dutch tombs at Kânkaria tank (p. 81, (No. 119)). It is engraved in Armenian capitals, and reads thus :—

JS + KS

Ays e dabanes Tarv-
iztzi Shamiri ortilo-
ussy hoki Tavout
Khanin ar ATZ pokhve-
tzau.. RJH Gamar ZA.

Literally :—" Jesus Christ : This is the tomb of the Tabrizian, Shamir's son, the illuminated soul of David Khân. To God he was removed . . in 1170, Gamar 11th " (30th July 1720).

Or more freely :—" This is the tomb of the illuminated soul Dawud Khân, son of Shamir of Tabriz. He was removed to God . . on the 11th of Gamar in 1170.[1]"

---

2. INSCRIPTIONS FROM CAMBAY.

No. 1. Over the north entrance of the Jâmi mosque (p. 96).

It appears from the date at the end of this inscription that this mosque was built in the first year of the 19th Pathân Sulṭân of Hindustân, before Gujarât had become independent and had its own kings.

After the usual *Bismillâh* comes *sûrah* LXXII., v. 18, of the *Qurân*, to which also the saying of the prophet, that "for him who builds a mosque for Allâh, Allâh will build a house in paradise," is added. Then the inscription continues as follows :—

هذا ما وقف الله وغايه بني هذا المسجد الجامع والمبارک ومكان الجمعيه وكله من خالص
ماله مما الله من فضله وكرمه خالصا لله تعالي في عهد السلطان العالم العادل محمد شاه بن
تغلق شاه السطان خلد الله ملكه و سلطانه العبد الضعيف الراجي الي رحمة الله تعالي و منته
محمد البوتماري حصل الله مرامه ودلل في الثامن عشر من المحرم سنه خمس و عشرين
و سبعمايه

---

[1] I owe this translation to the kindness of the Rev. S. Baromian, minister of the Armenian Congregation at Manchester, who supplied a transcript and the translation into French ; Mr. R. Martineau of the British Museum, through whose intermediation this was obtained, also favoured me with the transliteration given above.—J. B.

Translation.

"......This is a *waqf* [bequest] and dedication to Allâh. This blessed Jâmi' mosque and place for the congregation has all been built from the private property [*bestowed*] by the grace and bounty of Allâh and offered to Him, may He be exalted; in the reign of the learned and righteous Sulṭân Muhammad Shâh, son of Tughlaq Shâh the Sulṭân, may Allâh perpetuate his kingdom and his sovereignty by the feeble worshipper, who hopes for the mercy of Allâh, be He exalted! and for His grace, Muhammad Al-Bûtmârî may Allâh grant his wishes and guide him; on the eighteenth Muharram, in the year seven hundred and twenty-five" [*5th January* 1325].

No. 2. Over the central *mihrâb* in the Jâmi' mosque.

After the *Bismillâh* comes *sûrah* IX., v. 18, of *Qurân* complete, and nothing more.

No. 3. Over the south *mihrâb* in the Jâmi' mosque.

Sûrah III., v. 16, of *Qurân* beginning of v. 17. Exactly the same as in the set of inscriptions from Râjâpur Tomb, west side.

No. 4. Over the north *mihrâb* in the Jâmi' mosque.

Sûrah XXXIV., v. 36, complete, and nothing else.

No. 5. This is a Persian inscription and about the worst of the lot both in caligraphy and in style. It was written during the reign of the 20th Pathân Sulṭân of Hindûstân and pretends to be poetical. After the usual *Bismillâh* we have before the text the following superscription:—

بنا کرد این مسجد را بندهٔ حضرهٔ سلطنه سلطان فیروز

"This mosque was built by a servant of the majesty of sovereignty Sulṭân Fîrûz" [*a few words illegible of the title*].

بعهد سلطان ظفرخان گستری بانی • بنا کرد این مسجد عادل چون سلطانی
و سنه بخمس و سبعین و هفت صد از هجرهٔ محمد • که این مسجد مرمت کشت بر رونق سبحانی
خدا رحمت کند بر بندهٔ کواندر این مسجد • گوید بر جان و دل دعا خیر بربانی

Translation.

"In the reign of the [*above-named*] Sultân, Zafar Khân Gustarî,[2] the architect, built this mosque upright like royalty [*Sultâni*].

And in the year seven hundred seventy-five from the *Hijrah* of Muhammad [*Began 23rd June* 1373]

This mosque has been repaired for the worship of God [*lit., adornment of the glorious.*]

---

[1] This cognomen may be read also in several other ways on account of the absence of diacritical points.

[2] May also be read Al Shustari.

May God have mercy upon the worshipper who in this mosque
Utters from soul and heart a prayer for the architect."

No. 6. On the tomb at the Jâmi mosque, Cambay—upper and lower band together.

Contains *Qurân, sûrah* XXXVI, vv. 28—42 inclusive, complete—the upper beginning with v. 28 and the lower with v. 36.

No. 7. On a reservoir in the court of the Jâmi mosque, Cambay:—

فرغ من مرمة هذه البركة ومجري الماء الي الحوض في سنه الف وثلثين اقل عباد الله الهادي علي بن عبد النبي البغدادي

Translation.

"The repairing of this reservoir and of the water-channel to the basin was completed in the year one thousand and thirty [*Began 26th Nov.* 1620] by the meanest of the worshippers of Allâh, the director 'Alî the son of 'Abdu'n-nabî al-Baghdâdî."

No. 8. On a mosque in ruins at the back of Khâja Khezir's tomb (p. 96, No. (7.))

After the superscription بسم الله خير الاسماء "In the name of Allâh, the best of names," come the following seven Persian distiches in elegant Persian caligraphy:—

آن خديو زمانه مومن خان • حامی دين سيد کونين
بنده جان نثار او جاوید • گرد حامل سعادت ازين
برکه ساخت بهر تشنه لبان • تا شفيعش شود جناب حسين
خالق و خلق ز بنا خوشنود • وانکه زوگشت فتح بدر و حسين
لب دريا و چشمه شيرين • کن تماشای مجمع البحرين
سال تاريخ اين خجسته بنا • آمد بدلم بطرفه عين
کفت هاتف بگير نام امام • آب مائی بخور بياد حسين
۸۲ ۱۲۱۹

Translation.

"That Khidiv of the period Mumin Khân,
Defender of the religion of him who is prince of men and angels,
The servant who is always ready to sacrifice his life for him,
Attained felicity hereby that he
Constructed the reservoir for the thirsty-lipped
That the lord Husain may become his intercessor.
The creator and the creatures are pleased with the building
Whereby the victory of Badr and Husain is glorified.
The shore of the sea and the sweet fountain
Contemplate the union of the two seas
The chronogram of this auspicious edifice
Occurred to my heart in the twinkling of an eye;

The celestial herald said, take the name of the Imâm 82
And quaff limpid water to the memory of Husain 1219" [*Began* 12*th Apr.* 1804.]

No. 9. Tomb of Khâja Khezir, Cambay.

The upper portion of this inscription is wanting, since what is left contains only the beginning of *sûrah* II. v. 256, and the end of it. Also beginning of *sûrah* II. v. 285, and end of *sûrah* II. v. 289, completing *sûrah* II., the intermediate portions having no doubt been on a portion of the inscription, which is lost. The adjoining figure will better explain what is meant.

Upper portion wanting.

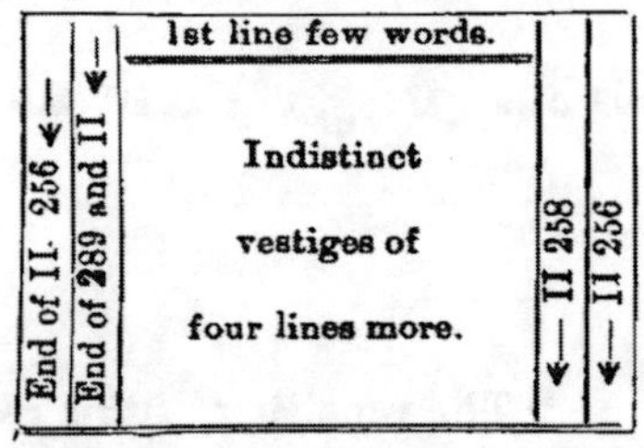

No. 10. Tomb of Khâja Khezir, Cambay, about a mile west of the town.

There is no *Bismillâh*, but only "Allâh has said, &c.," as before, *sûrah* LXXII, v. 18, with the saying already mentioned of the prophet, appended. Then :—

۸۲

صدق الله بنا هذا المکان المبارک وکان ذلک — خواجه خضر — سنه احد و سبعین و سبعمایه

Translation.

"Allâh is veracity. This blessed place was built which was [*illegible*] Khâja Khezir [*date of month illegible*] in the year seven hundred and seventy-one" [*Began* 5*th Aug.* 1369.]

No. 11. Tomb of Khâja Khezir, Cambay.

Like the preceding, namely *sûrah* LXXII., v. 18, and the saying of the prophet. Then comes a Persian inscription in the style of No. 5 consisting of the following six distiches :—

حد مقام خواجه خضر و کهمبایت • مهتر الیاس را از ابتدا
بود صد ساله اما قدیم خلد • یافته بود از باری تعالی سخت
بنده را قبور داد کرد کار • از حلال بمال خود کرد بنا
جوادو جود فرض آن نبد • ساخت از اساس نو بهر خدا
تا نیابد آزاد مرد جواب • اعمال نیست غیر رماد
عالم زمان بملا خزین • هفت صد و احد و سبعین

Translation.

"Boundary of the Maqâm of Khâja Khezir and of Cambay
The senior Elias from the beginning!
He was a centenarian, but had of yore eternity

Received decidedly from God, who be exalted.
The creator bestowed tombs upon His worshipper
Who built them up from his own legal property;
That beneficence and liberality was not a religious duty,
He built upon new foundations for the sake of God.
That a liberal man shall not get the reply :—
'Works are nothing but ashes.'
The people of the period grieve for the Mullâ.
Seven hundred and seventy-one" [*same as at the end of No.* 10.]

No. 12. Tomb of Hâjjî Yûsuf, Cambay :—

The actual epitaph is framed in by verses from the *Qurân*, as shown in the figure; namely :—

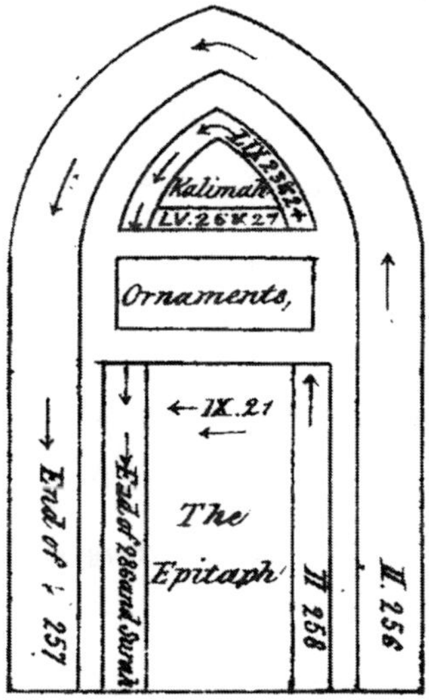

Outer frame *sûrah* II., vv. 256 and 257, large letters.

Inner arch *sûrah* LIX., vv. 23 and 24, completing the *sûrah*.

Base of ditto, *sûrah* LV., vv. 26 and 27.

Inside of ditto, *Kalimah* or confession :—

"No God but Allâh, Muḥammad messenger of Allâh."

On right and left side of the oblong parallelogram containing the epitaph, in smaller and more crowded characters, *sûrah* II., vv. 258 to 286 inclusive, completing the *sûrah*.

Above the epitaph, *sûrah* IX. v. 21.

The Epitaph.

هذا قبر المرحوم و المغفور العبد الراجي الي رحمة الله تعالي الكريم حاجي الحرمين الشريفين — يوسف ابن سيد احمد ابن محمد ابن عيسي ابن عبد السلام ابن احمد الحاجب القريشي يغفره الله بالرحمة و الرضوان في يوم الدين — الثالث عشر من ربيع الاخر سنه اربع و عشر و ثمانمايه من الهجرة النبوية

Translation.

"This is the tomb of one received into mercy and pardoned; the worshipper who hopes for the mercy of Allâh, be he exalted! the bountiful; a pilgrim to the two noble sanctuaries [3 *laudatory lines*] Yûsuf, son of Sayyid Ahmad, son of Muhammad, son of 'Isâ, son of 'Abdu's-sallâm, son of Ahmadu'l-Hâjab ul-Quraishî, may Allâh overwhelm him with mercy and approbation on the day of judgment [*a word not plain*]. Thirteenth Rabî' II. in the year eight hundred and fourteen [*6th Aug.* 1411] of the prophetic exile."

No. 13. Tomb of Fakhru'd-daulah wa'd-dîn Abû Bakr :—

Here we have on the outer margin *sûrah* II., vv. 256—258 inclusive, running round;

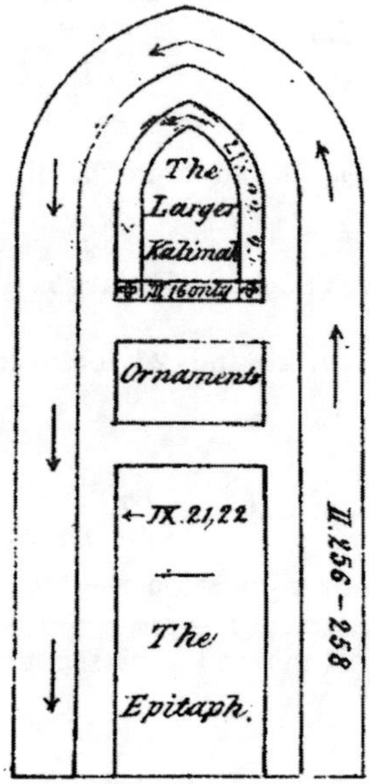

and a little space being left vacant after last-named verse, it was filled up by adding the words "Allâh the most high, verifier."

Sides of small pointed arch *sûrah* LIX., vv. 22—24, completing the *sûrah*. Base of arch, *sûrah* III. v. 16 only. Interior of arch, the larger *Kalimah* :—"I bear witness that there is no God but Allâh and that Muhammad is His worshipper and His messenger."

Oblong parallelogram, *sûrah* IX. vv. 21—22; then the saying of the prophet :—"Be thou in the world like a shadow, for thou art a stranger therein, and like a traveller," &c. Then comes

The Epitaph.

هذا قبر المرحوم الراجي الي رحمة الله تعالي مفخر لجار حزاين الاكابر والاحرار
فخر الدولة والدين ابوبكر ابن حسن ابن محمد ابن حسن ابن عيسي القريشي الحكيم يغفره الله
ابرحمته والرضوان في يوم الدين سبع عشر من صفر سنه ثمان وعشر وثمانمايه من الهجرة

Translation.

"This is the tomb of one received into mercy hoping for the mercy of Allâh the exalted, most glorious dispenser of treasures to the pious and the righteous; Fakhru'd-daulat wa'd-din Abu Bakr, son of Hasan, son of Muhammad, son of Hasan, son of 'Isiu'l-Quraishî u'l-Hakîm, may Allâh overwhelm him with His mercy and approbation on the judgment day. The seventeenth of Safar, year eight hundred eighteen of the *Hijrah*" [*29th April* 1415].

No. 14. Tomb of Ikhtyâru'd-daulat wa'd-dîn, treasurer of Cambay.

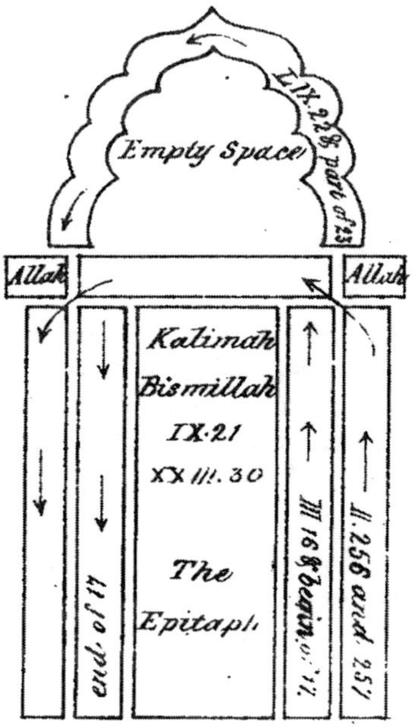

On the arch, *sûrah* LIX. v. 22, and part of v. 23.

Two outer bands and uppermost horizontal line, *sûrah* II. vv. 256-257.

Two inner bands, *sûrah* III. vv. 16-17.

Interior oblong parallelogram. The *Kalimah* and after it the *Bismillâh*, *i. e.*, the words "In the name of Allâh the merciful, the clement." Then *sûrah* IX. v. 21, and *sûrah* XXIII. v. 30. Lastly—

The Epitaph.

هذا قبر الامير الكبير المرحوم المغفور
السعيد الشهيد اختيار الدولة والدين مخزن
معمورة كهمبايت — برد الله مضجعه وايسره
في ليله حسبه — سابع عشر من شهر جمادي
الآخر سنه سادس عشر وسبعمايه

Translation.

"This is the tomb of the great Amîr, received into mercy, the pardoned, blessed, martyr, Ikhtyâru'd-daulat wa'd-dîn, treasurer of the city of Cambay...may Allâh cool his resting place and make it easy on the night of his reckoning...Seventeenth of the month Jumâdâ II, in the year seven hundred and sixteen" [*6th Sept.* 1316.]

No. 15. Tomb of the Vazîr 'Umr Ibn Ahmadu'l-Kâzerûnî (p. 135, No. 21).

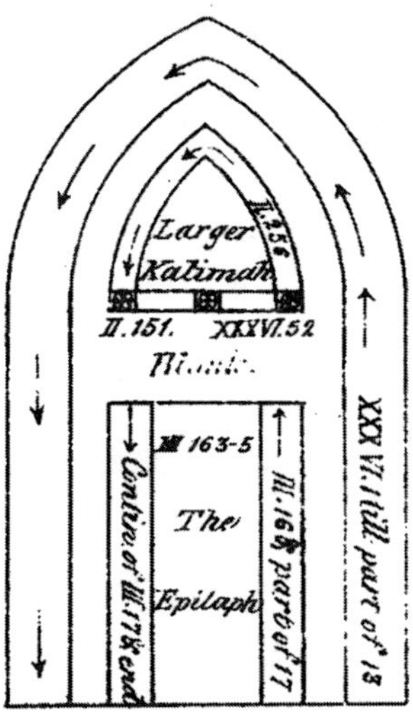

Exterior margin *sûrah* XXXII. v. 1, till part of v. 13. Interior arch only *sûrah* II. v. 256, but complete; the base of it is divided into two parts, containing the conclusion of v. 151 and of v. 52 of *sûrah* II. and XXXVI. respectively. The enclosed space of this arch is filled in with the larger *Kalimah* as in No. 13.

The oblong parallelogram has on one side *sûrah* III. v. 16 with part of v. 17, and on the other the continuation of the latter till its end. The upper portion of the parallelogram is occupied by *sûrah* III. vv. 163—165, given complete. Then comes—

The Epitaph.

هذا قبر العبد الضعيف السعيد الشهيد المرحوم المغفور ملك ملوك السرور الوزرا المشهور العرب والعجم ركن الدولة والدين عمر ابن احمد الكازروني المخاطب بزور الملك يغمده الله تعالي بالرحمة والمغفرة ورضوان الله في دار الجنان المتوفي الي رحمة الله تعالي في يوم الاربعا التاسع من صفر سنه اربع ثلثين وسبعمايه

Translation.

"This is the tomb of the feeble worshipper, blessed, martyr, received into mercy, chief of chiefs, prince [*server*] of the Vazîrs, celebrated in Arabia and Persia, pillar of the state and of the religion, 'Umar the son of Aḥmadu'l-Kâzerûnî, who bore the title of Zauru'l-Malik, may Allâh the most high overwhelm him with mercy, pardon, and the approbation of Allâh in the mansion of paradise. He departed to the compassion of Allâḥ, who be exalted, on Wednesday the ninth Safar, in the year seven hundred and thirty-four" [21*st October* 1333.]

No. 16. Tomb of Bibî Fâṭimah (p. 96, No. (2)):—

Oblong parallelogram with a band on each vertical side, both of which are occupied by *sûrah* II. v. 256 only.

The parallelogram itself has above the first four words of the *Kalimah*, "No God but Allâh"; then *sûrah* LV. vv. 26 and 27, and lastly—

The Epitaph.

هذا القبر المرحومه المغفوره فخر النسا تاج الخزاين بيبي فاطمه الخواجه الكبر ثلاني المرحوم حسين زوجه ... توفي الي رحمة الله في احد وعشر من شوال سنه ثلاث و ثمانين وسبعمايه

Translation.

"This is the tomb of one received into mercy, pardoned, the boast of women, crown of treasures, Bibî Fâtima who had performed the pilgrimage to Karbalâ...the deceased Husain, the wife.[1] Departed to the compassion of Allâh on the eleventh Shawwâl in the year seven hundred eighty-three" [30*th Dec.* 1381.]

No. 17. Four bands belonging to the preceding tomb No. 16 :—

1st band.—Part of first *sûrâh*.

2nd band.—Continuation and end of it. Then these words:

اللهم غفر لهذة المرحومة ونور قبرها بنور رحمتك يا ارحم الراحمين

---

[1] A whole line indistinct, but certainly containing the name 'Umar and probably also the title after it as in No. 15.

"O Allâh ! Pardon this deceased woman and illuminate her tomb with the light of Thy compassion, O most merciful of the merciful."

3rd band.—*Sûrah* III. v. 16, with part of v. 17.

4th band.—Only *sûrah* III. v. 182, but complete.

No. 18. Upper and lower bands along the west side of central tomb south of Jâmi Masjid.

The upper band contains *sûrah* XXXVI., vv. 65—71 inclusive; the lower contains *sûrah* XXXVI. vv. 72—79 inclusive.

No. 19. On a small pilaster to the left of the front face (head stone) of central tomb south of Jâmi Masjid. First half of v. 52 of *sûrah* XXXVI. flanked by ornaments and ends of bands, running at right angles with this line.

No. 20. One line without beginning or end, containing latter part of v. 20 and first part of v. 21 of *sûrah* XXXVI.

---

3. FROM SOJALI NEAR MAHMUDÂBÂD (*ante*, p. 93, No. (1)).

No. 1. On the large tomb is an inscription consisting of only the *Bismillâh* and four verses, *i. e. sûrah* II. vv. 256—259. Also on the tomb :—

فاصرف هواها و حاذر ان تولیه ان الهوي ما تولي يصم يصم وراعها وهي في الاعمال
سايمه وان هي استحبت المراعي فلا تسم كم لذة حسنت للمرء قاتر من حيث لم يدران
السم في الدواسم اخش الدسايس من جرع و من شبع فرب مخمصه من شرالتخمران
استفرغ الدمع من عين قد امتلات من المحار و من الزما حميه الندم وخالف النفس والشيطان
واعصهما و انهما محصال النصح ذاتهم ولا تطع منهما خصما ولا حكما وانت تعرف كيد الخصم
والحكم استغفر من الله قول بلا عمل لقد نسبت به نسلا الذي عقبه امر تلام اخر لكن فات
قمر استقمت ومات له قولي لک استقم رقبک ولا ودت الموت نافله ولم اصل سوي
فرض ولم اصم سنه ظلمت من احي الظلام الي ان اشتكت قد ماه الفرمن تندم ورم
سغب حشاوه وطوي تحت الحجار كشجاه مترف الادم

Translation.

"Then cultivate her passion and beware of neglect, because lust is not discarded with muteness and becomes dumb. And regard her whilst she is pleased with practical demonstrations; and if she desires to love the guardian, she will not poison. How many a pleasure which was delightful to a man is lethal, because he does not know that the poison in the medicine is the worst of treacheries in hunger and in repletion; and often wretchedness results from the evil of potations, because the flow of tears from an eye already saturated with heat and with music is a prohibition to restraint. Accordingly resist concupiscence and Satan, and disobey them, and they call for advice; therefore ponder. Obey neither their suggestions nor their behests, for thou knowest the fraud of altercations and judgments. I ask pardon from Allâh! Words without deeds are attributed to a progeny which is followed by consequences blamed at last. The fruit however which thou hast desired to cherish, perished and is dead. But are not my words to thee :—Endeavour to cherish thy neck, and not love death voluntarily. I allude only to matters established by command [*Farḍ*] and do not discard those sanctioned by usage [*Sonnat*] which has been transgressed. Who revives transgressions so that even his ancestors have suffered indignity; who repents but nevertheless dallies, his entrails are raked with pain, and he is buried under stones like a luxurious man who has abused his wealth unto his own destruction!"

2. On the same large tomb :—

خطي عبرة و شي مثل النهار علي خد...فاي فتي يعرض الحب للنسا لاله الاشي في الهوا تعدي معذري و متي البكا لولم تسلم تصفت عن شك حالي لا سري مستتر من الوشان ولا دابي بتختيم محنتي النصح لكن لست ان المحب يسمعه عز العدل في الضمير تهمت النصح...لكتمت سر بدا لي منه بالكتمه لي جماح غويتها من يرد مرا يرد كما جماح الخيل باللجم فلا ترم بالمعاصي كثير شهوتها ان الطعام يقوي شهوة التهم والنفس كالطفل تهمله شب علي حب الرضاع وان تفطمه ينفطم

Translation.

[1] "My writing is an admonition and something like daylight upon the face...[*some imperfect words*. And what youth is there who makes love to women, unless with some intentions of lust which pass my excuse; and when the shedding of tears although not given up, clears away, the doubt of my case has ceased. My secret is not hidden from slanderers, nor is it my custom to shirk the trouble of advice, and to conclude it, but the lover pays no attention to it. The nobility of justice is in the mind which has meditated on advice...[*again several imperfect sentences*]. I would have concealed with concealment a secret which appeared to me from him. I have a mettle which I subdued. Who restrains once, is restrained like the mettle of horses by bridling. Do not therefore augment her abundant lust by sins. Verily food strengthens sexual heat, and concupiscence is like an infant whom youthfulness impels to the love of sucking, but if thou weanest him he is weaned."

3. On the central grave-stone in the same tomb is a legend consisting of two lines :—

1st, the *Kalimah* with the *Bismillâh* prefixed.

2nd, "In the name of Allâh and by Allâh, and with the religion of the messenger of Allâh."

4. On the grave-stone east of the central one in the large tomb at Sôjâli is another exactly the same as the preceding, which, however, I here give in Arabic :—

بسم الله الرحمن الرحيم لا اله الا الله محمد رسول الله   بسم الله و بالله وعلي ملة رسول الله

---

[1] Beginning unintelligible although several words are plain.

4. INSCRIPTIONS FROM DHOLKÂ AND BROACH.

Of ten of the inscriptions from Dholkâ it is not worth while to give separate descriptions, as they contain only the profession of faith; each is inscribed within a kind of pointed arch resembling the top pieces of tomb-stones under which verses of the *Qurân* occur and the epitaphs; under these Dholkâ ones, however, there is nothing. All are more or less ornamental, and only one of them exceeds two feet in length, being more than five long, and contains, besides the central arch with the profession of faith, two lateral compartments with the word Allâh in large characters. All these are from the mosque of Qaḍhi Balol Khân at Dholkâ.

The six long slips marked K, M, N, O, P and Q, copied by hand from an inscription painted upon board panelling, now much obliterated, run round the inner walls of the mosque, beginning from the south end of the west or back wall.

K, at the south end of the west wall, ends with the words "Who is he that can intercede with him?" of *sûrah* II. v. 256 of the *Qurân*; a few words of the beginning of this verse are wanting. The remaining portion of the verse was no doubt on L, which is over the *mehrâb*.

M, on the north end of the back wall, contains the beginning of *sûrah* I, but the latter part of the slip is now blank.

N, on the west end of the north wall, bears the latter part of *sûrah* II. v. 251, and the remaining part is filled in with a benediction upon Muḥammad

O, on the central portion of the north wall, is almost totally blank; and the few letters at the beginning and end of the slip do not allow of identification with any verse from the *Qurân*.

P, on the east end of the north wall; on this are legible only a few letters at the end of the slip; the rest is now blank.

Q, on the north end of the east or front wall, still bears part of *sûrah* II. v. 285, which being towards the end of the *sûrah*, it may be presumed that the whole of it had been completed on some of the remaining panels, which could not be copied because the letters have disappeared, or nearly so.

1. From a stone built into a brick supporting wall in Qâḍhi Balol Khân's Masjid at Dholkâ :—

بسم الله الرحمن الرحيم قال الله تعالي ان المساجد لله فلا تدعوا مع الله احدا عمارت
این مسجد درعهد سلطان الاعظم ابو المجاهد محمد ابن تغلقشاه و بنوبت ملک الملوک
الشرق رکن الدولت والدین فتاح سرداریکدل خاص بنا کرده مفخر الامر مقرب الدولت
والدین هلال ملاي معمار بنده عبد الکریم لطیف في التاریخ السابع والعشرین من ذالحجه
سنه ثلاث وثلاثین وسبعمایه

Translation.

"In the name of Allâh, the merciful, the clement. Allâh, who be exalted, has said [*in the Qurân. LXXII.* 18] :—'Verily the mosques belong to Allâh, therefore do ye not invoke any one with Allâh.' The edifice of this mosque was—during the reign of his majesty the Sulṭân Abul-mujâhad Muḥammad, son of Toghluqshâh and during the period of Malek-ulmulûk-ushsharq Rokn-uddaulat-vuddyn-fattâḥ Sirdâr [or Server] yekdilkhâs—constructed by Mofakhr-ullomrâ muqarrab-uddaulat-vuddyn Hillâl Mollây [or Maleky] the architect being the slave A'bd-ulkarim Laṭif. Dated the twenty-seventh of the month Dilhejjah, in the year seven hundred and thirty-three" [8th September 1333.]

The following three inscriptions are from the Tanka Masjid at Dholkâ, and bear the same date in the reign of Firuz Shâh III, the 20th Sulṭân of the Pathân dynasty of Hindustân, whose name occurs also on each of them. The name of the individual at whose expense this mosque was constructed is also mentioned in each of the inscriptions and was Muffarraḥ [*exhilarator*], who is also called by the title of Mufakhr-ul-khovâs [*the boast of, or the chief of favourite courtiers*] and Mufarraḥ Sulṭâni. The first and second inscriptions are in Persian rhymes, and the third in Arabic prose.

2. From outside of court-wall [300] :—

بعهد دولت فیروز شاه اسکندر ثانی * مفرح مفخر الخواص خاص الخاص سلطانی
مصفا مسجد جامع بنا در دهولقه کرده * زمال خالص و خاصه بفضل الله ربانی
بعنبر خشت بر آورده گلست از مشک تاتاری * کسج از کافور خام آمد زهی فرخنده بانی
مروج همچو فردوس است و مردم بالاش خرام * بر پنج اوقات کند مسعود طای غارت سبحانی
تاریخ ظفر بود از مرمر ماسر تا مرتب شد * زهجرت هفصد و شست و دو بود از فیض یزدانی
مبارک باد براین بناش تا گردد محشر * همه دشوار رد گردد و شود پس جمله بر آسانی

Translation.

"In the reign of Firuz Shâh, another Alexander,
Mufarraḥ-Mufakhr ul-khovâs khâs-ulkhâs Sulṭâni
Built the pure Jâmi' mosque in Dhulqah
Of his own special private property by the divine favour of Allâh,
Upon amber bricks there are roses from musk of Tartary [i, e., *yellow tesselated pavement with black ornaments*]
The mortar is of pure camphor [*snowy whiteness*], Bravo to the fortunate builder!
The meadow [*surface*] is like paradise, and men walk thereon.
The five stated prayers are performed there by Masu'd Ṭâyi [*exemplar of liberality*].
The glorious date at its [*the mosque's*] completion of hard marble was
Of the *Hijrat* seven hundred and sixty-two [Began 11th Nov. 1360] by divine grace.

Benediction be upon this building of his, till the day of resurrection,
May all difficulties be repelled and general prosperity ensue."

3. Over the south gate of the court [301] :—

بنا کرد این مسجد این فضل داشت • بعهد دولت شاه جهان فیروز سلطانی
زمال خالص خود مفرح الخواص وامرا • زمفرح بندهٔ فیروز شاه اسکندر ثانی
دهم از شهر ربیع الاخر این جامع مرتب شد • بسال هفصد وشست ودو از تائید رحمانی
بعهد سکندر زمان شد امر • جهانگیر فیروز شاه نام دار
بنا جامع کرد که می خاست نیک نام • مفرح ملک شاه داد و تدبیر
بنا کرد در دهولقه مسجدی • بتوفیق از فال ز کردگار
ز هجرت بده هفصد و شست و دو • که این خیر شد در جهان پایدار
جز این مقام مقدس چنین عمارت جهان • ندیده دیده آن مه نو بر چرخ کردان
بدور دولت فیروز شاه روی زمین • که درجهان کردست سجده گاه سبحانی عظیم
بوقت مناسب اقطاع شد گاه منسک • دان که اخص دولت بندهٔ سلطان
مفرح ملک بعظم جهد مال خاص • بد امر اسکندر ثانی بعدل قوی و نشان
تمام کشت ز فضل الله از هجرت • بد سنه هفصد و شست و دو از دوران

Translation.

"He built this mosque, he obtained this favour,
In the reign of the Shâh of the world Firuz Sulṭân
Of his own private property ; [*he was the*] exhilarator among intimate courtiers and Amirs
Mufarreḥ [*exhilarator*] the slave of Firuz Shâh, another Alexander,
On the tenth of the month Rabi' II, this Jâmi [*mosque*] was completed,
In the year seven hundred and sixty-two [17*th Febr.* 1361] by divine aid.
In the reign of the Alexander of the period the command went forth,
The conqueror of the world, Firuz Shâh the celebrated.
He built the Jami for he desired a good name.
Mufarreḥ Melik the Shâh of liberality and deliberation,
Built this mosque in Dhulqah
By divine grace with a good omen from the Creator.
Of the *Hijrat* seven hundred and sixty-two had elapsed
When this good [*work*] had been established in the world.
Besides this sacred place an edifice like this in the world
The eye of the new moon had not beheld in the revolving sphere
During this period of the reign of Firuz, the Shâh of the surface of the earth
When a great place for divine worship was established in the world,
At the appropriate time the locality of piety was set apart.
Let it be known that [*this was done by*] a grandee of monarchy, the slave of the Sulṭân,
Mufarreḥ Melik, by a great expenditure of his private property.

At the command of one who is a second Alexander in justice, power and glory.

Completed by the grace of Allâh, when from the *Hijret*
It was the year seven hundred and sixty-two of the era."

4. Over the central *mehrâb* [302] :—

بسم الله الرحمن الرحيم شهد الله انه لا اله الا هو والملايكه و اولوا العلم قايما بالقسط
لا اله الا هو العزيز الحكيم ان الدين عند الله الاسلام المعبود هو الله فاحفظه قال رسول الله
والتراف سلام الله والجنة و رضوان الله عمر هذا المسجد الجامع الشريف في عهد السلطان
الاعظم و القهرمان المكرم ظل الله في الارض محيي السنه والفرض الواثق بتائيد الرحمن
فيروز شاه السلطان خلد الله ملكه و ابد دولته من خالص مال الملك المعظم صاحب السيف
والقلم والي العلم و العلم مفخر الخواص اختيار الدولة والدين مفرح السلطاني دومت له
خاص مكنه ولدّله ظلا البواب وكان ذلك في العاشر من ربيع الاخر سنه اثنين وستين وسبعمايه

Translation.

"In the name of Allâh, the merciful, the clement!" [*Qurân* 111, 16, *and part* 17]: "Allâh hath borne witness that there is no God but he; and the angels and those who are endowed with knowledge [*profess the same*]; who executeth righteousness; there is no God but he; the mighty, the wise. Verily the religion in the sight of Allâh is Islâm.' The object of adoration is Allâh, wherefore keep it. The prophet of Allâh has said :—'And mercifulness is the peace of Allâh, and paradise, and the approbation of Allâh.' This noble Jâmi mosque was built in the reign of the most great Sulṭân and the honoured Qaharmân; shadow of Allâh upon earth, vivifier of the Sonnah and the Fard confider in the aid of the merciful [Allâh]; Firuz Shâh the Sulṭân, may Allâh perpetuate his kingdom, and eternalize his monarchy, from the special property of his majesty the king, lord of the sword and of the pen, protector of [divine] knowledge and [*of secular*] knowledge, by Mufakhr-ulkhovâs âkhyâr-uddaulat-waddyn [paragon of the chief civil and religious dignitaries] Mufarreḥ-ussulṭâni, may his special dignity be permanent, and may the shadow of the [royal] portals be extended towards him. And this was on the tenth of Rabi' II, in the year seven hundred and sixty-two" [17*th Feb.* 1361.]

5. Also from the Tânka Masjid of Dholkâ: over *mehrâb* in the women's gallery (303):—

This is only LXXII. 18 from the *Qurân*, which is quoted many times in these inscriptions.

6. Over the central *mehrâb*, Jâmi mosque, Broach [304]:—

This inscription contains no date, but from the form and condition of the letters it can hardly be regarded as very old.

Transcript.

بسم الله الرحمن الرحيم قال الله تبارک و تعالي و ان المساجد لله فلا تدعوا مع الله
احدا و قال النبي صلي الله عليه و سلم من بني لله مسجدا يبتغي به وجه الله بني الله له
مثله في الجنة و عنه عليه السلام من بني لله مسجدا ولو كمفحص قطاة بني الله له بيتا في
الجنة و عنه عليه السلام بشر المشائين في الظلم الي المساجد بالنور التام يوم القيمة

Translation.

"In the name of &c., LXXII. 18. And the prophet, upon whom be the benediction of Allâh, and peace, has said :—'Who builds a mosque for Allâh, desiring thereby the face of Allâh; Allâh builds him one like it in paradise,' and the prophet also said :—'Who builds for Allâh a mosque, although it be only like the nest of the bird Qaṭah, Allâh builds him a house in paradise,' and the prophet also said :—'Give glad tidings unto those who walk in the dark to mosques, of full light on the day of resurrection.'"

7. Over the central *mehrâb*, Jâmi' mosque, Broach [305] :—

This is a paltry little inscription about three inches long, the first line of which contains the profession of faith, and the second is indistinct.

INSCRIPTIONS FROM GIRNÂR.

INSCRIPTION No. 1.

Over the west door of the temple of Vastupâla and Tejahpâla on mount Girnâr is an oblong slab containing the following thirteen lines with about 120 letters in each. The characters are mostly distinct, and the writing on the whole fairly correct.

॥ – नमः श्रीसर्वज्ञाय ॥ पायान्नेमिजिनः स यस्य क[थितः] स्वामीकृतागस्थितावग्रे रूपदिदृक्षया स्थितवते प्रीते सुराणां प्रभौ ॥ कार्ये भागवते [वनेव – क] – – – [द्विपोलाबिबे] शंसंताामिदशा – – – – – – मपि – – – [वनाजवे] ॥ १ ॥ स्वस्ति श्रीविक्रमसंवत् १२८८ वर्षे फागुणशुदी १० बुधे श्रीमदणहिल-

पुरवास्तव्यप्राग्वाटान्वयप्रसूत ठ. श्रीचंडपात्मज ठ श्रीचंडप्रसादांगज ठ. श्रीसोमतनुज ठ. श्रीआशाराजनंदनस्य ठ. श्रीकुमारदेवीकुक्षिसंभूतस्य ठ. श्रीलुणिगमहं श्रीमाल्देवयोरनुजस्यमहं. श्री तेजःपालाग्रजन्मनो महामात्यश्रीवस्तुपालस्यात्मजेमहं श्रीललितादेवीकुक्षिसरो-

वरराजहंसायमानेमहं. श्रीजयतसिंहे सं. ७९ वर्षपूर्वं स्तंभतीर्थमुद्राव्यापारान् व्यापृण्वति सति सं. ७७ वर्षे श्रीशत्रुंजयोज्जयंतप्रभृतिमहातीर्थयात्रोत्सवप्रभावाविर्भूतश्रीमद्देवाधिदेवप्रसादासादितसंघाधिपत्येन चौलुक्यकुलनभस्तलप्रकाशनैकमार्त्तंडमहाराजाधिराजश्रीलवणप्रसाददेवसु-

तमहाराजश्रीवीरधवलदेवप्रीतिप्रतिपन्नराज्यसर्वैश्वर्य्येण श्रीशारदाप्रतिपन्नापत्येन महामात्यश्रीवस्तुपालेन तथा अनुजेन सं. ७६ वर्षपूर्वं गुर्जरमंडले धवलक्ककप्रमुखनगरेषु मुद्राव्यापारान् व्यापृण्वतामहं श्रीतेजःपालेन च श्रीशत्रुंजयार्बुदाचलप्रभृतिमहातीर्थेषु श्रीमदणहिलपुरभृगुपु-

रस्तंभनकपुरस्तंभतीर्थदर्भवतीधवलक्ककप्रमुखनगरेषु तथा अन्यसमस्तस्थानेष्वपि कोटिशोभिनवधर्मस्थानानि प्रभूतजीर्णोद्धाराश्च कारिताः ॥ तथा सचिवेश्वरश्रीवस्तुपालेन इह स्वय निर्मापितश्रीशत्रुंजयमहातीर्थावतारश्रीमदादितीर्थंकरश्रीऋषभदेवस्तंभनकपुरावतारश्रीपार्श्वनाथदेवसत्यपु-

रावतारश्रीमहावीरदेवप्रशस्तिसहितकश्मीरावतारश्रीसरस्वतीमूर्तिदेवकुलिकाचतुष्टयजिनयुगलअम्बावलोकनाशाम्बप्रद्युम्नशिखरेषु श्रीनेमिनाथदेवालंकृत देवकुलिकाचतुष्टयतुरगाधिरूढस्वापितामहमहं. श्रीसोमानिजापितृठ. श्रीआशाराजमूर्त्तिद्वितयचारुतोरणत्रयश्रीनेमिनाथ-

देवआत्मीयपूर्वजाग्रजानुजपुत्रादिमूर्त्तिसमन्वितसुखोद्घाटनकस्तंभश्रीअष्टापदमहातीर्थप्रभृति अनेककीर्तनपरंपराविराजिते श्रीनेमिनाथदेवाधिदेवविभूषितश्रीमदुज्जयंतमहातीर्थे आत्मनस्तथा स्वधर्मचारिण्याः प्राग्वाटजातीयठ. श्रीकान्हडपुत्र्याः ठ. राणूकुक्षिसंभूतायामहं. श्रीललितादेव्याः

पुण्याभिवृद्धये श्रीनागेंद्रगच्छे भट्टारकश्रीमहेंद्रसूरिसंताने शिष्यश्रीशांतिसूरिशिष्यश्रीआणंदसूरिश्रीअमरसूरिपदे भट्टारकश्रीहरिभद्रसूरिपट्टालंकरणप्रभुश्रीविजयसेनसूरिप्रतिष्ठितश्रीअजितनाथदेवादिविंशतितीर्थंकरालंकृतोयमभिनवः समंडपः श्रीसंमेतमहातीर्थावतारप्रासादः कारितः ॥

पीयूषपूरस्य च वस्तुपालमंत्रीशितुश्चायमियान् विभेदः ॥ एकः पुनर्जीवयति प्रमीतं प्रमीयमाणं तु भुवि द्वितीयः ॥ १ ॥ श्रीदश्रीदयितेश्वरप्रभृतयः संतु क्वचित् तेपि ये प्रीणंति प्रभाविष्णवोपि विभवैर्नाकिंचनं कं च न ॥ सोयं सिंचति कांचनैः प्रतिदिनं दारिद्र्यदावानलप्रम्लानां पृथिवीं नवीनजलदः श्रीवस्तुपालः

पुनः ॥ २ ॥ भ्रातः पातकिनां किमत्र कथया दुर्मंत्रिणामेतया येषां चेतसि नास्ति किंचिदपरं लोकोपकारं विना ॥ नन्वस्यैव गुणान्गृणीहि गणशः श्रीवस्तुपालस्य यस्ताद्विश्वोपकृतिव्रतं चरति यत्कर्णेन चीर्णं पुरा ॥ ३॥ भीत्वा भानुं भोजराजे प्रयाते श्रीमुंजेपि स्वर्गसाम्राज्यभाजि ॥ एकः संप्रत्यर्थिनां वस्तुपालस्तिष्टत्यश्रु-

स्पंदनिष्कंदनाय ॥ ४ ॥ चौलुक्यक्षितिपालमौलसचिव त्वत्कीर्त्तिकोलाहलस्त्रैलोक्येपि विलोक्यमानपुलकानं-
दाश्रुभिः श्रूयते ॥ किं चैषा कलिदूषितापि भवता प्रासादवापीप्रपाकूपारामसरोवरप्रभृतिभिर्धात्री पवित्रीकृता ॥ ५ ॥
स श्रीतेजःपालः सचिवश्चिरकालमस्तु तेजस्वी ॥ येन वयं निश्चिताश्चितामणिने-

व नंदामः ॥ ६ ॥ लवणप्रसादपुत्रश्रीकरणे लवणसिंहजनकोसौ ॥ मंत्रित्वमत्र कुरुतां कल्पशतं कल्पतरु-
कल्पः ॥ ७ ॥ पुरा पादेन दैत्यारेर्भुवनोपरिवर्तिना ॥ अधुना वस्तुपालस्य हस्तेनाधःकृतो बलिः ॥ ८ ॥ दयिता ललि-
तादेवी तनयमवीतनयमाप सचिवेंद्रात् ॥ नाम्ना जयंतसिंहं जयंतमिन्द्रात्पुलोमपुत्रीव ॥ ९ ॥

[एते] श्रीगुर्जरेश्वरपुरोहित ठ. श्रीसोमेश्वरदेवस्य स्तंभतीर्थेत्र कायस्थवंशो वाजडनंदनः ॥ प्रशस्तिमेतामलिखत्
जैत्रसिंह ध्रुवः सुधीः ॥ १ ॥ वाहडस्य तनुजेन सूत्रधारेण धीमता ॥ एषा कुमारसिंहेन समुत्कीर्णा प्रयत्नतः ॥ २ ॥
श्रीनेमेस्त्रिजगद्भर्तुरम्बायाश्च प्रसादतः ॥ वस्तुपालान्वयस्यास्तु प्रशस्तिः स्वस्तिशालिनी ॥ ३ ॥

Translation.[1]

"Salutation to Sarvajña.[2] May Nemijina......... whose .... protect.......................

"In the auspicious year 1288[3] of Vikrama, Wednesday the 10th of the bright half of Phâlguna.

"Ṭhakur Chaṇḍapa, an inhabitant of Aṇahilapura and of the Prâgvâṭa family, begat Chaṇḍaprasâda, who begat Soma, whose son was Âśârâja—his son, by Kumâradevî, was the great minister Vastupâla, younger brother of Luṇiga and Mâladeva and elder brother of Tejaḥpâla,—his son was Jayatasiṁha, who was born like a royal goose in the lake-like womb of Lalitâdevî. Before the *Saṁvat* year 79 Jayatasiṁha was trading as a banker in Stambhatîrtha, *karors* of new temples were caused to be built and many old ones repaired at great and renowned places of pilgrimage, such as Śatruñjaya, Arbudâchala, &c., in the prosperous cities of Aṇahilapura, Bhṛigupura, Stambhanakapura, Stambhatîrtha, Darbhavatî, Dhavalakkaka and other places, by the great minister Vastupâla and by his younger brother Tejaḥpâla. In the year *Saṁ.* 77—Vastupâla, who had obtained the leadership of a pilgrim-party by the favour of the lord of gods, manifested in virtue of the solemnities at such holy places as Śatruñjaya, Ujjayanta, &c., who had obtained authority in the kingdom by the favour of Vîradhavala Mahârâja, son of Mahârâjâdhirâja Lavaṇaprasâda, who was shining like the Sun in the heaven of the Chaulûkya family and was blessed by the favour of Śâradâ (*Sarasvatî*) with a son, and his younger brother Tejaḥpâla was carrying on banking transactions with the cities of Gujarât of which Dhavalakkaka was the chief, in the year *Saṁ.* 76.

"Similarly the famous Vastupâla has caused to be built this new and splendid temple of the Mahâtîrthâvatâra with a *maṇḍapa* adorned by twenty Tîrthaṅkaras such as Ajitanâtha, which were religiously inaugurated by his holiness Vijayasenasûri the ornament of the sacred seat of Bhaṭṭâraka Haribhadrasûri who occupied the office of Amarasûri, and by Ânandasûri a pupil of Śântisûri, who again was a pupil and son of Bhaṭṭâraka Ma-

---

1 Translated by Mathurâdâs Amṛitalâl, Esq., High School, Junâgaḍ, and revised by Col. J. W. Watson. The translations are not critical, but give the general sense of the inscriptions.

2 This is an epithet of the Jinas, of the Buddhas and of Śiva,—meaning "all-knowing."

3 This date refers to *prâsâdah kâritah* in the last line.

hendrasûri, of the Nâgendra division,—for the augmentation of his own merit and that of his wife Lalitâdevî, the daughter of Kâhnaḍa by Rāṇû of the Prâgvâṭa family. On this great holy place, the famous Ujjayanta adorned by Neminâtha the lord of the gods, and graced by various traditionally recounted places of pilgrimage,—the famous Ashṭâpada, a pillar called Sukhodghâṭanaka containing the images of the happy Soma his grandfather, and of the venerable Âśârâja his father—both mounted on horses—of the famous Neminâtha with three decorated arches, and of his ancestors, elder brother, younger brother, sons, &c.; the gods graced by the worshipful Neminâtha on four summits known as Ambâ, Avalokanâ, Sâmba and Pradyumna; two Jinas and the four gods, *viz.* the famous Ṛishabhadeva the first Tîrthaṅkara, who was incarnate on the great holy place of Śatruñjaya, the famous god Pârśvanâtha, who appeared in the flesh at Stambhanakapura, the famous Mahâvîradeva, who established himself as a deity at Satyapura, and the famous image of Sarasvatî, who was incarnate in Kaśmîra, with a eulogistic inscription,—were established and all set up by him (*Vastupâla*)."

(*Ślôka.*) "There is this difference between a flood of nectar and Vastupâla, the best of ministers,—the first restores the dead, the other restores the dying on the earth.

"Let (Kubera) the giver of riches, (Vishṇu) the dear lord of Lakshmî, and Śiva the supreme ruler, be where they may—for though able, they do not satisfy the poor with treasures of enjoyment, while the famous Vastupâla every day sprinkles the earth, withered by the fire of poverty, like a fresh rain-cloud with golden riches. O brother, what is the use of talking about sinful and wicked ministers who have nothing in their mind but malice against the people? Sing then by hundreds the virtues of Vastupâla, who observes a vow of universal good as Karṇa did in times of yore. After Bhojarâja ascending above the sun was gone and Muñja became sole lord of the dominion in heaven, there now stands only the famous Vastupâla to wipe off the trickling tears of the needy.

"O chief minister of the Chaulûkya line, the sound of thy glory is heard with hairs visibly on end and tears of joy even in the three worlds—for though polluted by Kali the earth has been sanctified by thee with temples, wells, charitable places to give water to the thirsty, ponds, gardens, lakes, &c.

"May the celebrated minister Tejaḥpâla long be glorious—Tejaḥpâla by whom we pass our happy days free from anxieties as by a Chintâmaṇî gem.

"May this man, who is like a tree of paradise and a father to Lavaṇasiṁha, and in charge of the state seals of the son of Lavaṇaprasâda, enjoy the ministership for a hundred ages.

"In olden times Bali was pressed down by the foot of Vishṇu, the enemy of the demons, from the earth; now the same is done by the hand of Vastupâla.

"His wife Lalitâdevî had, by this best of ministers, a son named Jayantasiṁha, possessed of modest virtues, as Śachî, the daughter of Puloma, had Jayanta by Indra.

"These (*ślôkas*) are (*the composition*) of the Ṭhâkur Someśvaradeva, the priest of the king of Gurjara.

"Jaitrasiṁha surnamed Dhruva of good intelligence, son of Vâjaḍa and born in a Kâyastha family in Stambhatîrtha, has written the eulogistic inscription.

"This inscription has been carefully engraved by the ingenious Kumârasiṁha, the son of Vâhaḍa, a mason by profession.

"May this inscription by the favour of Ambâ and Nemi, the support of the three worlds, be fraught with blessing to the descent of Vastupâla."

INSCRIPTION No. 2.

This is on the west door of Vastupâla and Tejaḥpâla's temples. It is in 14 long lines. The first part is rather obliterated. The prose-text is the same as in the preceding with very slight modifications, but the *ślôkas* are new.

|| – – – – – – – – – – – यः पु – – – – – – तयदुकुलक्षीरार्णवेंदुर्जिनो यत्पादाब्जपवित्रमौलिरसमश्री- रुज्जयंतोप्ययं ॥ धत्ते मूर्ध्नि निजप्रभुप्रसृमरोद्दामप्रभामंडलो विश्वक्षोणिभृदाधिपत्यपदवीं नीलातपत्रोज्वलां ॥ १ ॥ स्वस्ति श्रीविक्रमसंवत् १२८८ वर्षे० लहि-

[लपुरवास्त]व्य० लुणिगमहं. ठ. श्रीमाल० ललितादेवी-

[कुक्षिसरोवरराजहं]साय० सं. ७९ पूर्वं स्तंभतीर्थमुद्राव्यापारं व्या० धिराजश्रीलवण-

[प्रसाददेवसुत]महारा० महातीर्थेषु

[श्रीमदणहिलपुर]श्रीभृगुपुर० श्रीऋषभदेव-

[स्तंभनकपुरावतार]श्रीपार्श्व० चतुष्टयजिनद्वंद्वअंबावलो० रुढनिजपितामहठ. श्रीसोमस्य निजपितृ ठ. श्रीआशाराज-

[मूर्तिद्वितय]चाद्धतो० श्रीउज्जयंतमहातीर्थे आत्मनस्तथा स्वभार्यायाः० ठ. कान्हडपुत्र्याः ठ.

[राणुकुक्षिसंभूताया] महंश्रीसोखुकायाः पुण्या० पट्टालंकरणश्रीविजय० ष्टितश्रीऋषभदेवप्रमुखचतुर्विंश- तितीर्थ० समंड-

[पः श्रीसमेतमहा]तीर्थावतारप्रधानप्रासादः कारितः ॥ छ ॥ ॥ चेतः किं कलिकाल सालसमहो किं मोह नो हस्यते तृष्णे कृष्णमुखासि किं कथय किं विघ्नौघ मोघो भवान् ॥ ब्रूमः किं नु सखे न खेलाति किमप्यस्माक- मुज्जृंभितं सैन्ये[1] यत्किल वस्तुपालकृतिना धर्मस्य संवर्धितं ॥ १ ॥ यं विधुं बंधवः सिद्धमर्थिनः शत्र-

– – – ॥ – – – – – – पश्यंति वर्ण्यतां किमयं मया ॥ २ ॥ वैरं विभूतिभारत्योः प्रभुत्वप्रणिपातयोः ॥ तेजस्विताप्रशमयोः शमितं येन मंत्रिणा ॥ ३ ॥ दीपः स्फूर्जति सज्जकज्जलमलस्नेहं मुहुः संहरन्निदुर्मंडलवृत्तखं- डनपरः प्रद्वेष्टि मित्रोदयं ॥ शूरः क्रूरकरः परस्य सहते तेजो न तेजस्विनस्तत्केन प्रतिमं ब्र-

[वीमि सचिवं श्री]वस्तुपालाभिधं ॥ ४ ॥ आयाताः कति नैव यांति कति नो यास्यंति नो वा कति स्थाने स्थाननिवासिनो भवपथे पांथीभवंतो जनाः ॥ अस्मिन् विस्मयनीयबुद्धिजलधिर्विध्वस्य दस्यून् करे कुर्वन् पुण्यनिधिं धिनोति वसुधां श्रीवस्तुपालः परं ॥ ५ ॥ दक्षस्य वीरधवलक्षितिपस्य राज्यभारे धुरंधरधुरं

– – – – – – – ॥ श्रीतेजपालसचिवे दधति स्वबंधुभारोद्धृतावविधुरैकधुरीणभावं ॥ ६ ॥ इह तेजपालसचिवो विमलितविमलाचलेंद्रममृतभृतं ॥ कृत्वानुपमसरोवरममरगणं प्रीणयांचक्रे ॥ ७ ॥ [एते] श्रीमलधारिश्रीनरचंद्रसूरिणां ॥ इह वालिगसुतसहजिगपुत्रानकं[2]तनुजबाजडतनूजः ॥ आलि-

[1] सैन्यं. [2] तक.

[खादिमां कायस्थस्तं]भपुरीयप्रभुर्वो जयतसिंहः ॥ ८ ॥ हरिमंडपनंदीश्वरशिल्पीश्वरसोमदेवपौत्रेण ॥ बकुलस्वामिसुतेनोत्कीर्णा पुरुषोत्तमेनेयं ॥ ९ ॥ श्रीनेमेस्त्रिजगद्भर्त्तु॰ शाकिनी ॥ १० ॥ महामात्य॰ रियं ॥ महामात्यश्रीवस्तुपालभार्यामहंश्रीसोखुकायाधर्मस्थानमिदं ॥

Translation.

"Jina......who purifies like the...moon in the milk ocean of the Yâdava family...... conquered............ Though this Ujjayanta has its summit sanctified by his lotus-feet and possesses unrivalled splendour of its own, yet being surrounded by the eminent lustre of its master, it wears on its head a dignity of superiority above all the mountains of the world—bright as a dark umbrella.

"In the auspicious year 1288 of Vikrama, Wednesday the 10th of the bright half of Phâlguna.

"Ṭhakur Chaṇḍapa, an inhabitant of Aṇahilapura and of the Prâgvâṭa family, begat Chaṇḍaprasâda, who begat Soma, whose son was Âśârâja—his son by Kumâradevî was the great minister Vastupâla, younger brother of Luṇiga and Mâladeva and elder brother of Tejaḥpâla—his son was Jayatasiṁha, who was born like a royal goose in the lake-like womb of Lalitâdevî. Before the *Saṁvat* year 79 Jayatasiṁha was trading as a banker in Stambhatîrtha, *karors* of new temples were caused to be built and many old ones repaired at great and renowned places of pilgrimage such as Śatruñjaya, Arbudâchala, &c., and in the prosperous cities of Aṇahilapura, Bhṛigupura, Stambhanakapura, Stambhatîrtha, Darbhavatî, Dhavalakkaka and other places by the great minister Vastupâla and by his younger brother Tejaḥpâla in the year *Saṁ.* 77—Vastupâla, who had obtained the leadership of a pilgrim-party by the favour of the lord of gods, manifested in virtue of the solemnities at such holy places as Śatruñjaya, Ujjayanta, &c., who had obtained authority in the kingdom by the favour of Vîradhavala Mahârâja, son of Mahârâjâdhirâja Lavaṇaprasâda, who was shining like the Sun in the heaven of the Chaulûkya family and was blessed by the favour of Śâradâ (*Sarasvatî*) with a son, and his younger brother Tejaḥpâla was carrying on banking transactions with the cities of Gujarât, of which Dhavalakkaka was the chief, in the year *Saṁ.* 76.

"Similarly the famous Vastupâla has caused to be built this new and splendid temple of the Mahâtîrthâvatâra with a *maṇḍapa* adorned by twenty-four Tîrthaṅkaras such as Ajitanâtha, religiously inaugurated by his holiness Vijayasenasûri, the ornament of the sacred seat of Bhaṭṭâraka Haribhadrasûri, who occupied the office of Amarasûri, and by Ânandasûri, a pupil of Śântisûri, who again was a pupil and son of Bhaṭṭâraka Mahendrasûri of the Nâgendra division—for the augmentation of his own merit and that of his wife Sokhukâ, the daughter of Kâhanaḍa by Râṇû of Prâgvâṭa caste, On this great holy place, the famous Ujjayanta, adorned by Neminâtha the lord of gods and graced by various traditionally recounted places of pilgrimage, the famous Ashṭâpada, a pillar called Sukhodghâṭanaka, containing the images of the happy Soma, his grandfather, and of the venerable Âśârâja his father—both mounted on horses,—of the famous Neminâtha with three decorated arches, and of his ancestors, elder brother, younger brother, sons, &c., the quadruple gods graced by the worshipful Neminâtha on four summits (*known as*) Ambâ, Avalokanâ, Sâmba and Pradyumna,—two Jinas and the four gods, *viz.* the famous Ṛishabhadeva, the first Tîrthaṅkara, who was incarnate on the great holy place of Śatruñjaya, the famous god Pârśvanâtha, who appeared in flesh at Stambhanakapura, the famous Mahâvîradeva, who established himself as a deity at Satyapura, and the famous image of Sarasvatî, who was incarnate in Kaśmîra, with eulogistic inscription,—were established, and all set up by him (*Vastupâla*)."

(*Ślôkas.*) "O Kalikâla, why is thy mind weary? O World-delusion, why dost thou not smile? O Thirst, why art thou with a blackened face? Why, O multitude of obstacles, is thy attempt not crowned with success? (They answer) what answer, friend, can we make but that our remedy does not progress well as the army of virtue has been greatly strengthened by the good deeds of Vastupâla.

"How can this man be described by me?—a man whom his relations look upon as the moon, the needy as the object accomplished, and enemies as the deity of destruction.

"He is a minister by whom the natural enmities between wealth and learning, superiority and subordination, and pride and humility, have been laid at rest.

"With what or whom can we compare the famous minister Vastupâla? For if (we compare him) with a lamp it continually sucks up oil (affection) and brings forth a sooty dirt; if (we compare him to) the moon it is always inclined to the diminution of his disk (circle) and envies the rise of the sun (friend), when the sun with torch-like rays does not bear the light of another luminous body.

"How many have not come in the course of this world like travellers making a temporary halt, how many do not go away, and how many will yet not go? But Vastupâla, the ocean of admirable genius, destroys all rogues, and keeping the treasures of merit in his hands, nourishes the earth.

"He, the best of ministers, bore the yoke of the king Vîradhavala's kingdom, and the famous Tejaḥpâla held a share in lifting the burden of his brother.........

"Here the minister Tejaḥpâla, making an unrivalled lake of nectarial water which purified Śatruñjaya, satisfied the host of the immortals.

"These are composed by Śrî Maladhâri Narachandrasûri.

"Kâyastha Jayatasiṁha surnamed Dhruva, of Stambhapura, the son of Vâjaḍa, the son of Âṭaka, who was the son of Sahajiga, the son of Vâliga, has written this (*inscription*).

"Engraved by Purushottama, the son of Bakula Svâmi, the grandson of Somadeva, head of the engravers of Vishṇu's temple and Śiva's bull.

"This is the eulogy of Vastupâla, the great minister.

"This is a temple of the virtuous Sokhukâ, the wife of Vastupâla, the great minister."

Inscription No. 3.

On the north door of the same temple in 18 lines. The prose text is very similar to that of the first and second inscriptions.

ॐ नमः सर्वज्ञाय ॥ प्रणमदमरप्रेंखन्मौलिस्फुरन्मणिधोरणी तरुणकिरणश्रेणीशोणीकृताखिलविग्रहः ॥ सुरपतिकरोन्मुक्तैः [स्ना]नोदकैर्घुसृणारुणः कृततनुरिवापायात् पायाज्जगांति शिवांगजः ॥ १ ॥ स्वस्ति श्री-विक्रम० व्यप्रा-

ग्वाटा० साधमाने-

महं० श्री० व्यापारंव्यापृ० वीरधव-

ल्देवप्री० दर्भवतीधव-

लक्कक० श्रीसत्यपु० रदेव-

प्रशस्ति० धिक्ढनिजपि० स्वपितृ० द्वितयकुंजराधिक्ढमहामात्यश्रीवस्तुपालअनुजमहं० श्रीतेजःपालमूर्तिद्वय-

चारुतोरणत्रय० स्तंभश्रीसंमेतमहातीर्थप्र० तथा स्वभार्यायाश्च प्रा० पुत्र्याः ठ.

राणुकाक्षि० श्रीसोलुकायाः पु० प्रतिष्ठितश्रीऋषभदेवप्रमुखदेवालंकृतोयमभिनवः समंडपः श्रीअष्टापदमहा-

तीर्थावतारनिरुपमप्रधानप्रासादः कारितः ॥ छ ॥ ॥ प्रासादैर्गगनांगणप्रणयिभिः पातालमूलंकषैः कासारैश्च सितैः सिताम्बरगृहैर्नीलैश्च लीलावनैः ॥ येनेयं नयनिर्जितेंद्रसचिवेनालंकृतालं क्षितिः क्षेमैकायतनं चिरायुरुदयी श्रीवस्तुपालोस्तु सः ॥ १ ॥ संदिष्टं तव वस्तुपाल बलिना विश्वत्रयीयात्रकान् मत्वा ना-

रदतश्चरित्रमिति ते हृष्टोस्मि नंद्याश्चिरं ॥ नार्थिभ्यः कुधमर्थितः प्रथयसि स्वल्पं न दत्से न च स्वश्लाघां बहु मन्यसे किमपरं न श्रीमदान्मुह्यसि ॥ २ ॥ अखिलदलनश्रीवीरनामायमुर्व्यां सुरपतिरवतीर्णस्तर्कयामस्तदस्य ॥ निवसति सुरशाखी वस्तुपालाभिधानः सुरगुरुरपि तेजःपालसंज्ञः समीपे ॥ ३ ॥ उदारः शूरो वा

रुचिरवचनो वास्ति न हि वा भवत्तुल्यः कोपि क्वचिदिति चुलुक्येंद्रसचिव ॥ समुद्भूतभ्रांतिर्नियतमवगंतुं तव यशस्ततिर्गेहे गेहे पुरि पुरि च याता दिशि दिशि ॥ ४ ॥ सा कुत्रापि युगत्रयी बत गता सृष्टा च सृष्टिः सतां सीद-त्साधुरसंवरत्सुचरितः खेलत्खलोभूत्कलिः ॥ तद्विश्वार्त्तिनिवर्त्तनैकमनसः प्रत्तोधुना शं-

भुना प्रस्तावस्तव वस्तुपाल भवते यद्रोचते तत्कुरु ॥ ५ ॥ के निधाय वसुधातले धनं वस्तुपाल न यमालयं गताः ॥ त्वं तु नंदसि निवेशयन्निदं दिक्षु धावति जने क्षुधावति ॥ ६ ॥ पोत्रेण धारय वराहपते धरित्रीं सूर्य प्रकाशय सदा जलदाभिषिंच ॥ विश्राणितेन परिपालय वस्तुपाल भारं भवत्सु यदिमं निदधे विधा-

ता ॥ ७ ॥ आत्मा त्वं जगतः सदागतिरियं कीर्तिर्मुखं पुष्करं मैत्री मंत्रिवरः स्थिरा घनरसः श्लोकस्तमोघ्नः शमः ॥ नोक्तः केन करस्तवामृतकरः कायश्च भास्वानिति स्पष्टं धूर्जटिमूर्त्तयः कृतपदाः श्रीवस्तुपाल त्वयि ॥ ८ ॥ विद्या यद्यपि वैदिकी न लभते सौभाग्यमेषा क्वचित् न स्मार्त्त कुरुते च कश्चन वचः कर्णद्वये य-

द्यपि ॥ राजानः कृपणाश्च यद्यपि गृहे यद्यप्ययं च व्ययार्थिता कापि तथापि तिष्ठाति न मे श्रीवस्तुपाले सति ॥ ९ ॥ कर्णे खलप्रलपितं न करोषि रोषं नाविःकरोषि न करोष्यपदे च लाभं ॥ तेनोपरि त्वमवनेरपि वर्त्तमानः श्रीवस्तुपाल कलिकालमधः करोषि ॥ १० ॥ सर्वत्र भ्रांतिमती सर्वविदस्त्वदभवत्कथं कीर्त्तिः ॥

श्रीवस्तुपालपैतृकमनुहरते संततिः प्रायः ॥ ११ ॥ सोपि बलेरवलेपः स्वल्पतरोभूत्तथैव कल्पतरोः ॥ श्रीवस्तु-पालसचिवे सिंचति दानामृतैर्जगतीं ॥ १२ ॥ नियोगिनागेषु नरेश्वराणां भद्रस्वभावः खलु वस्तुपालः ॥ उद्दामदान-प्रसरस्य यस्य विभाव्यते क्वापि न मत्तभावः ॥ १३ ॥ विबुधैः पयोधिमध्यादेको बहु-

भिः करींदुरुपलब्धः ॥ बहुवस्तु वस्तुपाल प्राप्ता विबुध त्वयैकेन ॥ १४ ॥ प्रथमं धनप्रवाहैर्वाहैरथनाथमा-त्मनः सचिवः ॥ अधुना तु सुकृतसिंधुः सिंधुरवृंदैः प्रमोदयति ॥ १५ ॥ श्रीवस्तुपाल भवता जलधेर्गभीरता किलाक-लिता ॥ आनीय ततो गजता स्वपतिद्वारे यदाकलिता ॥ १६ ॥ [९] ते श्रीमद्गुर्जरेश्वरपुरोहि-

तठ. श्रीसोमेश्वरदेवस्य ॥ इह वाल्मिगसुतसहजिग० जः ॥ अलिखदिमां कायस्थस्तंभपुरीयभुवो जयतसिंहः ॥ १ ॥ हरिमंडपनं० नेयं ॥ २ ॥ महामात्यश्रीवस्तुपालप्रशस्तिरियं निष्पन्ना ॥ शुभं भवतु ॥

श्रीनेमेञ्जिज० शालिनी ॥ महामात्यश्रीवस्तुपालभार्या महं श्रीसोखुकाया धर्मस्थानामिदं ॥ श्री कल्याणमस्तु ॥

Translation.

" Salutation to Sarvajña, May that son of Śiva whose whole body is red by the groups of tender rays proceeding from the bright gems in the chaplets of prostrated gods, and who looks red like saffron (?) as if washed by the bathing water poured by the hand of the lord of gods—May that son of the god protect the worlds from calamity !

" In the auspicious year of Vikrama 1288, Wednesday the 10th of the bright half of Phâlguna.

" Ṭhakur Chaṇḍapa, an inhabitant of Aṇahilapura and of the Prâgvâṭa family, begat Chaṇḍaprasâda, who begat Soma, whose son was Âśârâja—his son by Kumâradevî was the great minister Vastupâla, the younger brother of Luṇiga and Mâladeva and elder brother of Tejaḥpâla—his son was Jayatasiṁha who was born like a royal goose in the lake-like womb of Lalitâdevî. Before the *Saṁvat* year 79 Jayatasiṁha was trading as a banker in Stambhatîrtha, *karors* of new temples were caused to be built and many old ones repaired at great and renowned places of pilgrimage such as Śatruñjaya, Arbudâchala, &c., and in the prosperous cities of Aṇahilapura, Bhṛigupura, Stambhanakapura, Stambhatîrtha, Darbhavatî, Dhavalakkaka and other places, by the great minister Vastupâla, and by his younger brother Tejaḥpâla. In the year *Saṁ.* 77—Vastupâla, who had obtained the leadership of a pilgrim-party by the favour of the lord of gods, manifested in virtue of the solemnities at such holy places as Śatruñjaya, Ujjayanta, &c., who had obtained authority in the kingdom by the favour of Vîradhavala Mahârâja son of Mahârâjâdhirâja Lavaṇaprasâda, who was shining like the Sun in the heaven of the Chaulukya family and was blessed by the favour of Śâradâ (*Sarasvatî*) with a son, and his younger brother Tejaḥpâla was carrying on banking transactions with the cities of Gujarât of which Dhavalakkaka was the chief, in the year *Saṁ.* 76.

" Similarly the famous Vastupâla has caused to be built this new and splendid temple of the Mahâtîrthâvatâra with a *maṇḍapa* adorned by Tîrthankaras such as Ajitanâtha, religiously inaugurated by his holiness Vijayasenasûri, the ornament of the sacred seat of Bhaṭṭâraka Haribhadrasûri, who occupied the office of Amarasûri and by Ânandasûri a pupil of Śântisûri, who again was a pupil and son of Baṭṭâraka Mahendrasûri of the Nâgendra division—for the augmentation of his own merit and that of his wife Sokhukâ, daughter of Kâhnaḍa by Râṇû of the Prâgvâṭa caste. On this great holy place the famous Ujjayanta adorned by Neminâtha the lord of the gods, and graced by various traditionally recounted places of pilgrimage such as the famous Ashṭâpada,—a pillar called Sukhodghâṭanaka containing the images of the happy Soma his grandfather, and of the venerable Âśârâja his father—both mounted on horses, himself (Vastupâla) and his younger brother (Tejaḥpâla) being both mounted on the same elephant—of the famous Neminâtha with three decorated arches, and of his ancestors, elder brother, younger brother, sons, &c. ; the quadruple gods graced by the worshipful Neminâtha, on four summits (known as) Ambâ, Avalokanâ, Sâmba and Pradyumna, two Jinas and the four gods, *viz.* the famous

Ṛishabhadeva the first Tîrthaṅkara, who was incarnate on the great holy place of Śatruñjaya, the famous god Pârśvanâtha, who appeared in flesh at Stambhanakapura, the famous Mahâvîradeva, who established himself as a deity at Satyapura, and the famous image of Sarasvatî, who was incarnate at Kaśmîra, with eulogistic inscription,—were established and all set up by him (*Vastupâla*).

(*Ślôkas.*) "May this Vastupâla, the sole place of safety, be prosperous and long-lived—he who has surpassed the minister of Indra by prudence and has fully adorned the earth with palaces, whose foundations touched the very root of the earth and whose tops nodded in the sky, with lakes, and with white monasteries of Śvetâmbaras and with green gardens of pleasure.

"O Vastupâla, Bali has sent thee a message that he has been much pleased by hearing from Nârada, who visits the three worlds, that though frequently solicited thou dost not extend thy anger to the needy, dost not give them sparingly, and attachest no importance to thy praise; that, in short, thou art not intoxicated by the pride of riches, and thou mayest long be happy.

"We think the lord of gods has come to the earth under the name of Vîra (dhavala), the destroyer of his enemy's armies, and therefore the desire-fulfilling tree of paradise, under the disguise of Vastupâla, and Bṛihaspati, the preceptor of the gods, under that of Tejaḥpâla, dwell about him.

"O minister of the king of the Chaulukya line, thy glories, as if to ascertain whether there exists anywhere else a man who may be brave, generous and sweet-speaking like thee, have gone in all directions seeking in every house and every town.

"Alas, three *yugas* have somewhere departed and the production of virtuous men has ceased; the time now prevails of Kali, when the sages are harassed; men do not perform good deeds and rogues are plying at large. Under these circumstances, O Vastupâla, Śiva has now heard that thy attention is solely directed to the removal of universal distress—do as it may please you.

"Who have not gone to the place of Yama depositing their treasures in the ground? But, O Vastupâla, thou delightest in giving them (treasures) to hungry people roaming here and there in all directions.

"O lord of the boar, hold the earth in thy tusk! O sun, illumine her! O clouds, sprinkle water upon her, and O Vastupâla, protect her with thy charitable gifts; for the Creator has assigned these duties to you.

"O Vastupâla, images of Śiva visibly reside in thee; for thou art the soul of the world; thy glory is ever spreading (like the wind); thy face is lotus-like (like the sky); thy friendship, O best of ministers! is firm (like the earth); thy fame is sweet (like water); thy patience is dark-destroying (like the sun); and who has not declared thy hand to be of nectarial power (like the moon) and thy body bright (like Agni)?

"Though the Vedic knowledge fares not well in any place, though no one takes a word of *Smṛiti* into his ears, though kings are misers and there is so much expense in the house, yet I feel not the least concerned for all that so long as Vastupâla lives.

"That dost not listen to the word of the wicked, manifestest no anger and turnest not thy ambition to an improper object. By this, O Vastupâla ! though living on earth, thou treadest Kali underneath thy feet.

"As a rule, offsprings follow their father; how then, O Vastupâla, can thy glory be doubtful, sprung though she is from thy all-knowing self ?

"By the famous minister Vastupâla watering the earth with nectarial charities, the pride of Bali and Kalpataru has been greatly lowered.

"Among the elephant-like courtiers of the king, Vastupâla possesses the good qualities of a Bhadra ; for no intoxicated spirit ever comes out of him, though the profusion of gifts flows apace, just as a Bhadra is not maddened though rutting secretion flows profuse.

"Only one elephant was obtained from the ocean by many gods : while O Vastupâla, many elephants from the ocean (*i. e.*, countries on the seashore) by one wise man (*i. e.* yourself). Vastupâla, thou hast pleased thy master first with streams of wealth, then with horses, and now thou, who art the ocean of virtuous deeds, hast pleased him with numerous elephants.

"Vastupâla, thou hast indeed measured the depth of the ocean ; for having thence conveyed a number of elephants, thou hast placed them at the gates of thy master.

"These (*ślôkas*) are by Ṭhâkur Someśvara, priest to the king of Gujarât.

"Kâyastha Jayatasiṁha surnamed Dhruva, inhabitant of Stambhapura, the son of Vâjaḍa, the son of Âtaka, who was the son of Sahajiga, the son of Vâliga," &c., &c., &c.

Inscription No. 4.

This inscription is over the east door of the same temple. The letters are distinct and the stone is entire.

ॐ नमः श्रीनेमिनाथदेवाय ॥ ॥ तीर्थेशाः प्रणतेन्द्रसंहतिशिरःकोटीरकोटिस्फुटत्तेजोजालजलप्रवाहलहरीप्रक्षालितांघ्रिद्वयः ॥ ते वः केवलमूर्त्तयः कवलितारिष्टां विशिष्टाममी तामष्टादशशैलमौलिमणयोविश्राणयंतु श्रियं ॥ १ ॥ स्वस्ति श्री० फागुण

शुदि० पालस्यात्मजे

महं. श्रील० तीर्थवेलाकुलमुद्राव्यापारं व्यापृ० प्रकाशनैक-

मार्त्तं० पालेन च श्री-

शत्रुंज० कोटिशो धर्म्मस्थानानि० जयमहातीर्थाव-

तार० धिरूढानि-

जपिताम० सूपितृ० द्वितयतोरणत्रय० स्तंभश्रीसंमेतावतारमह० महातीर्थे आ-

त्मनस्तथा स्वभार्यायाः प्रा० महं० श्रीसोमुखकायाः पु० लंकरणश्रीविजयसे० ष्ठि-

तश्रीमदादिजिनराजश्रीऋषभदेवप्रमुखचतुर्विंशातितीर्थंकरालंकृतोयमभिनवः सर्मंडपः श्रीअष्टापदमहातीर्थावतारप्रधानप्रासादः कारितः ॥ ॥ छ ॥ ॥ स्वस्ति श्री बलये नमोस्तु नितरां कर्णाय दाने ययोरस्पष्टेपि द्वयां

यशः कियदिदं वंद्यास्तदेताः प्रजाः ॥ दृष्टे संप्रति वस्तुपालसचिवत्यागे कार्ष्यांति ताः कीर्तिं कांचन या पुनः स्फुटमियं विश्वेपि नो मास्याति ॥ १ ॥ कोटीरैः कटकांगुलीयतिलकैः केयूरहारादिभिः कौशेयैश्च. विभूष्यमाणवपुषो यत्पाणिविश्राणितैः ॥ विद्वांसो गृहमागताः प्रणयिनीरप्रत्यभिज्ञाभृतस्तैस्तैः स्वं शपथैः कथं कथमिव प्रत्याययांचक्रिरे ॥ २ ॥ न्यासं न्यातनुतां विरोचनसुत

स्त्यागं कवित्वश्रियं भासव्यासपुरःसराःपृथुरघुप्रायाश्च वीरव्रतं ॥ प्रज्ञां नाकपताकिनीगुरुरपिश्रीवस्तुपाल ध्रुवं जानीमो न विवेकमेकमकृतोत्सेकंतु कौतस्कुतं ॥ ३ ॥ वास्तवं वस्तुपालस्य वेत्ति कश्चरिताद्भुतं ॥ यस्य दानमविश्रांतमर्थिस्वपि रिपुस्वपि ॥ ४ ॥ स्तोतव्यः खलु वस्तुपालसचिवः कैर्नाम वाग्वैभवैर्यस्य

त्यागविधिर्विधूय विविधामू दारिद्र्यमुद्रां हठात् ॥ विश्वस्मिन्नखिलेप्यसूत्रयदसावर्थीति दातेति च द्वौ शब्दावभिधेयवस्तुविरहव्याहन्यमानस्थिती ॥ ९ ॥ आद्येनाप्यपवर्जनेन जनितार्थित्वप्रमाथान्पुनःस्तोकं दत्तमिति क्रमांतरगतानाहूययन्नर्थिनः ॥ पूर्वस्माद्गणसंख्ययापि गुणितं यस्तेष्वनावर्तिषु द्रव्यं

दातुमुदस्तहस्तकमलस्तस्थौ चिरं दुःस्थितः ॥ ६ ॥ विश्वस्मिन् कलि पंकपंकिलतले प्रस्थानवीर्थी विना सीदन्नेष पदे पदे न पुरतो गंतेति संचिंतयन् ॥ धर्मस्थानशतच्छलेन विदधे धर्मस्य वर्षीयसः संचाराय शिलाकलापपदवीं श्रीवस्तुपालस्फुटं ॥ ७ ॥ अंभोजेषु मरालमंडलरुचो डिंडीरपिंडत्विषः कासारे-

षु पयोधिरोधसि लुठन्निर्णिक्तमुक्ताश्रियः ॥ ज्योत्स्नाभाः कुमुदाकरेषु सदनोद्यानेषु पुष्पोल्वणाः स्फूर्तिं कामिव वस्तुपाल कृतिनः कुर्वंति नो कीर्त्तयः ॥ ८ ॥ देव स्वर्नाथ कष्टं ननु क इव भवान् नंदनोद्यानपालः खेदस्तत्कोद्य केनाप्यहह हतहतः काननात्कल्पवृक्षः ॥ हुं मा वादीस्तदेतत्किमपि

करुणया मानवानां मयैव प्रीत्यादिष्टोयमुर्व्यास्तिलकयतितलं वस्तुपालच्छलेन ॥ ९ ॥ श्रीमंत्रीश्वरवस्तुपालयशसामुक्तावचैर्वीचिभिः सर्वस्मिन्नपि लंभिते धवलतां कल्लोलिनीमंडले ॥ गंगैवेयमिति प्रतीतिविकलास्ताम्यंति कामं भुवि भ्राम्यंतस्तनुसादमंदितमुदो मंदाकिनीयात्रिकाः ॥ १० ॥ व-

त्कं निर्वासनाज्ञानयनपथगतं यस्य दारिद्र्यदस्योर्दृष्टिः पीयूषवृष्टिः प्रणयिषु परितः पेतुषी सप्रसादं ॥ प्रेमालापस्तु कोपि स्फुरदसमपरब्रह्मसंवादवेदीनेदीयान्वस्तुपालः स खलु यदि तदा को न भाग्यैकभूतिः ॥ ११ ॥ साक्षात् ब्रह्म परं धरागतमिव श्रेयोविवर्तैः सतां तेजःपाल इति प्रसिद्धमहिमा तस्यानु-

जन्माजयी ॥ यो धत्ते न दशां कदापि कलितावद्यामविद्यामयीं यं चोपास्य परिस्पृशंति कृतिनः सद्यः परां निर्वृतिं ॥ १२ ॥ आकृष्टे कमलाकुलस्य कुदशारंभस्य संस्तंभनं वश्यत्वं जगदाशयस्य यशसामासांतनिर्वासनं ॥ मोहः शत्रुपराक्रमस्य मृतिरप्यन्यायदस्योरिति स्वैरं षड्विधकर्मनिर्मितिमया मंत्रोस्य

मंत्रीशितुः ॥ १३ ॥ [ए] ते मलधारिनरेंद्रसूरिणां स्तंभतीर्थेत्र का० ध्रुवः सुधीः ॥ १ ॥ हरि मंडपनं० नेयं ॥ २ ॥ श्रीवस्तुपालप्रभोः प्रशस्तिरियं निष्पन्ना ॥ मंगलं महाश्रीः ॥ ॥ छ ॥ ॥

Translation.

"Salutation to the holy Neminâthadeva. May those gods of holy places who are jewels on the crests of the eighteen mountains, whose feet are washed by streams of radiant light proceeding from hundreds of coronets on the heads of prostrating gods and whose images are unrivalled—May those gods of holy places give excellent and evil devouring riches to you.

"In the auspicious year of Vikrama 1288, Wednesday the 10th of the bright half of Phâlguna.

"Ṭhakur Chanḍapa, an inhabitant of Aṇahilapura and an ornament of the Prâgvâṭa family, begat Chanḍaprasâda, who begat Soma, whose son was Aśârâja—his son by

Kumâradevî was the great minister Vastupâla, the younger brother of Luṇiga and Mâladeva and elder brother of Tejaḥpâla,—his son was Jayatasiṁha, who was born like a royal goose in the lake-like womb of Lalitâdevî. Before the *Saṁvat* year 79, Jayatasiṁha was trading as a banker in Stambhatîrtha, *karors* of new temples were caused to be built and many old ones repaired at great and renowned places of pilgrimage such as Śatruñjaya, Arbudâchala, &c., and in the prosperous cities of Aṇahilapura, Bhṛigupura, Stambhanakapura, Stambhatîrtha, Darbhavaṭî, Dhavalakkaka and other places by the great minister Vastupâla and by his younger brother Tejaḥpâla in the year *Saṁ.* 77—Vastupâla who had obtained the leadership of a pilgrim-party by the favour of the lord of gods, manifested in virtue of the solemnities at such holy places as Śatruñjaya, Ujjayanta, &c.—who had obtained authority in the kingdom by the favour of Vîradhavala Mahârâja, son of Mahârâjâdhirâja Lavaṇaprasâda, who was shining like the sun in the heaven of the Chaulukya family, and was blessed by the favour of Sâradâ (*Śarasvatî*) with a son, and his younger brother Tejaḥpâla was carrying on banking transactions with the cities of Gujarât of which Dhavalakkaka was the chief.

" Similarly the famous Vastupâla has caused to be built this new and splendid temple of the Mahâtîrthâvatâra with a *maṇḍapa* adorned by twenty Tîrthaṅkaras such as Ajitanâtha, religiously inaugurated by his holiness Vijayasenasûri, the ornament of the sacred seat of Bhaṭṭâraka Haribhadrasûri, who occupied the office of Amarasûri, and by Ânandasûri, a pupil of Śântisûri, who again was a pupil and son of Bhaṭṭâraka Mahendrasûri of the Nâgendra division. For the augmentation of his own merit and that of his wife Lalitâdevî, the daughter of Kânhaḍa by Râṇû of the Prâgvâta caste—on this great holy place, the famous (Ujjayanta) adorned by Neminâtha the lord of the gods and graced by various traditionally recounted places of pilgrimage such as the famous Ashṭâpada,—a pillar called Sukhodghâṭanaka containing the images of the happy Soma his grandfather, and of the venerable Aśârâja his father—both mounted on horses—of the famous Neminâtha with three decorated arches and of his ancestors, elder brother, younger brother, &c.; the quadruple gods graced by the worshipful Neminâtha on four summits (*known as*) Ambâ, Avalokanâ, Sâmba and Pradyumna; two Jinas and three gods, *viz.* the famous Ṛishabhadeva, the first Tîrthaṅkara who was incarnate on the great holy place of Śatruñjaya, the famous god Pârśvanâtha who appeared in flesh at Stambhanakapura, the famous Mahâvîradeva who established himself as a deity at Satyapura, and the famous image of Sarasvatî who was incarnate in Kaśmîra, were established with eulogistic inscription, all set up by himself (*Vastupâla*)."

(*Ślôkas.*) Let there be continuous salutation to holy Bali and Karṇa, whose charity though unseen has been the object of so much fame; consequently the people are worthy of worship, and the great minister Vastupâla's charity which the people see with their eyes so great that even the world itself can scarcely contain it.

" Many learned men adorned with diadems, bracelets, rings, frontal marks, armlets, garlands and silken robes presented by his (*Vastupâla's*) hands became so changed that they with great difficulty and many oaths could persuade their partners of their identity.

" The son of Virochana may extend (*give*) his gift of charity; Bhâsa, Vyâsa, &c., their riches of poetry; Pṛithu, Raghu, &c., their vow of bravery; and the instructor of the army of gods may lend his intelligence; but, Vastupâla, we know not from what source thou hast derived thy prideless manners.

"Who knows the extraordinary deeds of Vastupâla as they really are—Vastupâla whose *dânas* (*presents and punishments*) are unceasing equally upon his implorers and enemies?

"With what epithets of greatness should the great minister Vastupâla be praised, whose ways of giving alms, at once destroying the stamp of poverty, have strung together the words *giver* and *needy* in the whole world and made them useless!

"Thinking that he gave little to supplicants, who being satisfied by his first gift did not like to return, he stood calling after them with hands outstretched to give many times more than the first amount.

"Thinking that the world is soiled by the muddy vices of Kali, and that tottering virtue would stumble at every step without a path to walk on, he the great minister, has made places of charity as a pavement for the old religion to walk on.

"What new variety do not the glories of Vastupâla assume! They have the splendour of geese on the lotus; the brightness of a heap of foam on the lake, and beauty of spotless pearls on the sea shore; they look like moonlight in night-blowing lotuses and spreading white as flowers in gardens attached to the house.

"Alas, O lord of heaven, a great misfortune! 'Well, who are you?' (he says) 'a keeper of the garden of Paradise.' 'What is your affliction?' he asks; 'somebody has taken off the desire-fulfilling tree from the garden of your highness.' He replies: 'No, say not so; I have, out of special grace to men, sent it down to earth, which it now graces under the name of Vastupâla.'

"The whole river system being rendered white by the up-and-down waves of the great minister Vastupâla's glories, the pilgrims to the holy Ganges, mistaking every river for the real Ganges (*whose water is white*) wander here and there with minds very much perplexed and limbs exhausted and slackened with fatigue.

"Who is not fortunate when the minister Vastupâla is nigh? Vastupâla, whose face if once falling within the sight of stealing poverty, is a positive command for its departure, whose eyes if favourably cast are nectar showers to his friends, and whose kind conversation always turns upon the lucid and unrivalled discussion of the Supreme Being.

"His victorious younger brother, who never displays unholy anger in his eyes, and by whose shelter the virtuous at once get rid of their troubles, is known by the name of Tejaḥpâla, and he looks like the embodiment of final beatitude to the virtuous on this earth.

"He is the attraction of riches, hindrance of misfortune, restraint of worldly desires, and the cause of sending glories to the utmost boundary of the points of the compass. He causes the exploits of his enemy to swoon away and is death to the thief, injustice. These six qualities are self-existent in this minister.

"These are by Narendrasûri Maladhâri," &c., &c.

Inscription No. 5.

This is on the second east door of the same temple. The stone on which it is engraved is greenish in colour, and from the effect of the climate is now crumbling to dust. Hence some lines are obliterated and the characters are in many places faint and indistinct.

ॐ नमः सर्वज्ञाय ॥ येदुज्जयंत——————————जयाभूप्रजाकल्याणा ॥ स्वस्ति श्रीविक्रमसंवत् १२८८ वर्षे फागुणशुदी १० बुधे श्रीमदणहिलपुरवा-

स्तव्यप्राग्वाटान्वयप्रसूतठ. श्रीचंडपात्मजठ. श्रीचंडप्रसादांगजठ. श्रीसोमतनुजठ. श्रीआशाराजनंदनस्यठ. श्रीकुमारदेवीकुक्षिसंभूतस्यठ. श्रीलुणिगमहंश्रीमालदेवयोरनुजस्यमहं. श्रीतेजःपालाग्रजन्मनो महामात्यश्रीवस्तुपालस्यात्मजेमहं श्रीललिनादेवीकुक्षिसरोवरराजहंसाय-

मानेमहं. श्रीजयतसिंहे सं. ७९ वर्षपूर्वं स्तंभतीर्थे मुद्राव्यापारान् व्यापृण्वति सति सं. ७७ वर्षे शत्रुंजयोज्जयंतप्रभृतिमहातीर्थयात्रोत्सवप्रसादाविर्भूतश्रीमद्देवाधिदेवप्रसादासादितसंघाधिपत्येन चौलुक्यकुलनभस्तलप्रकाशनैकमार्त्तंडमहाराजाधिराजश्रीलवणप्रसाददेवसुतमहाराजश्रीवीरध-

वलदेवप्रीतिपन्नराज्यसर्वैश्वर्येण श्रीशारदाप्रतिपन्नापत्येन महामात्यश्रीवस्तुपालेन तथा अनुजेन सं. ७६ वर्षपूर्वं गुर्जरमंडले धवलक्ककप्रमुखनगरेषु मुद्राव्यापारान् व्यापृण्वतामहं. श्रीतेजःपालेन च श्रीशत्रुंजयार्बुदाचलप्रभृतिमहातीर्थेषु श्रीमदणहिलपुरभृगुपुरस्तं-

भनकपुरस्तंभतीर्थदर्भवतीधवलक्ककप्रमुखनगरेषु तथा अन्यसमस्तस्थानेष्वपि कोटिशोभिनवधर्मस्थानानि प्रभूतजीर्णोद्धाराश्च कारिताः ॥ तथा सचिवेश्वरश्रीवस्तुपालेनेह स्वयंनिर्मापितश्रीशत्रुंजयमहातीर्थावतारश्रीमदादितीर्थंकरश्रीऋषभदेवस्तंभनकपुरावतारश्रीपार्श्वनाथदेवसत्यपुरावतारश्री-

महावीरदेवप्रशस्तिसहितकश्मीरावतारश्रीसरस्वती मूर्तिदेवकुलिकाचतुष्टयजिनयुगलअम्बावलोकनाशाम्बप्रद्युम्नशिखरेषु श्रीनेमिनाथदेवालंकृतदेवकुलिकाचतुष्टयतुरगाधिरूढस्वपितामहमहंश्रीसोमनिजपितृठ. श्रीआशाराजमूर्त्तिद्वितयचारुतोरणत्रयश्रीनेमिनाथदेवआत्मी-

यपूर्वजाग्रजानुजपुत्रादिमूर्त्तिसमन्वितसुखोद्घाटनकस्तंभश्रीअष्टापदमहातीर्थप्रभृतिअनेककीर्त्तनपरंपराजिते श्रीनेमिनाथदेवाधिदेवविभूषितश्रीमदुज्जयंतमहातीर्थे आत्मनस्तथा स्वधर्मचारिण्याः प्राग्वाटजातीयठ. श्रीकान्हडपुत्र्याः ठ. राणुकुक्षिसंभूतायामहं. श्रीललितादेव्याः पुण्याभि-

वृद्धये श्रीनागेंद्रगच्छे भट्टारकश्रीमहेंद्रसूरिसंताने शिष्यश्रीशांतिसूरिशिष्यश्रीआणंदसूरिश्रीअमरसूरिपदे भट्टारकश्रीहरिभद्रसूरिपट्टालंकरणप्रभुश्रीविजयसेनसूरिप्रतिष्ठितश्रीअजितनाथदेवादिविंशतितीर्थंकरालंकृतोयमभिनवः समंडपः श्रीसंमेतमहातीर्थावतारप्रासादः कारितः ॥ छ ॥

सश्रीजिनाधिपतिधर्मधुराधुरीणः श्लाघास्पदं कथमिवास्तु न वस्तुपालः ॥ श्रीशारदासुकृतकीर्तिनयादिदेव्याः पुण्यः परिस्फुरति जंगमसंगमो यः ॥ १ ॥ विभुताविक्रमविद्या विदग्धतावित्तवितरणविवेकैः ॥ यः सतभिर्विकारैः कलितोपि बभार न विकारं ॥ २ ॥ यस्य भूः किमसावस्तु वस्तुपालसुतः सदा ॥ नावर्णासावथव्येतौ धर्मकर्मकृती कृती ॥ ३ ॥ कस्यापि कवितानविन-स्य हृदयामुखं ॥ वास्तव्यं वस्तुपालस्य पश्यामस्तद्द्वयं च यं ॥ ४ ॥ दुर्गैः स्वर्गगिरिः सकल्पतरुभिर्भेजे न चक्षुः पथे तस्थौ कामगवी जगाम जलधेरंतः स चिंतामणिः ॥ कालेस्मिन्नवलोक्य यस्य करुणं तिष्ठेत कोन्यः स्वतः पुंण्यः सोस्तु न वस्तुपालसुकृती दानैकवीरः कथं ॥ ५ ॥ सोयं मंत्री गुरुरतितरामुद्धरन् धर्मभारं श्लाघाभूमिं नयति न कथं वस्तुपालः सहेलं ॥ तेजःपालःस्व-लधवलः सर्वकर्माणबुद्धिर्द्वैतीयीकः कलयतितरां यस्य धौरेयकत्वं ॥ ६ ॥ एतस्मिन्वसुधासुधाजलधरे श्रीवस्तुपाले जगज्जीवातौ सित[योच्चयैनेकनवे]नेक्तं दिवं वर्ष-

ति आस्वातन्यजनाघनोश्छ्रितशशीज्योत्स्नाच्छवल्गद्गुणोद्भूतैरय— — — — — — — — — — — — — — — — — ॥. ७ ॥ लक्ष्मीर्मैथाचलेंद्रभ्रमणपरिचयादेवपारिप्लवेयं भ्रूभंगस्यैवभंगाच्चकितमृगदृशां प्रेमनस्थेतरस्या ॥ आयुर्निश्वासवायुप्रणयपरतयैवेवमस्थैर्यदुस्थं स्यात्स्तुर्धर्मोयमेकः परमिति हृदये

वस्तुपालेन मेने ॥ ८ ॥ तेजःपालस्य विष्णोश्च कः स्वरूपं निरूपयेत् ॥ स्थितं जगत्रयी—[पा]तुं यदा यो वरकंधरे ॥ ९ ॥ ललितादेवीनाम्ना सधर्मिणी वस्तुपालस्य ॥ अस्यामनिरस्तनयस्तनयोयं
जयतसिंहाख्यः ॥ १० ॥ दृष्ट्वा वपुश्च वृ — च परस्पराविरोधिनी ॥ विवादा. — — जैत्रसिंहस्तारुण्यवाद्रिकः ॥ ११ ॥ कृ-

तिरियं मलधारिश्रीसरचंद्रसूरीणां ॥ स्तंभतीर्थेत्र कायस्थवंशे वाजडनंदनः ॥ प्रशस्तिमेतामलिखत् जैत्रसिंहभुवः सुधीः ॥ १ ॥ वाडहस्य तनूजेन सूत्रधारेण धीमता ॥ एषा कुमारसिंहेन समुत्कीर्णा प्रयत्नतः ॥ २ ॥ श्रीनेमेस्त्रिजगद्भर्तुरम्बायाश्च प्रसादतः ॥ वस्तुपालान्वयस्यास्तु प्रशस्तिः स्वस्तिशालिनी ॥ छ ॥ शुभमस्तु ॥

Translation.

"Salutation to Sarvajña. Those ....to the mount of Ujjayanta..............for the benefit of the people.

"In the auspicious year of Vikrama 1288, Wednesday the 10th of the bright half of Phâlguna.

"Ṭhakur Chaṇḍapa, an inhabitant of Aṇahilapura and of the Prâgvâṭa family, begat Chaṇḍaprasâda, who begat Soma, whose son was Âśârâja—his son by Kumâradevî was the great minister Vastupâla, the younger brother of Luṇiga and Mâladeva and elder brother of Tejaḥpâla—his son was Jayatasiṁha, who was born like a royal goose in the lake-like womb of Lalitâdevî. Before the *Saṁvat* year 79, Jayatasiṁha was trading as a banker in Stambhatîrtha, *karors* of new temples were caused to be built and many old ones repaired at great and renowned places of pilgrimage such as Śatruñjaya, Arbudâchala, &c., and in the prosperous cities of Aṇahilapura, Bhṛigupura, Stambhanakapura, Stambhatîrtha, Darbhavatî, Dhavalakkaka and other places by the great minister Vastupâla and by his younger brother Tejahpâla. In the year *Saṁvat* 77—Vastupâla, who had obtained the leadership of a pilgrim-party by the favour of the lord of gods manifested in virtue of the solemnities at such holy places as Śatruñjaya, Ujjayanta, &c.—who had obtained authority in the kingdom by the favour of Vîradhavala Mahârâja son of Mahârâjâdhirâja Lavaṇaprasâda, who was shining like the sun in the heaven of the Chaulukya family, and was blessed by the favour of Śâradâ (*Sarasvatî*) with a son, and his younger brother Tejahpâla was carrying on banking transactions with the cities of Gujarât, of which Dhavalakkaka was the chief, in the year *Saṁvat* 76.

"Similarly the famous Vastupâla has caused to be built this new and splendid temple of the Mahâtîrthâvatâra with a *maṇḍapa* adorned by twenty Tîrthankaras such as Ajitanâtha, religiously inaugurated by his holiness Vijayasenasûri, ornament of the sacred seat of Bhaṭṭâraka Haribhadrasûri, who occupied the office of Amarâsûri, and by Ânandasûri, a pupil of Śântisûri, who again was a pupil of the Bhaṭṭâraka Mahendrasûri of the Nâgendra division. For the augmentation of his own merit and that of his wife Lalitâdevî, the daughter of Kânhaḍa by Rânû of the Prâgvâṭa caste—on this great holy place, the famous Ujjayanta adorned by Neminâtha the lord of the gods, and graced by various traditionally recounted places of pilgrimage such as the famous Ashṭâpada,—a pillar called Sukhodghâṭanka containing the images of Soma his grandfather, and of the venerable Âśârâja his father—both mounted on horses—of the famous Neminâtha with three decorated arches and of his ancestors, elder brother, younger brother, sons, &c.; the quadruple gods graced by the worshipful Neminâtha on four summits (*known as*) Ambâ, Avalokanâ, Sâmba and Pradyumna, two Jinas and the four gods, viz. the famous Rishabhadeva, the first Tîrthaṅkara who was incarnate on the great holy place of Śatruñjaya, the famous god Pârśvanâtha who appeared in flesh at Stambhanakapura, the famous Mahâvîradeva who established himself as a deity at Satyapura, and the famous image of Sarasvatî who was incarnate in Kaśmîra, with eulogistic inscription—were established and all set up by him (*Vastupâla*)."

(*Ślôkas.*) "How can this Vastupâla, a leading member of the religion of the lord of Jina, be not an object of praise? He shines like a moving combination of learning, virtue, glory, prudence and a crowd of other qualities.

"Though he is endowed with seven qualities,—nobility, valour, learning, wisdom, wealth, charity and judgment, all beginning with *Vs*[1], yet is influenced by no passion.

"May Vastupâla, this son, live for ever, created for the discharge of charitable duties, is not only the earth but even ships and oceans.

"We see in Vastupâla both the enjoyment of poetry and also other joys and happiness.

"The tree of paradise grew on the celestial mountain which is inaccessible, the cow of heaven fled out of sight, and the desire-fulfilling gem hid itself in the ocean; who else then can compete with Vastupâla's charity and solely call himself meritorious? If none, why should not Vastupâla be called the only unrivalled distributor of charities?

"How cannot this great minister Vastupâla, bearing as he does so much weight of religious duties, be the abode of praise (*in matters of politics*) when he has Tejaḥpâla white as......and possessed of intelligence to understand all things, to put himself to the administrative yoke as a partner? (literally, *as a second bull*).

"While Vastupâla, the bearer of ambrosial water and supporter of the people, is day and night raining with various silver plenties which are the results of his excellent good qualities, pure as moonlight cleared of clouds, the people are living through his protection.

"Vastupâla is fully convinced within himself that riches are restless because they had connection with the turning of the churning mountain; the love of women with eyes active like the gazelle is inconstant because it depends upon the amorous play of eyebrows; and that life is uncertain because it consists of the breath—and that therefore duty alone is firm.

"Who can well describe the proper form of Tejaḥpâla and Vishṇu, who protect the three worlds on their shoulder?

---

[1] This is a play on the word *Vikâra*.—J. W. W.

"The wife of Vastupâla was by name Lalitâdevî, who gave birth to a son named Jayatasiṁha, who was not wanting in justice.

"Jaitrasiṁha placed his youth immoveable, between his body and evil passions.

"This is the composition of Sarachandrasûri Maladhâri.

"Jaitrasiṁha, surnamed Dhruva, is the copyist, and Kumârasiṁha the engraver," &c., &c.

Inscription No. 6.

This is on the south entrance of the same temple. The characters are distinct.

ॐ नमः श्रीसर्वज्ञाय ॥ संमेताद्रिशिरःकिरीटमगयः स्मेरस्मराहंकृतिर्ध्वंसोल्लासितकीर्तयः शिवपुरप्राकारतार-श्रियः ॥ अनल्पश्रितसंविदादिविलसद्रत्नौघरत्नाकराः कल्याणावलिहेतवः प्रातिकलं ते संतु वस्तीर्थपाः ॥ १ ॥ स्वस्ति श्रीविक्रमसंवत् १२८८ वर्षे फागुणशुदी १० बुधे श्रीमदणहिलपुरवास्तव्यप्राग्वाटकुलालंकरणं

श्रीचंडपात्मजठ. श्रीचंडप्रसादांग्रजठ. श्रीसोमतनुजठ. श्रीआशाराजनंदनस्यठ. श्रीकुमारदेवीकुक्षिसंभूतस्यठ. श्रीलुणिगमहंश्रीमालदेवयोरनुजस्य महंश्रीतेजःपालाग्रजन्मनो माहामात्यश्रीवस्तुपालस्यात्मजे महंश्रीललितादेवीकुक्षि-सरोवरराजहंसायमाने महंश्रीजयतसिंहे सं० ७९ वर्षपूर्वं स्तंभती-

र्थमुद्राव्यापारान् व्यापृण्वति सति सं. ७७ वर्षे श्रीशत्रुंजयोज्जयंतप्रभृतिमहातीर्थयात्रोत्सवप्रभावाविर्भूतश्रीमद्देवा-धिदेवप्रसादासादितसंघाधिपत्येन चौलुक्यकुलनभस्तलप्रकाशनैकमार्तंडमहाराजाधिराजश्रीलवणप्रसाददेवसुतमहाराज-श्रीवीरधवलदेवप्रीतिप्रतिपन्नराज्यसर्वेश्वर्येण श्रीशारदाप्रतिपन्नापत्येन महामा-

त्य श्रीवस्तुपालेन तथा अनुजेन गुर्जरमंडले धवलक्ककप्रमुखनगरेषु मुद्राव्यापारान् व्यापृण्वता महं. श्रीतेजःपालेन च श्रीशत्रुंजयार्बुदाचलप्रभृतिमहातीर्थेषु श्रीमदणहिलपुरभृगुपुरस्तंभनकपुरस्तंभतीर्थदर्भवतीधवलक्ककप्रमुखनगरेषु तथा अन्यसमस्तस्थानेष्वपि कोटिशोभिनवधर्मस्थानानि प्रभूतजी-

र्णोद्धाराश्च कारिताः ॥ तथा श्रीशारदाप्रतिपन्नपुत्रसचिवेश्वरश्रीवस्तुपालेन .स्वधर्मचारिण्याः प्राग्वाटजातीयठ. श्रीकान्हडपुत्र्याः ठ. राणूकुक्षिसंभूतायामहं. श्रीललितादेव्यास्तथा आत्मनः पुण्याभिवृद्धये इह स्वयंनिर्मापितश्रीशत्रुं-जयमहातीर्थावतारश्रीमदादितीर्थंकरश्रीऋषभदेवस्तंभनकपुरावतारश्रीपार्श्वनाथदेवसत्यपुरा-

वतारश्रीमहावीरदेवप्रशस्तिसहितकश्मीरावतारश्रीसरस्वतीमूर्तिदेवकुलिकाचतुष्टयजिनयुगलअम्बावलोकना-शाम्बप्रद्युम्नशिखरेषु श्रीनेमिनाथदेवालंकृतदेवकुलिकाचतुष्टयतुरगाधिरूढनिजपितामहमहं. श्रीसोमस्वपितृठ. श्रीआ-शाराजमूर्तिद्वितयचारुतोरणत्रयश्रीनेमिनाथदेवआत्मीयपूर्वजाग्रजानुजपुत्रादि मूर्तिस-

मन्वितसुखोद्घाटनकस्तंभश्रीअष्टापदमहातीर्थप्रभृतिअनेककीर्तनपरंपराविराजिते श्रीनेमिनाथदेवाधिदेवविभू-षितश्रीमदुज्जयंतमहातीर्थे श्रीनागेंद्रगच्छे भट्टारकश्रीमहेंद्रसूरिसंताने शिष्यश्रीशांतिसूरिशिष्यश्रीआणंदसूरिश्रीअमरसूरिपदे भट्टारकश्रीहरिभद्रसूरिपट्टालंकरणप्रभुश्रीविजयसेनसूरिप्रातिष्ठितश्री-

मदजितनाथदेवप्रमुखविंशातितीर्थंकरालंकृतोयमभिनवः समंडपः श्रीसंमेतावतारमहातीर्थप्रासादः कारितः ॥ छ ॥

मुष्णाति प्रसभं वसु द्विजपते गौरीगुरूं लंघयन् नो धत्ते परलोकतो भयमहोहंसापलापे कृती ॥ उच्चैरास्तिक-चक्रवालमुकुटश्रीवस्तुपाल स्फुटं भेजे नास्तिकतामयं तव यशःपूरः कुतस्त्या-

मिति ॥ १ ॥ कोपाटोपपरैः परैश्चलच्चमूरंगत्तुरंगक्षतक्षोणीक्षोदवशादशोषि जलधिः श्रीस्तंभतीर्थे पुरे ॥ स्वेदांभ-स्तटिनीघटाघटनयाश्रीवस्तुपाल स्फुरत्तेजस्तिग्मगभस्तितसतनुभिस्तैरेव संपूरितः ॥ २ ॥ दिग्यात्रोत्सववीरवीरधवलक्षो-

णीधवाध्यासितं प्राज्यं राज्यरथस्य भारमभितः स्कंधे दधल्लीलया ॥ भाति भ्रातरि दक्षिणे समगुणे श्रीवस्तुपालः कथं न श्लाघ्यः स्वयमश्वराजतनुजः कामं सवामास्थितिः ॥ ३ ॥ लावण्यांग इति द्युतिव्यतिकरैः सत्याभिधानोभवद्भ्राता यस्य निशानिशांतविकसच्चंद्रप्रकाशाननः ॥ शंके शंकरकोपसंभ्रमभरादासीदनंगः स्मरः साक्षादंगमयोयमित्यपह्नुतः स्वर्गांगनाभिर्लघु ॥ ४ ॥ रक्तः सद्गतिभावभाजि चरणे श्रीमल्लदेवो परोयद्भ्राता परमेष्ठिवाहनतया प्राप्तः प्रतिष्ठां परां ॥ खेलन्निर्मलमानसे न समयं क्वापि श्रयन् पंकिलं विश्वे राजति राजहंस इव यः संशुद्धपक्षद्वयः ॥ ५ ॥ सोयं तस्य सुधारहस्य कवितानिष्ठः कनिष्ठः कृती बंधुर्बंधुरबुद्धिबोधमधुरः श्रीवस्तुपालाभिधः ॥ ज्ञानांभोरुहकोटरे भ्रमरतां सारंगसाम्यं यशः सोमे ऽशौरितुलां च यस्य महिमक्षीरोदधौ स्वं दधौ ॥ ६ ॥

इंदुर्बिंदुरपां सुरेश्वरसरिड्डिंडीरपिंडः पतिर्भासां विद्रुमकंदलः किल विभुः,श्रीवत्सलक्ष्मा नभः ॥ कैलासस्त्रिदशेभशंभुहिमवत्प्रायास्तु मुक्ताफलस्तोमः कोमलवालुकास्य च यशः क्षीरोदधौ कौमुदी ॥ ७ ॥ हस्ताग्रन्यस्तसारस्वतरसरसनप्राप्तमाहात्म्यलक्ष्मीस्तेजःपालस्ततोसौ जयति वसुभरैः पूरयन् दक्षिणाशां ॥ यद्बुद्धिः कल्पि-

[-मे]द्विपगहनपरक्षोणिभृद्वृद्धिसंपल्लोपामुद्राधिपस्य स्फुरति लसदिनस्फारसंचारहेतुः ॥ ८ ॥ पुण्यश्रीर्भुवि मल्लदेवतनयोभूत्पुण्यसिंहो यशोवर्यः स्फूर्जति जैत्रसिंह इति तु श्रीवस्तुपालात्मजः ॥ तेजःपालसुतस्त्वसौ विजयते लावण्यसिंहः स्वयं यैर्विश्वे भवदेकपादपि कलौ धर्मश्चतुष्पादयं ॥ ९ ॥ एते श्रीनागेंद्रगच्छे भट्टारकश्रीउद-

[यप्रभ]सूरीणां ॥ स्तंभतीर्थेत्र कायस्थवंशे वाजडनंदनः ॥ प्रशस्तिमेतामलिखत् जैत्रसिंहग्रुवः सुधीः ॥ १ ॥ वाहडस्य तनूजेन सूत्रधारेण धीमता ॥ एषा कुमारसिंहेन समुत्कीर्णा प्रयत्नतः ॥ २ ॥ श्रीनेमेस्त्रिजगद्भर्तुरम्बायाश्च प्रसादतः ॥ वस्तुपालान्वयस्यास्ति प्रशस्तिः स्वस्तिशालिनी ॥ ३ ॥ श्रीवस्तुपालप्रभोः प्रशस्तिरियं निष्पन्ना ॥ शुभ भवतु ॥

Translation.

"Salutation to Sarvajña. May those Tîrthaṅkaras be always the cause of manifold blessings to you—the Tîrthaṅkaras who are the jewels on the crown-like summit of Sâmeta mountain, whose glories are exalted by having humbled the pride of smiling Cupid, whose brilliant splendour is like that of the Fort of Śivapura, and who are mines of many excellent gems such as the knowledge connected with eternity.

"In the auspicious year of Vikrama 1288, Wednesday, the 10th of the bright half of Phâlguna.

"Ṭhakur Chaṇḍapa, an inhabitant of Aṇahilapura and of the Prâgvâṭa family, begat Chaṇḍaprasâda, who begat Soma, whose son was Âśârâja,—his son by Kumâradevî was the great minister Vastupâla, the younger brother of Luṇiga and Mâladeva and elder brother of Tejaḥpâla,—his son was Jayatasiṁha, who was born like a royal goose in the lake-like womb of Lalitâdevî. Before the *Saṁvat* year 79, Jayatasiṁha was trading as a banker in Stambhatîrtha, *karors* of new temples were caused to be built and many old ones repaired at great and renowned places of pilgrimage such as Śatruñjaya, Arbudâchala, &c., and in the prosperous cities of Aṇahilapura, Bhṛigupura, Stambhanakapura, Stambhatîrtha, Darbhavatî, Dhavalakkaka and other places by the great minister Vastupâla and by his younger brother Tejaḥpâla. In the year *Saṁ.* 77, Vastupâla who had obtained the leadership of a pilgrim-party by the favour of the lord of gods manifested in virtue of the solemnities at such holy places as Śatruñjaya, Ujjayanta, &c., who had obtained authority in the kingdom by the favour of Vîradhavala Mahârâja, son of Mahârâjâdhirâja Lavaṇaprasâda, who was shining like the sun in the heaven of the Chaulukya family and was blessed by the favour of Śâradâ (*Sarasvatî*) with a son, and his younger brother Tejaḥpâla was carrying on banking transactions with the cities of Gujarât, of which Dhavalakkaka was the chief in the year *Saṁ.* 76.

"Similarly the famous Vastupâla has caused to be built this new and splendid temple of the Mahâtîrthâvatâra with a *maṇḍapa* adorned by twenty Tîrthaṅkaras such as Ajitanâtha, religiously inaugurated by his holiness Vijayasenasûri, the ornament of the sacred seat of Bhaṭṭâraka Haribhadrasûri, who occupied the office of Amarasûri, and by Ânandasûri a pupil of Śântisûri, who again was a pupil and son of Bhaṭṭâraka Mahendrasûri of the Nâgendra division. For the augmentation of his own merit and that of his wife Lalitâdevî, the daughter of Kânhaḍa by Râṇn of Prâgvâṭa family—on this great holy place, the famous Ujjayanta adorned by Neminâtha the lord of the gods and graced by various traditionally recounted places of pilgrimage such as the famous Ashṭâpada,—a pillar called Sukhodghâṭanaka containing the images of the happy Soma his grandfather, and of the venerable Âśârâja his father—both mounted on horses—of the famous Neminâtha with three decorated arches, and of his ancestors, elder brother, younger brother, sons, &c.; the quadruple gods graced by the worshipful Neminâtha on four summits known as Ambâ, Avalokanâ, Sâmba and Pradyumna; two Jinas and the four gods, viz. the famous Ṛishabhadeva the first Tîrthaṅkara who was incarnate on the great holy place of Śatruñjaya, the famous god Pârśvanâtha who appeared in the flesh at Stambhanakapura, the famous Mahâvîradeva who established himself as a deity at Satyapura, and the famous image of Sarasvatî who was incarnate in Kaśmîra, with a eulogistic inscription,—were established and all set up by him (*Vastupâla*)."

(*Ślôkas.*) "O Vastupâla, the crown of the highly religious circle, whence does thy flood of glory partake of unholy character, for it deprives Brâhmaṇs of money and the moon of its light and surpasses the father of Pârvatî (or *stretches far beyond the Himâlaya*); it entertains no fear of heaven (*fears no enemy or rival*); it takes delight in despising the hermits (*considers to have achieved its object in surpassing the geese.*)

"Near the illustrious city of Stambhatîrtha the ocean had been dried up by the enemies making a grand display of their wrath, with dust raised by their war-horses in the army from the trodden earth. But the same was again filled up by the river flowing water of perspiration from their bodies, which were heated by the burning rays of Vastupâla's prowess.

"How should not Vastupâla, the son of Aśvarâja, be amply deserving of praise? For with his brother of equal ability shining on the right side and himself on the left, he bears on his shoulder as easily as in sport the heavy load of the administration chariot entrusted to him by King Vîradhavala, who is brave in making a triumphal march in all directions.

"His (*elder*) brother, having a face shining like the dark-destroying moon at night, was from the spread of his radiance called Luṇiga in the proper sense of the word (*of lovely body—'lâvaṇyâṅga'*) and I suspect he has been (*bodily*) carried off by celestial damsels simply because they thought the god Cupid had been made incorporeal by the anger of Śiva, while this man was Cupid incarnate.

"His second brother Malladeva shines like a royal goose in this world, for he is attached to virtuous deeds as the bird is red in feet with a graceful gait; he has attained great reputation by being a leader of those devoted to Brahmâ as the bird has by being a vehicle of the same deity; he takes delight in pure minds as the bird does in the pellucid lake of Mânasa without taking muddy ways; and he has two sides (*maternal and paternal*) unsullied as the bird has two white wings.

"The famous Vastupâla is virtuous, devoted to poetry of nectarial essence, and is sweet in giving instruction by his firm understanding. The heaven resembles a bee in the lotus cup of his knowledge; and is like a deer in the moon of his fame, and looks like Vishṇu in the ocean of his greatness.

"In the milky ocean of his glory the moon is a drop of water; the celestial river, a lump of foam; the lord of light is a spray of coral; and Vishṇu is the sky (*enveloping the ocean*). Kailâsa, heavenly elephant, Śiva, and the snowy mountains are the pearls, and the moonlight is its crystal sands.

"There shines Tejaḥpâla, who is richly great in possessing a taste for knowledge (?), who fills all the desires of Dakshiṇâ with abundant wealth, and whose genius may well compare with that of the lord of Lopâmudrâ who had been the cause of giving free course to the sun by stopping the huge increase of the Vindhya mountain infested with elephants, as it (*genius*) is a hindrance to the prosperity of his hostile king possessing many elephants.

"There are on earth the meritorious Puṇyasiṁha the son of Malladeva, Jaitrasiṁha of best renowned the son of Vastupâla, and Lâvaṇyasiṁha the son of Tejaḥpâla. These three make up as it were the four feet of merit, which is one-footed in Kali.

"These are by the famous Udayaprabhasûri Bhaṭṭâraka of the Nâgendra division.

"Jaitrasiṁha, &c., copyist.

"Kumârasiṁha, &c., engraver," &c., &c.

Inscription No. 7.

This is on a wall near the first entrance door of Nemiṅâtha's temple on the left side of the main road and a little way off from the fort-gate. The inscription is incomplete on the stone and the first parts of the first six lines are broken away. The characters are large and distinct, but the writing is very incorrect.

......मतेः श्रेष्ठं सधीमानसोसंबोधानयतिभ्मया भूपपरित्तागोनुरागाशयः ॥ पियूषपृतिवक्षिणादिजगती-

......दासारदा ॥ १ ॥ य[त्]कांतेः पुरतः समसमदचिप्र(द्यो) तनाद्या अमी खद्योता इव रेजिरे त्रिजगती-जाग्रत्प्रतापा आपि ॥ दासंति स्म यदीय सस्मर-

......वतस्वयच्छंततशीश्वर ॥ २ ॥ किं भूवध्वा प्रकरमुकुटानील्रत्नप्रकॄप्ताध्वितारत्नं जितपनीपतंनिमिदेधां-विदिंमीडटिवरममतरमिसिंभूंगेणदृतायदृष्टामेतिरिति भवे ॥

......तेचिविघ्नकरिणोदंतुं तथा प्रार्थनासाफल्याय बिभर्ति या फलतति माकंदजां धर्मिणां ॥ धत्तेंकंसुतसंयुतं सुतशतेच्छापूर्तये किं नृणां तां विश्वेकहि

– – – – – महाश्रीअंबिकां संस्तुवे ॥ ४ ॥ श्रीउज्जयंतगिरिराजमधिप्रतीते सद्धर्मकर्मकरणोद्यामिनां जनानां ॥ सांनिध्यमीहितममीगुदमेधनादाक्षेषाधिपप्रभृतय-

[त्रि]दशाःसृजंतु ॥ ९ ॥ अद्य च नानातीर्थोपवनतटिनीकानने रम्यहर्म्यैः पौरैर्भूमीपतिपृथुकृतात्यंतसौख्यैरसंख्यैः ॥ शश्वद्भूषाभृदपि विपुलां राष्ट्रवर्यः सुराष्ट्राराष्ट्रो दधेनुपमगिरिराट् रैवतालंकृतिंयः ॥ ६ ॥ मा गा गर्वममर्त्यपर्वत परां प्रीतिंभजंतस्त्वया भ्राम्यंते रविचंद्रमः प्रभृतयः के केन मुग्धाशयाः ॥ एको रैवतभूधरो विजयतां यद्दर्शनात्प्राणिनो यांति भ्रांतिविवर्जिताः किल महानंदं सुखश्रीजुषः ॥ ७ ॥ तत्र च ॥ गिरिस्फुरदुरुस्थितिर्विततभूरिशाखोदयः सुपर्वमहिमास्पदं जगति वं-

स आस्ते हरेः ॥ यदुद्भवशिवांगजाच्युतबलप्रमुख्या अलंकृतिं दधाति निर्मलामखिलसत्सु मुक्ता अपि ॥ ८ ॥ वंशेस्मिन्यदुनामकावरपतेरभ्युग्रशौर्यावलेरासीत् राजकु-

लं गुणौघविपुलं श्रीयादवख्यातिमत् ॥ अत्राभून्नृपमंडलीनतपदः श्रीमंडलीकः क्रमात् प्रासादं गुरुहेमपत्रततिभिर्योचीकरन्नेमिनः ॥ ९ ॥ नवघननृपतिस्तदीयसूनुर्नवघनमहितभ्रजोसिमादधानः ॥ नवघनवृष्टिः प्रजावतोधे नवघनसाररसदक्षयशोभिरामः ॥ १० ॥ महीमहेंद्रोमहिपालदेवः पुत्रस्तदीयोजनि यन्नृदेवः यद्दानदास्यं सुरधेनुरत्नद्रुमास्तदानीमगमन्नयत्नं ॥ श्रीप्रभासेसोमनाथप्रासादकृत् ॥ ११ ॥ षंगारनामा रिपुराज्यवृक्षेष्वंगार एवाजनि भूमिजानिः ॥ शृंगारकृत्तत्कुलराज्यलक्ष्म्याभृंगारधाराजगतीलतायाः ॥ १२ ॥ आसीत् श्रीजयसिंहदेवनृपतिस्तत्सद्भूभामिनी भास्वद्भोगरसालसार्द्रनयनो न्यायांबुधि श्वेतरुक् ॥ शत्रुत्रासनकृत् व्रतो च महिमा नम्रक्षगाभृत्ततिस्फूर्जन्मौलिमणीमयूषसलिलप्रक्षालितांघ्रिद्वयः ॥ १३ ॥ दिद्युते तदनु मोकलसिंहः शत्रुभूपगजभदनसिंहः ॥ यत्प्रतापमभजद्यादि हंसः सन्मनःसरसिने

कलहंसः ॥ १४ ॥ तदनुमेलगदेवनरेश्वरः सुकृततुष्टगरिष्टसुरेश्वरः ॥ समभवद्भव(नाथ) पदांबुजे भ्रमरतां कलयन्नमलांगवान् ॥ १५ ॥ तत्पादोदयभानुमभ्युदयकृत्प्रोद्यत्प्रतापाद्भुतो दिक्चक्रप्रसरत्करक्रमितभूभृच्छेखरे भासुरः ॥ आसीत् श्रीमहिपालदेवनृपतिर्निर्नाशितारिक्षमापालो लू-

कततिः कुनीतितिमिरप्रध्वंसनप्रत्पलः ॥ १६ ॥ तत्सूनुर्जयति द्विषत्करिकुलत्रासैकपंचाननः श्रीमन्मंडलिकः क्षितीश्वरशिरःकोटीरहीरप्रभः ॥ स्व(:) सिंधूर्म्युपलक्षिताक्षतगतिर्बभ्रम्यतेद्यापि यत् कीर्तिः स्मत्यमतीत्यवार्धिवलयं वर्द्धिष्णुसारत्वरां ॥ १७ ॥ नालंध्यः कुत उन्नतो नरपातिः कस्याः कुतो विश्व भूस्तंपात्रेकुरुतः किमत्र कृतिनो किं द्विट् कृतः स्वामिना ॥ सौराष्ट्राधिपातिः सुखाय रिपुभिश्चक्रेथ किंप्रीतितः कीदृक्मंडलिकः क्षितीश्वरइहश्रीराजराजिश्रितः ॥ १८ ॥ आलानस्तंभरूपो जयकलकलभस्यासुखांभोधिसेतुः केतुः शौर्यौघसौधे रणदधिमथनः सद्यसोमृक्षणोक्तः ॥ पूर्वाद्रिः (ख) द्रववश्वराकिरणरुचां वैरिराजांगनानां मुर्वैर्वैधव्यदीक्षो जयति नरपतेर्मंडलीकस्य बाहुः ॥ १९ ॥ रेरे प्रत्यर्थिनो वः किमपिहितवचः श्रावयेहं कृपातो यस्याश्वीयांघ्रिघातोस्थलितमृद्दुरजोप्युत्कटं सौरतेजः ॥ हत्वाभूल्लोकमेनंमालि नयतितमां तत्किमेतत्पुरस्तात् यूयं मुक्तामदश्राक् श्रयत नरपतेर्मंडलीकस्य सेवां ॥ २० ॥ चातुर्यं बत वेधसः सुरगवीरत्नद्रुमान्यत्पशुप्रोद्यत्कर्करकाष्टदुष्टवपुषश्चक्रेयमाजन्मतः ॥ सचैतन्यसुजन्मपाकुलद्वदो दानैकनिष्णाततां दृष्ट्वा मंडलीकप्रभोत्रभवतस्तेषां भविष्यन्कथं ॥ २१ ॥ इति श्रीराजवंशवर्णनं ॥ अथ श्रीशाणवर्णनं ॥ अस्ति स्वस्ति निधिः श्रियो निरवधिप्रेमास्पदं सेवधिः श्रीधर्मस्य वसुंधरोत्तमवधूमौलिस्फुरन्मंडनं वापीकूपतडागकान्नजिनप्रासादशैवालय ॥

Translation.[1]

"..............of genius....................best. He is intelligent..........................of the learned...........he..........................abode of compassion...................nectar.................. Before whose brilliancy, the sun, &c., of uneven lustre, though possessed of light (*sufficient*) to illumine the three worlds, are like fire-flies... ....4. I praise that great Ambikâ who..to kill the elephants of difficulty and to satisfy the desires of the meritorious, supplies many

[1] See another version in the *Report on the Antiquities of Kâthiâwâr and Kachh*, page 161.

mango fruits, and has a lap graced by a son, as if to fulfil the wishes of men for a hundred sons.

"5. May the gods Guru, Meghanâda, Indra, &c., give their desired proximity to those who busily engage themselves in the faithful performance of religious deeds on the great mountain-king Ujjayanta now-a-days.

"6. This country of Saurâshṭra, the best of lands, though perpetually adorned with various *tirthas*, gardens, rivers, forests and charming palaces and with countless citizens enjoying manifold comforts extended by kings, possesses an unrivalled ornament in the mountain-king Raivata.

"7. O mountain of the immortals, be not proud; for how many like the sun, moon, &c., have not been set wheeling round thee notwithstanding they bear thee infatuate love? Let therefore Raivata alone be praised, by whose very sight living beings become free from delusion and enjoy great happiness and pleasures.

"8. Furthermore on this mountain the family of Hari may be compared with bamboos; for the family had a great abode on this mountain as the bamboos have many stalks bending down; the family had celebrated Parvas as the bamboos have great knots. The great members of the Yâdava family Śivâṅgaja, Achyuta, Bala, &c., though themselves pearls among all saints, derive spotless beauty from this mountain.

"9. In the royal race of a king named Yadu, of terrible valour, there was a family which possessed many excellent qualities and was celebrated as the illustrious Yâdavas. There flourished, in the order of succession, the famous Maṇḍalîka who sat on the throne bowed down to by many kings, and who made a temple to Neminâtha with heavy plates of gold.

"10. His son was Râjâ Navaghana, who wielded a new strong sword against his enemy, who was a fresh cloud shower to his forest-like people, and who looked pleasing by his fame white as camphor.

"11. His son was Mahipâladeva, a great king, before whose liberality the heavenly cow, the desire-fulfilling jewel, and the tree of Paradise were easily reduced to submission, and who caused a temple of Somanâtha to be built at Prabhâsa.

"12. Afterwards there flourished a king called Khangâra, a fire in the trees of his enemies, an ornament in the splendour of his royal family, and a stream of water to the creeper-like world.

"13. Then succeeded the handsome king Jayasiṁhadeva, whose eyes were wet with the fatigue caused by the pleasure of the enjoyment of his crown land, which was as it were a beautiful woman; who was a moon of the ocean of justice, and the fear of his enemies; whose greatness was exalted by solemn vows, and whose feet were washed by the water of the rays issuing from the diamonds of the crowns of those kings who bowed before him.

"14. After him shone Mokaḷasiṁha like a lion to tear down the elephants of hostile kings. He was a royal goose in the mental-lake of the virtuous, and his light was borrowed by the sun in the sky.

"15. Next to him came the king Melagadeva, who satisfied the most worshipful lord of the gods by his virtuous deeds, and who resembled a bee in the lotus-foot of Bhavanâtha and possessed an unsullied body.

"16. Then came the king Mahipâladeva, who was like a sun to illuminate the dignity of his predecessor, a maker of prosperity and of extraordinary power by his excessive splendour. He overstepped the best of kings by imposing royal dues in all directions as the sun spreads his rays over mountain summits all about. He drove out the owls of hostile kings, and was prepared to destroy the darkness of immorality.

"17. The son of the above-named was the famous Maṇḍalîka, who was like the lion in creating fear among his elephant-like enemies, and whose splendour was like that of a diamond in the crown of the best of monarchs, and whose glory, comparable to the waves of a heavenly river uninterruptedly flowing and ready to go beyond the sea, is yet spreading in all directions.[1]

"19. The arm of king Maṇḍalîka desirous of gathering good renown, is ever victorious—arm which is a post to the circle of which to tie a young beautiful elephant of victory, a bridge to cross over the ocean of miseries and a banner on the house of bravery; it is a handle to churn the curd of the battle-field; an eastern mount to shoot the rays of the sword-like sun, and a cause of wholesale widowhood to the wives of his hostile kings.

"20. O enemies, out of compassion I will make you to hear a word of benefit. It is this—at once making yourself free from pride, seek the service of Maṇḍalîka, the king of men; for the tread of his horse's hoof raises so large quantity of fine dust, which at once concealing the sun obscures the face of the earth. Of what importance then are you before him?

"21. There is wisdom of Brahmâ in making the heavenly cow a senseless beast, the celestial gem a shining stone, and the tree of Paradise a lump of wood, from their very birth; for had they been made with the sensibilities of life, what would have been the state of their hearts troubled with shame at your liberality, O Maṇḍalîka!

---

[1] *Śloka* 18 is made out by Vallabhaji Âchârya to be a kind of acrostic, the last reply *Śrîrâjarâjiśritaḥ* containing the answer to the acrostic. The first reply is *Śrîtaḥ*, or the 1st and last syllables; the second is *Râtaḥ*, or the 2nd syllable and the final syllable; the third is *Ajataḥ*; the fourth, *Râtaḥ*; the fifth, *Jitaḥ*; the sixth, *Śrîtaḥ*; and the seventh, the entire answer *Śrîrâjarâjiśritaḥ*. The *ślôka* is as follows:—

18. Why can he not be surpassed?	On account of his beauty (*Śrîtaḥ*).
In what does his greatness consist?	In his wealth (*Râtaḥ*).
By whom was the universe created?	By Brahmâ (*Ajataḥ*).
What do two meritorious persons do with their riches?	They bestow gifts (*Râtaḥ*).
What did Maṇḍalika do to his enemies?	He conquered (them) (*Jitaḥ*).
What did the enemy to the lord of Saurâshṭra, in order to enjoy peace?	They did him service (*Śrîtaḥ*).
What sort of a Râjâ is Râjâ Maṇḍalîka?	He is a Râjâ served by many Râjâs (*Śrîrâjarâjiśritaḥ*)

"Thus ends the description of the family of the king.

"Now begins the description of the famous Sâṇa.

"He was a depository of welfare, an abode of unlimited affection of wealth, a treasure of religion, and a shining ornament on the crest-jewel of the earth, his best wife, and builder of wells, ponds, lakes, gardens, Jaina temples and Śaiva temples."

Inscription No. 8.

This inscription is on the wall of a chapel facing to the south, on the left side of the path leading to what is called the Hâthipagalâ (the elephant's foot). One of the corners of the stone is broken off. The characters are faint and indistinct; the middle part is entirely obliterated.

प्रभोमानंबभा
प्रसमदुपलब्धपरि
मालवंशमणिरुज्वकीर्ति
प्रभुरजायतावस्योदयनइत्यर्द्धिसं
कुहडनामधेयः ॥ श्रेयः पदं मंत्रिविभुर्बभूव
उक्ता सधर्मिणी निर्मलधर्मयुक्ता ॥ ४ ॥ त-
योः सतां – – – – – – मदोद्रमाः ॥ अजायत सुताः सप्तगोत्रोद्धारकुलाचलाः ॥ ५ ॥
पाल कुमार क्ष्मापालकोष्टागाराधिकारवान् ॥ कुमारसिंहः प्रथमोप्यु-
त्सगः पुरुषः सतां ॥ ६ ॥ जगत्सिंहोथ रम्यस्तु पद्मसिंहः श्रियः पदं ॥ ततो जयंत-
पाताकौ धीणिग – मिमप्रते ॥ ७ ॥ युग्मं ॥ श्रीपद्मसिंहदयिता [बिं]बीदेवी तनू-
रुहांश्चतुरः ॥ श्रीमहणसिंहसमरसिंह – सल्लक्षतेजाख्यान् ॥ ८ ॥ अथ सूमलाम-
नुपगांमहितेव बुधे दिवं प्रसुवे – यः ॥ जयंतकाकृति नगानधूतभी-
तां च सीतोदां ॥ ९ ॥ युग्मं ॥ सामतसिंह – – – – – – स्य विधू इव अध्यक्षौ सर्व-
देशेषु मुद्रुर्नाती ॥ १० ॥ – – – – – – – – – – – – – अणहिलपुरस्थकालाक-
विहितजेन – – – – – – – – – – – – – – – – – – – ॥ ११ ॥ घटपत्रकेचव-
मभूपरिमालि   कांमुक्कारसंसार-
सिंधुतरीः ॥ १२ ॥   शत्रंजयगिरौ
देवकुलिकांवालिः ॥   भवाधिवारिधिकि-
लीका या संल्पंतः   श्रीयाजयंतिजन – –
जयंति तेजल्लदे   भिधेयश्रीविल्ह – –
किवुणमंत्री   शांतनः ॥ सुः – –
चरंन्यधयसुं   . वशं न्यान्याय – – –
नः ॥ अनुवि   तनकेपा – – –
नेगफणमंडपः   विभूषितः ॥ १८ ॥ वर्द्धमा-
नपुरे येन वा   मनाथवाथरवत्तकं ॥ १९ ॥
पुरे च पेथलापा   सद्दलानामजामेः श्री

वीरवित्तकौ ॥ २० ॥ नेमिवेश्मंत ॥ मंडपश्रे-
मसे क्षाड – प्राधि देवकुलिकाद्वारि द्वारि च
महातीर्थेऽथ तीर्थे – लिंगं मे देवकुलिकाकलिता-
द्भुता ॥ २३ ॥ तत्रादिबंधोः पुण्या-
य सवसनस्यादितीर्थकृत् ॥ मन – – – क – ।किःश्रीवीरस्य विनि-
र्ममे ॥ २४ ॥ – – – – जयानंदसूरिपट्टप्रतिष्ठितैः ॥ व्यधि-
यंत प्रतिष्टा च श्रीम – दनसूरिभिः ॥ २९ ॥ बृहद्गणोपद्गतपि-
प्पलशाखायां श्रीधनेश्वरविनेयः मसिंहसूरिः प्र-
शस्तिमेतामिति व्यतनोत् ॥ २६ ॥ ऊर्ध्वसिनिप्रभाः ॥ संवदा-
स्तामसौशस्ताप्रशस्तिः स्व स्छिठ. हरिपालेनमालेयमु-
त्कीर्णोति ॥

Traslation.

"O lord of.........at once obtained.........a jewel in the family of Mâla......possessed of unsullied fame............had two sons named Udayana and.........Kuhaḍa, an abode of fortune, became minister..................was a wife of perfect duty. Seven sons raised up their family like the celebrated mountain, were born to them. The first and the best was Kumârasiṁha, who was a treasure of an officer of the king Kumârapâla, then the pleasant Jagatsiṁha and then Padmasiṁha the place of riches, then Jayanta and Pâṭâka, Dhîṇiga and...mimaprata. Bimbîdêvî the wife of the famous Padmasiṁha. Padmasiṁha had four sons—the famous Mahaṇasiṁha, Samarasiṁha,......sallaksha and Teja...possessing a mountain the size of Jayanta (the son of Indra) and also an unrivalled daughter Sumalâ who was............Sâmatasiṁha and.........were at the head of all countries like the moon and possessed.........from Lâlâka living in Aṇahilapura......in Ghaṭapadra.........a ship to cross the worldly ocean............on Śatruñjaya mountain with his hand folded before the idol Deva......of the ocean of the miseries of the world......the people are happy by the wealth of......the son of Tejallade(va) by name the famous Vilha.........adorned by.........by whom in Wadhwân and in the town of Pethalâpâ (was caused to be built) a temple of Nemi; and trees were planted for the good of the *maṇḍapa* ....a curious group of idols were set up.........for the merit of his elder brother the famous Krasûri, who performed a pilgrimage of Savana.........consecration was made by the famous............danasûri who had been nominated to the sacred seat of Jayânandasûri.........On a *Pippala* branch brought by a large multitude......Jayasiṁhasûri, revered by the famous Dhaneśvara, has written this eulogistic inscription......This eulogistic inscription has been engraved by Ṭhakur Haripâla."

INSCRIPTION No. 9.

There are two pillars at the north entrance to Neminâtha's temple. Both have inscriptions. The following is from that on the east side:—

संवत् १३३९ वर्षे ज्येष्टसुदि ८ बुधे श्रीउज्ज-
यंतमहातीर्थे श्रयवाणावास्तव्यप्रग्वाटज्ञा-
तीयमहं जिसधरसुतमहं पूनासिंहभा-

र्यो. गुनसिरिश्रेयोर्थनेचकेद्रा ३०० त्रीणिशता-
निनेचके कारितानि दिनंप्रतिपुष्फ. १०५० ॥
संवत् १३३५ वर्षे वैशाख शुदि ८
गुरौ श्रीमदुज्जयंतमहातीर्थे देव – – –
च श्रीनेमिनाथपूजार्थं धवलक्ककवास्तव्य-
श्रीमालजातीयसंघ० वील्हणत – – – –

Translation.

"On Wednesday, the 8th of the bright half of Jyeshṭha in *Saṁ.* 1339; three hundred *dra.* have been given towards the daily *pûjâ* on the great holy place of Ujjayanta for the special benefit of Gunasiri, the wife of Punasiṁha the son of Jisadhara of the Prâgvâṭa family and an inhabitant of Śrayavâṇa. Every day 3,050 flowers to be used in the *pûjâ*.

Thursday, the 8th of the bright half of Vaiśâkha *Saṁ.* 1335; a Saṁgha... Vîlhaṇata of the Śrîmâla caste and an inhabitant of Dhavalakkaka............for the worship of the holy Neminâtha of the great holy place of this famous Ujjayanta........."

INSCRIPTION No. 10.

The following is on the adjoining pillar :—

संवत् १३३३ वर्षे ज्येष्ठ वदि १४ भौमश्री-
जिनप्रबोधसूरिसुगुरूपदेशात् उच्चा-
पुरीवास्तव्येन श्रे० आसपालसुतश्रे० हरिपा-
लेन आत्मनः स्वमातृहरिलायाश्च श्रेयोर्थं
श्रीउज्जयंतमहातीर्थे श्रीनेमिनाथदेवस्य नित्यपू-
जार्थं द्र. २०० शतद्वयं प्रदत्तं । अमीषां व्याजेन पुष्प-
सहस्र २००० द्वयेन प्रतिदिनं पुजा कर्तव्या श्रीदे-
वकीयआरामवाटिकासत्कपुष्पानि श्रीदेवक-
– पंचकुलेन श्रीदेवायऊटापनीयानि ॥

Translation.

"Tuesday, the 14th of the dark half of Jyeshṭha *Saṁ.* 1333. 200 *dra.* have been given towards the daily worship of the famous Neminâtha on the great holy place of Ujjayanta by the great merchant Haripâla, son of Âsapâla and an inhabitant of Uchchâpurî, in accordance with the instruction of a holy preceptor named Jinaprabodhasûri, for the spiritual benefit of his mother Harilâ............Out of the interest of this sum every day worship with 2,000 flowers should be performed. The flowers should be gathered by the *Deva's Pancha* from the *Deva's* garden for the *Deva's* worship alone."

INSCRIPTION No. 11.

This is on the wall of a small temple to the west of an enclosure near the south entrance to Neminâtha's temple. The stone is broken.

॥ स्वस्ति श्रीधृति
॥ नमः श्रीनेमिनाथाय ज
॥ वर्षे फाल्गुन शुदि ५ गुरौ श्री
॥ तिलकमहाराज श्रीमहीपाल
॥ वयरसिंहभार्या फाउसुतसा
॥ सुतसा० साईआसा० मेलामेला
॥ जसुताऽऽ्डीगांगीप्रभृती
॥ नाथप्रासादा कारिता प्रतिष्ट
॥ द्रसूरितत्पट्टे श्रीमुनिसिंह
॥ – – – – – – – कल्याणत्रय

Translation.

"With auspicious beginning the famous, courageous............Salutation to the holy Neminâtha......year......5th of the bright half of Phâlguna, Thursday, the famous...... ....the well-known Mahîpâla, the great king and the crest of ....the wife of Vayarasimha by name Phâu; his son the respectable...........his sons the respectable Sâyiâ and Melâmelâ............his daughters Rudî, Gâṅgî, &c.—all these caused a temple of Neminâtha to be built—which was consecrated by the famous Munisimha on the holy seat of........ drasûri.................May three merits............"

INSCRIPTION No. 12.

On a broken pillar at the same spot just under the two images the following inscription occurs :—

ओं नमः सर्वज्ञाय ॥ संवत् १४८५ वर्षे कार्ति शुदि
पंचमी ५ बुधे श्रीगिरिनारिमहातीर्थे सापषेतासिंह-
निर्वाणं श्रीमंत्रिद्रलियवंशे श्रीमतसुनामडगो-
त्रो मरुतीयाणाठपजहा पुत्रठापलाखूतत्सूत-
ठापकट्ट-तदन्वयवीसल तदंग (भू) ठापसुरातदंगभूठाप
माथूठापभीमसिंहठपमाला भीमसिंहभार्याठापभी-
मापुत्री बाईमोहणकुक्षिसमुत्पन्न ठापषेतासिंहभा-
र्या बाइचंदागह श्रीनेमिनाथचरणप्रणमति
॥ शुभं ॥

Translation.

"Salutation to Sarvajña—Wednesday, the 5th of the bright half of Kârtika, *Samvat* 1485. In the famous line of Ilia and the well-known family of Sunâmaḍa there was one Marutîyâṇâthapa Jahâ; his son was Lâkhû whose son was Jeṭha; his son was Vîsala; his son Surâ had three sons Mâthû, Bhîmasimha and Mâlâ—of these Bhîmasimha's wife named Bhîmî had a daughter named Mohâṇa who gave birth to Khetasimha. The wife of this

Khetasimha named Chandâgaha bows down to the feet of the holy Neminâtha on this great holy place of Girinâri."

Inscription No. 13.

This is on a wall to the east of the same entrance as No. 11 :—

संवत् १४९६ वर्षे आषा-
ढशुदि १३ गुरी जंझणपुरि-
वास्तव्या महतीआणीषु
रतरगछागोत्रनन्हडे
साहचादूणसंतानसाह-
गुणसजतस्यहजाजावीर·
मदेवापुत्रमाणकचंदभ्रा-
त्रीसंघवीरायिमलश्रीगिरि-
जात्राकरीश्रीनेमि·

Translation.

"Thursday, the 13th of the bright half of Âshâḍha 1496. In the Khadatara division and Nahnaḍa family there was one named Sâha Châḍhûṇa; his son was Sâha......whose son was Sâha Jâjâvîra naturally possessed of good qualities............Madeva and his son Mâṇakachanda and his brother Saṅghavî Râyimala, inhabitants of Janjhaṇapuri and who bore the surname of Mahatiânâ, performed a pilgrimage to this holy mountain, the famous Neminâtha............"

On a wall to the west of the inscription No. 12 :—

संवत् १९२२ श्रीमूलसंघे श्रीहर्षकीर्ति श्रीपद्मकीर्ति भुवनकीर्ति – – – – –

"*Saṁ.* 1522, the famous Mûlasaṅgha, the famous Harshakîrti, Padmakîrti, Bhuvanakîrti," &c.

Inscription No. 14.

This is on the eastern wall of a room near a small gate into Ghadi Ghaṭukâ's temple at the north gate of the temple of Neminâtha.

श्रीमत्सूरिधनेश्वरः समभवन्नीशीरभट्टात्मजः ॥ शिष्यस्त[त्प] दपंकजे मधुकरक्रीडाकरो योभवत् ॥ [शि]ष्यः सोभितवेत्रनेमिसदने श्रीचंद्र [सू] रि – – ॥ श्रीमद्रेवतके चकार शुभदे कार्यं प्रतिष्ठादिकं ॥ १ ॥ श्रीसड्गात-महामात्यपृष्टार्थविहितोत्तरः भं० [उ]द्भूतवशादेव चंडादिजनतान्वितः ॥ स०

Translation.

"There was a son of Nîśîrabhaṭṭa, who playing the part of a bee on the lotus-like feet of Dhaneśvarasûri became his pupil; his pupil Chandrasûri performed religious ceremonies, such as *Pratishṭha,* on the auspicious mountain Revata in the splendid temple of Neminâtha......Chandrasûri who answered a question put to him by the great minister Saḍgâta, and who by miraculous power was accompanied by Chaṇḍa," &c.

INSCRIPTION No. 15.

On a pillar at the same place :—

– नेदयगच्छविभूषणमंसिदसूरिसरामकइसिस्सो संवच्छरतेण उपवंदह नेमिस्सपयकमके ॥

Translation.

"Mamsidasûri, the ornament of .....the Nedaya division, with Râmakasimha, built in three years...I bow to Nemi's lotus-like feet. (?)"

INSCRIPTION No. 16.

In the same place on the western wall to the south :—

संवत् १२१९ वर्षे चैत्रशुदि ८ रवावद्येह श्रीमदुज्जयंततीर्थे जगतीसमस्तदेवकुलिकासत्कछाजाकुवा लिसंविरणसंघविठ. सालवाहणप्रतिपत्या सू० जसहडउ० सावदवेन परिपूर्णा कृता ॥ तथा ठ. भरथसुत ठ. पंडि[त] सालिवाहणेन नागजरिसिरायापरितः कारित [भाग] चत्वारि बिंबीकृत कुंडकर्मांतर तदधिष्ठात्री श्रीअंबिकादेवीप्रतिमा देवकुलिका च निष्पादिता ॥

Translation.

"On an auspicious Sunday, the 8th of Chaitra *Śudi*, *Sam*. 1215.

"Here to-day on this famous holy place of Ujjayanta a row of all the Jaina-god-images have been completed by the mason Jasahada and Sâvadeva with the consent of the Sangbavî Ṭhâkura Sâlivâhana; likewise a Nâgajhari Śirâ or an elephant fount has been enclosed (*by a wall*) by Paṇḍita Sâlivâhana the son of Bharatha, in which four idols have been placed.

"After the above-named *kuṇḍa* an image of the famous Ambikâ upon it and a group of idols have been erected."

INSCRIPTION No. 17.

This is in the north of the same locality :—

.........राजदेवप[ति]सिधचक्रपतिश्रीजयसिंघदेव .....विजय

....पारकरणायनतापिताभे.....................घातेन

.........केन उपायेन...जादवकुलतिलक......तीर्थंकर श्रीने-

मिनाथपाद.........ठ. कीकाच ठ. वाता.....................

सूत्राविक्रममारुति.......................................

Translation.

"For the spiritual benefits of Râjadevapa(ti) Siddhachakrapati, the famous Jayasimhadeva Vijaya.........caused to be built a *Pâdukâ* of the famous Tîrthankara Neminâtha, a crest-jewel of the Jâdava family, with...............mason Vikrama Mâruti."

INSCRIPTION No. 18.

This is on one of the stone slabs on the ground floor in the *maṇḍapa* of the Girinâri temple close to the southern entrance.

श्रीसुभकीर्तिदेवसाहुजाजासुतसाहुतेजकीर्तिदेव.

"The famous Subhakîrtideva and Sâhu Tejakîrtideva, the son of Sâhu Jâjâ."

INSCRIPTION No. 19.

On entering the first gate of the fort there is a temple in the south-east on the right side of the main road. On the back of the temple which is on the *kuṇḍa* or pool is a broken pillar, on which there are five images, one in the middle and four on the upper part. The middle one bears the following name :—

महामात्यश्रीगेल्लक

"The famous Gellaka, the great minister."

Of the upper four images the first bears

श्रीसल्खण

"The famous Salakhaṇa."

The second has

श्रीरास्वदेव

"The famous Râsvadeva."

The third and fourth have the names obliterated. There are some *ślokas* too, but they are hopelessly illegible.

INSCRIPTION No. 20.

There is a raised square-seat under a tree in the compound of what is called Humada's holy place. On the edge of the seat the following occurs :—

सं. ५८ वर्षे चैत्रवदी २
सोमे धारागंजे
पं० नेमिचंदशिष्य
पंचाणचंदमूर्ति.

Translation.

"In the year *Saṁ.* 58, Monday, 2nd of Chaitra *Vadi*, the image of Pañchâṇachanda, the pupil of Nemichanda in the Dhârâ division."

INSCRIPTIONS NOS. 21 AND 22.

Of the temples of Vastupâla the one in the middle contains an image of Pârśvanâtha. In the *maṇḍapa* of this temple are two niches opposite to each other. The following occurs in the upper part of the niche in the north :—

महामात्यश्रीवस्तुपालमहं० श्रीललितादेवीमूर्ति.

"This is an image of Lalitâdevî, the wife of Vastupâla, the great minister."

In the upper part of the southern niche of the same temple :—

महामात्यश्रीवस्तुपाल महं. श्रीसोखुकामूर्ति...

"This is an image of Sokhukâ, the wife of Vastupâla, the great minister."

INSCRIPTION No. 23.

At the base of Pârśvanâtha's statue in the same temple as No. 21 :—

ई० संवत् १३०९ वर्षे वै-
शाखशुदि ३ शनौ श्रीपत्तनवास्त-
व्यश्रीमालज्ञातीयठ. वाहड-
सुतमहंपद्मसिंहपुत्रठ.
पथिमिदेवीअंगज – – – –
– नुजमहं श्रीसामतसिंह
तथा महामात्यश्री-
सलखणसिंहाभ्यां श्रीपार्श्वनाथ-
बिंबं पित्रोः श्रेयसेऽत्रका-
रितं ततो बृहद्गच्छे श्रीप्रद्युम्नसूरि
पटोद्धरणश्रीमानदेव
सूरिशिष्यश्रीजयानं[द] – – – प्रतिष्ठितं [शुभं भवतु]

Translation.

"Oṁ ! Saturday, the 3rd of the white half of Vaiśâkha, *Saṁ.* 1305 ; this statue of Pârśvanâtha is caused to be set up by Ṭhakur Vâhaḍa and the famous Salakhaṇasiṁha, the great minister of the Śrîmâla caste, and inhabitants of Paṭṭana for the spiritual benefit of their father and mother. Jayânanda, the pupil of the venerable Mânadevasûri, who was an ornament of the sacred seat of Sâmatasiṁha, the younger brother of ....and who by Pathimidevî was the son of Padmasiṁha, who was again the son of Pradyumnasûri of the Bṛihat division........................"

INSCRIPTION No. 24.[1]

Under a broken image in the compound of Soni Saṅgram's temple the following line occurs :—

चांपसिंहमूर्ति

"An image of Châṁpasiṁha."

INSCRIPTION No. 25.

On a rock near Suvâvaḍi-paraba :—

......पालविहारेण......

[1] See inscription No. 34.

यशैलराजो विराजते

" By Vâlvisar.........Vâsala .....shines."

Inscription No. 26.

On a stone in a raised seat near the same Paraba :—

सुबिवाअराय – सिंघभार्या

तेपंचमी टुके काल कीधो तेनी पादुका

" Footprints of Tejâ, the wife of the famous ......siṁha and who died on the 5th summit."

Inscription No. 27.

Above the stone-quarry known as the Khabutrîkhâṇa and below the Paraba of No. 25, the following inscription is found on a wall on the northern side of a mountain-path :—

संवत् १२२२ श्री श्रीमालज्ञाती-

यमहं. श्रीराणिगसूतमहं

श्रीआंबाकेन पद्या कारिता

" *Saṁvat* 1222 ; these holy feet have been set up by Âmbâka, the son of Râṇiga, of the Śrîmâla caste."

Inscriptions Nos. 28, 29, and 30.[1]

In the stone-quarry called Khabutrikhâna are three inscriptions, of which the first is :—

– – विहारेण– – ॥ शैलराजो विराजते ॥

– – हरिणेवो[ज्वल]श्रिया

उपकंठस्थितेनायं

" By a convent established by.........white as a garland and occupying the entrance as the garland occupies the neck, this mountain-king looks more beautiful."

The second :—

सं० १५३५

"*Saṁ*. 1535."

The third :—

सं. १२२३ महं. श्रीराणिगसुत[महं] श्रीआबा-

केन पद्या कारिता.

" *Saṁvat* 1223; these holy feet have been placed by Âbâka, the son of Râṇiga."

---

[1] See inscription No. 34.

INSCRIPTION No. 31.

This is near the sacred place called Hâthîpaglâṅ (Elephant's Foot) :—

स्वस्तिश्री १६८३ वर्षे कार्तिक
वदि ६ सोमे श्रीगिरनारतीर्थ-
नी पूर्वपाजनो उद्धार श्री-
दिवने संघे षोर्प्यानिप्रज्ञ (पुण्यनिमित्त) श्री-
मालज्ञातीयमां सिंघजी
मेघजीने उद्यमे कराव्यो
सं. १२२३ महं. श्रीराणि.

Translation.

" Monday, the 6th of Kârtika *Vadi, Saṁvat* 1683 ; the repair of the old road on this sacred place of Girnâr has been made by the exertion of tho meritorious Mânsiṁhaji Meghaji of the Śrîmâli caste in a pilgrim-party from Dîva."

INSCRIPTION No. 32.

On the threshold of the eastern door of Bhavanâtha's temple :—

लि. त्रवाडी...
महादेवमुकुंद.

षोमाविश्व......
वो। नाग.........
दयर.........
...काजा......
नागरवो। विश्वनाथ
नाभ। नाकाजागं...

Translation.

वोरा (Vorâ) नागर (Nâgara) विश्व (Viśva)......

Writer Travâdi Mahâdeva Mukunda.

वो. नाग...
दयर (Dayârâm)
नागर वोरा विश्वनाथ
नागर ब्राह्मण नाका जागम

INSCRIPTION No. 33.

In the fort of the town there is a fallen temple containing a yellow slab with twenty-four Jina images where the following is found :—

संवत् १३१० वर्षे वैशाख सुदि ९ शुक्रे पल्लीवाल [ज्ञा] तीयसाडुवणदासुतसाडुव
सहजूमादोरिषेतलहासलधांधल देवि कामलदे वि...
पाल्हणिग · – वयजूभावलसहरलीलाडी [ज्ञांज्ञ] णमं...

Translation.

"*Saṁ.* 1350, Friday the 5th of Vaiśâkha *Śudi,* Vasahabhûma, &c., the sons of Vanadâ of the Pallivâla caste, Rikhetala, Hâṅsala, Dhâṅdhaladêvî, Kâmaladevî………… Luniga, Vayajû, Bhâval………"

INSCRIPTION No. 34.

On the rock to the east of Râjala and Vejala caves and west of the road leading to Gaumukha :—

वस्तुपालविहारेण हारेणेवोज्वलश्रिया उपकंठस्थितेनायं शैलराजो विराजते ॥
श्रीविक्रम संवत् १२८९ वर्षे आश्विन वदी १५ सोमे महामात्यश्रीवस्तुपालेन आत्मश्रेयोर्थं
पश्चाद्भागे श्रीकपर्दियक्षप्रासादसमलंकृतः श्रीशत्रुंजयाव [तार] श्रीआदिनाथप्रासादस्तदग्रतो वामपक्षे
स्वीयसध्धर्मचारिणीमहंश्रीललितादेविश्रेयोर्थं विंशतिजिनालंकृतः श्रीसम्मेतशिखरप्रा-
सादस्तथा दक्षिणपक्षे द्वि० भार्यामहंश्रीसोखुश्रेयोर्थं चतुर्विंशतिजिनोपशोभितः श्रीअष्टा-
पदप्रासादः ० अपूर्वघाटरचनारुचिरतरमभिनवप्रासादचतुष्टयं निजद्रव्येण कारयांचक्रे ॥

Translation.

"This mountain shines by a *Vihâra* of Vastupâla, white as a garland and gracing the entrance as the garland graces the neck.

"Monday the 15th of Âśvina *Vadi,* Vikrama *Saṁ.* 1289. The great minister Vastupâla caused four new and beautiful temples of rare construction to be built—one of the famous Kaparadîyaksha on the western side; the second of the famous Âdinâtha of Śatruñjaya-descent on the left side of the above for his own spiritual benefit; the third with ornamented top and adorned with twenty Jinas for the spiritual benefit of his virtuous wife Lalitâdevî; and the fourth of Ashṭâpada adorned with twenty-four Jinas for the heavenly good of his second wife Sokhukâ—all these with his own money."

INSCRIPTION No. 35.

This is on a wall of the sacred seat of the head-priest of the Vaishṇavas, at the Revatîkuṇḍa near the south entrance gate :—

ओं नमो विनायकाय ॥ योगींद्रैर्मुनिपुंगवैरनिमिषैर्यो भक्तिवश्यः परं न ध्यानेन न चेज्यया न तपसा
धर्तुं ह्रदाप्याप्यते ॥ गोप्यासौ नवनीततस्करपरो बद्धो गवां दामभिः स्थाणुत्वं निरमोचयद्वरयोर्दामो-
दरोव्यात् जगत् ॥ १ ॥ मंडलीकनृपातिर्यदुवंशे यो बभूव युधि मुद्गलजेता ॥ श्रीकरीसहितभूपतिसेव्य-
स्तस्य सूनुरभवन्महिपालः ॥ २ ॥ तत्तनयोवनिभर्त्ता खंगारोनाद वेदमुद्धर्त्ता ॥ द्वीपनवद्वयहर्त्ता सोमेश-
स्थापनाकर्त्ता ॥ ३ मुरुक्मदानपरितोषितभूमिदेवस्तं नंदनः समभवत्जयसिंहदेवः ॥ वर्णाश्रमस्थि
तिकरो नृपमुक्तसिंहस्तस्मादरिद्विरदविक्रममुक्तसिंहः ॥ ४ ॥ मधुपनृपतिशुद्धेस्तीर्थराडन्यना-
र्यां जनितनिजजनित्रीतुल्यबुद्धिर्वदान्यः ॥ समितिसुभटमुख्यो मंडलीकस्तदीयोजनि च त-
मनुजन्मा मेलिगः स्थूललक्षः ॥ ५ ॥ भीताभयदव्रतवरनृपमेलिगनंदनश्च जयसिंहः ॥ अस्ति च
तस्य तु राज्ये यदुसामतसैन्यपेसमये ॥ ६ ॥ अभिषेणयितुमुपेतं झिझरकोटस्य परिसरे स-
[म]रे ॥ यो हत्वा यवनबलं मुमोच धर्मोध्य नाशेषं ॥ ७ ॥ संवद्रामतुरंगसागरमहीसंख्येथ शा-

क्रे सिते पंचम्यां भृगुवासरे व्यरचयत् षट्कृष्णषट्कर्मकृत् ॥ पाटिश्रीनरसिंहदेवतनयो दा-
मोदरः पूर्वजानुद्धर्तुं यतियात्रिकोपकृतये तिष्टत्वखंडं मठं ॥ ८ ॥ नागराभ्यंतरज्ञातिद्विजधांधलनंदनः ॥
मंत्रिसिंहस्तस्य सुतः प्रशस्तेः सामलः कविः ॥ ९ ॥ इति सं० १४७३ वर्षे सूत्रजाल्हासुतसूत्र० करणा-
केन ॥ ॥

Translation.

" Salutation to Vinâyaka ; he, who, being solely won by devotion, is not accessible to the best of sages, hermits or gods with all their contemplations, sacrifices and charities—may he protect the world!

" There was a king named Maṇḍalîka in the family of the Yâdavas, who conquered the Mudgala (*Moghal*) and was served by many friendly kings with rich tributes. His son was Mahîpâla. His son Khangâra, the nourisher of the world, was a great supporter of musical science. He conquered twice nine islands (*continents*) and established a great idol of Somanâtha. His son was Jayatasiṁha-deva, who satisfied the Brâhmaṇs with land, gold and other gifts. After him came the king Muktasiṁha, who properly controlled the rules of social divisions and acted by exploits like a lion let loose upon his elephant-enemies.

" The son of the above was Maṇḍalîka, who was a holy place for the purification of wine-drinking Yâdavas, who looked upon the wives of others as his mother and who was a warlike soldier in the battle-field.

" His younger brother Meliga was of large intelligence. His son was Jayasiṁha, whose vows consisted of the pledges of security to the terrified. At one time in his reign, which protected many members of the Yâdava family, a large army of the Yavanas came to the frontier of Jiñjharakâta. This he defeated and spared the remainder according to the rules of justice: and Dâmodara, the son of the famous Pâti Narasiṁhadeva, who daily performed six ceremonies of the six Kṛishṇas, constructed this unbroken mansion for the good of the pilgrims and hermits to save his own ancestors. Friday the 5th of Chaitra Sudî, *Saṁ.* Râma (3), Turanga (7), Sâgara (4), Mahi (1) (*i.e.* 1473).

" Sâmala the son of Mantrîsiṁha, who was the son of Dhândhala, a Brâhmaṇ in the Nâgara division, has composed this inscription ; Karaṇâka, the son of Jhâla, a mason, has cut this inscription in the year 1473."

INSCRIPTION No. 36.

This is on a finely sculptured marble-slab in the library of Mr. Narasiṁhaprasâd Hariprasâd :—

संवत् १३७० वर्षे वैसाखशुदि २ गुरु
लीलादिविश्रेयोर्थं श्रीआदिनाथबिंबं थथिरपाल

" Wednesday, the 2nd of the bright half of Vaiśâkha, *Saṁvat* 1370. For the spiritual safety of Lîlâdevî, Thathirapâla has.........this sacred image of Âdinâtha."

INSCRIPTION No. 37.

॥ ९० ॥ संवत् १३९६ वर्षे जेष्टशुदि १९ शुक्रे श्रीपल्ली-
वालज्ञातीय श्रेष्ठिपासूसुतसाहुपदमभार्यातिजला......
हेनकुलगुरुश्रीस्मनिमुनिआदेशेन श्रीमुनिसुव्रत-
स्वामिबिंबं देवकुलियां पितामह श्रेया

Translation.

" ....Friday the 15th of the bright half of Jyêshṭha, *Saṁ.* 1356............Tejalâ, the wife of the famous Padama, who was the son of Pâsû and a Pallîvâla by caste has set up this image of the famous ascetic Suvratasvâmi amid the idol-group for the spiritual benefit of her grandfather."

INSCRIPTIONS NOS. 38 AND 39.

There is a blocked-up gate in the east wall of the town-fort, where there are some hand-prints of virtuous women. There are also some nineteen inscriptions, seven in the east and twelve in the west walls. The place is accessible from the side of a stone-quarry.

On the west wall :—

ए स्वस्ति संवत् १९२१ वर्षे श्रावणशुदि १९ भोमे ठा-
कुरश्रीसा[जण] सुतपरिक्ष
ठाकुर [श्री]सतीबाइरणादे ॥ देवमतीसिंहमहंमक्षं–व्ह – – –

Translation.

"Tuesday, the 15th of Śrâvaṇa *Śudi Saṁ.* 1521 ; a virtuous woman named Raṇâde the wife of Pariksha, the son of Ṭhâkur Sâjada......dêva, Matisiṁh and Maksha........."

On the east wall :—

स्वस्ति संवत् १९१९ वर्षे ज्येष्ट शुदि १० शुक्रे जालहराज्ञा-
तिमांडवियाजयता भार्यासतीबाई [रयण]

Translation.

"Friday the 10th of Jyeshṭha *Śudi, Saṁ.* 1590 ; a chaste woman by name Rayaṇa the wife of Jayatâ, a custom-master and Jâlaharâ by caste........."*

* These inscriptions are without verbs. Probably *Satî*, which is an adjective, may be made the predicate with a copula understood, and then the inscriptions would mean that those women sacrificed themselves or became *Satî*.

GLOSSARY OF TERMS AND PROPER NAMES.

ABHINANDA, one of the twenty-four Tîrthankaras of the Jains.

Abru, honour, credit.

Achaleśvara, a name of Śiva (lord of the earth).

Âchârya, a spiritual guide.

Âdibuddhâji Ṛishabhadeva, the first Tîrthankara.

Âdike-Nârâyaṇa, a name of Vishṇu.

Âdi-Keśava, a name of Vishṇu (the primeval being).

Âdinâtha or Âdinâthaji, Ṛishabhadeva.

Âdîśvara Bhagavân, the first of the twenty-four Tîrthankaras of the Jains.

Aeśvara, an epithet of Śiva.

Aguada (Port.), a place where ships obtain water.

Agni, god of fire, and guardian of the south-east point of the compass.

Agraśâlâ, the front hall or verandah.

Ajakasambhava, one of the twenty-four Tîrthankaras of the Jains.

Ajitanâtha, one of the twenty-four Tîrthankaras of the Jains.

Alpa, small, little.

Ambâbâi or Ambâmâtâ, a name of Durgâ. Goddess of wealth.

Ambârkhânâ, a granary.

Ambikâ, same as Ambâbâi.

Amṛitalinga, same as Amṛiteśa.

Amṛiteśa, a name of Śiva (the lord of the nectar).

Amṛiteśvara, same as last.

Ananta, one of the twenty-four Tîrthankaras of the Jains; another name of Sumati; a snake.

Ândhra, name of an ancient dynasty.

Ângirasa, the name of one of the years in the Hindu cycle of sixty years.

Anjanî, name of the mother of Mâruti.

Ankuśeśvara. An epithet of Śiva (ankuśa, goad).

Annachhatra, a house where cooked food is given away once or twice a day, especially to Brâhmaṇs.

Annapûrṇâ, a form of Durgâ; the Goddess of Plenty.

Anasûyâ, name of the wife of Atri *ṛishi*, mother of Dattâtreya.

Ara, one of the twenty-four Tîrthankaras of the Jains.

Araṇeśvara, an epithet of Śiva (Aran, name of a village).

Arbudeśvara. An epithet of Śiva (arbuda, one hundred millions).

Arjuna, name of the third Pâṇḍava, son of Kuntî by Indra.

Arvattukhambaḍa basti, temple of sixty pillars.

Âsana, a seat, a throne.

Âśâpûrâ Mâtâ, Devî, Goddess who fulfills desires.

Âshâḍha, name of the fourth lunar month (June-July).

Ashṭabhujâ, a goddess having eight hands; Durgâ.

Ashṭadikpâlas, the eight guardians of the points of the compass.

Ashṭamangala, a collection of eight lucky things.

Ashṭa-mâtarah, the eight Mothers, namely, Brâhmî, Mâheśvarî, Chaṇḍî, Vârâhî, Vaishṇavî, Kaumârî, Châmuṇḍâ, and Charchikâ.

Ashṭa Vinâyaka, eight avatâras of Gaṇeśa.

Aśvathara, an architectural term: horse moulding.

Âśvina, name of the seventh lunar month (Sept.-Oct.).

Âtmalinga, the phallic emblem of Śiva as worshipped.

Avatâra, an incarnation.

BADEŚVARA, an epithet of Śiva.

Bâgh or bagichâ, a flower garden.

Bahudhânya, the name of one of the years in the Hindu cycle of sixty years.

Bala, Baladeva, or Balarâma, name of the elder brother of Kṛishṇa, the eighth incarnation of Vishṇu.

Bâlâji, a term used by the Gujarâtis for Kṛishṇa in childhood.

Baleśvara, an epithet of Śiva (god of might).

Bâleśvara, an epithet of Śiva (Bâla, a child).

Bali, name of a celebrated demon sent to Pâtâla by Vâmana or the dwarf *avatâra* of Vishṇu.

Ballâlatîrtha, the name of a holy place.

Banadaśaṁkarî, same as Banaśaṁkarî.

Banaśaṁkara, a name of Śiva (bana or vana, a forest).

Banaśaṁkarî, name of Pârvatî (bana or vana, a forest).

Bând, or band (Hind.), a retaining wall of earth, a dam.

Baneśvara, epithet of Śiva (lord of the forest).

Bârav, a well or tank.

Basâppâ, same as Basavâ.

Basavâ or Basavâṇṇâ, the sacred bull Nandi. Also the name of the founder of the Lingâyata religion.

Basaveśvara, an epithet of Śiva (Basavâ, the sacred bull).

Basti, a temple (term used in the Kânarese districts).

Bauddha. Adjectival form of Buddha.

Bava, a karaṇa of the same name.

Bâva or Bâvadi, a well with steps.

Bhâdeśvara, an epithet of Śiva.

Bhadrakâlî, a name of Durgâ (Pârvatî).

Bhadrakâlî-Śaṁkara, Pârvatî and Śiva.

Bhâdrapada, the sixth lunar month (Aug.-Sept.)

Bhadreśvara, an epithet of Śiva (bhadra, happiness, prosperity).

Bhagavân, a name of Vishṇu.

Bhairava, the terrific form of Śiva.

Bhairavanâtha, the same as the last.

Bhadra, happiness, fortune.

Bhâleśvara, an epithet of Śiva (bhâla, the brow).

Bhâmatî, cloisters.

Bhânu, the name of one of the years in the Hindu cycle of sixty years.

Bharateśvara, an epithet of Śiva.

Bhârgavarâma, the sixth incarnation of Vishṇu, that is, Paraśurâma.

Bhâskarâchârya, name of the great astronomer who wrote several works on astronomy. He flourished about the tenth or eleventh century.

Bhaṭṭâraka, venerable, worshipful.

Bhavanâtha, a name of Śiva (lord of the world).

Bhavânî, a name of Pârvatî.

Bhavânî-Śaṁkara, Pârvatî and Śiva.

Bhâvi, a well.

Bhîdabhanjana, an epithet of Śiva.

Bhikshuka, a beggar, a mendicant.

Bhîma, name of one of the Pâṇḍavas.

Bhîmaka, mythical King of Ayodhyâ.

Bhîmâśaṁkara, name of a Śiva-linga near the source of the Bhîmâ.

Bhogamaṇḍapa, the inner hall of a temple.

Bhogeśalinga, name of a liṅga of Mahâdeva or Śiva.

Bhogeśa, same as Bhogeśvara (bhoga, a snake).

Bhogeśvara, epithet of Śiva.

Bhṛigu Ṛishi, name of the sage Jamadagni.

Bhṛingî, name of a skeleton attendant of Śiva.

Bhûta, a spirit.

Bhûtanâtha, a name of Śiva (lord of spirits).

Bhuvaneśvara, epithet of Śiva (bhuvana, the world).

Bichu-kâṇṭâ, scorpion's sting.

Bighâ, a certain measurement of land almost equal to an acre.

Bileśvara, an epithet of Śiva.

Bilveśvara, an epithet of Śiva; Bilva, name of a tree (*Ægle Marmelos*).

Bin, "son of".

Bommappa, the god Brahmâ.

Brahmâṇḍeśvara, epithet of Śiva (lord of the universe).

Brahmadeva, the first deity of the Triad—the creator.

Bṛihaspati, name of the preceptor of the gods.

CHÂDARA, a covering cloth, a sheet.

Chaitra, the first lunar month (March-April).

Chaitya, name applied to the arched-roofed caves of the Buddhists.

Chakra, a disc, especially that of Vishṇu.

Chakreśvarî Mâtâ, a name of Lakshmî.

Chameśvara, an epithet of Śiva.

Champâ, name of a tree (Mesua ferrea).

Chaṇḍikâ, a name of Durgâ.

Chandrakaleśvara, an epithet of Śiva (moon-crested).

Chandramaulîśvara, an epithet of Śiva (moon-crested).

Chandranâtheśvara, name of one of the Tîrthankaras.

Chandraprabhu, same as above.

Chandraśâlâ, an open verandah.

Chandravâra, Monday (the day of the moon).

Chandravîraprabhu, same as Chandraprabhu.

Châṅgadeva, a name of an ancient Sâdhu.

Changalâdevî, name of a goddess.

Changalova (Devî), name of a devî.

Chankeśvara, an epithet of Śiva.

Chaturbhujarâya, a name of Vishṇu.

Chaukaṇḍi, a walled enclosure without a roof.

Chauki, a police station.

Chaumukha, Chaturmukha, four Jaina images placed on a pedestal back to back so as to face the four cardinal points of the compass (four faces).

Chauri, a fly-brush, generally made of yak tail in a silver-mounted handle.

Châvadi, the open court-house of the village officials.

Chyavana, name of an ancient Ṛishi.

Chyavaneśvara, an epithet of Śiva (Chyavana, name of an ancient Ṛishi).

Chelâ, a disciple.

Chhatra or chhatri, an umbrella; a pavilion.

Chikkeśvara, an epithet of Śiva.

Chinha, a symbol.

Chintâmaṇi-Pârśvanâtha, one of the twenty-four Tîrthankaras.

Cholâmaṇḍala, name of a country.

Choleśvara, epithet of Śiva (Chola, name of a country).

Chovivattu, temple with images of the twenty-four Tîrthankaras.

Chûḍâśekhara, a name of Śiva (Chûḍâ, the matted hair, and Śekhara, the head, that is, a god having matted hair on his head).

DÂGOBA, a representation of the stûpa or burial mound originally erected over the ashes or relics of Buddha.

Damaru, a small drum.

Daftardâr, a record officer.

Dakshiṇâ, gift, donation; the south.

Dâmodara, a name of Vishṇu.

Dâna, charity, present.

Daṇḍeśvara, an epithet of Śiva (daṇḍa, a stick).

Darbâr, a king's court.

Dargâh, a Musalmân tomb or rest-house.

Darwâjâ, gateway.

Daśameśvara, an epithet of Śiva.

Daśaratha, name of a king of Ayodhyâ, father of Râma, hero of the Râmâyaṇa.

Daśâśvamedha tîrtha, a holy place (a place where the ten horse sacrifices were performed).

Datta or Dattâtreya, name of the son of Atri by Anasûyâ, considered to be an incarnation of Brahmâ, Vishṇu, and Maheśa.

Dâvrâ, three-cornered small well.

Dayâleśvara, epithet of Śiva (lord of mercy).

Deva, a god.

Devâlaya, Devala, } a temple.

Devanâgarî, the character in which Sanskṛit and its derived languages are usually written.

Devasthâna, a temple (abode of a god).

Devî, applied to Durgâ, Sâvitrî, and Sarasvatî (goddess).

Dhâkleśvara, an epithet of Śiva.

Dhaneśvara, an epithet of Śiva (dhana, wealth).

Dhâreśvara, an epithet of Śiva.

Dharmanâthaji, one of the twenty-four Tîrthankaras.

Dharmaśâlâ, a charitable rest-house.

Dharvarâya (Dharmarâya ?), name of the first Pâṇḍava

Dhâtṛi, the Creator; also the name of a year in the Hindu cycle of sixty years.

Dhed, a man of the lowest caste.

Dhobi, a washerman.

Dhokeśvara, an epithet of Śiva (Dhoke, name of a village.)

Dhûtapâpa, name of a holy place (freed from sin).

Dhvajastambha, a pillar for a flag.

Digambara, one of the sects of the Jainas whose images are nude; also a name of Śiva.

Dikpâla, a guardian of one of the points of the compass. (See "Ashṭadikpâlas").

Dîpakhâmba, dîpadakhâmba, or dîpastambha, a lamp pillar.

Dîpamâlâ, a lamp pillar.

Divâṇa, prime minister.

Divâṇkhâna, a hall.

Dodda-Basâppâ. Same as Basavâ.

Draupadî, the common wife of the five Pâṇḍavas.

Dudheśvara, an epithet of Śiva (lord of milk).

Dundubhi, a drum; also the name of a year in the Hindu cycle of sixty years.

Durgâ, a name of Pârvatî.

Durmukha, name of a year in the Hindu cycle of sixty years.

Dvârakânâtha, a name of Kṛishṇa (lord of the city of Dvârakâ).

Dvârapâla, a door-keeper; also a name of Vishṇu.

EKÂDAŚI, eleventh day of each fortnight of the Hindu month, being a fast day.

Ekanâtha, name of an ancient Sâdhu.

FAQIR, a Muhammadan religious mendicant.

Feringâbâi, name of a goddess at Nânoli.

GÂBHÂRÂ, the inner shrine of a temple.

Gachchina-Basâppâ, a name of Basavâ.

Gaḍ, a fort.

Gâdi, a throne.

Gaja-Lakshmî, Lakshmî with two elephants, one on either side of her, which pour water upon her from vessels held in their trunks.

Galageśvara or Galaganâtha, an epithet of Śiva (Galaganâth, name of a village).

Galteśvara, an epithet of Śiva.

Gaṇapati, Gaṇâppâ, or Gaṇeśa. Son of Śiva and Pârvatî (god of wisdom). Gaṇâppâ is the Kânarese form.

Gaṇeśa chaturthî, the fourth day of the month of Bhâdrapada.

Gangâdhareśvara, epithet of Śiva (he who holds the river Gangâ or Ganges).

Gangâ-Râmeśvara, same as above.

Gangânâtha, a name of Śiva.

Ganjikhânâ, a place for storing grass.

Gargeśvara, an epithet of Śiva (Garga, name of an ancient Ṛishi).

Garuḍa, son of Kaśyapa by his wife Vinatâ; the Vâhana of Vishṇu.

Gaurava, the pujâri or temple servant in a Śiva temple whose particular duty is to remove the offerings.

Gaurî, a name of Pârvatî.

Gavareśvara (Gaurîśvara ?), an epithet of Śiva.

Gautama, a great sage; the propounder of the Nyâya philosophy; also the name of Buddha.

Gautama Svâmi, same as Gautama.

Ghât, a flight of steps at the side of a river or tank; a mountain pass.

Girijâpati, Śiva (Girijâ, name of Pârvatî).

Gokaleśvara, an epithet of Śiva.

Gokarṇeśvara, an epithet of Śiva.

Gokhalâ, an outer verandah. A niche.

Gomukhayaksha, a demi-god having the head of a cow.

Gopadevamuni, Kṛishṇa.

Gopâla Kṛishṇa, Kṛishṇa as the son of a cowherd.

Gopî, a cowherd's wife, a milkmaid.

Gopinâtha, Kṛishṇa, who sported with the Gopîs, the wives of the cowherds of Vṛindâvana.

Gopura, a lofty many-storied gateway to a temple enclosure. Very common in Southern India.

Gosâvi, a Hindu religious mendicant.

Govardhananâtha, Kṛishṇa, who raised the hill Govardhana.

Govindarâja, Vishṇu.

Gṛihastha, a householder.

Guhâ, a cave; a cavern.

Gumbaz, a domed tomb of the Muhammadans.

Gumti, a small domed tomb.

Guṇavanteśvara, an epithet of Śiva (guṇavat, meritorious).

Gupteśvara, epithet of Śiva (the invisible god).

HAIGA BRÂHMANA, a Brâhmaṇ well versed in the performance of sacrifices.

Halevûra-Basavânnâ, a name of Basavâ.

Hammâmkhânâ, bath room.

Hanumân, Hanumanta, } the monkey chief and warrior.

Hara-Nareśvara, an epithet of Śiva (Hara, Śiva, and Nara, the supreme spirit).

Harideva, a name of Vishṇu.

Hari-Hara, Vishṇu and Śiva combined.

Hari-Vijaya-Sûri, name of a Jaina pontiff.

Hâṭakeśvara, epithet of Śiva (hâṭaka, gold).

Haveli, a building.

Hauda, a cistern.

Hemâḍpant, or Hemâdri, a minister to one of the Yâdava kings of Devagiri in the thirteenth century, who is supposed to have been a great temple builder, and to whom all temples of that period and style are ascribed.

Homa-kuṇḍa, a hole in the ground to hold the sacrificial fire.

Hiḍimba, name of a demon slain by Bhîma.

Hiri Hanumanta, same as Hanumân.

Hoṇḍa, a tank.

Hrîṃkâra, one of the sacred spells of the Devî.

Huṁkâreśvara, an epithet of Śiva (huṁ or huṁkâra, a sound signifying assent).

IDGÂH, a Musalmân place of prayer.

Inâm, a grant of land or a village generally for services performed.

Inâmdâr, one who holds inâm land.

Indra, the lord of gods, and guardian of the east.

Îśa, an epithet of Śiva; guardian of the north-east.

Iśvaradeva, Śiva.

JAGADAMBÂ, a name of Durgâ (mother of the universe).

Jagadîśa, an epithet of Śiva (lord of the universe).

Jagannâtha, name of Vishṇu (lord of the universe).

Jâgîr, land held for services given.

Jâgirdâr, one who holds a jâgîr.

Jahâj, a ship.

Jakhaṇâchârya, the mythical architect of South Indian architecture.

Jala (trees), water plants.

Jâmbul, a tree bearing a plum-like fruit (*Eugenia Jambolana*).

Jaina, a religious sect, whose doctrines are a compromise between Buddhism and Hinduism.

Janhu, name of a mythical king.

Janjâl, small iron gun.

Jaṭâśaṁkara, Śiva with matted hair (jaṭâ, matted hair).

Jatiga. Term used for certain stones set up in groves in the Kânarese country.

Jatrâ, a fair.

Jayanta, name of Indra's son.

Jayarâma Svâmi, the famous sâdhu of Vadgâon, Sâtâra.

Jayantipura, name of an ancient city.

Jina, term applied to each of the twenty-four holy teachers or Tîrthankaras of the Jains.

Jnâneśvara, Jnânobâ. { The famous sâdhu of Âḷandi. Jnâneśvara is also an epithet of Śiva (jnâna, knowledge).

Jogeśvarî, a name of Durgâ.

Jogi, a religious mendicant, a sâdhu.

Jotibâ, name of a deity.

Jyesṭha, the third lunar month (May-June).

Jyotirlinga, any one of the twelve most celebrated liṅgas.

Jyotiśaṁkara, a name of Śiva.

KACHHÂ, raw, unfinished, rough, temporary.

Kacheri, office, court-house.

Kacheśvara, an epithet of Śiva (Kacha, name of the son of Bṛihaspati, preceptor of the gods).

Kadambeśvara, epithet of Śiva (Kadamba, name of a tree).

Kailâsa, Śiva's mountain home or Paradise.

Kaiṭabheśvara, an epithet of Śiva (Kaiṭabha, name of a demon slain by Vishṇu).

Kâlabhairava, Śiva in his terrific forms.

Kalahasteśvara, epithet of Śiva (Kalâ, a digit of the moon).

Kalameśvara, epithet of Śiva (Kalama, rice).

Kalaśa, a pot; also the pot-like finial of the spire of a temple.

Kâleśvara, an epithet of Śiva (Kâla, the destroyer of the universe).

Kâlikâdevî, a name of Durgâ.

Kalimah, Muhammadan confession of faith.

Kaliyuga, the fourth age of the world.

Kallâppâ, a deity worshipped by thieves.

Kallavasaveśvara, the bull Nandi (Vasavâ or Basavâ, the sacred bull Nandi).

Kallideva, name of a deity in the Kânarese districts.

Kalomeśvara, epithet of Śiva.

Kalyâṇeśvara, epithet of Śiva (kalyâṇa, happiness, prosperity).
Kâmadâr, an officer.
Kâmadhenu, the heavenly cow yielding all desires.
Kamaleśvara, an epithet of Śiva (kamala, a lotus).
Kamâvisdâr, a magistrate.
Kanakeśvara, an epithet of Śiva (kanaka, gold).
Kânaphâtâ, a Śaiva religious sect who wear large and heavy rings on their ears.
Kandugiri, name of a mountain.
Kântâreśvara, epithet of Śiva (lord of the forest).
Kânteśvara, epithet of Śiva (kânta, beautiful).
Kanthadanâtha, name of a deity.
Kapâleśvara, an epithet of Śiva (Śiva with skulls).
Kapileśvara, an epithet of Śiva. (Kapila, name of a Ṛishi).
Kâtareśvara, an epithet of Śiva.
Kaṭeśvara, an epithet of Śiva.
Karaṇa, a division of the day (in astronomy). The Karaṇas are eleven in number.
Kârbhâri, a minister.
Kardameśvara, an epithet of Śiva (Kardama, name of a Ṛishi).
Karṇa, name of a celebrated warrior on the side of the Kauravas. He was famous for his charity.
Karṇeśvara, an epithet of Śiva (karṇa, the ear; also the name of a celebrated warrior).
Kârtika, the eighth lunar month (Oct.-Nov.).
Kârtikasvâmi, son of Śiva (the god of war).
Kâseśvara, an epithet of Śiva (Kâsa, name of a village).
Kâśîliṅga, the celebrated liṅga at Kâśî (Benâres).
Katyâra or kaṭâra, a dagger.
Kauśagîya, a standing image.
Kâyastha, a sub-caste of the Brâhmaṇs.
Kedâranâtha, name of Śiva (Kedâra, name of mountain).
Kedâreśvara, an epithet of Śiva.
Keribasâppâ, same as Basavâ (keri, a tank).
Keśara, saffron.
Keśavarâya, a name of Vishṇu.
Khabutra, a pigeon.
Khabutrakhâṇâ, a pigeon-house.
Khaḍataragachcha, a sect of the Jains.
Khaḍâva, wooden pattens.
Khageśvara, epithet of Śiva (khaga, a bird).
Khâlsâ, land or village, of the revenue of which the State is sole proprietor.
Khâmba, a pillar.
Khaṇḍeśvara, an epithet of Śiva. Same as Khaṇḍobâ.
Khaṇḍi, a weight equal to 20 maunds or 1,600 lbs.
Khaṇḍobâ, a name of deity.

Khara, name of a year in the Hindu cycle of sixty years.
Khimeśvara, an epithet of Śiva.
Khiṇḍ, a pass through hills.
Khodiar Mâtâ, name of a deity.
Khola Nâtha, name of a deity.
Khole'svara, an epithet of Śiva (khol, deep).
Khunyâ Muralîdhara, Muralîdhara Kṛishṇa with a flute in his hand and Khunyâ (so called because a murder was perpetrated when the image was set up).
Kibla, same as mehrâb.
Kîlaka, name of a year in the Hindu cycle of sixty years.
Killedâr, an officer in charge of a fort.
Kîrtistambha, pillar of victory.
Koleśvara, an epithet of Śiva.
Komanâtha, (Kâmanâtha ?), name of Śiva.
Kopeśvara, an epithet of Śiva (kopa, anger).
Koreśvara, an epithet of Śiva (Kore, name of a village, short form of Koregâon).
Kotavâla, a village official.
Koṭeśvara, an epithet of Śiva.
Koṭitîrtha, name of a holy place.
Kṛishṇa, one of the incarnations of Vishṇu.
Kṛishṇâbâi, name of deity of villages on the Kṛishṇa river.
Kṛishṇeśvara, an epithet of Śive (Kṛishṇa, probably the name of the builder of the temple: an avatâra of Vishṇu.)
Krodhana, name of a year in the Hindu cycle of sixty years.
Krodhi, name of a year in the Hindu cycle of sixty years.
Kror or Karor, 1,00,00,000.
Kshatrapa, Satrap; a viceroy or ruler.
Kshatriya, a member of the military or second caste.
Kshaya, a name of a year in the Hindu cycle of 60 years.
Kshetrapâla, another name of Bhairava.
Kubâ, a tomb.
Kubera, god of wealth and guardian of the north.
Kubereśvara, an epithet of Śiva (Kubera, name of god of wealth).
Kukadeśvara, an epithet of Śiva.
Kuladevatâ, a tutelary deity.
Kulkarṇi, a village official under the Pâtil whose duty it is to keep the accounts.
Kuṃbhâragirîśvara, epithet of Śiva (Kumbâragiri, name of a hill).
Kumbheśvara, epithet of Śiva (kumbha, a water pot).

Kuṇḍa, a small masonry tank for water; also a place for sacrifices or to hold sacred fire.

Kunthi, one of the twenty-four Tîrthankaras of the Jains.

Kurund, red stone.

Kuvâ, a well.

LÂKHA, 1,00,000.

Lakshmaṇa, step-brother of Râma, king of Ayodhyâ.

Lakshmeśvara, epithet of Śiva (Lakshma, a mark).

Lakshmî, wife of Vishṇu and goddess of wealth.

Lakshmî-Narasiṁha, Lakshmî and Narasiṁha.

Lakshmî-Nârâyaṇa, Lakshmî and Nârâyaṇa.

Lankâ, Ceylon, the abode of the demon king Râvaṇa.

Lankeśvara, Râvaṇa (lord of Lankâ). An epithet of Śiva.

Liṅga, the genital organ of Śiva, worshipped in the form of a Phallus.

Lingâyata, a religious sect who especially dedicate themselves to the worship of Basavâ, an incarnation of Nandi.

Lokanâtha, a name of Śiva.

Lokapâla, guardian of one quarter of the world.

MACHCHA-KANDERÂYA, name of a hermit.

Mâdhavarâja, Vishṇu (husband of Lakshmî).

Madhukeśvara, epithet of Śiva (Madhu or Madhuka, name of a demon slain by Vishṇu).

Madhyaranga, the central hall of a temple.

Madhyameśvara, an epithet of Śiva.

Madressa, a Muhammadan school or college.

Mâgha, the eleventh lunar month (Jan.-Feb.).

Mahâbaleśvara, epithet of Śiva (mahâbala, great might).

Mahâbhârata, a celebrated epic poem.

Mahâdeva, favourite name of Śiva (the great god).

Mahâkâleśvara, an epithet of Śiva (Mahâkâla, the destroyer).

Mahâkâlî, Durgâ in her terrible form.

Mahâkûṭeśvara, an epithet of Śiva (kûṭa, summit of a mountain).

Mahâlakshmî, the Śakti or female counterpart of Nârâyaṇa.

Mahâmantri, a great minister.

Mahâmâyâ, a name of Durgâ.

Mahâmâyî, a name of Śiva.

Mahanta, the head of a monastery.

Mahârâja, great king, a title.

Mahârâjâdhirâja, paramount sovereign.

Mahârudra Śaṁkara, Śaṁkara or Śiva in his most terrific form.

Mahâsâmanta, a tributary prince.

Mahâsarasvatî, or Sarasvatî, the goddess of speech and learning.

Mahâtmya, description (traditional or historical).

Mahâvîrasvâmi, the last of the twenty-four Tîrthankaras.

Mahishamardanî, Durgâ, who killed the demon Mahisha.

Mahishâsuramardanî, same as the last.

Mailâradeva, Khaṇḍoba or Mallâri.

Mailâra-liṅga, same as above.

Makâm, a place.

Makara, conventional beast in Hindu decoration, probably the tapir or rhinoceros, not the "maggar" or alligator as generally supposed.

Makara-toraṇa, an arch flanked by makaras.

Maḷâ, a garden.

Mâleśvara, an epithet of Śiva.

Mâlakeśvara, an epithet of Śiva.

Mallammâ, name of a devî.

Mallappâ, name of a deity.

Mallaya, same as last.

Malleśvara, an epithet of Śiva (Malla, name of a demon slain by Śiva).

Malli, one of the twenty-four Tîrthankaras.

Mallikârjuna, name of Śiva-liṅga.

Mâlsâbâi, wife of Khaṇḍobâ.

Mâṇḍalîka, a subordinate ruler.

Maṇḍapa, the large open hall of a temple.

Mândhâtâ, name of a king of the solar race.

Mandir, a temple.

Mâṇḍvi, a custom house.

Mânga, a man of the lowest caste.

Mâṇikyeśvara, an epithet of Śiva (mâṇikya, a ruby).

Maṇî-Malla, names of two demons killed by Mallâri (Khaṇḍobâ).

Maṇinâga, name of a hill (a snake with a jewel).

Mansâpurî, name of a village deity.

Mantra, a vedic hymn; also a formula sacred to any deity.

Mârgaśîrsha, the ninth lunar month (Nov.-Dec.).

Mârkaṇḍeśvara, an epithet of Śiva (Mârkaṇḍa, the name of a Ṛishi).

Mârtaṇḍa, the sun, Khaṇḍobâ.

Marudevî, the wife of Nâgarâjâ.

Mâruti or Hanumân, the monkey chief and warrior.

Masabati, a village deity.

Masjid, a Musalmân place of worship.

Masnad, a throne, dais.

Mastikal, a memorial stone.

Maṭha, a monastery.

Maulavi, doctor of learning.

Mehallâ or Mohallâ, a portion of a town or city.

Mehrâb, niche in a mosque towards which worshippers turn to pray.

Meḷa, a fair.

Meru Śikhara, Mount Meru; image of in Jaina temples

Mimbâr, pulpit in a masjid.

Minâr, a minaret.

Mokshanâtha, name of Śiva (moksha, final emancipation).

Moṭ, a ramp leading to a well upon which bullocks draw up the water.

Muchakunda, son of king Mândhâtâ.

Muktâbâi, sister of Jnâneśvara (see "Âlandi").

Mukteśvara, epithet of Śiva (mukta, one finally emancipated).

Mukuṭa, a crown.

Munisuvrata, one of the twenty-four Tîrthankaras.

Mukarbâ, a Muhammadan tomb.

Mujâvara, a servant or caretaker of a masjid.

Mukâm, a place.

Muralidhara, Kṛishṇa with the flute.

Murḍeśvara, epithet of Śiva.

Mur-Gopinâtha-Kṛishṇa, a name of Kṛishṇa.

Murum, soft disintegrated rock.

NÂGA, chief of the Serpent race, generally represented by a man with the tail of a serpent said to inhabit Pâtâla, the nether world.

Nâganâtha, an epithet of Vishṇu and Śiva; also of Śesha as lord of serpents.

Nâgapanchamî the fifth day of the month of Śrâvaṇa, on which is performed the snake worship.

Nagârakhâna, the place where drums are beaten.

Nagareśa, name of a liṅga.

Nâgârjuna, a Jaina deity (Arjuna) with a snake's hood above the head.

Nagendragachha, a religious sect of the Jains.

Nageśvara, name of a liṅga, epithet of Śiva (Naga, a mountain).

Nâgobâ, same as Nâga.

Nakshatra, asterism.

Nala, name of a year in the Hindu cycle of sixty years.

Naḷa, a water pipe.

Nâlâ, a stream.

Nama or Nemi, one of the twenty-four Tîrthankaras of the Jains.

Nandana, name of a year in the Hindu cycle of sixty years.

Nandi, the attendant and vehicle of Śiva: the bull.

Nandyâvarta, a particular symbol.

Nâneśvara, epithet of Śiva (the god of manifold forms).

Nârada, one of the ten mind-born sons of Brahmâ and the messenger of the gods.

Narakeśvara, epithet of Śiva (the god that saves from hell).

Narasiṁha, the man-lion incarnation of Vishṇu.

Narasobâ, same as Narasiṁha.

Nârâyaṇa, Vishṇu.

Nârâyaṇa-Nâgabali. A special sacrifice to be performed alone by those who have no son.

Nârâyaṇeśvara, epithet of Śiva.

Naṭeśvara, an epithet of Śiva (naṭa, a dancer).

Navadurgâ, the nine forms of Durgâ. (They are (1) Śailaputrî, (2) Brahmachâriṇî, (3) Chandraghaṇṭa, (4) Kûshmâṇḍâ, (5) Skandamâtâ, (6) Kâtyâyanî, (7) Kâlarâtri, (8) Mahâgaurî, and (9) Siddhidâ).

Navagraha, the nine planets. (They are (1) Ravi, (2) Soma, (3) Mangala, (4) Budha, (5) Guru, (6) Śukra, (7) Śani, (8) Râhu, and (9) Ketu).

Navasiddhi, the nine superhuman powers.

Nemi or Neminâtha, one of the twenty-four Tîrthankaras of the Jains.

Nîlakaṇṭheśvara, an epithet of Śiva (Nîlakaṇṭha, dark-blue throated).

Nîlammâ, name of a devî.

Nîm or Nimba (Melia azadirachta), a sacred tree.

Nivriti, a brother of Jnâneśvara (see "Âḷandi)".

OṀKÂRA, the sacred syllable ओम्, which is uttered as a holy exclamation at the beginning and end of the reading of the Vedas, or previous to the commencement of a prayer or sacred work.

Oṁkâreśvara, an epithet of Śiva.

Oṭa, a podium or platform.

Ovâra, a flight of steps.

PADASALI, a verandah.

Padma, the lotus.

Padmaprabhu, one of the twenty-four Tîrthankaras of the Jains.

Padmâvatî, a name of Lakshmî.

Pâdukâ, holy foot-prints.

Pagalâna, holy foot-prints.

Paggi, a watchman.

Paliyâ, a memorial stone.

Panch, an assembly usually of five members, a jury.

Pânchâleśvara, an epithet of Śiva. (Pânchâla, name of an ancient country.)

Panchaliṅga, a collection of five liṅgas.

Panchatîrthi, a collection of five holy things.

Panchâyatana, five deities, namely Śiva, Vishṇu, Gaṇapati, Sûrya, and Devî.

Pâṇḍavadarâ, place of residence of the Pâṇḍavas,

Pâṇḍavas, the five sons of king Pâṇḍu, namely Dharma, Bhîma, Arjuna, Nakula, and Sahadeva.

Pândhari, the name of a river (*lit.* white).

Panjâ, palm of the hand used as a symbol; it is an object of reverence among the Muhammadans.

Pâouli, an open space.

Pâpanâtha, an epithet of Śiva (lord of sin).

Parama-Bhaṭṭâraka, an epithet applied to great men.

Parameśvara, an epithet of Śiva (the Supreme Being).

Paraśurâma, the celebrated Brâhman warrior, son of the sage Jamadagni and the sixth incarnation of Vishṇu.

Pargaṇâ, a province.

Paridhâvi, name of a Hindu year in the cycle of sixty years.

Parigraha, retinue.

Pârśva or Pârśvanâtha, one of the twenty-four Tîrthankaras of the Jains.

Pârśvanâtheśvara, same as Pârśvanâtha.

Pârtheśvara, an epithet of Śiva (Pârtha, a term applicable to any of the five Pâṇḍavas).

Parvateśvara, epithet of Śiva (Parvata, a hill or mountain).

Pârvatî, the wife of Śiva.

Pâshâṇa, a stone.

Pâṭeśvara, an epithet of Śiva.

Pâṭil, a village official.

Pâtia, a flat stone or slab.

Pâvakeśvara, an epithet of Śiva (god of fire).

Pausha, the tenth lunar month (Dec.-Jan.).

Pawrah, an agricultural implement, a hoe.

Peshvâ, originally Prime Minister or first of the eight principal officers of State established by Śivâji, and, later, a ruler of almost independent power with his seat at Poona.

Phâlguna, the twelfth lunar month (Feb.-Mar.).

Phirnal, a well.

Phuleśvara, an epithet of Śiva (phula, a flower).

Pimpareśvara, an epithet of Śiva (Pimpri, name of a village.)

Piṇḍi, same as "liṅga."

Pingaleśvara, an epithet of Śiva (Pingalâ, name of a courtezan).

Pippala (*Ficus religiosa*), a tree sacred to Vishṇu.

Pîr, a Musalmân saint.

Plavanga, name of a Hindu year in the cycle of sixty years.

Prabhava, name of a Hindu year in the cycle of sixty years.

Pradakshiṇâ, circumambulation from left to right, so that the right side is always towards the object circumambulated.

Prâgvâṭa, a sub-caste of the Śrâvaka Baniâ.

Pralhâda, name of a son of the demon Hiraṇyakaśipu, slain by Narasiṁha.

Pramâthi, name of a Hindu year in the cycle of sixty years.

Pramodi, name of a Hindu year in the cycle of sixty years.

Prâsâda, a temple, mansion.

Pratishṭhâ, installation.

Pratyangirâ, name of a devî or goddess.

Pratimâ, a likeness, an image.

Pṛithu, the name of a mythological king of the solar race.

Pujâri, a worshipper, temple attendant.

Pûjâ, worship.

Puloma, name of the father of Śachî, Indra's wife.

Puṇḍarîka, name of a great sage of the Jains.

Puṇḍarîkanâthaji, same as Puṇḍarîka.

Purâṇas, old traditional stories, eighteen in number.

Purandareśvara, an epithet of Śiva (he who killed the demon Pura).

Pûrnimâ, full-moon.

QÂZI, Muhammadan priest.

Qurân, the Muhammadan scriptures.

RÂFADÂ, mound of earth.

Raghu, name of a mythical king of the solar race; great-grandfather of Râma.

Raghunâtha, a name of Râma.

Râjâ, king.

Râjâdhirâja, same as Mahârâjâdhirâja.

Rainchalis, heavenly she-goats.

Rakheśvara, an epithet of Śiva.

Rakhmâi, wife of Viṭhoba.

Râkshasa, a demon.

Raktâkshi, the name of a Hindu year in the cycle of sixty years.

Râma, the seventh incarnation of Vishnu.

Râmachandra, same as last.

Râmakuṇḍa, the name of a tîrtha.

Râmalinga, an epithet of Śiva.

Râmâyaṇa, the celebrated epic by Vâlmiki in seven *kâṇḍas* or books.

Râmeśvara, an epithet of Śiva.

Raṇachhodji, Kṛishṇa.

Râneśvara, an epithet of Śiva.

Rânjan, an earthen pot.

Ratha, a chariot, generally applied to those huge constructions on wheels in which the god of a temple is drawn at high festivals.

Rauza, a Muhammadan tomb.

Râvaṇa, the celebrated king of Lankâ, or Ceylon, who was killed by Râma.

Râyaṇa, a sacred tree with the Jains.

Rayata, subjects.

Reṇukâ, wife of Jamadagni and mother of Paraśurâma.

Revalanâtha, the name of a deity (Śiva).

Rishabhadeva, the first of the twenty-four Tîrthankaras of the Jains.

Rishabhanâtha, same as Rishabhadeva.

Rishi, a sage.

Rokḍeśvara, an epithet of Śiva.

Rudhirodgâri, the name of a year in the Hindu cycle of sixty years.

Rudra, name of a year in the Hindu cycle of sixty years; also a form of Śiva.

Rudramâlâ, group of eleven gods.

Rûpeśvara, an epithet of Śiva (rûpa, beauty).

SABHÂMANḌAPA, the principal hall before the shrine of a temple; in the case of two halls, the outer open one.

Śachî, the name of Indra's wife

Sadâvarta, alms-house, or place where uncooked provision is given.

Sâdhâraṇa, the name of one of the sixty years of the Hindu cycle.

Sâdhu, a holy man.

Sâgaragachha, a religious sect of the Jains.

Sâgareśvara, an epithet of Śiva (sâgara, an ocean).

Sahasrakûṭa. A pedestal in Jaina temples covered with a thousand little images of Jinas.

Sahasra-liṅga, a thousand liṅgas.

Śaiva, relating to Śiva.

Śaka, a Hindu era (of Śalivâhana).

Śakreśvara, an epithet of Śiva, (Śakra, name of Indra).

Śâlivâhana, the name of a king, founder of the era of the same name.

Sâḷunkâ, the stone within which the liṅga is placed made to represent the female counterpart of the liṅga.

Samâdhi Kallu, a tomb-stone.

Śâmba Śiva, Śamba, Śiva with Pârvatî.

Śambhavanâtha, one of the twenty-four Tîrthankaras of the Jains.

Śambhu, Śiva (*lit.* granting prosperity).

Śambhu-liṅga, Śiva's liṅga.

Sâmeta Śikhara, the pinnacle of the mountain Sâmeta.

Śaṁkara-liṅga, name of a liṅga.

Śaṁkara-Nârâyaṇa, same as Hari-Hara.

Saṁsthâna, a holy place.

Saṁvat, the Hindu era of Vikrama.

Saṁvatsara, a year.

Sandhyâmaṇḍapa, a maṇḍapa or pavilion on the bank of a tank or river in which to perform Sandhyâ ceremonies.

Sangama, confluence of two rivers.

Sangameśvara, epithet of Śiva (sangama, see above.)

Sangha, a collection of people (pilgrims); a fair.

Sankaleśvara, an epithet of Śiva.

Śani, the planet Saturn.

Śanivâra, Saturday.

Śaṅkarâchârya, the celebrated teacher of the Vedânta philosophy and reformer of the Hindu religion.

Śankha, a conch shell.

Śânteśvara, an epithet of Śiva. (Śânta, free from passion).

Śântinâtha, one of the twenty-four Tîrthankaras of the Jains.

Sanyâsi, an ascetic; a Brâhmaṇ, in the fourth order of his religious life.

Saptamâtṛis, the seven mothers, namely Brâhmî, Mâheśvarî, Kaumârî, Vaishṇavî, Mâhendrî or Aindrî, Vârâhî, and Châmuṇḍî.

Saptaśṛingî, the devî on the hill of Saptaśṛingi.

Sapta-Rishi, the seven sages.

Śâradâ, name of Sarasvatî.

Sarâi, caravansary, a rest-house.

Saranjâm, villages or lands granted in inâm for services required.

Sarasvatî, goddess of learning and letters represented as the wife of Brahmâ; also a name of Durgâ.

Sarvajit, name of one of the Hindu years in the cycle of sixty.

Sarvajña, the name of Buddha (all-knowing).

Sarveśvara, an epithet of Śiva (sarva, entire).

Śâsanam, an order, edict.

Śaśivâra, Monday.

Satî, the name of Durgâ; a wife who immolates herself on her husband's pyre.

Satyayuga, the first of the four Yugas or ages of the world.

Sâvkâr or **Sâhukâr**, a moneylender.

Saumya, the name of a Hindu year in the cycle of sixty years.

Śeshaphaṇâ, the hood of a snake.

Śeshaśâyi, Vishṇu represented as lying upon the serpent Śesha.

Shajeśvara, an epithet of Śiva.

Shâhid, martyr.

Siddhachakra, a circular slab with siddhas (demi-gods) engraved upon it.

Siddhaliṅga, name of a liṅga.

Siddhanâtha, Śiva. Buddha.

Siddhânta Śiromaṇi, a work on astronomy by Bhâskarâchârya.

Siddhâppâ, the name of a liṅga.

Siddharâmeśvara, an epithet of Śiva.

Siddhi, a yoga of the same name.

Siddhârthi, the name of a Hindu year in the cycle of sixty years.

Siddheśvara, an epithet of Śiva (siddha, perfected).

Śikhara, top of a mountain or spire of a temple.

Śilâśâsanaṁ, a stone or slab on which a grant of land is inscribed.

Siṁhâsana, a throne; a decorated seat of an image.

Śiśir, the cold season.

Sîtâ or Sîtâbâi, the wife of Râma, and daughter of Janaka, king of Mithalâ.

Sitakalânâthaji. A name of Śiva (Sitakala, the moon).

Sîtala, one of the twenty-four Tîrthankaras of the Jains.

Sitalâ, name of goddess of small-pox, who is generally represented as seated on an ass and is nude, has in her hands a broom and water-pot and over her head a winnowing basket.

Sîtâ's Nhâṇi, Sîtâ's bathroom.

Śiva, the third deity of the Triad (Brahmâ, Vishṇu, and Śiva).

Śivaliṅga, the liṅga of Śiva.

Śivâlaya, temple of Mahâdeva.

Śivarâtri, the fourteenth day of the dark half of the month of Mâgha, when a fast in honour of Śiva is observed.

Śloka, a stanza or verse.

Smârta-Brâhmaṇa, a Brâhmaṇ following "Smṛiti."

Smṛiti, code of laws (civil or religious).

Solabeśvara, an epithet of Śiva.

Śobhakratu, name of a Hindu year in the cycle of sixty years.

Somanâtha, Śiva with the moon upon his head.

Somappâ, Śiva.

Somavâra, Monday.

Someśvara, same as Somanâtha (Soma, the moon).

Sopâna, brother of Jñâneśvara.

Sphaṭika, a crystal.

Śrâvaṇa, the fifth lunar month (July-Aug.)

Śrâvaka, a name generally applied to the Jains.

Sreyânsa, one of the twenty-four Tîrthankaras of the Jains.

Śrî, Lakshmî; also as a prefix to works or writings and to the names of great persons

Śrîmâlî or Mâlî, a sub-caste of the Śrâvaka Baniâ.

Śṛingâra, decoration.

Srîvatcha, a mark on the breast of Vishṇu and the Jaina Tîrthankaras.

Stambha, a pillar.

Stûpa, a Buddhist monument erected to hold sacred relics.

Subhedâr, a district officer.

Sudarśana, the name of the bow in Vishṇu's hand.

Śuddha, the bright half of the month, from new to full-moon.

Śukleśvara, an epithet of Śiva (śukla, white; also the bright half of a lunar month).

Śukravâra, Friday.

Sumatinâtha, one of the twenty-four Tîrthankaras of the Jains.

Sundar-Nârâyaṇa, Vishṇu.

Supârśvanâtha, one of the twenty-four Tîrthankaras of the Jains.

Sûrya-Nârâyaṇa, the sun god.

Suvarṇeśvara, an epithet of Śiva (lord of gold).

Suvrata or Muṇi Suvrata, one of the twenty-four Tîrthankaras of the Jains.

Svâmi-Nârâyaṇa, name of a religious sect.

Svastika, a particular symbol.

Svayaṁbhu, self-born.

Śvetâmbara, a religious sect of the Jaina wearing white clothes.

Śyâmji or Śyâmalji, Kṛishṇa (syâma, the sky colour).

Tâkâ, a cistern.

Tâkaleśvara, an epithet of Śiva.

Taksâl or tanksâl, mint.

Talâva, a tank.

Talavar, a watchman.

Tali, a round piece of gold.

Tâlukâ, sub-division of a district.

Tâmbdi, red.

Tâmragaurî, Pârvatî.

Tâmraparṇî, name of a river.

Tâṇḍava, an extraordinary dance of Śiva.

Tanka, a stamped old coin, especially of silver.

Tapâgachcha, a religious sect of the Jains.

Tapascharyâ, religious austerity.

Tâpasi, men who practise religious austerity.

Tapeśvara, an epithet of Śiva (tapah, religious austerity).

Târakeśvara, an epithet of Śiva (târaka, saviour).

Taṭeśvara, an epithet of Śiva.

Temblâi, a goddess who holds a lamp in her hand.

Thadagi, tombs.

Thânâ, the head station of a tâlukâ.

Thâṇedâr, the officer in charge of a thânâ.

Thul, a tower.

Tîrtha, a holy place, especially where there is a holy well, tank, or spring.

Tîrthankara, the twenty-four celebrated Jaina saints were called Tîrthankaras.

Todavîrabhadra, the being created by Śiva from his hair to kill Daksha.

Trikûṭeśvara, an epithet of Śiva (Trîkûṭa, name of a mountain).

Trimûrti, a triad incarnation of Brahmâ, Vishṇu, and Śiva.

Trinetra, an epithet of Śiva (he who has three eyes).

Tripiṇḍi, a collection of three *piṇḍis* or liṅgas.

Trîpurâutakeśvara, an epithet of Śiva (Tripura, a demon slain by Śiva).

Tripurâsura, name of a particular demon slain by Śiva.

Triśûla, a trident.

Triveṇî, a term applied to the confluence of three rivers.

Trivikrama, the dwarf or Vâmana Avatâra of Vishṇu.

Tryambakeśvara, Śiva (the god with three eyes).

Tuk, a great walled court, enclosing a number of temples.

Tukâi (Devî), goddess of the village Tukâi Vâdi.

Tukobâ or Tukârâma, name of a famous sâdhu of Dehu (Poona). He is famous for his verses in the Abhanga metre.

Tulasi, a sacred plant very commonly worshipped by the followers of Vishṇu. The *Ocimum sanctum.*

Tulasikuṇḍa, a basin round the tulasi plant.

UDDHÂRA, restoration.

Ujali, name of a river.

Umâ-Maheśvara, Pârvati-Śiva.

Utkaṇṭheśvara, epithet of Śiva.

Uttarâ, a lunar mansion.

Uttarâbhâdrapadâ, an asterism of the same name.

Uttareśvara, an epithet of Śiva.

VÂDÂ, a palace.

Vadâr, a stone-cutter.

Vaddâra, a stone-dresser. The caste name of people who quarry stone.

Vadya, the dark fortnight of the lunar month.

Vâgheśvarî Mâtâ, a goddess who sits upon a tiger.

Vâhana, a vehicle.

Vidyânâtha, name of one of the twenty-four Tîrthankaras of the Jains.

Vaijanâtha, a name of Śiva.

Vaiśâkha, the second month of the lunar year (April-May).

Vaishṇava, relating to Vishṇu.

Vajramâtâ, name of a goddess (mother with the thunderbolt).

Vâlukeśvara, an epithet of Śiva.

Vâpikâ, a well.

Varâhakâleśvara, an epithet of Śiva.

Varâha, the third or the boar incarnation of Vishṇu.

Varâha-Narasiṁha, the third and fourth incarnations of Vishṇu.

Vardhmânasvâmi, one of the twenty-four Tîrthankaras.

Varuṇa, god of water; guardian of the West.

Vâsuki, name of a celebrated snake, king of snakes.

Vâsukinâtha, Vishṇu.

Vâsupûjya, one of the twenty-four Tîrthankaras of the Jains.

Vâyu, god of wind; guardian of the north-west.

Vazir, prime minister, same as Divâna.

Vedâ Râjâ, mad king.

Vedas, the Hindu scriptures.

Vedî, a part of the basement of a temple; an altar.

Venkaṭaramaṇa, Vishṇu (Venkaṭa, name of a mountain).

Venkaṭeśa, Vishṇu.

Vibhava, name of one of the sixty years of the Hindu cycle.

Vidyâdhara, a class of demi-gods.

Vihâra, a Buddhist or Jaina monastery or temple.

Vijaya, name of one of the sixty years of the Hindu cycle; name of Arjuna.

Vikrama, name of one of the sixty years of the Hindu cycle; name of a king.

Vilambi, name of one of the sixty years of the Hindu cycle.

Vimalanâtha, one of the twenty-four Tîrthankaras of the Jains.

Vimâna, a heavenly or aërial car.

Vinâyaka, Gaṇapati.

Vîrabhadra, a demon created by Śiva from his hair to kill Daksha.

Viragal or virakal, memorial stones set up in commemoration of warriors.

Vîrakshetrapâla, same as Kshetrapâla.

Vîra-Nârâyaṇa, Vishṇu as a warrior.

Vîreśvara, an epithet of Śiva (vîra, a warrior).

Virochana, name of the father of the demon Bali.

Virodhi, name of one of the sixty years of the Hindu cycle.

Virûpâksha, Śiva (having an unusual number of eyes).

Vishaparihâreśvara, a name of Śiva (Vishaparihâra, destroyer of poison).

Vishṇu, the second deity of the Triad (Brahmâ, Vishṇu, and Śiva).

Viśvanâtha, Śiva (lord of the universe).

Visvâvasú, name of one of the sixty years of the Hindu cycle.

Viśveśvara, an epithet of Śiva (lord of the universe).

Viṭṭhala, a form of Vishṇu; the celebrated god of Paṇḍharpur.

Viṭhobâ, same as above.

Vyâghreśvarî Mâtâ or Vâgheśvarî Mâtâ, a goddess who sits on a tiger.

Vyâsa, name of a great sage, author of the Mahâbhârata.

Vṛiddheśvara, an epithet of Śiva (Vṛiddha, old).

Vṛindâvana, name of a forest near Gokula. A raised mound of earth round a tulasi plant.

Vṛishabha, the first of the twenty-four Tîrthankaras of the Jains.

Vyâsamuni, the great sage and author of Hindu mythological works, Mahâbhârata, etc.

WALLAD, "son of", (a term used among the lower classes and Muhammadans).

Wâlli, supporter.

YÂDAVA, surname of the family of Kṛishṇa.

Yaksha, a class of demi-gods who attend on Kubera.

Yakshabrahmakambha, name of a pillar.

Yama, the god of death.

Yellammâ, name of a goddess.

Yoga, a particular astronomical division of time. The Yogas are twenty-seven in number.

Yogeśvara, an epithet of Śiva. (Yoga, deep and abstract meditation, concentration of the mind and contemplation of the supreme spirit.)

Yoginidevî, a name of Durgâ.

Yudhishṭhira, name of the eldest Pâṇḍava, also called Dharma and Dharmarâja.

Yuga, an age of the world.

Yuva, name of a Hindu year in the cycle of sixty years.

ZILLA, a division of a province.

CLASSIFIED LIST FOR CONSERVATION PURPOSES

OF REMAINS IN THE

BOMBAY PRESIDENCY.

(For explanation of Classes see Preface.)

CLASS I*a*.

District.	Tâlukâ.	Locality.	Description.
Poona ...	... Mâval...	... Kârle	... The cave-temples and inscriptions.
,, ...	... ,, ...	... Bhâja	... Do. do.
,, ...	... ,, ...	... Bedsa	... Do. do.
,, ...	... Junnar	... Junnar	... Caves and inscriptions.
Sâtârâ ...	... Jâvli ...	... Râjpuri	... A Devanâgari inscription slab.
Ahmadnagar	... Śrigonda	.. Pedgâon	... The temple of Lakshmî-Nârâyaṇa.
Nâsik ...	... Nâsik ...	.. Pâṇḍu Lena Hill.	The caves in Pâṇḍu Lena Hill.
,, ...	... Sinnar	... Sinnar	... The temple of Âeśvara.
Khândesh	... Châlisgâon	... Pâtan	... The temple of Maheśvara with its inscription slab.
,,	... ,,	... Pitalkhora	... The series of Buddhist caves.
Ahmadâbâd	... Daskroi	... Ahmadâbâd	... Azam Khân's palace.
,,	... ,,	... ,,	... Ahmad Shâh's Mosque in the Bhadr.
,,	... ,,	... ,,	... The Jami Masjid.
,,	... ,,	... ,,	... Sidi Sayyid's Masjid.
,,	... ,,	... ,,	... The Moti Shâhi Bâgh.
,,	... ,,	... ,,	... Dâdâ Harir's well.
,,	... ,,	... ,,	... The Dutch tombs.
,,	... ,,	... Adâlaj	... The step-well with its inscription.
Panch Mahâls...	Hâlol	... Champânir	... The Jami Masjid.
,,	... ,,	... ,,	... The Naginâ Masjid.
,,	... ,,	... ,,	... The Kevadâ Masjid.
Thânâ ...	... Sâlsette	... Kânheri	... The Buddhist caves at Kânheri.
Belgaum	... Gokâk	... Konnur	... Three groups of dolmens.
Dhârwâr	... Bankâpur	... Bankâpur	... The Arvattukhambaḍa temple in the fort.
,,	... ,,	... ,,	... Old Kânarese and Sanskṛit inscription slabs.
Bijâpur	... Bijâpur	... Bijâpur	... The walls and fortifications.
,,	... ,,	... ,,	... The Jami Masjid.
,,	... ,,	... ,,	... 'Ali Shâhid Pîr's Masjid.
,,	... ,,	... ,,	... The Andu Masjid.
,,	... ,,	... ,,	... The Zangiri Masjid.
,,	... ,,	... ,,	... The Zamrud Musjid.
,,	... ,,	... ,,	... The Makkâ Masjid.
,,	... ,,	... ,,	... Mosque No. 257.
,,	... ,,	... ,,	... The Gagan Mahâl.
,,	... ,,	... ,,	... The Sât Manzli.
,,	... ,,	... ,,	... A small structure on the north of the Sât Manzli.
,,	... ,,	... ,,	... The 'Asâr Mahâl.
,,	... ,,	... ,,	... The Mihtari Mahâl.
,,	... ,,	... ,,	... The Gol Gumbaz.
,,	... ,,	... ,,	... 'Ali (I) Rauza.
,,	... ,,	... ,,	... Tombs 35 to 39.
,,	... ,,	... ,,	... The Kamrakhi Gumbaz.
,,	... ,,	... ,,	... The Chând Bâori.
,,	... ,,	... ,,	... The Tâj Bâori.
,,	... ,,	... ,,	... Ibrâhim Rauza.
,,	... ,,	... Kumatgi	... The pavilion with frescoes.
,,	... Bâdâmi	... Bâdâmi	... Caves and inscriptions.
Kârwâr	... Honâvar	... Bhatkal	... European graves.
,,	... ,,	... Gersâppâ	... Images.

District.	Tâlukâ.	Locality.	Description.
Kârwâr	... Honâvar	... Gersâppâ	... Old Kânarese and Sanskṛit Inscriptions.
„	... „	... „	... Images.
Ratnâgiri	... Dâpoli...	... Dâbhol	... Old Mosque.
Kolâba...	... Panvel	... Ghârâpuri	... The Elephanta caves.
„ ...	... Mângâon	... Kuda ...	... Buddhist caves.
Karâchi	... Tattâ ...	... Tattâ	... Jâm-Nizâm-u-din's tomb.
„	... „ ...	... „	... Divân Shurfa Khân's tomb.
„	... „ ...	... „	... Nawâb Isâ Khân's tomb.
„	... „ ...	... „	... Navâb Isâ Khân's *zanana* tombs.
„	... „ ...	... „	... Mirzâ Jâni Beg's tomb.
„	... „ ...	... „	... Grave of Edward Cooke.
„	... „ ...	... „	... The Jami Masjid.
Hyderâbâd	... Hyderâbâd	... Hyderâbâd	... Ghulâm Shâh Kalhora's tomb.
„	... Moro ...	... Thul Rukhân...	A Buddhist *stûpa*.
„	... „ ...	...	... The tomb of Nûr Muhammad Kalhora.
„	... Shâhdâdpur	... Bumbra-ke-thul	The ruins of the ancient city of Brâhmanâbâd.
Shikârpur	... Rohri ...	... Hakrâh	... The ruins of an ancient town.

CLASS II*a*.

District.	Tâlukâ.	Locality.	Description.
Poona ...	... Haveli	... Poona...	... Old European tombs.
„	... Mâval	... Selârvâdi	... Excavations and inscriptions.
„	... „	... Lohagaḍ	... Fort.
„	... „	... Visâpur	... Fort.
„	... „	... Râjmâchi	... Fort.
„	... Junnar	... Junnar	... Fort of Śivneri.
Sâtâra ...	... Karâd	... Karâd	... Caves near Karâd.
„ ...	... Pâtan	... Pâtan ...	... Caves.
Ahmadnagar	... Ahmadnagar	... Ahmadnagar	... The Fariabâgh, the tomb of Nizâm Ahmad Shâh, the Bihisti Bâgh, Alamgir's Dargâh.
„	... „	... Mehekri	... Salâbat Khân's tomb.
„	... Pârner	... Dhoke	... Dhokeśvara cave.
„	... Akolâ	... Harischandra-gaḍ.	Caves and temple.
Sholâpur	... Sholâpur	... Sholâpur	... Inscriptions in the fort.
„	... „	... Begampur	... Tomb of a daughter of Aurangzib.
Nâsik	... Yeola	... Ankâi	... Caves.
Khândesh	... Shirpur	... Thâlner	... Muhammadan tombs.
„	... Châlisgâon	... Pâtan	... Caves.
Ahmadâbâd	... Daskroi	... Ahmadâbâd	... Gâikvâd Haveli, tomb of Mir Abu Turab, Dâdâ Harir's mosque and tomb.
„	... „	... Batwâ	... Burhân-ud-din Qutbu'l Alam's tomb.
„	... Dholkâ	... Dholkâ	... Khân Masjid.
Panch Mahâls...	Hâlol	... Pâvâgaḍ	... The fort of Pâvâgaḍ.
Broach	... Broach	... Broach	... The Dutch tombs.
Surat	... Chorâsi	... Surat	... Old English and Dutch tombs.
„	... Olpâd	...	... Vaux's tomb.
Thânâ	... Sâlsette	... Thânâ	... Graves of John Halsey and George Page.
„	... „	... Kondivte	... Caves.
„	... Bassein	... Bassein	... Fort and old Portuguese remains.
Belgaum	... Belgaum	... Belgaum	... Asad Khân's Dargâh and inscriptions.
Bijâpur	... Bijâpur	... Bijâpur	... Batula Khân's Masjid.
„	... „	... „	... Yusuf's old Jami Masjid.
„	... „	... „	... Mustâ â Khân's mosque.
„	... „	... „	... Karîm-ud-din's mosque.
„	... „	... „	... Mosque No. 294.
„	... „	... „	... The Chinch Diddi Masjid.
„	... „	... „	... Ibrâhim's Jami Masjid.
„	... „	... „	... Ikhlâs Khân's mosque.
„	... „	... „	... The Chhotâ 'Asâr mosque.
„	... „	... „	... The Rangi Masjid.

District.	Tâlukâ.	Locality.	Description.
Bijâpur (*contd.*)	Bijâpur (*contd.*)	Bijâpur (*contd.*)	The small pavilion in front of the 'Arash Mahâl.
" ...	" ...	" ...	Mubârak Khân's Mahâl.
" ...	" ...	" ...	Tomb No. 56.
" ...	" ...	" ...	Ali (II) Rauza.
" ...	" ...	" ...	Malik Sandal's tomb.
" ...	" ...	" ...	Sikandar Shâh's tomb.
" ...	" ...	" ...	Kishwar Khân's tomb.
" ...	" ...	" ...	Hâji Hassan Sâheb's tomb.
" ...	" ...	" ...	Water towers.
" ...	" ...	" ...	A ruined gateway with an inscription.
" ...	" ...	" ...	The Bari Kamân.
Kârwâr ...	Kârwâr ...	Kârwâr ...	European tombs.
" ...	Honâvar ...	Gersâppâ ...	The Chaturmukha basti.
Kolâba ...	Mahâd ...	Pâl ...	Caves.
" ...	Karjat ...	Kondâne ...	Caves.
" ...	" ...	Ambivali ...	Cave.
" ...	" ...	Kotali Fort ...	Old guns.
Karâchi ...	Tattâ ...	Tattâ ...	Makli's tomb.
" ...	" ...	" ...	Tomb of Nawâb Amîr Khalîl Khân.
" ...	" ...	" ...	Nawâb Amîr Mîr Abul Bakr.
" ...	" ...	" ...	Mirzâ Baki Khân's tomb.
" ...	" ...	" ...	Mirzâ Tugral Beg's tomb.
" ...	" ...	" ...	A 12-pillared pavilion.
" ...	" ...	" ...	Old Dabgir Masjid.
" ...	Dâdu ...	Khudâbâd ...	The Jami Masjid.
Hyderâbâd ...	Shâhdâdpur ...	Depur ...	Old brick *thul.*
" ...	Guni ...	Tândo Muhammad Khân.	Old brick *thul.*
Shikârpur ...	Ubauro ...	Vijnot ...	Site of an old city.
Thar and Pârkar.	Nagar Pârkar .	Bhodesar ...	Old Jaina temples.

CLASS I.*b*.

District.	Tâlukâ.	Locality.	Description.
Ahmadnagar ...	Ahmadnagar ...	Ahmadnagar ...	The Damri Masjid.
Nâsik ...	Sinnar ...	Sinnar ...	The temple of Gondeśvara.
Khândesh ...	Pimpalner ...	Balsâne ...	Two Hindu temples.
" ...	Erandol ...	Erandol ...	Sculptured *mehrâbs* in Pâṇḍava's Vâdâ.
" ...	Châlisgâon ...	Pâtan ...	Inscription slab in wall of temple of Ai Bhavânî.
" ...	" ...	Vâghli ...	Three inscribed slabs in the temple of Kṛishṇa.
Ahmadâbâd ...	Daskroi ...	Ahmadâbâd ...	The Tin Darawâjâ.
" ...	" ...	" ...	Râni Rûpwanti's mosque in Mirzâpur.
" ...	" ...	" ...	Râni Sipri's mosque and tomb.
" ...	" ...	" ...	Muhâfiz Khân's mosque.
" ...	" ...	" ...	Ahmad Shâh's tomb.
" ...	" ...	" ...	Tombs of the Queens of Ahmad Shâh.
" ...	" ...	" ...	Haibat Khân's Masjid.
" ...	" ...	" ...	Dastur Khân's Masjid.
" ...	" ...	" ...	Sayyid Alam's Masjid.
" ...	" ...	" ...	The Shâhpur or Qizi M. Chisti's Masjid.
" ...	" ...	" ...	The Queen's mosque in Sârangpur.
" ...	" ...	" ...	Kutb Shâh's mosque.
" ...	" ...	" ...	Sayyid Usmân's mosque and tomb.
" ...	" ...	" ...	Shâh Âlam's tomb.
" ...	" ...	" ...	Bibi Ji's Masjid at Râjpur Hirpur.
" ...	" ...	Sarkhej ...	The tomb of Shekh Ahmad Khattu Ganj Baksh.
" ...	" ...	" ...	Pavilion before the last.
" ...	" ...	" ...	The great mosque.
" ...	" ...	" ...	Tomb of Mahmud Bîgârah.
" ...	" ...	" ...	Tomb of Bîbî Râjbâi.
" ...	Dholkâ ...	Dholkâ ...	Mosque of Balol Khân Qâzi.
" ...	" ...	" ...	Jami Masjid.

District.	Tâlukâ.	Locality.	Description.
Kaira	... Kaira	... Mahmudâbâd...	Tomb of Mubârak Sayyîd.
„	... Kapadvanj	... Kapadvanj ...	A sculptured arch.
Broach	... Broach	... Broach ...	The Jami Masjid.
Thânâ	... Sâlsette	... Borivli ...	A group of Memorial Stones.
„	... Kalyân	... Ambarnâth ...	The temple of Ambarnâtha.
Belgaum, Dharwâr, Bijâpur	... .	......	All old Sanskṛit and Kânarese inscriptions earlier than 15th century.
Belgaum	... Śampgâon	... Degâon ...	Old temple.
Dhârwâr	... Hubballi	... Unkal... ...	Old temple of Chandramaulîśvara.
„	... Gadag	... Gadag... ...	The temples of Sarasvatî and Someśvara.
„	... „	... Lakkundi ...	The temples of Kâśiviśveśvara, Nanneśvara and the large Jaina *basti*.
„	... „	... Dambal ...	The temple of Dodda Basâppâ.
Nizâm's Territory.	Yelburga	... Ittagi	Old Hindu temple.
„	... „	... Kukkanur ...	Temples of Kalleśvara and Navalinga.
Dhârwâr	... Bankâpur	... Ganjigatti ...	A sculptured slab.
„	... Hângal	... Hângal ...	Temple of Târakeśvara.
„	... Karajgi	... Haveri ...	The temple of Siddheśvara.
„	... Rânebennur	... Chandâdampur.	The temple of Mukteśvara.
Miraj	... Lakshmeśvar...	Lakshmeśvar ..	Temples and the Kâli Masjid.
Bijâpur	... Bijâpur	... Bijâpur ...	Tomb of Pîr Shekh Hamid Qâdir.
„	... „	... „ ...	A small tomb, No. 47.
„	... „	... „ ...	Tomb No. 48.
„	... „	... „ ...	The Sonbâri Masjid.
„	... „	... „ ...	The Ainâpur Mahâl.
„	... „	... „ ...	Haidar Khân's tomb.
„	... „	... „ ...	Afzul Khân's cenotaph.
„	... Hungund	... Aihole ...	Caves and temples.
„	... Bâdâmi	... Pattadakal ...	Old temples.
Kârwâr...	... Honâvar	... Bhatkal ...	Ketapai Nârâyaṇa Devasthâna.
„	... „	... „ ...	Śantâppâ Nâyaka Tirumal Devasthâna.
„	... „	... „ ...	Jattâpâ Nâyakana Chandranâtheśvara Basti.
Thar and Pârkar.	Nagar...	... Gori	An old Jaina temple.
Baroda...	... Dabhoi	... Dabhoi ...	Old fortifications and temples.
„ ...	... Paṭṭan	... Paṭṭan ...	Images and carved slab.
„ ...	... Siddhapur	... Siddhapur ...	The remains of the Rudra Mâlâ.
„ ...	... Vadnagar	... Vadnagar ...	Remains of old temples.
„ ...	... Kadi ...	... Mudherâ ...	The temple of Sûrya.
„ ...	... „	... Jhinjuvâdâ ...	The old fort and gateways.
„ ...	... „	... Sandera ...	Two old temples.
„ ...	... „	... Sunâk ...	The temple of Nîlakaṇṭha Mahâdeva.
„ ...	... „	... Kasera ...	The old triple-shrined temple.
Kâthiâwâd	... Jhâlâwâd Prânt.	Kodinâra ...	An old inscribed stone.
„	... „	... Junâgaḍ ...	Old inscriptions.
„	... „	... Verâval Pattan.	The old temple of Somanâtha and the Jami masjid.
Kolhâpur	... Kolhâpur	... Kolhâpur ...	Old Kânarese and Sanskṛit Inscriptions.
„	... „	... Herle ...	Do. do.
„	... „	... Bamni ...	Do. do.

Class II. *b*.

District.	Tâlukâ.	Locality.	Description.
Poona	... Haveli	... Poona ...	The cave temple at Bhâmburde.
„	... Junnar	... Junnar ...	The Jami Masjid.
„	... „	... Pur ...	The temple of Kukadeśvara.
Sâtârâ	... Karâd	... Karâd ...	The Jami Masjid.
Ahmadnagar	... Śrigonda	... Śrigonda ...	Old wood carving.
„	... „	... Mândavgân Katrâbâd.	The temple of Devî.

District.	Tâluka.	Locality.	Description.
Ahmadnagar—(*contd.*)	Kopargâon ...	Kokamthân ...	An old temple.
,, ...	Akolâ ...	Akolâ ...	The temple of Siddheśvara.
,, ...	,, ...	Ratanvâdi ...	Temple of Amṛiteśvara.
Sholâpur ...	Mâdha ...	Wapha ...	An inscription slab.
,, ...	Mâlsiras ...	Velâpur ...	A Hemâḍpanti temple.
Nâsik ...	Nâsik ...	Anjaneri ...	Old temples.
,, ...	Malegâon ...	Jhodga ...	The temple of Mâṇikeśvara.
Khândesh ...	Pimpalner ...	Balsâne ...	Old temples.
,, ...	Erandol ...	Erandol ...	The Pâṇḍava's Vâḍâ.
,, ...	Bhusâval ...	Chângadeva ...	The temple of Chângadeva.
,, ...	Pâchora ...	Sangameśvara .	The old temple of Mahâdeva.
Ahmadâbâd ...	Daskroi ...	Ahmadâbâd ...	Shâh Khupâi Masjid.
,, ...	,, ...	,, ...	Sakar Khân's masjid.
,, ...	,, ...	,, ...	Phuti masjid.
,, ...	,, ...	,, ...	Daryâ Khân'stomb.
,, ...	,, ...	,, ...	Achyut Bibi masjid and tomb.
,, ...	,, ...	,, ...	Malik Âlam's mosque.
,, ...	,, ...	,, ...	Bâbâ Lului's masjid.
,, ...	,, ...	,, ...	Mâlik Îsan-ul-Mulk's mosque.
,, ...	,, ...	,, ...	Mâtâ Bhavânî's well.
,, ...	,, ...	Sarkhej ...	The great tank, palace, and harem.
,, ...	Sânand ...	Sânand ...	The rauzas of Bâvâ Alisâr and Bâvâ Ganj Baksh.
,, ...	Viramgâm ...	Viramgâm ...	The Monsar *talâv* and shrines.
,, ...	,, ...	Mândal ...	The Jami, Sayyid, Qâzi, and Ganjni masjid.
,, ...	Dholkâ ...	Dholkâ ...	Tânka masjid and Multâv *talâv*.
Kaira ...	Kaira ...	Mahmudâbâd...	Tombs of Saifu'd-din and Nizâmu'd-din, and the Pîr or Bhâmaria well.
,, ...	Thâsra ...	Sarnal ...	Temple of Galeśvara.
Panch Mahâls .	Hâlol ...	Champânir ...	Sakar Khân's Dargâh.
,, ...	,, ...	Hâlol ...	Tomb of Sikandar Shâh.
,, ...	,, ...	Desar ...	The Rudra Mâlâ.
,, ...	,, ...	Bhavka ...	An old ruined temple of Mahâdeva.
Thânâ ...	Sâlsette ...	Borivli ...	Old Portuguese churches, watch tower and caves.
,, ...	,, ...	Mâgâthâna ...	A sculpured slab.
,, ...	,, ...	Amboli ...	The Jogeśvarî caves.
,, ...	,, ...	Mandapeśvara .	Caves.
,, ...	Kalyân ...	Kalyân ...	The Kâli masjid.
,, ...	Bassein ...	Pelâr ...	Temple and inscription slabs.
Belgaum ...	Bidi ...	Nandigaḍ ...	Old temple.
,, ...	Sampgâon ...	Sampgâon ...	A small mosque.
Belgaum } Dhârwâr }	......	......	Old Kânarese and Sanskṛit inscription slabs later than the 14th century.
Belgaum ...	Sampgâon ...	Wakkund ...	Old temple of Mukteśvara.
,, ...	Gokâk ...	Konnur ...	Old temples near the falls.
Dhârwâr ...	Dhârwâr ...	Dhârwâr ...	Four sculptured slabs.
,, ...	Hubballi ...	Amargol ...	The temple of Śankaralinga.
,, ...	Navalgund ...	Annigeri ...	The temple of Amṛiteśvara.
,, ...	Ron ...	Naregal ...	Old temples.
,, ...	Gadag ...	Nilgund ...	The temple of Nârâyaṇa.
,, ...	,, ...	Mulgund ...	The temple of Siddheśvara.
,, ...	Gadag ...	Gadag ...	The temple of Trikûṭeśvara.
,, ...	,, ...	Lakkundi ...	The temple of Mallikârjuna.
,, ...	,, ...	,, ...	The temple of Someśvara.
,, ...	Hângal ...	Hângal ...	The old temples in the fort.
,, ...	,, ...	Tilivalli ...	The temple of Ŝânteśvara.
,, ...	,, ...	Balambida ...	Temples of Râmeśvara and Kallameśvara.
,, ...	Karajgi ...	Haralahalli ...	Temples of Someśvara and Kâleśvara.
,, ...	,, ...	Galaganâth ...	Temple of Gargeśvara.
,, ...	Kod ...	Rattihalli ...	Temple of Kadambeśvara.
,, ...	,, ...	Balambid ...	Temple of Vishaparihâreśvara.
Miraj ...	Lakshmeśvar...	Lakshmeśvar...	Old temples.
,, ...	,, ...	Sirhatti ...	The palace.

District.		Tâlukâ.		Locality.		Description.
Jamkhandi	...	Kundgol	...	Kundgol	...	An old temple.
Bijâpur	...	Bijâpur	...	Bijâpur	...	The Nau Gumbaz.
"	...	"	...	"	...	The Bukhâri Masjid.
"	...	"	...	"	...	Mosque No. 21.
"	...	"	...	"	...	Dhâi Wâdi Masjid.
"	...	"	...	"	...	The Gumat Bâori.
"	...	"	...	"	...	The Ambar Khânâ.
"	...	"	...	"	...	The old guns.
"	...	"	...	"	...	The Mulla mosque.
"	...	"	...	"	...	The Khidaki Masjid.
"	...	"	...	"	...	The Îbrâhîmpur Masjid.
"	...	"	...	"	...	Mosque No. 366.
"	...	"	...	"	...	The Sangat and Nari mahâls at Torweh.
"	...	"	...	"	...	Afzal Khân's wives' tombs.
"	...	"	...	"	...	Jahân Begam's tomb.
"	...	"	...	"	...	'Ain-ul-mulk's tomb.
"	...	"	...	"	...	Certain miscellaneous buildings.
Kârwâr	...	Sirsi	...	Banavâsi	...	The temple of Madhukeśvara.
"	...	Siddhâpur	...	Bilgi	...	The Jain *basti* of Pârśvanâtha.
"	...	Honâvar	...	Bhatkal	...	Raghunâtha Devasthân.
Ratnâgiri	...	Sangameśvara	.	Sangameśvara	.	The temple of Karṇeśvara.
Kolâbâ	...	Alibâg	...	Alibâg	...	Certain old inscriptions.
"	...	Pen	...	Nâgothana	...	Old Muhammadan bridge.
"	...	Mahâd	...	Râyagaḍ Fort	.	Old inscription in the temple of Mahâdeva.
Karâchi	...	Sehwan	...	Sehwan	...	The tomb of Lâl Shâh Bhâz.
Hyderâbâd	...	Hâlâ	...	Matiari	...	The Jami Masjid.
Shikârpur	...	Sakar	...	Sakar	...	Mir Masum's Minâr and tomb and the Masumi Sayyids' tombs.
Thar and Pârkar.		Nagar	...	Virâvâh	...	Old temple ruins.
Baroda	...	Paṭṭan	...	Paṭṭan	...	Old Hindu remains.
"	...	Mehsâna	...	Akhaj	...	Remains of a *kîrttistambha*.
Pâlanpur	...	......		Sarotra	...	An old Jaina temple.
Baroda	...	"	...	Dilmâl	...	Old temple.
"	...	"	...	Kanoda	...	Old temple.
Kâthiâwâd	...	Jhâlâwâd Prânt.		Thân	...	The temples of Muni Bâvâ and Tarnetar.
"	...	"	...	Ânandapura	...	An old temple.
"	...	"	...	Junâgaḍ	...	The caves of Khâprâ Kodiâ.
"	...	"	...	Girnâr	...	Jaina temples.
Kachh	...	......		Bhuvad	...	The temple of Bhuvaneśvara.
"	...	......		Kotâi	...	An old temple.
"	...	......		Kheda	...	The *vimâna* of an old temple.
Kolhâpur	...	Kolhâpur	...	Kolhâpur	...	The temple of Ambâbâi.
"	...	"	...	Panhâla Fort	...	Ruined buildings.
"	...	"	...	Khedrâpur	...	The temple of Kopeśvara.

INDEX.

List of Volumes constituting the New Imperial Series of the Reports of the Archæological Survey of India.

Prescribed Number in New Series.	Name of Book.	Author or Editor.	Date of Publication.	Existing Provincial Number. Western India.	Southern India.	Northern India.
I.	Report of the first season's Operations in the Belgaum and Kalâdgi Districts.	Burgess	1874	I.	...	...
II.	Report on the Antiquities of Káthiáwár and Kachh.	Burgess	1876	II.	...	...
III.	Report on the Antiquities of the Bidar and Aurangâbâd Districts.	Burgess	1878	III.	...	...
IV.	The Buddhist Caves and their Inscriptions.	Burgess	1883	IV.	...	...
V.	The Caves of Elura and the other Bráhmanical and Jaina Caves in Western India.	Burgess	1884	V.	...	...
VI.	The Buddhist Stûpas of Amarâvti and Jaggayyapeta.	Burgess	1887	...	V.	...
VII.	Lists of Antiquarian Remains in the Presidency of Madras (Volume I.)	Sewell	1882	...	I.	...
VIII.	Lists of Inscriptions and Sketch of Dynasties of Southern India (Volume II.)	Sewell	1884	...	II.	...
IX.	South Indian Inscriptions (Volume I.) ...	Hultzsch	1890	...	III.	...
X.	South Indian Inscriptions (Volume II.)...	Hultzsch	1891-92-95.	...	IV.	...
XI.	Report on the Sharqi Architecture of Jaunpur.	Burgess and Führer.	1889	...	...	I.
XII.	Monumental Antiquities and Inscriptions in the North-Western Provinces and Oudh.	Führer	1891	...	...	II.
XIII.	Epigraphia Indica (Volume I.) ...	Burgess	1891	...	...	...
XIV.	Epigraphia Indica (Volume II.) ...	Burgess	1894	...	...	...
XV.	South Indian Buddhist Antiquities ...	Rea	1894	...	VI.	...
XVI.	Revised Lists of Antiquarian Remains in the Bombay Presidency.	Cousens	1897	VIII.	...	...
XVII.	Lists of Architectural and Archæological Remains in Coorg.	Rea	1894	...	VII.	...
XVIII.	Report on the Moghul Architecture of Fathpur-Sikri, Parts I and II.	Smith	1895-96	...	...	} III.
,,	Fathpur-Sikri, Part III	Smith	1897	...	...	} III.
XIX.	Lists of Antiquarian Remains in the Central Provinces and Berars.	Cousens	1897	...	...	...
XX.	Monograph on Ancient Jaina Art and Architecture.	Führer	1897	...	...	IV.
XXI.	Châlukyan Architecture, including examples from the Bellary District, Madras Presidency.	Rea	1896	...	VIII.	...
XXII.	Bower Manuscripts	Hœrnle	1893-94-95.	...	...	...
XXIII.	The Muhammadan Architecture of Bharoch, Cambay, Dholkâ, Champânir, and Mahmudâbâd, in Gujarât.	Burgess	1896	VI.	...	...
XXIV.	The Muhammadan Architecture of Ahmadâbâd.	Burgess	In preparation.	VII.	...	...
XXV.	Monumental Remains of the Dutch East India Company in the Presidency of Madras.	Rea	1897	...	...	...

List of Volumes constituting the New Imperial Series of the Reports of the Archæological Survey of India—*continued.*

Prescribed Number in New Series.	Name of Book.	Author or Editor.	Date of Publication.	Existing Provincial Number.		
				Western India.	Southern India.	Northern India.
XXVI.	Monograph on Buddha Śâkyamuni's Birthplace in the Nepalese Tarai.	Führer.	1897	...	...	V
XXVII.	The Monumental Antiquities and Inscriptions in Râjputânâ and Central India.	Führer.	In preparation.	...	...	VI
XXVIII.	The Monumental Antiquities and Inscriptions in the Panjab.	Führer.	"	...	...	VII

Mysore Archæological Series.

Number of Volume.	Name of Book.	Author or Editor.	Date of Publication.
I	Coorg Inscriptions	Rice.	1886
II	Inscriptions at Sravana Belgola (Epigraphia Carnatica) ...	Do.	1889
III	Inscriptions in the Mysore District, Part I	Do.	1894
IV	Do. do. Part II	Do.	In the Press
V	Do. Hassan District	Do.	Do.
VI	Do. Kadur District	Do.	Do.
VII	Do. Shemoga District, Part I	Do.	Do.
VIII	Do. do. Part II	Do.	Do.
IX	Do. Bangalore District	Do.	Do.
X	Do. Kolar District	Do.	Do.
XI	Do. Chitaldroog District	Do.	Do.
XII	Do. Tunkur District	Do.	Do.